maran

illustrated™

Microsoft®

Access 2003

maranGraphics®

&

THOMSON™

COURSE TECHNOLOGY

Professional ■ Trade ■ Reference

MARAN ILLUSTRATED™ Microsoft® Access 2003

Distributed in the U.S. and Canada by Thomson Course Technology PTR. For enquiries about Maran Illustrated™ books outside the U.S. and Canada, please contact maranGraphics at international@maran.com

For U.S. orders and customer service, please contact Thomson Course Technology at 1-800-354-9706. For Canadian orders, please contact Thomson Course Technology at 1-800-268-2222 or 416-752-9448.

ISBN: 1-59200-872-0

Library of Congress Catalog Card Number: 2005921493

Printed in the United States of America

05 06 07 08 09 BU 10 9 8 7 6 5 4 3 2 1

Trademarks

maranGraphics is a registered trademark of maranGraphics Inc. Maran Illustrated, the Maran Illustrated logos and any trade dress related to or associated with the contents or cover of this book are trademarks of maranGraphics Inc. and may not be used without written permission.

The Thomson Course Technology PTR logo is a trademark of Course Technology and may not be used without written permission.

All other trademarks are the property of their respective owners.

Permissions

Microsoft

Important

maranGraphics and Thomson Course Technology PTR cannot provide software support. Please contact the appropriate software manufacturer's technical support line or Web site for assistance.

maranGraphics and Thomson Course Technology PTR have attempted throughout this book to distinguish proprietary trademarks by following the capitalization style used by the source. However, we cannot attest to the accuracy of the style, and the use of a word or term in this book is not intended to affect the validity of any trademark.

Copies

Educational facilities, companies, and organizations located in the U.S. and Canada that are interested in multiple copies of this book should contact Thomson Course Technology PTR for quantity discount information. Training manuals, CD-ROMs, and portions of this book are also available individually or can be tailored for specific needs.

DISCLAIMER: PURCHASERS, READERS OR USERS OF THIS BOOK AGREE TO BE BOUND BY THE FOLLOWING TERMS.

INFORMATION CONTAINED IN THIS BOOK HAS BEEN OBTAINED BY MARANGRAPHICS AND FROM SOURCES BELIEVED TO BE RELIABLE. HOWEVER, NEITHER MARANGRAPHICS INC. NOR THOMSON COURSE TECHNOLOGY PTR NOR ANY OF THEIR RESPECTIVE AFFILIATES, DISTRIBUTORS, EMPLOYEES, AGENTS, CONTENT CONTRIBUTORS OR LICENSORS, IF ANY, MAKE ANY REPRESENTATION, WARRANTY, GUARANTEE OR ENDORSEMENT AS TO THE INFORMATION CONTAINED IN THIS BOOK OR AS TO THIRD-PARTY SUPPLIERS REFERENCED IN THIS BOOK, INCLUDING WITHOUT LIMITATION REGARDING THEIR ACCURACY, CORRECTNESS, TIMELINESS, RELIABILITY, USEFULNESS OR COMPLETENESS, OR THE RESULTS THAT MAY BE OBTAINED FROM THE USE OF THIS BOOK, AND DISCLAIM ALL EXPRESS, IMPLIED OR STATUTORY WARRANTIES, INCLUDING IMPLIED WARRANTIES OF MERCHANTABILITY, FITNESS OR SUITABILITY FOR A PARTICULAR PURPOSE, TITLE AND NON-INFRINGEMENT. THE SUBJECT MATTER OF THIS BOOK IS CONSTANTLY EVOLVING AND THE INFORMATION PROVIDED IN THIS BOOK IS NOT EXHAUSTIVE. IT SHOULD NOT BE USED AS A SUBSTITUTE FOR CONSULTING WITH A QUALIFIED PROFESSIONAL WHERE PROFESSIONAL ASSISTANCE IS REQUIRED OR APPROPRIATE, INCLUDING WHERE THERE MAY BE ANY RISK TO HEALTH OR PROPERTY, AND THE PURCHASER, READER OR USER UNDERSTANDS AND ACKNOWLEDGES THAT THE AFOREMENTIONED PARTIES ARE NOT HEREBY PROVIDING ANY PROFESSIONAL ADVICE, CONSULTATION OR OTHER SERVICES.

IN NO EVENT WILL ANY OF MARANGRAPHICS INC., THOMSON COURSE TECHNOLOGY PTR, OR ANY OF THEIR RESPECTIVE AFFILIATES, DISTRIBUTORS, EMPLOYEES, AGENTS, CONTENT CONTRIBUTORS OR LICENSORS BE LIABLE OR RESPONSIBLE FOR ANY DAMAGES INCLUDING ANY DIRECT, INDIRECT, SPECIAL, CONSEQUENTIAL, INCIDENTAL, PUNITIVE OR EXEMPLARY LOSSES, DAMAGE OR EXPENSES (INCLUDING BUSINESS INTERRUPTION, LOSS OF PROFITS, LOST BUSINESS, OR LOST SAVINGS) IRRESPECTIVE OF THE NATURE OF THE CAUSE OF ACTION, DEMAND OR ACTION, INCLUDING BREACH OF CONTRACT, NEGLIGENCE, TORT OR ANY OTHER LEGAL THEORY.

maranGraphics®

maranGraphics Inc.
5755 Coopers Avenue
Mississauga, Ontario
L4Z 1R9
www.maran.com

THOMSON
COURSE TECHNOLOGY™
Professional ■ Trade ■ Reference

Thomson Course Technology PTR, a division of Thomson Course Technology
25 Thomson Place ■ Boston, MA 02210 ■ http://www.courseptr.com

maranGraphics is a family-run business.

At **maranGraphics**, we believe in producing great computer books—one book at a time.

Each maranGraphics book uses the award-winning communication process that we have been developing over the last 30 years. Using this process, we organize screen shots, text and illustrations in a way that makes it easy for you to learn new concepts and tasks.

We spend hours deciding the best way to perform each task, so you don't have to! Our clear, easy-to-follow screen shots and instructions walk you through each task from beginning to end.

Our detailed illustrations go hand-in-hand with the text to help reinforce the information. Each illustration is a labor of love—some take up to a week to draw!

We want to thank you for purchasing what we feel are the best computer books money can buy. We hope you enjoy using this book as much as we enjoyed creating it!

Sincerely,

The Maran Family

We would love to hear from you! Send your comments and feedback about our books to family@maran.com

Please visit us on the Web at:

www.maran.com

CREDITS

Author:
Ruth Maran

Access 2003 Update Director:
Kelleigh Johnson

Project Manager:
Judy Maran

Editing and Screen Captures:
Raquel Scott
Roderick Anatalio
Adam Giles

Layout Designer:
Richard Hung

Illustrator & Screen Artist:
Russ Marini

Illustrator, Screen Artist & Assistant Layout Designer:
Steven Schaerer

Indexer:
Raquel Scott

Post Production:
Robert Maran

President, Thomson Course Technology:
David R. West

Senior Vice President of Business Development, Thomson Course Technology:
Andy Shafran

Publisher and General Manager, Thomson Course Technology PTR:
Stacy L. Hiquet

Associate Director of Marketing, Thomson Course Technology PTR:
Sarah O'Donnell

National Sales Manager, Thomson Course Technology PTR:
Amy Merrill

Manager of Editorial Services, Thomson Course Technology PTR:
Heather Talbot

ACKNOWLEDGMENTS

Thanks to the dedicated staff of maranGraphics, including Roderick Anatalio, Adam Giles, Richard Hung, Kelleigh Johnson, Wanda Lawrie, Jill Maran, Judy Maran, Robert Maran, Ruth Maran, Russ Marini, Steven Schaerer, Raquel Scott and Roxanne Van Damme.

Finally, to Richard Maran who originated the easy-to-use graphic format of this guide. Thank you for your inspiration and guidance.

TABLE OF CONTENTS

Chapter 1

GETTING STARTED

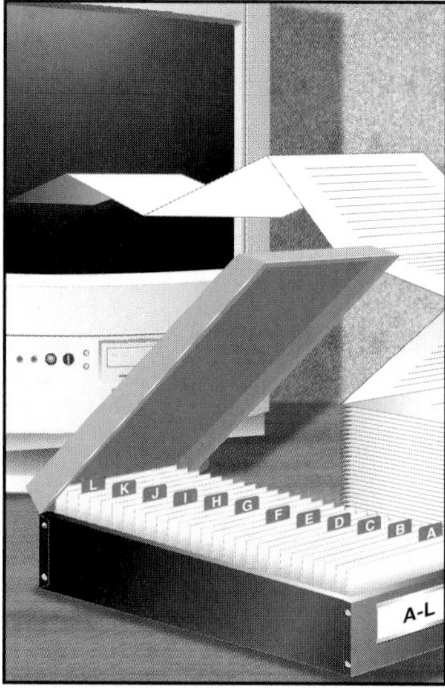

Chapter 2

CREATE TABLES

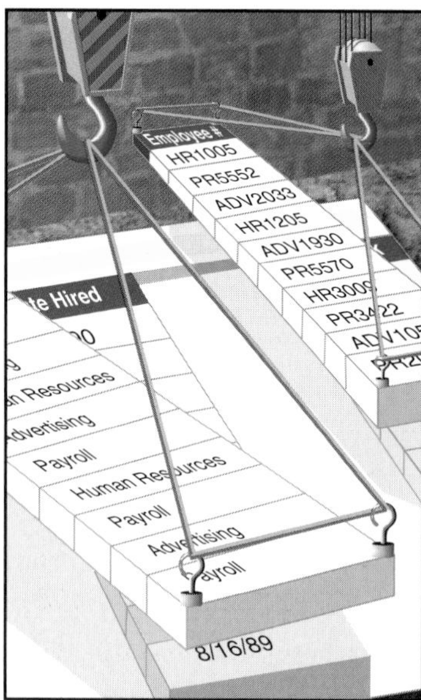

Chapter 3

EDIT TABLES

Chapter 4

DESIGN TABLES

TABLE OF CONTENTS

Chapter 5 ESTABLISH RELATIONSHIPS

Chapter 6 CREATE FORMS

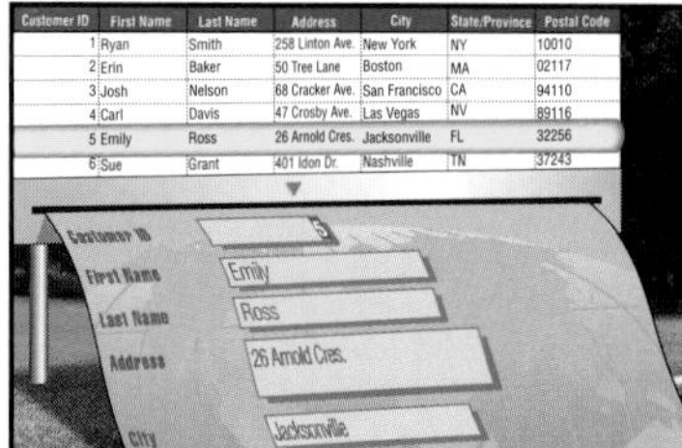

Chapter 7 DESIGN FORMS

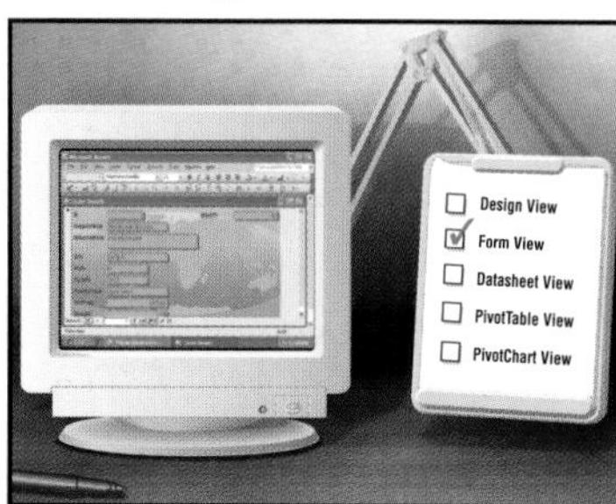

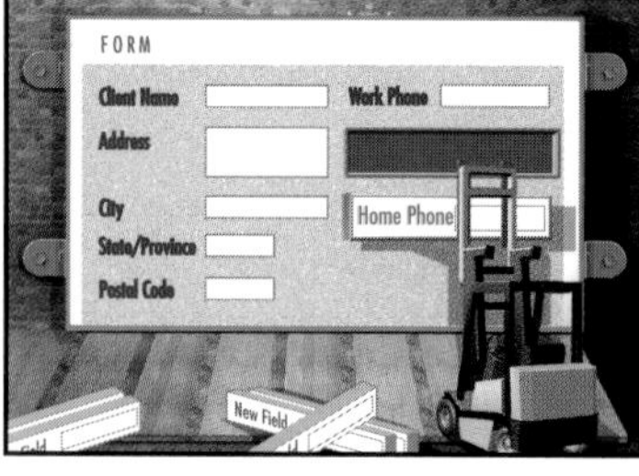

Chapter 8

FIND DATA

Chapter 9

CREATE QUERIES

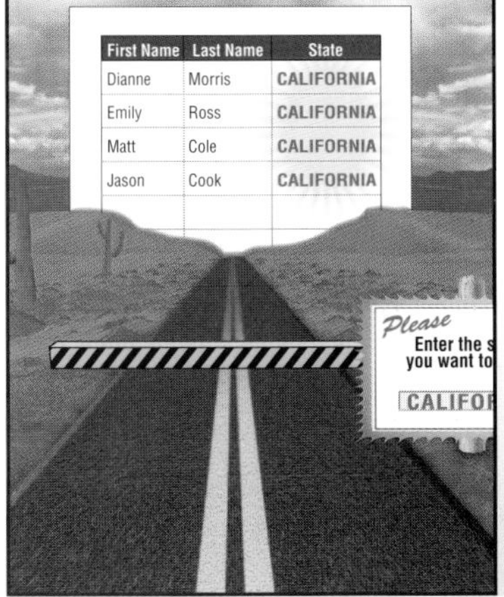

TABLE OF CONTENTS

Chapter 10

USING THE PIVOTTABLE AND PIVOTCHART VIEWS

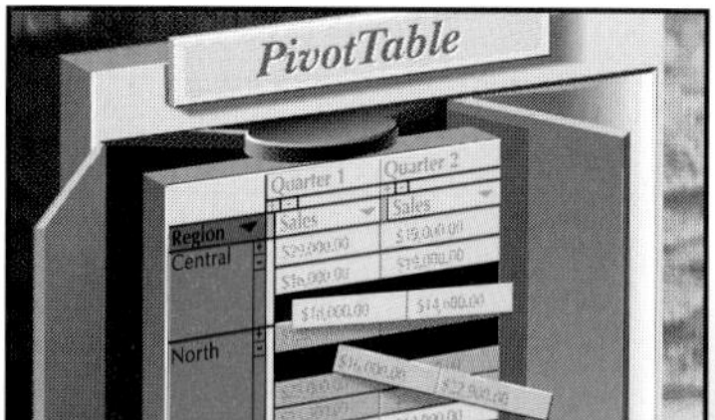

Chapter 11

CREATE REPORTS

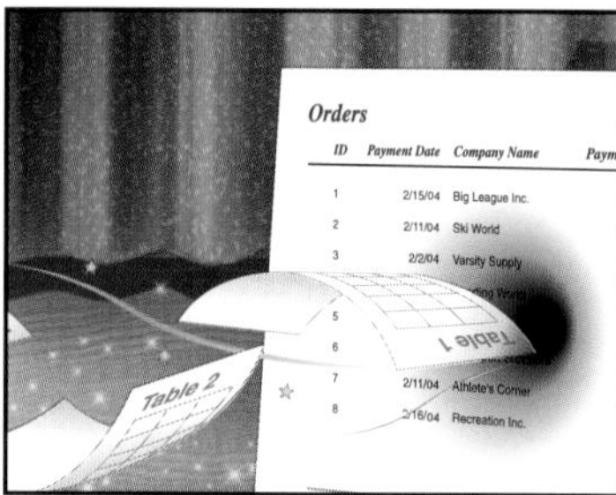

Chapter 12

PRINT INFORMATION

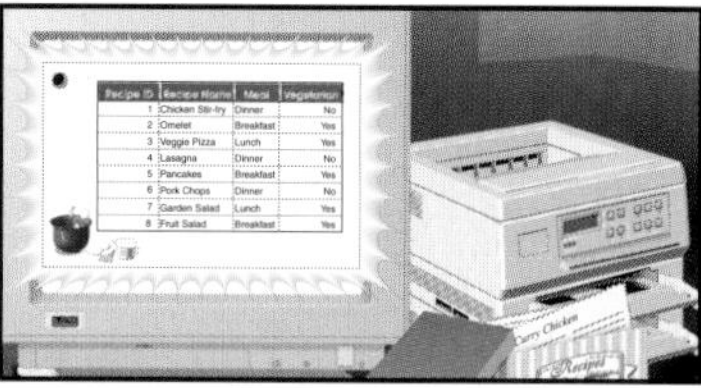

Chapter 13

CREATE DATA ACCESS PAGES

TABLES
FORMS
QUERIES
REPORTS
PAGES
ID
Company
Product
Unit Price

CHAPTER 1

Getting Started

Are you ready to begin using Microsoft Access 2003? This chapter will help you get started.

INTRODUCTION TO ACCESS

Microsoft® Access 2003 is a database program that allows you to store and manage large collections of information. Access provides you with all the tools you need to create an efficient and effective database.

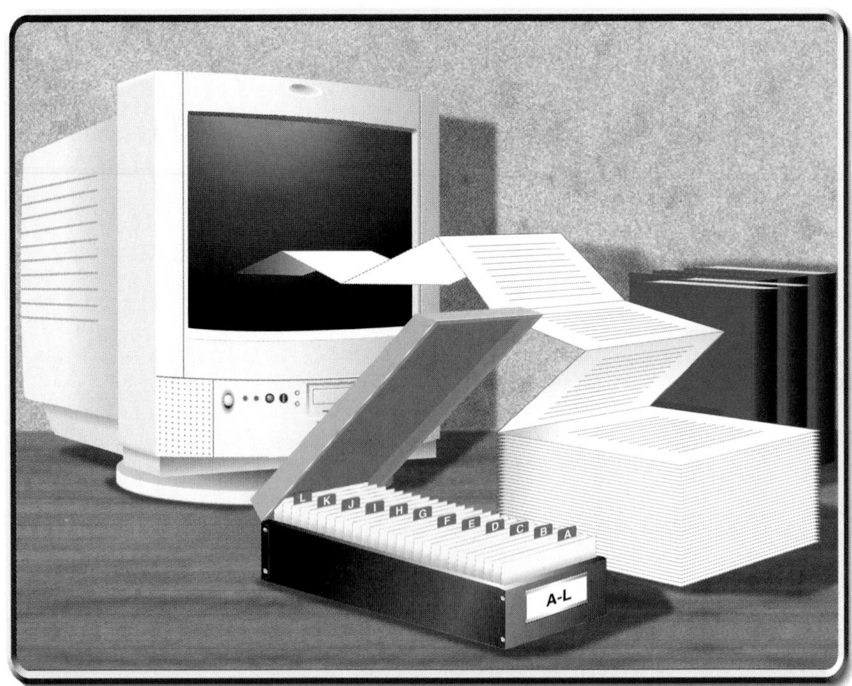

Many individuals use databases to store personal information such as addresses, music collections, recipes and wine lists.

Companies use databases to store information such as mailing lists, client orders, expenses, inventory and payroll.

DATABASE APPLICATIONS

Store Information

A database stores and manages a collection of information related to a particular subject or purpose. You can efficiently review, add, update and organize the information stored in a database.

Find Information

You can instantly locate information of interest in a database. For example, you can find all clients with the last name "Smith." You can also perform more advanced searches, such as finding all clients living in California who purchased more than $1,000 of your products last year.

Analyze and Print Information

You can perform calculations on the information in a database to help you make quick, accurate and informed decisions. You can neatly present the information in professionally designed reports.

START ACCESS

You can start Access to create a new database or work with a database you previously created.

When you finish using Access, you can exit the program. You should always exit all open programs before turning off your computer.

START ACCESS

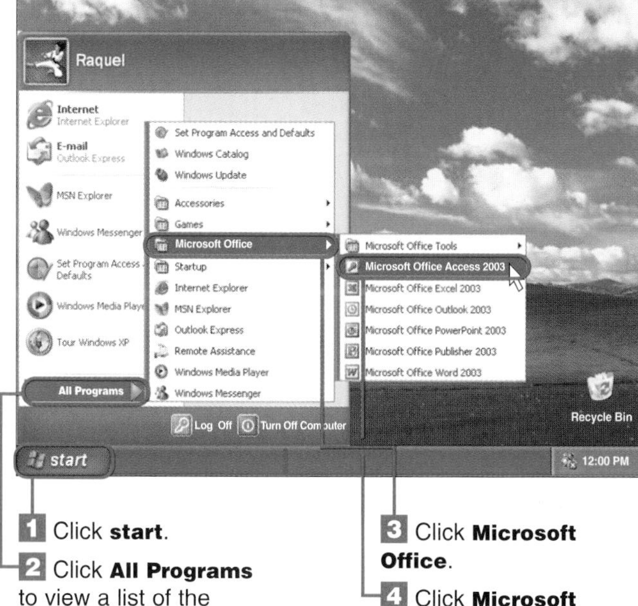

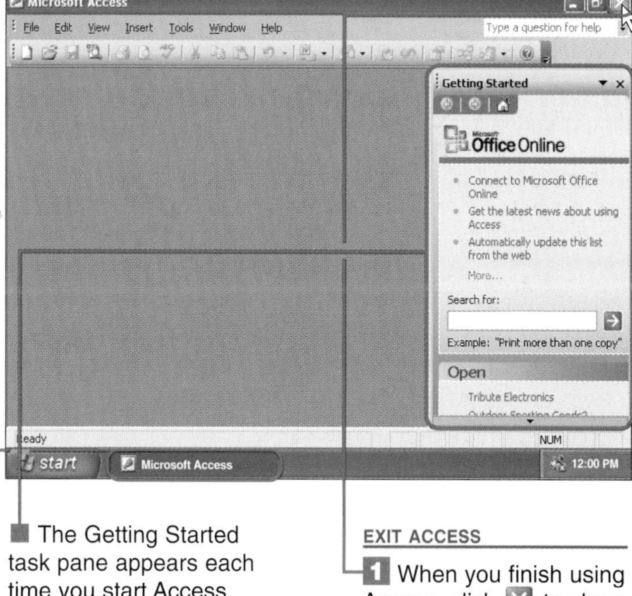

1 Click **start**.

2 Click **All Programs** to view a list of the programs on your computer.

*Note: If you are using an earlier version of Windows, click **Programs** in step 2.*

3 Click **Microsoft Office**.

4 Click **Microsoft Office Access 2003**.

■ The Microsoft Access window appears.

■ The Getting Started task pane appears each time you start Access, allowing you to quickly perform common tasks.

■ A button for the Microsoft Access window appears on the taskbar.

EXIT ACCESS

1 When you finish using Access, click ☒ to close the Microsoft Access window and exit Access.

PARTS OF A DATABASE

A database consists of objects such as tables, forms, queries, reports and pages.

Tables

A table stores a collection of information about a specific topic, such as a mailing list. You can have one or more tables in a database. A table consists of fields and records.

Address ID	First Name	Last Name	Address	City	State/Province	Postal Code
1	Janet	Smith	258 Linton Ave.	New York	NY	10010
2	Mark	Taylor	50 Tree Lane	Boston	MA	02117
3	Nancy	King	68 Cracker Ave.	San Francisco	CA	94110
4	Jack	Adams	47 Crosby Ave.	Las Vegas	NV	89116
5	Amy	Martin	26 Arnold Cres.	Jacksonville	FL	32256
6	Kevin	Turner	401 Idon Dr.	Nashville	TN	37243
7	Julie	Brown	10 Heldon St.	Atlanta	GA	30375
8	Matt	Cole	36 Buzzard St.	Boston	MA	02118
9	Frank	Hill	15 Bizzo Pl.	New York	NY	10020
10	Erin	Baker	890 Apple St.	San Diego	CA	92121

Field

A field is a specific category of information in a table, such as the first names of all your customers.

Record

A record is a collection of information about one person, place or thing in a table, such as the name and address of one customer.

Forms

Forms provide a quick way to view, enter and edit information in a database by presenting information in an attractive, easy-to-use format. Forms display boxes that clearly show you where to enter and/or edit information. Forms usually display one record at a time.

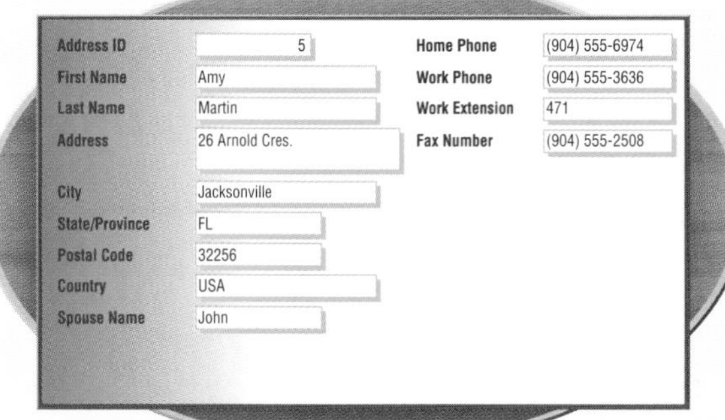

Queries

Queries allow you to find information of interest in a database. You can enter criteria in a query to specify what information you want to find. For example, you can create a query to find every customer who lives in California.

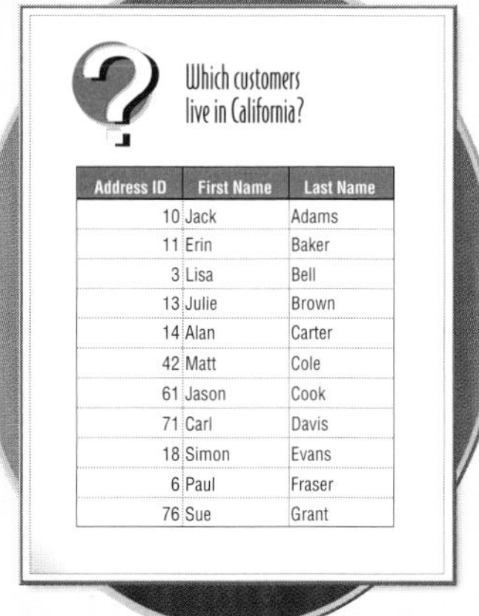

Address ID	First Name	Last Name
10	Jack	Adams
11	Erin	Baker
3	Lisa	Bell
13	Julie	Brown
14	Alan	Carter
42	Matt	Cole
61	Jason	Cook
71	Carl	Davis
18	Simon	Evans
6	Paul	Fraser
76	Sue	Grant

Reports

Reports are professional-looking documents that summarize information from a database. You can perform calculations in a report to help you analyze the data. For example, you can create a report that displays the total sales for each product.

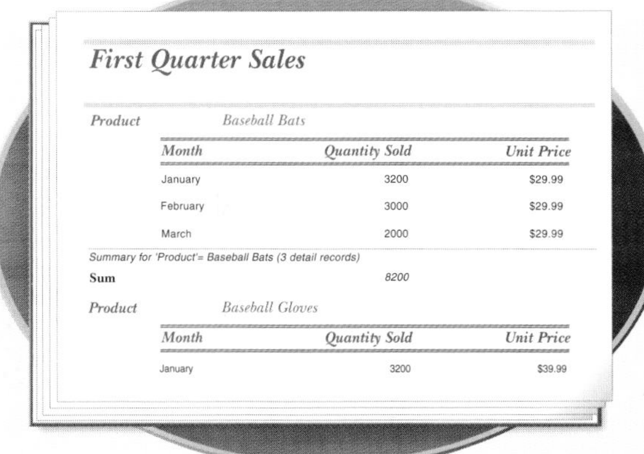

First Quarter Sales

Product *Baseball Bats*

Month	Quantity Sold	Unit Price
January	3200	$29.99
February	3000	$29.99
March	2000	$29.99

Summary for 'Product'= Baseball Bats (3 detail records)

Sum *8200*

Product *Baseball Gloves*

Month	Quantity Sold	Unit Price
January	3200	$39.99

Pages

Data access pages are Web pages that connect directly to the information in your database. You can use these pages to view, enter, edit and analyze data in your database from the Internet or your company's intranet.

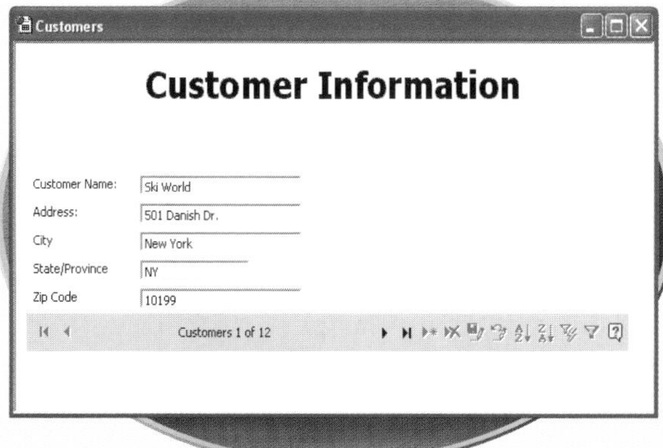

PLAN A DATABASE

You should take the time to plan your database. A well-planned database helps ensure that you will be able to perform tasks efficiently and accurately.

Determine the Purpose of Your Database

Decide what information you want your database to store and how you plan to use the information. If colleagues, friends or family members will use the database, you should consult with them to determine how they plan to use the database.

Determine the Tables You Need

Gather all the information you want to store in your database and then divide the information into separate tables. Each table should contain information for only one subject, such as a list of customer addresses.

The same information should not appear in more than one table in your database. You can work more efficiently and reduce errors if you only need to update information in one table.

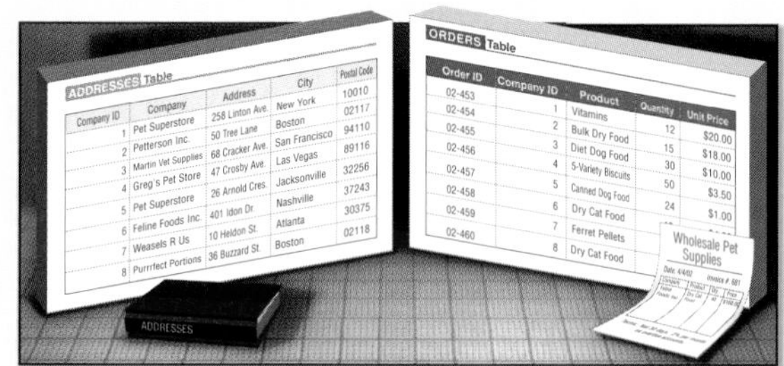

Determine the Fields You Need

A field is a specific category of information in a table, such as the last name of every client.

➢ Each field should relate directly to the subject of a table.

➢ Make sure you break information in a table into its smallest parts. For example, break down names into two fields called First Name and Last Name.

➢ Try to keep the number of fields in a table to a minimum. Tables with many fields increase the time Access takes to process information.

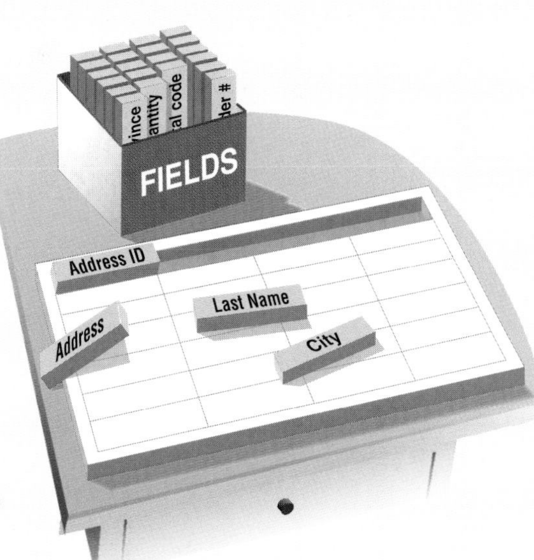

➢ Do not include a field that contains data you can calculate using other fields. For example, if a table includes a Unit Price field and a Quantity field, do not include a field that multiplies the values in these two fields. Access can perform the calculations for you and will update the calculations each time you change values in the fields.

Determine the Primary Key in Each Table

Each table in your database should have a primary key. A primary key is one or more fields that uniquely identifies each record in a table. For example, the primary key in a table containing employee information can be the social security number for each employee.

Social Security #	First Name	Last Name	Address	City	State/Province	Postal Code
11-1111	Jack	Adams	258 Linton Ave.	New York	NY	10010
2-22-2222	Frank	Hill	50 Tree Lane	Boston	MA	02117
3-33-3333	Kevin	Turner	68 Cracker Ave.	San Francisco	CA	94110
444-44-4444	Linda	Harris	47 Crosby Ave.	Las Vegas	NV	89116
600-60-6000	Carl	Davis	26 Arnold Cres.	Jacksonville	FL	32256
777-77-7777	Alan	Carter	401 Idon Dr.	Nashville	TN	37243
888-88-8888	Mary	Wilson	10 Heldon St.	Atlanta	GA	30375
999-99-9999	Janet	Young	36 Buzzard St.	Boston	MA	02118
000-00-0000	Lisa	Bell	15 Bizzo Pl.	New York	NY	10020
000-11-2222	Paul	Fraser	890 Apple St.	San Diego	CA	92121

Determine the Relationships Between Tables

Relationships between tables allow Access to bring together related information stored in separate tables in your database. For example, you can create a relationship between the Customers table and the Orders table. You usually relate the primary key in one table to a matching field in another table to create a relationship.

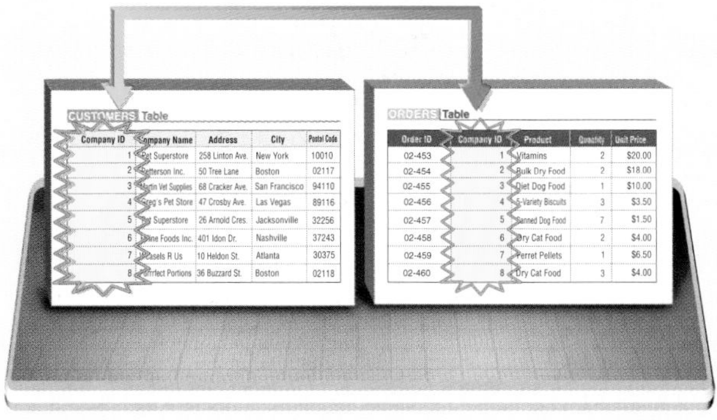

CREATE A DATABASE USING THE DATABASE WIZARD

You can use the Database Wizard to quickly and easily create a database. The wizard saves you time by creating the tables, forms, queries and reports for your database.

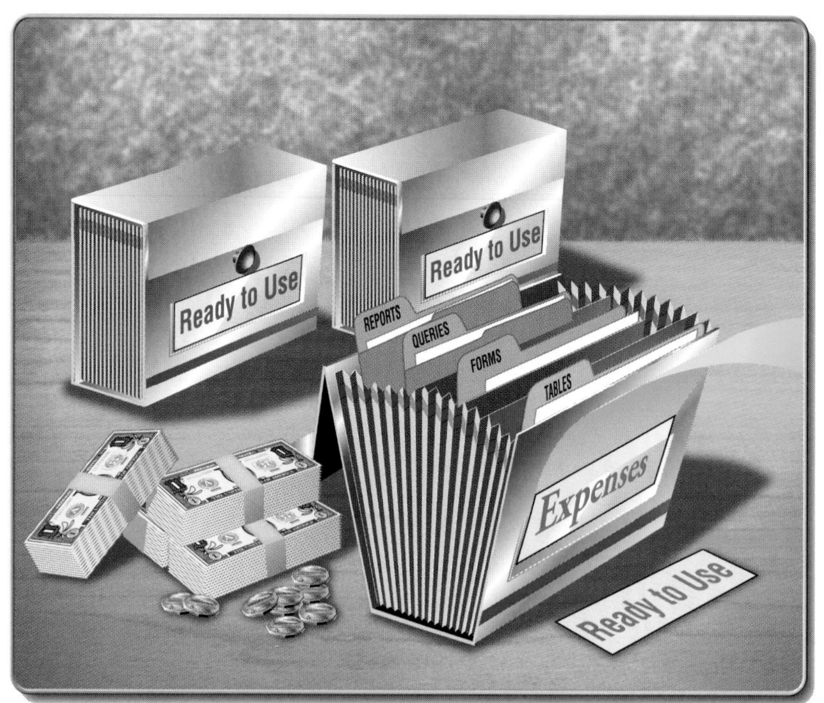

You can use the Database Wizard to create many types of databases, such as databases for contact management, expenses, inventory control and order entry.

You can have only one database open at a time. Access will close a database displayed on your screen when you create a new database.

CREATE A DATABASE USING THE DATABASE WIZARD

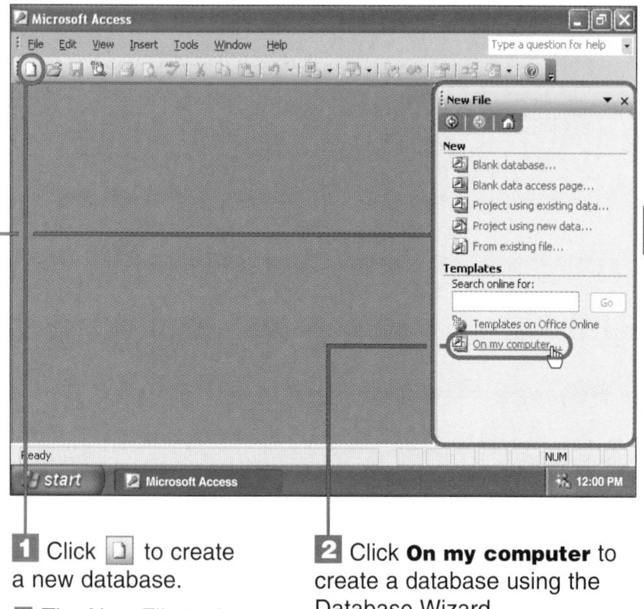

1 Click [new] to create a new database.

■ The New File task pane appears.

2 Click **On my computer** to create a database using the Database Wizard.

■ The Templates dialog box appears.

3 Click the **Databases** tab.

4 Click the database template that best describes the type of database you want to create.

5 Click **OK** to create the database.

■ The File New Database dialog box appears.

How can I quickly select a database template I recently used?

The New File task pane displays the names of the last four database templates you used. To display the New File task pane, perform step 1 on page 10.

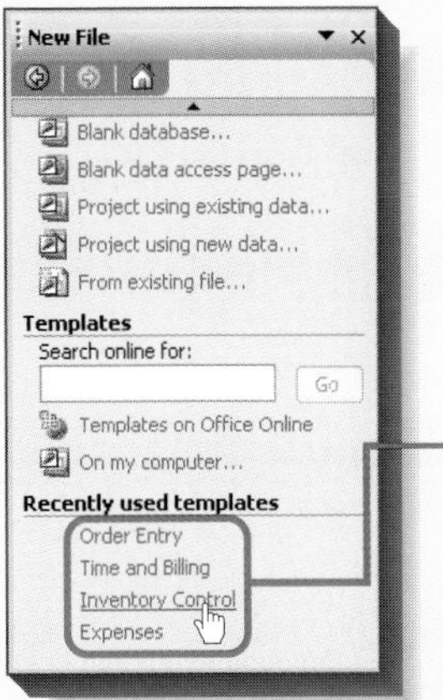

1 To select a database template you recently used, click the name of the template.

How can I get more database templates?

When you are connected to the Internet, click **Templates on Office Online** on the New File task pane. To display the New File task pane, perform step 1 on page 10. A Web page will appear, allowing you to obtain more database templates that you can use.

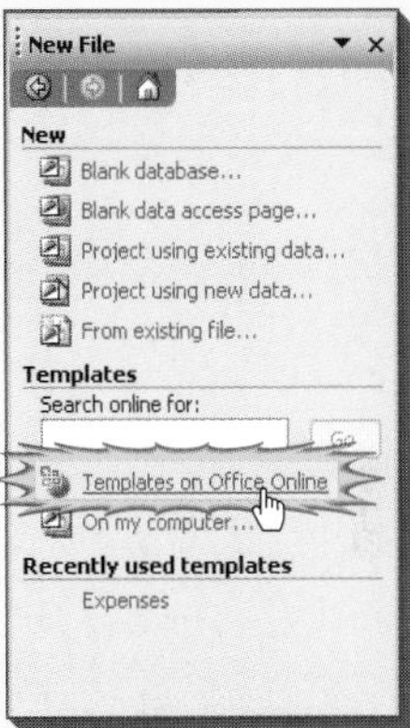

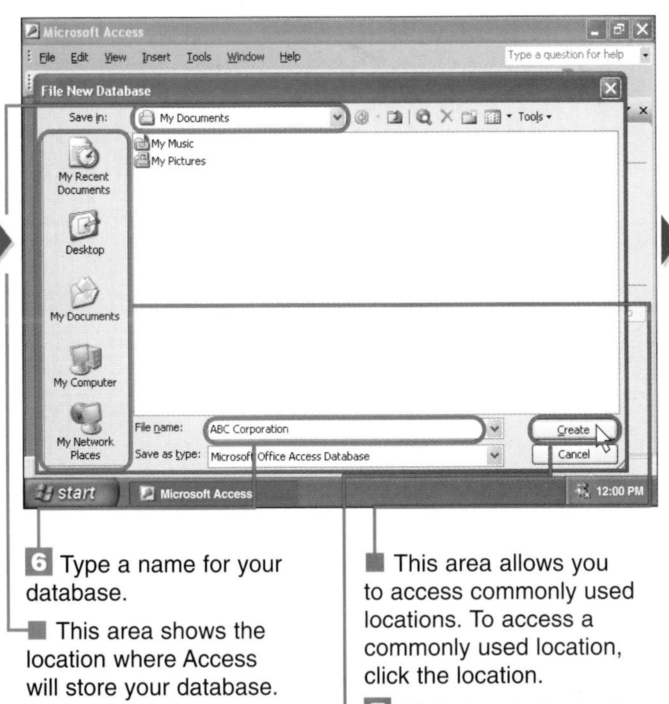

6 Type a name for your database.

■ This area shows the location where Access will store your database. You can click this area to change the location.

■ This area allows you to access commonly used locations. To access a commonly used location, click the location.

7 Click **Create** to create the database.

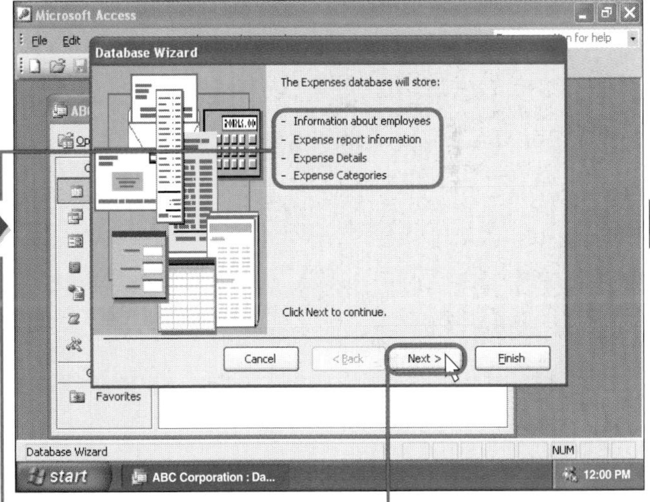

■ The Database Wizard appears.

■ This area describes the type of information the database will store.

8 Click **Next** to continue.

CONTINUED

CREATE A DATABASE USING THE DATABASE WIZARD

The Database Wizard displays the fields that each table in your database will include. You can choose to include additional fields in each table.

A field is a specific category of information in a table, such as the last names of all your customers.

CREATE A DATABASE USING THE DATABASE WIZARD (CONTINUED)

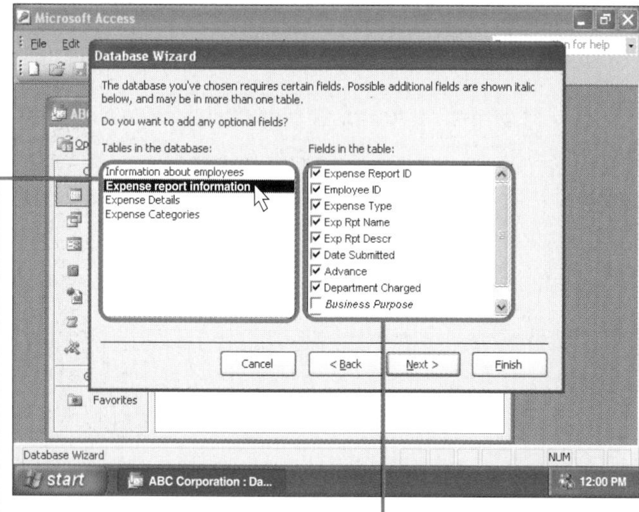

- This area displays the tables Access will include in your database.

9 Click a table to display the fields in the table.

- This area displays the fields in the table you selected. The fields displaying a check mark (✔) are required fields and must be included in the table. The fields shown in *italics* are optional.

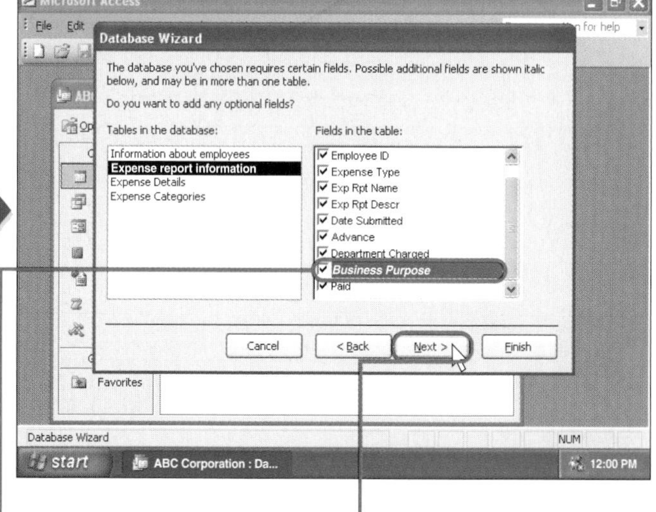

10 To add an optional field to the table, click the box (☐) beside the field (☐ changes to ☑). Repeat this step for each optional field you want to include in the table.

- To add optional fields to other tables in the database, repeat steps **9** and **10** for each table.

11 Click **Next** to continue.

Can I remove a required field from a table in the Database Wizard?

No. You can remove a required field from a table only after you finish creating the database. When you try to remove a required field in the Database Wizard, a message will appear, stating that the field is required and must be selected. To remove a field from a table after you finish creating the database, see page 47.

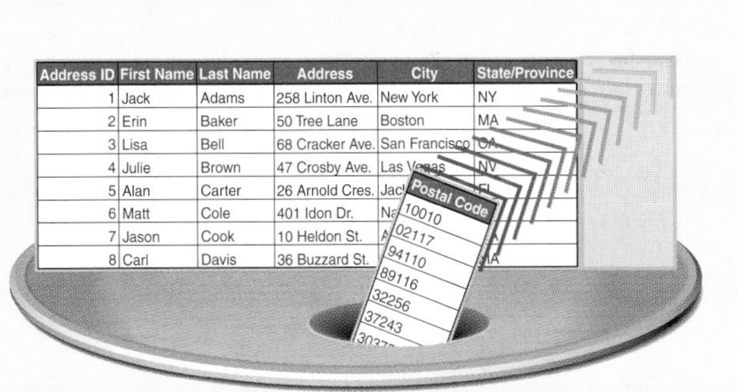

Address ID | First Name | Last Name | Address | City | State/Province
1 | Jack | Adams | 258 Linton Ave. | New York | NY
2 | Erin | Baker | 50 Tree Lane | Boston | MA
3 | Lisa | Bell | 68 Cracker Ave. | San Francisco
4 | Julie | Brown | 47 Crosby Ave. | NV
5 | Alan | Carter | 26 Arnold Cres.
6 | Matt | Cole | 401 Idon Dr.
7 | Jason | Cook | 10 Heldon St.
8 | Carl | Davis | 36 Buzzard St.
Postal Code
10010
02117
94110
89116
32256
37243

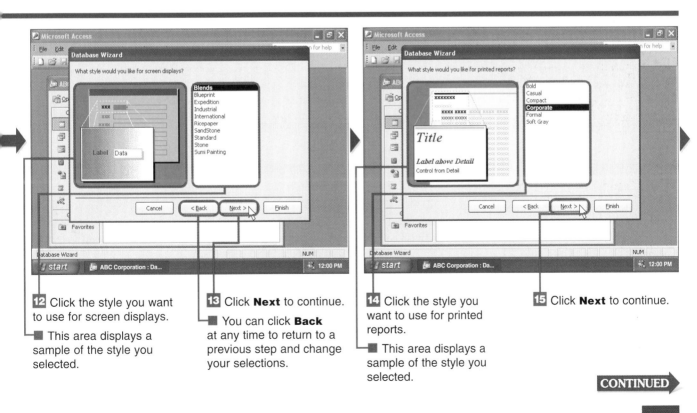

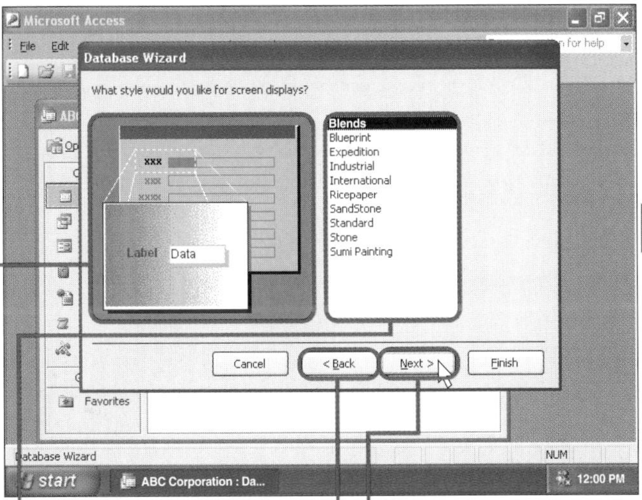

12 Click the style you want to use for screen displays.

- This area displays a sample of the style you selected.

13 Click **Next** to continue.

- You can click **Back** at any time to return to a previous step and change your selections.

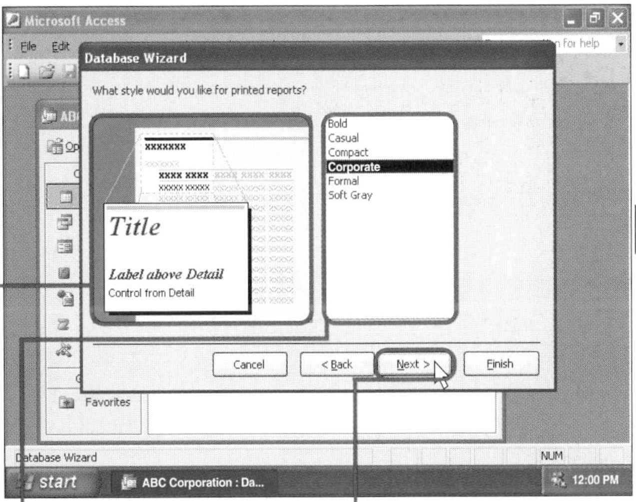

14 Click the style you want to use for printed reports.

- This area displays a sample of the style you selected.

15 Click **Next** to continue.

CONTINUED

CREATE A DATABASE USING THE DATABASE WIZARD

When the Database Wizard finishes creating your database, Access displays a switchboard that you can use to perform common tasks in the database.

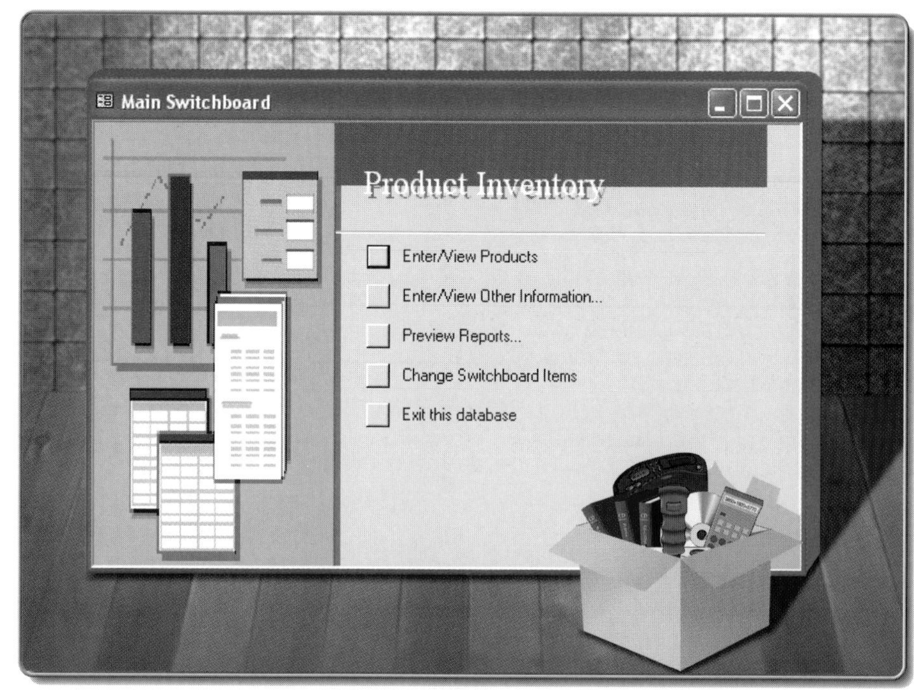

A switchboard is a menu that offers a list of choices.

CREATE A DATABASE USING THE DATABASE WIZARD (CONTINUED)

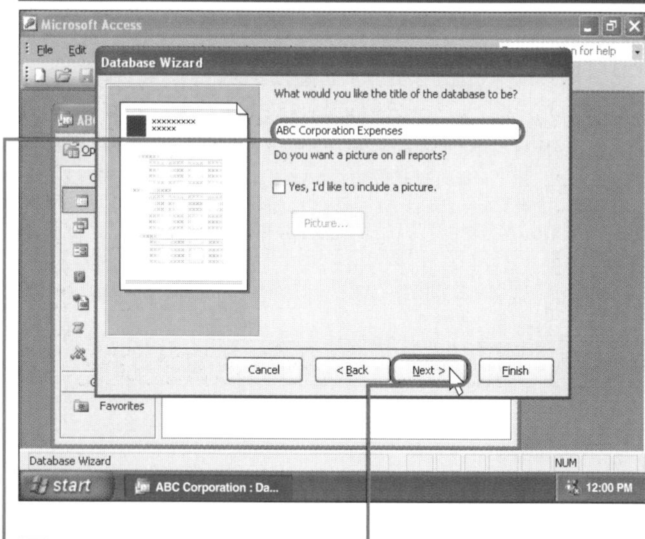

16 This area displays the title of your database. To use a different title, type the title.

17 Click **Next** to continue.

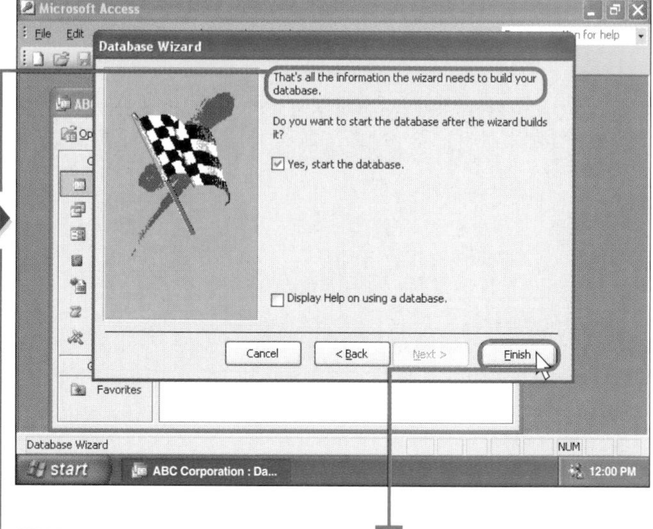

■ The Database Wizard indicates that you have provided all the information needed to create your database.

18 Click **Finish** to create your database.

Why does this dialog box appear when I finish using the Database Wizard?

Access needs you to enter information, such as your company name and address, to finish setting up the database.

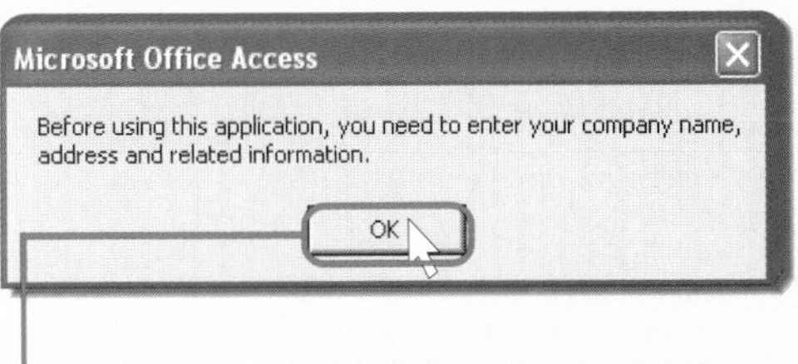

■ To close the dialog box and display a form that provides areas for you to enter your information, click **OK**. To enter data into a form, see page 148.

Do I have to use the Main Switchboard to work with my database?

No. Instead of using the Main Switchboard window, you can use the Database window to work with your database. To quickly display the Database window at any time, press the F11 key. For more information on the Database window, see page 20.

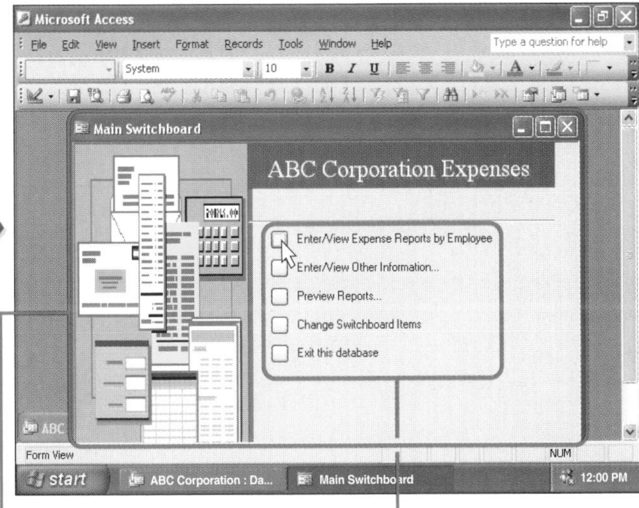

■ Access creates the objects for your database, including tables, forms, queries and reports.

■ The Main Switchboard window appears, displaying options you can select to perform common tasks in the database.

19 To perform a task, click the task you want to perform.

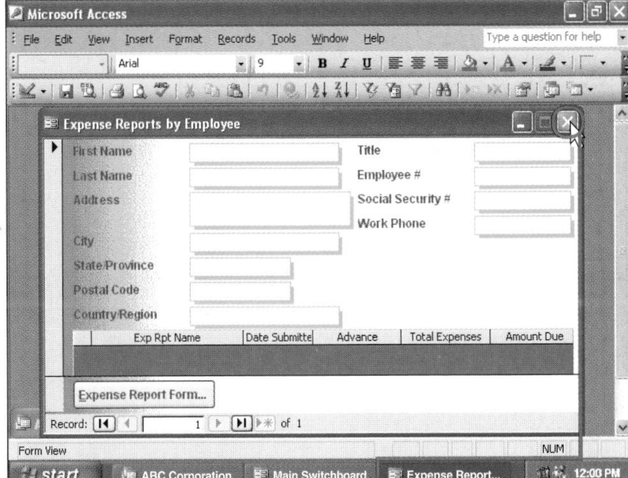

■ The database object that allows you to perform the task appears.

*Note: If a list of additional tasks appears, repeat step **19** to select the task you want to perform.*

20 When you finish using the database object, click ☒ to close the object and return to the switchboard.

CREATE A BLANK DATABASE

If you want to design your own database, you can create a blank database. Creating a blank database gives you the most flexibility and control when designing a database.

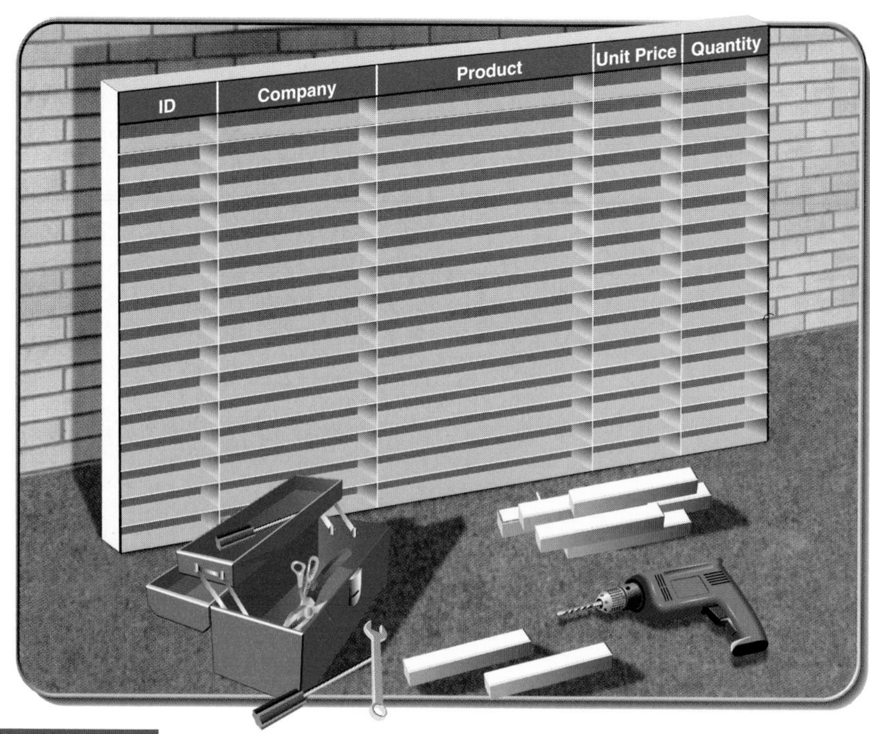

You can have only one database open at a time. Access will close a database displayed on your screen when you create or open another database.

CREATE A BLANK DATABASE

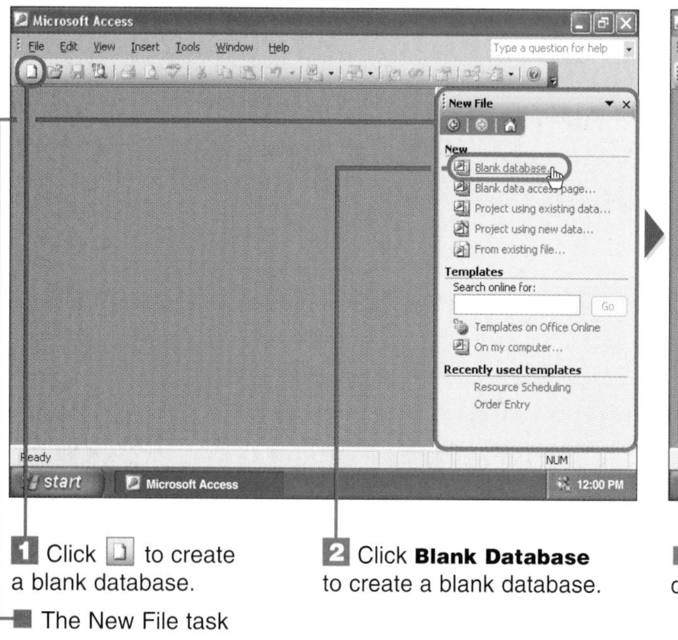

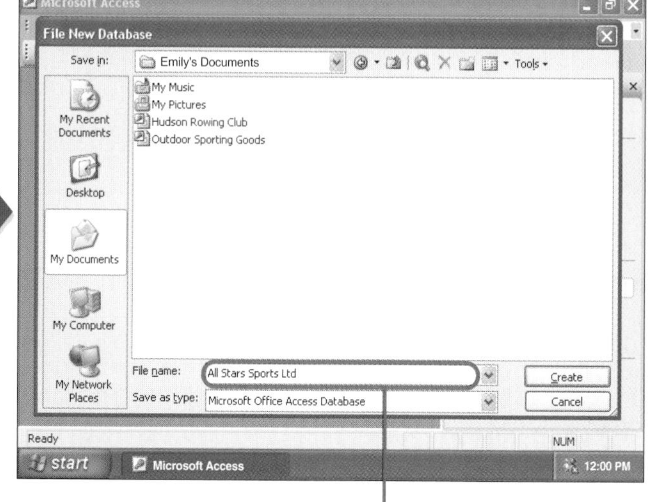

1 Click [New] to create a blank database.

■ The New File task pane appears.

2 Click **Blank Database** to create a blank database.

■ The File New Database dialog box appears.

3 Type a name for your database.

What are the commonly used locations that I can access when saving a blank database?

Provides access to databases and folders you recently worked with.	Allows you to store a database on the Windows desktop.	Provides a convenient place to store a database.	Allows you to store a database on a drive on your computer, such as a floppy or external hard drive.	Allows you to store a database on your network.

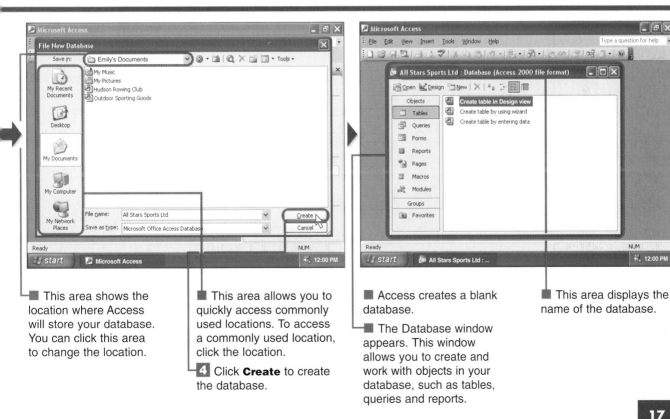

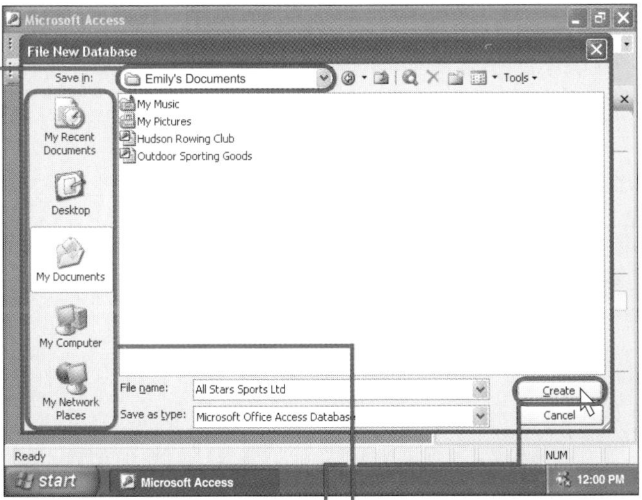

- This area shows the location where Access will store your database. You can click this area to change the location.
- This area allows you to quickly access commonly used locations. To access a commonly used location, click the location.

4 Click **Create** to create the database.

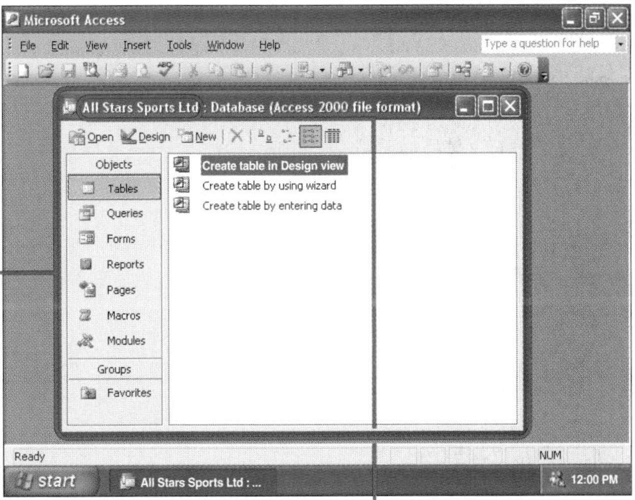

- Access creates a blank database.
- The Database window appears. This window allows you to create and work with objects in your database, such as tables, queries and reports.
- This area displays the name of the database.

OPEN A DATABASE

You can open a database to view the database on your screen. Opening a database allows you to review and make changes to the database.

You can have only one database open at a time. Access will close a database displayed on your screen when you open another database.

OPEN A DATABASE

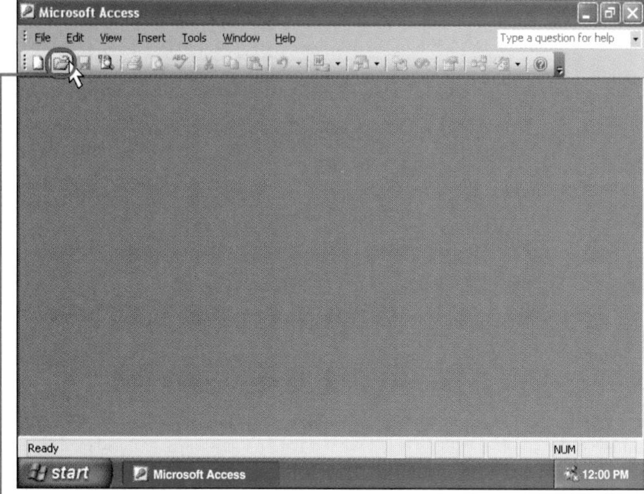

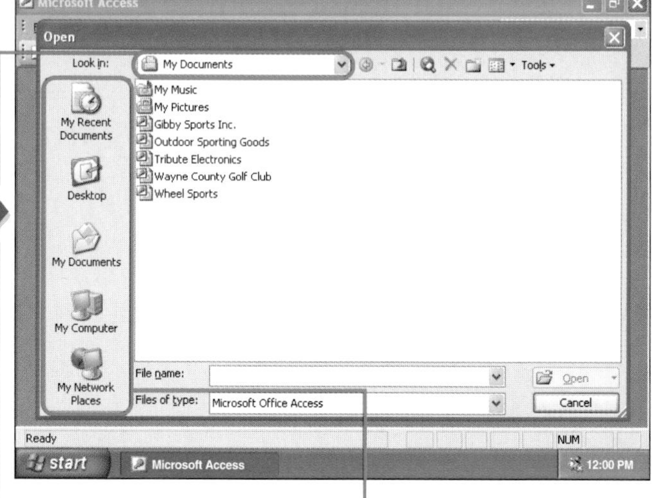

1 Click to open a database.

■ The Open dialog box appears.

■ This area shows the location of the displayed databases. You can click this area to change the location.

■ This area allows you to access databases in commonly used locations. You can click a location to display the databases in the location.

Note: For information on the commonly used locations, see the top of page 17.

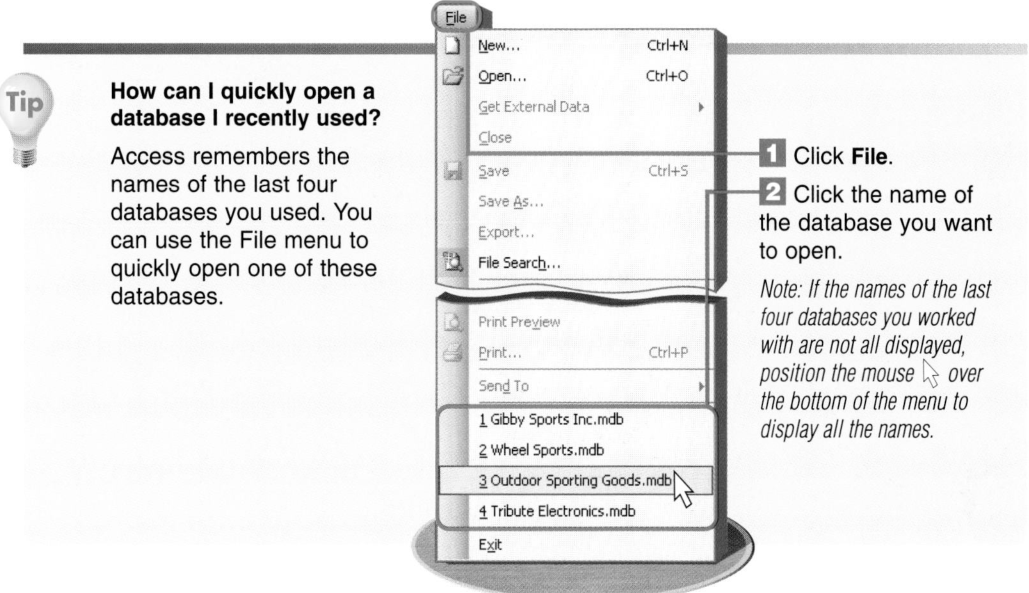

Tip

How can I quickly open a database I recently used?

Access remembers the names of the last four databases you used. You can use the File menu to quickly open one of these databases.

1 Click **File**.

2 Click the name of the database you want to open.

Note: If the names of the last four databases you worked with are not all displayed, position the mouse over the bottom of the menu to display all the names.

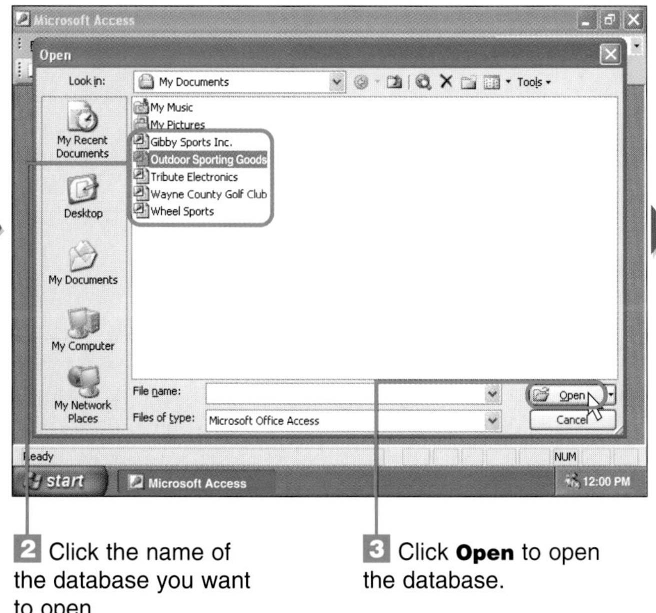

2 Click the name of the database you want to open.

3 Click **Open** to open the database.

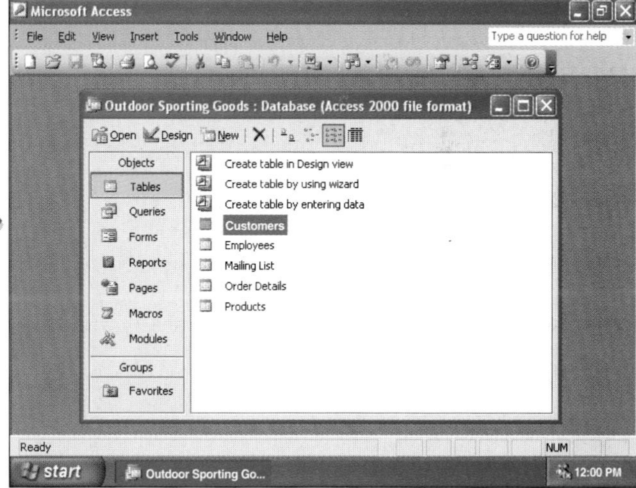

■ The database opens and appears on your screen. You can now review and make changes to the database.

Note: A Security Warning dialog box may appear, asking you to confirm that you want to open the database. To open the database, click ***Open***.

USING THE DATABASE WINDOW

You can use the Database window to open and work with objects in your database, such as tables, queries, forms, reports and pages.

USING THE DATABASE WINDOW

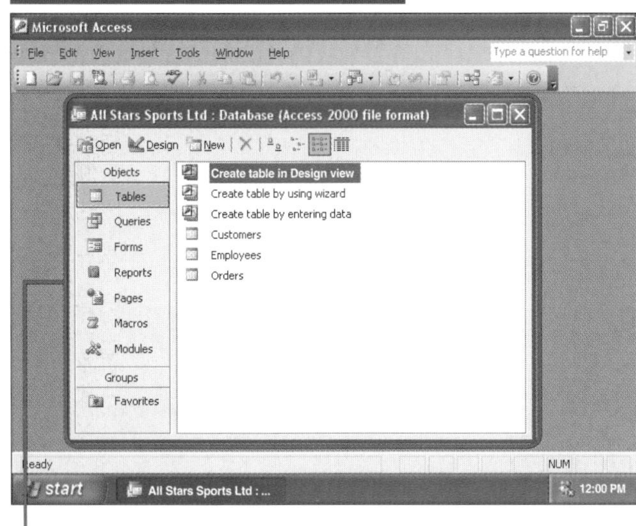

■ Each table, query, form, report and data access page in your database appears in the Database window.

■ If the Database window is hidden behind other windows, press the F11 key to display the Database window.

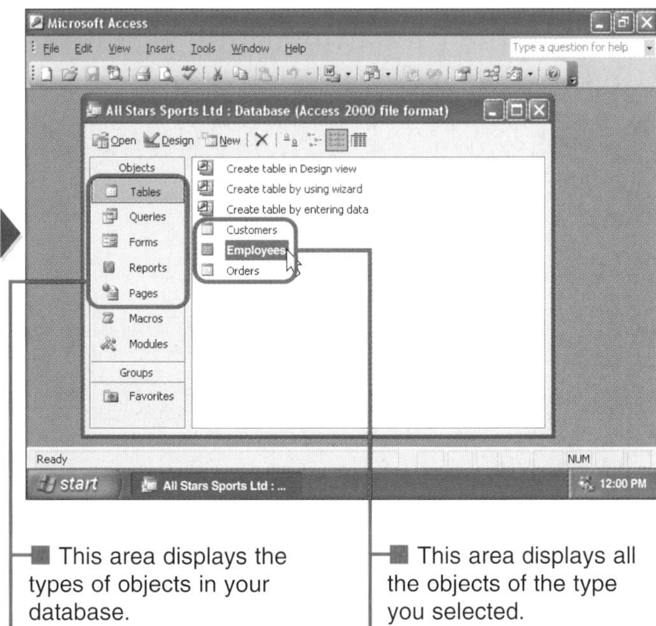

■ This area displays the types of objects in your database.

1 Click the type of object you want to work with.

■ This area displays all the objects of the type you selected.

2 To open an object, double-click the object.

What types of objects will I find in the Database window?

Tables

Tables store information about a specific topic, such as a mailing list.

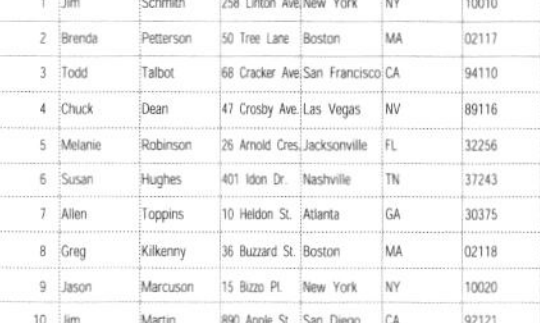

Address ID	First Name	Last Name	Address	City	State/Province	Postal Code
1	Jim	Schmith	258 Linton Ave.	New York	NY	10010
2	Brenda	Petterson	50 Tree Lane	Boston	MA	02117
3	Todd	Talbot	68 Cracker Ave.	San Francisco	CA	94110
4	Chuck	Dean	47 Crosby Ave.	Las Vegas	NV	89116
5	Melanie	Robinson	26 Arnold Cres.	Jacksonville	FL	32256
6	Susan	Hughes	401 Idon Dr.	Nashville	TN	37243
7	Allen	Toppins	10 Heldon St.	Atlanta	GA	30375
8	Greg	Kilkenny	36 Buzzard St.	Boston	MA	02118
9	Jason	Marcuson	15 Bizzo Pl.	New York	NY	10020
10	Jim	Martin	890 Apple St.	San Diego	CA	92121

Queries

Queries allow you to find information of interest in your database.

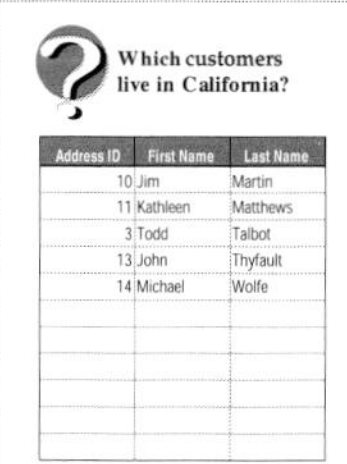

Address ID	First Name	Last Name
10	Jim	Martin
11	Kathleen	Matthews
3	Todd	Talbot
13	John	Thyfault
14	Michael	Wolfe

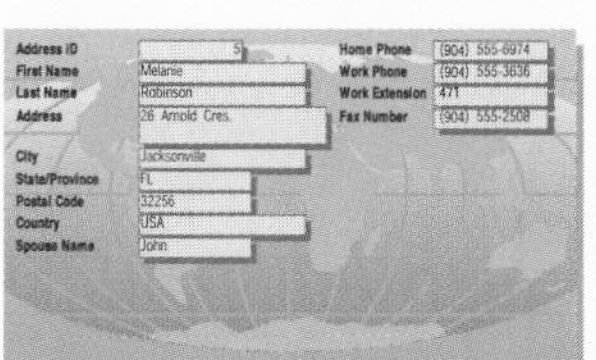

Forms

Forms provide a quick way to view, enter and edit data in your database.

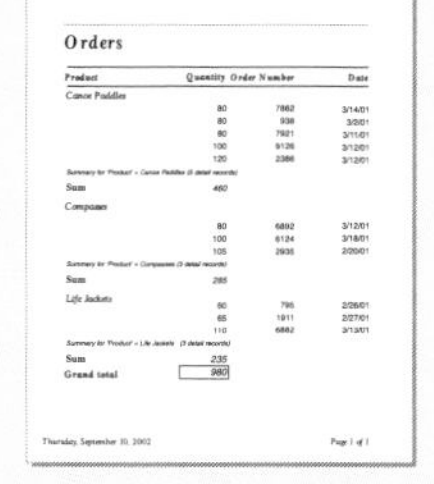

Reports

Reports summarize and print the data from your database in professional-looking documents.

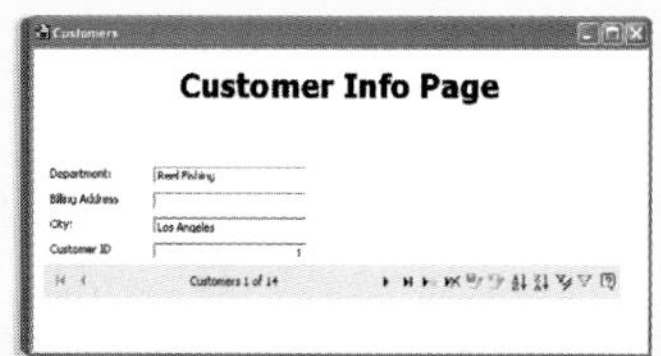

Pages

Data access pages allow you to view, enter, edit and analyze data in your database from the Internet or your company's intranet.

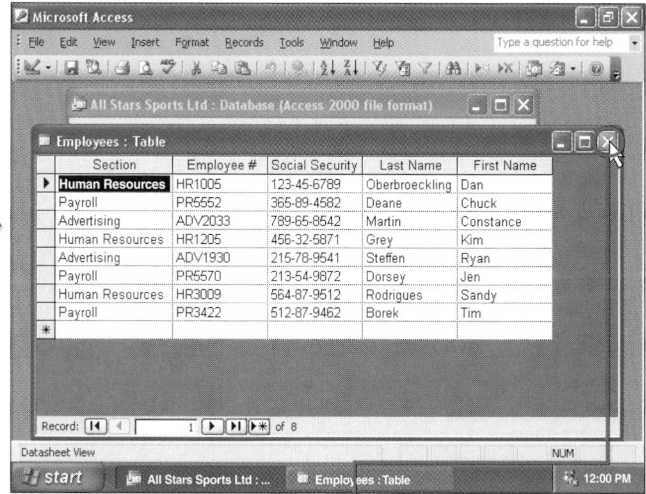

■ The object opens and appears on your screen.

3 When you finish working with the object, click ☒ to close the object and return to the Database window.

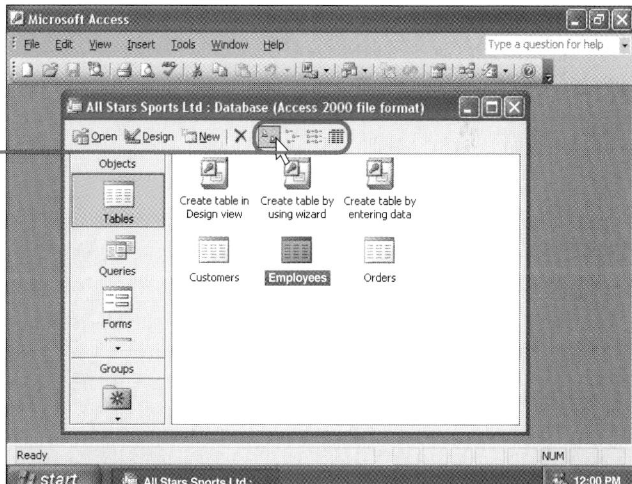

CHANGE APPEARANCE OF OBJECTS

1 To change the appearance of the objects in the Database window, click one of the following buttons.

- Large Icons
- Small Icons
- List
- Details

RENAME A DATABASE OBJECT

You can change the name of a database object, such as a table, form, query or report, to better describe the information stored in the object.

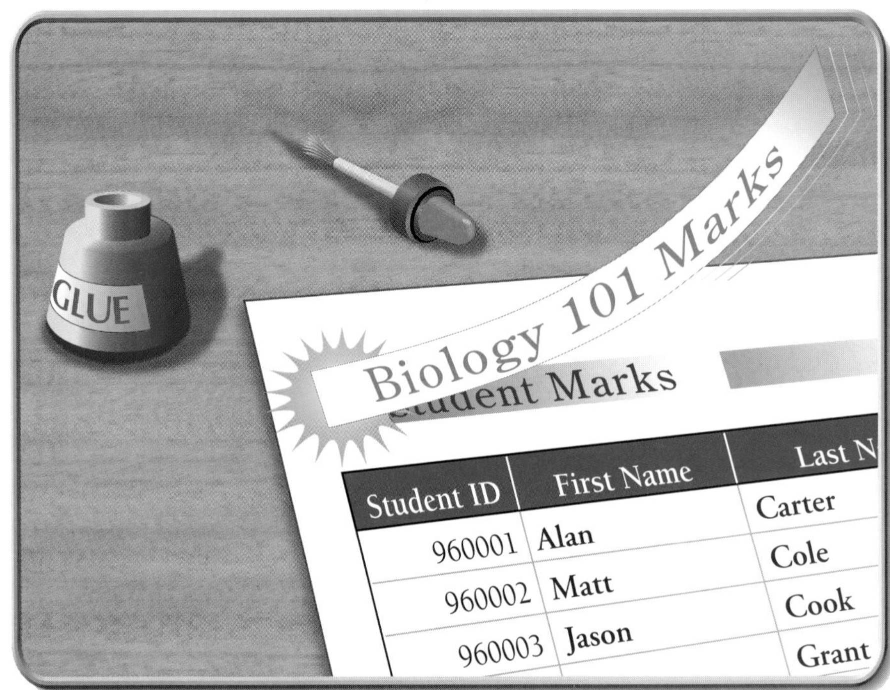

For information on renaming a data access page, see page 294.

RENAME A DATABASE OBJECT

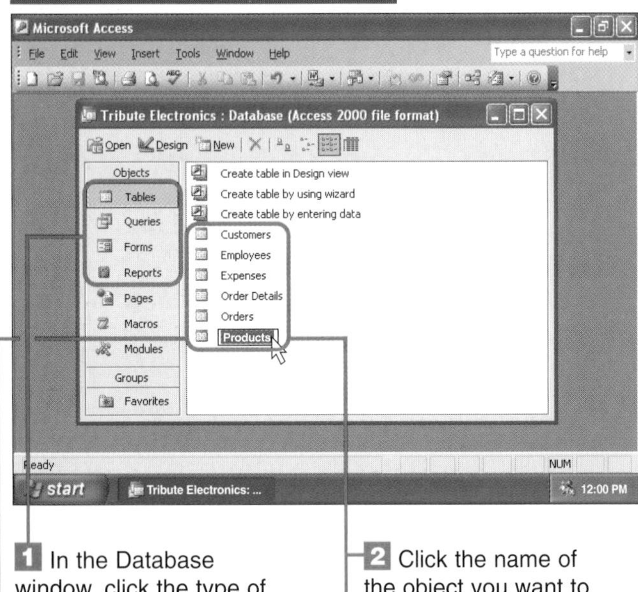

1 In the Database window, click the type of database object you want to rename.

■ This area displays all the objects of the type you selected.

2 Click the name of the object you want to rename.

3 After a few seconds, click the name again or press the F2 key. A black border appears around the name.

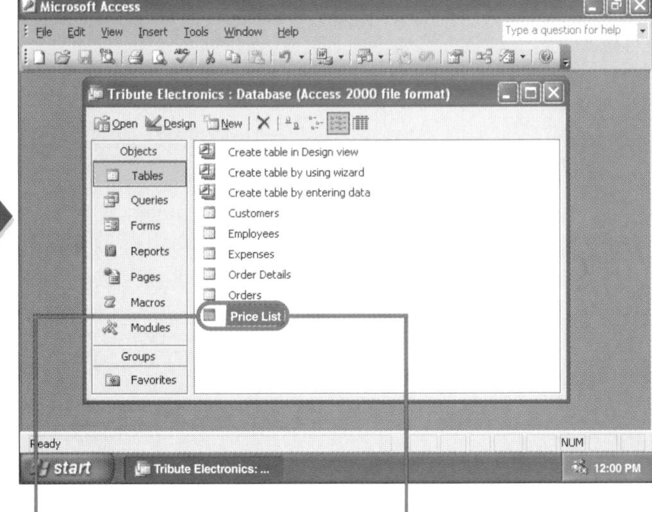

4 Type a new name for the object and then press the Enter key.

■ The object displays the new name.

DELETE A DATABASE OBJECT

If you no longer need a database object, such as a table, form, query or report, you can permanently delete the object from your database.

Before you delete an object, make sure other objects in your database do not depend on the object. For information on object dependencies, see page 124.

For information on deleting a data access page, see page 295.

DELETE A DATABASE OBJECT

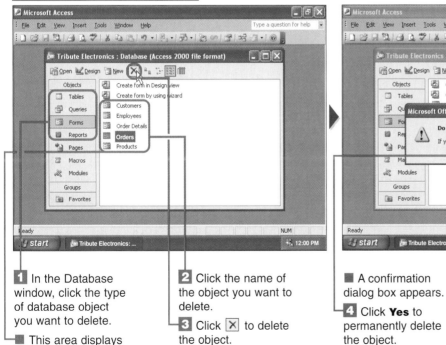

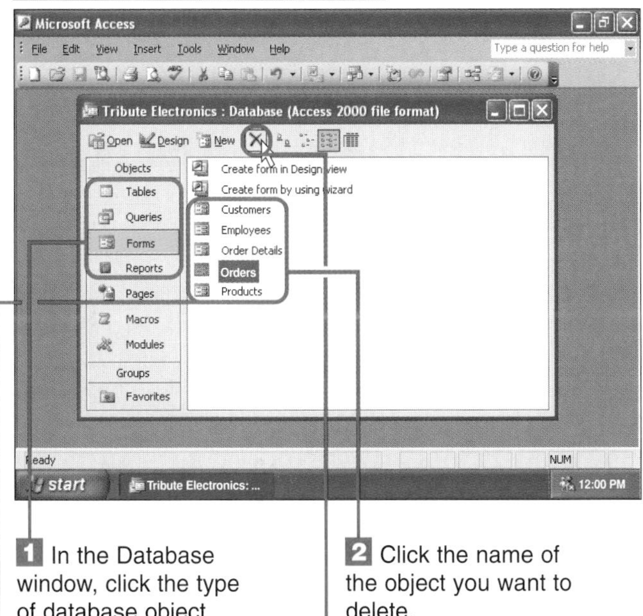

Microsoft Access
File Edit View Insert Tools Window Help
Type a question for help
Tribute Electronics : Database (Access 2000 file format)
Open Design New
Objects
Tables
Create form in Design view
Create form by using wizard
Microsoft Office Access
Do you want to permanently delete the form 'Orders'?
If you click Yes, you won't be able to undo the deletion.
Yes No
Modules
Groups
Favorites
Ready
NUM
start
Tribute Electronics: ...
12:00 PM

1 In the Database window, click the type of database object you want to delete.

■ This area displays all the objects of the type you selected.

2 Click the name of the object you want to delete.

3 Click ☒ to delete the object.

■ A confirmation dialog box appears.

4 Click **Yes** to permanently delete the object.

■ The object disappears from the Database window.

MINIMIZE A WINDOW

If you are not using a window, you can minimize the window to temporarily remove it from your screen. You can redisplay the window at any time.

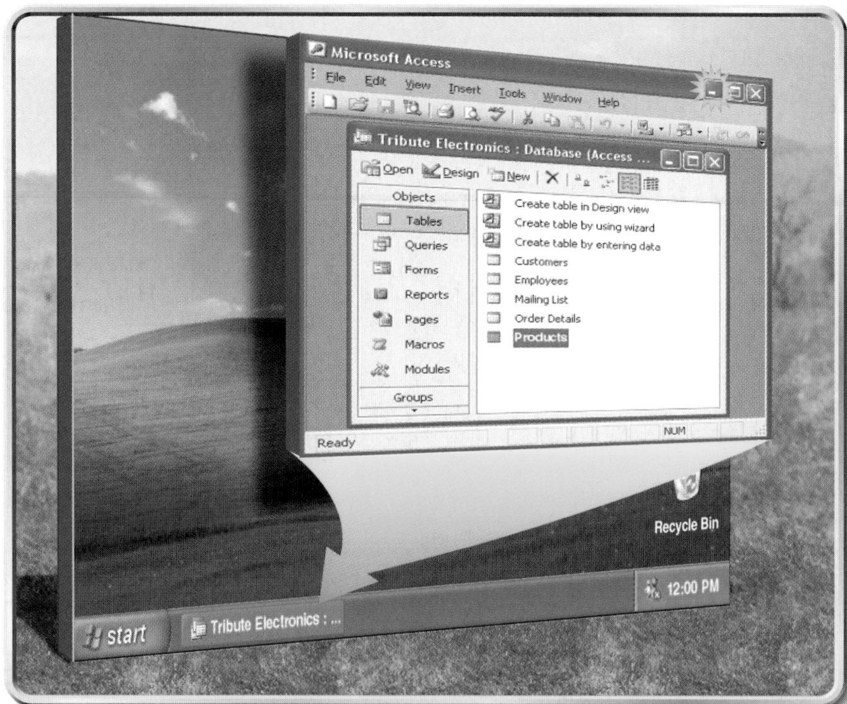

Minimizing a window allows you to temporarily put a window aside so you can work on another task.

MINIMIZE A WINDOW

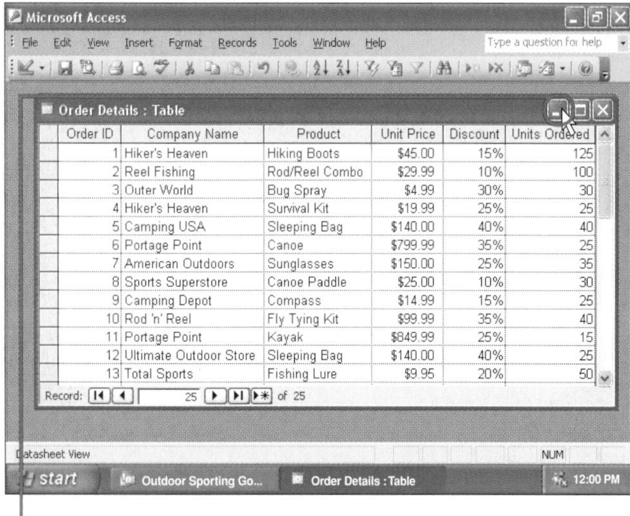

Order ID	Company Name	Product	Unit Price	Discount	Units Ordered
1	Hiker's Heaven	Hiking Boots	$45.00	15%	125
2	Reel Fishing	Rod/Reel Combo	$29.99	10%	100
3	Outer World	Bug Spray	$4.99	30%	30
4	Hiker's Heaven	Survival Kit	$19.99	25%	25
5	Camping USA	Sleeping Bag	$140.00	40%	40
6	Portage Point	Canoe	$799.99	35%	25
7	American Outdoors	Sunglasses	$150.00	25%	35
8	Sports Superstore	Canoe Paddle	$25.00	10%	30
9	Camping Depot	Compass	$14.99	15%	25
10	Rod 'n' Reel	Fly Tying Kit	$99.99	35%	40
11	Portage Point	Kayak	$849.99	25%	15
12	Ultimate Outdoor Store	Sleeping Bag	$140.00	40%	25
13	Total Sports	Fishing Lure	$9.95	20%	50

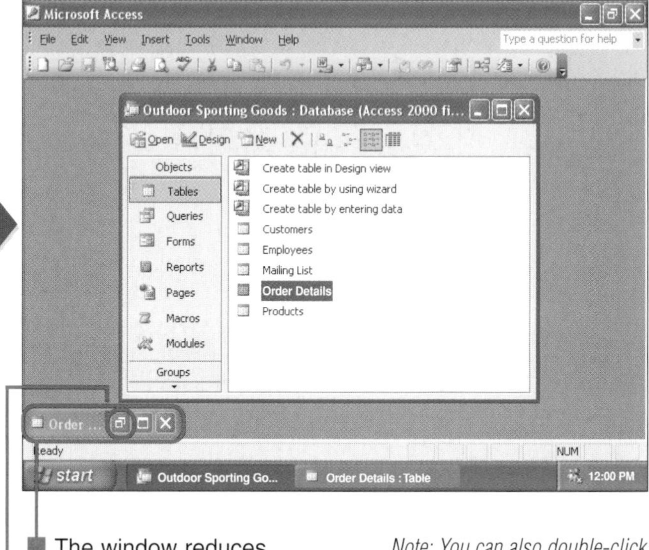

1 Click ▬ in the window you want to minimize.

■ The window reduces to a bar at the bottom of your screen.

■ To once again show the contents of the window, click ⧉ to restore the window to its original size.

Note: You can also double-click a blank area on the bar to once again show the contents of the window.

DISPLAY OR HIDE A TOOLBAR

Access offers several toolbars that you can display or hide at any time. Each toolbar contains buttons that you can use to perform common tasks.

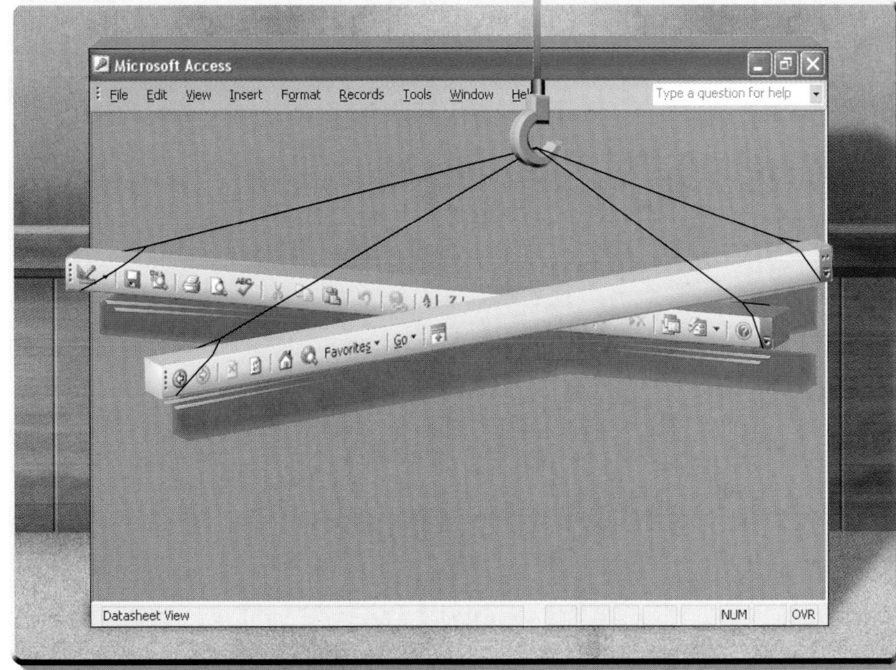

The available toolbars depend on the task you are performing.

DISPLAY OR HIDE A TOOLBAR

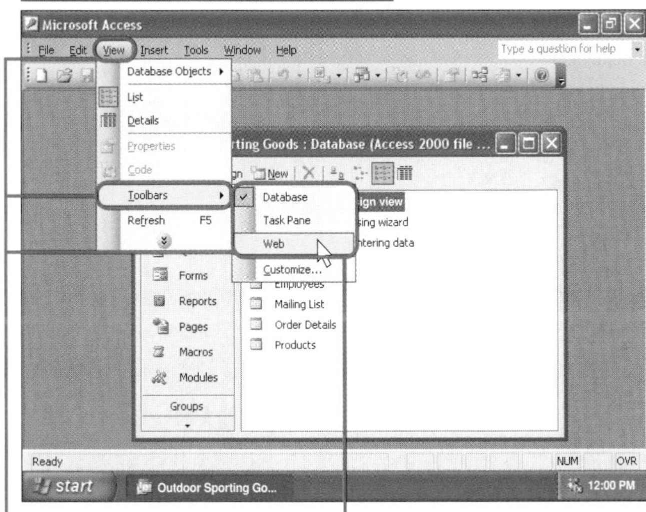

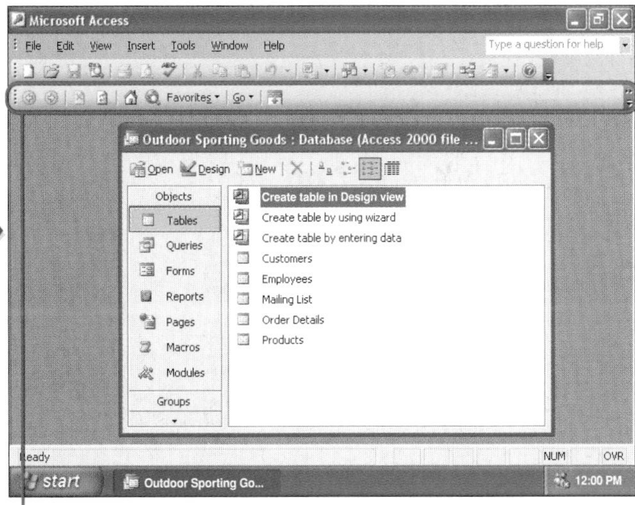

1 Click **View**.

2 Click **Toolbars**.

■ A list of toolbars appears. A check mark (✓) beside the name of a toolbar indicates that the toolbar is currently displayed.

Note: The Task Pane also appears in the list of toolbars. Like a toolbar, the Task Pane allows you to perform common tasks.

3 Click the name of the toolbar you want to display or hide.

■ Access displays or hides the toolbar you selected.

SEARCH FOR A DATABASE

If you cannot find a database you want to work with, you can search for the database.

SEARCH FOR A DATABASE

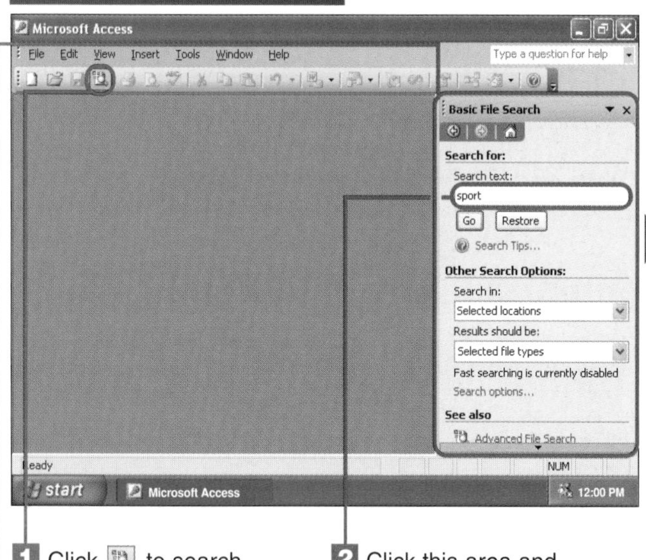

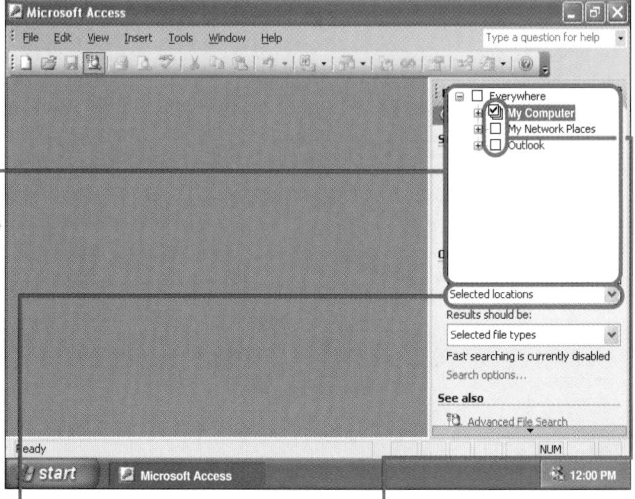

1 Click 🔍 to search for a database.

■ The Basic File Search task pane appears.

2 Click this area and type all or part of the name of the database you want to find.

*Note: If the area already contains text, drag the mouse I over the existing text before performing step **2**.*

3 Click ▾ in this area to select the locations you want to search.

■ A check mark (✔) appears beside each location that Access will search.

Note: By default, Access will search all the drives and folders on your computer.

4 You can click the box beside a location to add (☑) or remove (☐) a check mark.

5 Click outside the list of locations to close the list.

When selecting the locations I want to search, how can I display more locations?

Each location that displays a plus sign (⊞) contains hidden locations. To display hidden locations, click the plus sign (⊞) beside a location (⊞ changes to ⊟). To once again hide the locations, click the minus sign (⊟) beside a location.

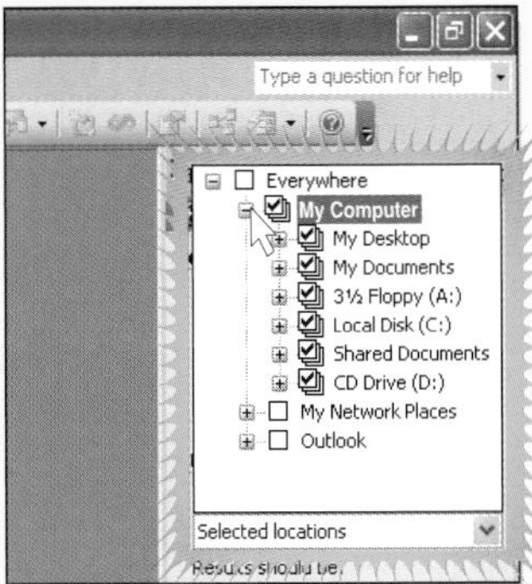

Can I view information about the databases that Access found?

Yes. To view information about a database that Access found, position the mouse over the database. A yellow box will appear, displaying the location of the database and the date you last made changes to the database.

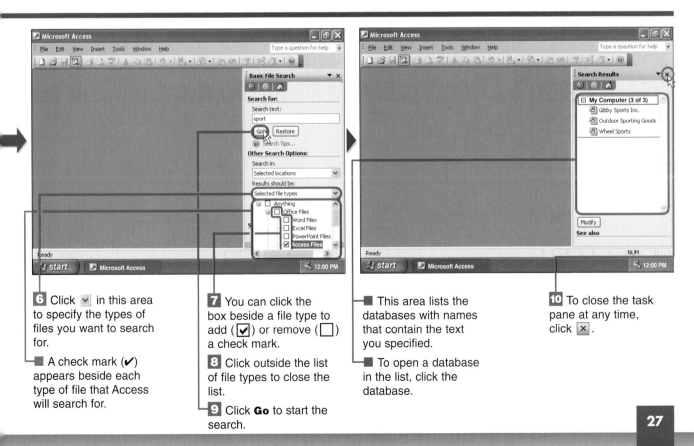

6 Click ▾ in this area to specify the types of files you want to search for.

■ A check mark (✔) appears beside each type of file that Access will search for.

7 You can click the box beside a file type to add (☑) or remove (☐) a check mark.

8 Click outside the list of file types to close the list.

9 Click **Go** to start the search.

■ This area lists the databases with names that contain the text you specified.

■ To open a database in the list, click the database.

10 To close the task pane at any time, click ✕.

BACK UP A DATABASE

You can make a backup copy of your database. Regularly making a backup copy helps minimize any loss of information that may be caused by fire, computer viruses or the theft of your computer.

Making a backup copy of your database allows you to copy the information from your computer to a storage medium, such as a floppy disk, for safekeeping.

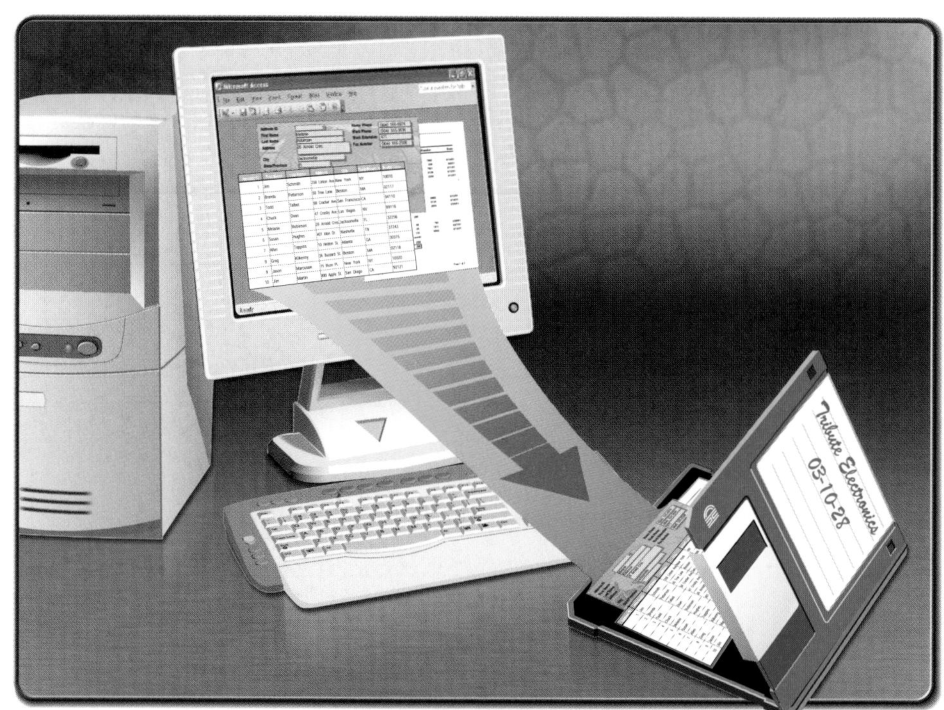

BACK UP A DATABASE

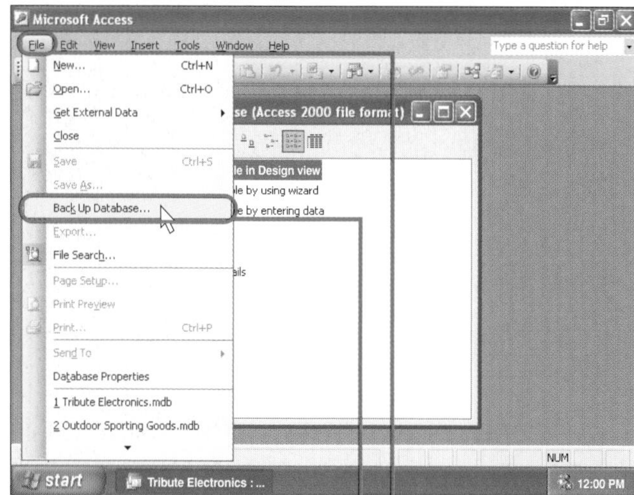

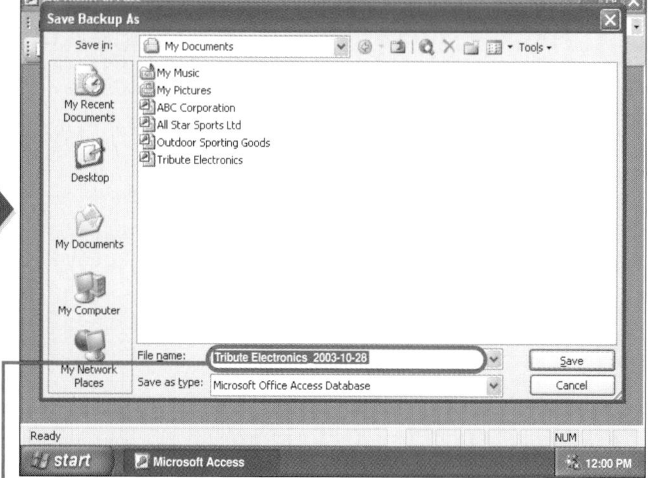

1 Insert the disk that you want to back up your information on into a drive.

2 Close all your open database objects. For information on closing a database object, see page 21.

3 Click **File**.

4 Click **Back Up Database**.

Note: If Back Up Database does not appear on the menu, position the mouse over the bottom of the menu to display the menu option.

■ The Save Backup As dialog box appears.

■ This area displays the name Access will use to save your backup copy of the database.

Note: To save the backup copy with a different name, drag the mouse I over the existing name to highlight the name and then type the new name.

Can I store a backup copy of a database on a CD-R or CD-RW disc?

You cannot back up your database directly to a CD-R or CD-RW disc. To store a backup copy of a database on a CD, perform the steps below to back up the database to a location on your computer. Then copy the backup file from your computer to a CD-R or CD-RW disc. For information on copying a file to a CD-R or CD-RW disc, see your Windows documentation.

How can I restore my database using the backup copy?

If your database is lost or damaged, you can use the backup copy to restore the database to your computer.

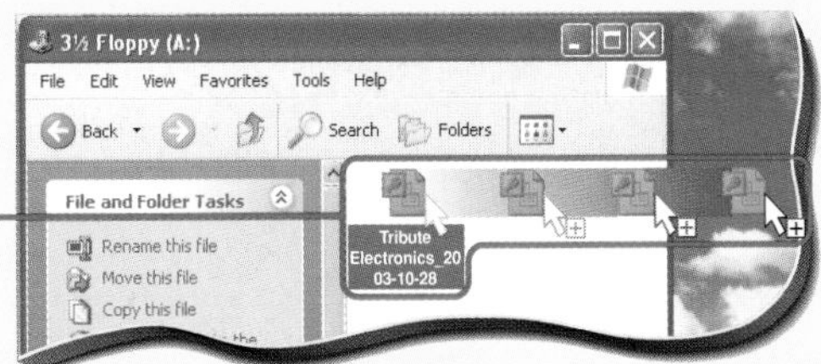

1 Insert the disk that contains the backup copy of the database you want to restore into a drive and display the contents of the disk.

2 Drag the backup copy of the database onto your Windows desktop.

■ The backup copy of the database is now copied to your computer. You can rename and work with the backup copy as you would work with the original database.

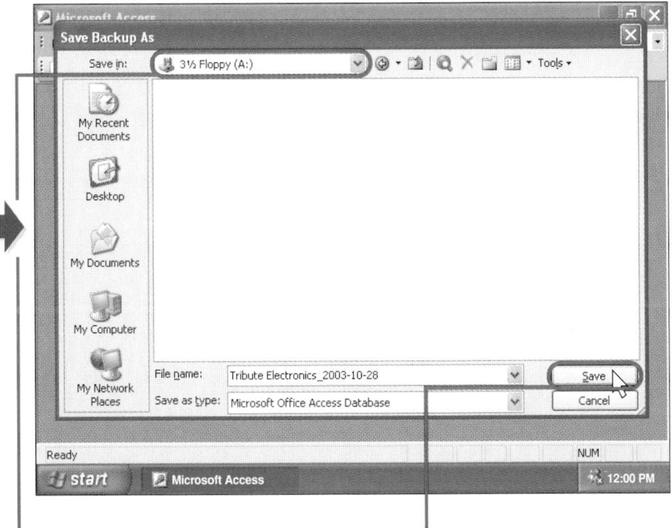

■ This area shows the location where Access will store the backup copy of your database. You can click this area to change the location.

5 Click **Save** to save the backup copy of your database.

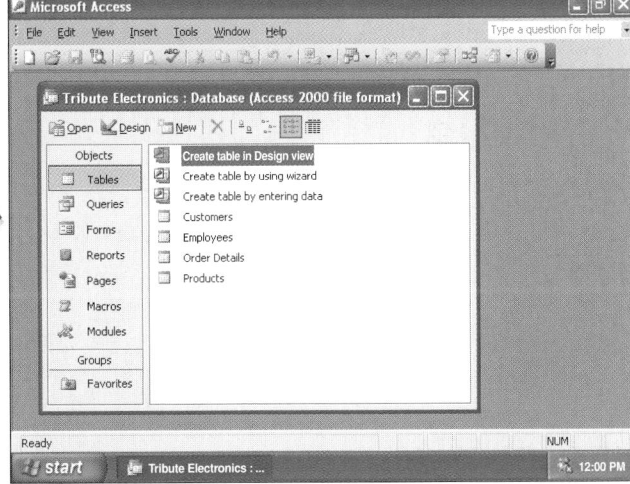

■ Access saves the backup copy of the database in the selected location.

■ When the backup is complete, Access redisplays the Database or Main Switchboard window for your original database. You can continue working with the database objects as you normally would.

GETTING HELP

If you do not know how to perform a task in Access, you can search for help information on the task.

Some help information is only available on the Internet. You must be connected to the Internet to access online help information.

GETTING HELP

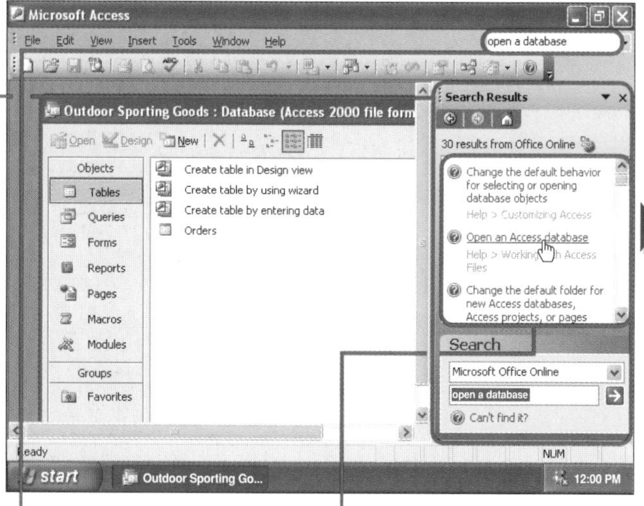

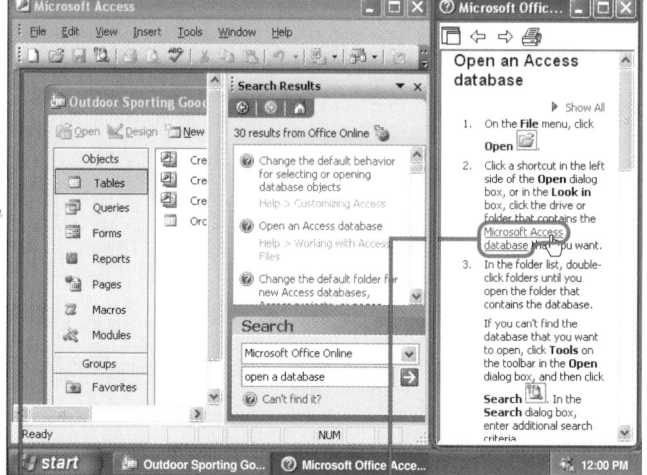

1 Click this area and type the task you want to get help information on. Then press the Enter key.

■ The Search Results task pane appears.

■ This area displays a list of related help topics. You can use the scroll bar to browse through the available topics.

2 Click the help topic of interest.

■ A window appears, displaying information about the help topic you selected.

3 To display additional information for a word or phrase that appears in color, click the word or phrase.

What do the icons beside each help topic represent?

Here are some icons you will see beside help topics.

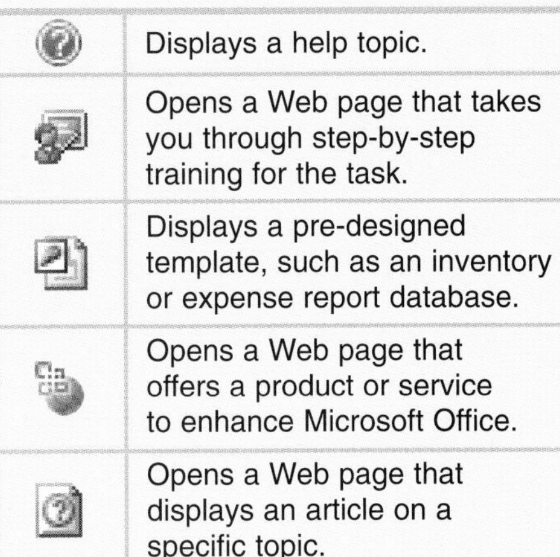

	Displays a help topic.
	Opens a Web page that takes you through step-by-step training for the task.
	Displays a pre-designed template, such as an inventory or expense report database.
	Opens a Web page that offers a product or service to enhance Microsoft Office.
	Opens a Web page that displays an article on a specific topic.

How can I get help information when working with a dialog box?

You can click ? in the top right corner of a dialog box (⇖ changes to ⇖?). Then click an area of the dialog box you want to view help information for. A box will appear, displaying help information for the area you selected.

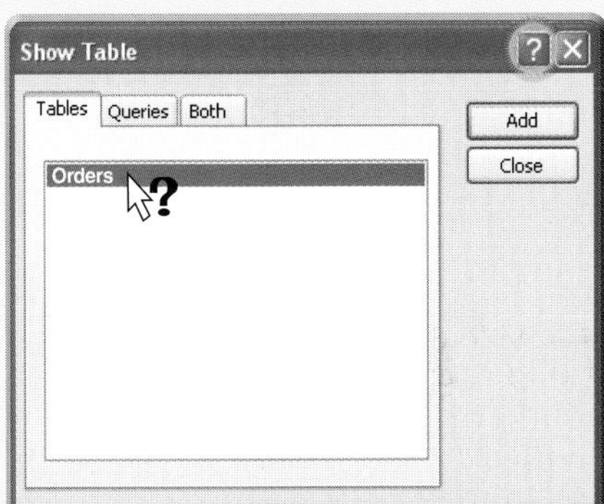

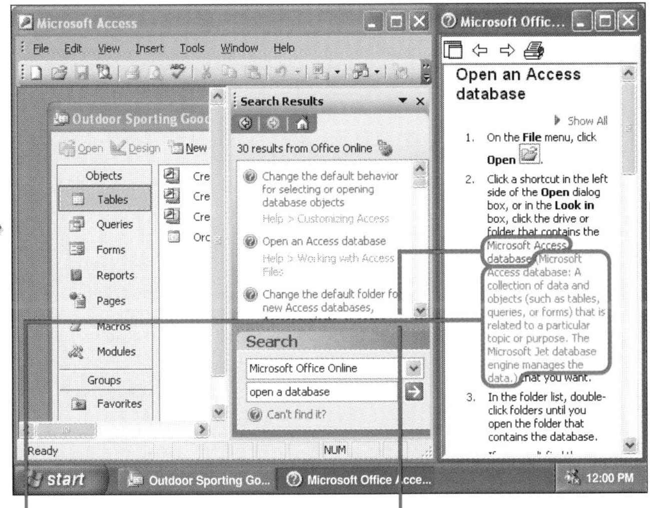

■ The additional information appears.

Note: Selecting a colored word or phrase will display information such as a definition, tip or a list of steps.

■ To once again hide the information, click the colored word or phrase.

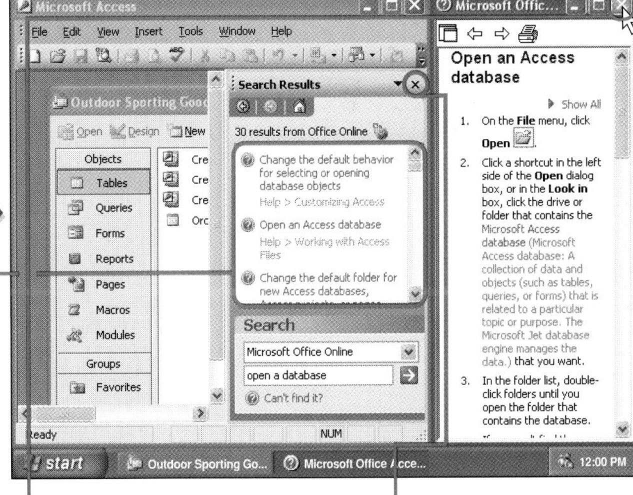

4 When you finish reviewing the help information, click ✕ to close the window.

■ To display the information for another help topic, click the help topic.

5 When you are finished getting help, click ✕ to close the Search Results task pane.

Database
Department
ID
Human Resources
Payroll
Advertising
Human Resources
Advertising
Payroll
Payroll
1
2
3
4
5
6
7
8
9
10

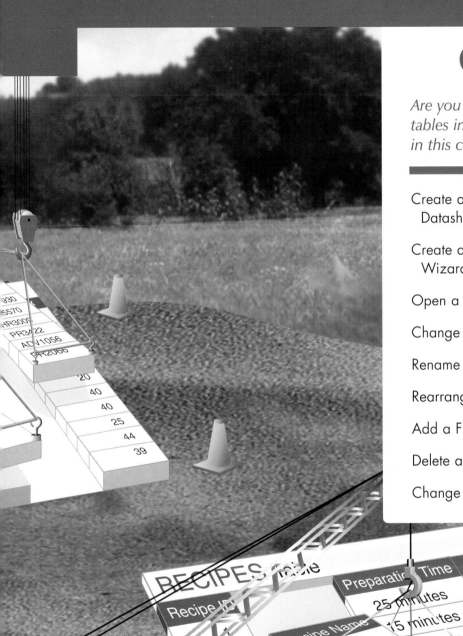

CHAPTER 2

Create Tables

Are you wondering how to create tables in your database? Learn how in this chapter.

CREATE A TABLE IN THE DATASHEET VIEW

You can create a table to store new information in your database.

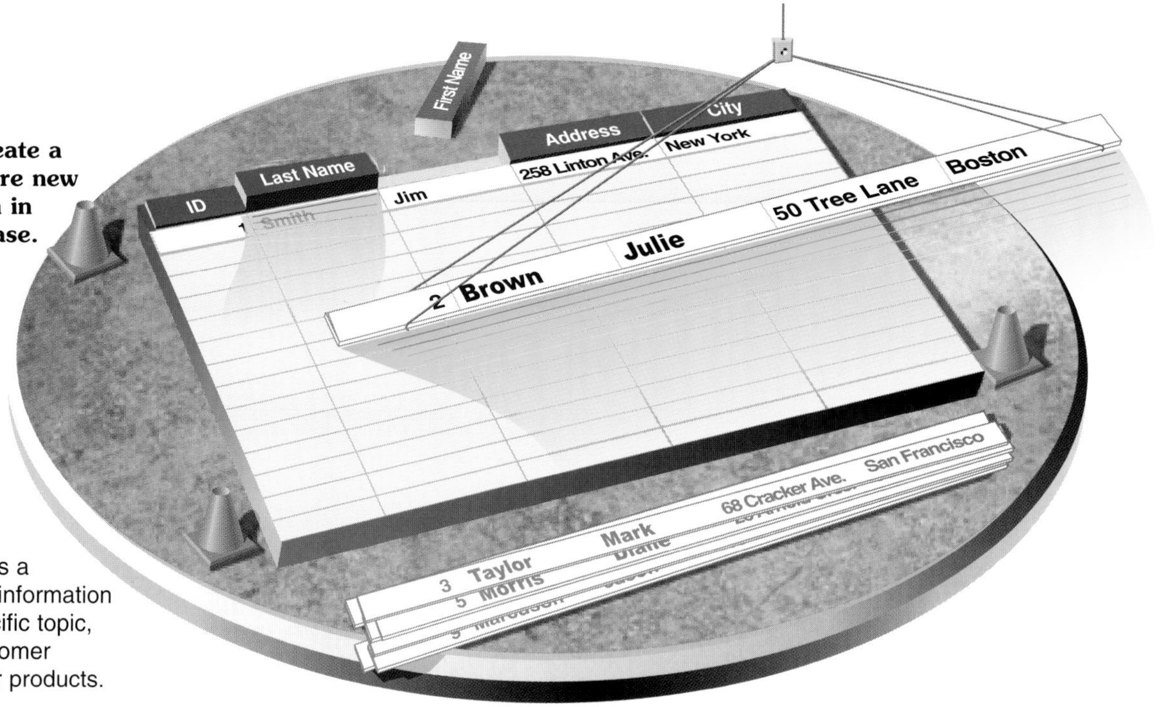

A table stores a collection of information about a specific topic, such as customer addresses or products.

CREATE A TABLE IN THE DATASHEET VIEW

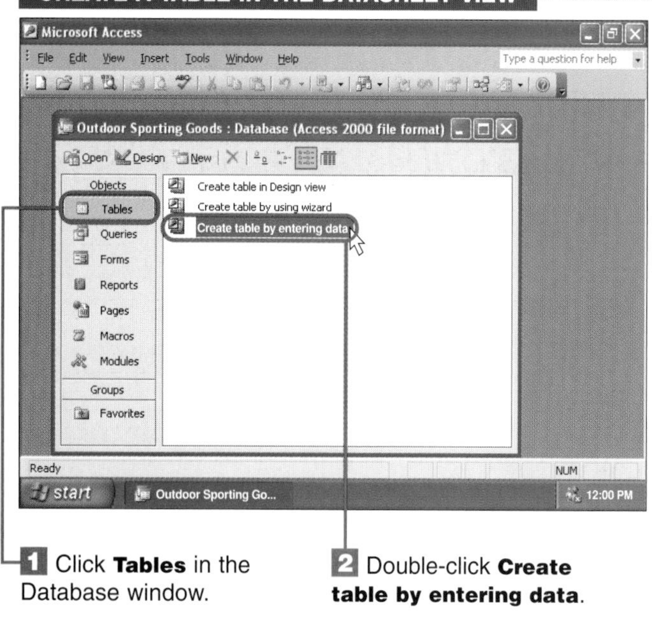

1 Click **Tables** in the Database window.

2 Double-click **Create table by entering data**.

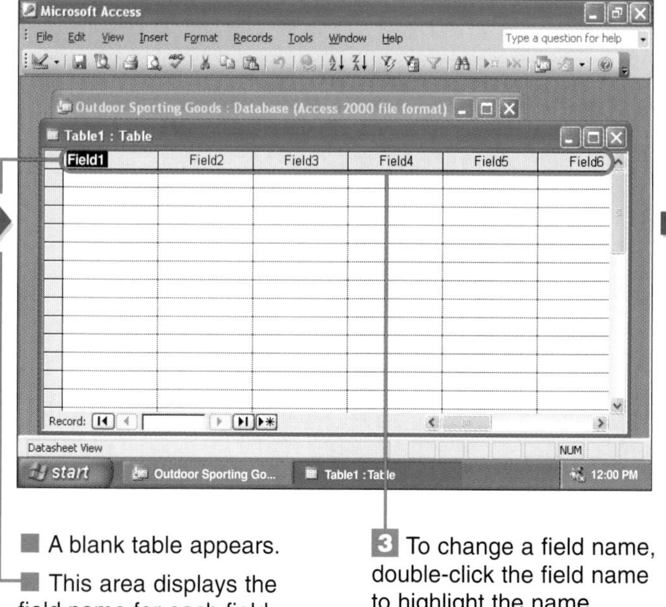

■ A blank table appears.

■ This area displays the field name for each field in your table.

3 To change a field name, double-click the field name to highlight the name.

What are the parts of a table?

Mailing List : Table

Mailing List ID	First Name	Last Name	Address	City	State
1	Jack	Adams	104 Sunset Ave.	Phoenix	AZ
2	Erin	Baker	223 Beach St.	Denver	CO
3	Lisa	Bell	27 Oak Dr.	Miami	FL
4	Julie	Brown	114 Jordan Dr.	Dallas	TX
5	Alan	Carter	558 Colburg Rd.	Manhattan	NY
6	Matt	Cole	48 Montana Ave.	Little Rock	AR
7	Jason	Cook	89 Springhill Ave.	Chicago	IL
8	Carl	Davis	6283 Main St.	Dallas	TX
9	Simon	Evans	56 Palm St.	Columbus	OH
10	Paul	Fraser	75 Ranch Blvd.	Denver	CO
11	Sue	Grant	93 Crane St.	Phoenix	AZ
12	Linda	Harris	4 Cherry Cres.	Miami	FL
13	Frank	Hill	12 Mozart Dr.	Chicago	IL
(AutoNumber)					

Record: 1 of 13

Field

A field is a specific category of information and contains the same type of information for every record. For example, a field can contain the last name of every client.

Field Name

A field name identifies the information in a field.

Record

A record is a collection of information about one person, place or thing. For example, a record can contain a client's name and address.

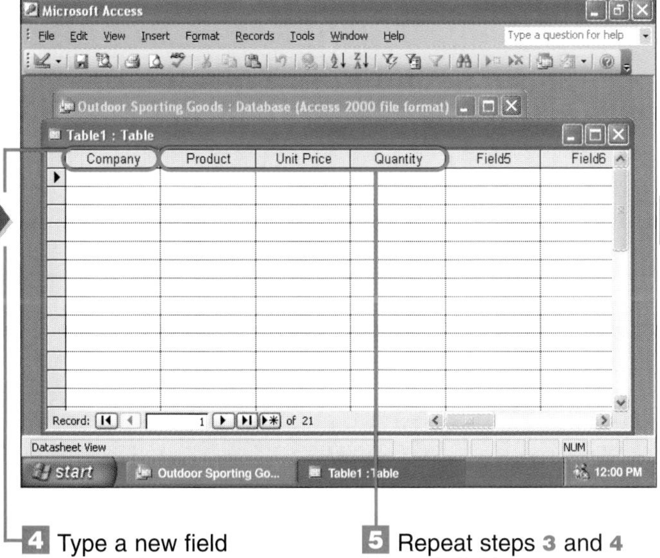

4 Type a new field name and then press the Enter key.

5 Repeat steps **3** and **4** for each field you want to include in your table.

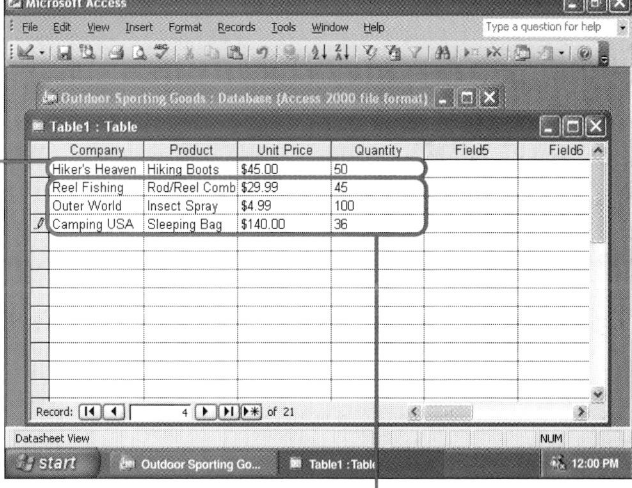

6 To enter the data for a record, click the first empty cell in the table.

7 Type the data that corresponds to the field and then press the Enter key to move to the next field. Repeat this step until you finish entering all the data for the record.

8 Repeat steps **6** and **7** for each record you want to add to your table.

CONTINUED

CREATE A TABLE IN THE DATASHEET VIEW

When creating a table, you can have Access create a primary key for the table.

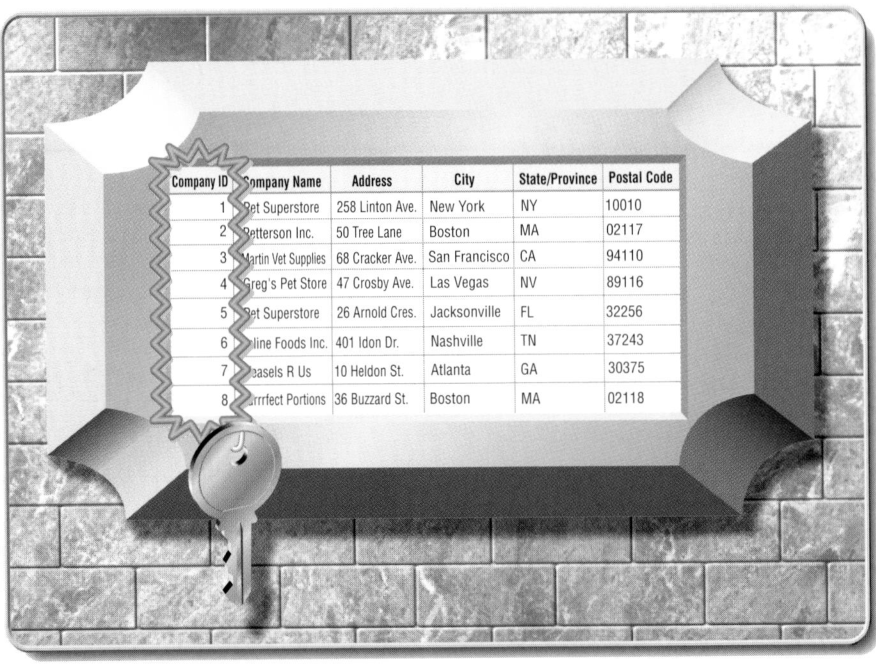

Company ID | ompany Name | Address | City | State/Province | Postal Code
1 | et Superstore | 258 Linton Ave. | New York | NY | 10010
2 | etterson Inc. | 50 Tree Lane | Boston | MA | 02117
3 | artin Vet Supplies | 68 Cracker Ave. | San Francisco | CA | 94110
4 | reg's Pet Store | 47 Crosby Ave. | Las Vegas | NV | 89116
5 | et Superstore | 26 Arnold Cres. | Jacksonville | FL | 32256
6 | line Foods Inc. | 401 Idon Dr. | Nashville | TN | 37243
7 | asels R Us | 10 Heldon St. | Atlanta | GA | 30375
8 | rrrfect Portions | 36 Buzzard St. | Boston | MA | 02118

A primary key is one or more fields that uniquely identifies each record in a table, such as a field containing ID numbers. Each table in your database should have a primary key.

CREATE A TABLE IN THE DATASHEET VIEW (CONTINUED)

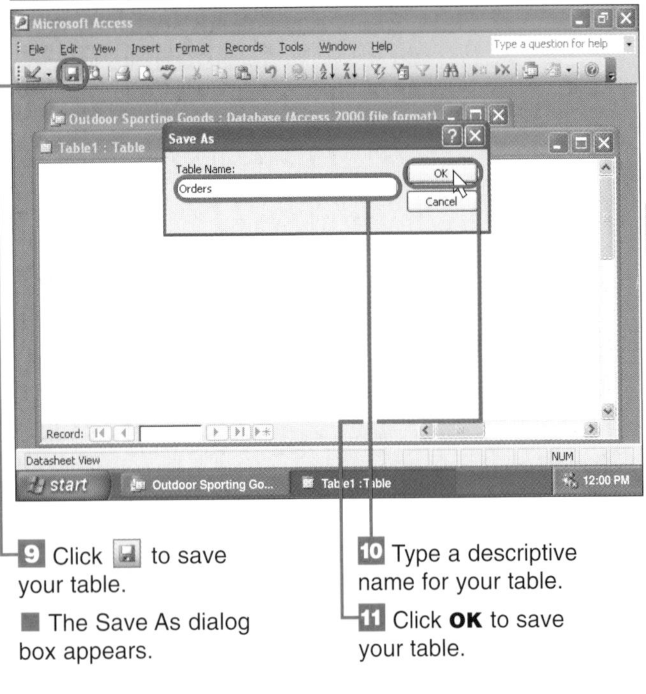

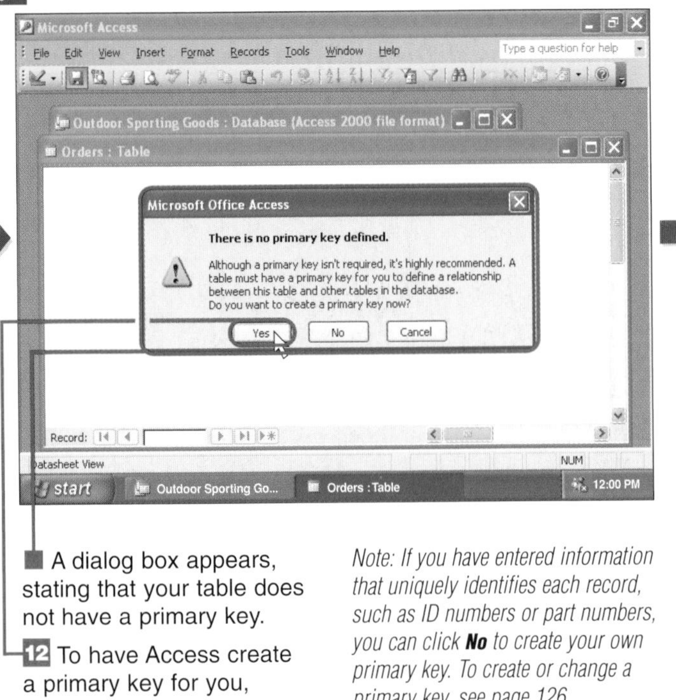

9 Click 💾 to save your table.

■ The Save As dialog box appears.

10 Type a descriptive name for your table.

11 Click **OK** to save your table.

■ A dialog box appears, stating that your table does not have a primary key.

12 To have Access create a primary key for you, click **Yes**.

*Note: If you have entered information that uniquely identifies each record, such as ID numbers or part numbers, you can click **No** to create your own primary key. To create or change a primary key, see page 126.*

Why should each table in my database have a primary key?

Access uses the primary key in each table to establish relationships between the tables in your database. Relationships between tables allow Access to bring together related information in the tables. For more information on relationships, see page 128.

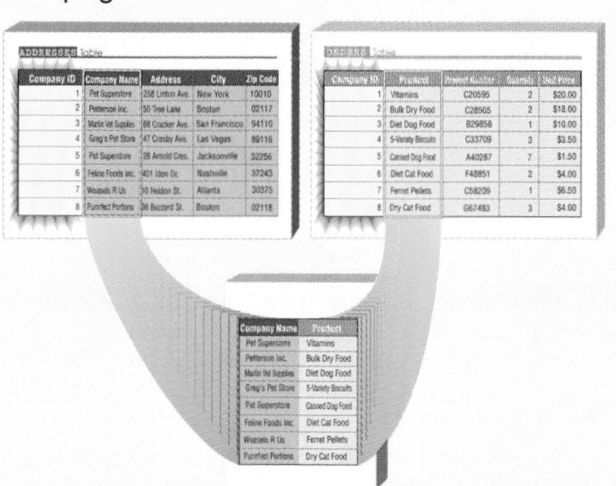

Will Access analyze the information I enter in a table?

When you save a table, Access analyzes the information you have entered and assigns a data type to each field. A data type determines the kind of information you can enter in a field, such as text, numbers or dates. For more information on data types, see page 82.

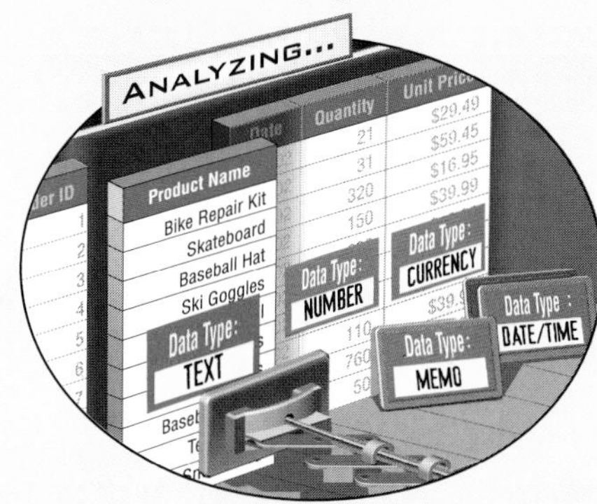

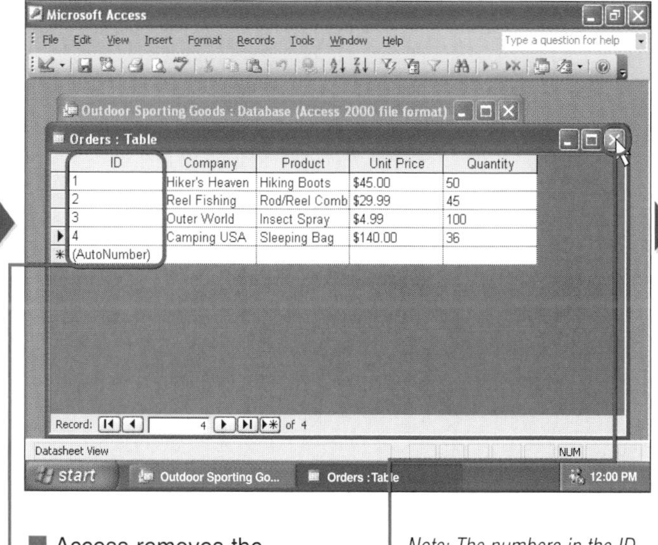

■ Access removes the rows and columns that do not contain data.

■ If you selected Yes in step **12**, Access adds an ID field to your table to serve as the primary key. The ID field automatically numbers each record in your table.

Note: The numbers in the ID field may not begin at 1.

13 When you finish reviewing your records, click ☒ to close your table.

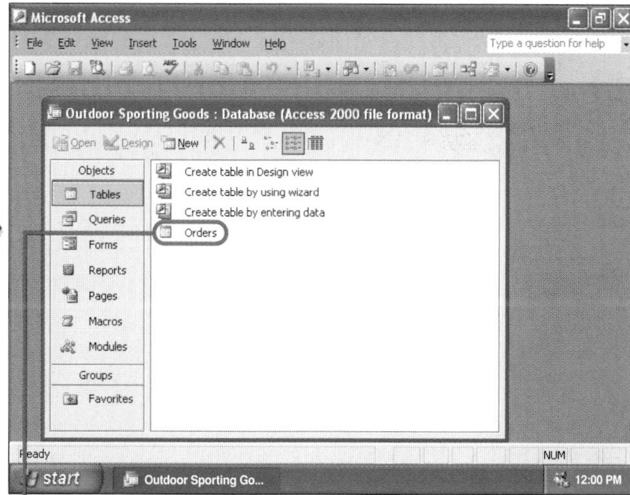

■ The name of your table appears in the Database window.

CREATE A TABLE USING THE TABLE WIZARD

You can use the Table Wizard to quickly create a table. The wizard asks you a series of questions and then sets up a table based on your answers.

The wizard can help you create a table for business or personal use. You can use the wizard to create tables that store information about specific topics, such as Customers, Products, Orders, Recipes and Investments.

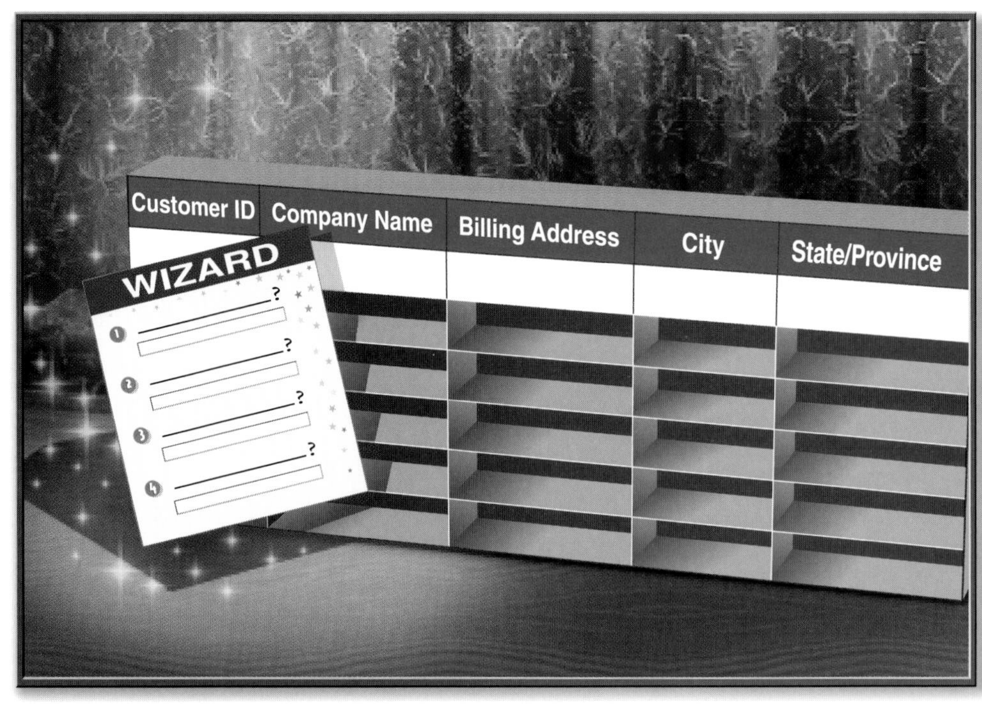

CREATE A TABLE USING THE TABLE WIZARD

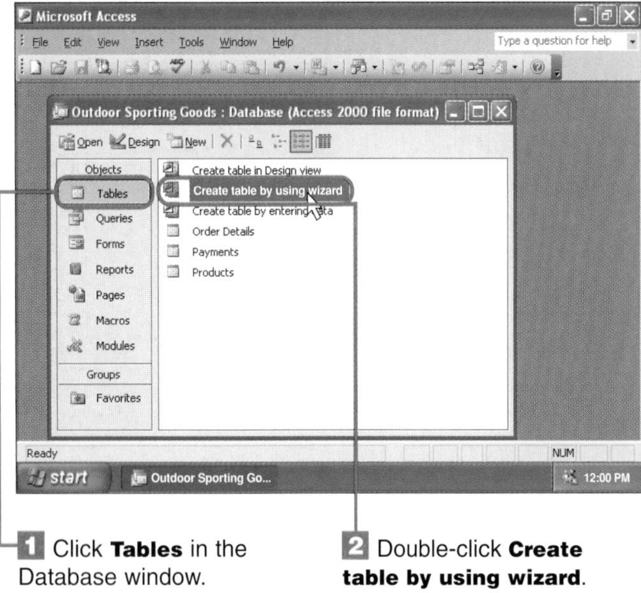

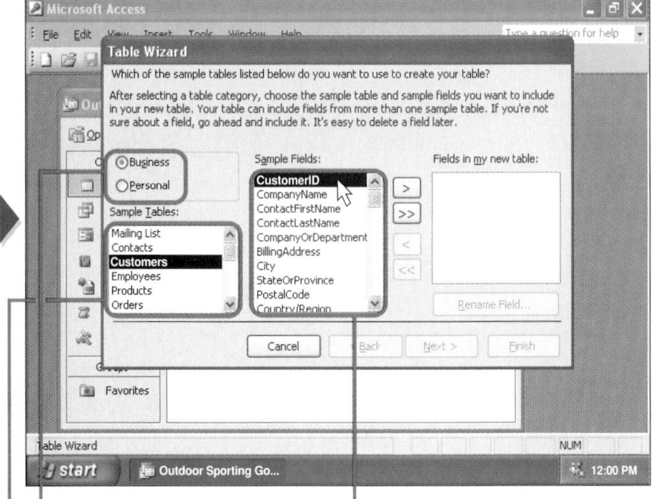

1 Click **Tables** in the Database window.

2 Double-click **Create table by using wizard**.

■ The Table Wizard appears.

3 Click an option to specify whether the table is for business or personal use (○ changes to ◉).

4 Click the sample table you want to use.

*Note: The available sample tables depend on the option you selected in step **3**.*

■ This area displays the available fields for the sample table you selected.

5 Double-click each field you want to include in the table.

Note: To select all the fields at once, click >>.

What is a primary key?

A primary key is one or more fields that uniquely identifies each record in a table, such as a field containing ID numbers. Each table in your database should have a primary key. When using the Table Wizard to create a table, you can have Access set a primary key for you. Access will create a field that automatically numbers each record in your table. To later change the primary key, see page 126.

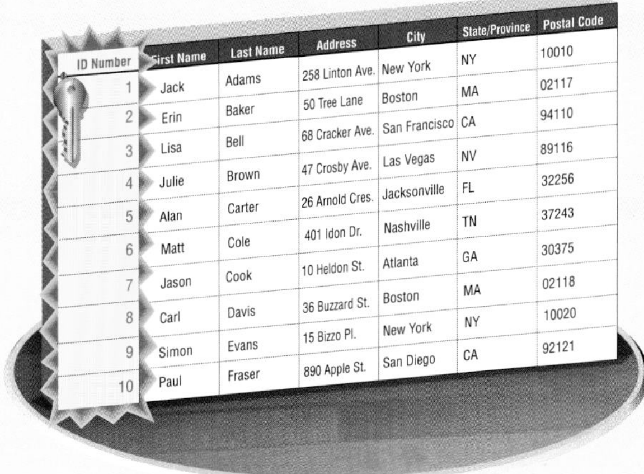

ID Number	First Name	Last Name	Address	City	State/Province	Postal Code
1	Jack	Adams	258 Linton Ave.	New York	NY	10010
2	Erin	Baker	50 Tree Lane	Boston	MA	02117
3	Lisa	Bell	68 Cracker Ave.	San Francisco	CA	94110
4	Julie	Brown	47 Crosby Ave.	Las Vegas	NV	89116
5	Alan	Carter	26 Arnold Cres.	Jacksonville	FL	32256
6	Matt	Cole	401 Idon Dr.	Nashville	TN	37243
7	Jason	Cook	10 Heldon St.	Atlanta	GA	30375
8	Carl	Davis	36 Buzzard St.	Boston	MA	02118
9	Simon	Evans	15 Bizzo Pl.	New York	NY	10020
10	Paul	Fraser	890 Apple St.	San Diego	CA	92121

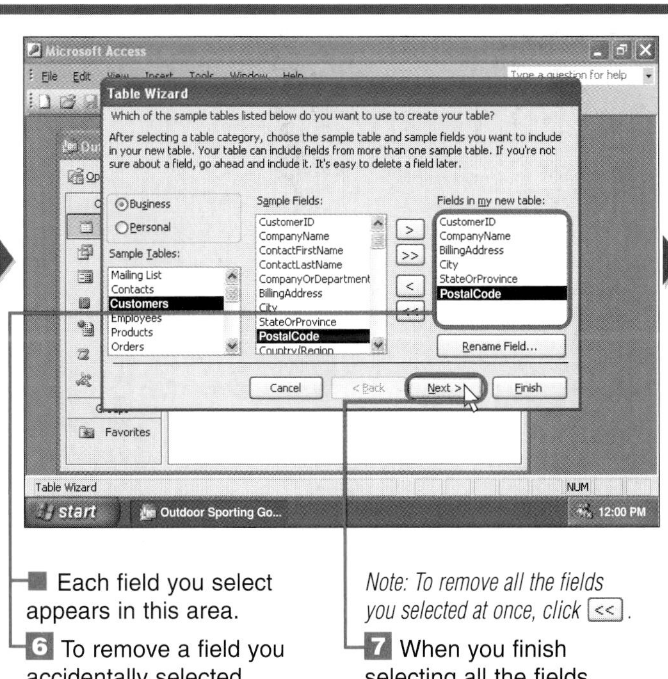

■ Each field you select appears in this area.

6 To remove a field you accidentally selected, double-click the field in this area.

Note: To remove all the fields you selected at once, click <<.

7 When you finish selecting all the fields you want to include in the table, click **Next** to continue.

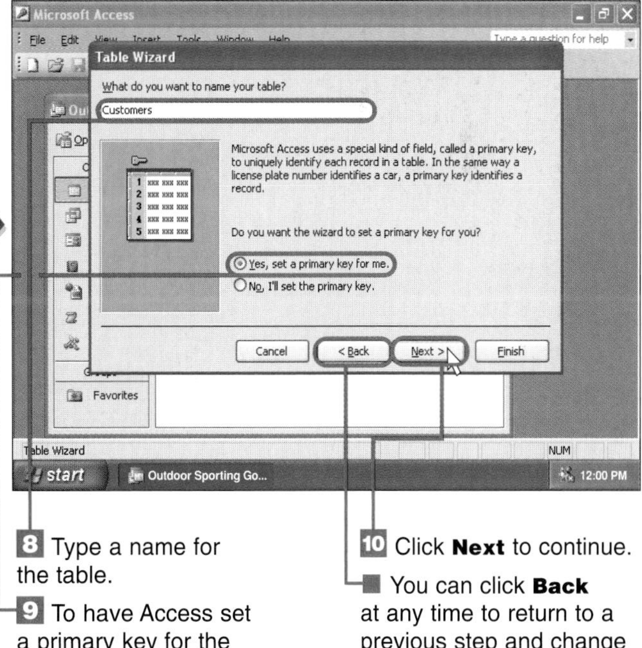

8 Type a name for the table.

9 To have Access set a primary key for the table, click this option (○ changes to ◉).

Note: For information on the primary key, see the top of this page.

10 Click **Next** to continue.

■ You can click **Back** at any time to return to a previous step and change your selections.

CONTINUED

CREATE A TABLE USING THE TABLE WIZARD

The Table Wizard shows how your new table relates to the other tables in your database.

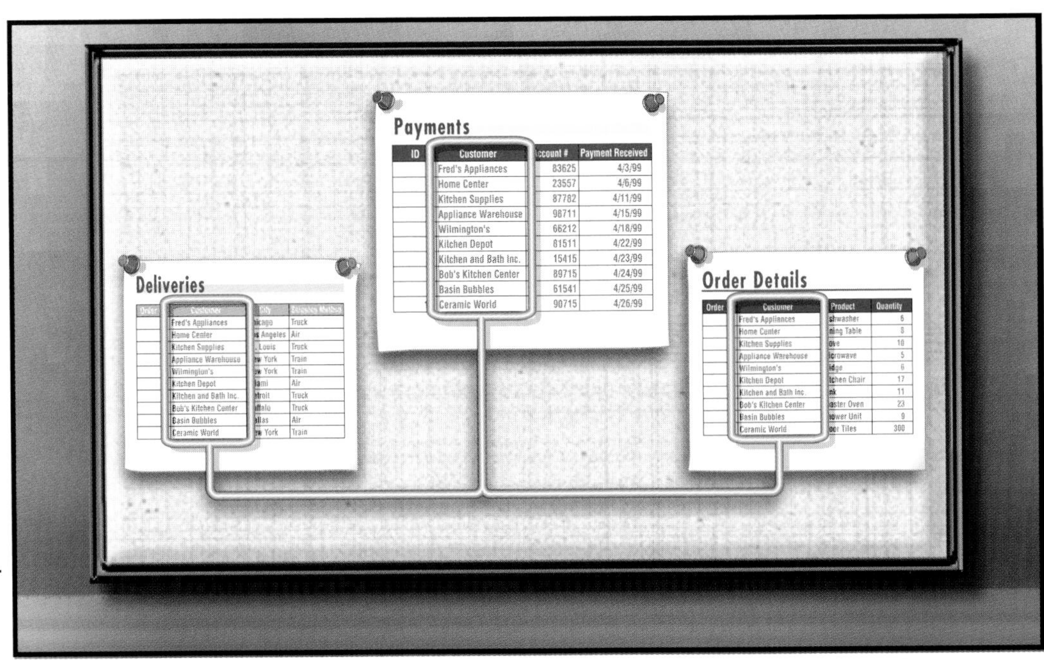

Relationships between tables allow Access to bring together related information in the tables. For more information on relationships, see page 128.

CREATE A TABLE USING THE TABLE WIZARD (CONTINUED)

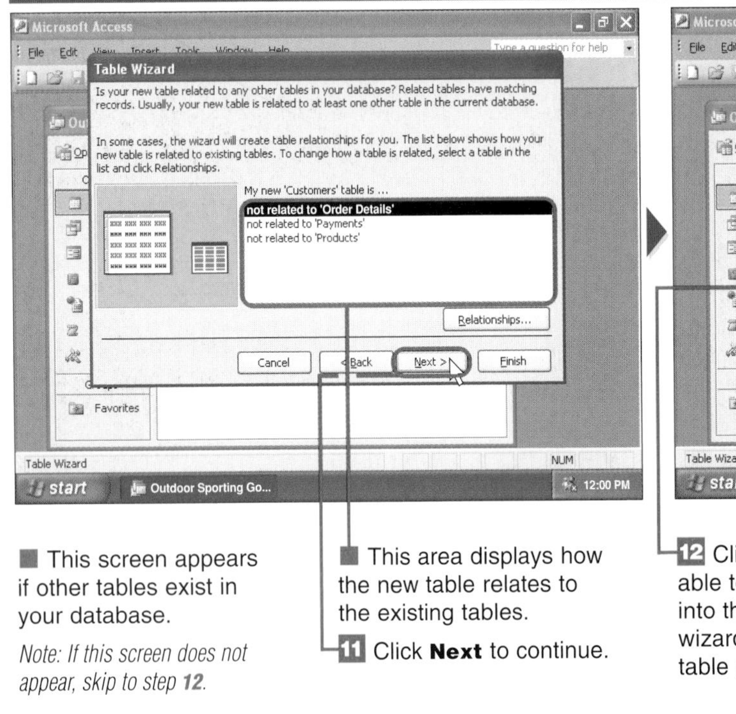

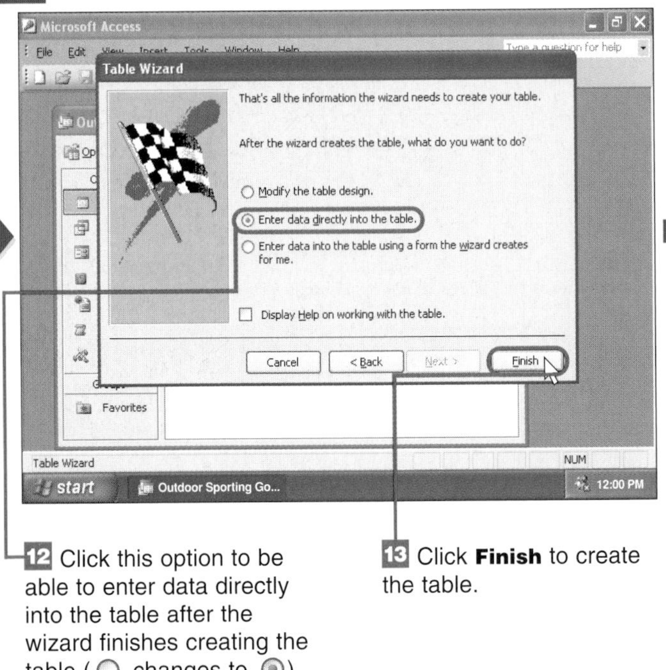

■ This screen appears if other tables exist in your database.

*Note: If this screen does not appear, skip to step **12**.*

■ This area displays how the new table relates to the existing tables.

11 Click **Next** to continue.

12 Click this option to be able to enter data directly into the table after the wizard finishes creating the table (○ changes to ◉).

13 Click **Finish** to create the table.

Can I make changes to a table?

Yes. After you create a table using the Table Wizard, you can make changes to the table. For example, you can change the width of columns, rename a field, rearrange fields, add a new field or delete a field. To make changes to a table, see pages 43 to 49.

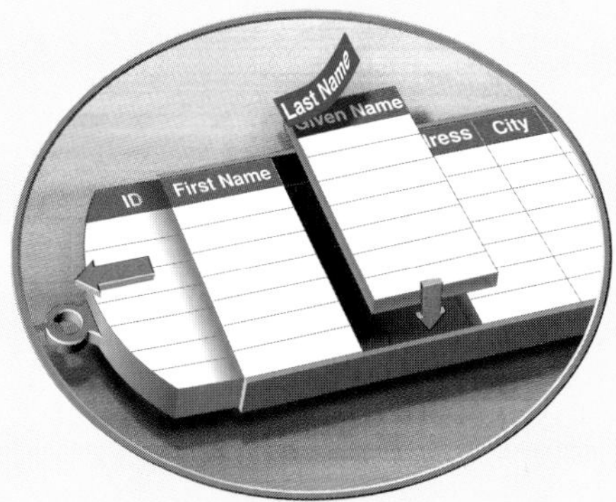

Can I later add records to a table?

After you create a table, you can add new records to the table at any time. For example, you may want to add information about a new customer to a table containing customer information. To add new records to a table, see page 64.

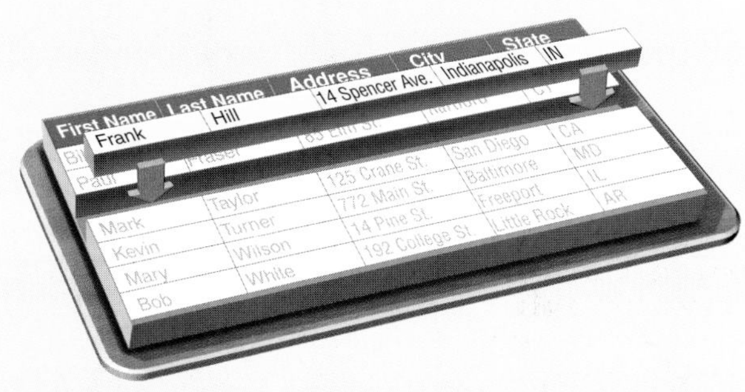

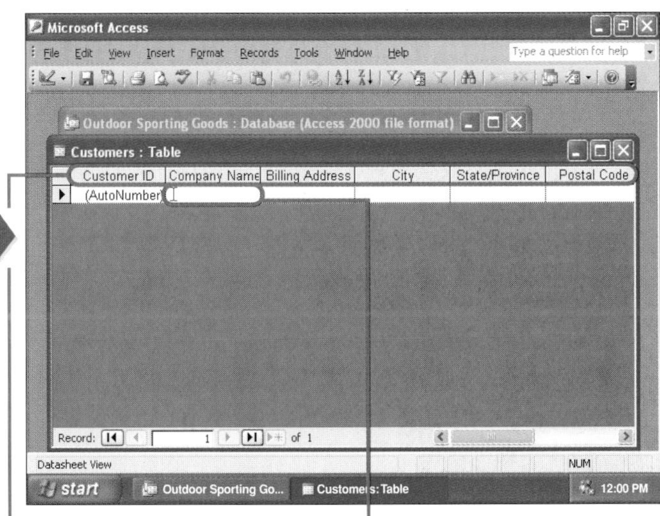

■ This area displays the field names for the table.

■ If you selected Yes in step 9, Access adds an ID field to the table to serve as the primary key. The ID field will automatically number each record you add to the table.

Note: The numbers in the ID field may not begin at 1.

14 To enter the data for a record, click the first empty cell in the table.

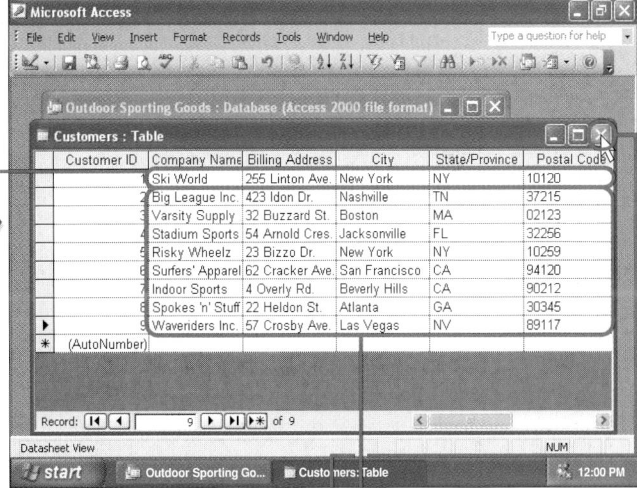

15 Type the data that corresponds to the field and then press the Enter key to move to the next field. Repeat this step until you finish entering all the data for the record.

16 Repeat steps 14 and 15 for each record you want to add to your table. Access automatically saves each record you enter.

17 When you finish entering records, click ☒ to close the table.

OPEN A TABLE

You can open a table to display its contents on your screen. Opening a table allows you to review and make changes to the table.

OPEN A TABLE

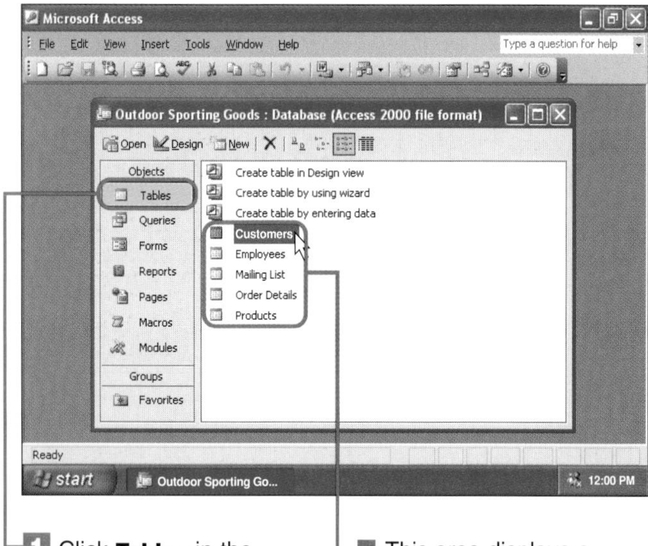

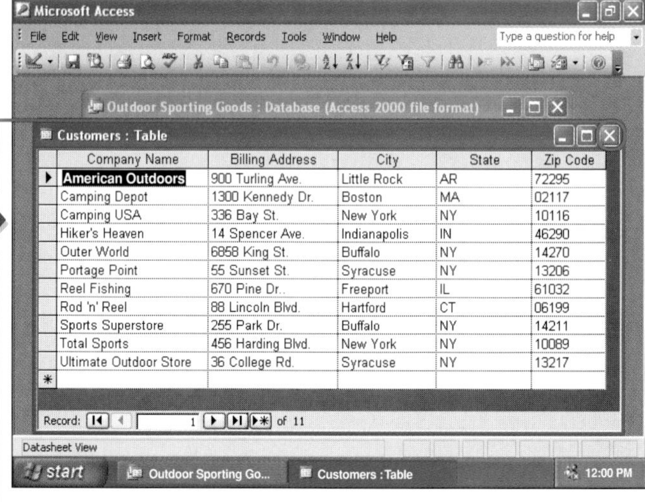

1 Click **Tables** in the Database window.

■ This area displays a list of the tables in your database.

2 Double-click the table you want to open.

■ The table opens. You can now review and make changes to the table.

■ When you finish working with the table, click ☒ to close the table.

*Note: A dialog box will appear if you did not save changes you made to the layout of the table. To specify if you want to save the changes, click **Yes** or **No**.*

CHANGE A COLUMN WIDTH

You can change the width of a column in a table. Increasing the width of a column allows you to view data that is too long to display in the column.

Reducing the width of columns allows you to display more fields on your screen at once.

CHANGE A COLUMN WIDTH

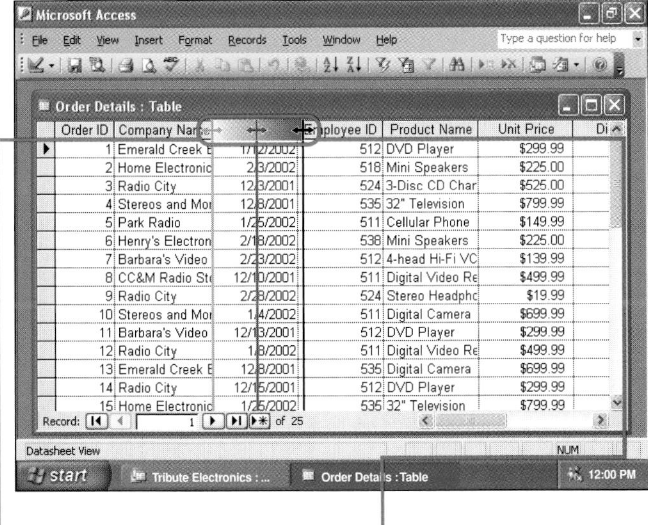

1 To change the width of a column, position the mouse I over the right edge of the column heading (I changes to ↔).

2 Drag the column edge until the line displays the column width you want.

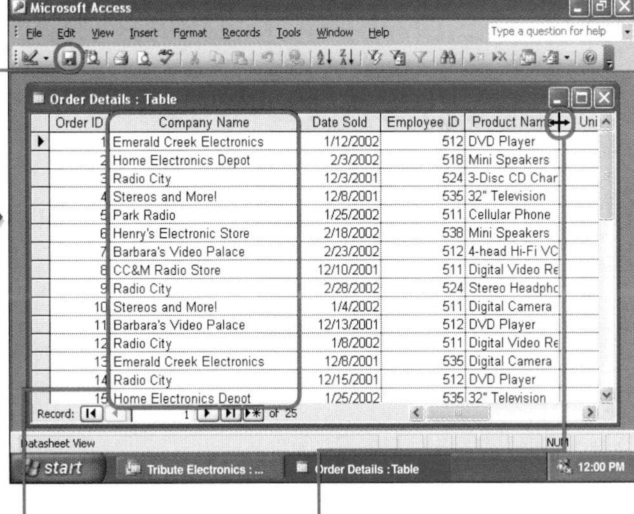

■ The column displays the new width.

3 Click 💾 to save your change.

FIT LONGEST ITEM

1 To change a column width to fit the longest item in the column, double-click the right edge of the column heading.

RENAME A FIELD

You can give a field a new name to more accurately describe the contents of the field.

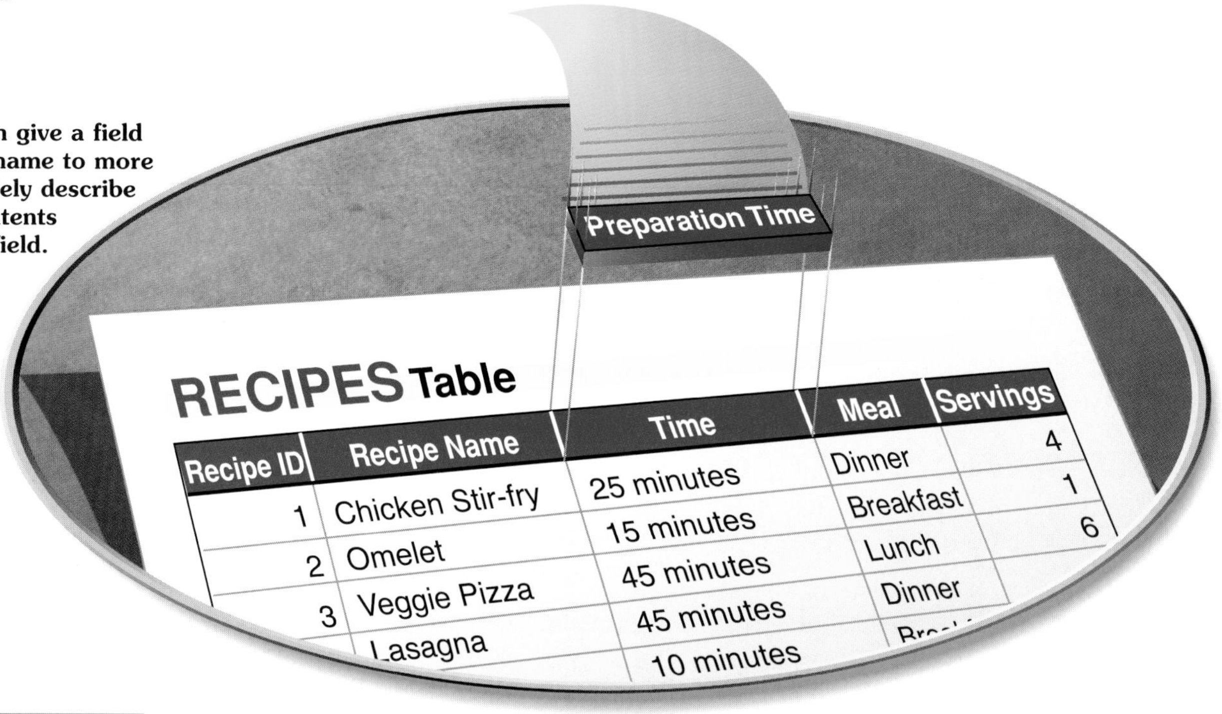

RENAME A FIELD

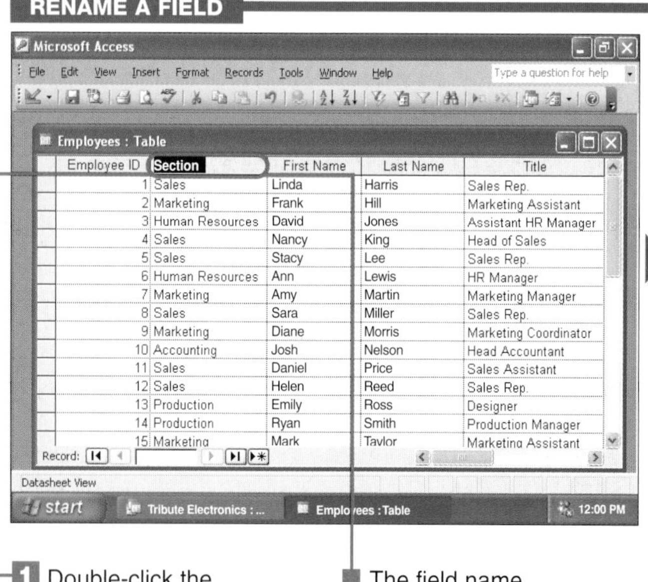

1 Double-click the field name you want to change.

■ The field name is highlighted.

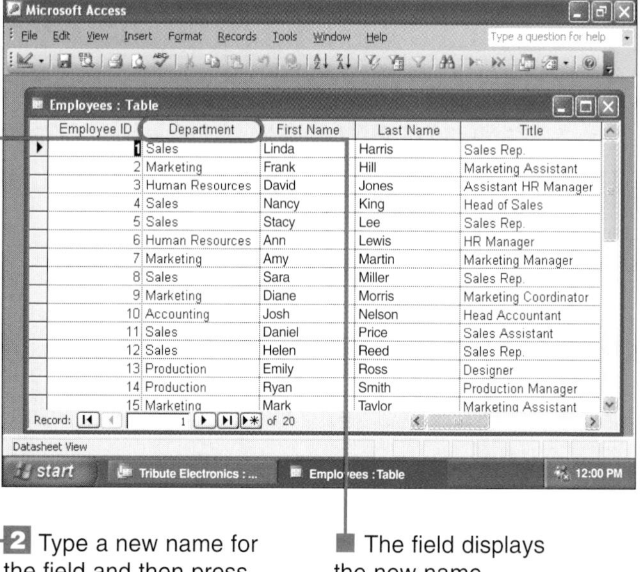

2 Type a new name for the field and then press the Enter key.

■ The field displays the new name.

REARRANGE FIELDS

You can change the order of fields to better organize the information in a table.

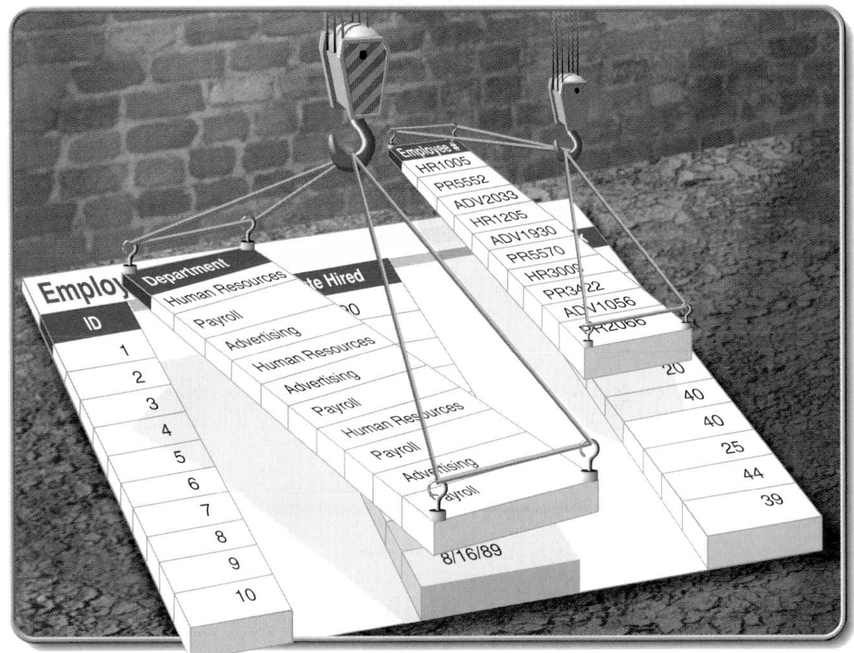

Rearranging fields in the Datasheet view will not affect how the fields appear in the Design view of a table. For information on the views of a table, see page 74.

REARRANGE FIELDS

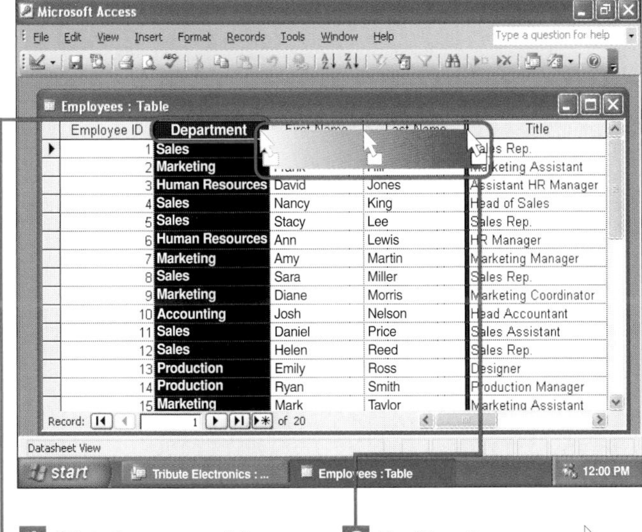

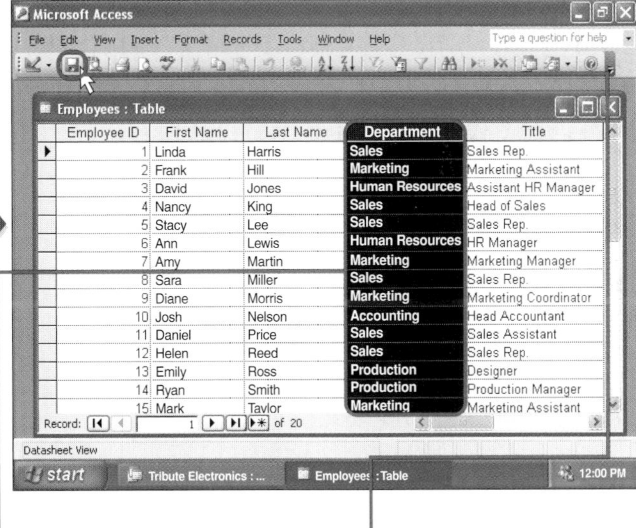

1 Click the name of the field you want to move. The field is highlighted.

2 Position the mouse over the field name and then drag the field to a new location.

■ A thick line shows where the field will appear.

■ The field appears in the new location.

3 Click to save your change.

ADD A FIELD

You can add a field to a table when you want the table to include an additional category of information.

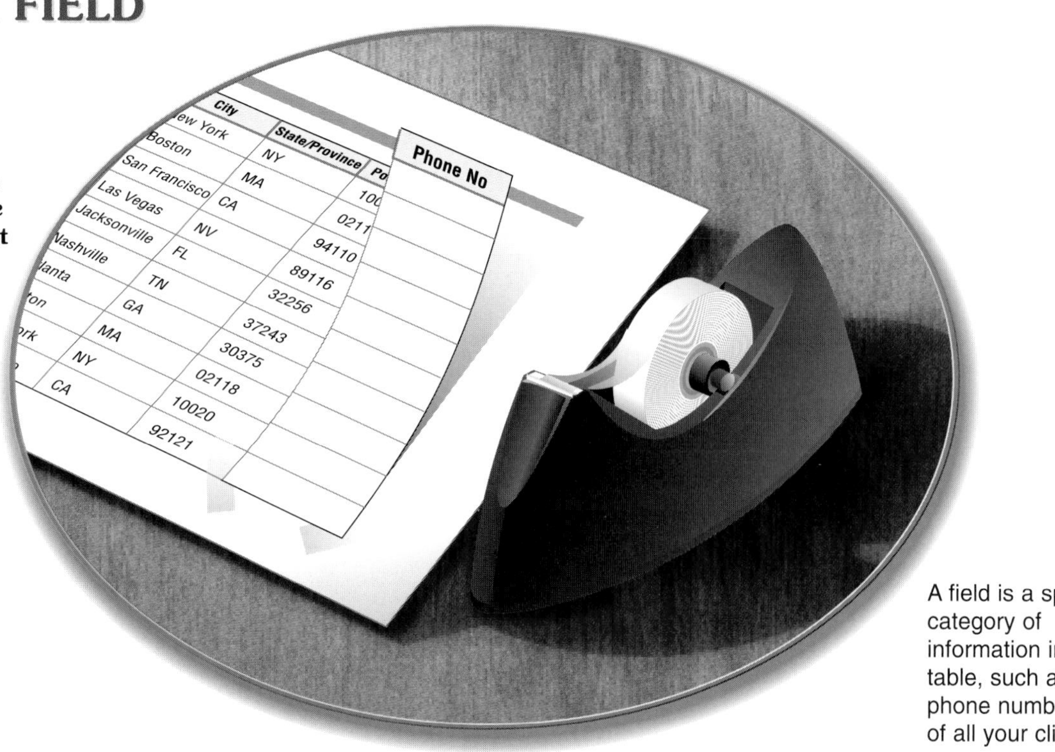

A field is a specific category of information in a table, such as the phone numbers of all your clients.

ADD A FIELD

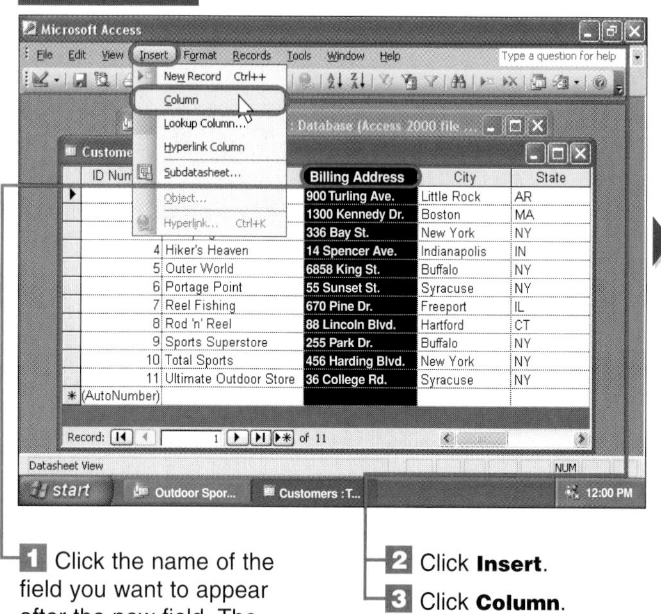

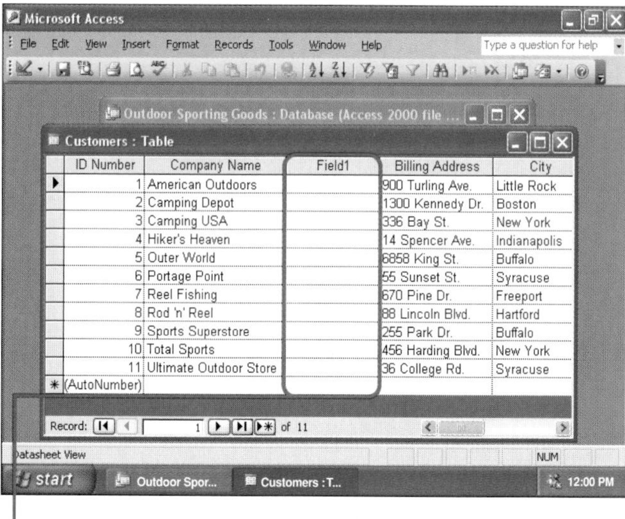

1 Click the name of the field you want to appear after the new field. The field is highlighted.

2 Click **Insert**.

3 Click **Column**.

■ The new field appears in your table.

■ Access assigns a name to the new field. To give the field a descriptive name, see page 44 to rename the field.

DELETE A FIELD

If you no longer need a field, you can permanently delete the field from a table.

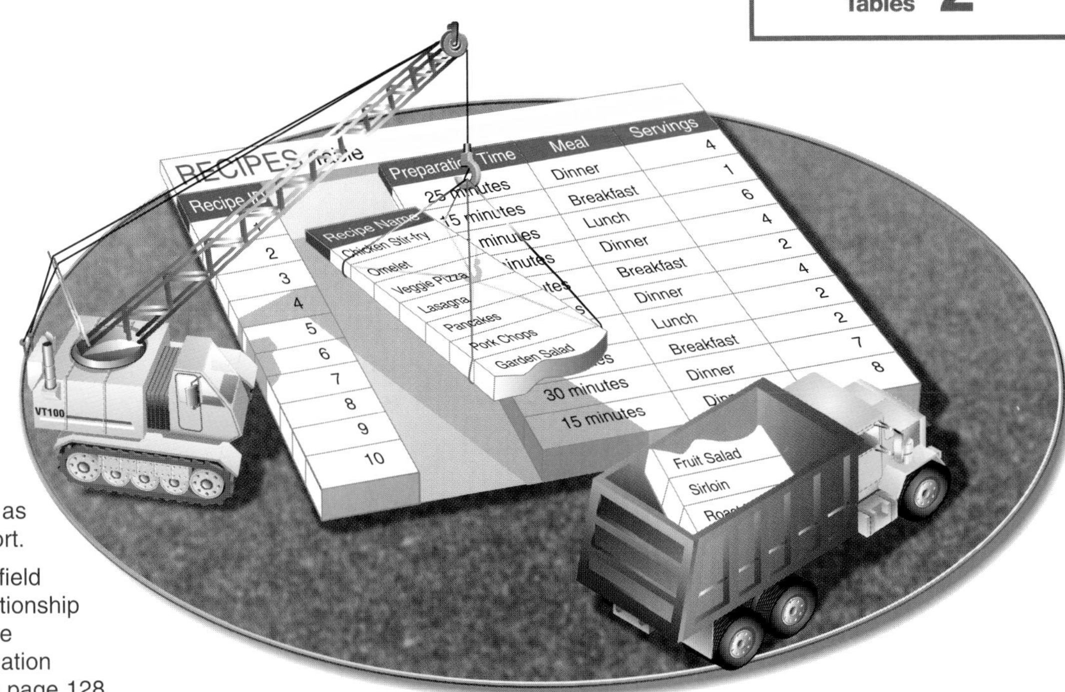

Before you delete a field, make sure the field is not used in any other objects in your database, such as a form, query or report.

You cannot delete a field used to create a relationship to another table in the database. For information on relationships, see page 128.

DELETE A FIELD

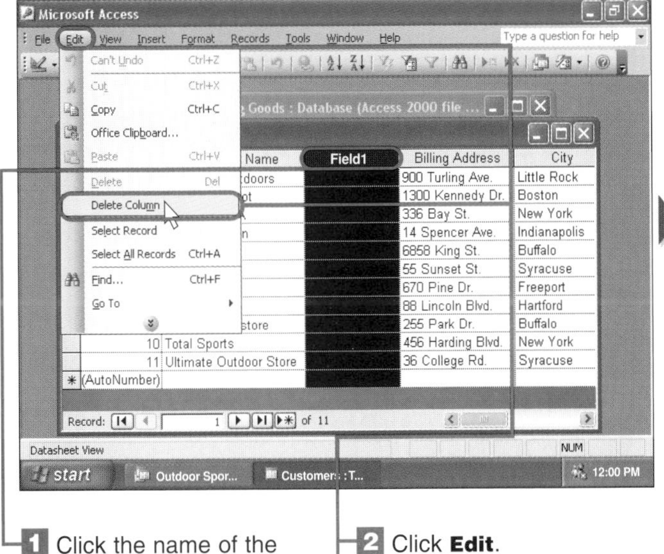

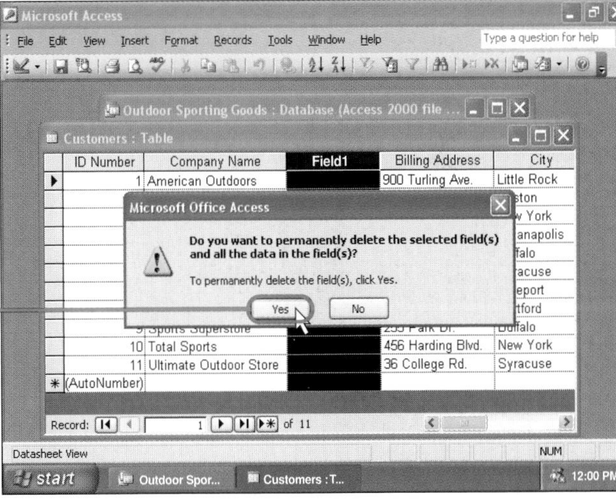

1 Click the name of the field you want to delete. The field is highlighted.

2 Click **Edit**.

3 Click **Delete Column**.

■ A confirmation dialog box appears.

4 Click **Yes** to permanently delete the field.

■ The field disappears from your table.

CHANGE THE APPEARANCE OF A TABLE

You can change the cell style and colors in a table to enhance the appearance of the table.

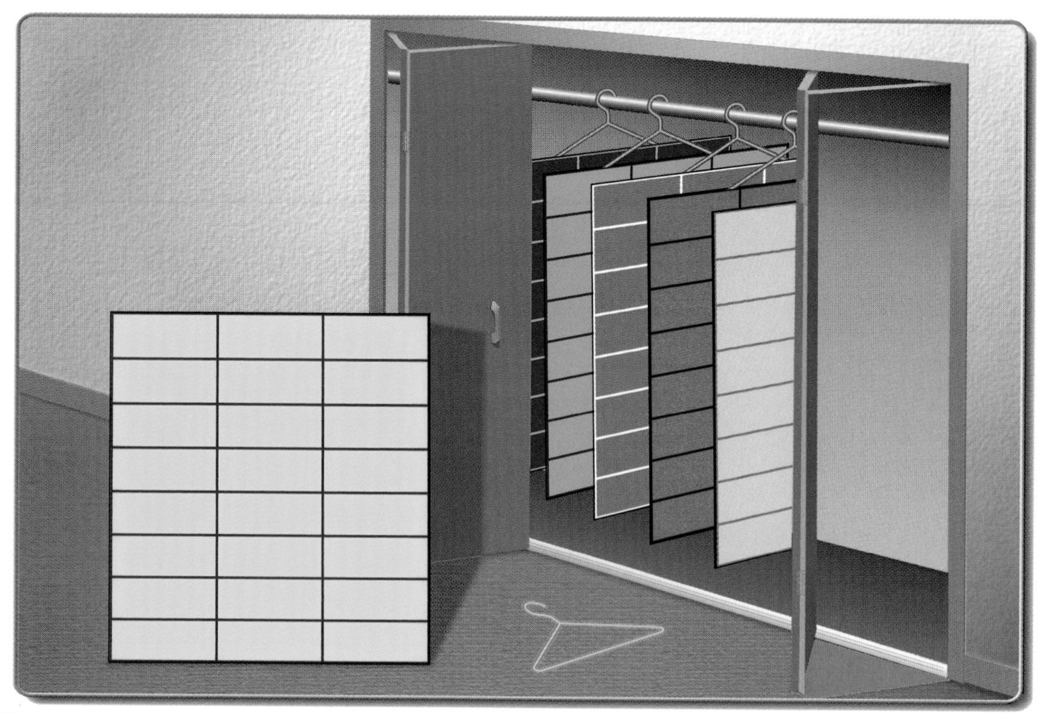

CHANGE THE APPEARANCE OF A TABLE

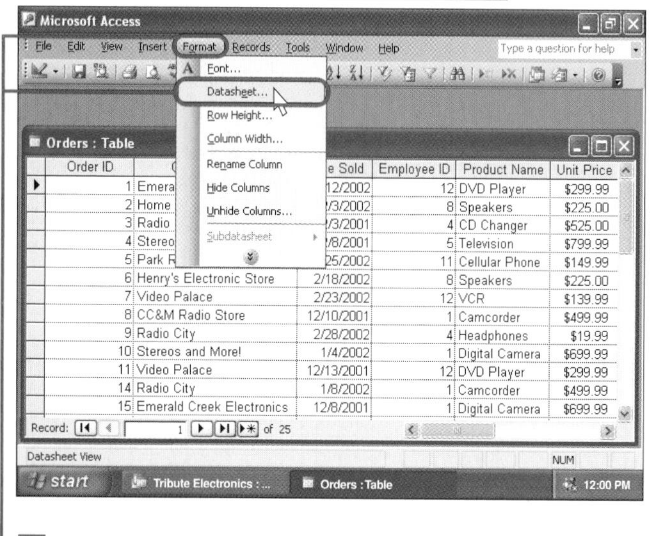

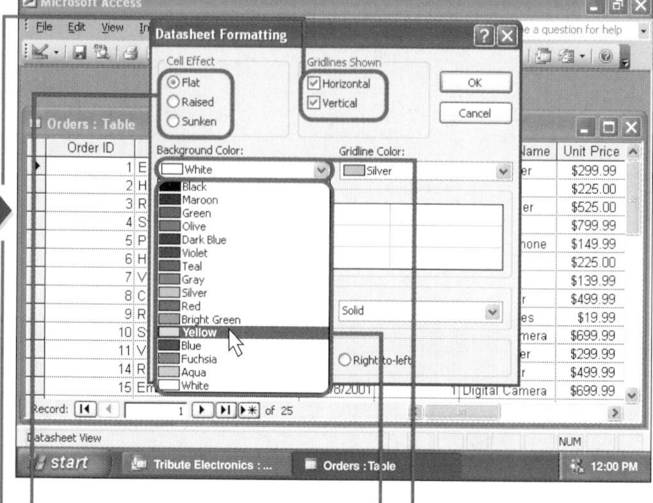

1 Click **Format**.

2 Click **Datasheet**.

■ The Datasheet Formatting dialog box appears.

3 Click the cell effect you want to use (○ changes to ◉).

*Note: If you selected Raised or Sunken in step **3**, skip to step **9**.*

4 To remove the horizontal or vertical gridlines, click each gridline you want to remove (☑ changes to ☐).

5 To change the background color, click this area to display a list of the available colors.

6 Click the background color you want to use.

How can I change the border or line styles in a table?

In the Datasheet Formatting dialog box, you can change the border and line styles in a table.

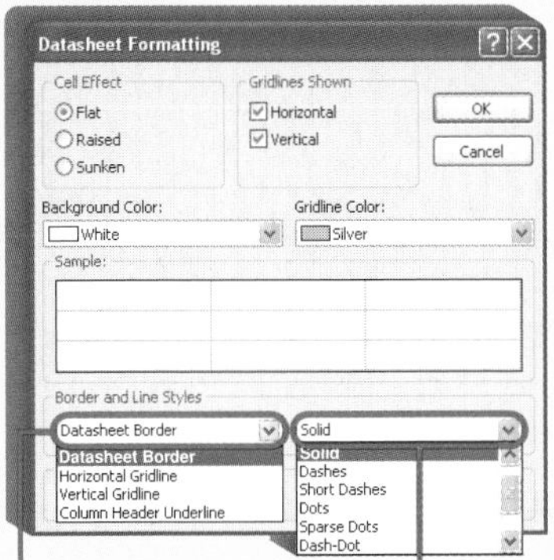

■ You can click this area to select the type of border or line you want to change.

■ You can click this area to select a style for the type of border or line you selected.

Can I change the appearance of a form or query?

You can also perform the steps shown below to change the appearance of a form or a query displayed in the Datasheet view. To change the view of a form or query, see page 152 or 202.

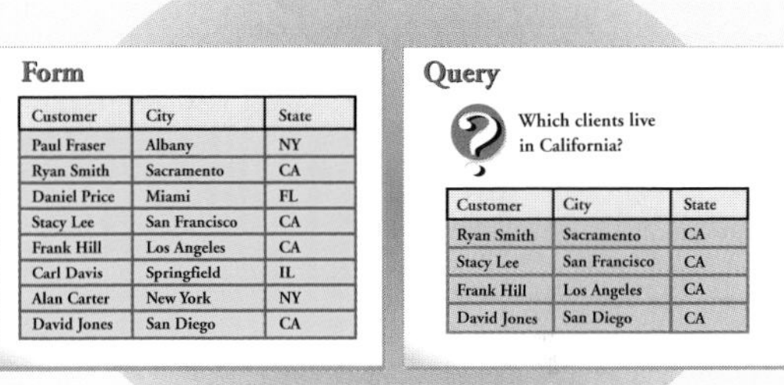

Form

Customer	City	State
Paul Fraser	Albany	NY
Ryan Smith	Sacramento	CA
Daniel Price	Miami	FL
Stacy Lee	San Francisco	CA
Frank Hill	Los Angeles	CA
Carl Davis	Springfield	IL
Alan Carter	New York	NY
David Jones	San Diego	CA

Query

Which clients live in California?

Customer	City	State
Ryan Smith	Sacramento	CA
Stacy Lee	San Francisco	CA
Frank Hill	Los Angeles	CA
David Jones	San Diego	CA

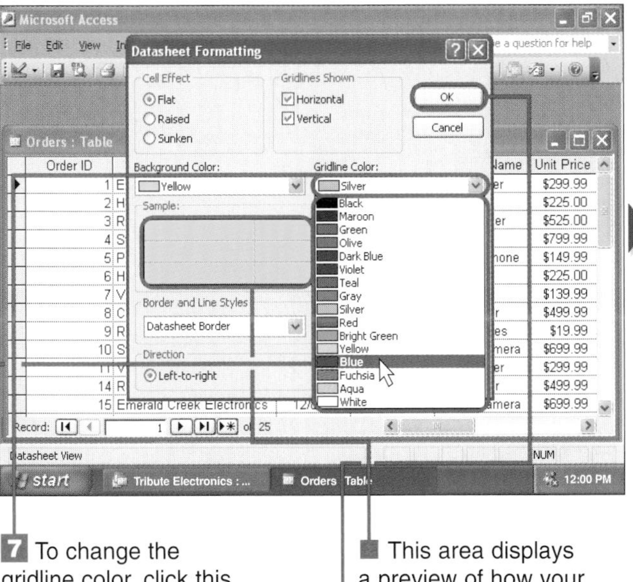

7 To change the gridline color, click this area to display a list of the available colors.

8 Click the gridline color you want to use.

■ This area displays a preview of how your table will appear.

9 Click **OK** to apply your changes to the table.

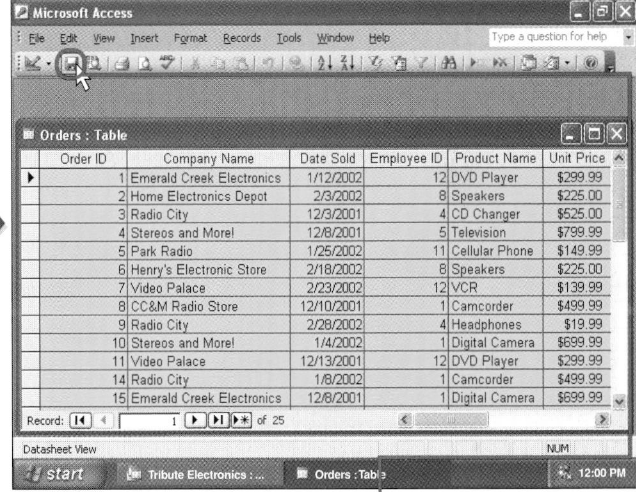

■ The table displays the changes you selected.

10 Click 💾 to save your changes.

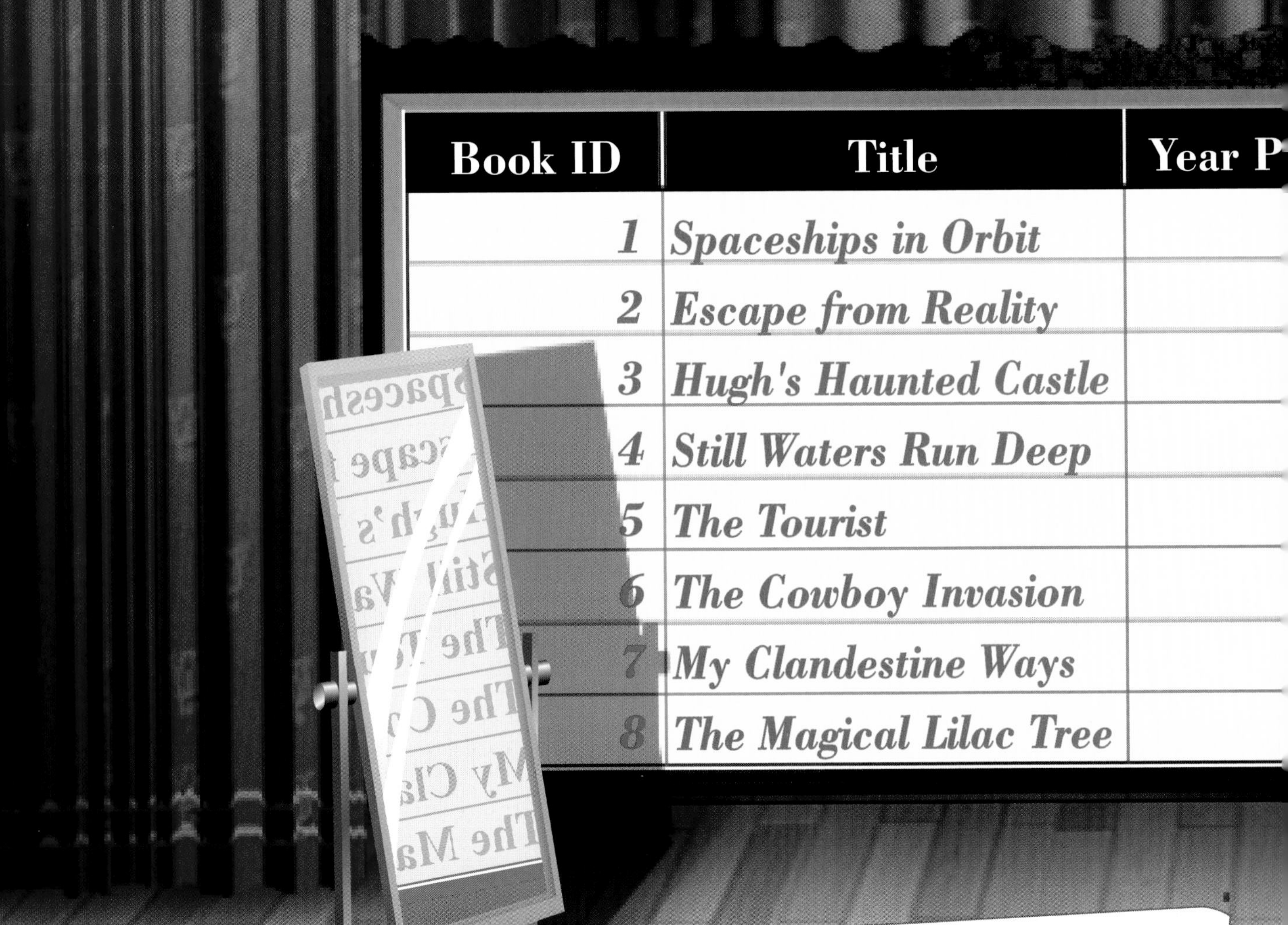

Customer ID	First Name	Last Name	Phone Number	Fax Number
1064	Carol	Barclay	(201) 555-4591	(201) 555-1264
5469	Mark	Dunn	(201) 555-1278	(201) 555-1287
3570	Peter	Lejcar	(201) 555-1975	(201) 555-1064
2146	Tim	Matthews	(201) 555-1946	(201) 555-1953
7521	Deborah	Peterson	(201) 555-1976	(201) 555-1967
2368	John	Smith	[illegible] 1944	(201) 555-1994
3494	Tina	[illegible]	[illegible]	[illegible] 555-1424
7321	Frank	Dawson	(201) 555-1479	(201) 555-1462

CHAPTER 3

Edit Tables

Do you want to work with and edit the data in your tables? This chapter teaches you how to add and remove records, hide and freeze fields in your tables and more.

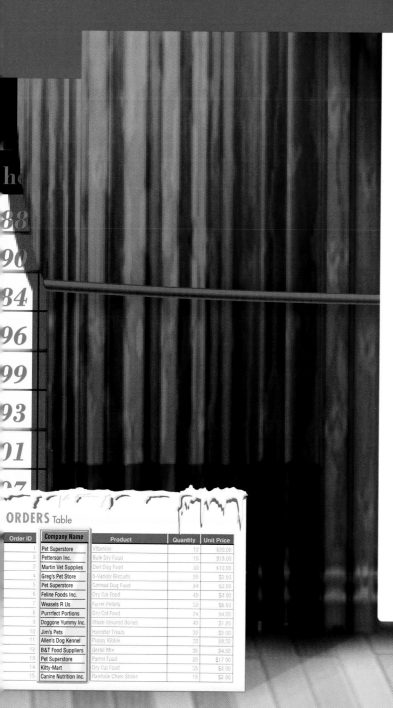

ORDERS Table

Order ID	Company Name	Product	Quantity	Unit Price
1	Pet Superstore	Vitamins	12	$20.00
2	Petterson Inc.	Bulk Dry Food	15	$13.00
3	Martin Vet Supplies	Diet Dog Food	30	$10.00
4	Greg's Pet Store	5-Variety Biscuits	50	$3.50
5	Pet Superstore	Canned Dog Food	24	$3.00
6	Feline Foods Inc.	Dry Cat Food	40	$4.00
7	Weasels R Us	Ferret Pellets	30	$6.50
8	Purrrfect Portions	Dry Cat Food	24	$4.00
9	Doggone Yummy Inc.	Steak-flavored Bones	40	$1.25
10	Jim's Pets	Hamster Treats	30	$5.00
11	Allen's Dog Kennel	Puppy Kibble	20	$3.50
12	B&T Food Suppliers	Gerbil Mix	35	$4.50
13	Pet Superstore	Parrot Food	25	$17.00
14	Kitty-Mart	Dry Cat Food	35	$4.00
15	Canine Nutrition Inc.	Rawhide Chew Sticks	15	$2.00

MOVE THROUGH DATA

You can move through the data in a table to review and edit information.

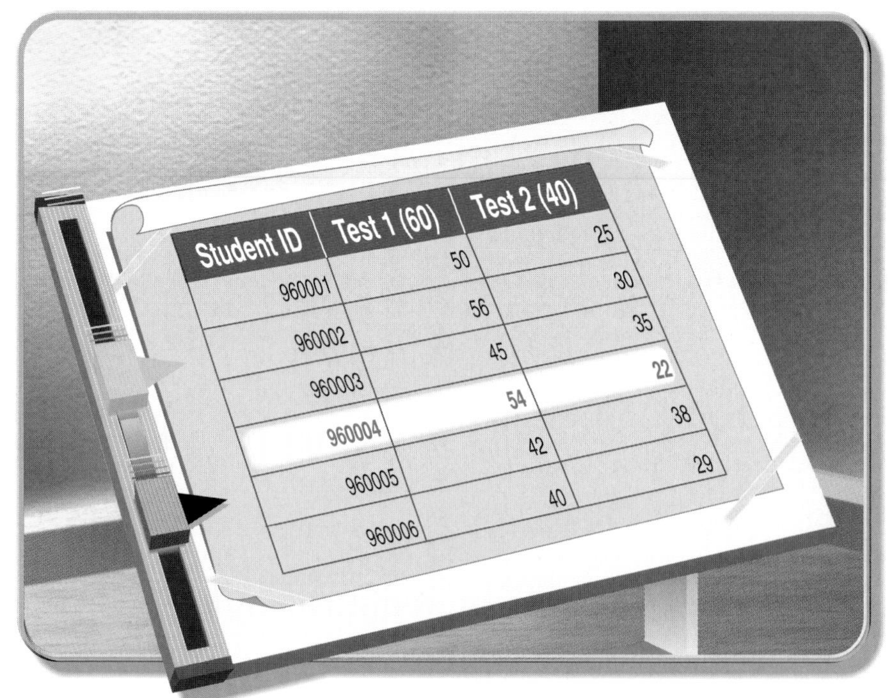

If a table contains a lot of data, your computer screen may not be able to display all the data at once. You can scroll through records and fields to display data that does not appear on your screen.

MOVE THROUGH DATA

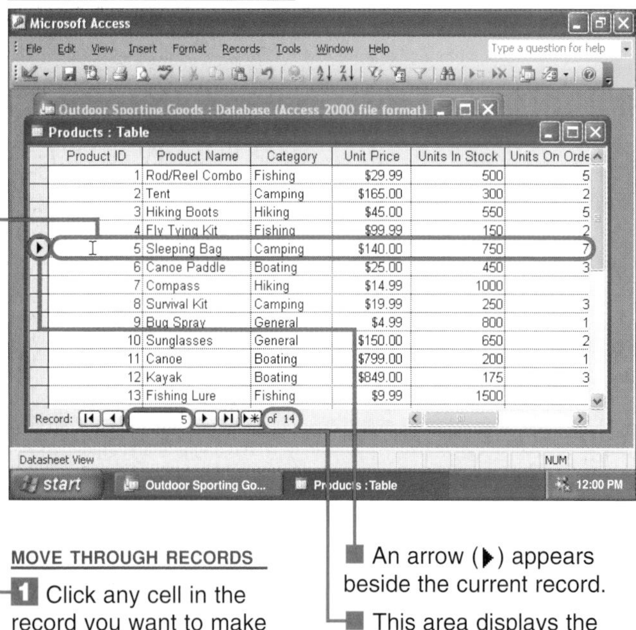

MOVE THROUGH RECORDS

1 Click any cell in the record you want to make the current record.

■ An arrow (▶) appears beside the current record.

■ This area displays the number of the current record and the total number of records in the table.

2 To move through the records, click one of the following buttons.

- ⏮ First record
- ◀ Previous record
- ▶ Next record
- ⏭ Last record

■ To quickly move to a specific record, double-click this area and then type the number of the record you want to display. Then press the Enter key.

How do I use my keyboard to move through data in a table?

To Move:	Press on Keyboard:
Up one screen of records	Page Up
Down one screen of records	Page Down
To the next field in the current record	Tab
Up one record in the same field	↑
Down one record in the same field	↓

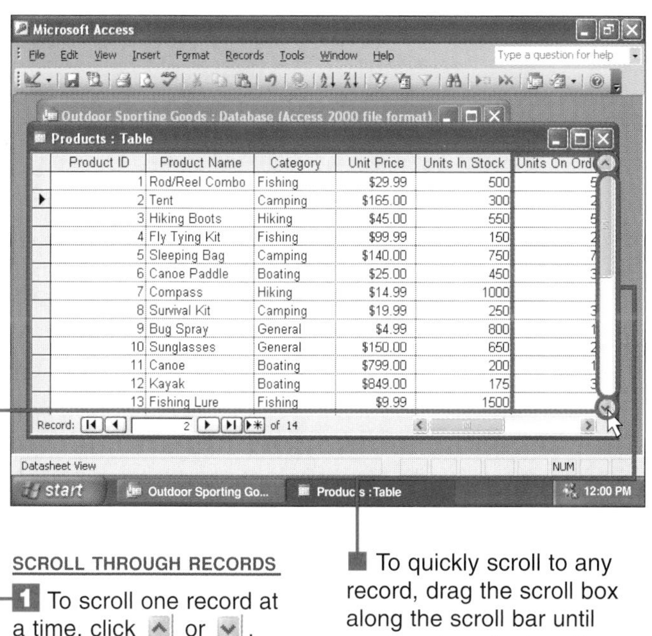

SCROLL THROUGH RECORDS

1 To scroll one record at a time, click ˄ or ˅.

Note: You cannot scroll through records if all the records appear on your screen.

■ To quickly scroll to any record, drag the scroll box along the scroll bar until a yellow box displays the number of the record you want to view.

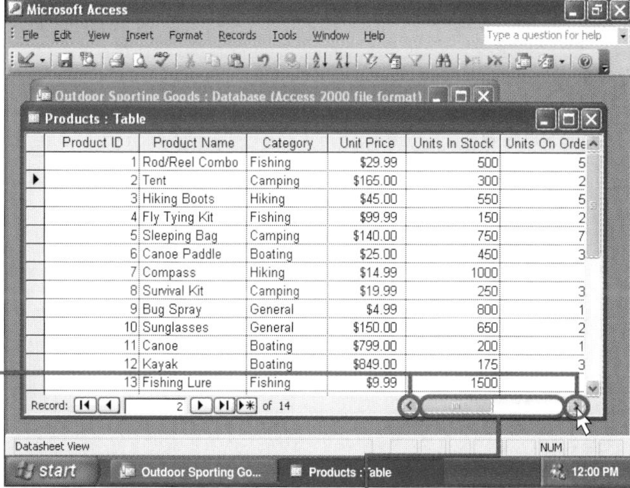

SCROLL THROUGH FIELDS

1 To scroll one field at a time, click ‹ or ›.

Note: You cannot scroll through fields if all the fields appear on your screen.

■ To quickly scroll to any field, drag the scroll box along the scroll bar until the field you want to view appears.

SELECT DATA

Before performing many tasks in a table, you must select the data you want to work with. Selected data appears highlighted on your screen.

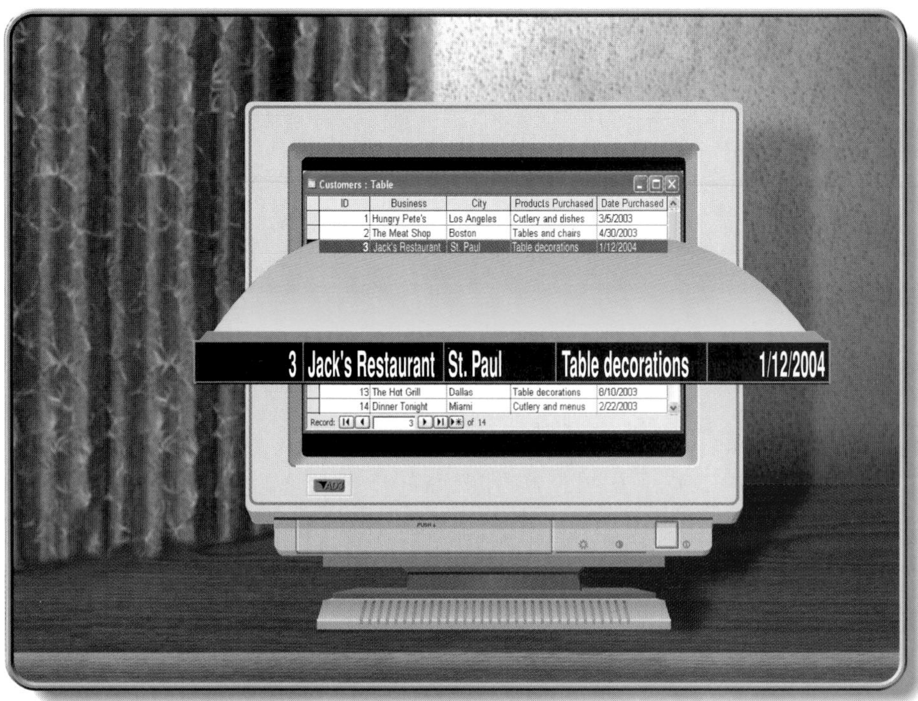

SELECT DATA

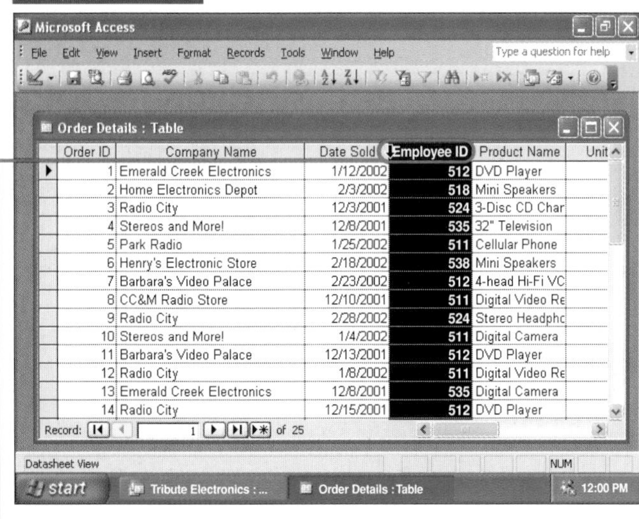

Order ID	Company Name	Date Sold	Employee ID	Product Name	Unit
1	Emerald Creek Electronics	1/12/2002	512	DVD Player	
2	Home Electronics Depot	2/3/2002	518	Mini Speakers	
3	Radio City	12/3/2001	524	3-Disc CD Char	
4	Stereos and More!	12/8/2001	535	32" Television	
5	Park Radio	1/25/2002	511	Cellular Phone	
6	Henry's Electronic Store	2/18/2002	538	Mini Speakers	
7	Barbara's Video Palace	2/23/2002	512	4-head Hi-Fi VC	
8	CC&M Radio Store	12/10/2001	511	Digital Video Re	
9	Radio City	2/28/2002	524	Stereo Headphc	
10	Stereos and More!	1/4/2002	511	Digital Camera	
11	Barbara's Video Palace	12/13/2001	512	DVD Player	
12	Radio City	1/8/2002	511	Digital Video Re	
13	Emerald Creek Electronics	12/8/2001	535	Digital Camera	
14	Radio City	12/15/2001	512	DVD Player	

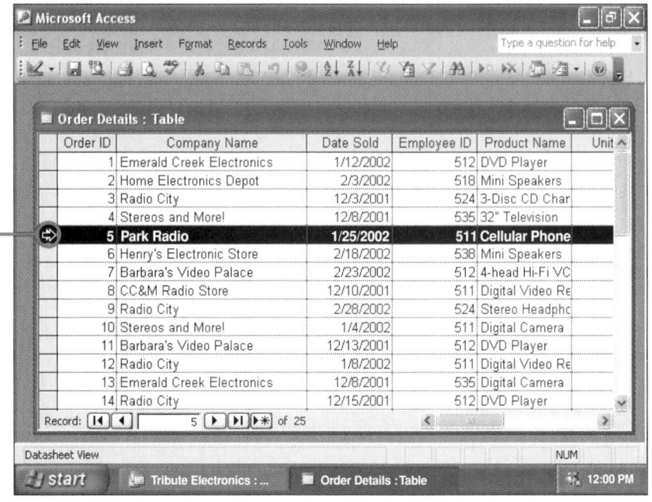

Order ID	Company Name	Date Sold	Employee ID	Product Name	Unit
1	Emerald Creek Electronics	1/12/2002	512	DVD Player	
2	Home Electronics Depot	2/3/2002	518	Mini Speakers	
3	Radio City	12/3/2001	524	3-Disc CD Char	
4	Stereos and More!	12/8/2001	535	32" Television	
5	Park Radio	1/25/2002	511	Cellular Phone	
6	Henry's Electronic Store	2/18/2002	538	Mini Speakers	
7	Barbara's Video Palace	2/23/2002	512	4-head Hi-Fi VC	
8	CC&M Radio Store	12/10/2001	511	Digital Video Re	
9	Radio City	2/28/2002	524	Stereo Headphc	
10	Stereos and More!	1/4/2002	511	Digital Camera	
11	Barbara's Video Palace	12/13/2001	512	DVD Player	
12	Radio City	1/8/2002	511	Digital Video Re	
13	Emerald Creek Electronics	12/8/2001	535	Digital Camera	
14	Radio City	12/15/2001	512	DVD Player	

SELECT A FIELD

1 Position the mouse I over the name of the field you want to select (I changes to ⬇) and then click to select the field.

■ To select multiple fields, position the mouse I over the name of the first field (I changes to ⬇). Then drag the mouse ⬇ until you highlight all the fields you want to select.

SELECT A RECORD

1 Position the mouse I over the area to the left of the record you want to select (I changes to ➡) and then click to select the record.

■ To select multiple records, position the mouse I over the area to the left of the first record (I changes to ➡). Then drag the mouse ➡ until you highlight all the records you want to select.

How do I select all the information in a table?

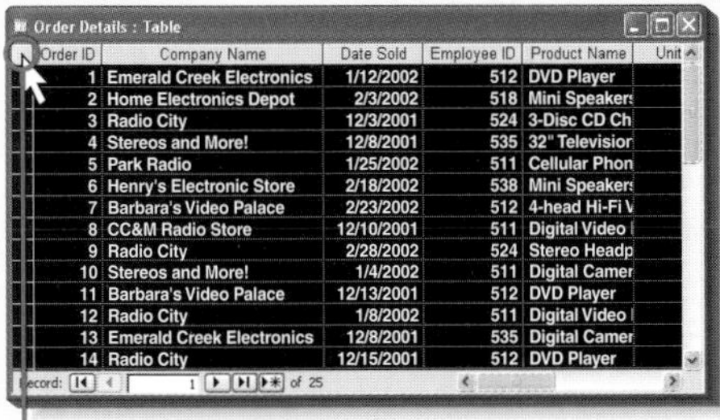

■ To select all the information in a table, click the blank area (□) to the left of the field names.

How do I deselect data?

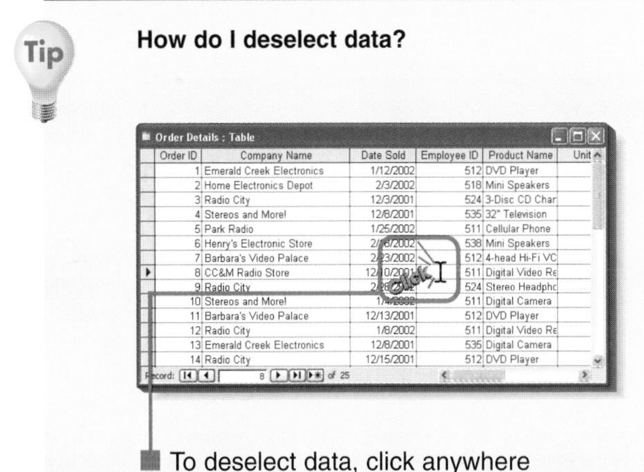

■ To deselect data, click anywhere in the table.

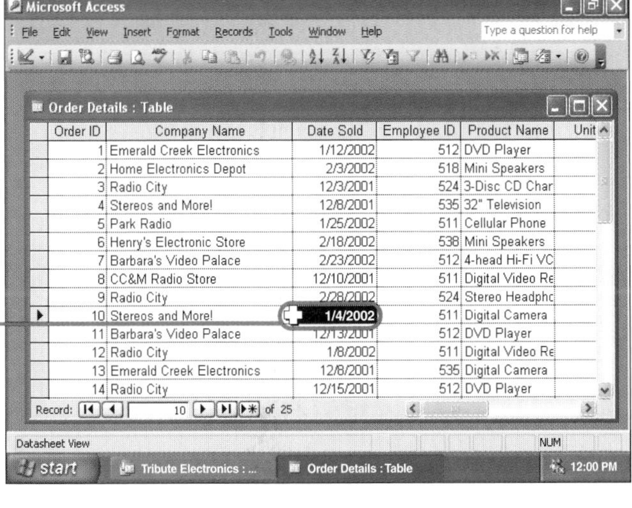

SELECT A CELL

1 Position the mouse I over the left edge of the cell you want to select (I changes to ✚) and then click to select the cell.

■ To select multiple cells, position the mouse I over the left edge of the first cell (I changes to ✚). Then drag the mouse ✚ until you highlight all the cells you want to select.

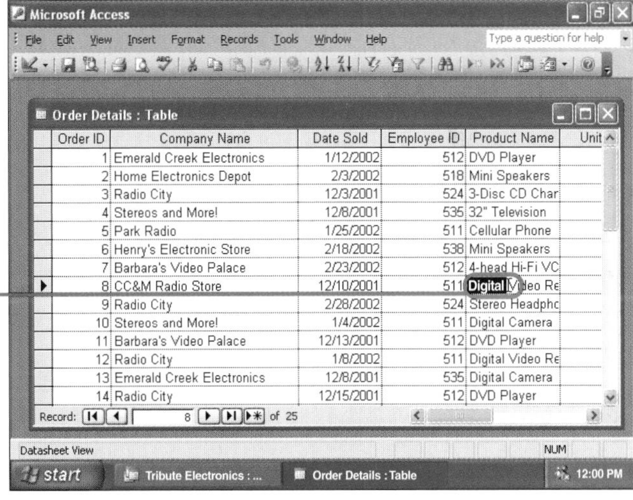

SELECT DATA IN A CELL

1 Position the mouse I over the left edge of the data and then drag the mouse I until you highlight all the data you want to select.

■ To quickly select a word, double-click the word.

EDIT DATA

You can edit the data in a table to correct a mistake or update the data.

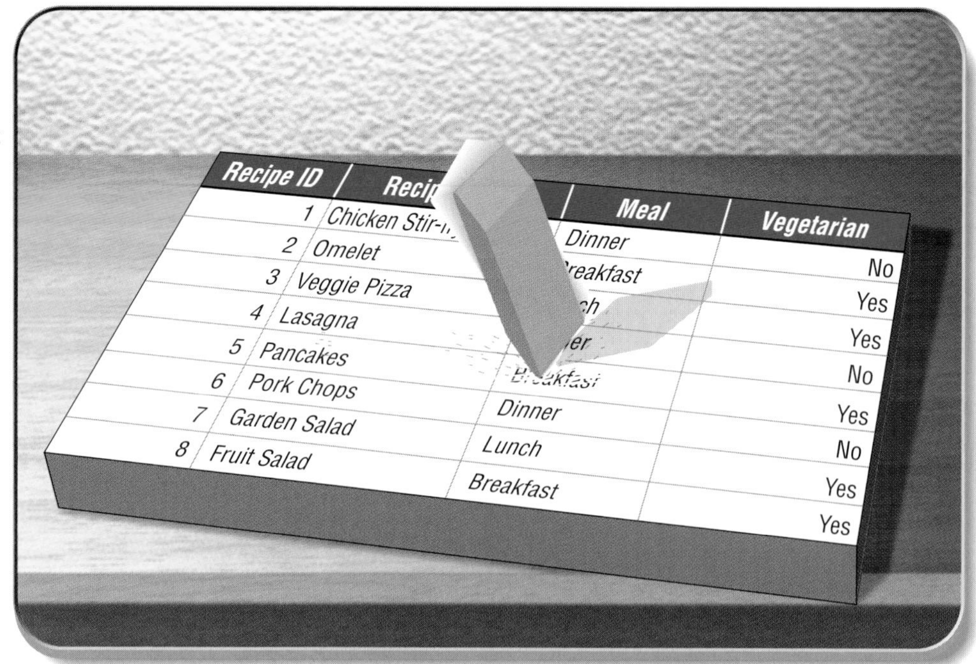

Access automatically saves the changes you make to the data in a table.

EDIT DATA

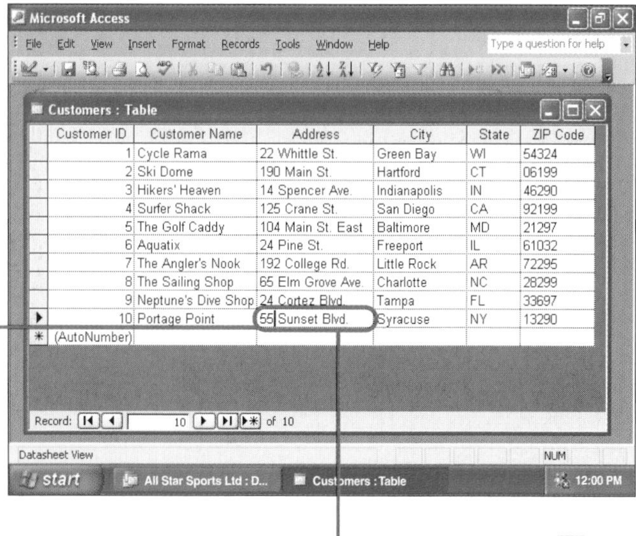

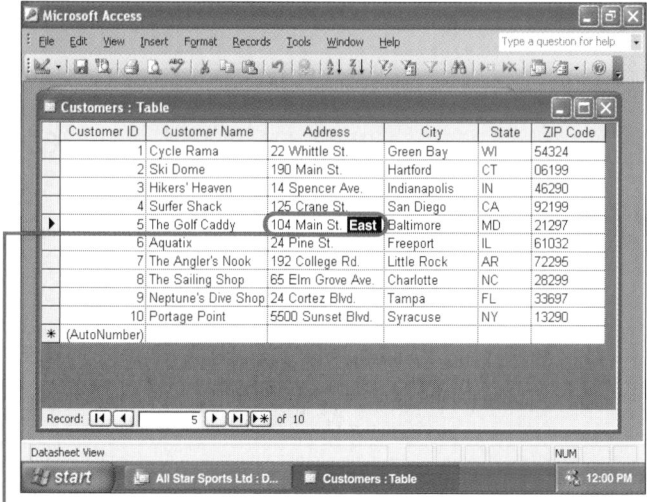

INSERT DATA

1 Click the location in the cell where you want to insert data.

■ A flashing insertion point appears in the cell, indicating where the data you type will appear.

Note: You can press the ← or → key to move the insertion point.

2 Type the data you want to insert.

DELETE DATA

1 Drag the mouse I over the data you want to delete to highlight the data.

2 Press the Delete key to delete the highlighted data.

Note: To delete a single character, click the location where you want to delete the character. To remove the character to the left of the insertion point, press the ←Backspace key. To remove the character to the right of the insertion point, press the Delete key.

What are the symbols that appear to the left of the records in a table?

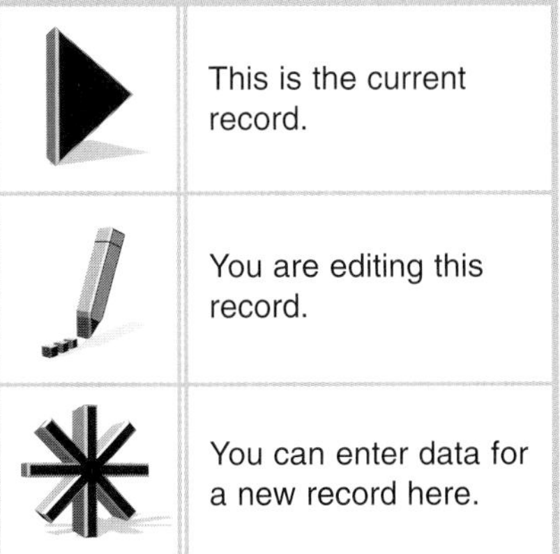

▶	This is the current record.
✎	You are editing this record.
✱	You can enter data for a new record here.

Why can't I edit the data in a cell?

You may be trying to edit data in a field that has the AutoNumber data type. A field that has the AutoNumber data type automatically numbers each record for you to uniquely identify each record. For more information on data types, see page 83.

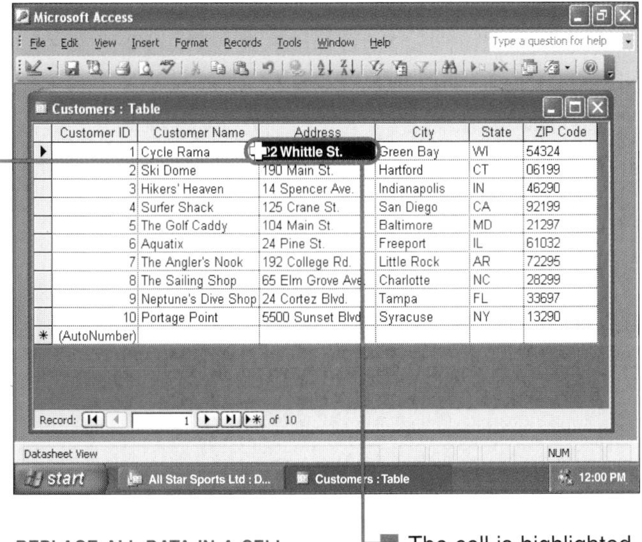

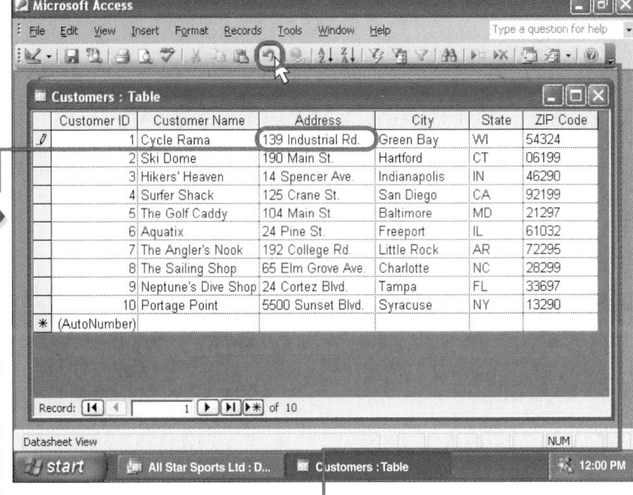

REPLACE ALL DATA IN A CELL

1 Position the mouse I over the left edge of the cell containing the data you want to replace with new data (I changes to ✚) and then click to select the cell.

■ The cell is highlighted.

2 Type the new data and then press the Enter key.

UNDO CHANGES

1 Click ↶ to immediately undo your most recent change.

ZOOM INTO A CELL

You can zoom into any cell in a table to make the contents of the cell easier to review and edit.

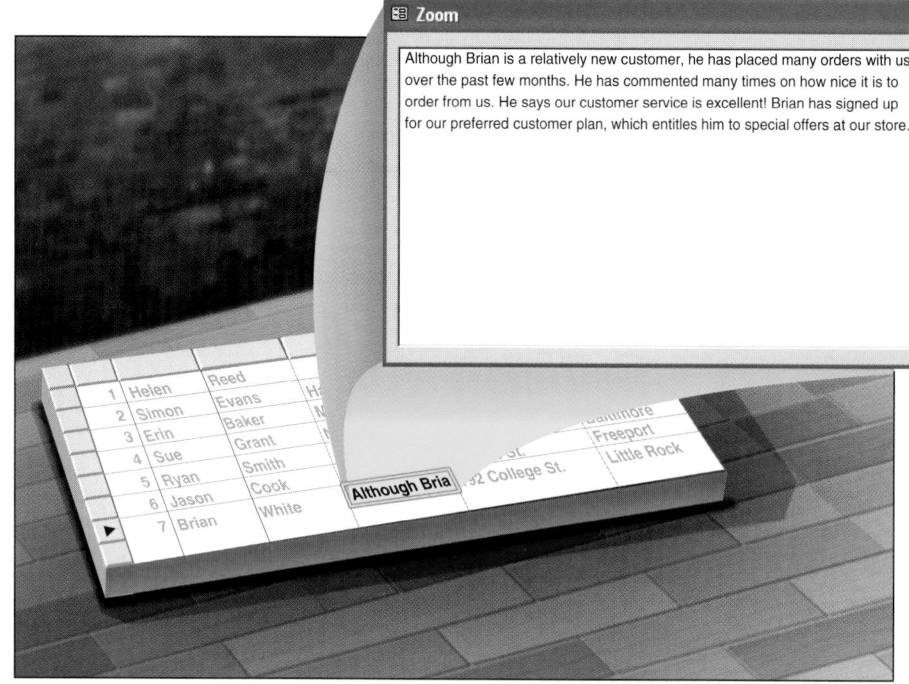

Zooming into a cell is useful when a cell contains a large amount of information, such as notes about a customer.

ZOOM INTO A CELL

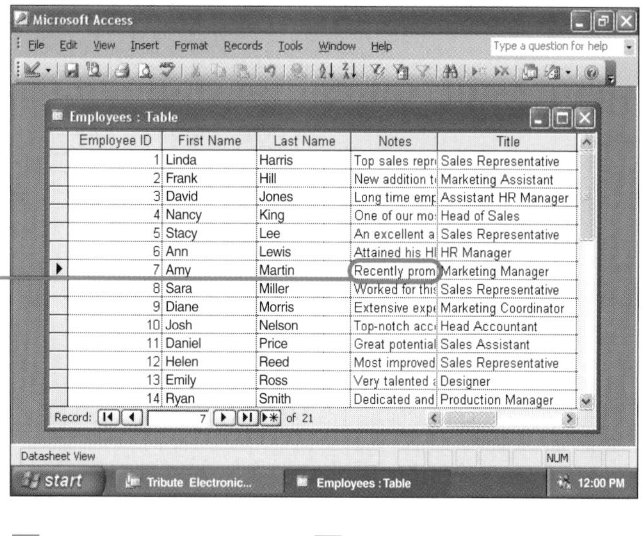

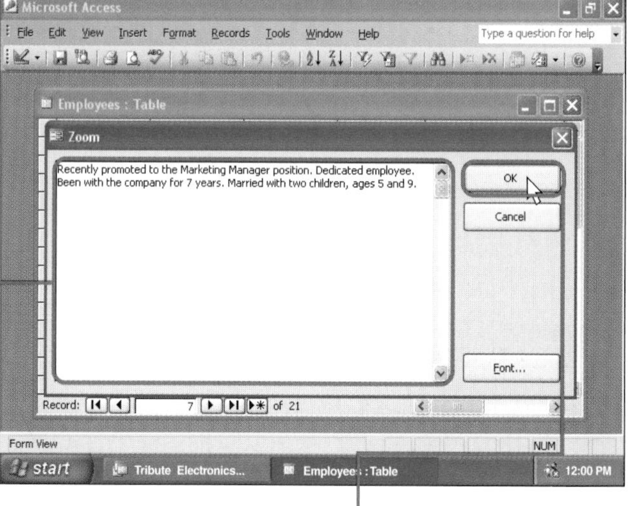

1 Click the cell you want to zoom into.

2 Press and hold down the **Shift** key as you press the **F2** key.

■ The Zoom dialog box appears.

■ This area displays all the data in the cell. You can review and edit the data. To edit data, see page 56.

3 When you finish reviewing and editing the data, click **OK** to close the dialog box.

■ The table will display any changes you made to the data.

DISPLAY A SUBDATASHEET

When viewing the information in a table, you may be able to display a subdatasheet to view and edit related data from another table.

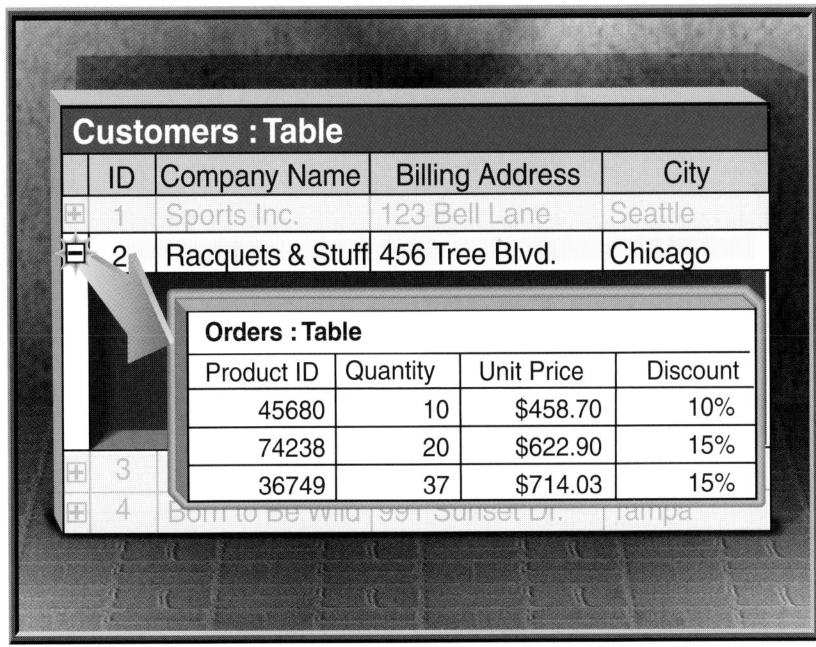

For example, when viewing a table containing customer information, you can display a subdatasheet to view the orders placed by a customer.

You can display a subdatasheet only when a table is related to another table. For information on relationships, see page 128.

DISPLAY A SUBDATASHEET

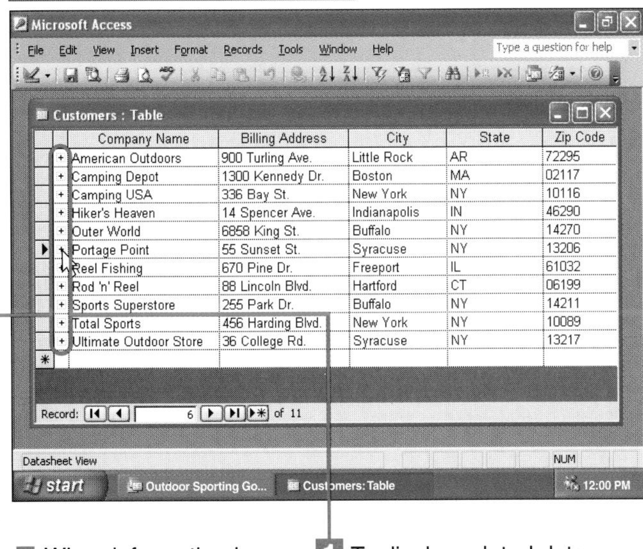

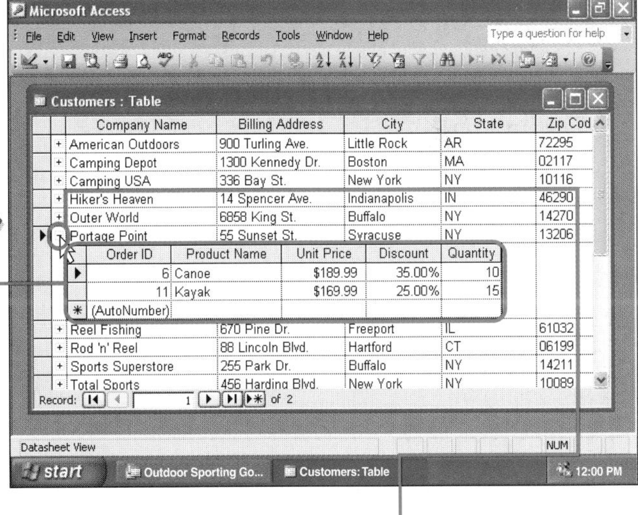

■ When information in a table relates to data in another table, a plus sign (+) appears beside each record.

1 To display related data from the other table, click the plus sign (+) beside a record (+ changes to −).

■ A subdatasheet appears, displaying the related data from the other table. You can review and edit the data. To edit data, see page 56.

2 To once again hide the subdatasheet, click the minus sign (−) beside the record.

CHECK SPELLING

You can find and correct all the spelling errors in a table.

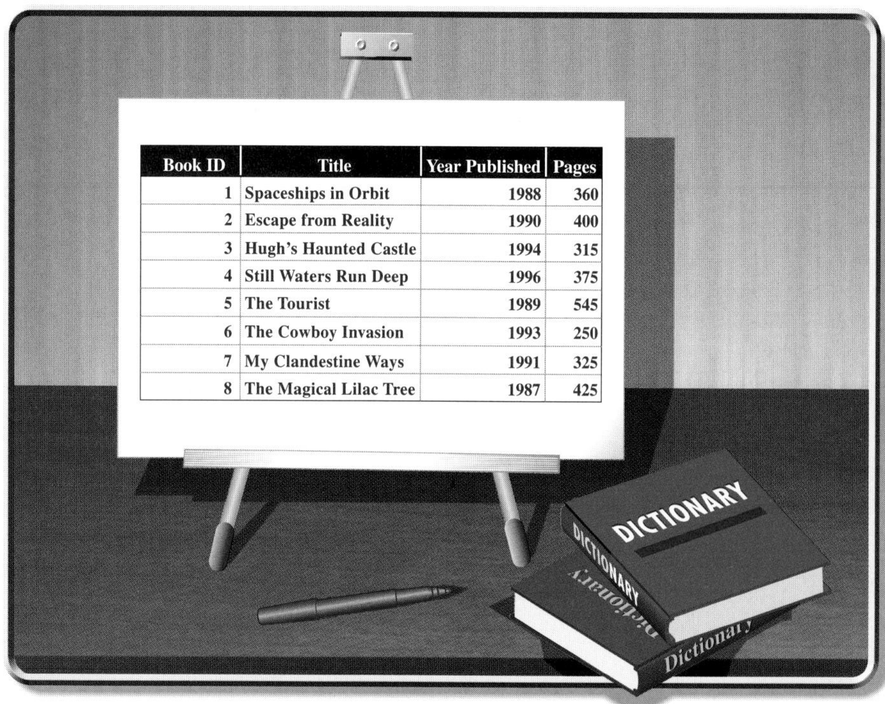

Book ID	Title	Year Published	Pages
1	Spaceships in Orbit	1988	360
2	Escape from Reality	1990	400
3	Hugh's Haunted Castle	1994	315
4	Still Waters Run Deep	1996	375
5	The Tourist	1989	545
6	The Cowboy Invasion	1993	250
7	My Clandestine Ways	1991	325
8	The Magical Lilac Tree	1987	425

Access compares every word in your table to words in its dictionary. If a word in your table does not exist in the dictionary, Access considers the word misspelled.

CHECK SPELLING

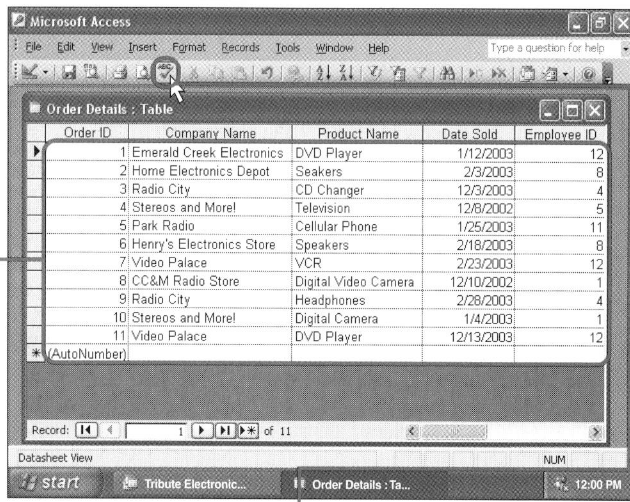

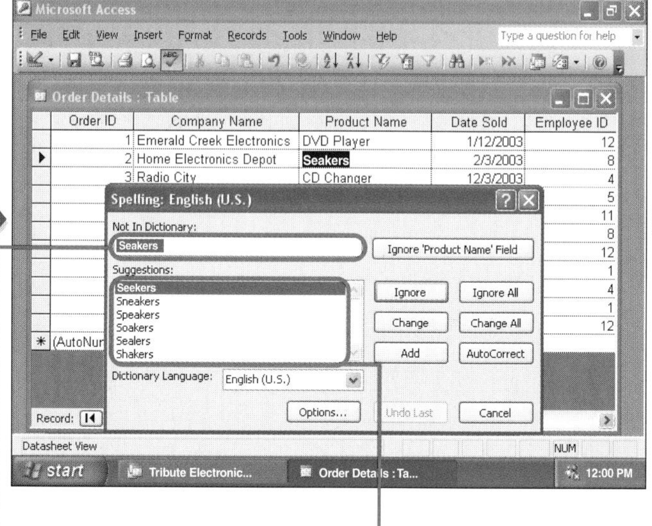

1 To spell check your entire table, click any cell in the table.

Note: To spell check only part of your table, select the field, record or cell you want to check in the table. To select data in a table, see page 54.

2 Click the spelling button to start the spell check.

■ The Spelling dialog box appears if Access finds a misspelled word in your table.

■ This area displays the misspelled word.

■ This area displays suggestions for correcting the word.

Can Access automatically correct my typing mistakes?

Yes. Access automatically corrects common spelling errors as you type. Here are a few examples:

adn → and
alot → a lot
comittee → committee
don;t → don't
nwe → new
occurence → occurrence
recieve → receive
seperate → separate
teh → the

Will a spell check find all the errors in my table?

No. A spell check will find only spelling errors. Access will not find correctly spelled words used in the wrong context, such as "blew" in a Product Color field. You should carefully review your table to find this type of error.

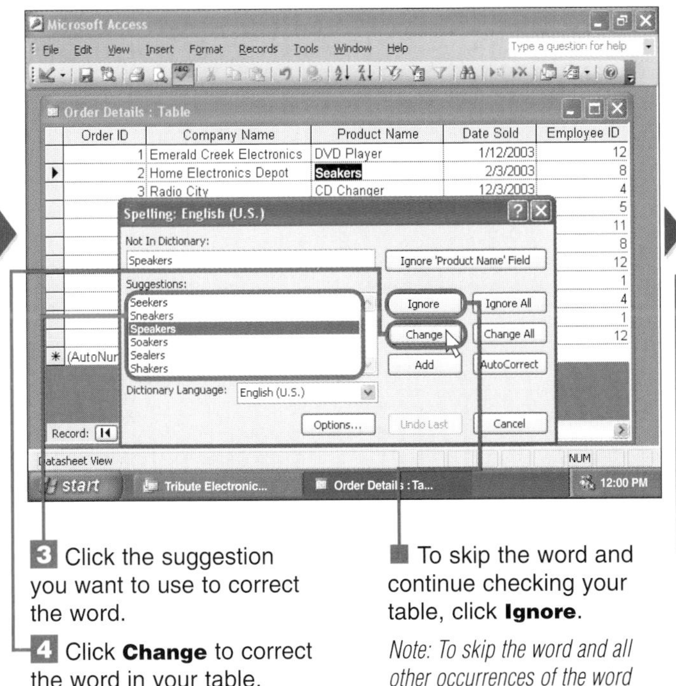

3 Click the suggestion you want to use to correct the word.

4 Click **Change** to correct the word in your table.

■ To skip the word and continue checking your table, click **Ignore**.

*Note: To skip the word and all other occurrences of the word in your table, click **Ignore All**.*

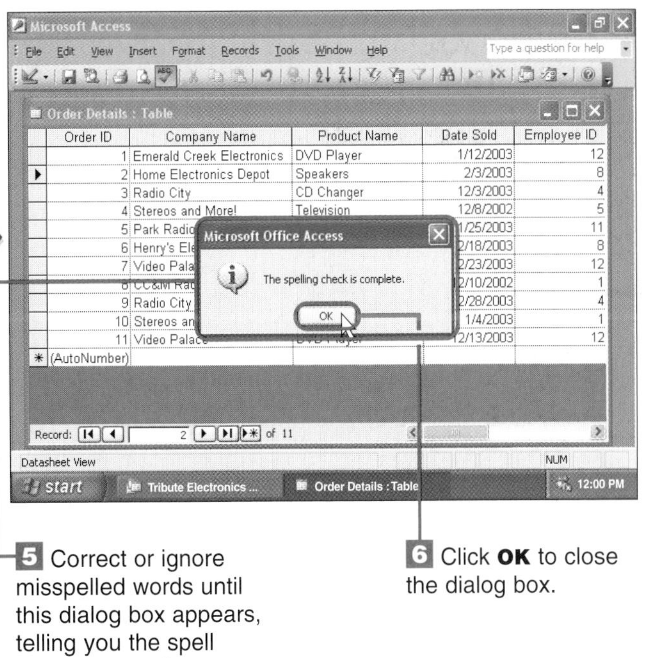

5 Correct or ignore misspelled words until this dialog box appears, telling you the spell check is complete.

6 Click **OK** to close the dialog box.

MOVE OR COPY DATA

You can move or copy data to a new location in your table.

Moving data allows you to rearrange data in your table. When you move data, the data disappears from its original location.

Copying data allows you to repeat data in your table without having to retype the data. When you copy data, the data appears in both the original and new locations.

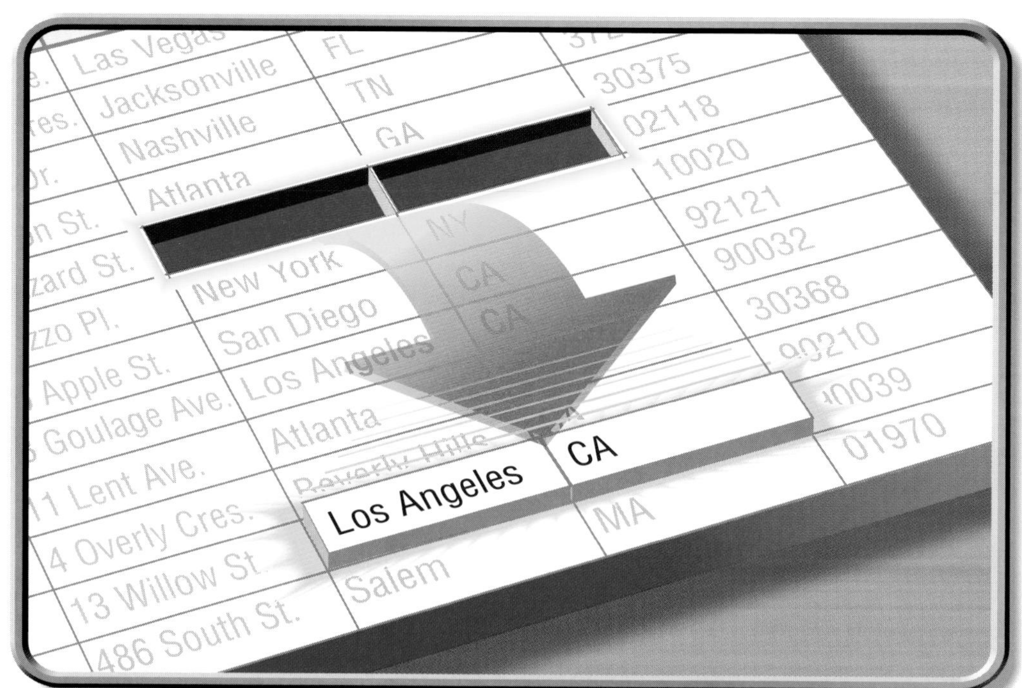

MOVE OR COPY DATA

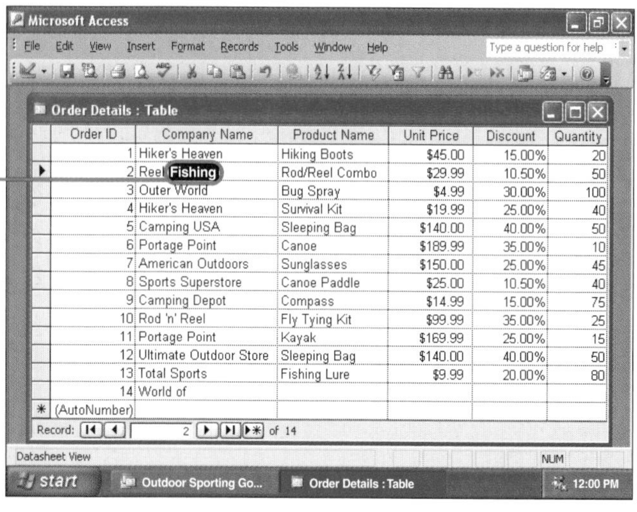

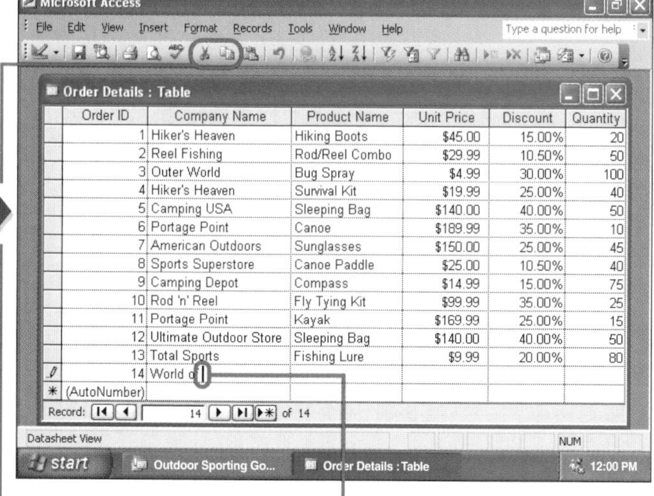

1 To move or copy data in a cell, drag the mouse I over the data until you highlight the data you want to move or copy.

■ To copy the entire contents of one or more cells, select the cell(s) containing the data you want to copy. To select cells, see page 55.

2 Click one of the following buttons.

- ✂ Move data
- 📋 Copy data

3 Click the location in the table where you want to place the data.

■ If you copied the entire contents of one or more cells, select the cell(s) where you want to place the data.

Tip

Why does the Clipboard task pane appear when I move or copy data?

When you move or copy data, the Clipboard task pane may appear. The Clipboard task pane displays the last items you have selected to move or copy. To place a clipboard item in your table, click the location where you want to place the item and then click the item in the task pane.

Note: To close the Clipboard task pane, click ✕ at the top of the task pane.

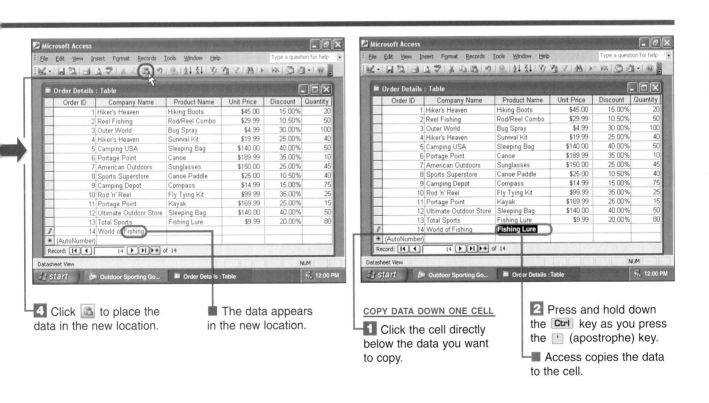

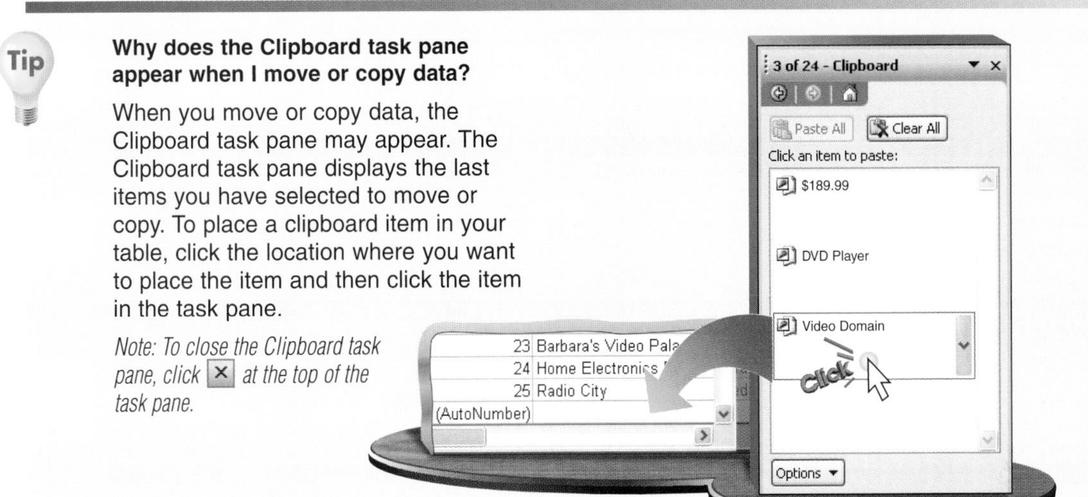

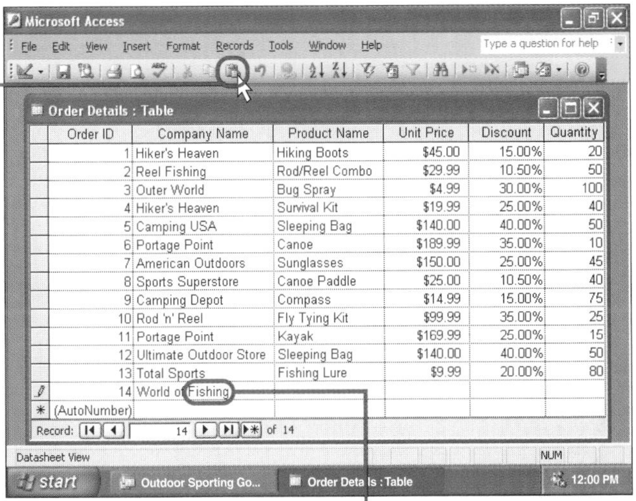

3 of 24 - Clipboard
Paste All
Clear All
Click an item to paste:
$189.99
DVD Player
Video Domain
Click
Options
23 Barbara's Video Pala
24 Home Electronics
25 Radio City
(AutoNumber)

Microsoft Access
File Edit View Insert Format Records Tools Window Help
Type a question for help
Order Details : Table
Order ID | Company Name | Product Name | Unit Price | Discount | Quantity
1 Hiker's Heaven | Hiking Boots | $45.00 | 15.00% | 20
2 Reel Fishing | Rod/Reel Combo | $29.99 | 10.50% | 50
3 Outer World | Bug Spray | $4.99 | 30.00% | 100
4 Hiker's Heaven | Survival Kit | $19.99 | 25.00% | 40
5 Camping USA | Sleeping Bag | $140.00 | 40.00% | 50
6 Portage Point | Canoe | $189.99 | 35.00% | 10
7 American Outdoors | Sunglasses | $150.00 | 25.00% | 45
8 Sports Superstore | Canoe Paddle | $25.00 | 10.50% | 40
9 Camping Depot | Compass | $14.99 | 15.00% | 75
10 Rod 'n' Reel | Fly Tying Kit | $99.99 | 35.00% | 25
11 Portage Point | Kayak | $169.99 | 25.00% | 15
12 Ultimate Outdoor Store | Sleeping Bag | $140.00 | 40.00% | 50
13 Total Sports | Fishing Lure | $9.99 | 20.00% | 80
14 World of Fishing
(AutoNumber)
Record: 14 of 14
Datasheet View
NUM
start
Outdoor Sporting Go...
Order Details : Table
12:00 PM

4 Click 📋 to place the data in the new location.

■ The data appears in the new location.

Microsoft Access
File Edit View Insert Format Records Tools Window Help
Type a question for help
Order Details : Table
Order ID | Company Name | Product Name | Unit Price | Discount | Quantity
1 Hiker's Heaven | Hiking Boots | $45.00 | 15.00% | 20
2 Reel Fishing | Rod/Reel Combo | $29.99 | 10.50% | 50
3 Outer World | Bug Spray | $4.99 | 30.00% | 100
4 Hiker's Heaven | Survival Kit | $19.99 | 25.00% | 40
5 Camping USA | Sleeping Bag | $140.00 | 40.00% | 50
6 Portage Point | Canoe | $189.99 | 35.00% | 10
7 American Outdoors | Sunglasses | $150.00 | 25.00% | 45
8 Sports Superstore | Canoe Paddle | $25.00 | 10.50% | 40
9 Camping Depot | Compass | $14.99 | 15.00% | 75
10 Rod 'n' Reel | Fly Tying Kit | $99.99 | 35.00% | 25
11 Portage Point | Kayak | $169.99 | 25.00% | 15
12 Ultimate Outdoor Store | Sleeping Bag | $140.00 | 40.00% | 50
13 Total Sports | Fishing Lure | $9.99 | 20.00% | 80
14 World of Fishing | Fishing Lure
(AutoNumber)
Record: 14 of 14
Datasheet View
NUM
start
Outdoor Sporting Go...
Order Details : Table
12:00 PM

COPY DATA DOWN ONE CELL

1 Click the cell directly below the data you want to copy.

2 Press and hold down the Ctrl key as you press the ' (apostrophe) key.

■ Access copies the data to the cell.

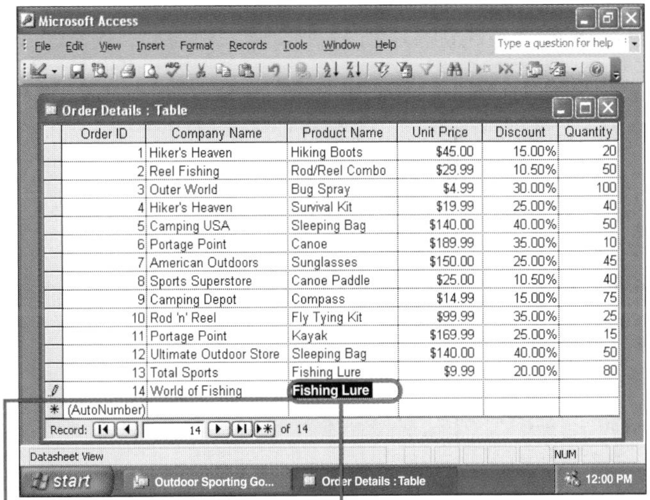

ADD A RECORD

You can add a new record to include additional information in your table. For example, you may want to add information about a new customer.

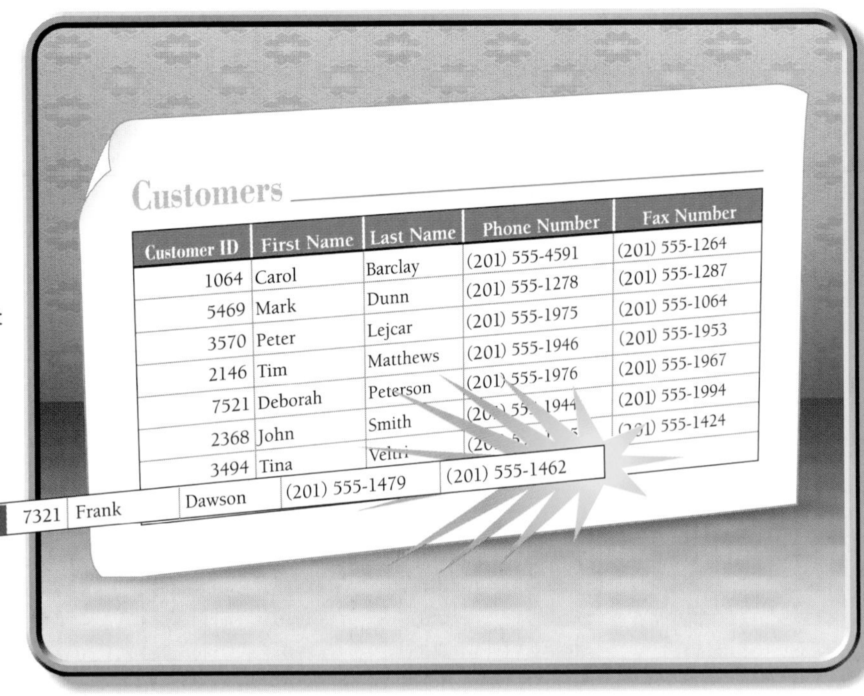

You can add a new record only to the end of your table. If you later want to change the order of the records in the table, you can sort the records. To sort records, see page 176.

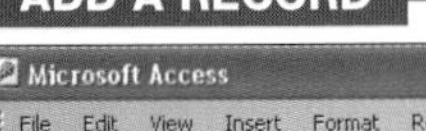

ADD A RECORD

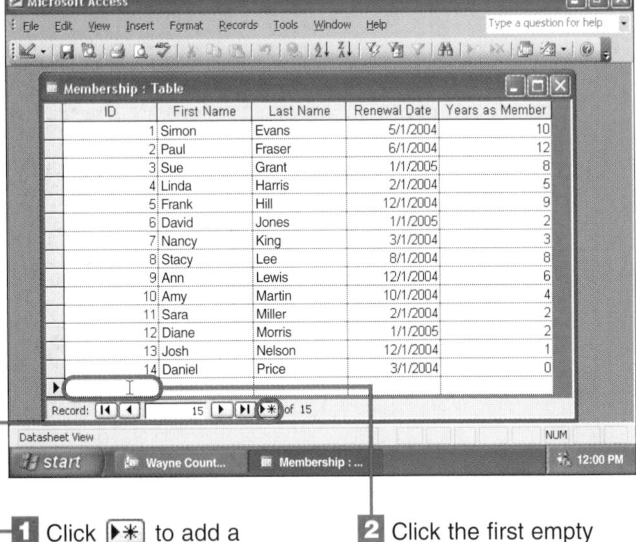

ID	First Name	Last Name	Renewal Date	Years as Member
1	Simon	Evans	5/1/2004	10
2	Paul	Fraser	6/1/2004	12
3	Sue	Grant	1/1/2005	8
4	Linda	Harris	2/1/2004	5
5	Frank	Hill	12/1/2004	9
6	David	Jones	1/1/2005	2
7	Nancy	King	3/1/2004	3
8	Stacy	Lee	8/1/2004	8
9	Ann	Lewis	12/1/2004	6
10	Amy	Martin	10/1/2004	4
11	Sara	Miller	2/1/2004	2
12	Diane	Morris	1/1/2005	2
13	Josh	Nelson	12/1/2004	1
14	Daniel	Price	3/1/2004	0

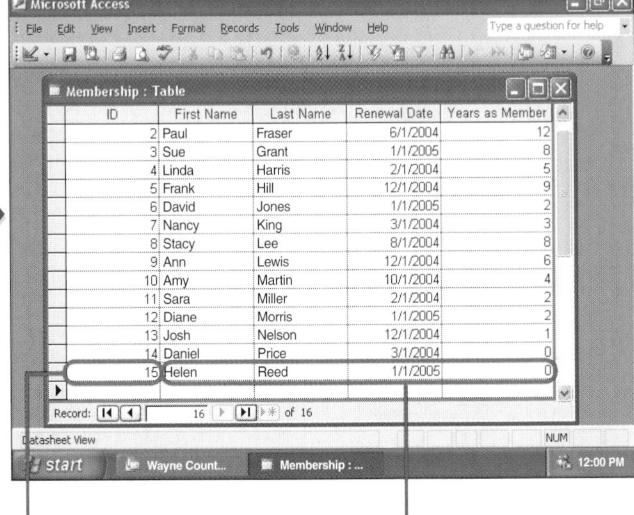

ID	First Name	Last Name	Renewal Date	Years as Member
2	Paul	Fraser	6/1/2004	12
3	Sue	Grant	1/1/2005	8
4	Linda	Harris	2/1/2004	5
5	Frank	Hill	12/1/2004	9
6	David	Jones	1/1/2005	2
7	Nancy	King	3/1/2004	3
8	Stacy	Lee	8/1/2004	8
9	Ann	Lewis	12/1/2004	6
10	Amy	Martin	10/1/2004	4
11	Sara	Miller	2/1/2004	2
12	Diane	Morris	1/1/2005	2
13	Josh	Nelson	12/1/2004	1
14	Daniel	Price	3/1/2004	0
15	Helen	Reed	1/1/2005	0

1 Click ▶* to add a new record to your table.

2 Click the first empty cell in the row.

3 Type the data that corresponds to the field and then press the Enter key to move to the next field.

4 Repeat step **3** until you finish entering all the data for the record.

■ Access automatically saves each new record you add to the table.

DELETE A RECORD

You can delete a record from a table to permanently remove information you no longer need. For example, you may want to remove information about a customer who no longer orders your products.

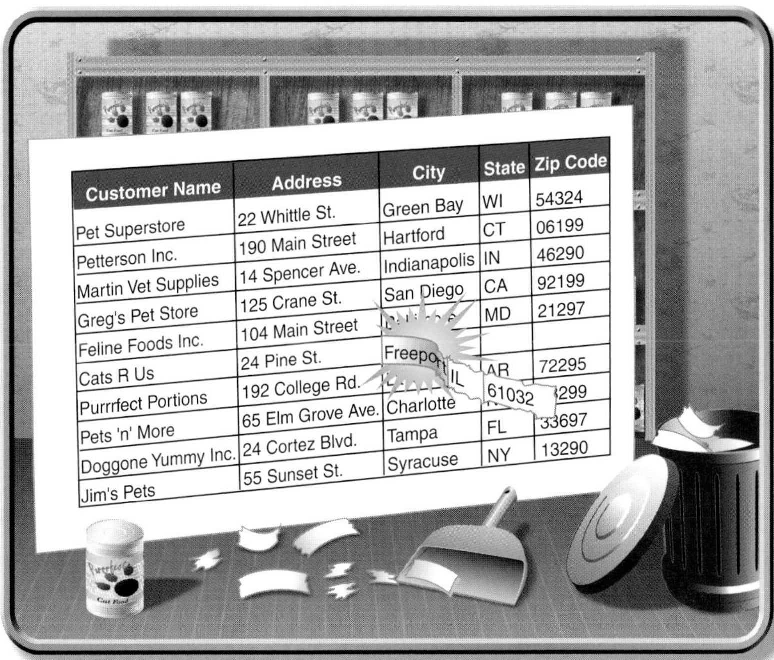

Deleting records saves storage space on your computer and keeps your database from becoming cluttered with unnecessary information.

When you delete a record, you may also want to delete any related records in other tables. For example, if you delete a company from your supplier table, you may also want to delete the company's products from your products table.

DELETE A RECORD

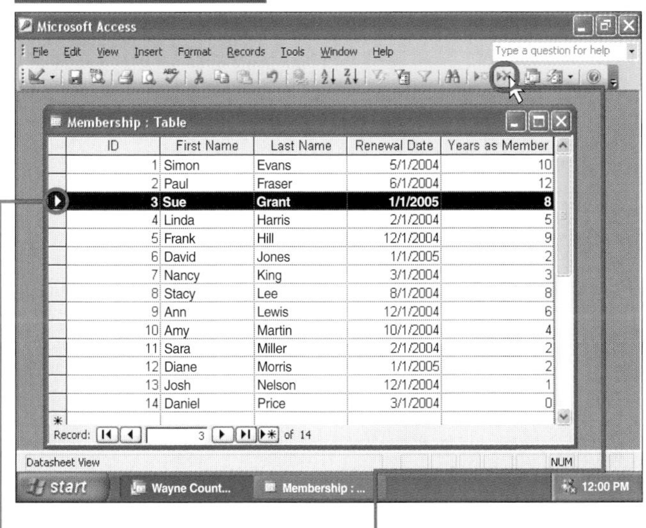

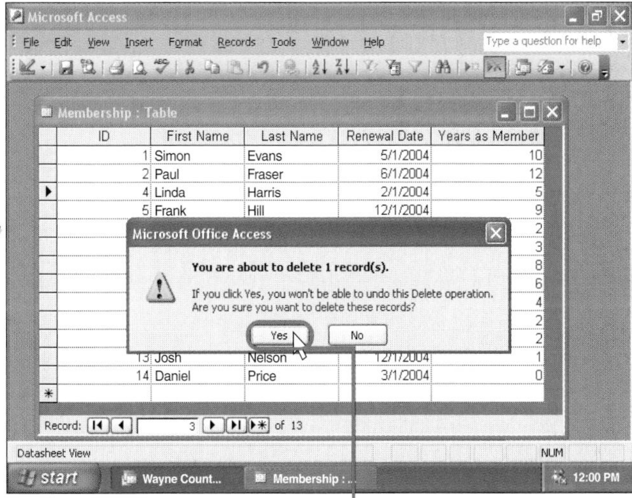

1 Position the mouse I over the area to the left of the record you want to delete (I changes to ➡) and then click to select the record.

2 Click ▶✕ to delete the record.

■ The record disappears.

■ A warning dialog box appears.

3 Click **Yes** to permanently delete the record.

CHANGE THE FONT OF DATA

You can change the font, style, size and color of data in a table to customize the appearance of the table.

For example, you may want to use a smaller font size for your data to display more information on the screen at once. When you change the font of data, all the data in the table will display the change.

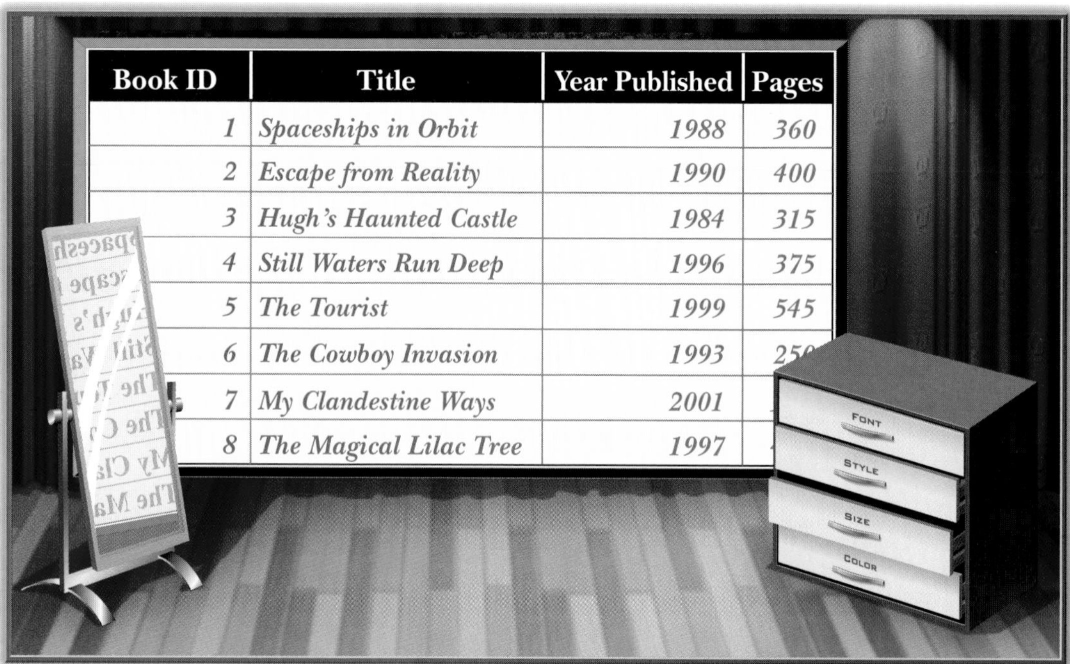

Book ID | Title | Year Published | Pages
1 | Spaceships in Orbit | 1988 | 360
2 | Escape from Reality | 1990 | 400
3 | Hugh's Haunted Castle | 1984 | 315
4 | Still Waters Run Deep | 1996 | 375
5 | The Tourist | 1999 | 545
6 | The Cowboy Invasion | 1993
7 | My Clandestine Ways | 2001
8 | The Magical Lilac Tree | 1997
Font
Style
Size
Color

CHANGE THE FONT OF DATA

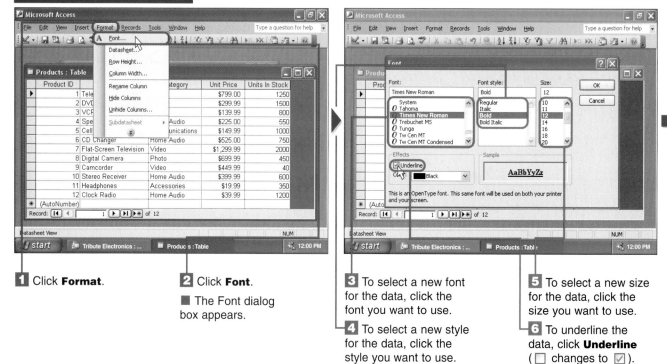

1 Click **Format**.

2 Click **Font**.

■ The Font dialog box appears.

3 To select a new font for the data, click the font you want to use.

4 To select a new style for the data, click the style you want to use.

5 To select a new size for the data, click the size you want to use.

6 To underline the data, click **Underline** (☐ changes to ☑).

What determines which fonts are available on my computer?

The fonts available on your computer depend on the programs installed on your computer, the setup of your computer and the printer you are using. You can obtain additional fonts at stores that sell computer software and on the Internet.

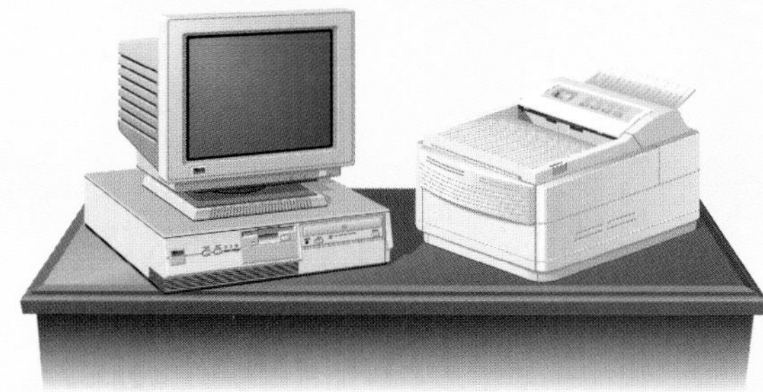

Why do some fonts display the O symbol in the Font dialog box?

In the Font dialog box, the O symbol beside a font indicates an OpenType font. An OpenType font will print exactly as it appears on your screen. A font that does not display the O symbol in the Font dialog box may not print exactly as it appears on your screen.

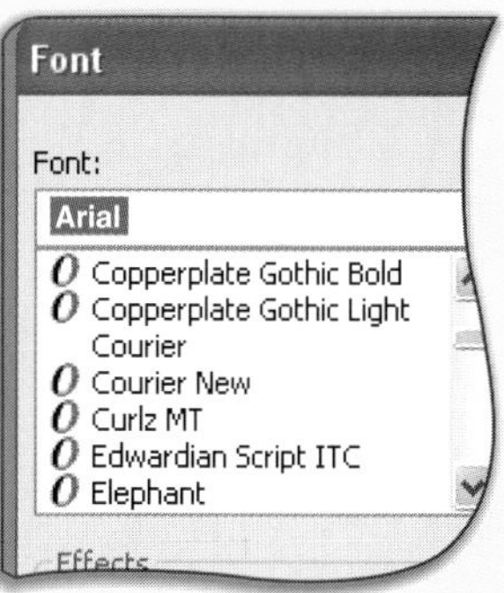

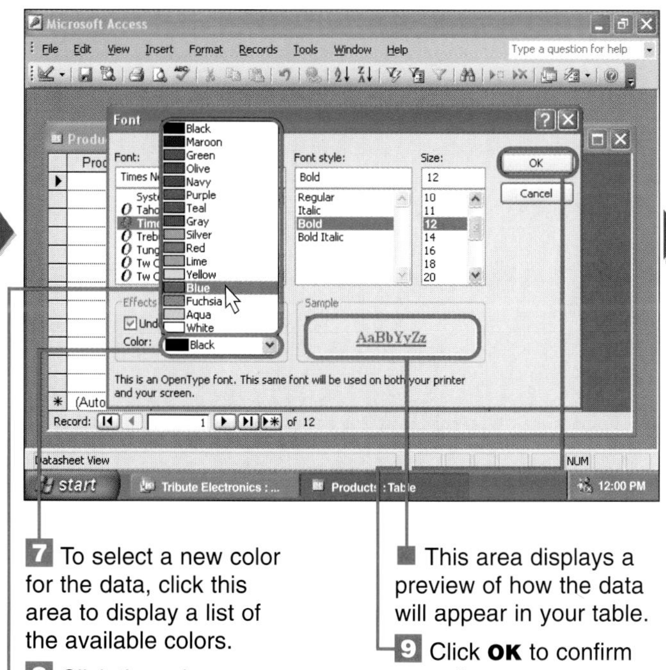

7 To select a new color for the data, click this area to display a list of the available colors.

8 Click the color you want to use.

■ This area displays a preview of how the data will appear in your table.

9 Click **OK** to confirm your changes.

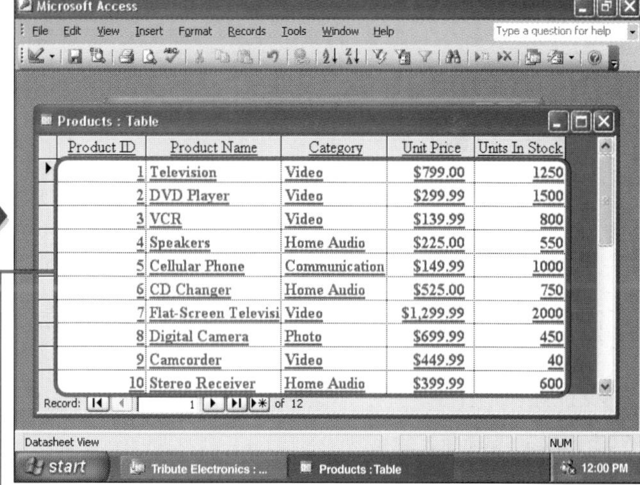

■ The data in your table displays the changes.

HIDE A FIELD

You can temporarily hide a field in a table to reduce the amount of information displayed on your screen.

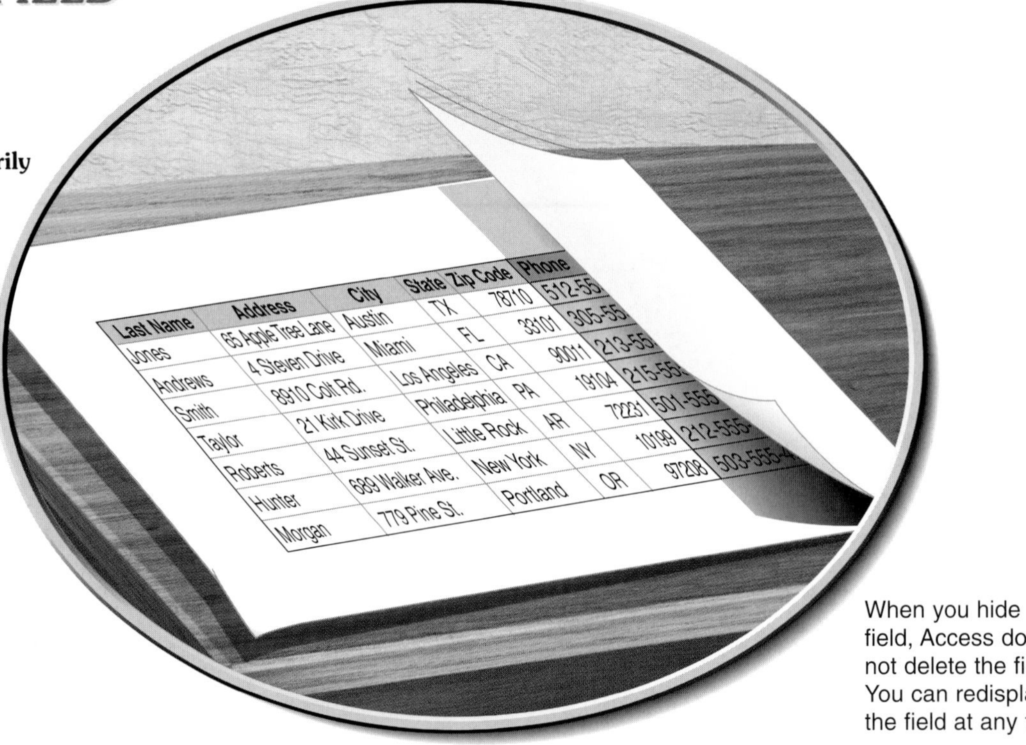

When you hide a field, Access does not delete the field. You can redisplay the field at any time.

HIDE A FIELD

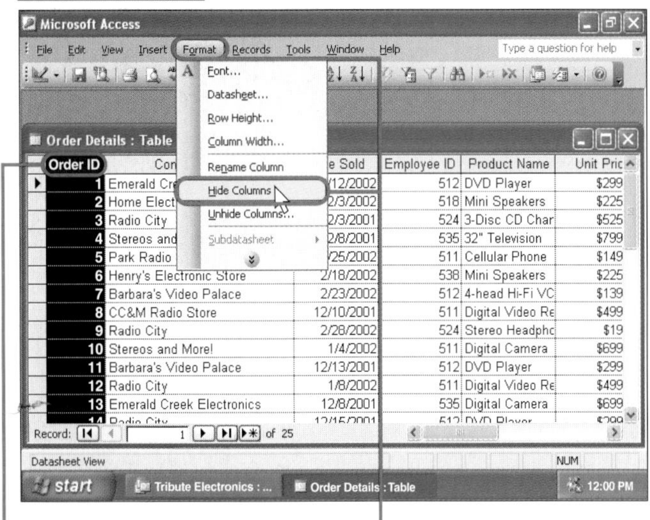

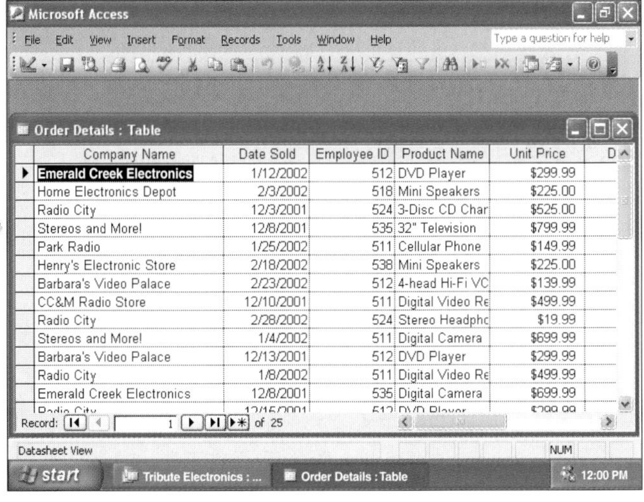

1 Click the name of the field you want to hide. The field is highlighted.

2 Click **Format**.

3 Click **Hide Columns**.

■ The field disappears from your table.

When would I hide a field?

Hiding a field can help you review information of interest in a table by removing unnecessary data from your screen. For example, if you want to browse through only the names and telephone numbers of your customers, you can hide the fields that display other information in your table.

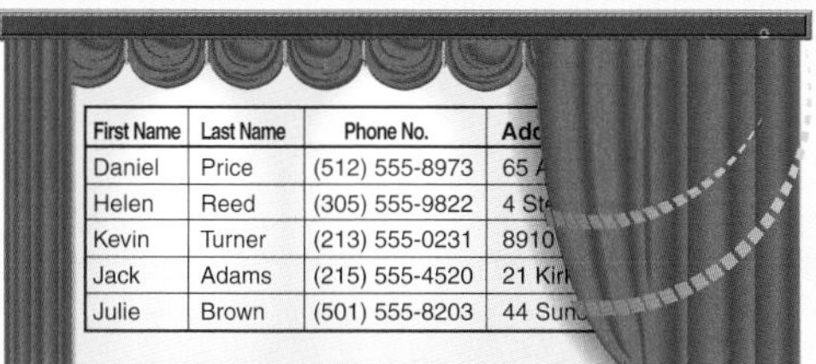

How can I hide multiple fields in my table?

To hide more than one field at the same time, you must first select all the fields you want to hide. Position the mouse I over the name of the first field you want to hide (I changes to ⬇). Then drag the mouse ⬇ until you highlight all the fields you want to hide. To hide the selected fields, perform steps **2** and **3** on page 68.

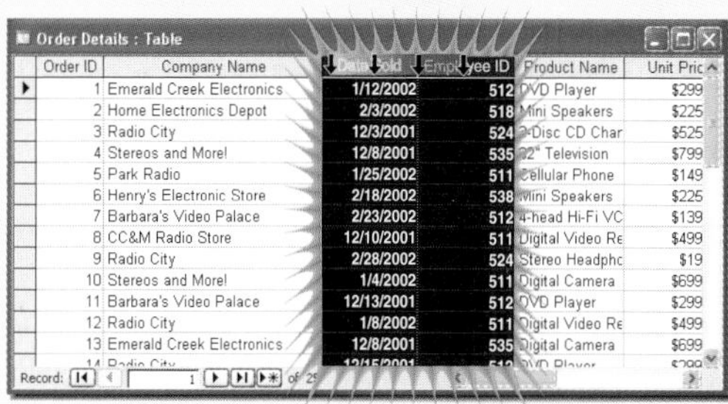

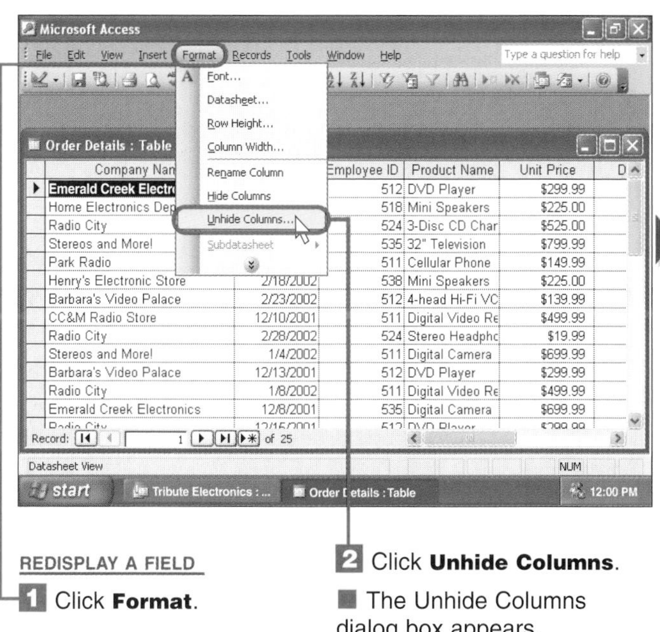

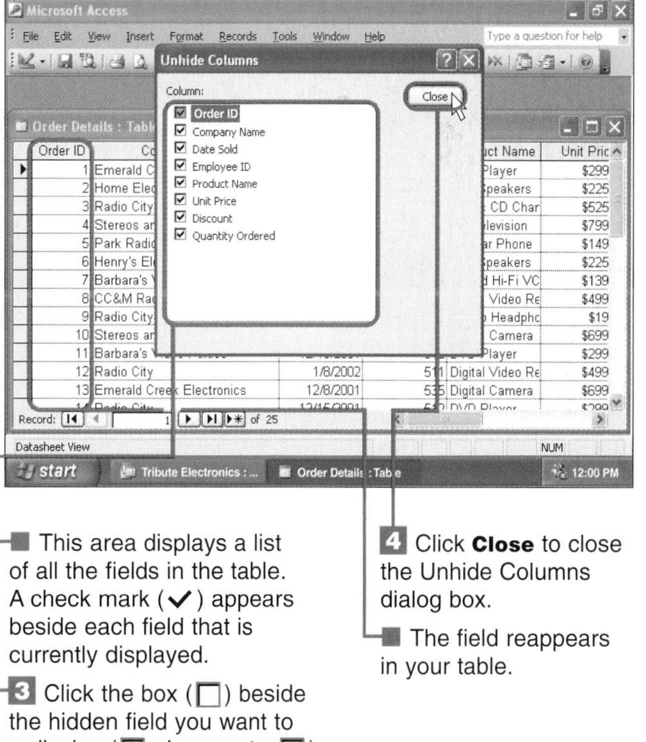

REDISPLAY A FIELD

1 Click **Format**.

2 Click **Unhide Columns**.

■ The Unhide Columns dialog box appears.

■ This area displays a list of all the fields in the table. A check mark (✔) appears beside each field that is currently displayed.

3 Click the box (☐) beside the hidden field you want to redisplay (☐ changes to ☑).

4 Click **Close** to close the Unhide Columns dialog box.

■ The field reappears in your table.

FREEZE A FIELD

You can freeze a field in a table so the field will remain on your screen at all times.

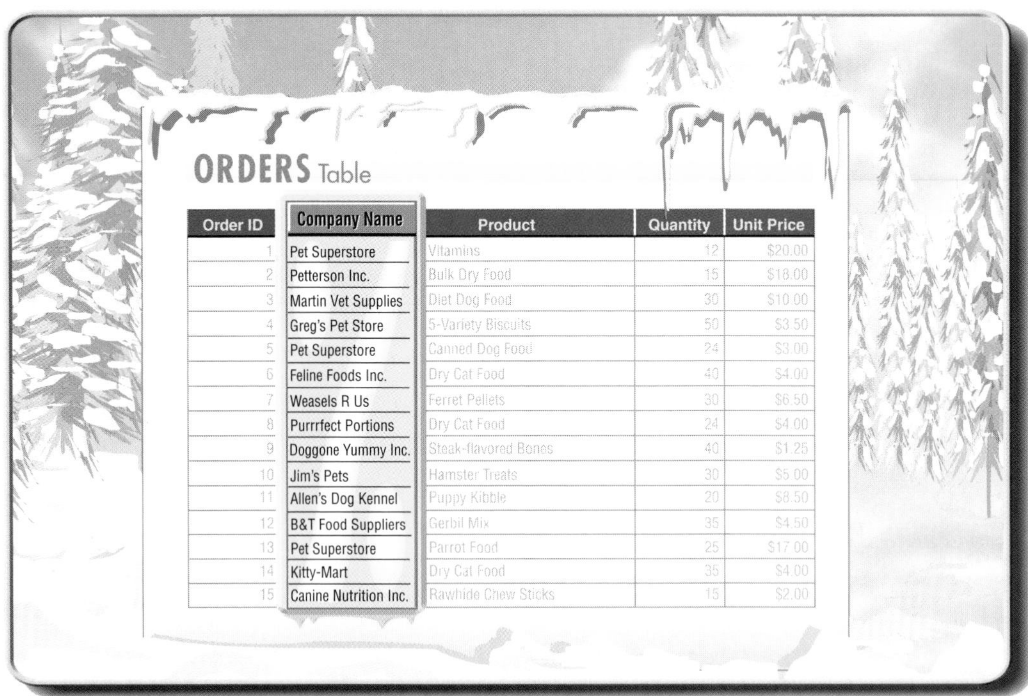

ORDERS Table

Order ID	Company Name	Product	Quantity	Unit Price
1	Pet Superstore	Vitamins	12	$20.00
2	Petterson Inc.	Bulk Dry Food	15	$18.00
3	Martin Vet Supplies	Diet Dog Food	30	$10.00
4	Greg's Pet Store	5-Variety Biscuits	50	$3.50
5	Pet Superstore	Canned Dog Food	24	$3.00
6	Feline Foods Inc.	Dry Cat Food	40	$4.00
7	Weasels R Us	Ferret Pellets	30	$6.50
8	Purrrfect Portions	Dry Cat Food	24	$4.00
9	Doggone Yummy Inc.	Steak-flavored Bones	40	$1.25
10	Jim's Pets	Hamster Treats	30	$5.00
11	Allen's Dog Kennel	Puppy Kibble	20	$8.50
12	B&T Food Suppliers	Gerbil Mix	35	$4.50
13	Pet Superstore	Parrot Food	25	$17.00
14	Kitty-Mart	Dry Cat Food	35	$4.00
15	Canine Nutrition Inc.	Rawhide Chew Sticks	15	$2.00

FREEZE A FIELD

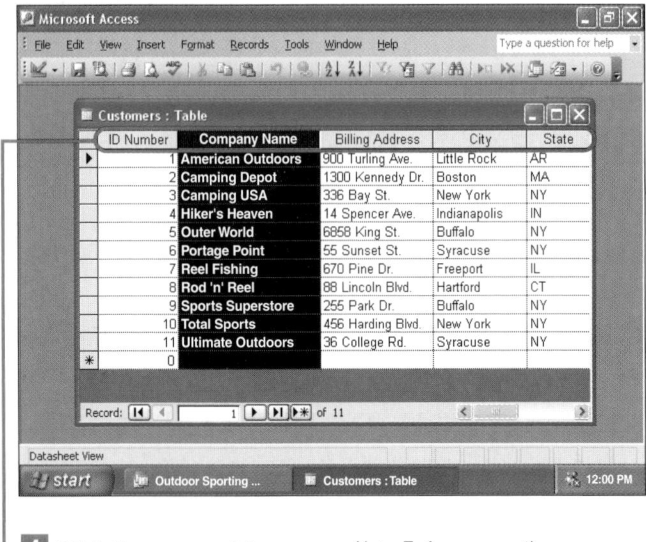

1 Click the name of the field you want to freeze.

The field is highlighted.

Note: To freeze more than one field at the same time, select the fields you want to freeze. To select multiple fields, see page 54.

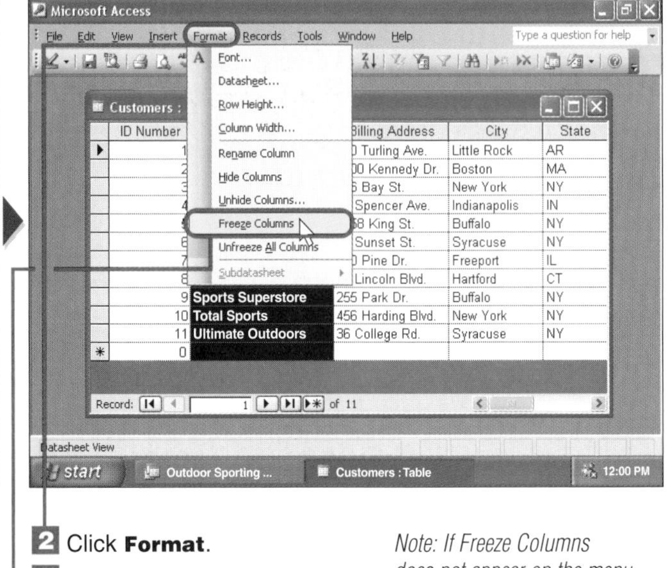

2 Click **Format**.

3 Click **Freeze Columns**.

Note: If Freeze Columns does not appear on the menu, position the mouse over the bottom of the menu to display the menu option.

When would I freeze a field?

Freezing a field allows you to keep important data displayed on your screen as you move through data in a large table. For example, you can freeze a field that contains the product numbers in a table so the numbers will remain on your screen while you scroll through the product information.

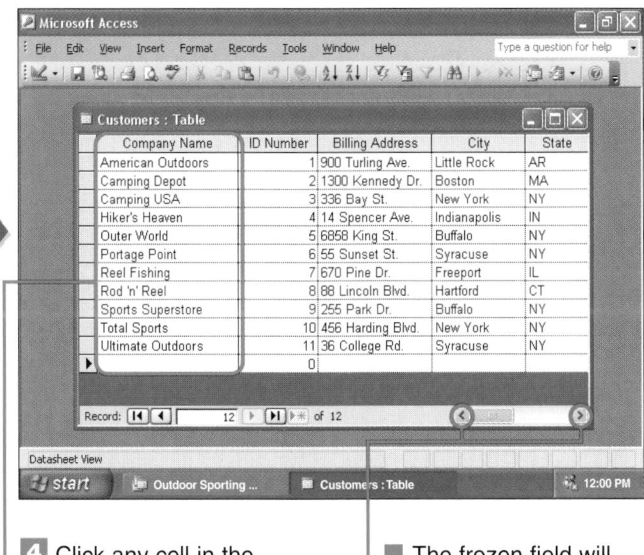

4 Click any cell in the table to deselect the field.

■ Access moves the field to the left side of the table. The black vertical line to the right of the field indicates that the field is frozen.

■ The frozen field will remain on your screen as you move through the other fields in the table.

■ To move through the other fields in the table, click ◀ or ▶.

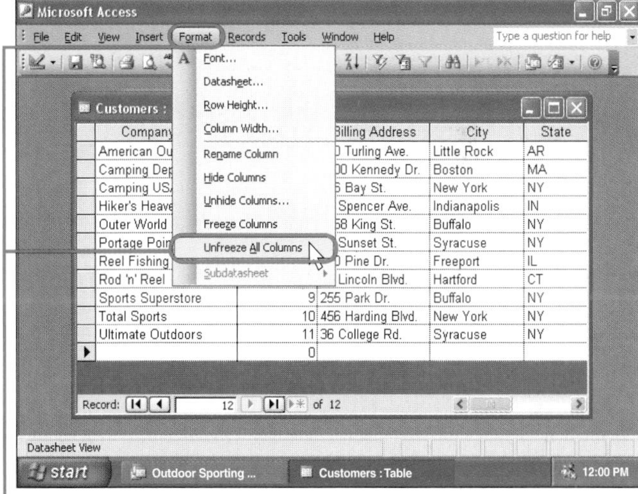

UNFREEZE ALL FIELDS

1 Click **Format**.

2 Click **Unfreeze All Columns**.

Note: If Unfreeze All Columns does not appear on the menu, position the mouse ↖ over the bottom of the menu to display the menu option.

■ When you unfreeze a field, Access will not return the field to its original location in the table. To rearrange fields in a table, see page 45.

DATA
REQUIRED
Text
Text
Text
State
City
WI
CT
IN
NY
MD
IL
AR
NC
220 Whittle St.
190 Milverton Blvd.
14 Spencer Ave.
125 Crane St.
772 Main St.
24 Pine St.
193 College St.
85 Elm Grove Ave.
24 Cortez Blvd.
55 Sunset St.
87 Atlantic Ave.
14 King St.
145 Alpine St.
Hartford
Buffalo
Charlotte
Buffalo
Syracuse
Seattle
San Jose
The Golf Caddy
Aquatix
The Angler's Nook
The Sailing Shop
Neptune's Dive Shop
Portage Point
Hikers' Paradise
Canoes Inc.
Camping Superstore
Outdoor World

CHAPTER 4

Design Tables

Would you like to customize your tables to better suit your needs? In this chapter, you will learn how to add and delete fields, create a lookup column and much more.

CHANGE THE VIEW OF A TABLE

You can view a table in four different ways. Each view allows you to perform different tasks.

CHANGE THE VIEW OF A TABLE

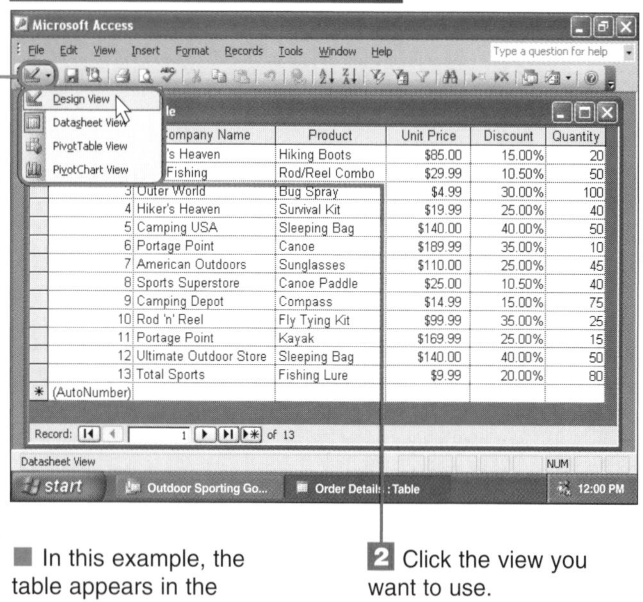

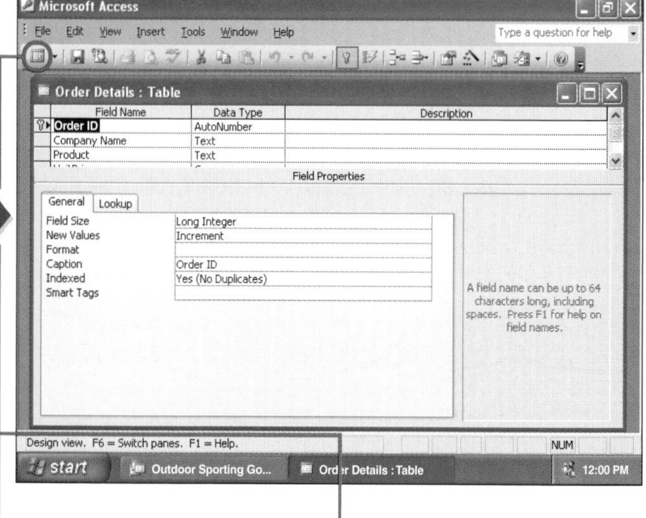

■ In this example, the table appears in the Datasheet view.

1 Click ▾ in this area to display the table in a different view.

2 Click the view you want to use.

■ The table appears in the view you selected.

■ In this example, the View button changed from ✎ to ▦.

■ To quickly switch between the Datasheet (▦) and Design (✎) views, click the View button.

THE TABLE VIEWS

Design View

The Design view displays the structure of a table. You can change the settings in this view to specify the kind of information you can enter into a table.

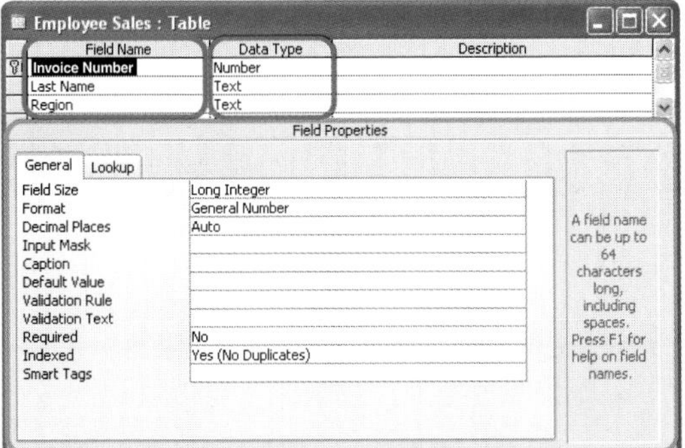

The **Field Name** area displays the name of each field in a table.

The **Data Type** area displays the type of data you can enter into each field, such as text or numbers.

The **Field Properties** area shows the properties for the current field.

Datasheet View

The Datasheet view displays all the records in a table. The field names appear across the top of the window and the information for one record appears in each row. You can review, enter and edit records in this view.

Employee Sales : Table

Invoice Number	Last Name	Region	Period	Sales
23452	Grant	North	Quarter 1	$15,000.00
23453	Lewis	South	Quarter 3	$12,400.00
23454	Smith	Central	Quarter 2	$19,000.00
23455	Grant	North	Quarter 2	$22,900.00
23456	Lewis	South	Quarter 1	$28,900.00
23457	Smith	Central	Quarter 3	$18,000.00
23458	Grant	North	Quarter 3	$21,000.00
23459	Lewis	South	Quarter 2	$19,500.00
23460	Smith	Central	Quarter 1	$29,000.00
23461	Fraser	Central	Quarter 1	$16,000.00
23462	Turner	North	Quarter 1	$16,800.00
23463	Fraser	South	Quarter 3	$18,200.00
23464	Turner	North	Quarter 2	$23,000.00
23465	Morris	South	Quarter 1	$17,300.00
23466	Fraser	Central	Quarter 3	$14,600.00

Record: 1 of 18

PivotTable View

The PivotTable view allows you to summarize and analyze the data in a table. When you first display a table in this view, the PivotTable is empty and you must add the fields you want the PivotTable to display. For information on using the PivotTable view, see page 232.

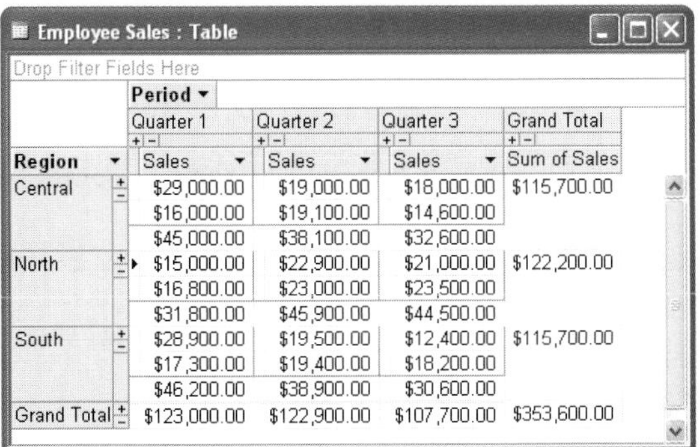

Employee Sales : Table

Drop Filter Fields Here

Region	Quarter 1 Sales	Quarter 2 Sales	Quarter 3 Sales	Grand Total Sum of Sales
Central	$29,000.00	$19,000.00	$18,000.00	$115,700.00
	$16,000.00	$19,100.00	$14,600.00	
	$45,000.00	$38,100.00	$32,600.00	
North	$15,000.00	$22,900.00	$21,000.00	$122,200.00
	$16,800.00	$23,000.00	$23,500.00	
	$31,800.00	$45,900.00	$44,500.00	
South	$28,900.00	$19,500.00	$12,400.00	$115,700.00
	$17,300.00	$19,400.00	$18,200.00	
	$46,200.00	$38,900.00	$30,600.00	
Grand Total	$123,000.00	$122,900.00	$107,700.00	$353,600.00

PivotChart View

The PivotChart view allows you to display a graphical summary of the data in a table. When you first display a table in this view, the PivotChart is empty and you must add the fields you want the PivotChart to display. For information on using the PivotChart view, see page 238.

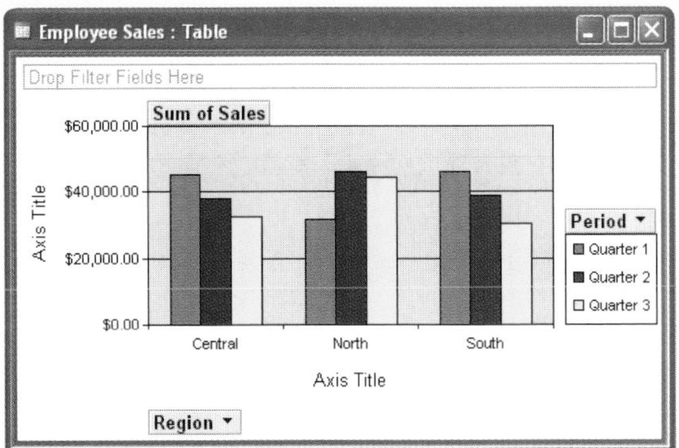

ADD A FIELD

You can add a field to a table when you want the table to include an additional category of information.

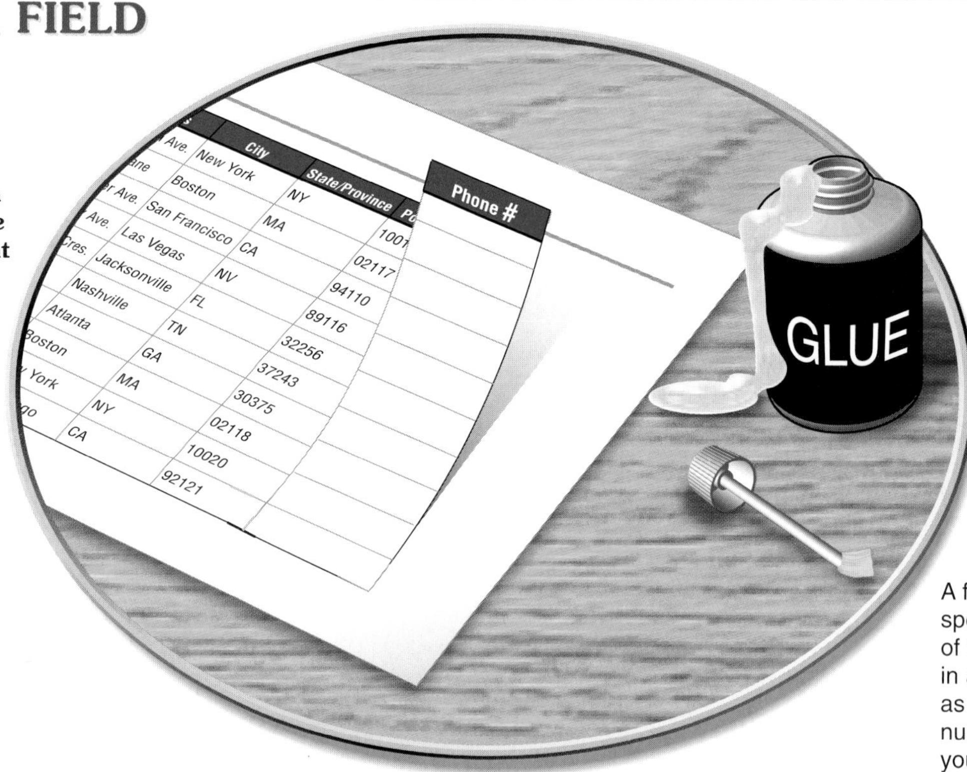

A field is a specific category of information in a table, such as the phone numbers of all your clients.

ADD A FIELD

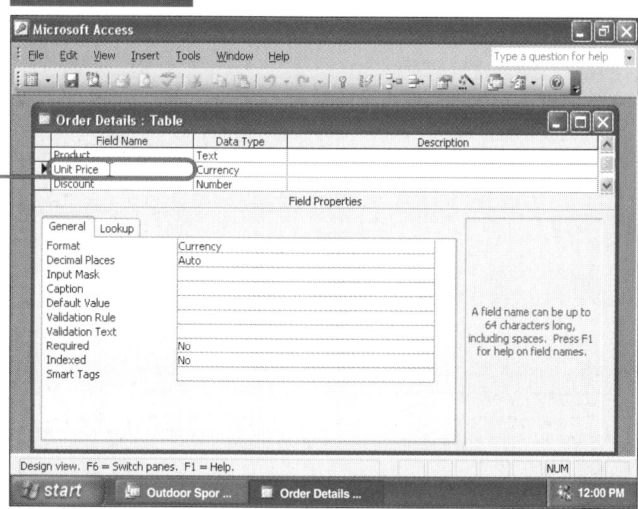

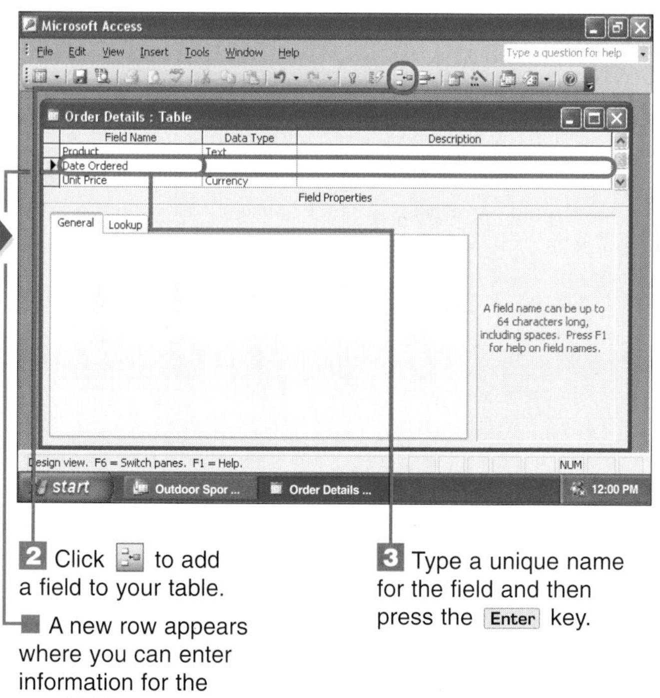

1 Click the name of the field you want to appear after the new field. A triangle (▶) appears beside the field name.

■ To add a field to the end of your table, click the area directly below the last field name. Then skip to step 3.

2 Click [icon] to add a field to your table.

■ A new row appears where you can enter information for the new field.

3 Type a unique name for the field and then press the Enter key.

What should I consider when adding fields to a table?

Make sure each field you add to a table relates directly to the subject of the table. You should also make sure you separate the information you want to include in a table into its smallest parts, such as First Name and Last Name.

What data type should I select for my new field?

The data type you should select depends on the type of information you want to enter in the field. For example, you can choose the Currency data type for a field you want to contain monetary values, such as the prices of products. For more information on data types, see page 82.

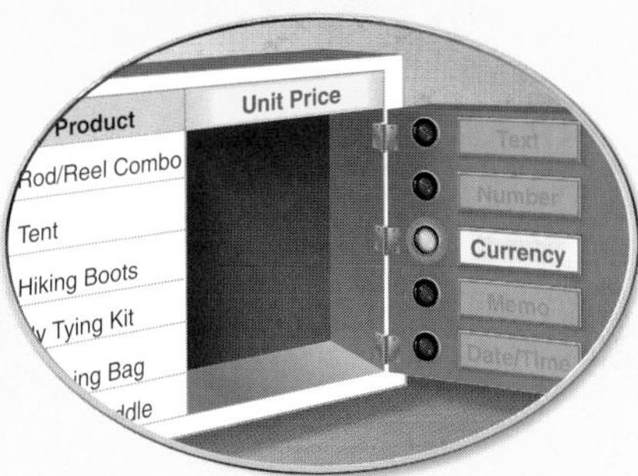

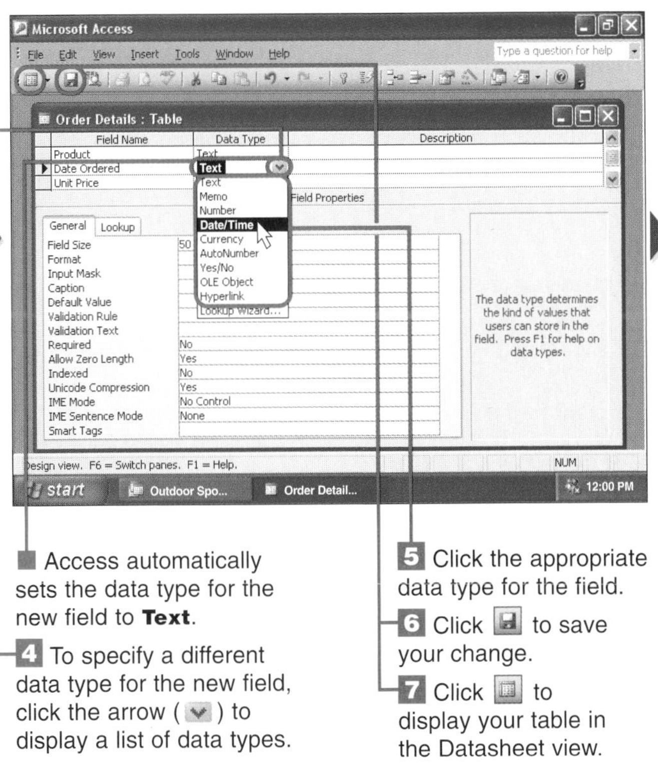

■ Access automatically sets the data type for the new field to **Text**.

4 To specify a different data type for the new field, click the arrow ( ) to display a list of data types.

5 Click the appropriate data type for the field.

6 Click to save your change.

7 Click to display your table in the Datasheet view.

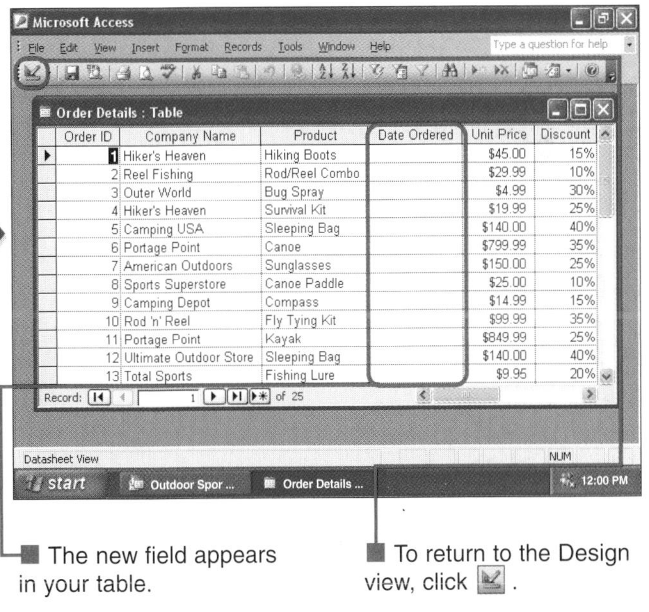

■ The new field appears in your table.

■ To return to the Design view, click .

DELETE A FIELD

If you no longer need a field, you can permanently delete the field from a table.

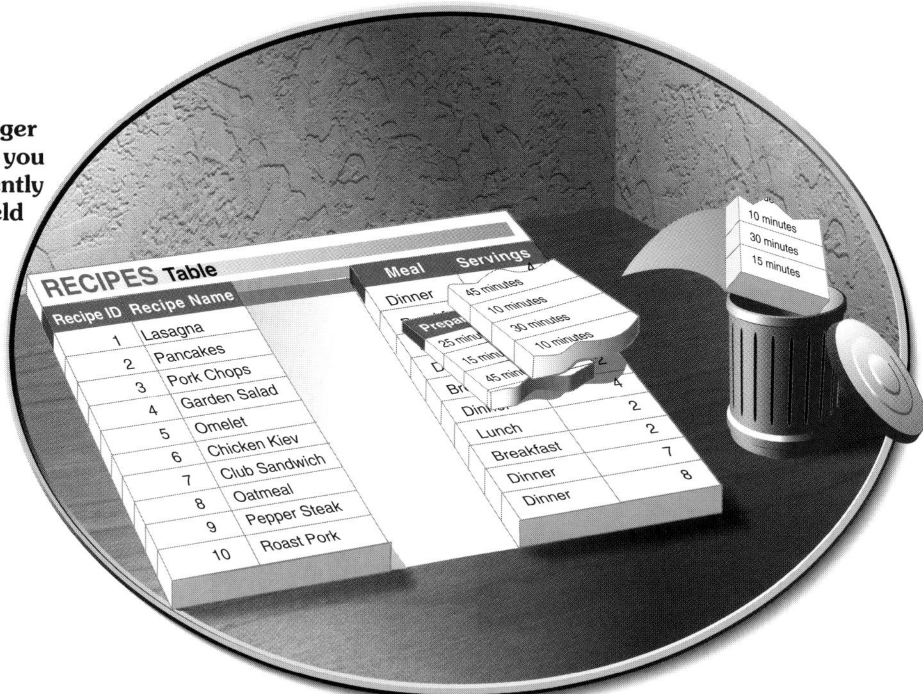

Before you delete a field, make sure the field is not used in any other objects in your database, such as a form, query or report.

You cannot delete a field used to create a relationship with another table in your database. For information on relationships, see page 128.

DELETE A FIELD

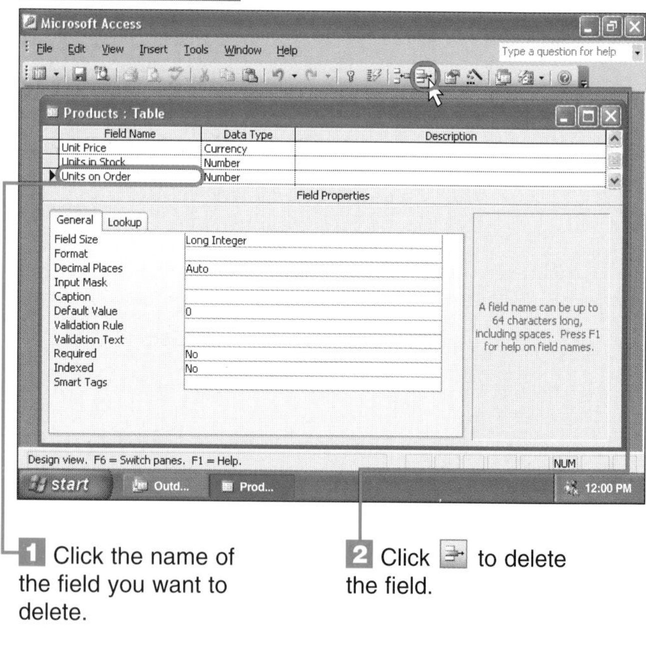

1 Click the name of the field you want to delete.

2 Click ![icon] to delete the field.

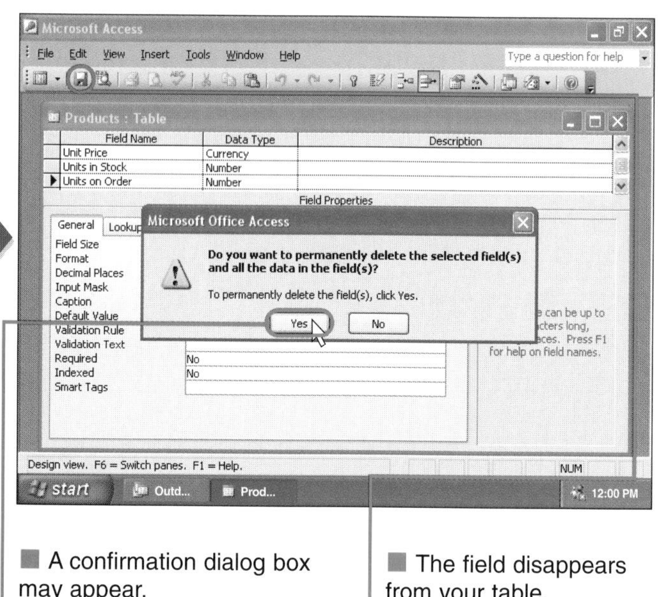

■ A confirmation dialog box may appear.

3 Click **Yes** to permanently delete the field.

■ The field disappears from your table.

4 Click ![icon] to save your change.

REARRANGE FIELDS

You can change the order of fields to better organize the information in a table.

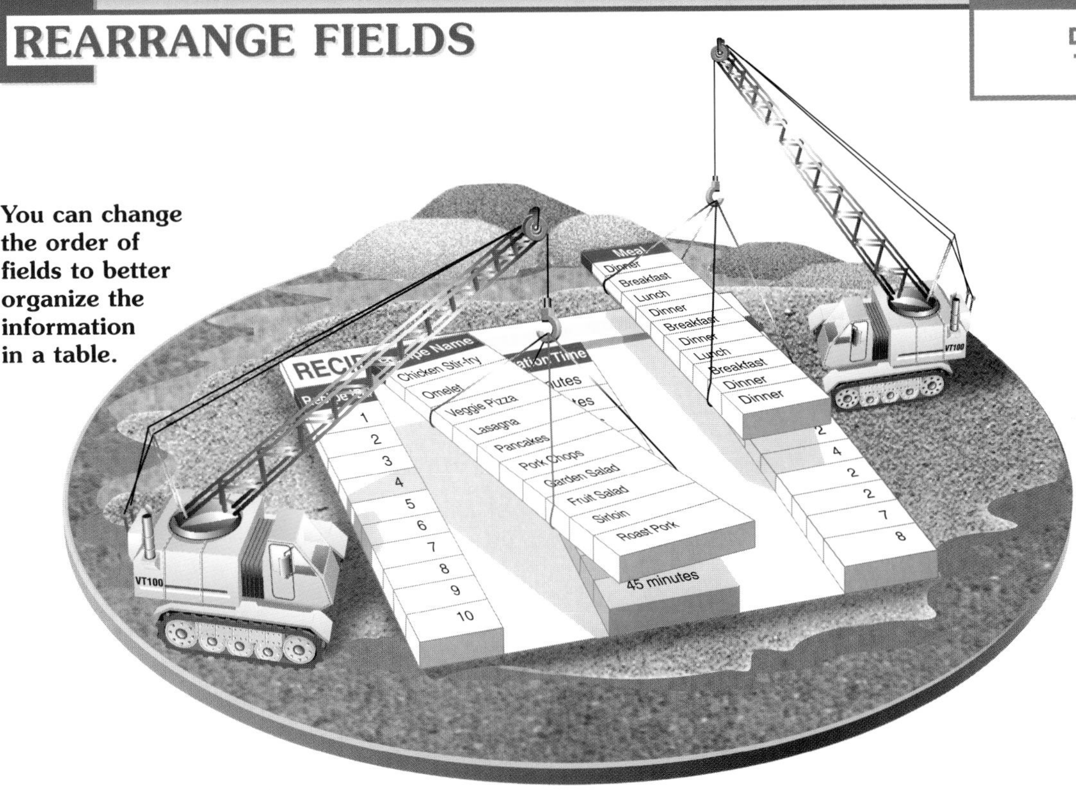

When you rearrange fields in the Design view, Access also displays the changes in the Datasheet view of a table. For information on the views of a table, see page 74.

REARRANGE FIELDS

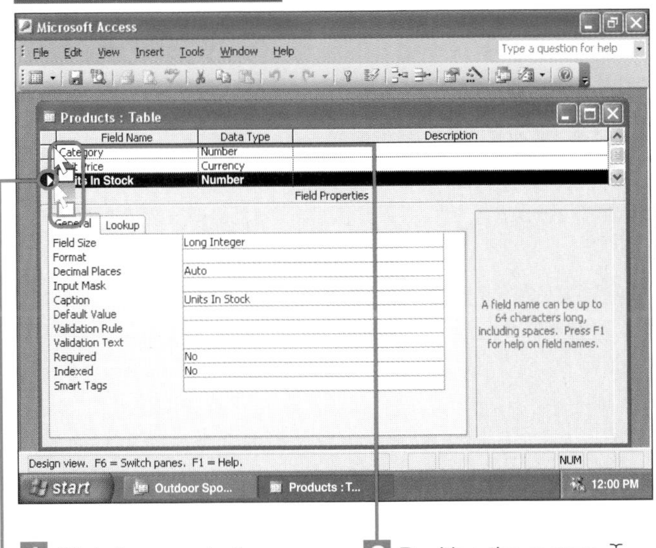

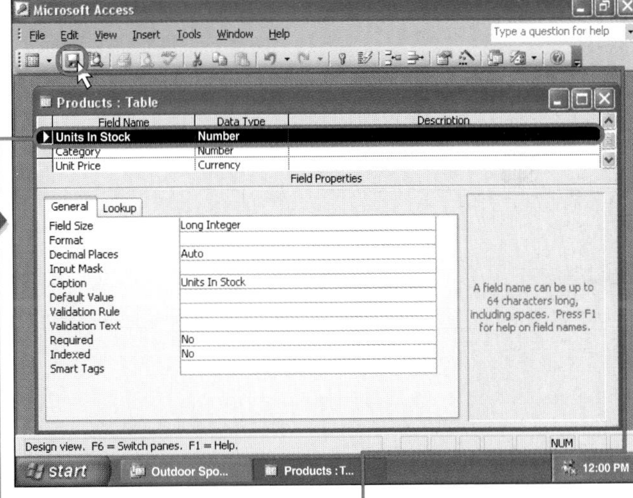

1 Click the area to the left of the field you want to move. The field is highlighted.

2 Position the mouse I over the area to the left of the field (I changes to ↖) and then drag the field to a new location.

■ A thick line shows where the field will appear.

■ The field appears in the new location.

3 Click 💾 to save your change.

DISPLAY FIELD PROPERTIES

You can display the properties for each field in a table. The field properties are a set of characteristics that control how data is entered, displayed and stored in a field.

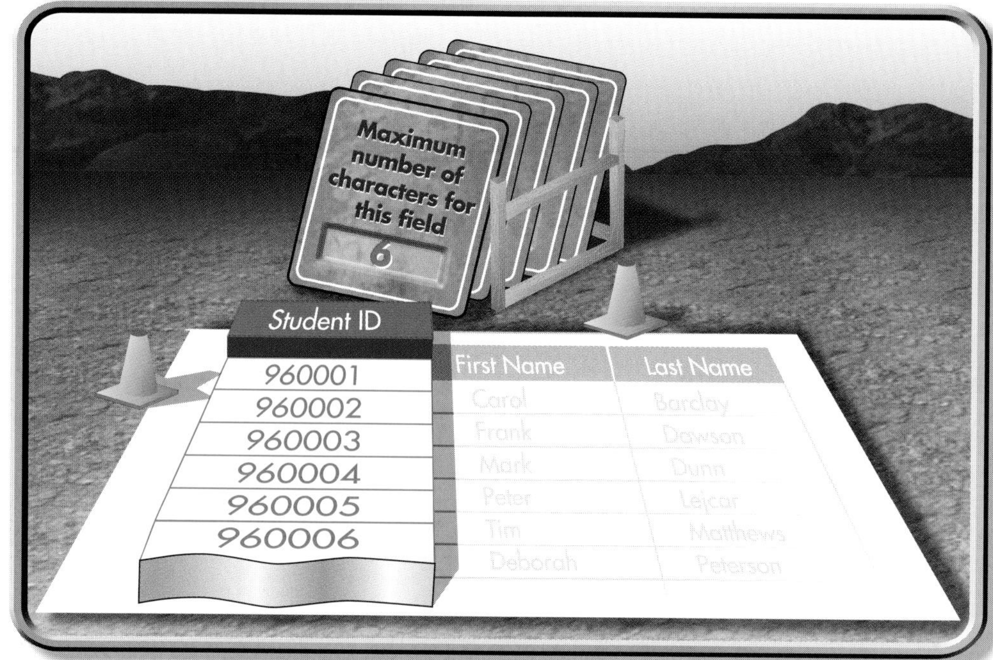

For example, a field property can specify the maximum number of characters a field can accept.

DISPLAY FIELD PROPERTIES

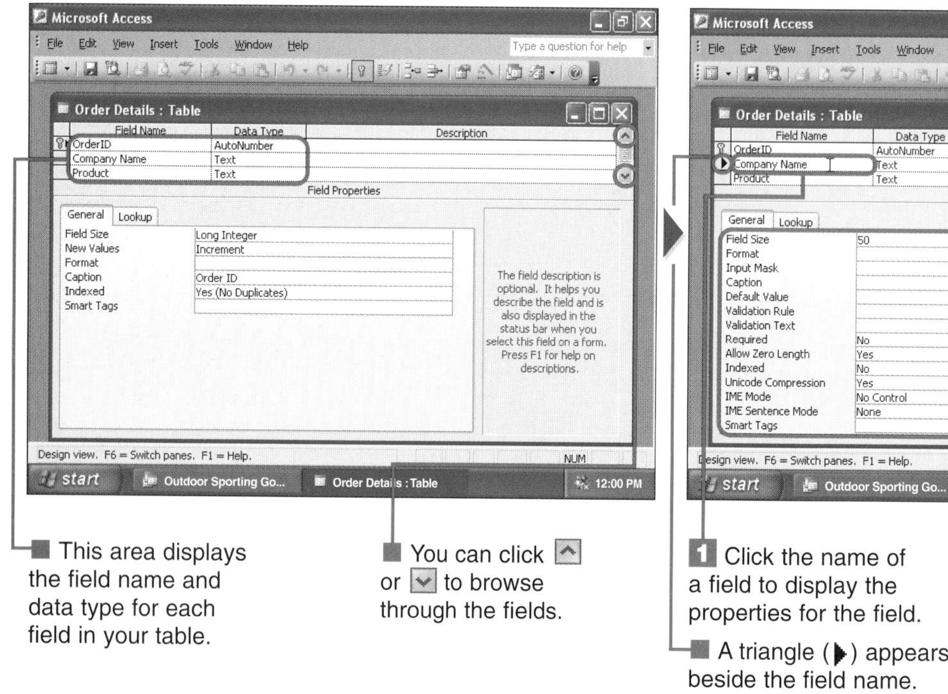

■ This area displays the field name and data type for each field in your table.

■ You can click ⌃ or ⌄ to browse through the fields.

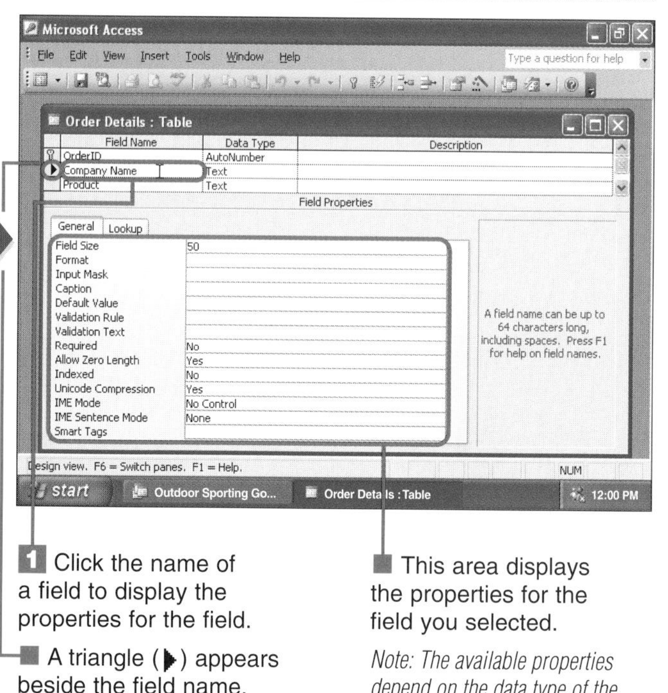

1 Click the name of a field to display the properties for the field.

■ A triangle (▶) appears beside the field name.

■ This area displays the properties for the field you selected.

Note: The available properties depend on the data type of the field. For information on data types, see page 83.

ADD A FIELD DESCRIPTION

You can add a description to a field to help you determine the kind of information you should enter in the field.

You can use up to 255 characters to describe a field.

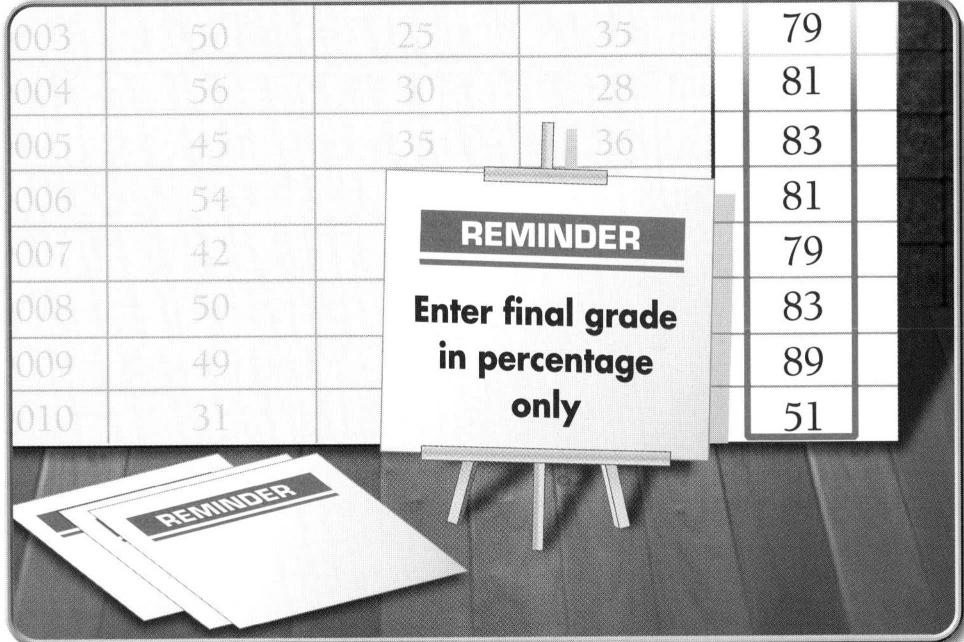

REMINDER
Enter final grade in percentage only
REMINDER

ADD A FIELD DESCRIPTION

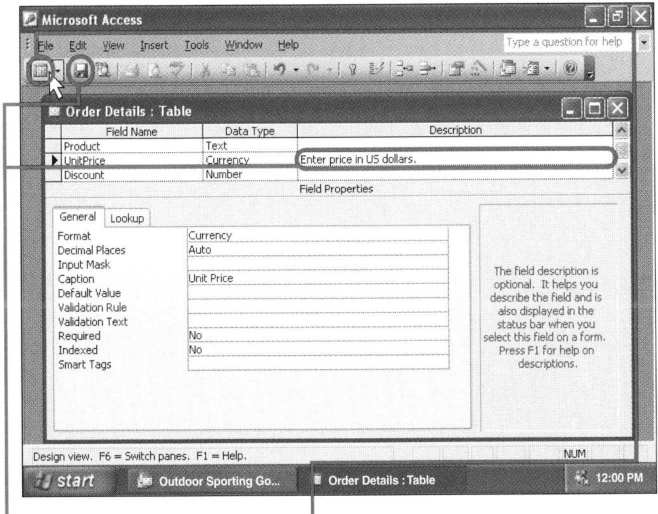

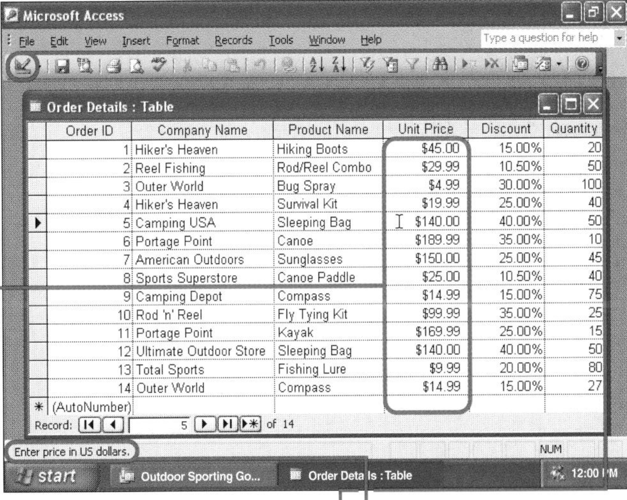

1 Click the Description area for the field you want to add a description to.

2 Type the description.

3 Click the save button to save your change.

Note: The Property Update Options button may appear, allowing you to automatically add the field description to all your forms or reports that display the field. For more information, see the top of page 85.

4 Click the Datasheet view button to display your table in the Datasheet view.

5 Click anywhere in the field you added the description to.

■ The description for the field appears in this area.

■ To return to the Design view, click the Design view button.

CHANGE A DATA TYPE

You can change the type of data you can enter into a field.

Changing the data type for a field helps prevent errors when entering data in the field. Access will not accept data that does not match the data type you specify. For example, you cannot enter text into a field with the Number data type.

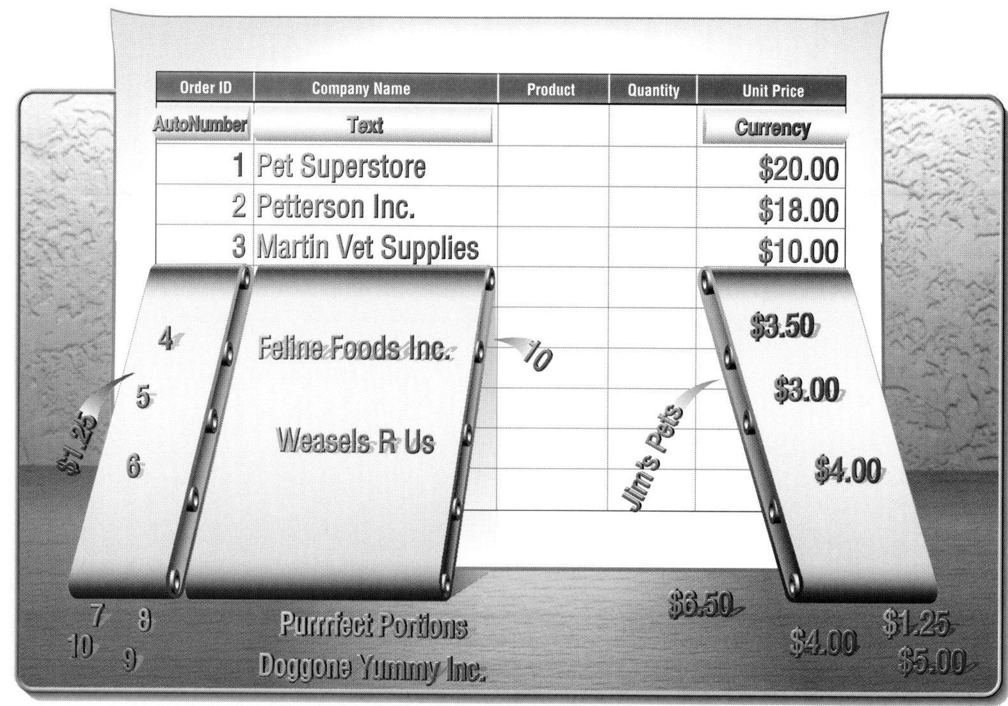

Order ID
Company Name
Product
Quantity
Unit Price
AutoNumber
Text
Currency
1 Pet Superstore $20.00
2 Petterson Inc. $18.00
3 Martin Vet Supplies $10.00
Feline Foods Inc.
Weasels R Us
Jim's Pets
Purrrfect Portions
Doggone Yummy Inc.

CHANGE A DATA TYPE

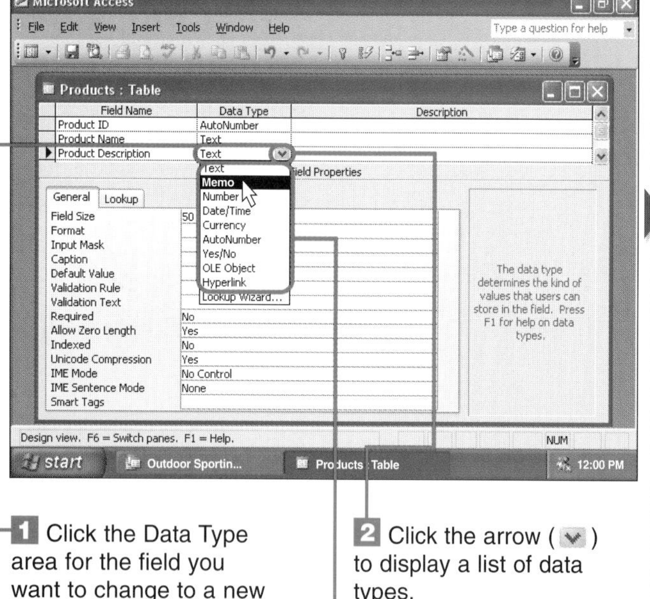

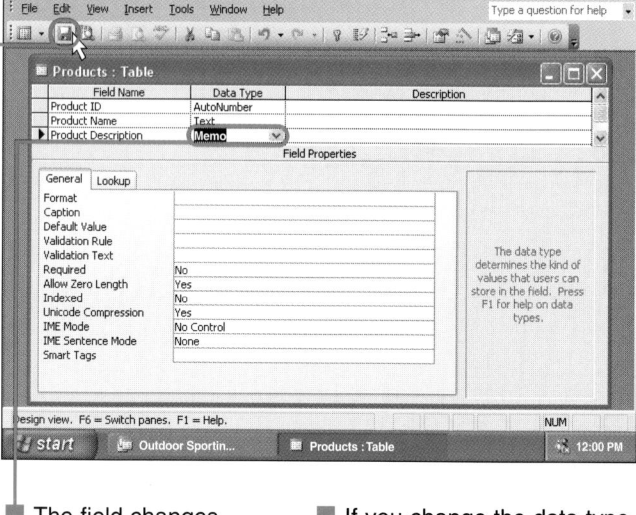

1 Click the Data Type area for the field you want to change to a new data type. An arrow ( ) appears.

2 Click the arrow ( ) to display a list of data types.

3 Click the data type you want the field to use.

■ The field changes to the new data type.

4 Click to save your change.

■ If you change the data type for a field that contains data, Access will display an error message if it encounters errors while converting the data. To delete the data that is causing the errors, click **Yes**. To cancel the change, click **No**.

DATA TYPES

Text

Accepts entries up to 255 characters long that include any combination of text and numbers, such as names or addresses. Make sure you use this data type for numbers you will not use in calculations, such as phone numbers, product numbers or zip codes.

Memo

Accepts entries up to 65,535 characters long that include any combination of text and numbers, such as notes, comments or descriptions.

Number

Accepts numbers you want to use in calculations. For calculations that involve monetary values, use the Currency data type.

Date/Time

Accepts only dates and times.

Currency

Accepts monetary values.

AutoNumber

Automatically numbers each record for you. The numbers may not begin at 1.

Yes/No

Accepts only one of two values—Yes/No, True/False or On/Off.

OLE Object

Accepts OLE objects. An OLE object is an item created in another program, such as a document, spreadsheet, picture or sound.

Hyperlink

Accepts hyperlinks you can select to jump to a document or Web page.

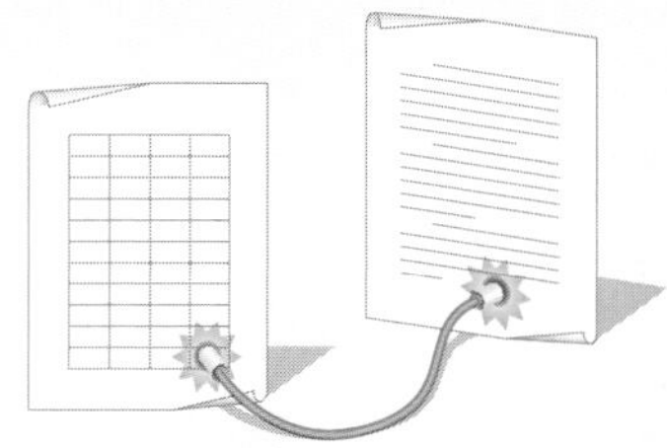

SELECT A FORMAT

You can select a format to customize the way information appears in a field. For example, you can select the way you want numbers or dates to appear.

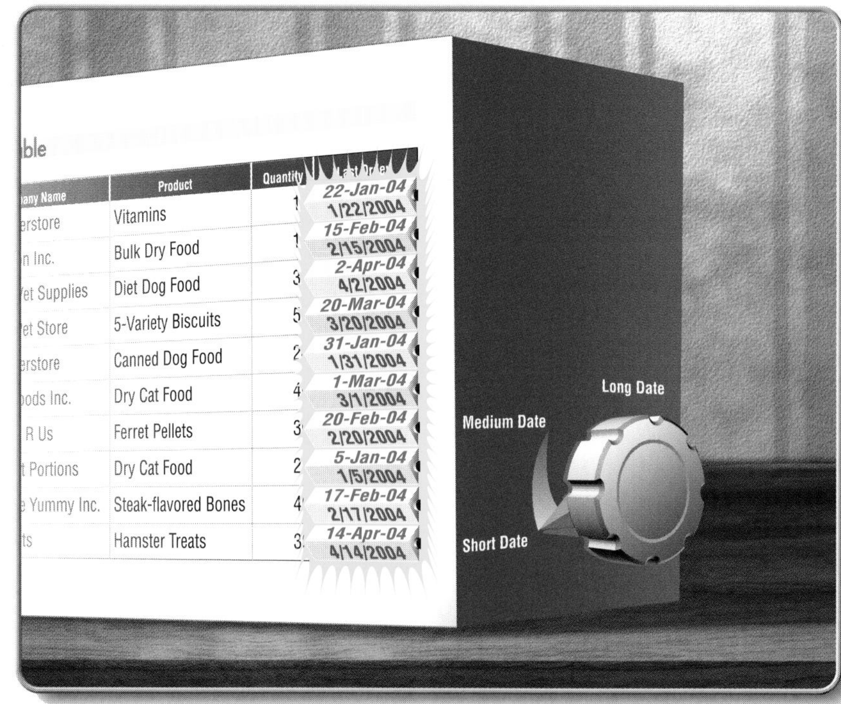

Selecting a format will not change how information is stored in a table.

SELECT A FORMAT

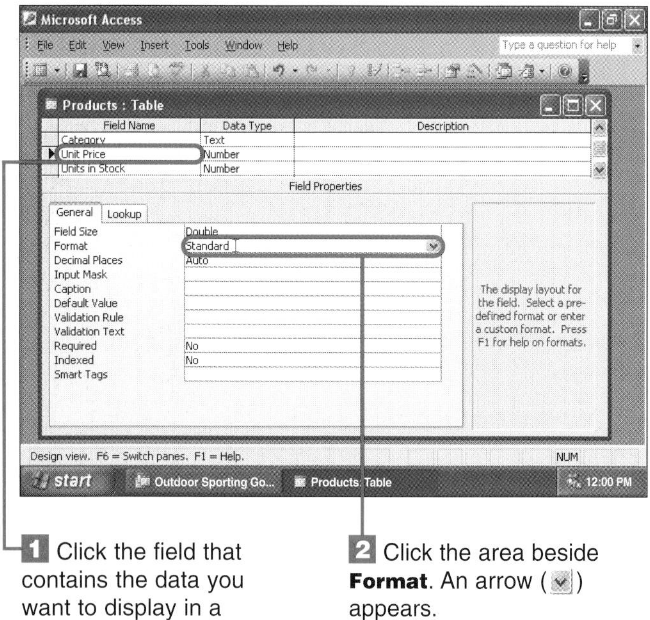

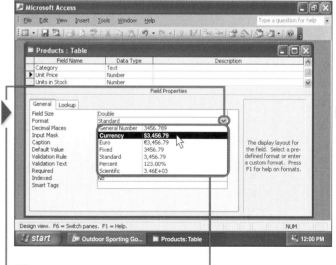

1 Click the field that contains the data you want to display in a new format.

2 Click the area beside **Format**. An arrow ( ) appears.

3 Click the arrow ( ) to display a list of formats.

Note: A list of formats only appears for fields with the Number, Date/Time, Currency, AutoNumber or Yes/No data type. For information on data types, see page 82.

4 Click the format you want to use.

What formats are available?

There are several different formats that you can choose from. For example, you can format numbers as currency using the dollar ($) or Euro (€) symbol, as a percentage, or as scientific notation. You can also format dates and times using many different styles, such as "Saturday, June 19, 2004" or "5:34:23 PM."

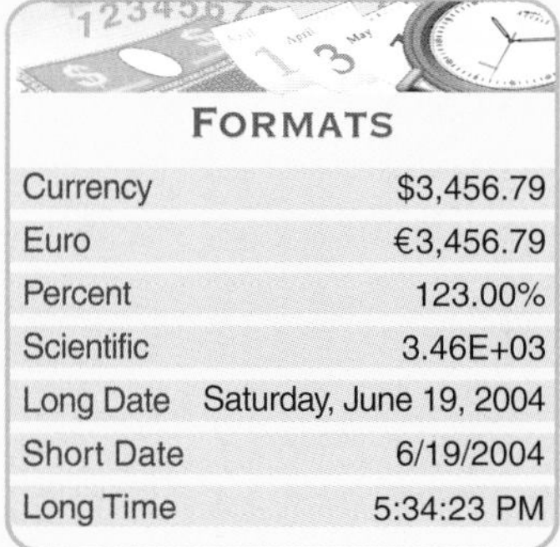

FORMATS

Format	Example
Currency	$3,456.79
Euro	€3,456.79
Percent	123.00%
Scientific	3.46E+03
Long Date	Saturday, June 19, 2004
Short Date	6/19/2004
Long Time	5:34:23 PM

Why does the Property Update Options button ( ) appear when I change the format of a field?

You can use the Property Update Options button ( ) to automatically change the format of the current field in all your forms or reports that display the field. Click the Property Update Options button to display a list of options and then select the option you want to use. The Property Update Options button is available only until you perform another task.

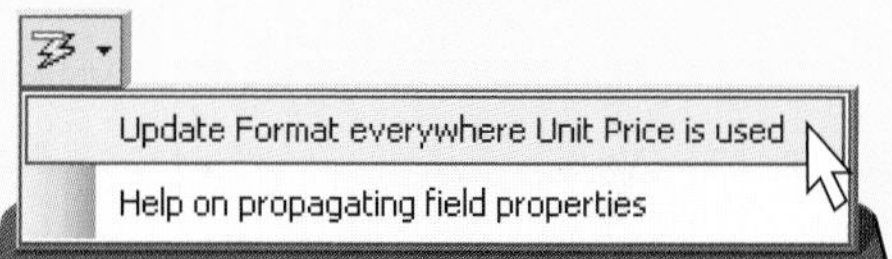

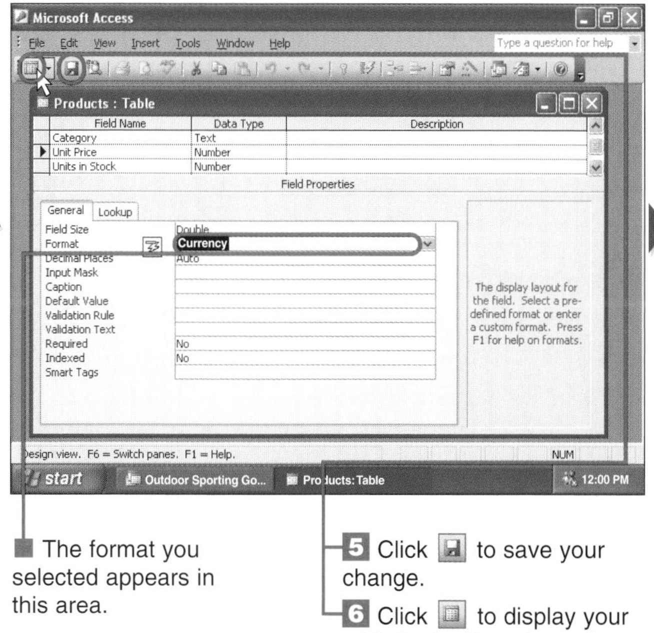

■ The format you selected appears in this area.

5 Click to save your change.

6 Click to display your table in the Datasheet view.

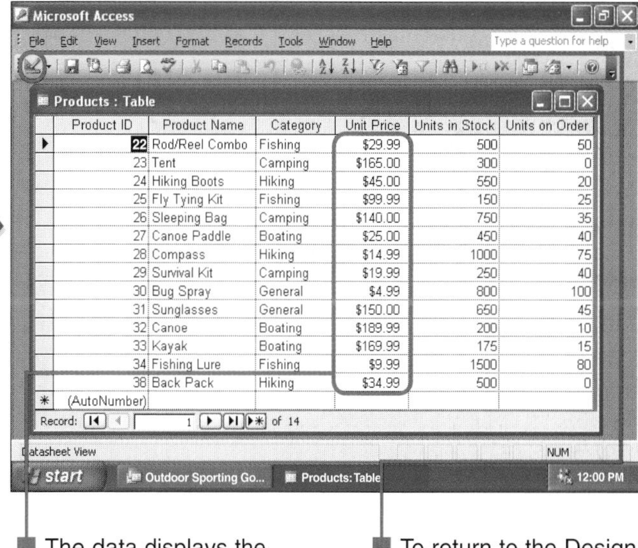

Product ID	Product Name	Category	Unit Price	Units in Stock	Units on Order
22	Rod/Reel Combo	Fishing	$29.99	500	50
23	Tent	Camping	$165.00	300	0
24	Hiking Boots	Hiking	$45.00	550	20
25	Fly Tying Kit	Fishing	$99.99	150	25
26	Sleeping Bag	Camping	$140.00	750	35
27	Canoe Paddle	Boating	$25.00	450	40
28	Compass	Hiking	$14.99	1000	75
29	Survival Kit	Camping	$19.99	250	40
30	Bug Spray	General	$4.99	800	100
31	Sunglasses	General	$150.00	650	45
32	Canoe	Boating	$189.99	200	10
33	Kayak	Boating	$169.99	175	15
34	Fishing Lure	Fishing	$9.99	1500	80
38	Back Pack	Hiking	$34.99	500	0
(AutoNumber)					

■ The data displays the format you selected.

■ Access will automatically change any data you enter in the field to the new format. For example, Access will automatically change 1234 to $1,234.00.

■ To return to the Design view, click .

CHANGE THE FIELD SIZE

First Name
Last Name
City
State
Jack
Adams
New York
N Y
Ryan
Smith
Boston
M A
Jason
Cook
San Diego
C A
Ann
Lewis
Jacksonville
F L
Paul
Fraser
Nashville
T N
Janet
Young
Atlanta
G A

You can change the size of a text or number field to specify the maximum size of data that you can enter in the field.

You should select the smallest possible field size for data. Smaller field sizes can be processed faster, require less memory and use less storage space.

Changing the field size also helps you reduce errors when entering data. For example, if you set the size of a text field to 2, you can enter CA but not California.

TEXT FIELDS

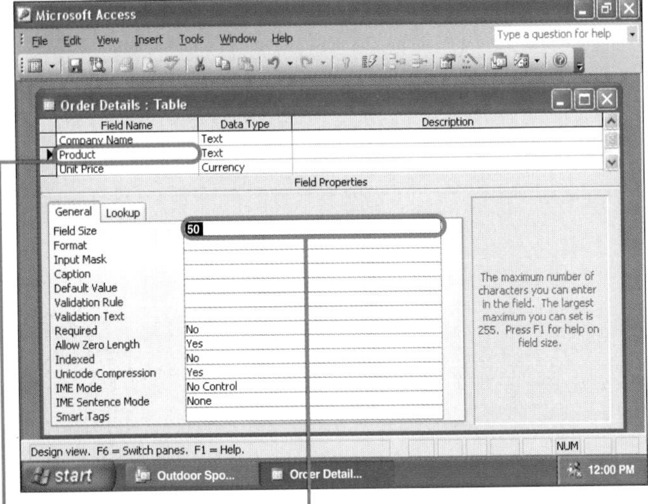

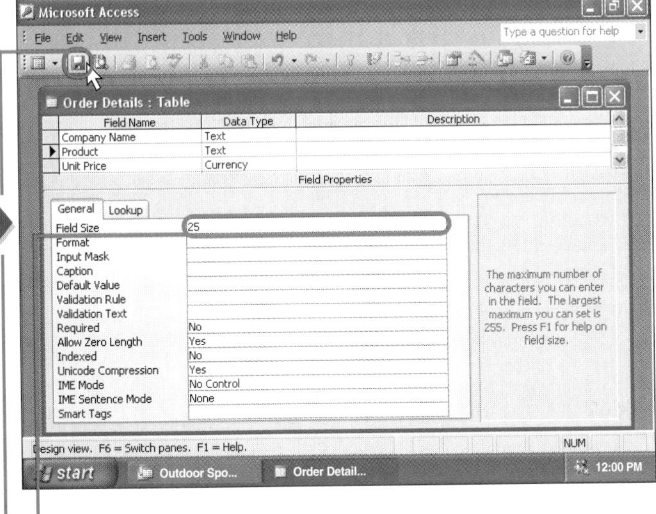

1 Click the field you want to accept a maximum number of characters.

■ The area beside Field Size displays the maximum number of characters you can currently type in the field. The default setting is 50.

2 Double-click the number to highlight the number.

3 Type the maximum number of characters you want the field to accept.

Note: You can enter a number from 0 to 255.

4 Click 💾 to save your change.

■ A warning dialog box appears if you are reducing the size of a text field that contains data. Access will shorten any data that is longer than the new field size. To continue, click **Yes**.

What field sizes are available for number fields?

Access offers several field sizes for number fields. Some field sizes allow you to only enter whole numbers. If you want to be able to enter numbers with decimal places, such as 1.23, you must select the Single, Double or Decimal field size.

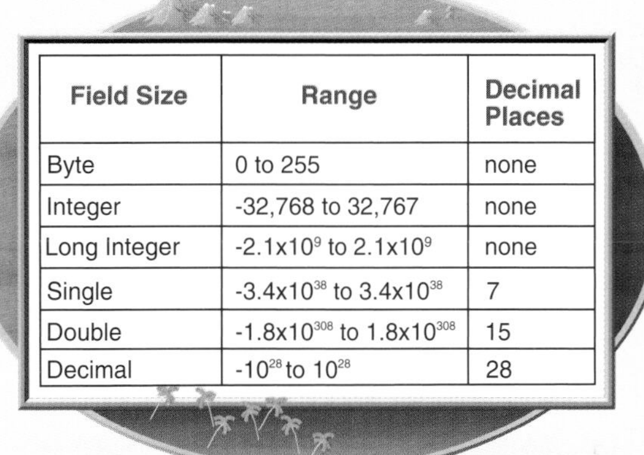

Field Size	Range	Decimal Places
Byte	0 to 255	none
Integer	-32,768 to 32,767	none
Long Integer	-2.1×10^{9} to 2.1×10^{9}	none
Single	-3.4×10^{38} to 3.4×10^{38}	7
Double	-1.8×10^{308} to 1.8×10^{308}	15
Decimal	-10^{28} to 10^{28}	28

NUMBER FIELDS

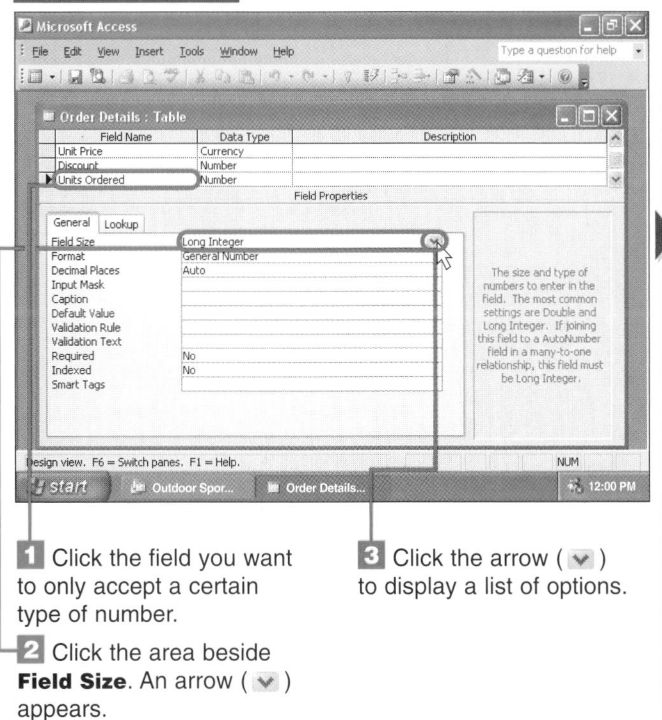

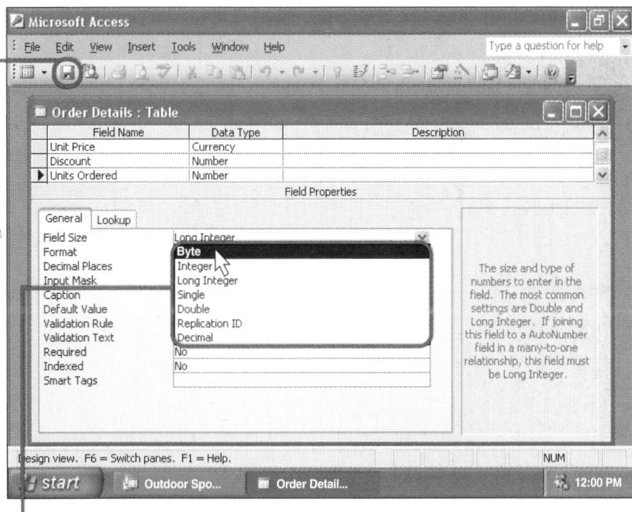

1 Click the field you want to only accept a certain type of number.

2 Click the area beside **Field Size**. An arrow (⌄) appears.

3 Click the arrow (⌄) to display a list of options.

4 Click the type of number you want the field to accept.

Note: For information on the types of numbers available, see the top of this page.

5 Click (save icon) to save your change.

■ A warning dialog box appears if you are reducing the size of a number field that contains data. Access will change or delete data that is larger than the new field size. To continue, click **Yes**.

CHANGE THE NUMBER OF DECIMAL PLACES

You can specify how many decimal places you want numbers to display in a field.

You can display up to 15 decimal places after the decimal point.

Changing the number of decimal places will not affect the way numbers are stored or used in calculations.

CHANGE THE NUMBER OF DECIMAL PLACES

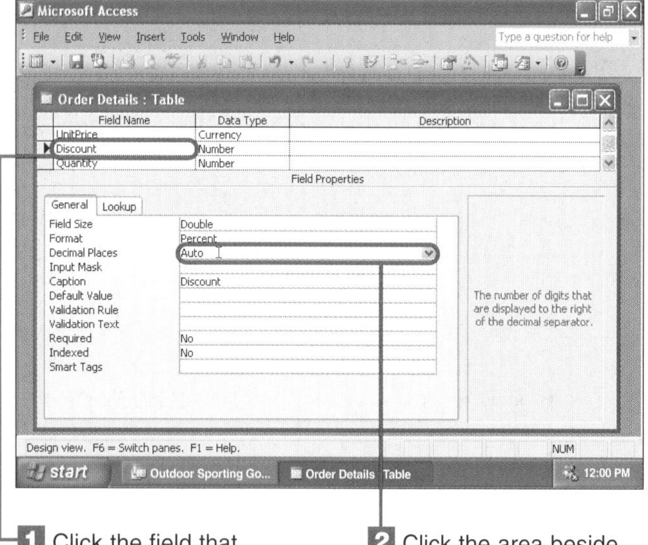

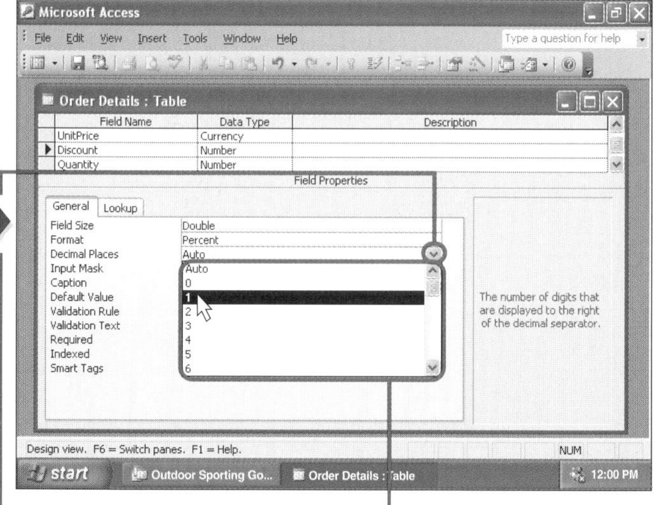

1 Click the field that contains the data you want to display a specific number of decimal places.

2 Click the area beside **Decimal Places**. An arrow (⌄) appears.

3 Click the arrow (⌄) to display a list of decimal place options.

4 Click the number of decimal places you want the data in the field to display.

Note: The Auto option will usually display numbers with two decimal places.

Why does the Property Update Options button () appear when I change the number of decimal places for a field?

You can use the Property Update Options button to automatically update the number of decimal places for the field in all your forms or reports that display the field. Click the Property Update Options button to display a list of options and then select the option you want to use. The Property Update Options button is available only until you perform another task.

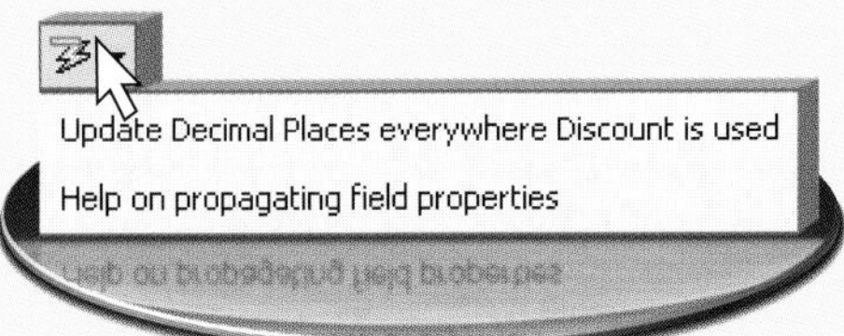

Why doesn't my data display the number of decimal places I specified?

Changing the number of decimal places will not change the appearance of numbers if the Format property of the field is blank or set to General Number. To change the Format property of a field, see page 84.

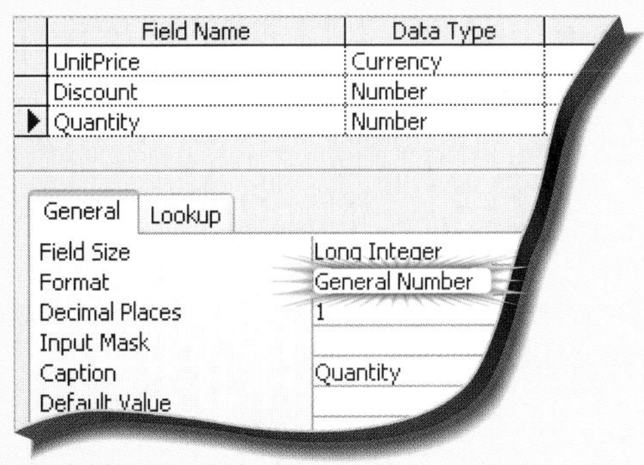

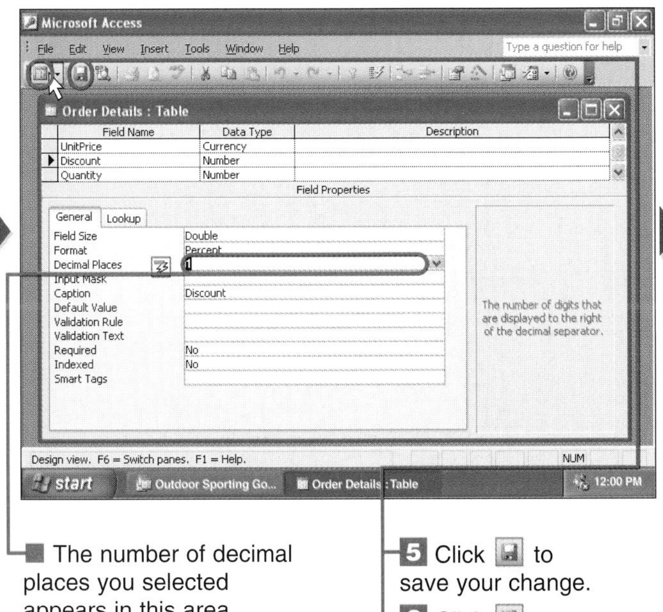

■ The number of decimal places you selected appears in this area.

5 Click the Save button to save your change.

6 Click the View button to display your table in the Datasheet view.

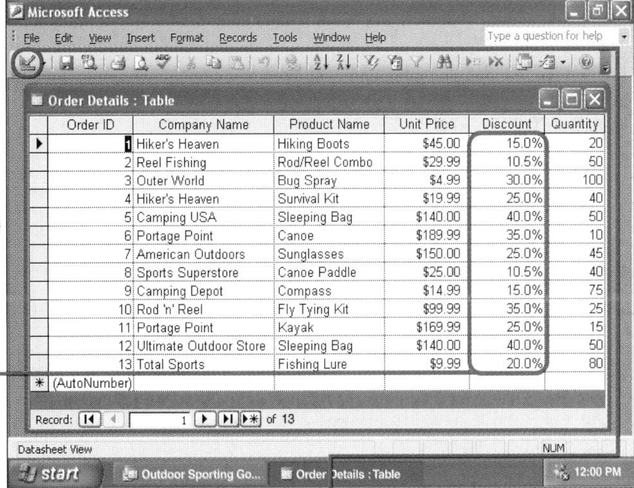

Order ID	Company Name	Product Name	Unit Price	Discount	Quantity
1	Hiker's Heaven	Hiking Boots	$45.00	15.0%	20
2	Reel Fishing	Rod/Reel Combo	$29.99	10.5%	50
3	Outer World	Bug Spray	$4.99	30.0%	100
4	Hiker's Heaven	Survival Kit	$19.99	25.0%	40
5	Camping USA	Sleeping Bag	$140.00	40.0%	50
6	Portage Point	Canoe	$189.99	35.0%	10
7	American Outdoors	Sunglasses	$150.00	25.0%	45
8	Sports Superstore	Canoe Paddle	$25.00	10.5%	40
9	Camping Depot	Compass	$14.99	15.0%	75
10	Rod 'n' Reel	Fly Tying Kit	$99.99	35.0%	25
11	Portage Point	Kayak	$169.99	25.0%	15
12	Ultimate Outdoor Store	Sleeping Bag	$140.00	40.0%	50
13	Total Sports	Fishing Lure	$9.99	20.0%	80
(AutoNumber)					

■ The data displays the number of decimal places you specified.

■ When you enter data in the field, Access will automatically display the data with the correct number of decimal places.

Note: If Access changes decimal places you type to zeros (example: 12.34 changes to 12.00), you need to change the field size. To change the field size, see page 86.

■ To return to the Design view, click the View button.

ADD A CAPTION

You can add a caption to a field. The caption will appear as the heading for the field instead of the field name.

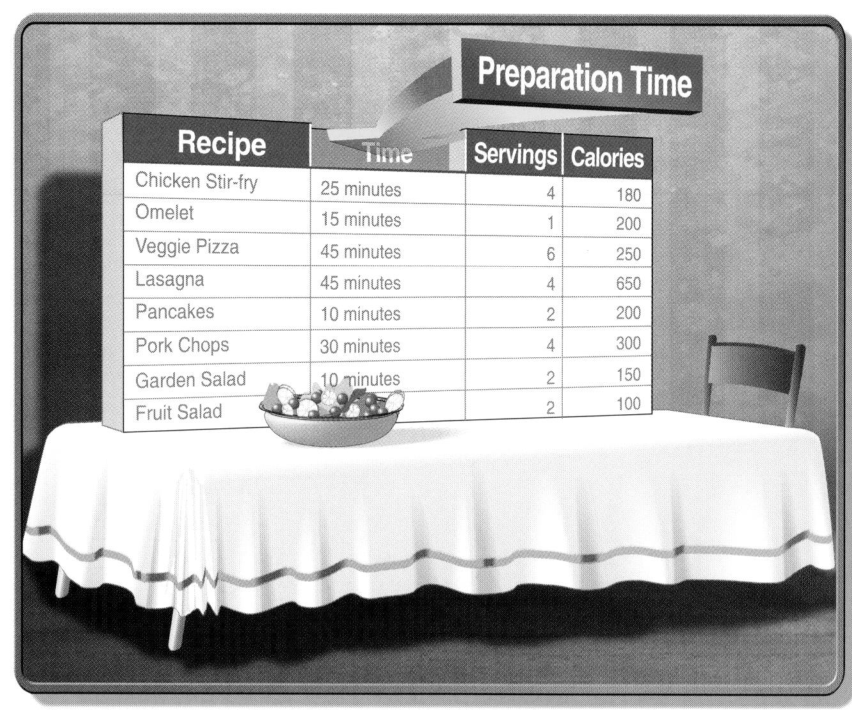

A caption can be longer and more descriptive than a field name.

After you add a caption to a field, any forms, reports or queries you create that include the field will display the caption instead of the field name.

ADD A CAPTION

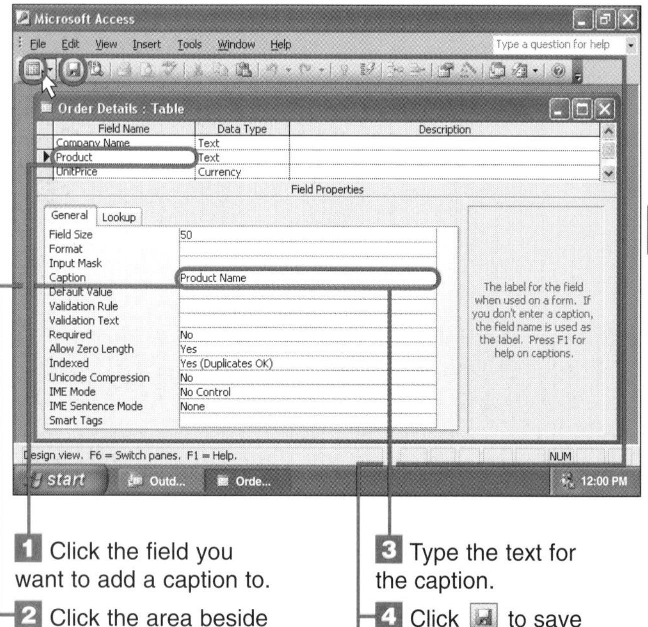

1 Click the field you want to add a caption to.

2 Click the area beside **Caption**.

Note: If a caption already exists, drag the mouse I over the caption to highlight the text.

3 Type the text for the caption.

4 Click [save icon] to save your change.

5 Click [view icon] to display your table in the Datasheet view.

■ The caption you entered replaces the field name in your table.

■ To return to the Design view, click [design icon].

SET A DEFAULT VALUE

You can specify a value that you want to appear automatically in a field each time you add a new record. Setting a default value saves you from having to repeatedly type the same data.

For example, if most of your customers live in California, you can set "California" as the default value for the State field.

In a field that contains dates, such as an Order Date field, you can set the current date as the default value for the field.

SET A DEFAULT VALUE

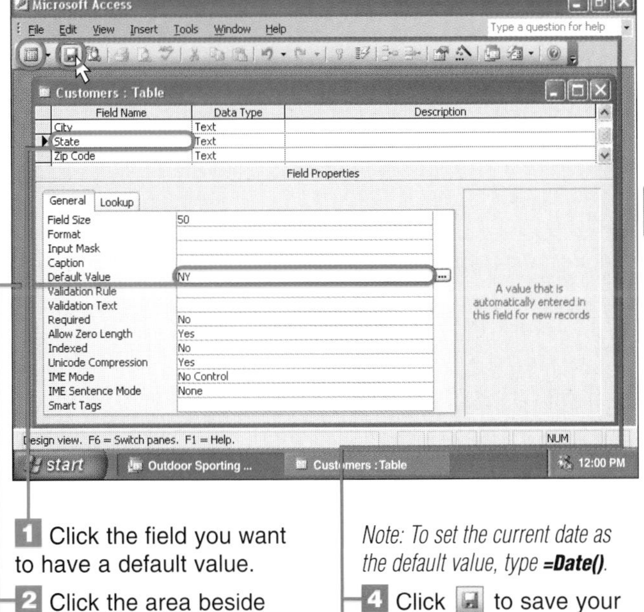

Company Name	Billing Address	City	State	Zip Code
Camping Depot	1300 Kennedy Dr.	Boston	MA	02117
Rod 'n' Reel	88 Lincoln Blvd.	Hartford	CT	06199
Total Sports	456 Harding Blvd.	New York	NY	10087
Camping USA	336 Bay St.	New York	NY	10116
Portage Point	55 Sunset St.	Syracuse	NY	13206
Ultimate Outdoor Store	36 College Rd.	Syracuse	NY	13217
Sports Superstore	255 Park Dr.	Buffalo	NY	14211
Outer World	6858 King St.	Buffalo	NY	14270
Hiker's Heaven	14 Spencer Ave.	Indianapolis	IN	46290
Reel Fishing	670 Pine Dr.	Freeport	IL	61032
American Outdoors	900 Turling Ave.	Little Rock	AR	72295
			NY	

1. Click the field you want to have a default value.
2. Click the area beside **Default Value**.
3. Type the text or number you want to set as the default value.

Note: To set the current date as the default value, type ***=Date()****.*

4. Click the save button to save your change.
5. Click the view button to display your table in the Datasheet view.

■ The default value automatically appears in the field each time you add a new record. You can accept the default value or type another value.

Note: Setting a default value will not affect existing data in the field.

■ To return to the Design view, click the design view button.

DATA ENTRY REQUIRED

You can specify that a field must contain data for each record. This prevents you from leaving out important information when entering data.

For example, a table containing invoice information can require data in the Invoice Number field.

DATA ENTRY REQUIRED

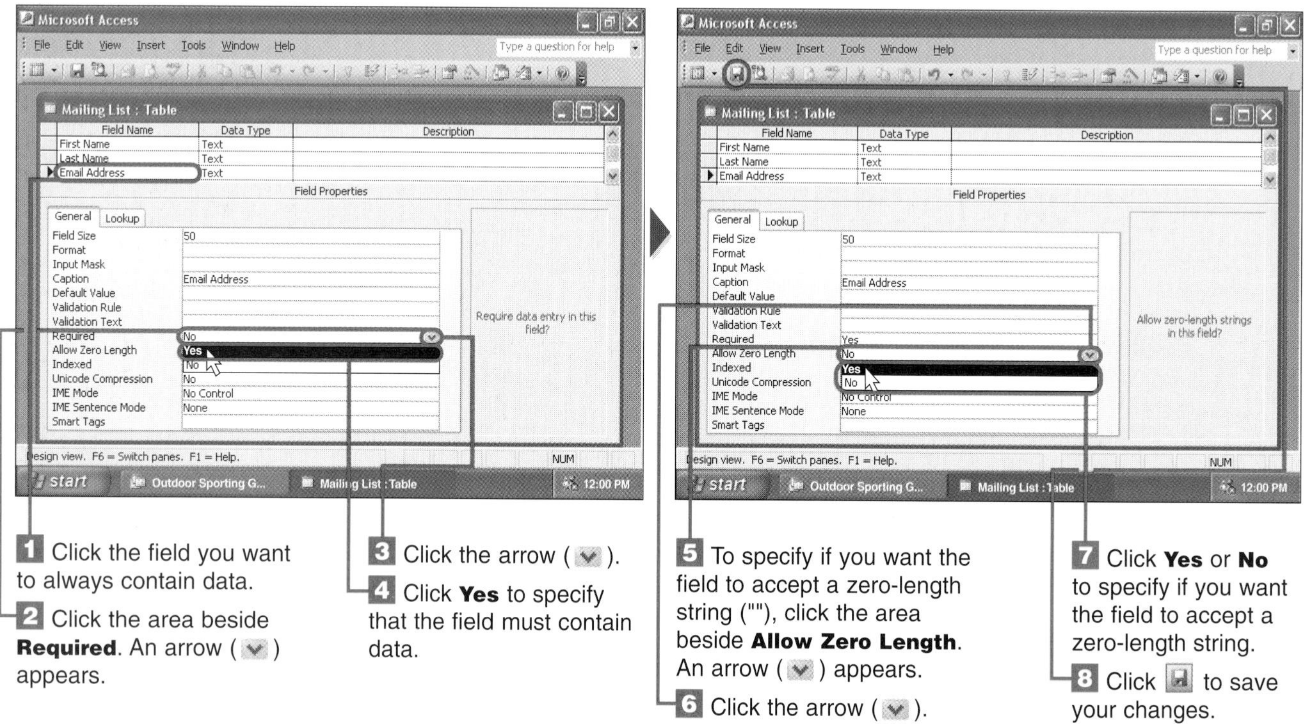

1 Click the field you want to always contain data.

2 Click the area beside **Required**. An arrow ( ) appears.

3 Click the arrow ( ).

4 Click **Yes** to specify that the field must contain data.

5 To specify if you want the field to accept a zero-length string (""), click the area beside **Allow Zero Length**. An arrow ( ) appears.

6 Click the arrow ( ).

7 Click **Yes** or **No** to specify if you want the field to accept a zero-length string.

8 Click to save your changes.

What is a zero-length string?

A zero-length string ("") indicates that no data exists for the field. A zero-length string is useful when a field is set to require data, but no data exists. For example, if the Fax Number field must contain data, but a customer does not have a fax number, you can enter a zero-length string in the field. You can allow zero-length strings only in fields with the Text, Memo or Hyperlink data type. For information on data types, see page 82.

To enter a zero-length string, type "" in a cell. When you enter a zero-length string, the cell will appear empty.

ID	First Name	Last Name	Phone	Fax
1	Linda	Harris	555-4433	555-4434
2	Frank	Hill	555-1234	
3	David	Jones	555-6677	555-6678
4	Nancy	King	555-1215	555-1216
5	Stacy	Lee	555-2200	
6	Ann	Lewis	555-1543	555-1550
7	Amy	Martin	555-6235	555-6236
8	Sara	Miller	555-8976	

CAN CONTAIN ZERO-LENGTH STRINGS

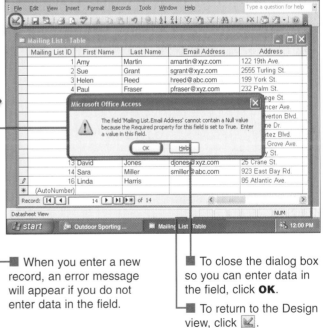

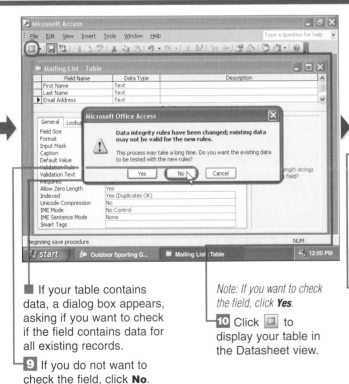

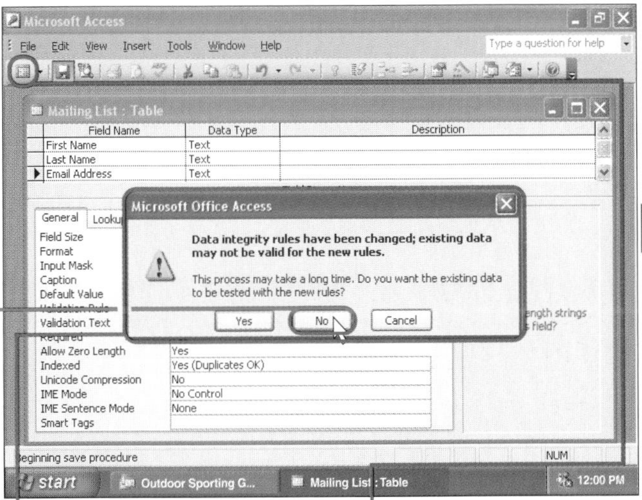

■ If your table contains data, a dialog box appears, asking if you want to check if the field contains data for all existing records.

9 If you do not want to check the field, click **No**.

*Note: If you want to check the field, click **Yes**.*

10 Click ▦ to display your table in the Datasheet view.

■ When you enter a new record, an error message will appear if you do not enter data in the field.

■ To close the dialog box so you can enter data in the field, click **OK**.

■ To return to the Design view, click ▦.

ADD A VALIDATION RULE

You can add a validation rule to help reduce errors when entering data in a field. A field that uses a validation rule can only accept data that meets the requirements you specify.

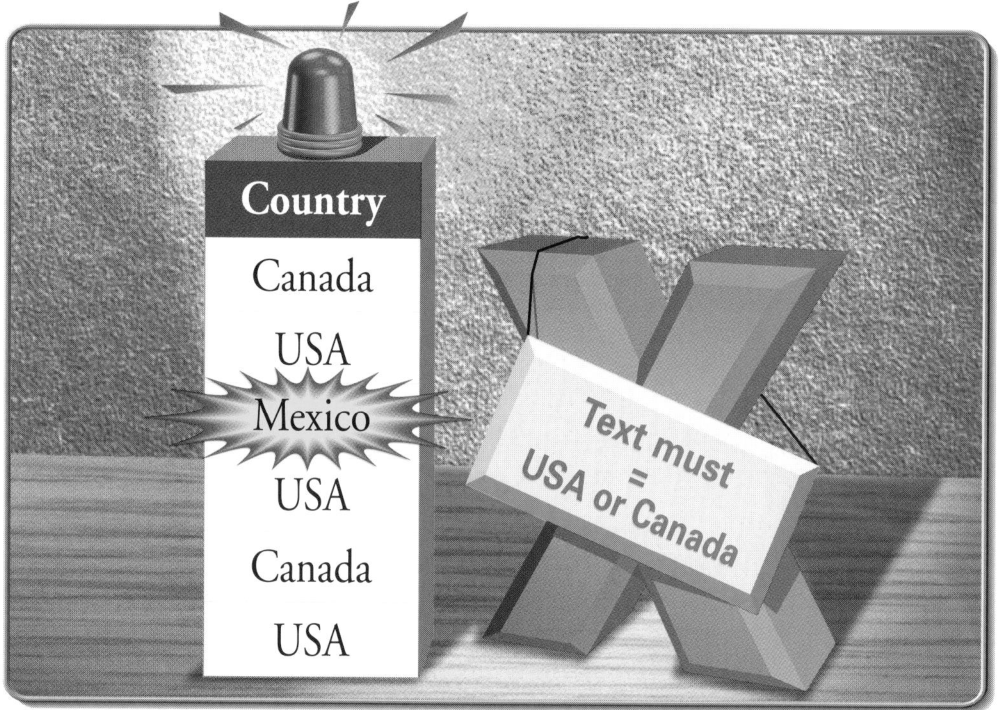

ADD A VALIDATION RULE

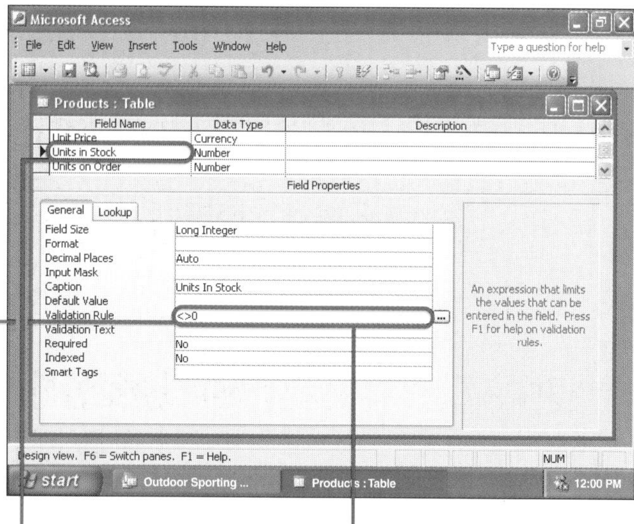

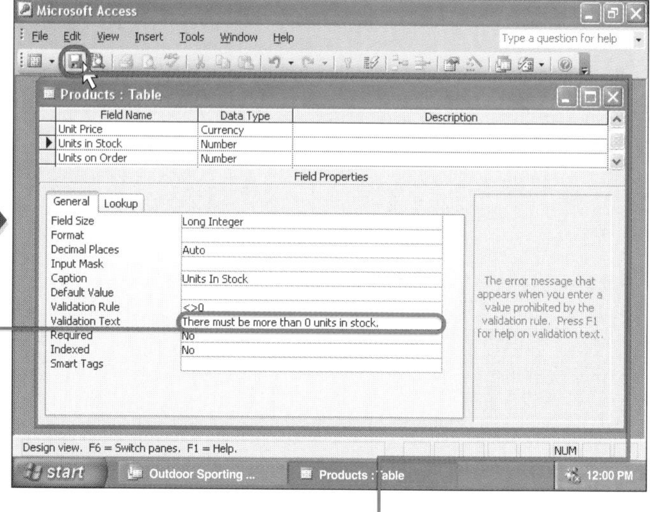

1 Click the field you want to use a validation rule.

2 Click the area beside **Validation Rule**.

3 Type the validation rule you want to use to limit the data you can enter into the field.

Note: For examples of validation rules, see the top of page 95.

4 To create the error message you want to appear when incorrect data is entered, click the area beside **Validation Text**.

5 Type the error message you want to appear.

Note: If you do not specify an error message, Access will display a standard message.

6 Click the save button to save your changes.

What validation rules can I use?

Here are some examples of validation rules that you can use. For more examples, see page 214.

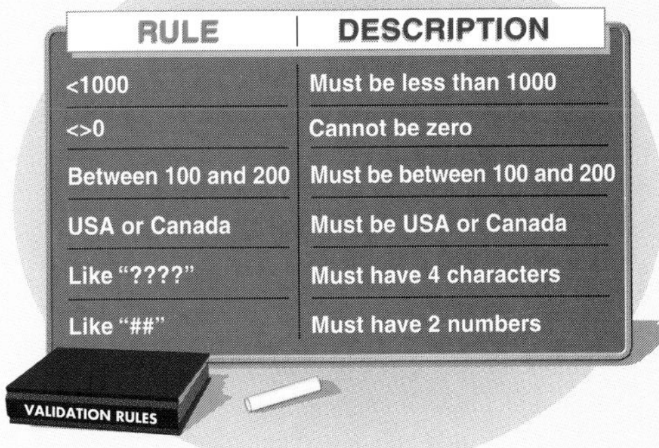

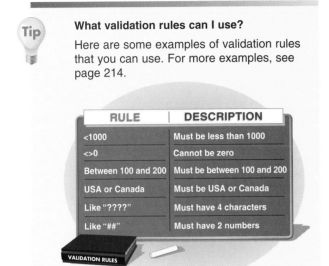

RULE	DESCRIPTION
<1000	Must be less than 1000
<>0	Cannot be zero
Between 100 and 200	Must be between 100 and 200
USA or Canada	Must be USA or Canada
Like "????"	Must have 4 characters
Like "##"	Must have 2 numbers

What should my error message contain?

When you enter incorrect data, the error message that appears should clearly explain why the data you entered is incorrect. For example, the error message "You must enter a number between 1 and 100" is more informative than the message "Data Rejected."

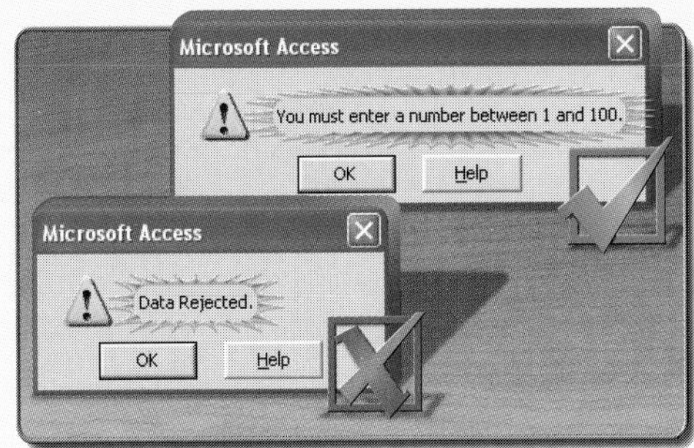

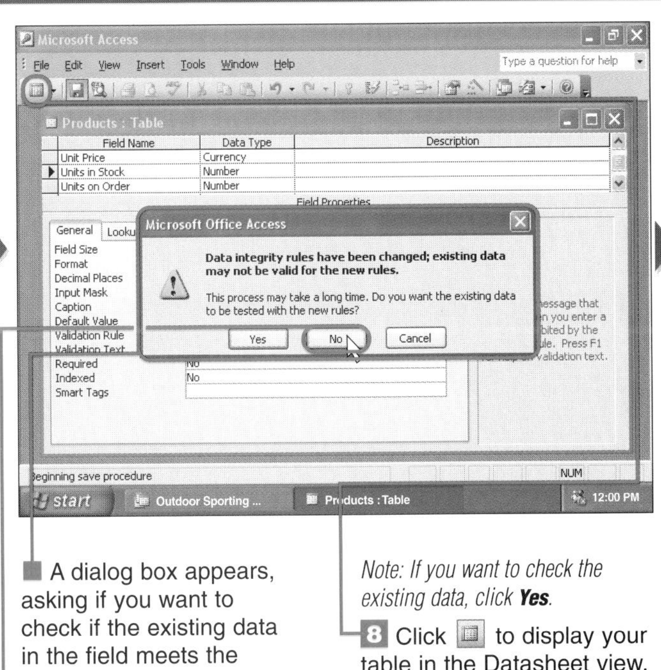

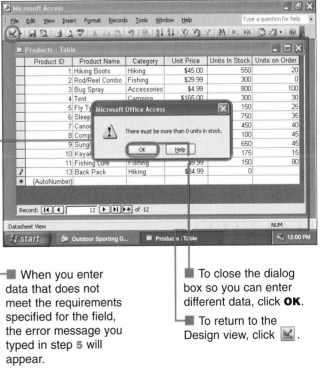

■ A dialog box appears, asking if you want to check if the existing data in the field meets the requirements you specified.

7 If you do not want to check the existing data, click **No**.

*Note: If you want to check the existing data, click **Yes**.*

8 Click ▦ to display your table in the Datasheet view.

■ When you enter data that does not meet the requirements specified for the field, the error message you typed in step **5** will appear.

■ To close the dialog box so you can enter different data, click **OK**.

■ To return to the Design view, click ▦.

CREATE AN INPUT MASK

You can create an input mask to control the type of information you can enter in a field. Input masks reduce errors and ensure data has a consistent appearance.

The Input Mask Wizard provides commonly used input masks that you can choose from.

You can use the Input Mask Wizard only in fields with the Text or Date/Time data type. For information on data types, see page 82.

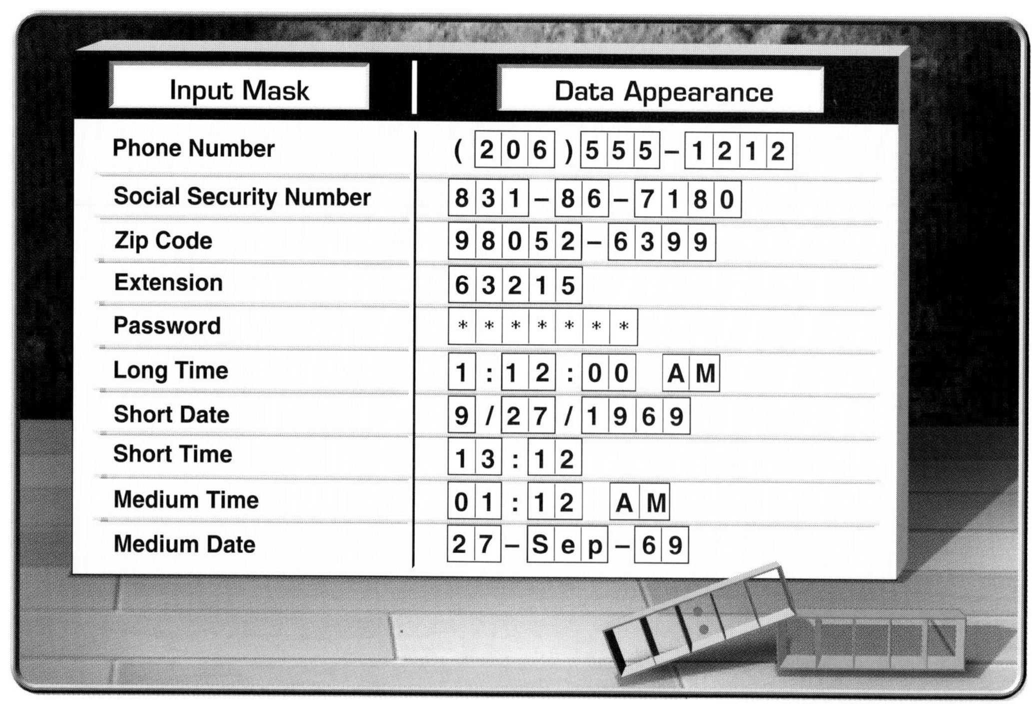

Input Mask	Data Appearance
Phone Number	(206)555-1212
Social Security Number	831-86-7180
Zip Code	98052-6399
Extension	63215
Password	*******
Long Time	1:12:00 AM
Short Date	9/27/1969
Short Time	13:12
Medium Time	01:12 AM
Medium Date	27-Sep-69

CREATE AN INPUT MASK USING THE WIZARD

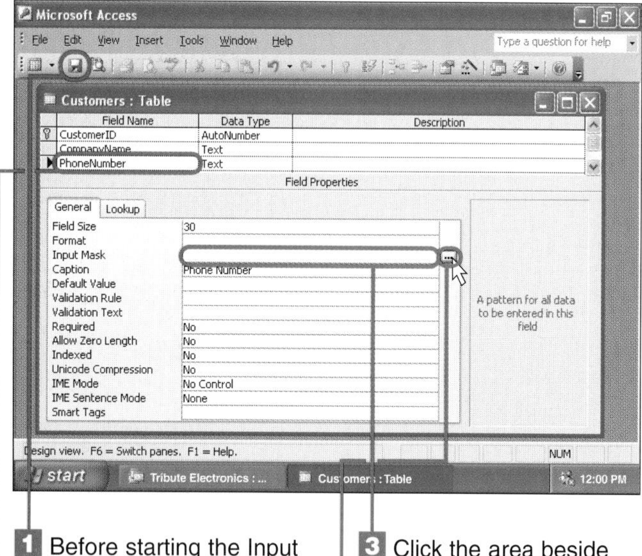

1 Before starting the Input Mask Wizard, you must save your table. To save your table, click 💾.

2 Click the name of the field you want to use an input mask.

3 Click the area beside **Input Mask**. A button (...) appears.

4 Click the button (...) to start the Input Mask Wizard.

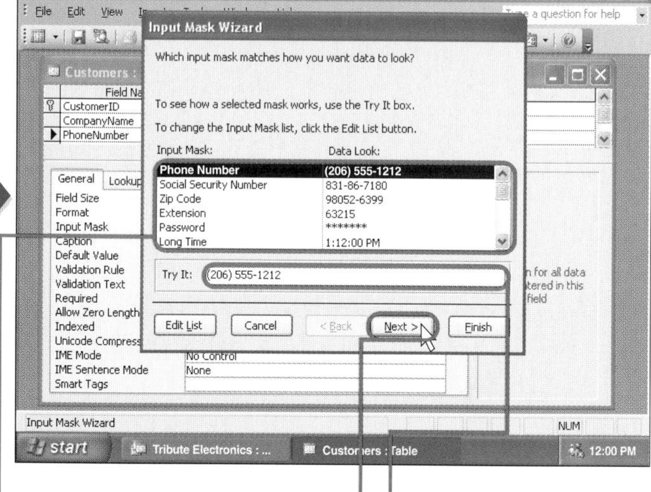

■ The Input Mask Wizard appears.

■ This area displays the available input masks and how the data will appear in the field.

5 Click the input mask you want to use.

6 To try the input mask you selected, press the Tab key and then type the appropriate data.

7 Click **Next** to continue.

Why does a dialog box appear when I try to start the Input Mask Wizard?

When you try to start the Input Mask Wizard for the first time, a dialog box appears, stating that the wizard is not installed on your computer. To install the wizard, click **Yes**.

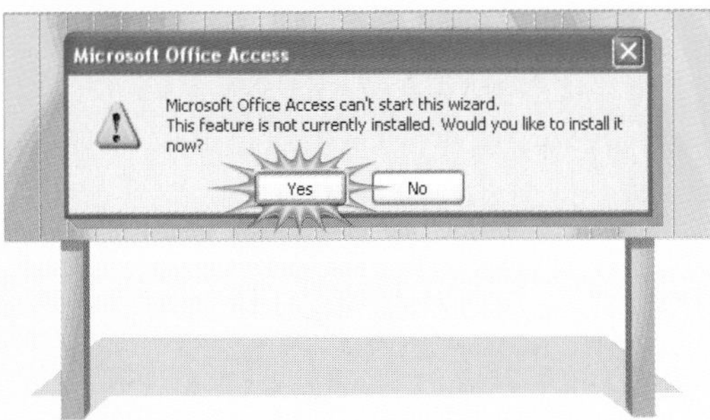

How can an input mask save me time when I enter data in a field?

Input masks can save you time by automatically entering characters for you, such as brackets ( ), hyphens (-) and slashes (/). For example, when you type **2015551234** in a field that uses the Phone Number input mask, Access will change the data to **(201) 555-1234**.

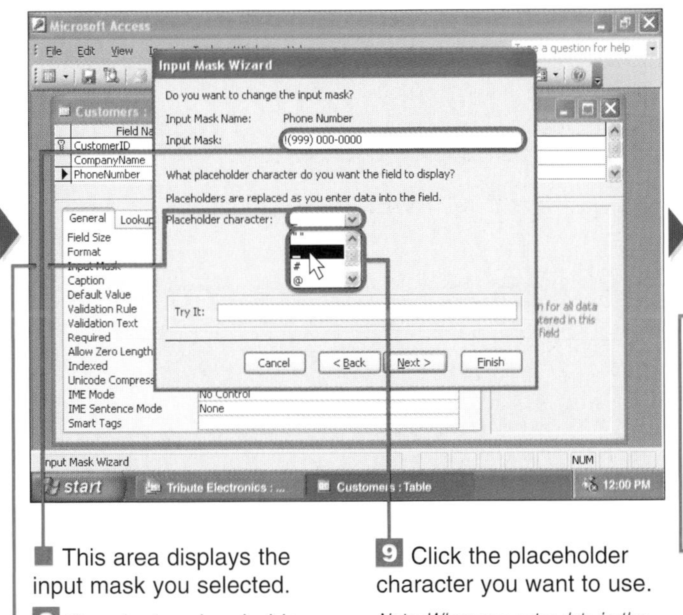

■ This area displays the input mask you selected.

8 To select a placeholder character for the input mask, click ▾ in this area.

9 Click the placeholder character you want to use.

Note: When you enter data in the field, the data you type will replace the placeholder characters. For example, (___) ___-____ will change to (555) 555-3874.

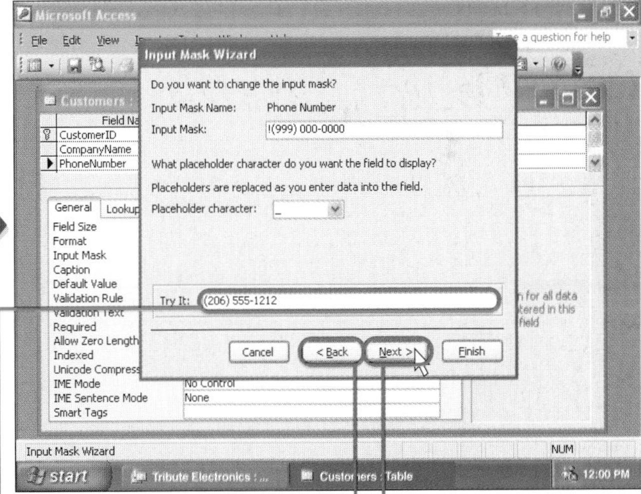

10 To try the input mask with the placeholder character you selected, press the Tab key and then type the appropriate data.

11 Click **Next** to continue.

■ You can click **Back** at any time to return to a previous step and change your selections.

CONTINUED

CREATE AN INPUT MASK

When you create an input mask, the wizard may ask how you want to store the data you enter in the field.

You can store data with or without symbols. Storing data without symbols saves storage space on your computer.

CREATE AN INPUT MASK USING THE WIZARD (CONTINUED)

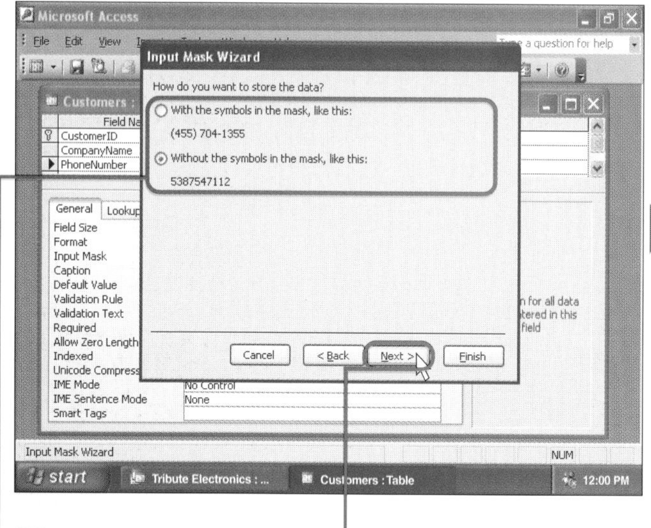

12 Click an option to specify how you want to store the data in the field (○ changes to ◉).

*Note: This screen does not appear for some input masks. If the screen does not appear, skip to step **14**.*

13 Click **Next** to continue.

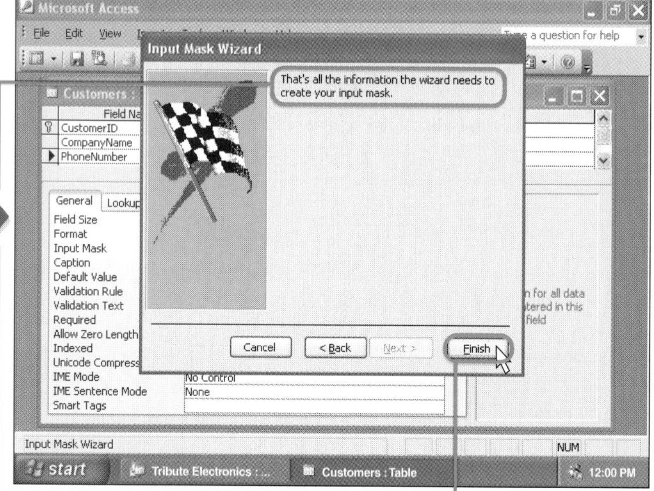

■ This message appears when you have provided all the information the wizard needs to create the input mask.

14 Click **Finish** to close the wizard.

After creating an input mask, why doesn't the data I enter appear the way I expect?

After you use an input mask to enter data in a field, Access will display the data using the format set for the field. For example, if you enter the date **01/25/2004** in a field that uses the Short Date input mask and the Long Date format, the date will automatically change to **Sunday, January 25, 2004** after you press the Enter key. To select a format for a field, see page 84.

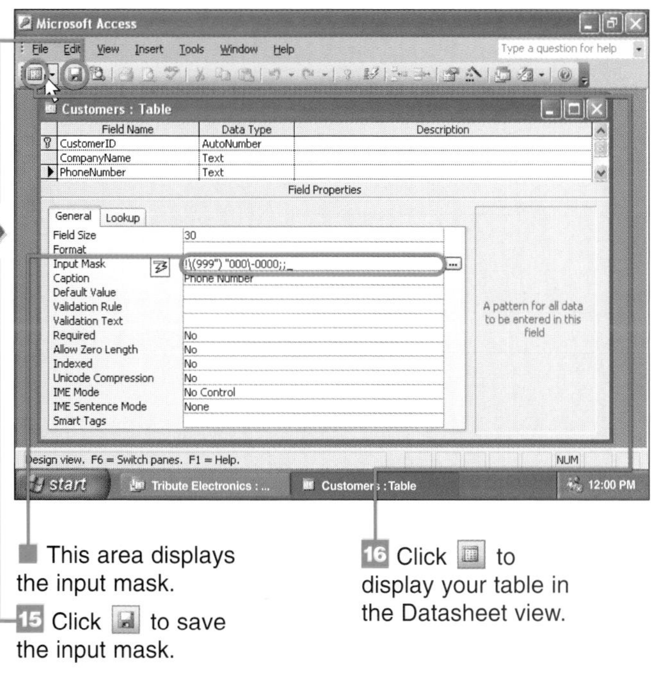

■ This area displays the input mask.

15 Click 💾 to save the input mask.

16 Click ▦ to display your table in the Datasheet view.

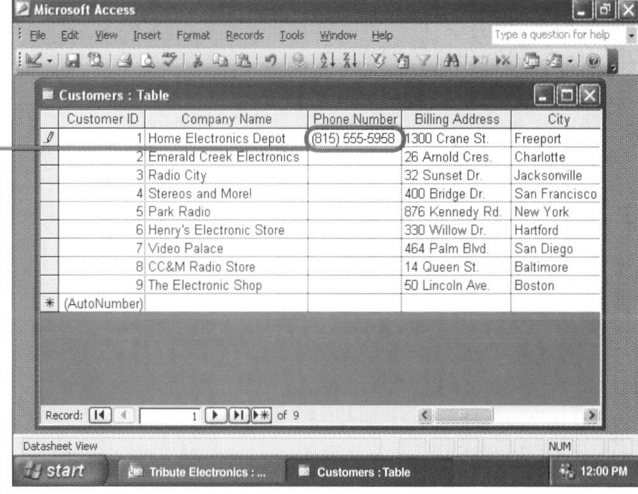

USE AN INPUT MASK

1 Click an empty cell in the field that uses the input mask.

2 To move to the beginning of the cell, press the Home key.

3 Type the appropriate data and then press the Enter key.

Note: Access will only accept characters specified by the input mask. For example, you can only enter numbers in a field that uses the Phone Number input mask.

CONTINUED

CREATE AN INPUT MASK

You can create your own input mask to establish a pattern for data you can enter in a field.

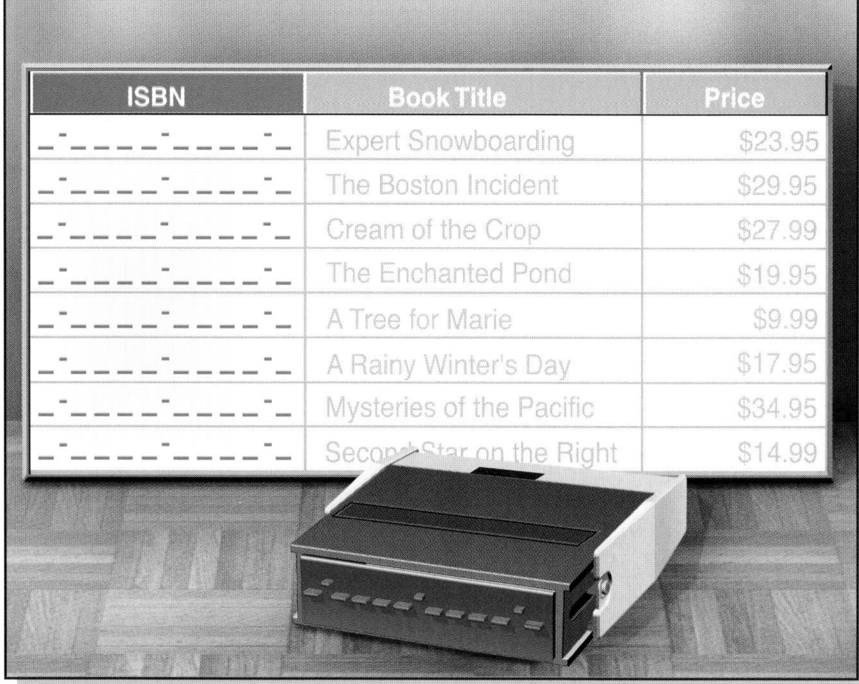

ISBN
Book Title
Price
Expert Snowboarding
$23.95
The Boston Incident
$29.95
Cream of the Crop
$27.99
The Enchanted Pond
$19.95
A Tree for Marie
$9.99
A Rainy Winter's Day
$17.95
Mysteries of the Pacific
$34.95
$14.99

You may want to create your own input mask if the Input Mask Wizard does not offer an input mask that suits the data you want to enter in a field. To create an input mask using the wizard, see page 96.

CREATE YOUR OWN INPUT MASK

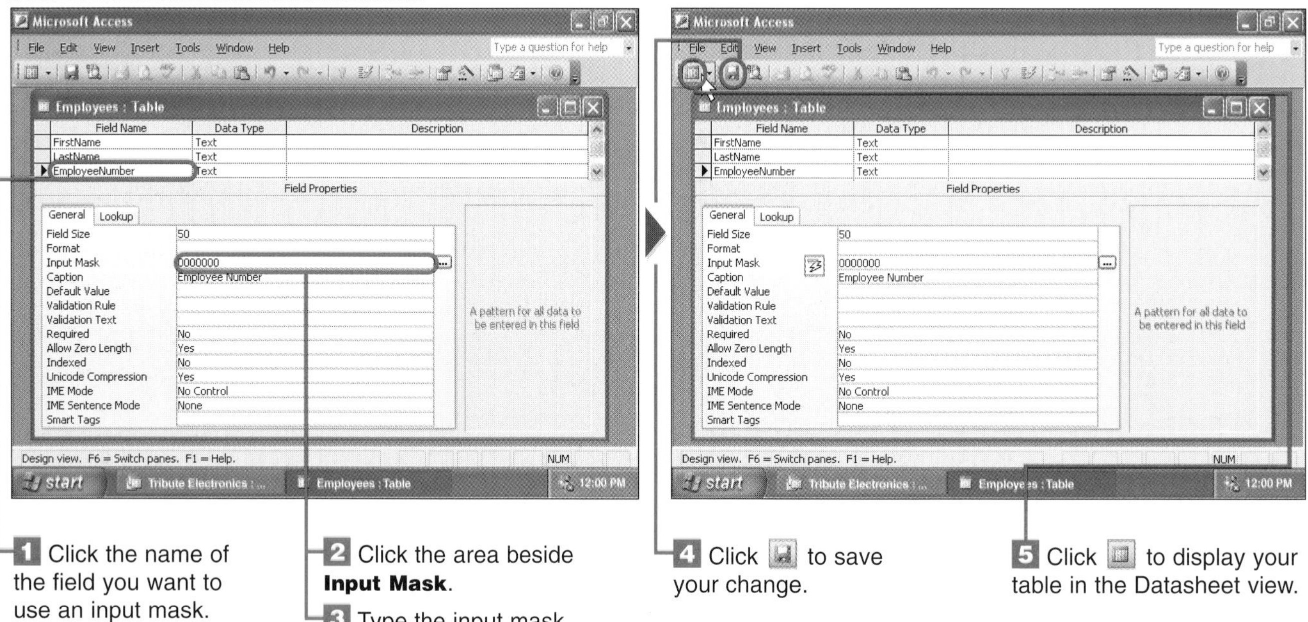

1 Click the name of the field you want to use an input mask.

2 Click the area beside **Input Mask**.

3 Type the input mask you want to use.

4 Click [save icon] to save your change.

5 Click [view icon] to display your table in the Datasheet view.

How do I remove an input mask?

If you no longer want a field to use an input mask, you can delete the input mask. In the Input Mask area for the field, position the mouse I to the left of the input mask and then drag the mouse I until you highlight the entire input mask. Then press the Delete key to delete the input mask.

Why does the Property Update Options button ( ) appear when I create an input mask?

You can use the Property Update Options button ( ) to automatically update the format of the field in all your forms or reports that display the field. Click the Property Update Options button to display a list of options and then select the option you want to use. The Property Update Options button is available only until you perform another task.

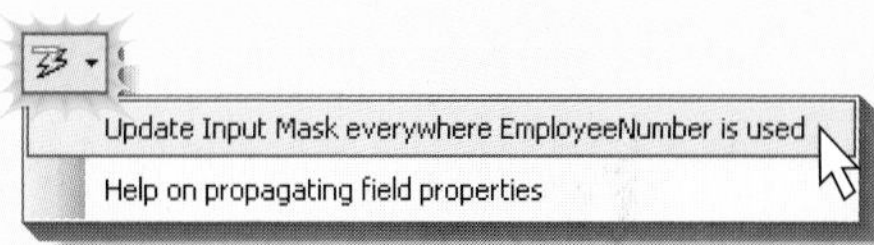

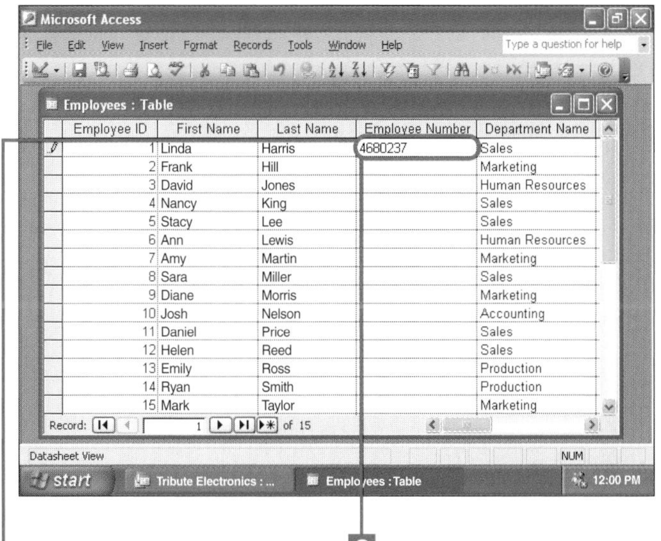

USE AN INPUT MASK

1. Click an empty cell in the field that uses the input mask.
2. To move to the beginning of the cell, press the Home key.
3. Type the appropriate data.

Note: Access will only accept characters specified by the input mask. In this example, you can enter only 7 digits in the field.

INPUT MASK CHARACTERS

You can use these characters to create an input mask.

0
Numbers 0 to 9, required. Plus (+) and minus (-) signs not allowed.

9
Number or space, optional. Plus (+) and minus (-) signs not allowed.

#
Number or space, optional. Plus (+) and minus (-) signs allowed.

L
Letters A to Z, required.

?
Letters A to Z, optional.

A
Letter or number, required.

a
Letter or number, optional.

&
Character or space, required.

C
Character or space, optional.

. , : ; - /
Decimal point and thousands, date and time separators.

<
Convert the following characters to lowercase.

>
Convert the following characters to uppercase.

!
Display characters from right to left, rather than from left to right.

****
Display the following input mask character. For example, **\&** will display **&**.

Password
Display an asterisk (*) for each character you type.

CREATE A FIELD TO STORE PICTURES

You can create a field that allows you to add a picture to each record in a table.

For example, you can create a field to store pictures of employees, houses for sale, artwork, recipes or products.

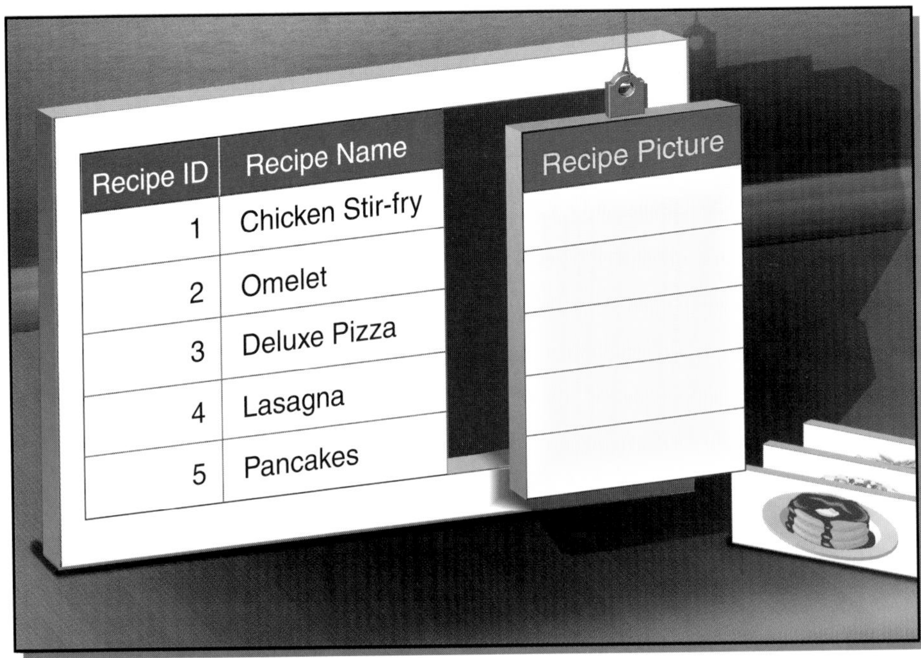

Access allows you to include pictures stored in several popular file formats, such as Bitmap (.bmp) and Windows Metafile (.wmf).

CREATE A FIELD TO STORE PICTURES

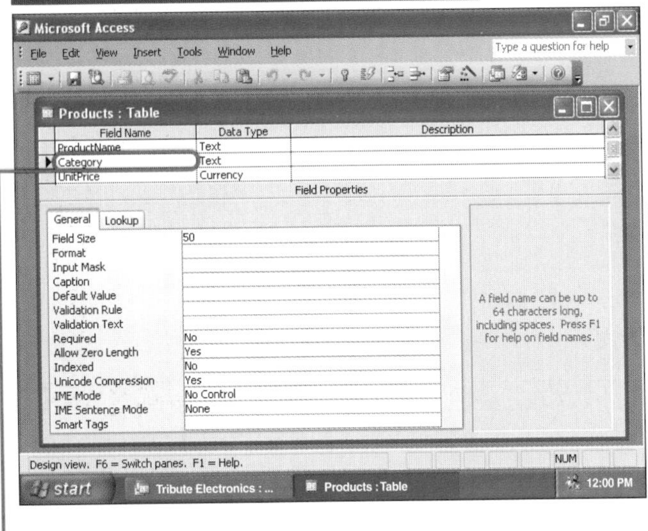

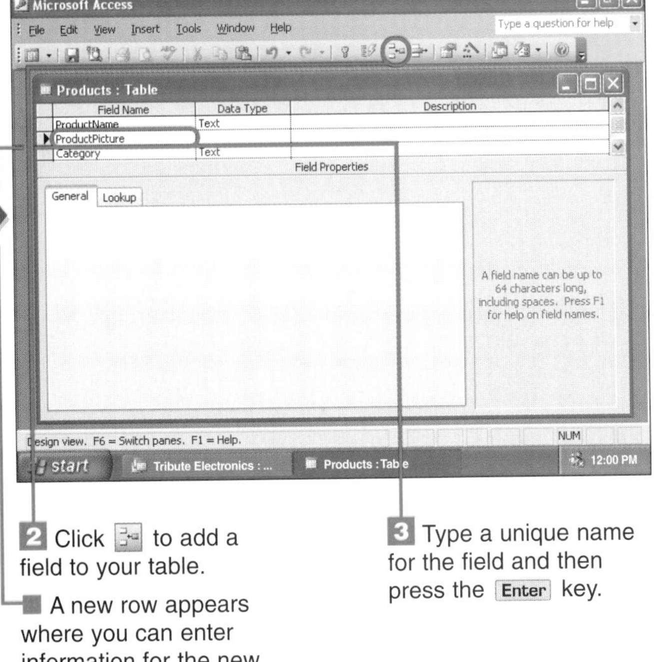

1 To create a field that will store pictures, click the name of the field you want to appear after the new field. A triangle (▶) appears beside the field name.

■ To add a field that will store pictures to the end of your table, click the area directly below the last field name. Then skip to step **3**.

2 Click [icon] to add a field to your table.

■ A new row appears where you can enter information for the new field.

3 Type a unique name for the field and then press the **Enter** key.

Will the pictures I add to my table appear on a form?

When you create a form using a table that includes pictures, the form will display the pictures.

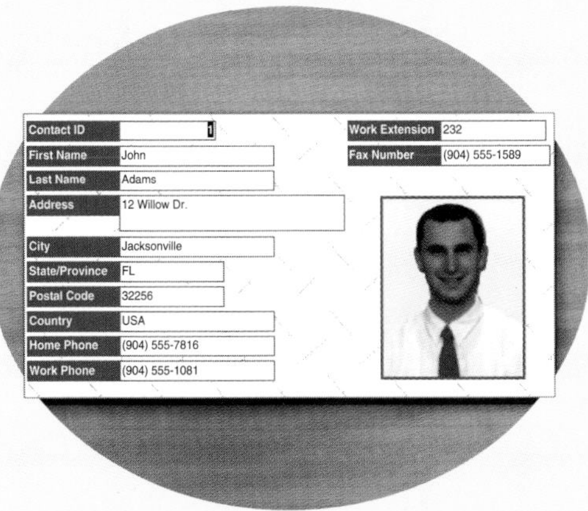

Can I add other types of files to a table?

You can add files such as documents, spreadsheets, sounds and videos to a table as you would add pictures to a table. When you double-click the cell containing a file in a table, the appropriate program will open and display or play the file.

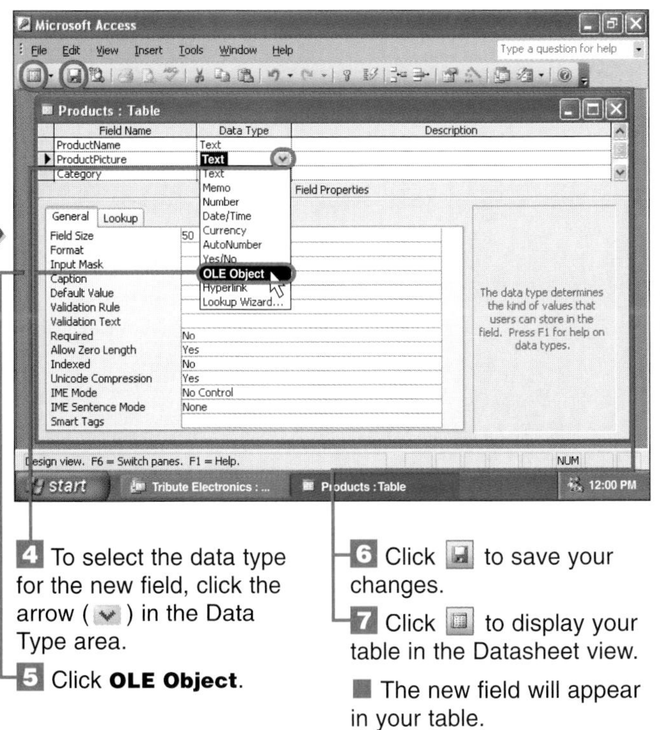

4 To select the data type for the new field, click the arrow ( ) in the Data Type area.

5 Click **OLE Object**.

6 Click to save your changes.

7 Click to display your table in the Datasheet view.

■ The new field will appear in your table.

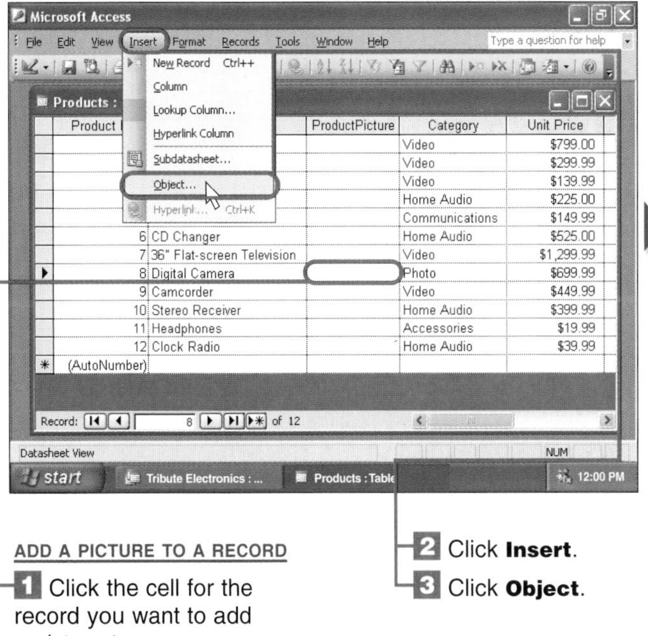

ADD A PICTURE TO A RECORD

1 Click the cell for the record you want to add a picture to.

2 Click **Insert**.

3 Click **Object**.

CONTINUED

CREATE A FIELD TO STORE PICTURES

When adding a picture to a record in a table, you must specify where the picture is stored on your computer.

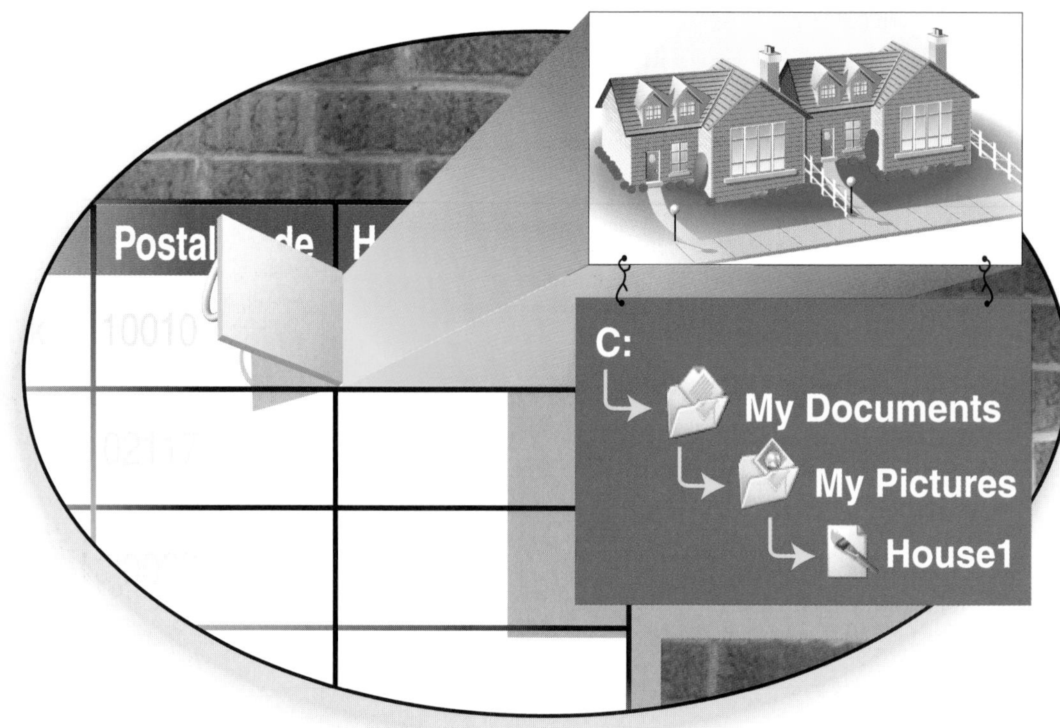

CREATE A FIELD TO STORE PICTURES (CONTINUED)

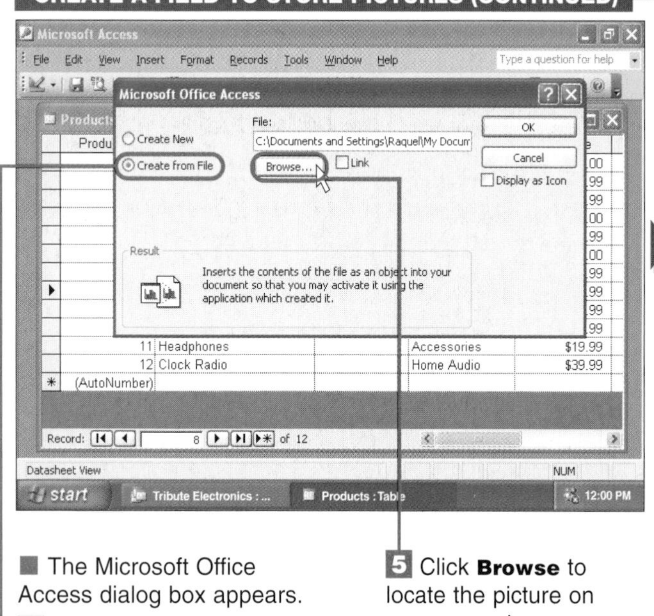

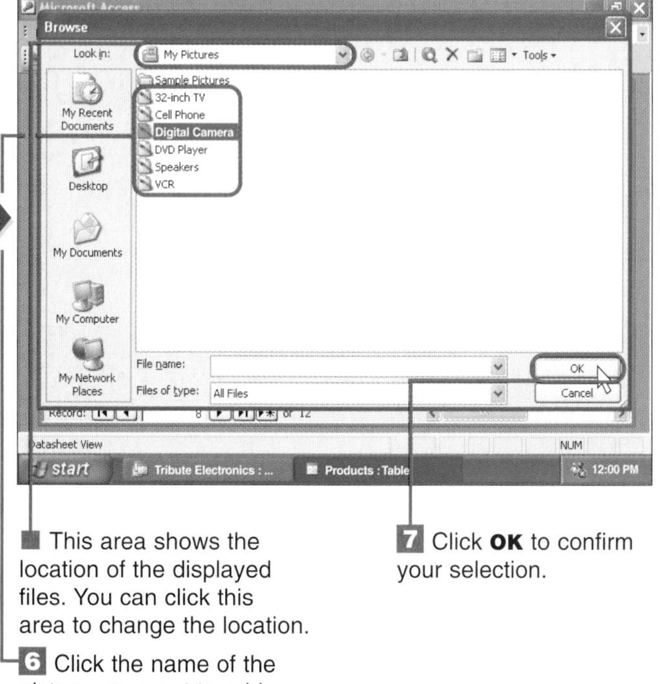

■ The Microsoft Office Access dialog box appears.

4 Click **Create from File** to add a picture stored on your computer to the record (○ changes to ◉).

5 Click **Browse** to locate the picture on your computer.

■ This area shows the location of the displayed files. You can click this area to change the location.

6 Click the name of the picture you want to add to the record.

7 Click **OK** to confirm your selection.

Why would I add a link to a picture to my table?

When you add a link to a picture, Access creates a connection to the original picture on your computer. Changes you make to the original picture will affect the picture in the table. If you choose not to add a link to a picture, Access stores a copy of the picture in your database. Changes you make to the original picture will not affect the picture in the table.

Recipe ID	Recipe Name	Recipe Picture
1	Pepper Stir-fry	Bitmap Image
2	Omelet	Bitmap Image
3	Deluxe Pizza	Bitmap Image
4	Lasagna	Bitmap Image
5	Pancakes	Bitmap Image

How do I remove a picture I added to my table?

To remove a picture from a table, click the cell containing the picture and then press the Delete key. Access will not delete the original picture stored on your computer.

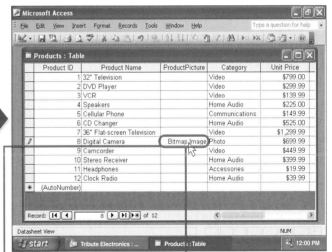

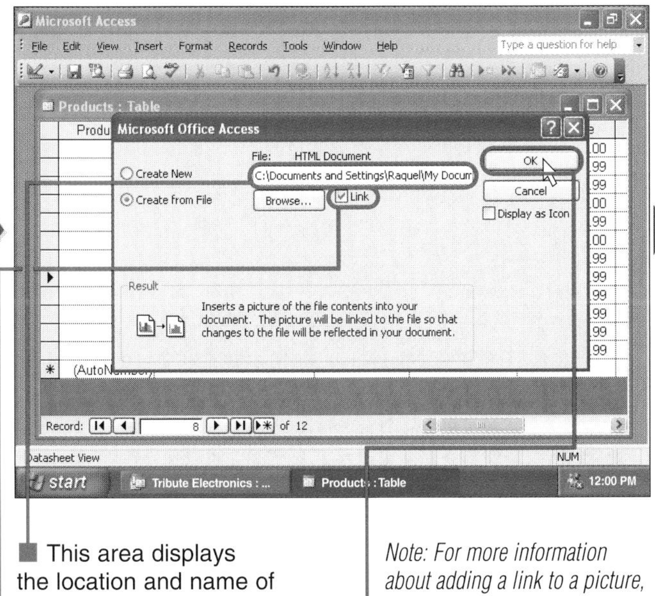

Product ID	Product Name	ProductPicture	Category	Unit Price
1	32" Television		Video	$799.00
2	DVD Player		Video	$299.99
3	VCR		Video	$139.99
4	Speakers		Home Audio	$225.00
5	Cellular Phone		Communications	$149.99
6	CD Changer		Home Audio	$525.00
7	36" Flat-screen Television		Video	$1,299.99
8	Digital Camera	Bitmap Image	Photo	$699.99
9	Camcorder		Video	$449.99
10	Stereo Receiver		Home Audio	$399.99
11	Headphones		Accessories	$19.99
12	Clock Radio		Home Audio	$39.99
(AutoNumber)				

■ This area displays the location and name of the picture you selected.

8 To add a link to the picture, click **Link** (☐ changes to ☑).

Note: For more information about adding a link to a picture, see the top of this page.

9 Click **OK** to add the picture to the record.

■ The cell displays information about the picture you added to the record.

■ To add pictures to other records, repeat steps 1 to 9 starting on page 103 for each record.

VIEW A PICTURE

1 To view a picture, double-click the cell containing the picture you want to view.

*Note: A warning dialog box may appear. Click **Open** to continue.*

CREATE A LOOKUP COLUMN

You can create a lookup column, which displays a list of values that you can choose from when entering information in a field.

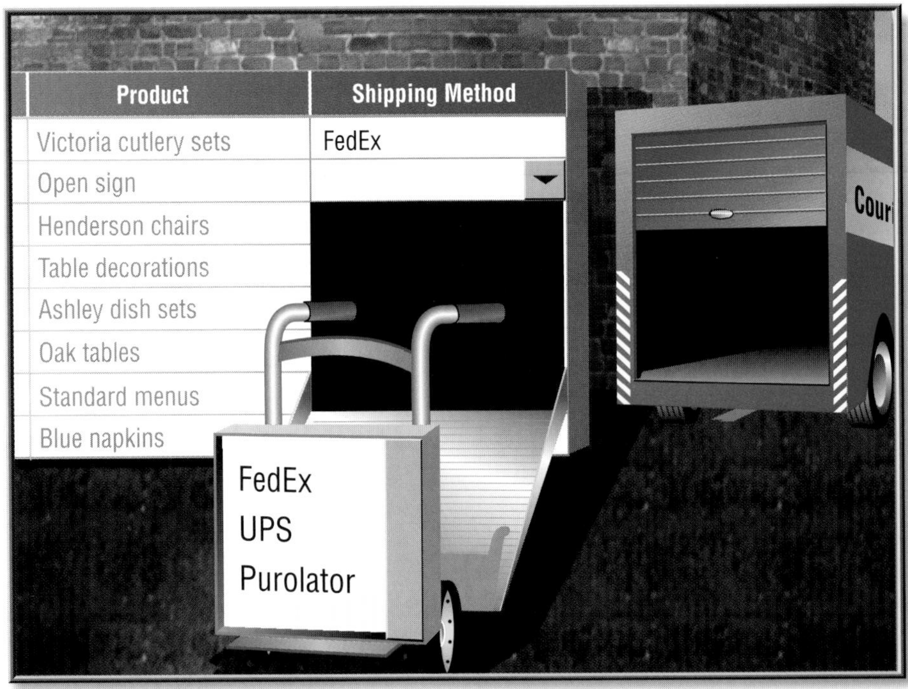

CREATE A LOOKUP COLUMN

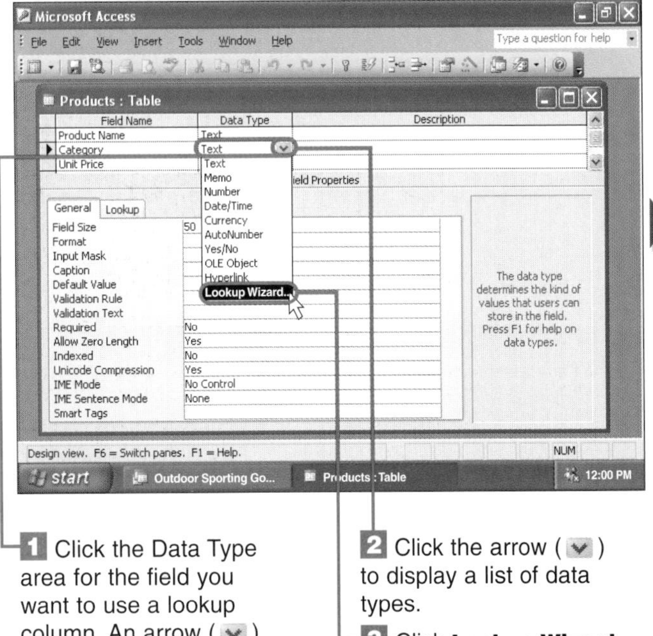

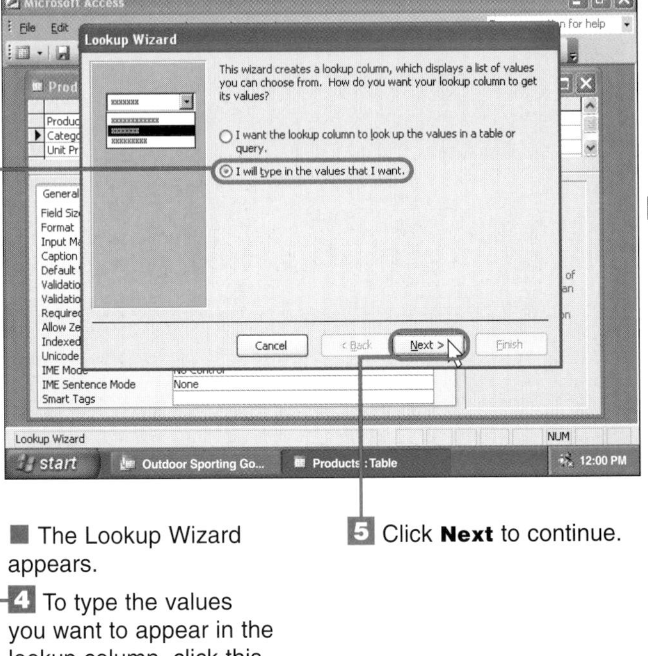

1 Click the Data Type area for the field you want to use a lookup column. An arrow (▾) appears.

2 Click the arrow (▾) to display a list of data types.

3 Click **Lookup Wizard**.

■ The Lookup Wizard appears.

4 To type the values you want to appear in the lookup column, click this option (○ changes to ◉).

5 Click **Next** to continue.

Why would I create a lookup column?

Creating a lookup column is useful if you repeatedly enter the same values in a field. For example, if your customers reside in three states, you can create a lookup column that displays the three states, such as CA, TX and IL.

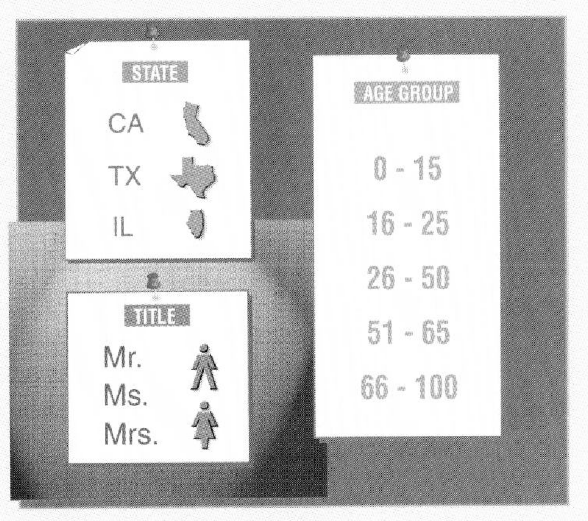

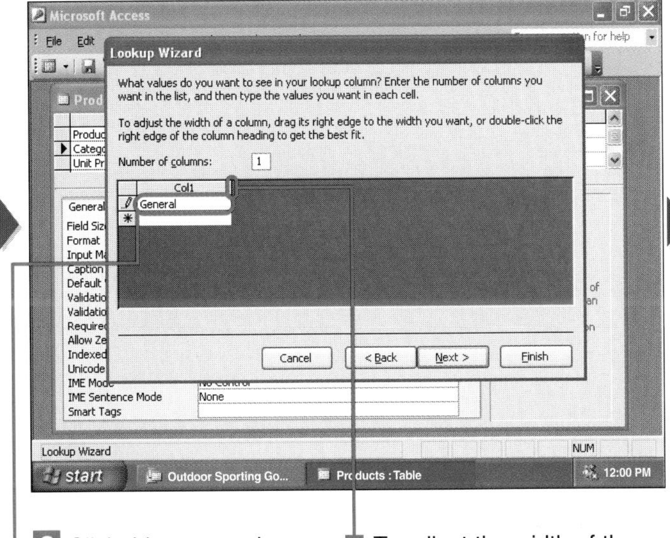

6 Click this area and then type the first value you want to appear in the lookup column.

■ To adjust the width of the lookup column, position the mouse ⇖ over the right edge of the column heading (⇖ changes to ✥) and then drag the column edge to the width you want.

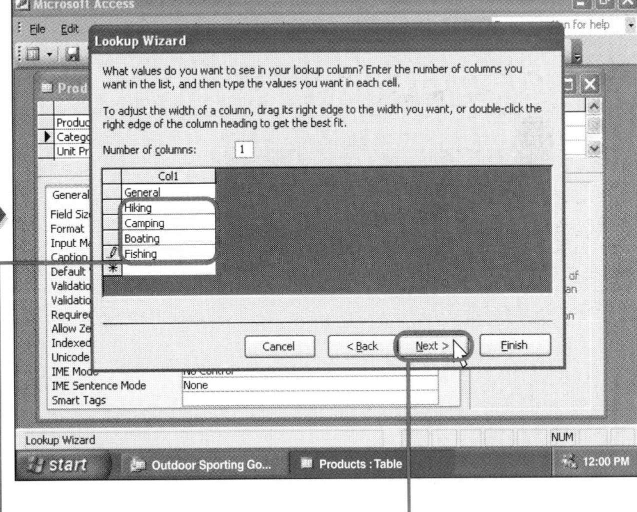

7 To enter the next value, press the Tab key and then type the value.

8 Repeat step 7 for each value you want to appear in the lookup column.

9 When you finish entering all the values for the lookup column, click **Next** to continue.

CONTINUED

CREATE A LOOKUP COLUMN

When entering data in a field, you can select a value from a lookup column to save time.

Selecting a value from a lookup column can also prevent errors such as typing mistakes and ensure that you enter the correct type of data in a field.

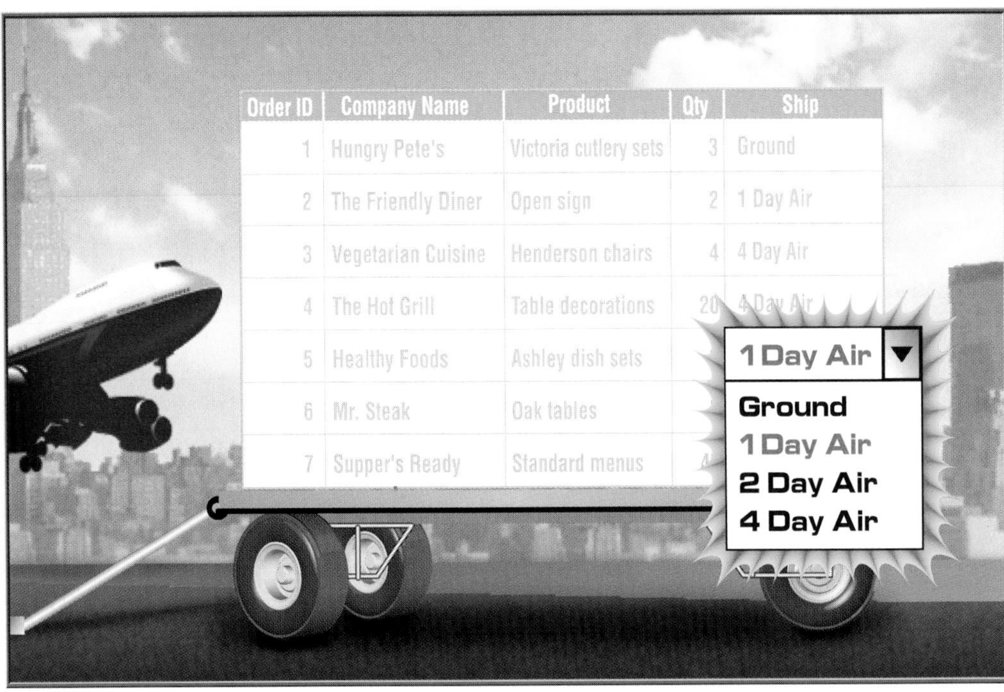

CREATE A LOOKUP COLUMN (CONTINUED)

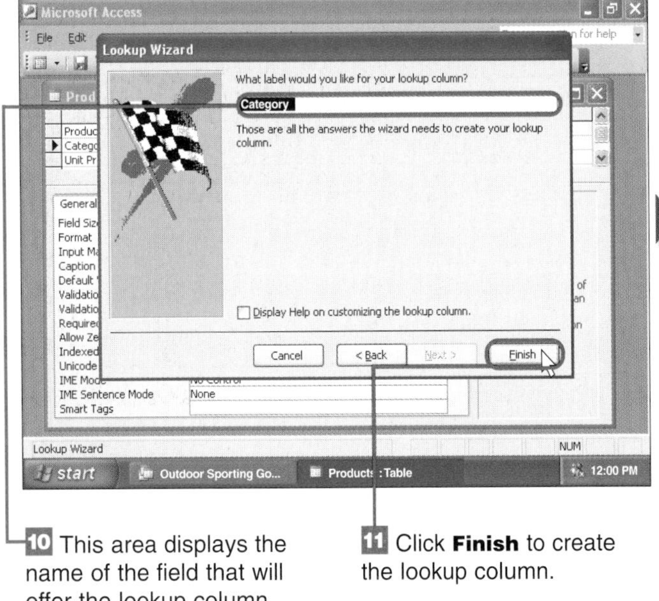

10 This area displays the name of the field that will offer the lookup column. To change the field name, type a new name.

11 Click **Finish** to create the lookup column.

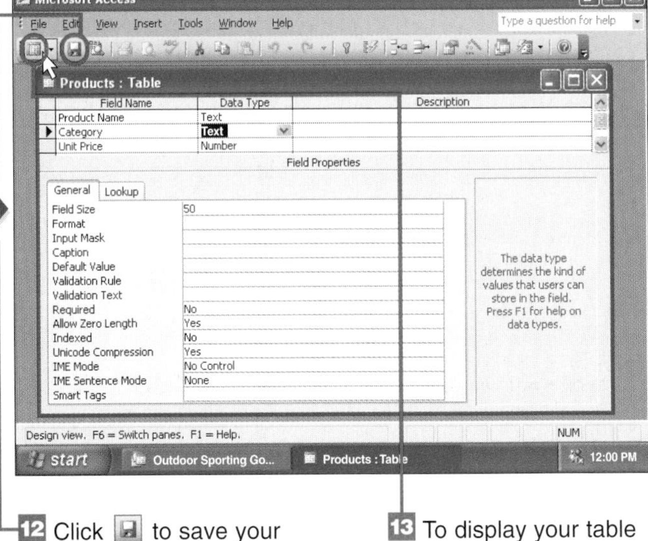

12 Click ![save] to save your changes.

13 To display your table in the Datasheet view, click ![datasheet].

Do I have to select a value from a lookup column?

No. If a lookup column does not display the value you want to use, you can type a different value. To hide a lookup column you displayed without selecting a value, click outside the lookup column. You can then type your own value.

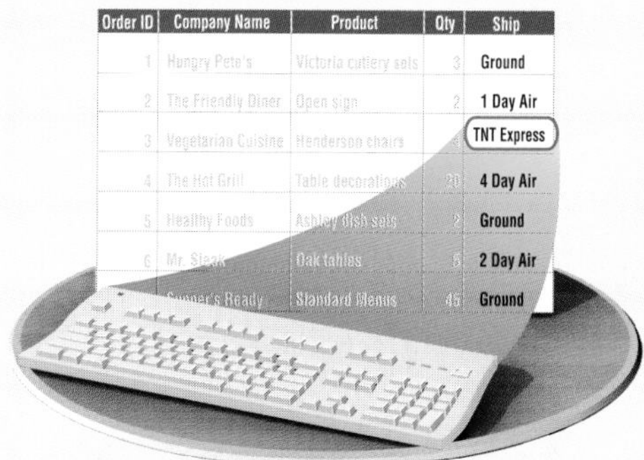

Can I change the values in a lookup column?

If you want to change the values that a lookup column displays, you can recreate the lookup column. To recreate a lookup column, repeat the steps starting on page 106.

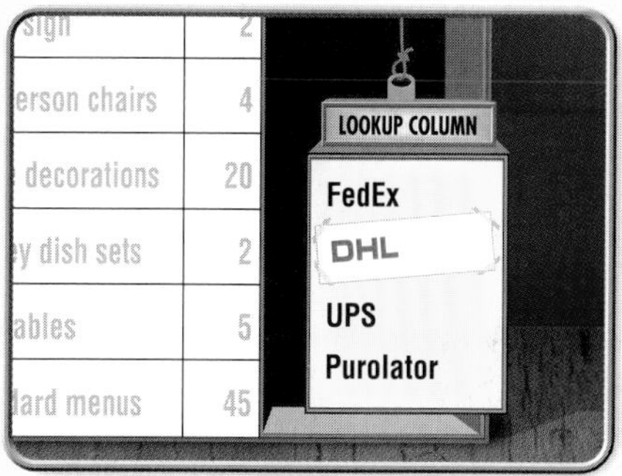

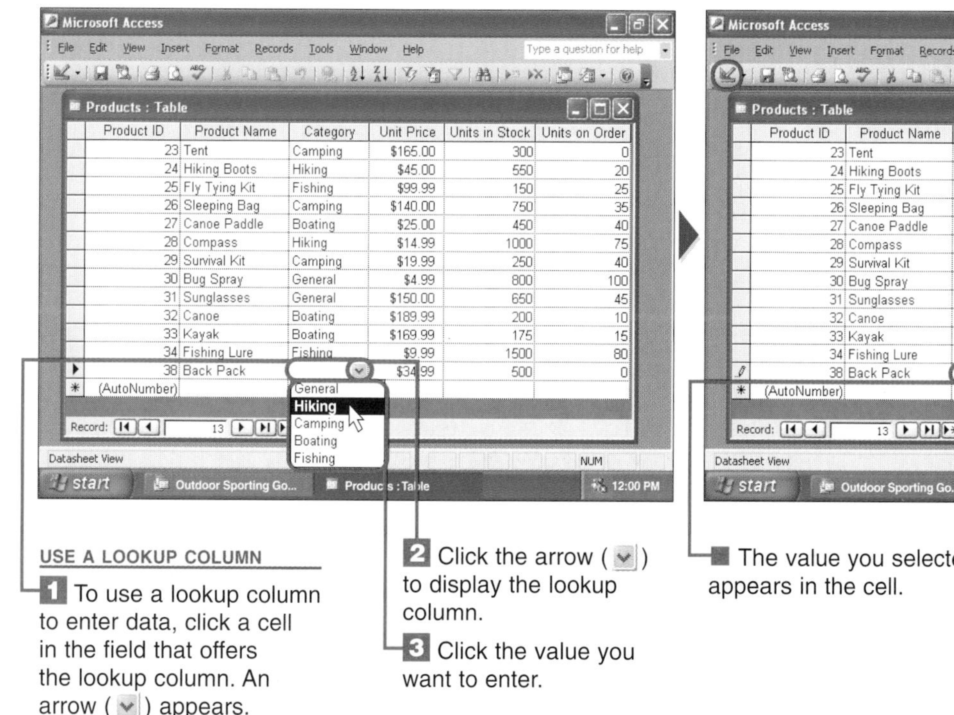

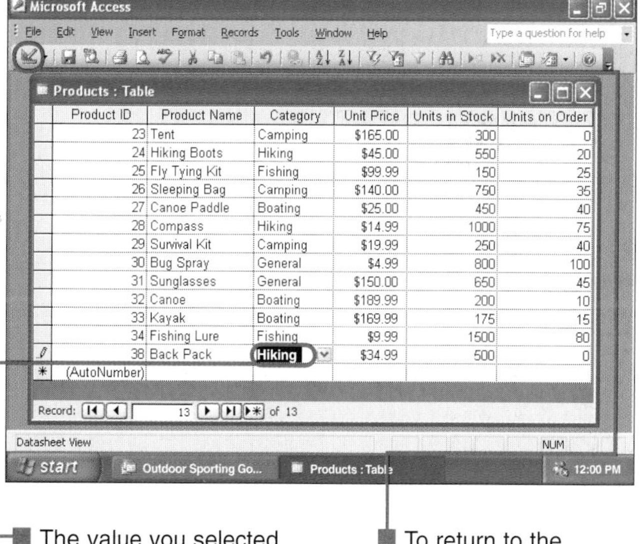

USE A LOOKUP COLUMN

1 To use a lookup column to enter data, click a cell in the field that offers the lookup column. An arrow (▾) appears.

2 Click the arrow (▾) to display the lookup column.

3 Click the value you want to enter.

■ The value you selected appears in the cell.

■ To return to the Design view, click ☐.

CREATE A YES/NO FIELD

You can create a field that accepts only one of two values—Yes/No, True/False or On/Off.

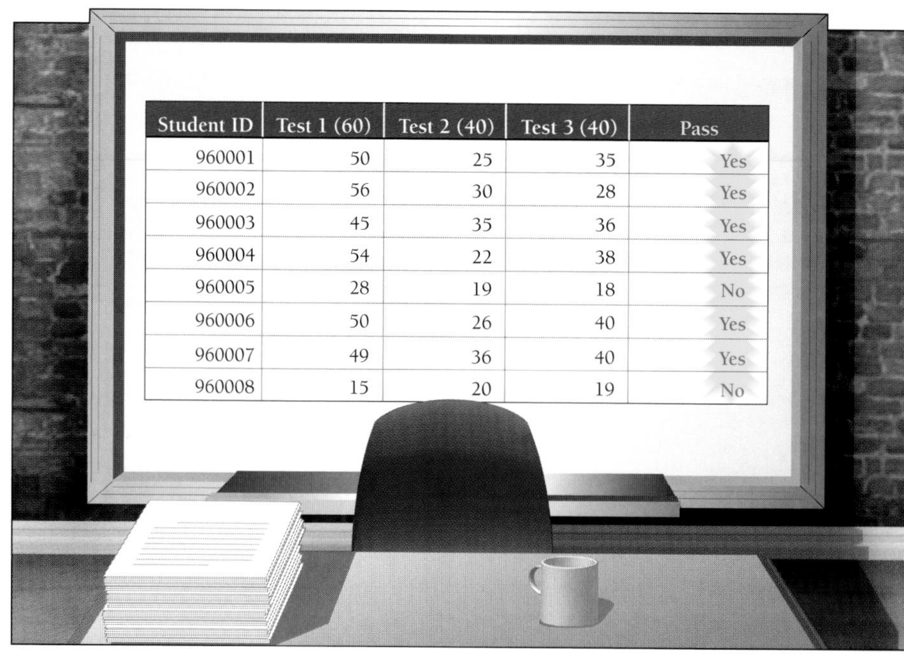

Student ID	Test 1 (60)	Test 2 (40)	Test 3 (40)	Pass
960001	50	25	35	Yes
960002	56	30	28	Yes
960003	45	35	36	Yes
960004	54	22	38	Yes
960005	28	19	18	No
960006	50	26	40	Yes
960007	49	36	40	Yes
960008	15	20	19	No

For example, you can create a Yes/No field to specify whether each student passed a course.

CREATE A YES/NO FIELD

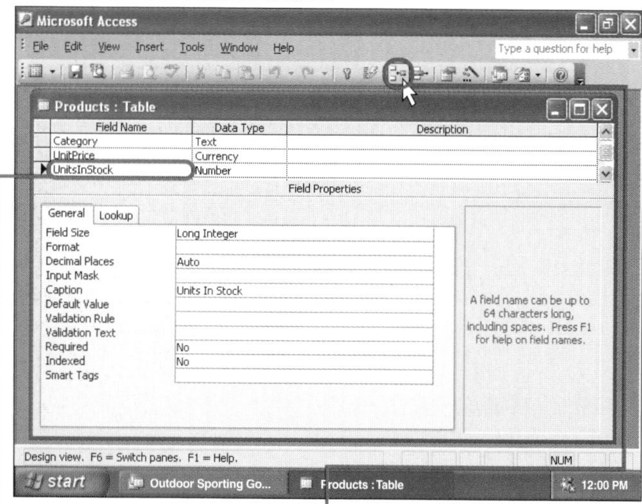

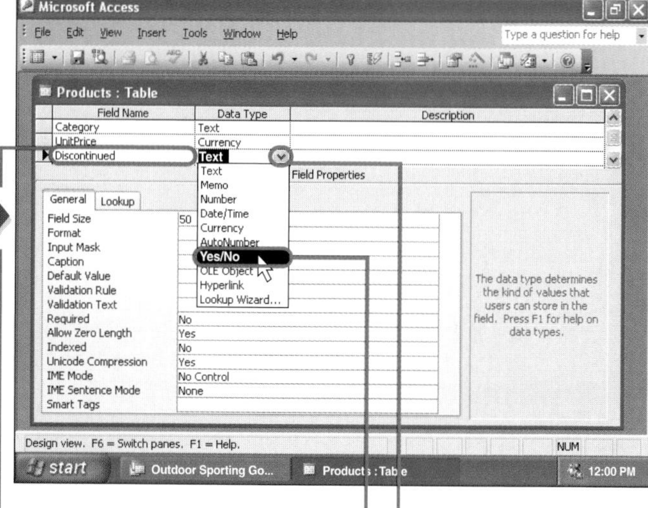

1 Click the field you want to appear after the new Yes/No field. A triangle (▶) appears beside the field name.

■ To add a Yes/No field to the end of your table, click the area directly below the last field name. Then skip to step **3**.

2 Click [icon] to add a field to your table.

■ An area appears where you can enter information for the new field.

3 Type a unique name for the new field and then press the Enter key.

4 To select the data type for the new field, click the arrow ([icon]) in the Data Type area.

5 Click **Yes/No**.

How can I display data in a Yes/No field?

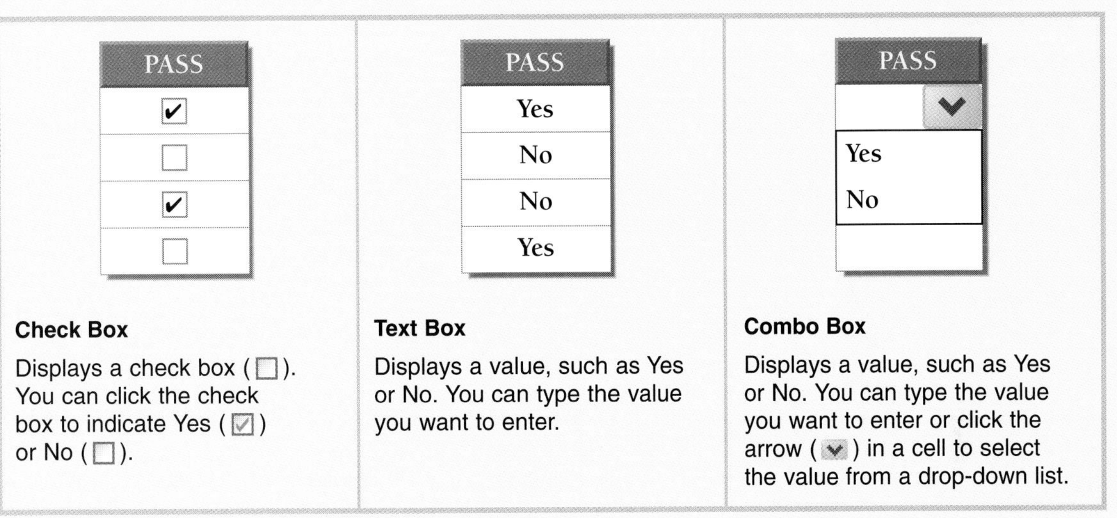

Check Box

Displays a check box (☐). You can click the check box to indicate Yes (☑) or No (☐).

Text Box

Displays a value, such as Yes or No. You can type the value you want to enter.

Combo Box

Displays a value, such as Yes or No. You can type the value you want to enter or click the arrow (⌄) in a cell to select the value from a drop-down list.

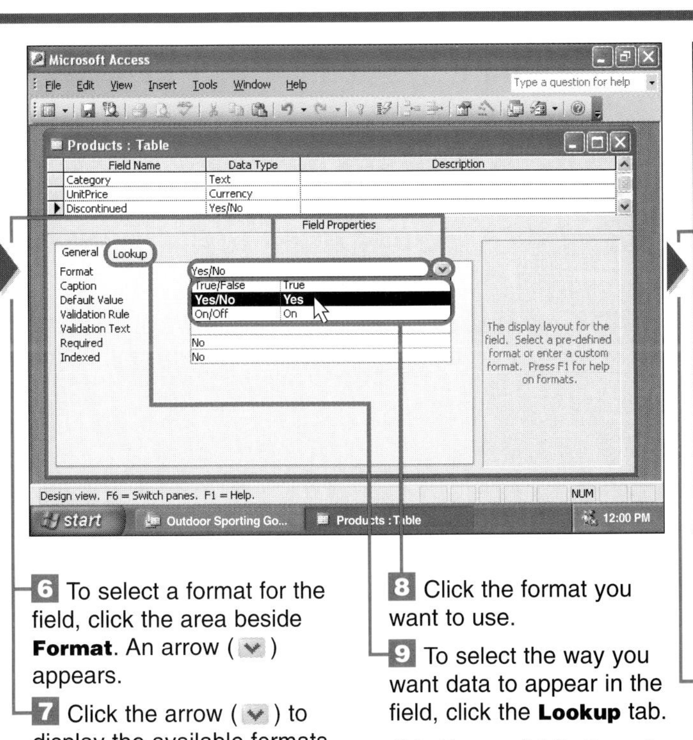

6 To select a format for the field, click the area beside **Format**. An arrow (⌄) appears.

7 Click the arrow (⌄) to display the available formats.

8 Click the format you want to use.

9 To select the way you want data to appear in the field, click the **Lookup** tab.

Note: You can click the ***General*** *tab at any time to return to the General properties.*

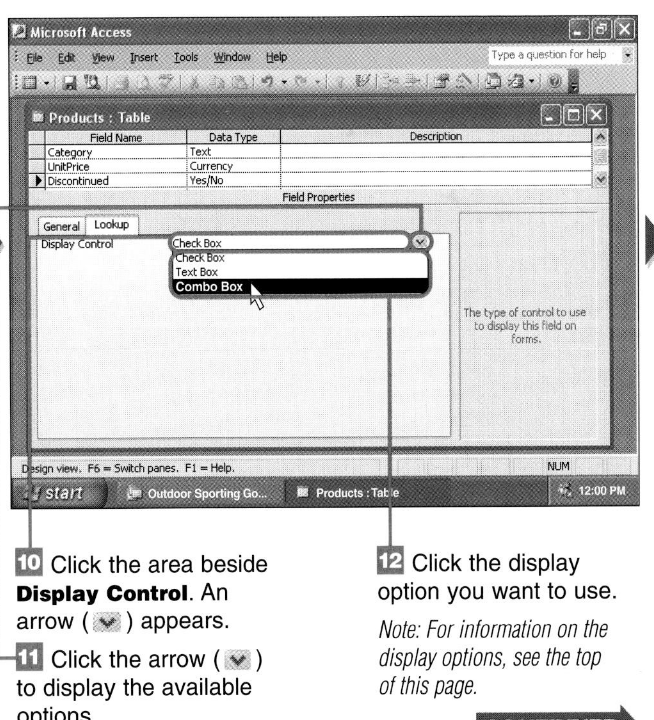

10 Click the area beside **Display Control**. An arrow (⌄) appears.

11 Click the arrow (⌄) to display the available options.

12 Click the display option you want to use.

Note: For information on the display options, see the top of this page.

CONTINUED

CREATE A YES/NO FIELD

If you are creating a Yes/No field that uses a Combo Box, you can specify the values you want to appear in the drop-down list for the field.

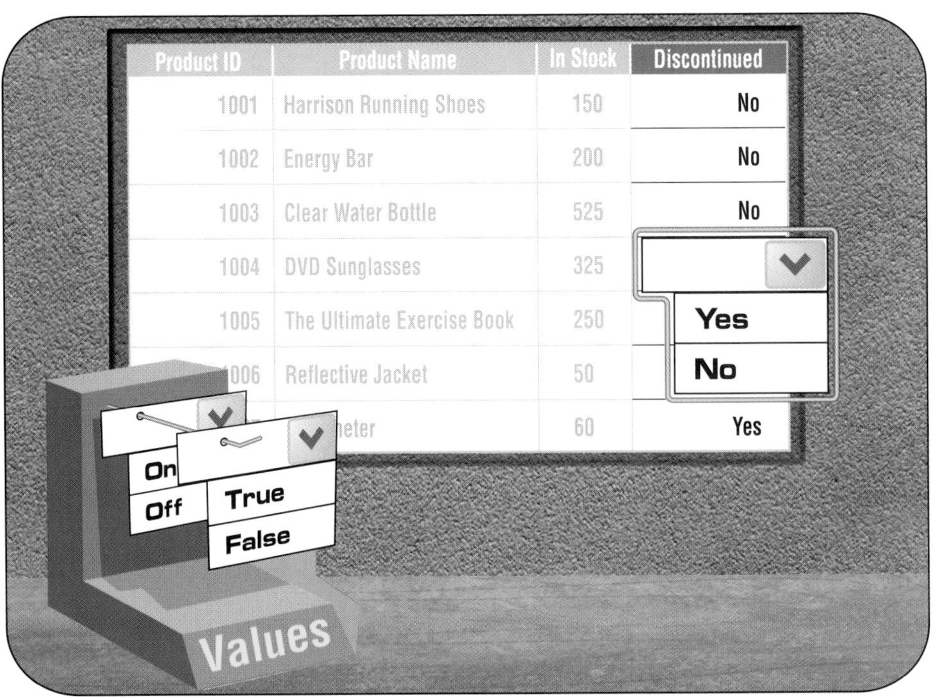

Product ID
Product Name
In Stock
Discontinued
1001 Harrison Running Shoes 150 No
1002 Energy Bar 200 No
1003 Clear Water Bottle 525 No
1004 DVD Sunglasses 325
1005 The Ultimate Exercise Book 250
Reflective Jacket 50
60 Yes
Yes
No
On
Off
True
False
Values

CREATE A YES/NO FIELD (CONTINUED)

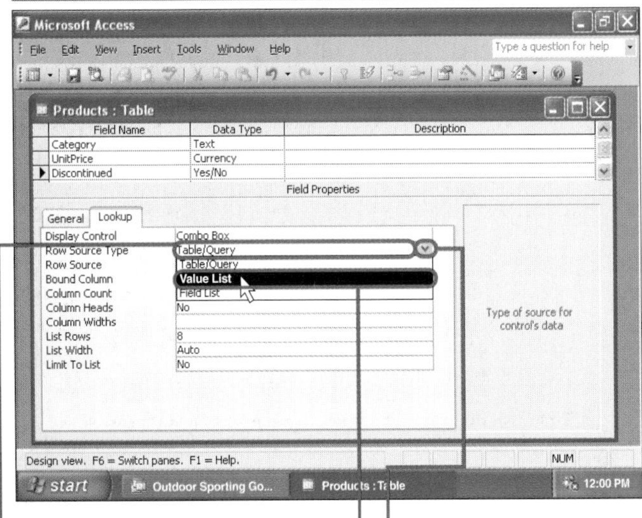

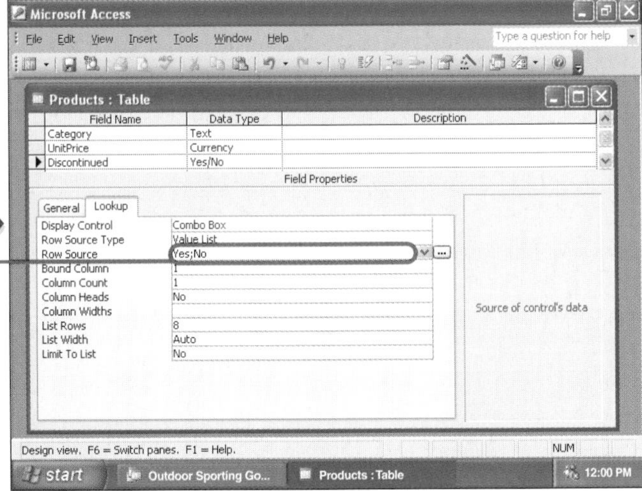

13 If you selected Combo Box in step **12**, click the area beside **Row Source Type**. An arrow ( ) appears.

*Note: If you selected Check Box or Text Box in step **12**, skip to step **18**.*

14 Click the arrow ( ) to display the available options.

15 Click **Value List** to be able to type the values you want to appear in the drop-down list for the field.

16 Click the area beside **Row Source**.

17 Type the two values you want to appear in the drop-down list for the field. Separate the values with a semicolon (;).

*Note: The values you type should match the format you selected in step **8** on page 111.*

How can I speed up entering data in a Yes/No field?

When you add a new record to your table, Access automatically displays the **No**, **False** or **Off** value in a Yes/No field. The value Access displays depends on the format you selected in step **8** on page 111. If most of your records will require a **Yes**, **True** or **On** value, you can change the default value to **Yes**, **True** or **On**. To set the default value for a field, see page 91.

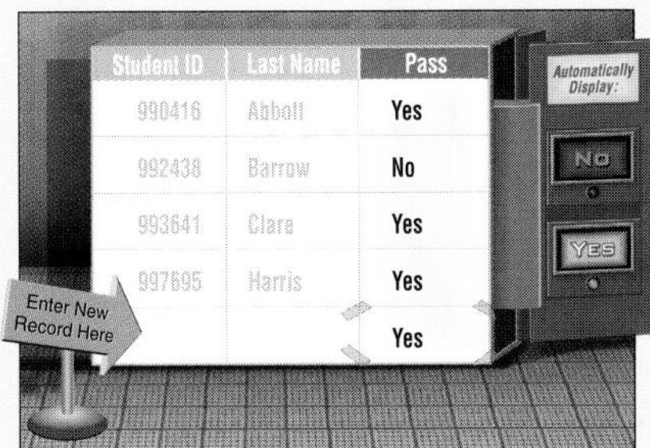

Why does the Property Update Options button ( ) appear when I create a Yes/No field?

You can use the Property Update Options button ( ) to automatically update the format of the Yes/No field in all your forms or reports that display the field. Click the Property Update Options button to display a list of options and then select the option you want to use. The Property Update Options button is available only until you perform another task.

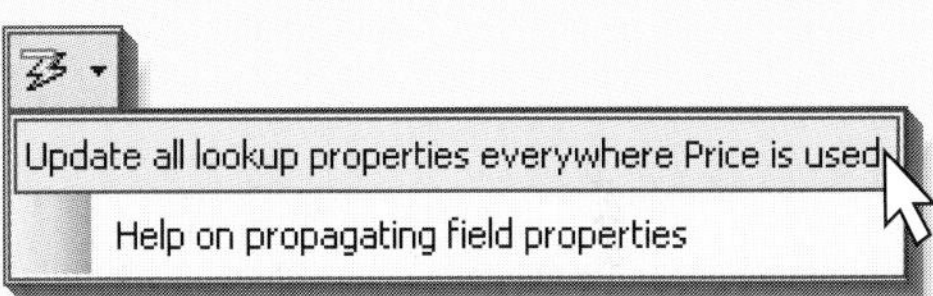

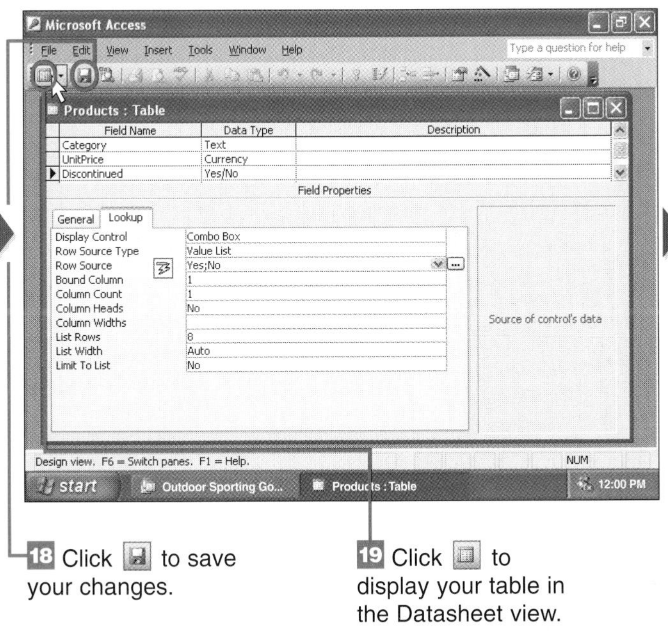

18 Click to save your changes.

19 Click to display your table in the Datasheet view.

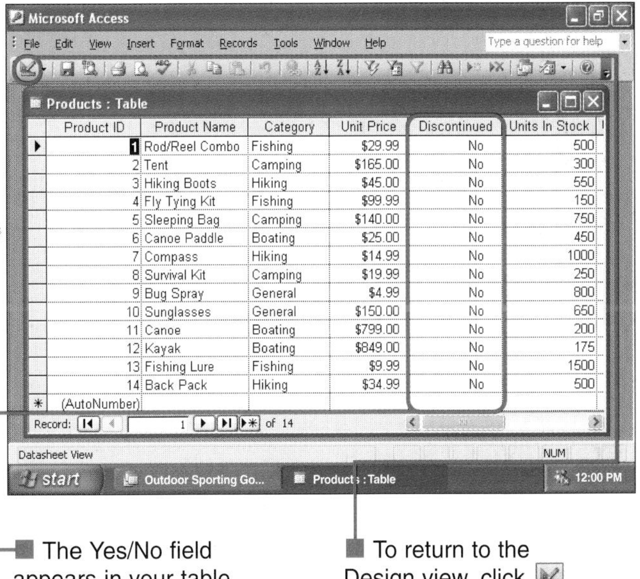

■ The Yes/No field appears in your table.

■ To return to the Design view, click .

CREATE A HYPERLINK FIELD

You can create a field that allows you to add a hyperlink to each record in a table. A hyperlink, also called a link, allows you to quickly display a Web page or file or send an e-mail message.

For example, you can create a Hyperlink field to store the Web page addresses or e-mail addresses of your suppliers. You can then select a hyperlink to quickly display a supplier's Web page or send the supplier an e-mail message.

CREATE A HYPERLINK FIELD

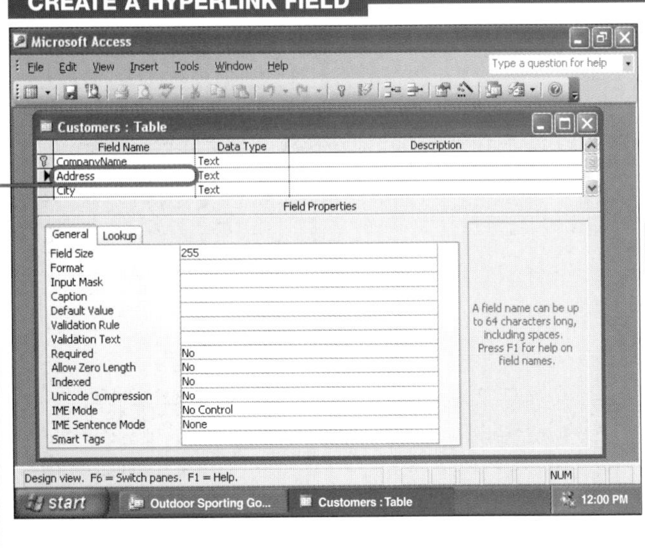

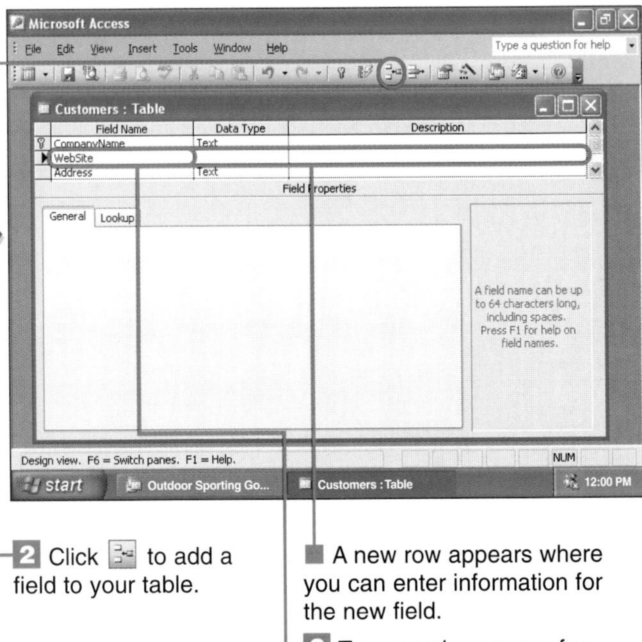

1 To create a field that will store hyperlinks, click the name of the field you want to appear after the new field. A triangle (▶) appears beside the field name.

■ To add a Hyperlink field to the end of your table, click the area directly below the last field name. Then skip to step **3**.

2 Click (Insert Rows) to add a field to your table.

■ A new row appears where you can enter information for the new field.

3 Type a unique name for the field and then press the **Enter** key.

What types of files can I create hyperlinks to?

You can create hyperlinks to files such as documents, pictures, spreadsheets and sounds. When you select a hyperlink to a file, the appropriate program will open and display or play the file. To select a hyperlink to a file, see page 117.

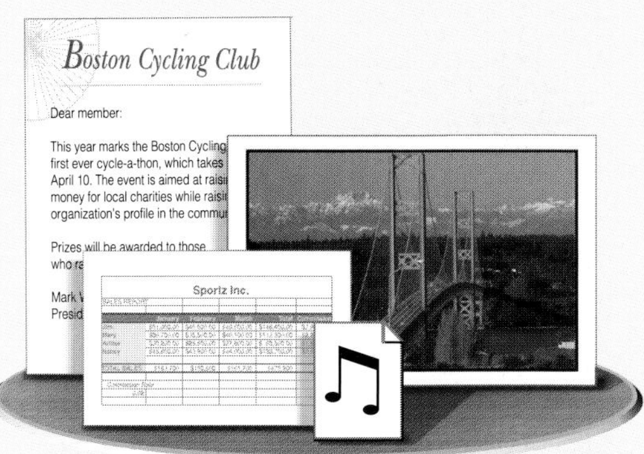

Will the Hyperlink field I add to my table appear on a form?

When you create a form using a table that contains a Hyperlink field, the form will display the Hyperlink field. You can select a hyperlink on a form as you would select a hyperlink in a table. To select a hyperlink in a table, see page 117.

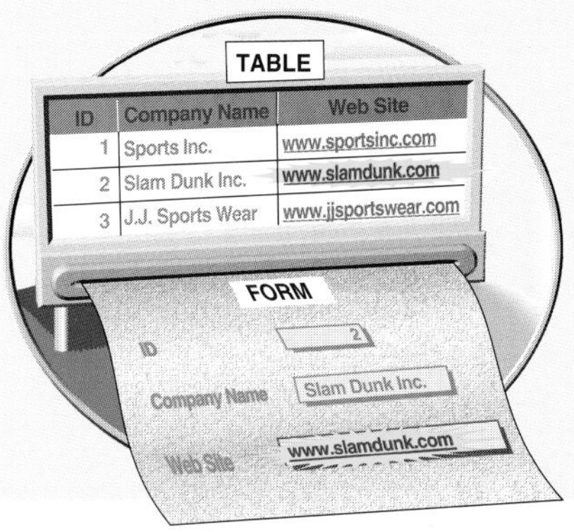

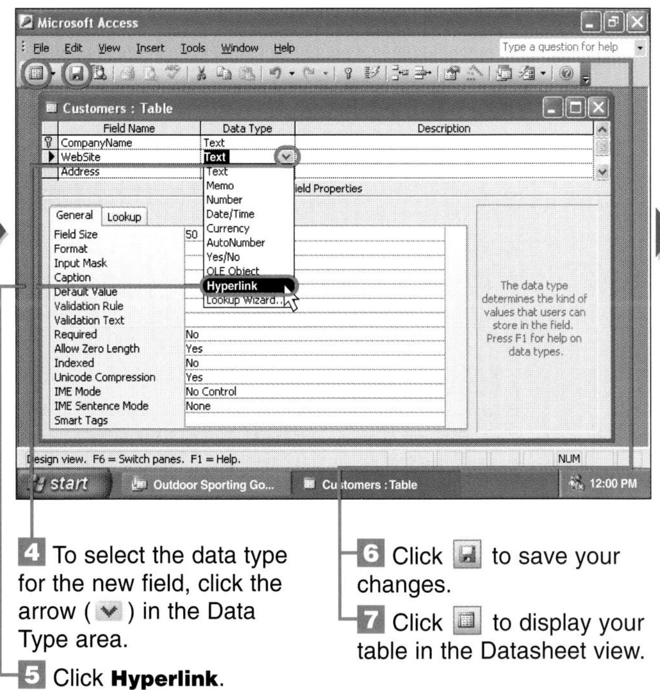

4 To select the data type for the new field, click the arrow ( ) in the Data Type area.

5 Click **Hyperlink**.

6 Click to save your changes.

7 Click to display your table in the Datasheet view.

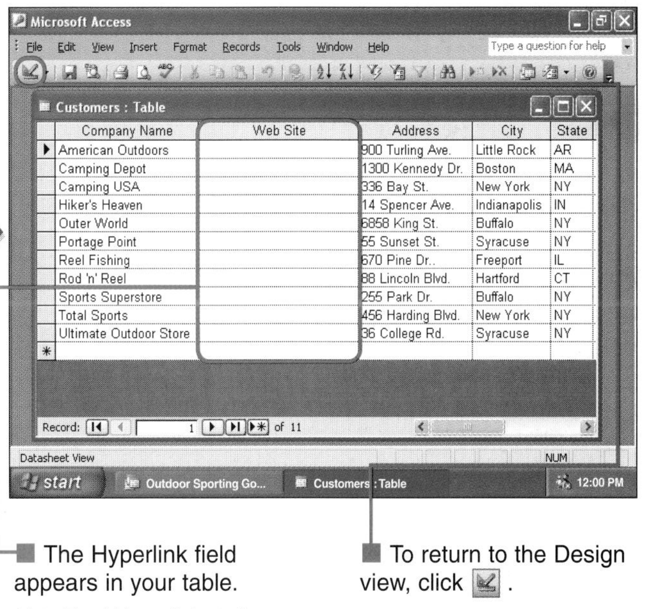

■ The Hyperlink field appears in your table.

Note: To add hyperlinks to the field, see pages 116 to 119.

■ To return to the Design view, click .

CONTINUED

CREATE A HYPERLINK FIELD

After you create a field that will store hyperlinks, you can add hyperlinks to the field that will allow you to quickly display Web pages or files stored on your computer, network, corporate intranet or the Internet.

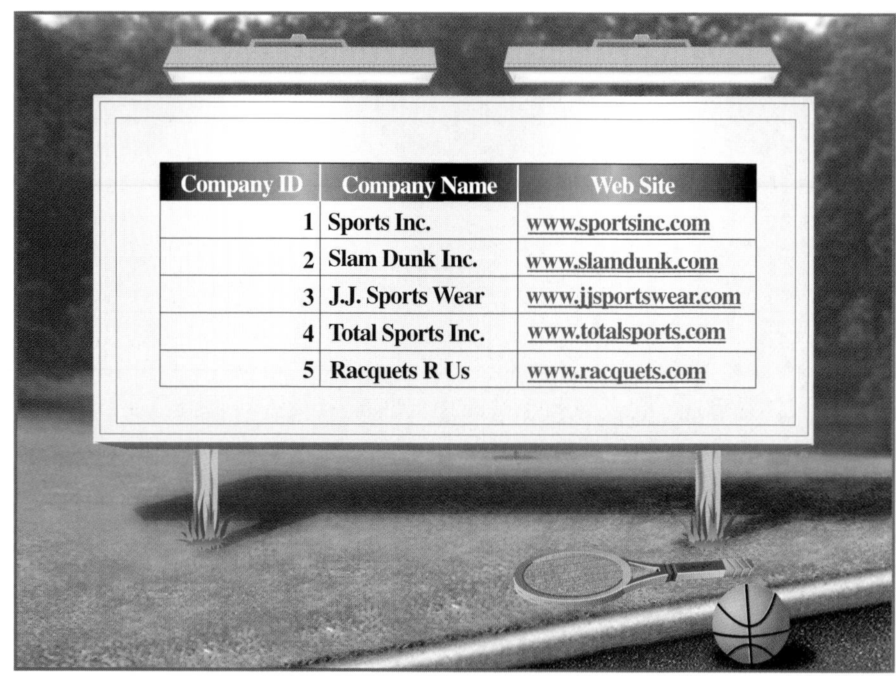

An intranet is a small version of the Internet within a company.

CREATE A HYPERLINK TO A WEB PAGE OR FILE

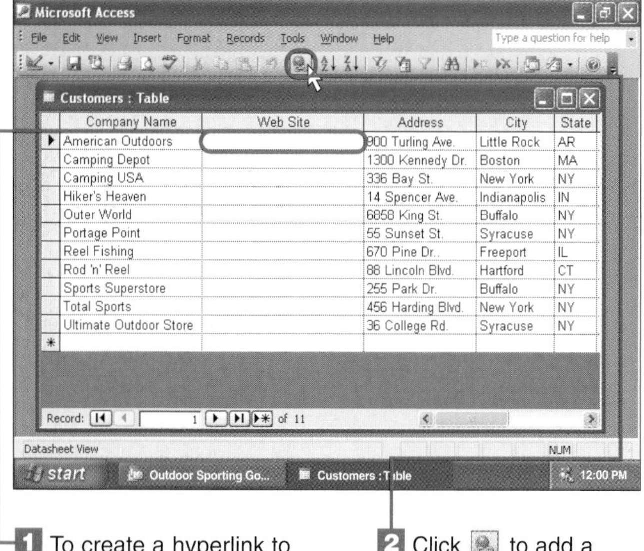

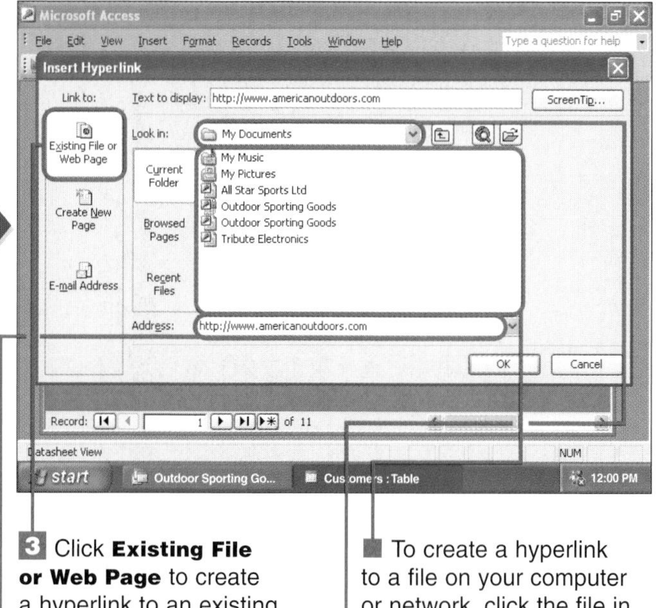

1 To create a hyperlink to a Web page or file, click the cell for the record you want to add the hyperlink to.

Note: To create a field that will store hyperlinks, see page 114.

2 Click (icon) to add a hyperlink.

■ The Insert Hyperlink dialog box appears.

3 Click **Existing File or Web Page** to create a hyperlink to an existing file or Web page.

4 To create a hyperlink to a Web page, click this area and type the address of the Web page.

■ To create a hyperlink to a file on your computer or network, click the file in this area.

■ This area shows the location of the displayed files. You can click this area to change the location.

Is there a faster way to create a hyperlink to a Web page or file?

Yes. When you type the address of a Web page or the location and name of a file into a field that stores hyperlinks, Access will automatically change the address or location and name to a hyperlink for you.

How do I remove a hyperlink to a Web page or file?

To select the hyperlink you want to remove, position the mouse I over the left edge of the cell that contains the hyperlink (I changes to ✚) and then click to select the contents of the cell. To delete the hyperlink, press the Delete key.

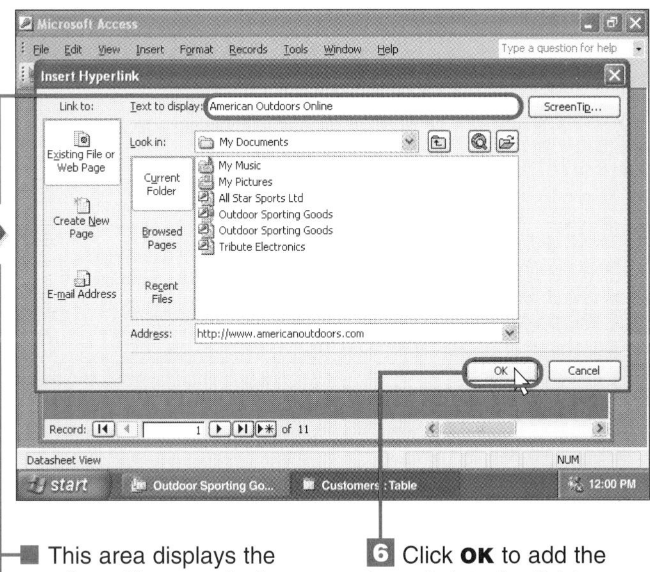

■ This area displays the text that will appear in the Hyperlink field.

5 To change the text, drag the mouse I over the text until you highlight all the text. Then type the text you want to appear in the field.

6 Click **OK** to add the hyperlink to the field.

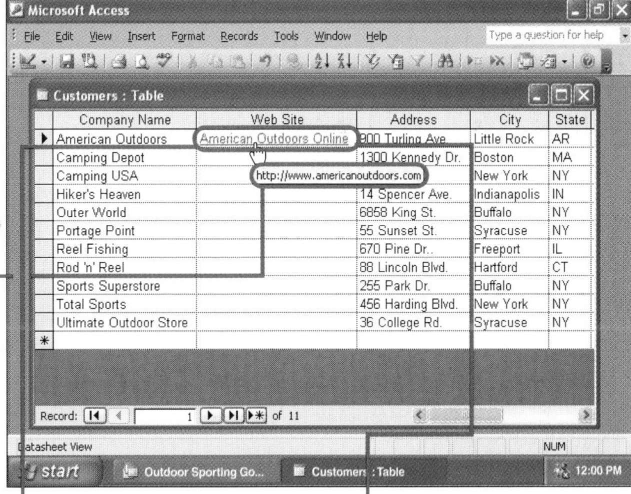

■ Access adds the hyperlink to the field. A hyperlink appears underlined and in color.

■ When you position the mouse over a hyperlink, a yellow box appears, displaying the Web page address or the location and name of the file that the hyperlink will display.

SELECT A HYPERLINK

1 To select a hyperlink to display the Web page or file connected to the hyperlink, click the hyperlink.

CONTINUED

CREATE A HYPERLINK FIELD

After you create a field that will store hyperlinks, you can add hyperlinks to the field that will allow you to quickly send e-mail messages.

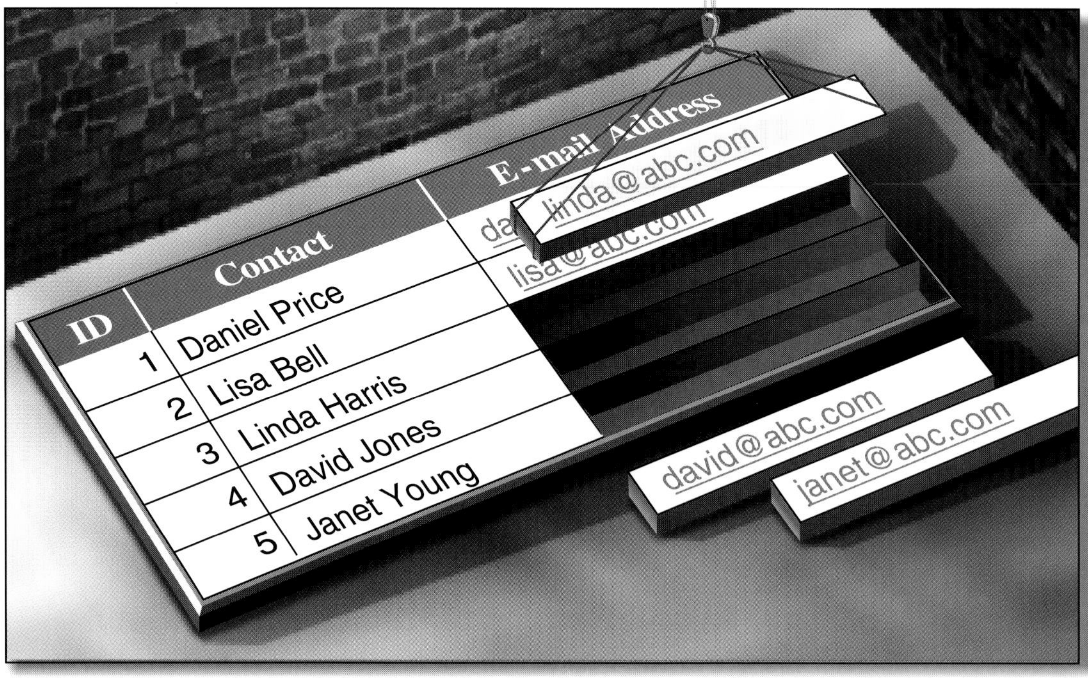

CREATE A HYPERLINK TO AN E-MAIL ADDRESS

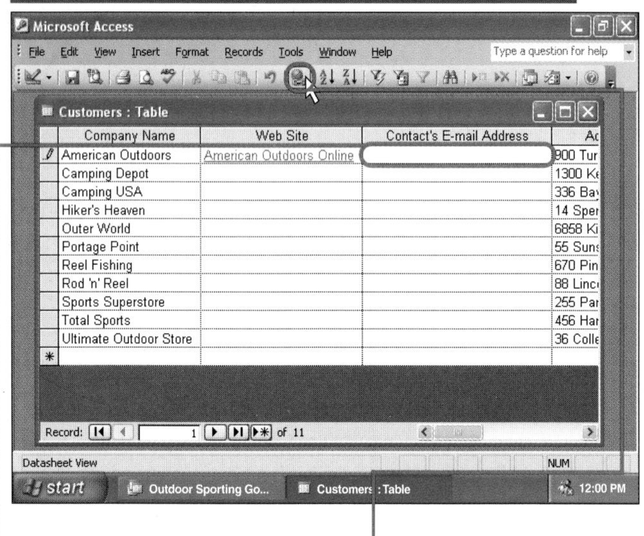

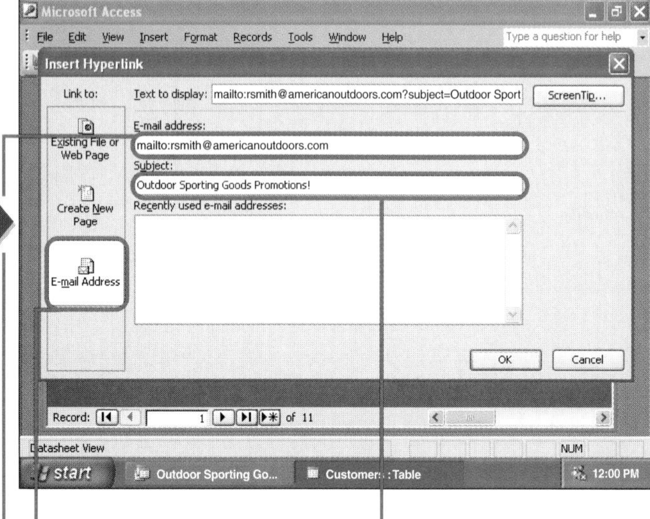

1 To create a hyperlink to an e-mail address, click the cell for the record you want to add the hyperlink to.

Note: To create a field that will store hyperlinks, see page 114.

2 Click [icon] to create a hyperlink.

■ The Insert Hyperlink dialog box appears.

3 Click **E-mail Address** to create a hyperlink to an e-mail address.

4 Click this area and type the e-mail address of the person you want to receive the e-mail messages.

Note: Access automatically adds ***mailto:*** *to the beginning of the e-mail address you type.*

5 If you want specific information to appear in the Subject area of the e-mail messages, click this area and type the subject.

Is there a faster way to create a hyperlink that will allow me to send e-mail messages?

Yes. In a field that stores hyperlinks, you can type **mailto:** followed by the e-mail address of the person you want to send messages to. For example, you can type **mailto:shawn@abccorp.com**. Access will automatically change the text you type to a hyperlink.

How do I remove a hyperlink to an e-mail address?

To select the hyperlink you want to remove, position the mouse I over the left edge of the cell that contains the hyperlink (I changes to ✚) and then click to select the contents of the cell. To delete the hyperlink, press the Delete key.

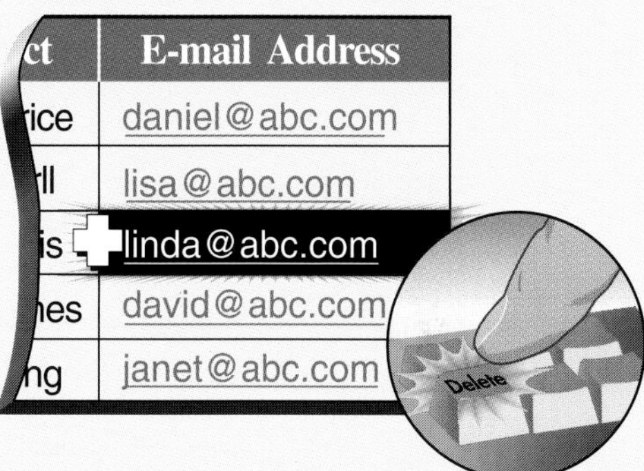

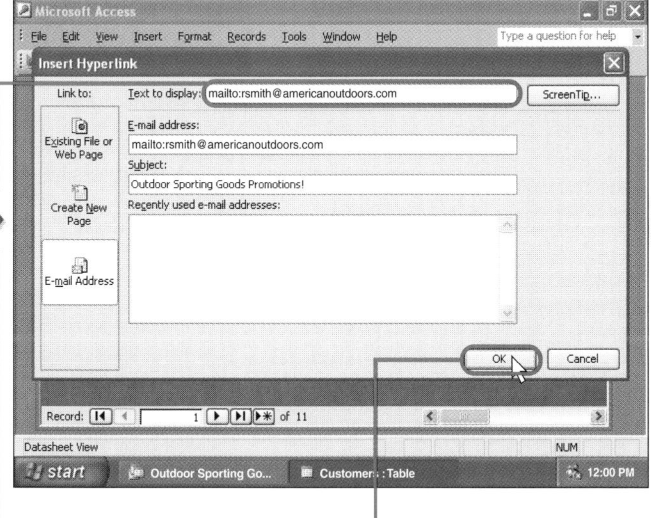

■ This area displays the text that will appear in the Hyperlink field.

6 To change the text, drag the mouse I over the text until you highlight all the text. Then type the text you want to appear in the field.

7 Click **OK** to add the hyperlink to the field.

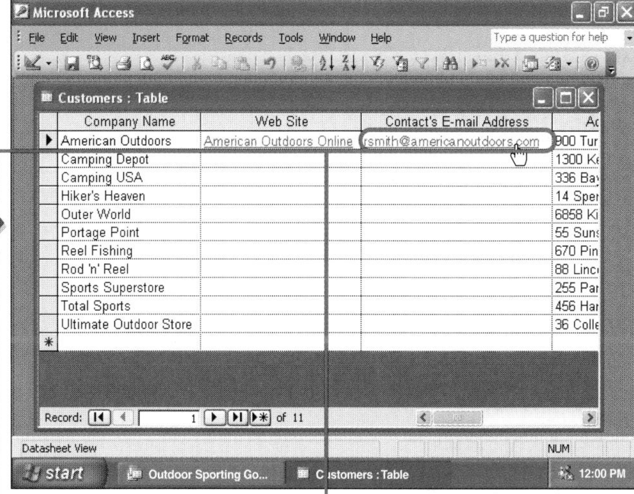

■ Access adds the hyperlink to the field. A hyperlink appears underlined and in color.

SELECT A HYPERLINK

1 To select a hyperlink to send an e-mail message to a person, click the hyperlink.

■ Your e-mail program will open, displaying a new message addressed to the person you specified.

USING SMART TAGS

You can use smart tags to quickly perform tasks while working in Access. A smart tag is information, such as a date, which Access recognizes and labels.

For example, you can have Access label dates in a field to allow you to quickly display your Microsoft Outlook calendar for a date of interest.

USING SMART TAGS

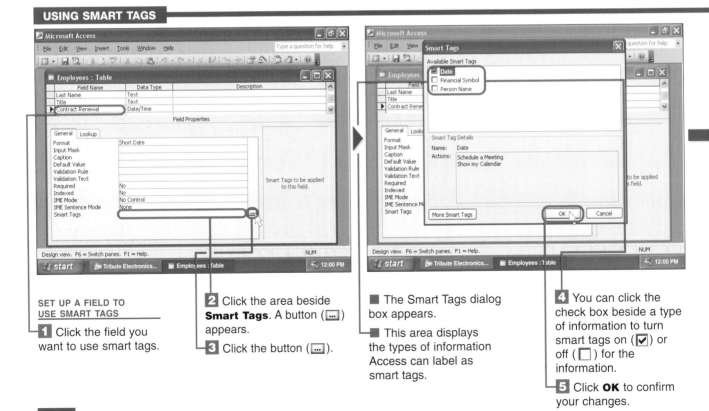

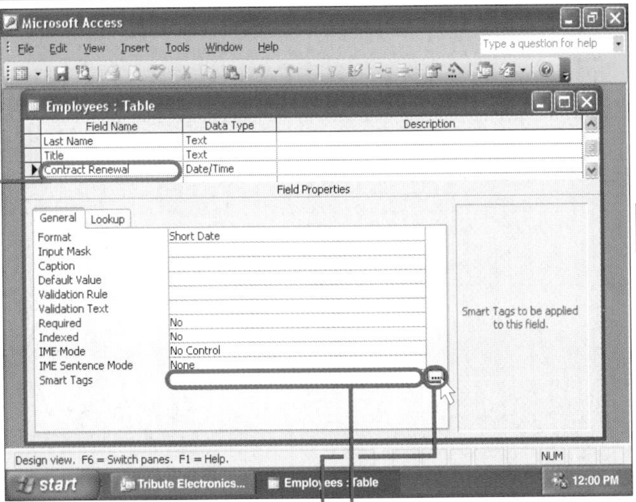

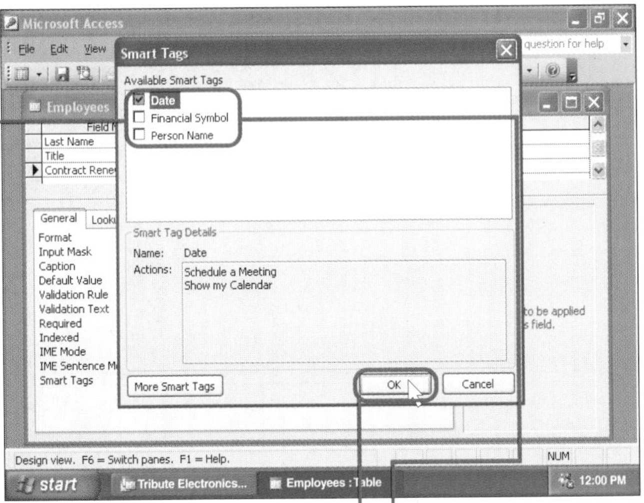

SET UP A FIELD TO USE SMART TAGS

1 Click the field you want to use smart tags.

2 Click the area beside **Smart Tags**. A button (...) appears.

3 Click the button (...).

■ The Smart Tags dialog box appears.

■ This area displays the types of information Access can label as smart tags.

4 You can click the check box beside a type of information to turn smart tags on (☑) or off (☐) for the information.

5 Click **OK** to confirm your changes.

What actions can I perform for data labeled with a smart tag?

Date

When a date in your table is labeled with a smart tag, you can display your Microsoft Outlook calendar or schedule a meeting for the date.

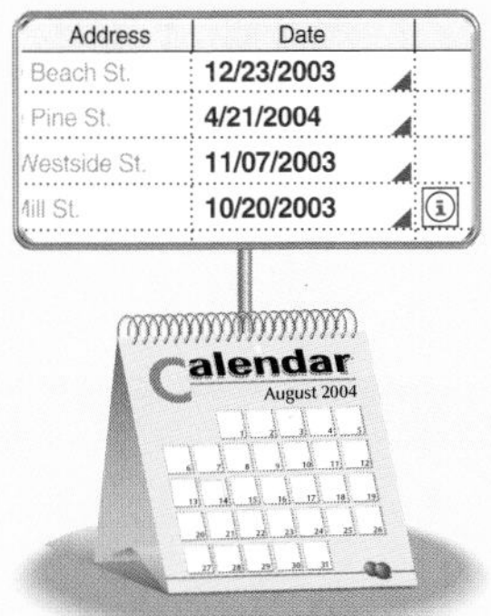

Financial Symbol

When a company's financial symbol in your table is labeled with a smart tag, you can get a stock price or display information about the company, such as a company report or a recent news item.

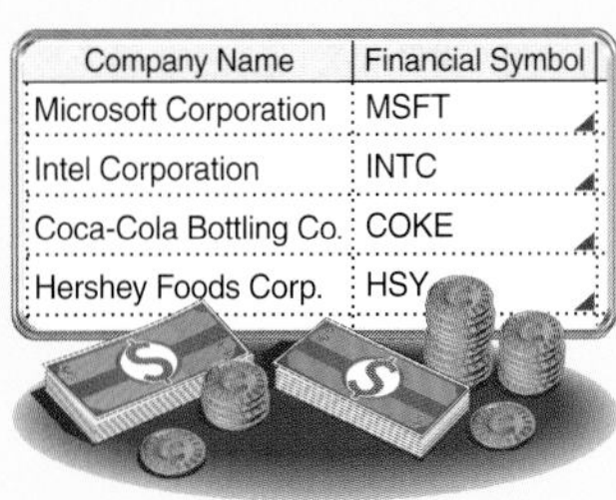

Person's Name

When a person's name or e-mail address is labeled with a smart tag in your table, you can send the person an e-mail message, schedule a meeting with the person, view the person's contact information or add the person to your list of contacts in Microsoft Outlook.

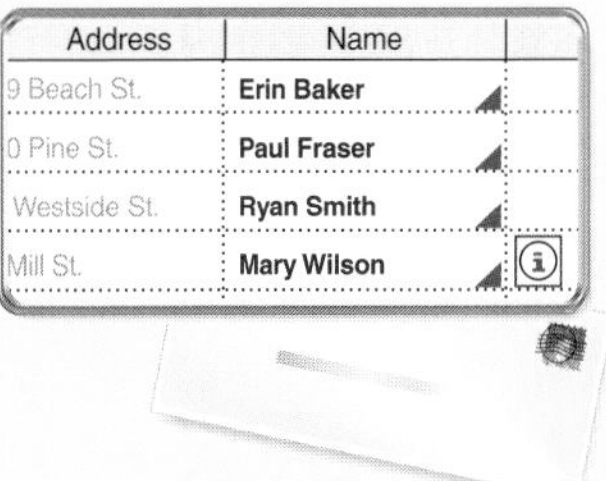

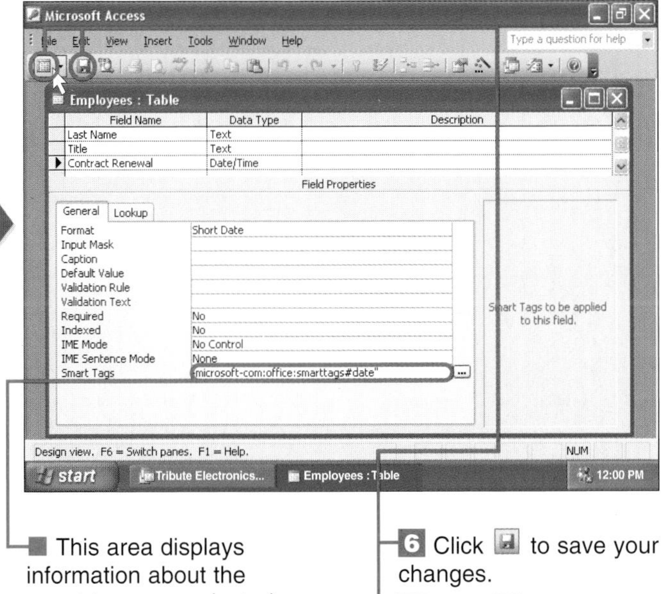

■ This area displays information about the smart tags you selected.

6 Click [save icon] to save your changes.

7 Click [datasheet icon] to display your table in the Datasheet view.

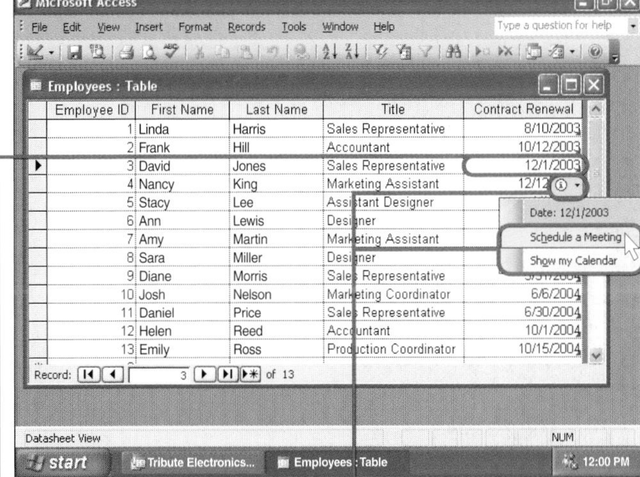

USE A SMART TAG

■ A purple triangle appears in the bottom right corner of a cell containing data that Access labels with a smart tag.

1 To perform an action using a smart tag, click a cell containing a purple triangle.

■ The Smart Tag Actions button ([smart tag icon]) appears.

2 Click the button to display a list of actions you can perform using the smart tag.

3 Click the action you want to perform.

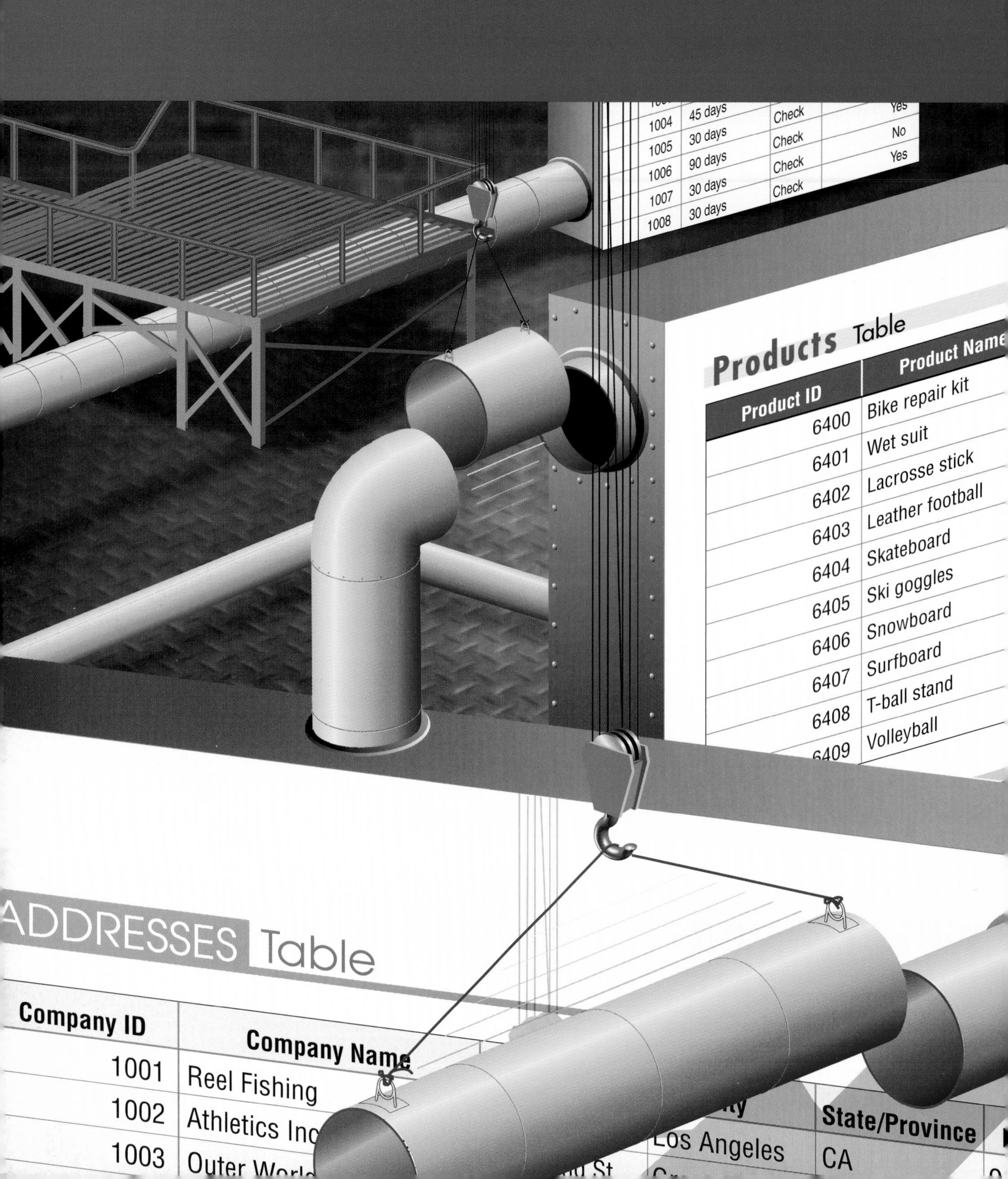
1004 45 days Check Yes
1005 30 days Check No
1006 90 days Check Yes
1007 30 days Check
1008 30 days
Products Table
Product ID
Product Name
6400 Bike repair kit
6401 Wet suit
6402 Lacrosse stick
6403 Leather football
6404 Skateboard
6405 Ski goggles
6406 Snowboard
6407 Surfboard
6408 T-ball stand
6409 Volleyball
ADDRESSES Table
Company ID
Company Name
State/Province
1001 Reel Fishing
1002 Athletics Inc
1003
Los Angeles
CA

CHAPTER 5

Establish Relationships

Do you want to establish relationships between the tables in your database? This chapter teaches you how.

VIEW OBJECT DEPENDENCIES

You can view a list of objects, such as tables, forms, queries and reports, that depend on a specific object in your database. This allows you to quickly see which items require data from an object of interest.

For example, if you are considering deleting a table from your database, you may want to first view a list of the objects that depend on the table. If other objects depend on the table, you should not delete the table.

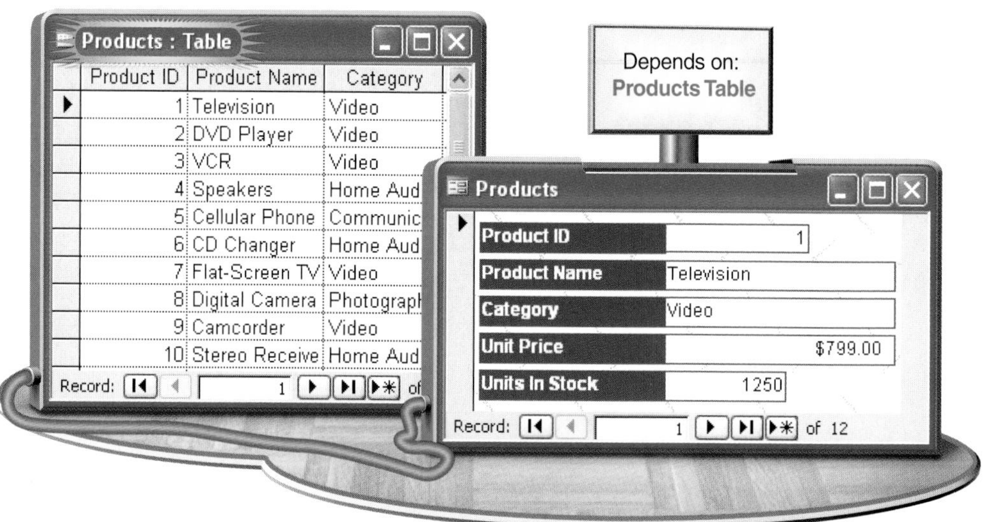

VIEW OBJECT DEPENDENCIES

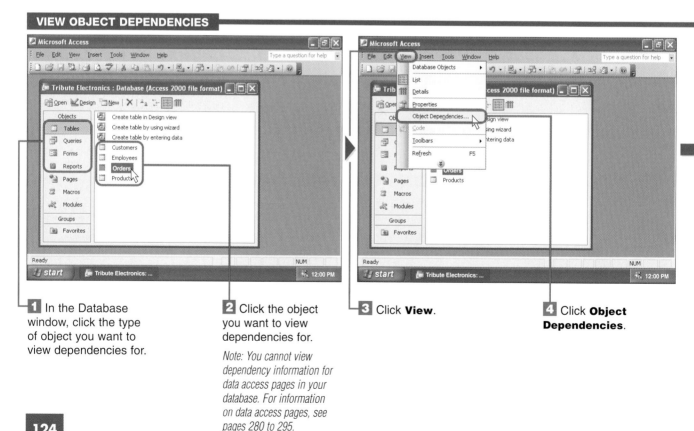

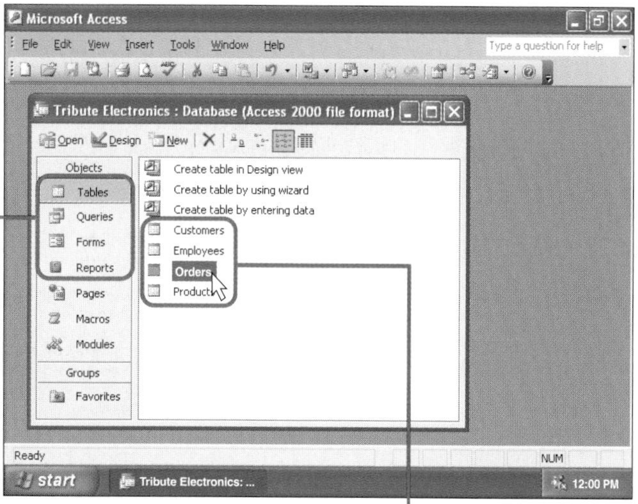

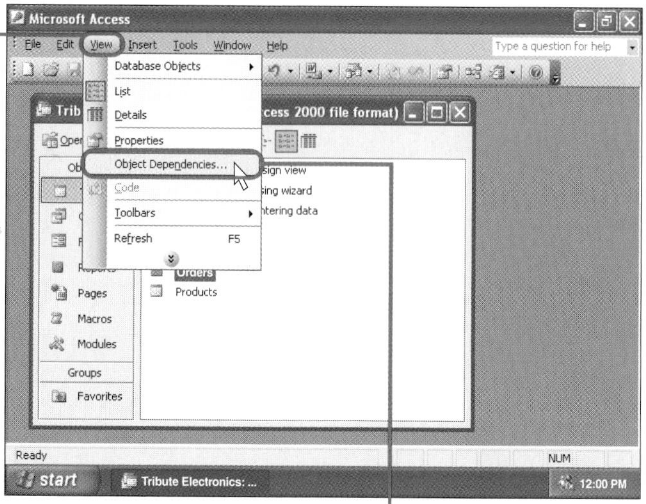

1 In the Database window, click the type of object you want to view dependencies for.

2 Click the object you want to view dependencies for.

Note: You cannot view dependency information for data access pages in your database. For information on data access pages, see pages 280 to 295.

3 Click **View**.

4 Click **Object Dependencies**.

Why does this dialog box appear when I view object dependencies in my database?

The first time you view dependency information for a database, Access must first gather and update the dependency information. Click **OK** in the dialog box to continue.

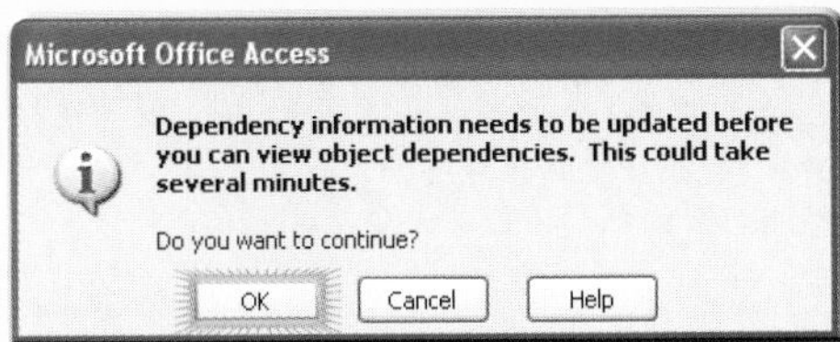

Can I view a list of tables, forms, queries and reports that contain data required by an object of interest?

Yes. For example, you can quickly view a list of tables that contain data required by a form of interest. Perform steps **1** to **6** below, except select **Objects that I depend on** in step **5**.

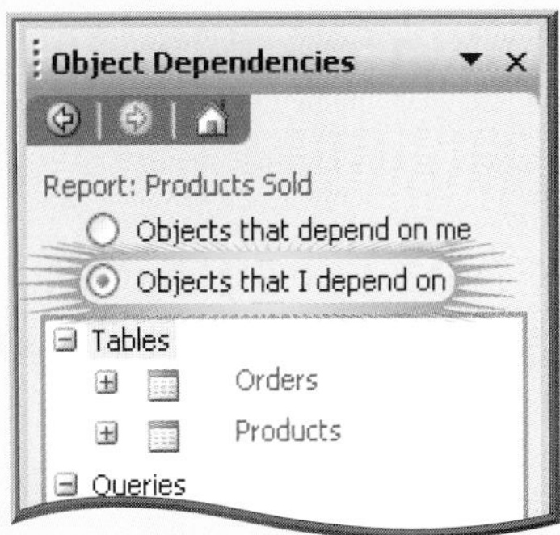

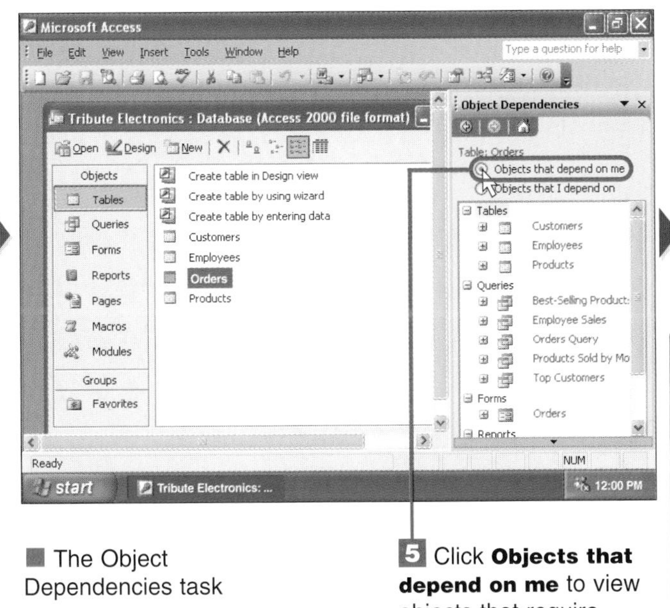

■ The Object Dependencies task pane appears.

5 Click **Objects that depend on me** to view objects that require data stored in the object you selected (◯ changes to ◉).

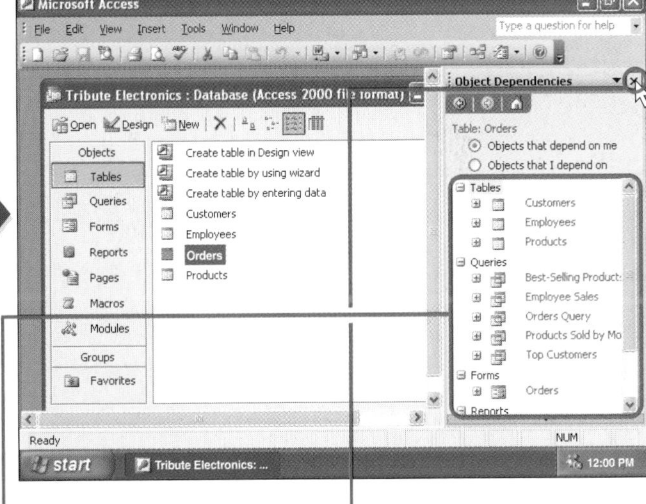

■ This area displays the objects of interest.

■ To quickly open an object displayed in the task pane, click the name of the object.

■ To view dependency information for another object in the database, repeat steps **1** to **4**.

6 When you finish viewing dependency information, click ✕ to close the Object Dependencies task pane.

SET THE PRIMARY KEY

You can set the primary key for a table. A primary key is one or more fields that uniquely identifies each record in a table. Each table in your database should have a primary key.

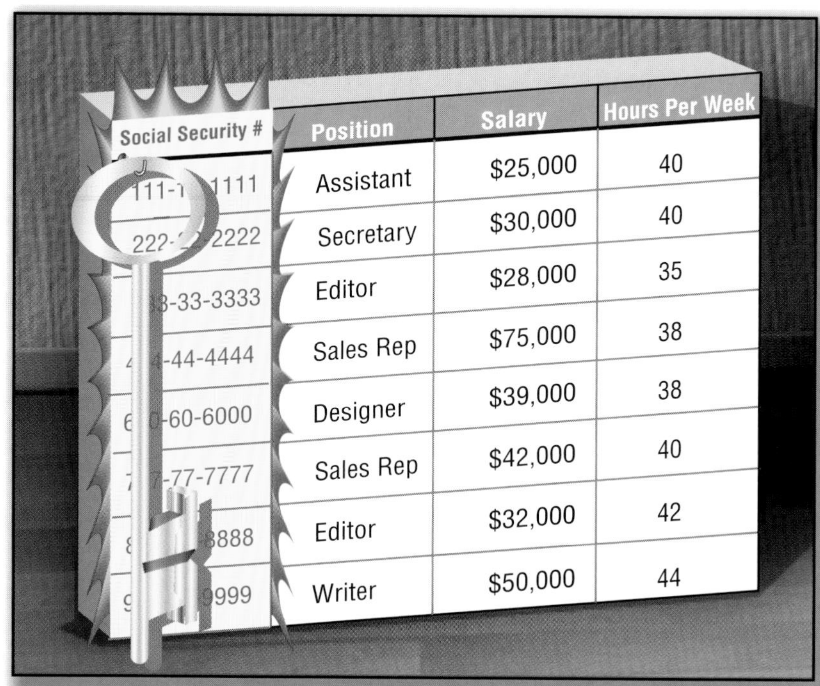

Access uses the primary key in each table to create relationships between the tables in your database. Relationships between tables allow Access to bring together related information in the tables. For information on relationships, see page 128.

SET THE PRIMARY KEY

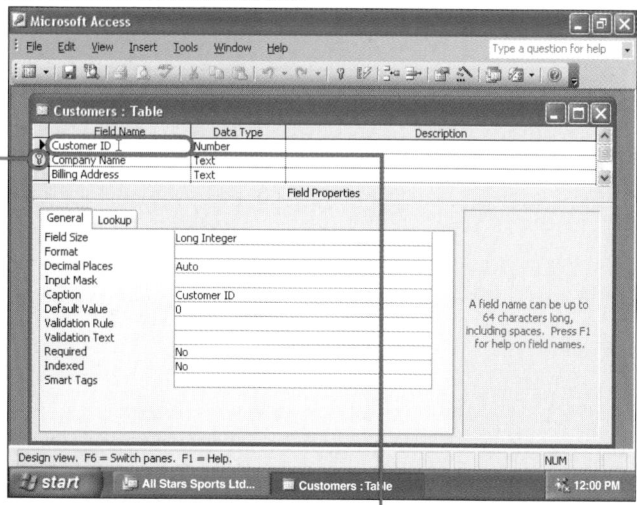

1 Display the table you want to change in the Design view. To change the view of a table, see page 74.

■ The field that is currently set as the primary key displays a key symbol (🔑).

Note: You may have had Access set a primary key for you when you created the table.

2 Click the name of the field you want to set as the primary key.

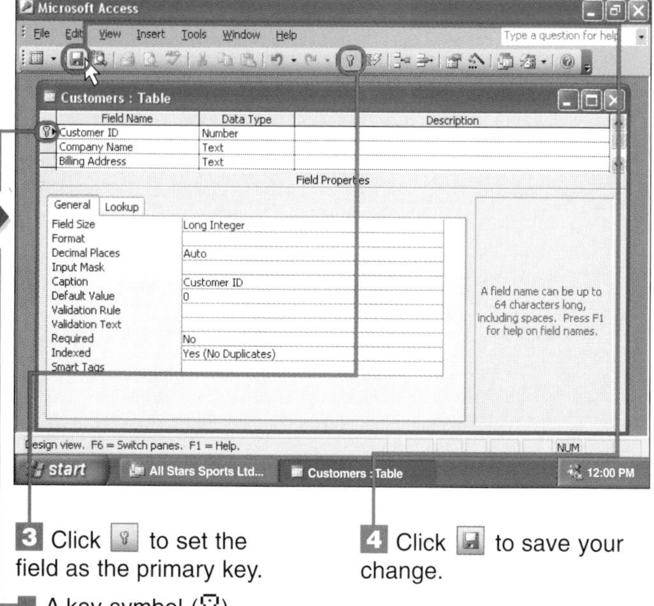

3 Click 🔑 to set the field as the primary key.

■ A key symbol (🔑) appears beside the field.

4 Click 💾 to save your change.

What types of primary keys can I create?

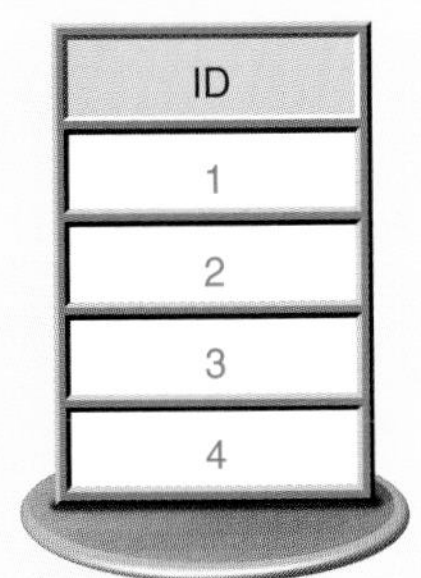

AutoNumber

A field that automatically assigns a unique number to each record you add. When you create a table, Access can create an AutoNumber primary key for you.

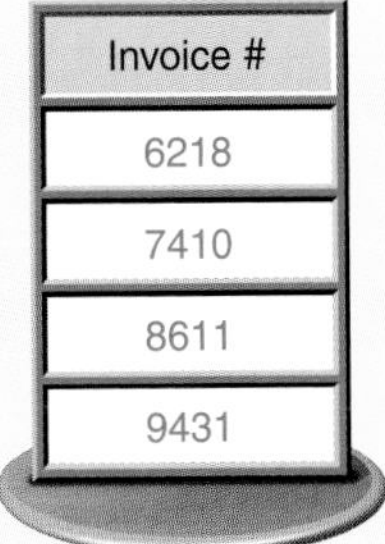

Single-Field

A field that contains a unique value for each record, such as an invoice number, social security number or product number.

Last Name
Date of Birth
Abbott
6/19/1970
Smith
3/1/1967
Smith
12/18/1980
Turner
2/5/1954

Multiple-Field

Two or more fields that together make up a unique value for each record, such as a last name and date of birth.

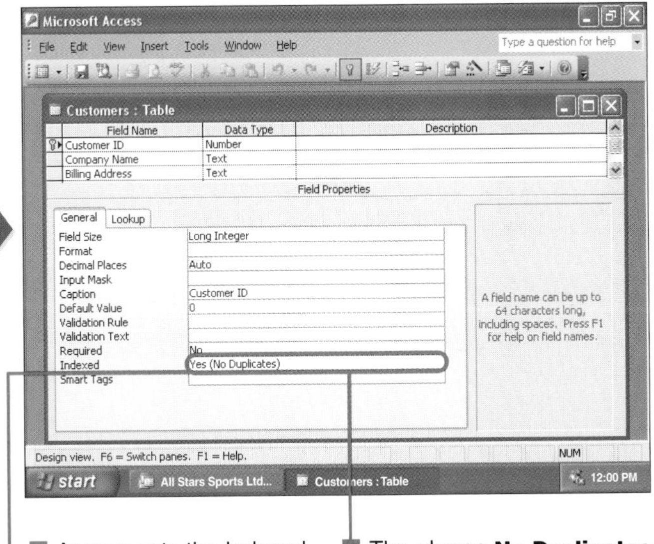

■ Access sets the Indexed property of the field to **Yes (No Duplicates)**. Access will index the data in the field so you can quickly sort and search for data in the field.

■ The phrase **No Duplicates** indicates that Access will not allow you to enter the same value more than once in the field.

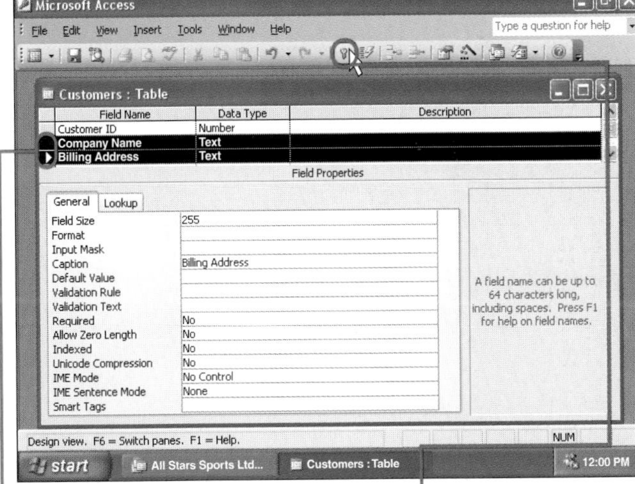

CREATE A MULTIPLE-FIELD PRIMARY KEY

1 To set more than one field as the primary key, press and hold down the Ctrl key as you click the area to the left of each field you want to set as the primary key.

2 Click the primary key button to set the selected fields as the primary key.

■ A key symbol appears beside each field.

CREATE RELATIONSHIPS BETWEEN TABLES

You can create relationships between tables. Relationships between tables allow you to bring together related information in your database.

Relationships between tables are essential for creating a form, query or report that uses information from more than one table in your database.

CREATE RELATIONSHIPS BETWEEN TABLES

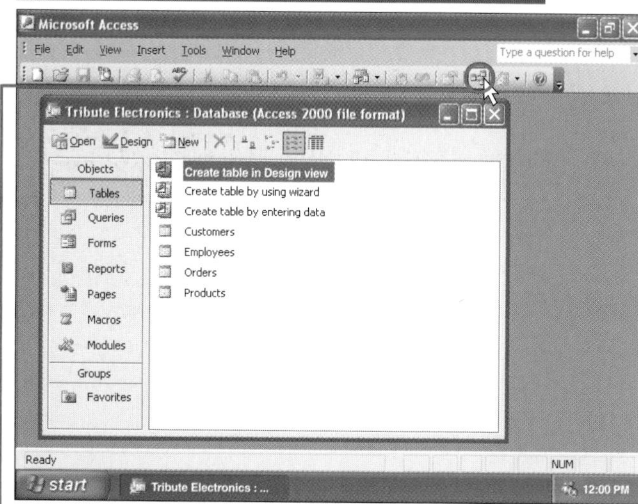

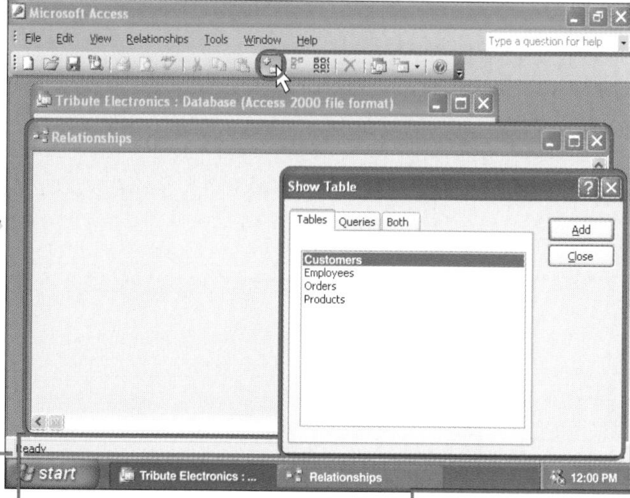

1 Click to display the Relationships window.

*Note: If is not available, press the **F11** key to display the Database window and toolbar.*

■ The Relationships window appears. If any relationships exist between the tables in your database, a box for each table appears in the window.

■ The Show Table dialog box may also appear, listing all the tables in your database.

2 If the Show Table dialog box does not appear, click to display the dialog box.

Why do relationships already exist between the tables in my database?

If you used the Database Wizard to create your database, the wizard automatically created relationships between the tables for you. For information on the Database Wizard, see page 10.

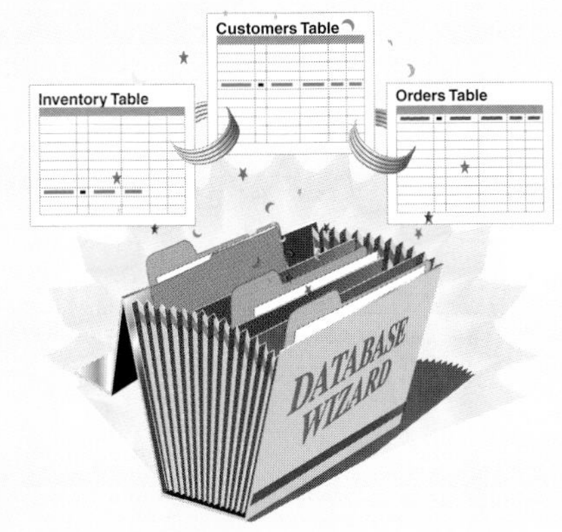

How do I remove a table from the Relationships window?

To remove a table from the Relationships window, click the box for the table and then press the Delete key. Removing a table from the Relationships window will not delete the table from your database or affect the table's relationships with other tables.

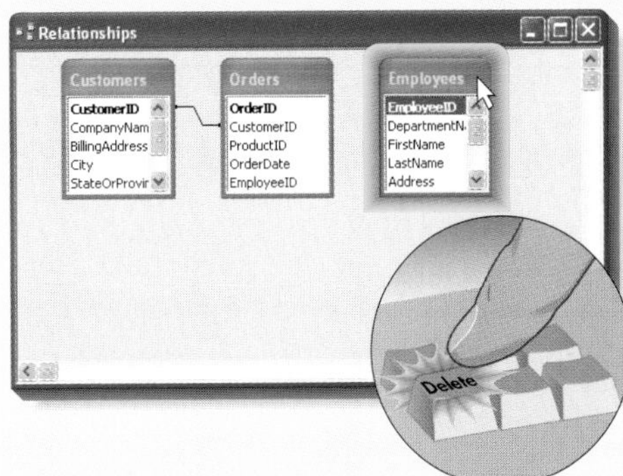

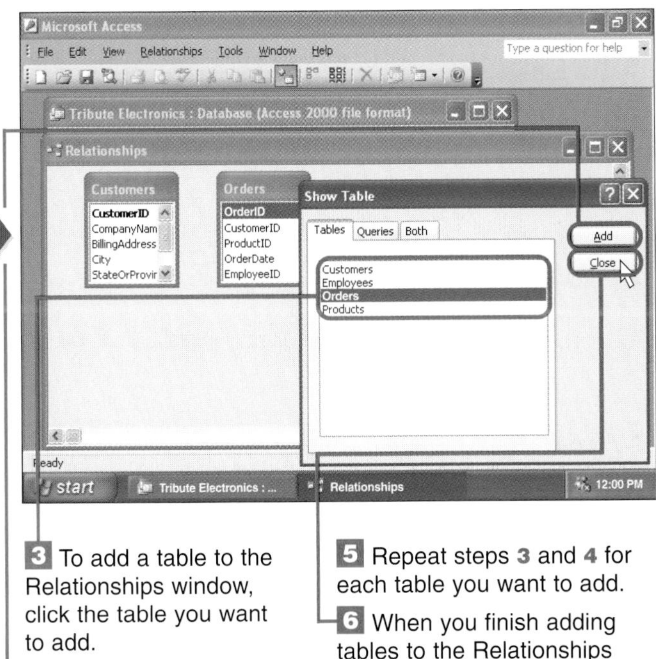

3 To add a table to the Relationships window, click the table you want to add.

4 Click **Add** to add the table to the window.

5 Repeat steps 3 and 4 for each table you want to add.

6 When you finish adding tables to the Relationships window, click **Close** to remove the Show Table dialog box.

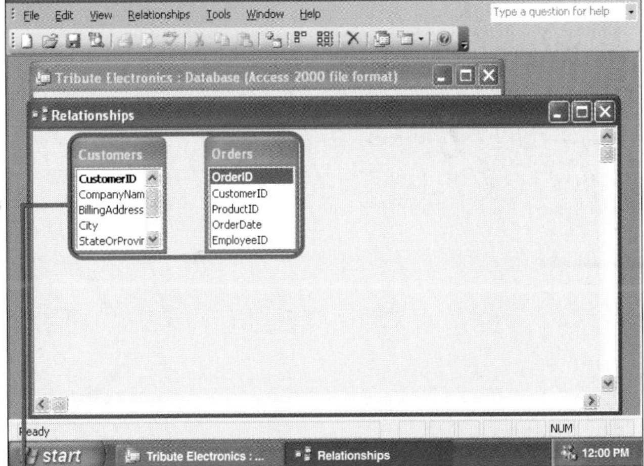

■ Each box in the Relationships window displays the fields for one table.

■ The primary key in each table appears in **bold**. The primary key uniquely identifies each record in a table.

CONTINUED

CREATE RELATIONSHIPS BETWEEN TABLES

You create a relationship between tables in your database by identifying the matching fields in the tables.

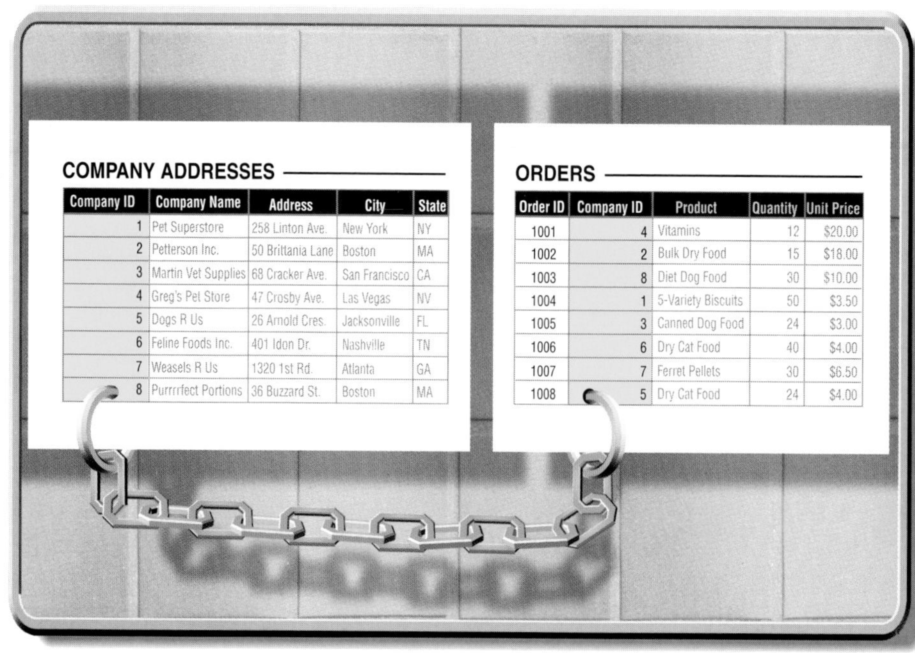

COMPANY ADDRESSES

Company ID	Company Name	Address	City	State
1	Pet Superstore	258 Linton Ave.	New York	NY
2	Petterson Inc.	50 Brittania Lane	Boston	MA
3	Martin Vet Supplies	68 Cracker Ave.	San Francisco	CA
4	Greg's Pet Store	47 Crosby Ave.	Las Vegas	NV
5	Dogs R Us	26 Arnold Cres.	Jacksonville	FL
6	Feline Foods Inc.	401 Idon Dr.	Nashville	TN
7	Weasels R Us	1320 1st Rd.	Atlanta	GA
8	Purrrfect Portions	36 Buzzard St.	Boston	MA

ORDERS

Order ID	Company ID	Product	Quantity	Unit Price
1001	4	Vitamins	12	$20.00
1002	2	Bulk Dry Food	15	$18.00
1003	8	Diet Dog Food	30	$10.00
1004	1	5-Variety Biscuits	50	$3.50
1005	3	Canned Dog Food	24	$3.00
1006	6	Dry Cat Food	40	$4.00
1007	7	Ferret Pellets	30	$6.50
1008	5	Dry Cat Food	24	$4.00

You will usually relate the primary key in one table to a matching field in the other table. In most cases, the fields will have the same name.

The fields you use to create a relationship between tables should contain the same type of data, such as text, numbers or dates.

CREATE RELATIONSHIPS BETWEEN TABLES (CONTINUED)

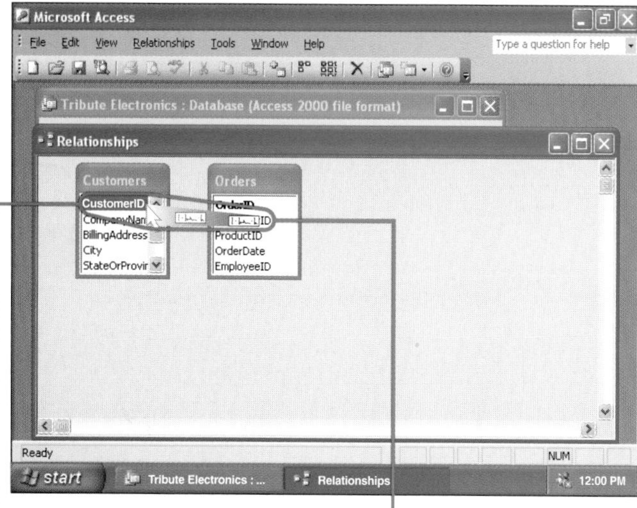

7 To create a relationship between two tables, position the mouse over a field you want to use to create the relationship.

8 Drag the field to the matching field in the other table.

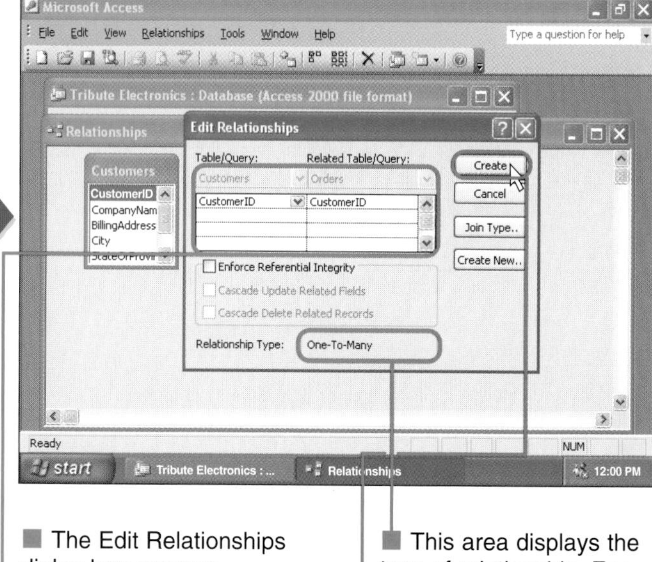

■ The Edit Relationships dialog box appears.

■ This area displays the names of the tables you are creating a relationship between and the names of the matching fields.

■ This area displays the type of relationship. For information on the types of relationships, see the top of page 131.

9 Click **Create** to create the relationship.

What types of relationships can I create between tables?

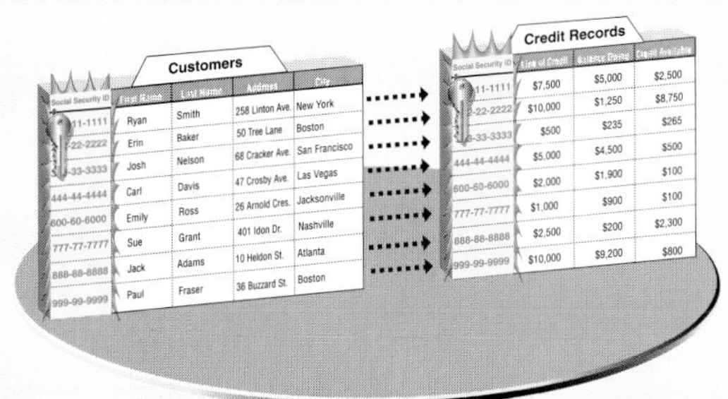

One-to-One

Each record in a table relates to one record in another table. For example, each customer has only one credit record. Access creates a one-to-one relationship between tables if the matching fields are both primary keys.

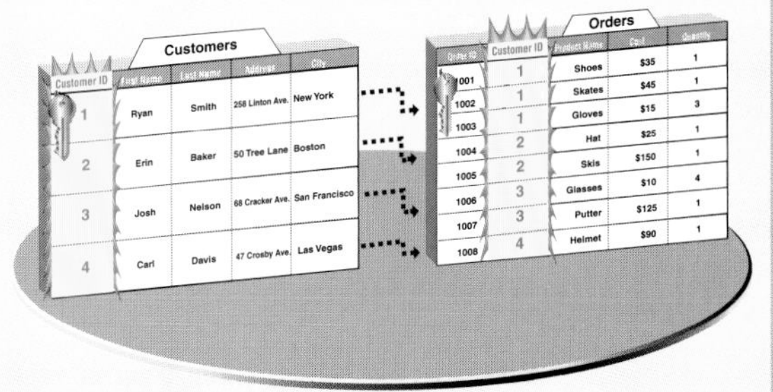

One-to-Many

Each record in a table relates to one or more records in another table. This is the most common type of relationship. For example, each customer can have more than one order. Access creates a one-to-many relationship between tables if only one of the matching fields is a primary key.

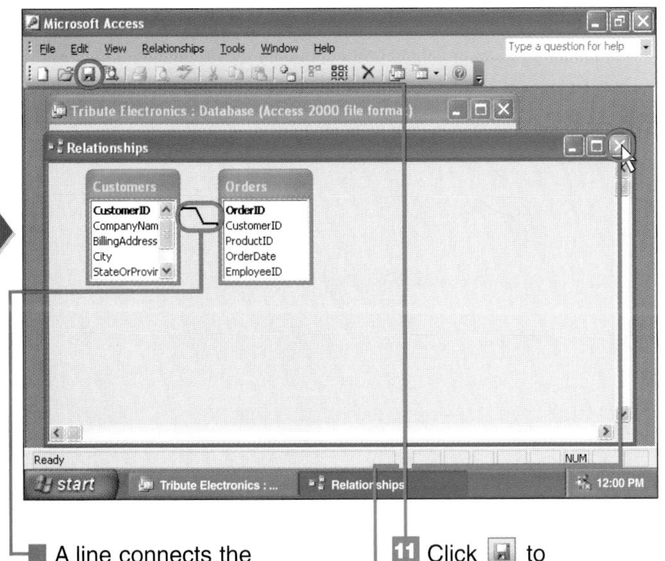

■ A line connects the fields in the two tables to show the relationship.

10 To create a relationship between other tables in your database, repeat steps **7** to **9** for each relationship you want to create.

11 Click 💾 to save your changes.

12 When you finish working in the Relationships window, click ☒ to close the window.

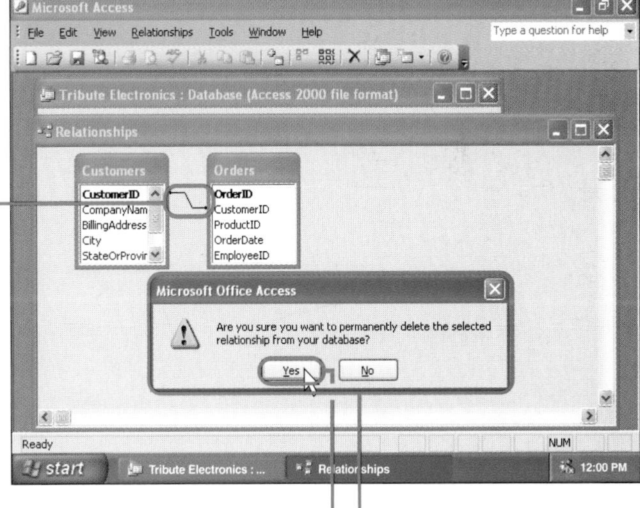

DELETE A RELATIONSHIP

1 In the Relationships window, click the line for the relationship you want to delete.

2 To delete the relationship, press the Delete key.

■ A confirmation dialog box appears.

3 Click **Yes** to permanently delete the relationship.

ENFORCE REFERENTIAL INTEGRITY

Referential integrity is a set of rules that prevents you from changing or deleting a record if matching records exist in a related table.

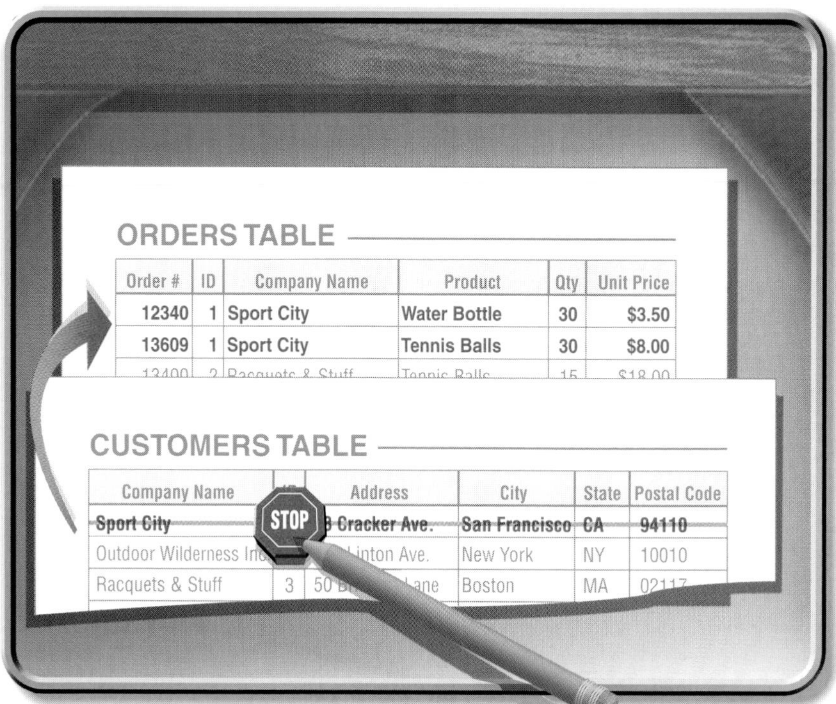

ORDERS TABLE
Order # | ID | Company Name | Product | Qty | Unit Price
12340 | 1 | Sport City | Water Bottle | 30 | $3.50
13609 | 1 | Sport City | Tennis Balls | 30 | $8.00
CUSTOMERS TABLE
Company Name | Address | City | State | Postal Code
Sport City | Cracker Ave. | San Francisco | CA | 94110
Outdoor Wilderness Inc. | New York | NY | 10010
Racquets & Stuff | 3 | Boston | MA
STOP

For example, you cannot delete a customer from the Customers table if the related Orders table contains orders for the customer.

Referential integrity also prevents you from entering a record in one table if a matching record does not exist in a related table. For example, if a customer does not exist in the Customers table, you cannot enter an order for the customer in the Orders table.

ENFORCE REFERENTIAL INTEGRITY

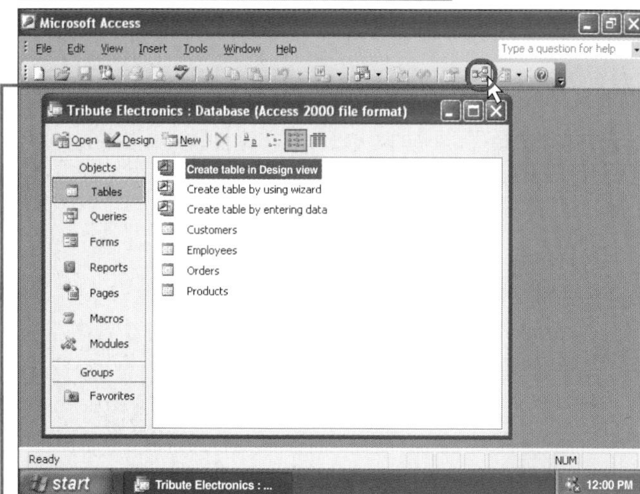

1 Click to display the Relationships window.

Note: If is not available, press the F11 key to display the Database window and toolbar.

■ The Relationships window appears.

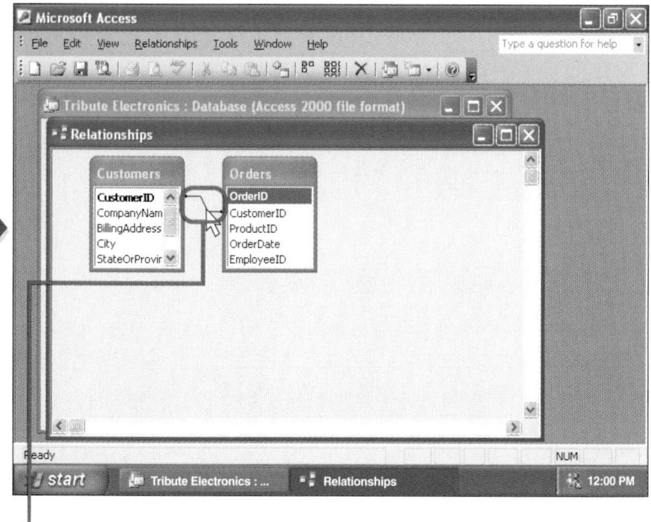

2 To enforce referential integrity between two tables in your database, double-click the line showing the relationship between the tables.

Note: If a line does not appear between the tables, you must create a relationship between the tables. To create a relationship, see page 128.

■ The Edit Relationships dialog box appears.

How can I change or delete a record after I enforce referential integrity between two tables?

Access provides two options that allow you to perform updating and deleting tasks that would normally be prevented by referential integrity.

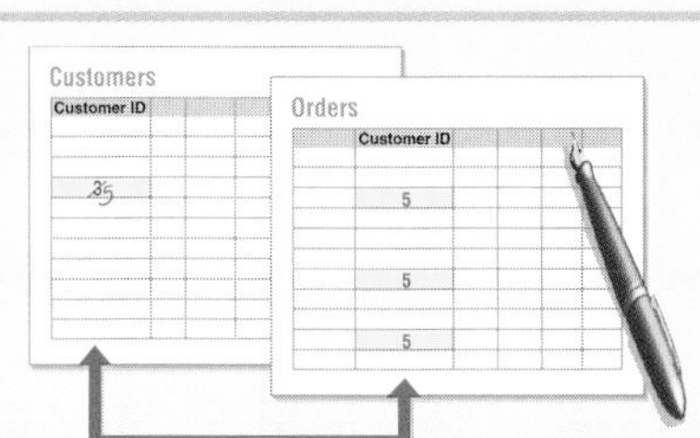

Cascade Update Related Fields

When you change data in the primary key in a table, Access automatically updates the matching data in the related table(s). For example, if you change a customer ID in the Customers table, the customer ID will automatically change for all the customer's orders in the Orders table.

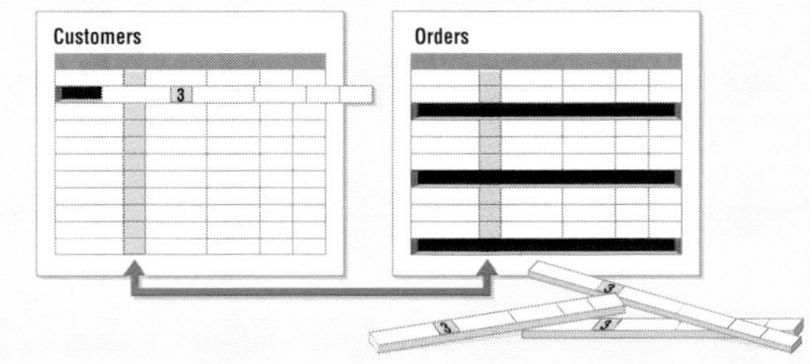

Cascade Delete Related Records

When you delete a record in a table, Access automatically deletes matching records in the related table(s). For example, if you delete a customer from the Customers table, all the customer's orders will automatically be deleted from the Orders table.

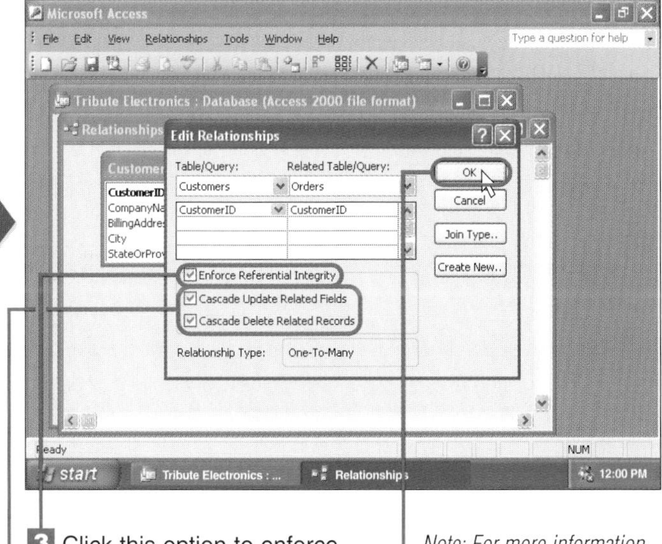

3 Click this option to enforce referential integrity between the tables (☐ changes to ☑).

4 To have Access automatically update related fields or delete related records in the tables, click each option you want to use (☐ changes to ☑).

Note: For more information on the options, see the top of this page.

5 Click **OK** to confirm your changes.

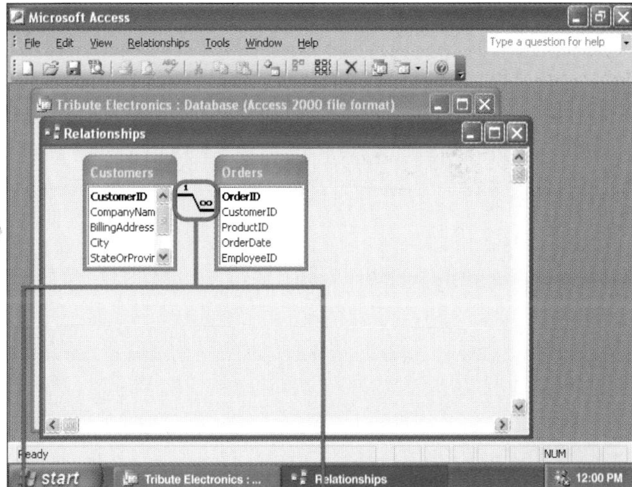

■ When you enforce referential integrity between two tables, the line showing the relationship between the tables becomes thicker.

■ The symbols above the line indicate the type of relationship. In this example, each record in the Customers table (**1**) relates to one or more records in the Orders table (**∞**).

Note: For information on the types of relationships, see the top of page 131.

Columnar
Order Details
Order ID 1
Company Name Emerald Creek Electronics
Product Name DVD Player
Unit Price $299.99
Date Ordered 1/12/2002
Employee ID 512
Discount 25%
Quantity Ordered 350
Record: 1 of 25
Tabular
Order Details
Order ID Company Name Product Name Unit Price
1 Emerald Creek E DVD Player $299.99
2 Home Electronic: Mini Speakers $225.00
3 Radio City 3-Disc CD Chang $525.00
4 Stereos and Mor 32" Television $799.99
5 Park Radio Cellular Phone $149.99
6 Henry's Electroni Mini Speakers $225.00
7 Barbara's Video I 4-head Hi-Fi VCF $139.99
8 CC&M Radio Sto Digital Video Rec $499.99
Record: 1 of 25
Datasheet
Order Details
Order ID Company Name Product Name
1 Emerald Creek Electronic DVD Player
2 Home Electronics Depot Mini Speakers
3 Radio City 3-Disc CD Changer
4 Stereos and More! 32" Television
5 Park Radio Cellular Phone
6 Henry's Electronic Store Mini Speakers
7 Barbara's Video Palace 4-head Hi-Fi VCR
8 CC&M Radio Store Digital Video Recorder
9 Radio City Stereo Headphones
10 Stereos and More! Digital Camera
11 Barbara's Video Palace DVD Player
12 Radio City Digital Video Recorder
Record: 1 of 25
Which Style?
Specify a Name

CHAPTER 6

Create Forms

Would you like to use forms to work with data in your database? In this chapter, you will learn how to create forms to help you present data in an organized, easy-to-use format.

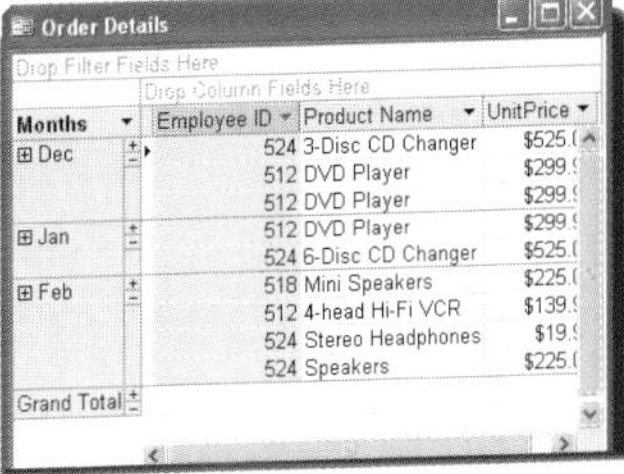

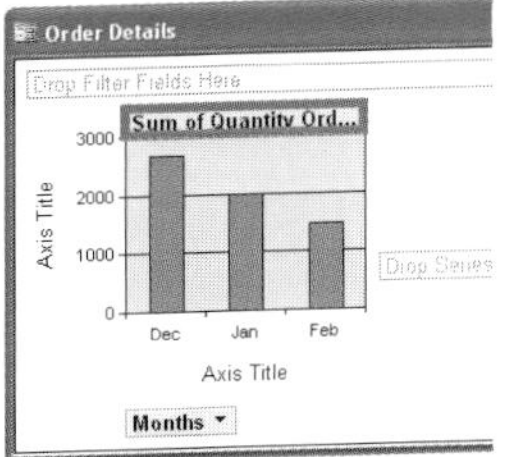

CREATE A FORM USING AN AUTOFORM

You can use the AutoForm Wizard to quickly create a form that displays the information from one table in your database.

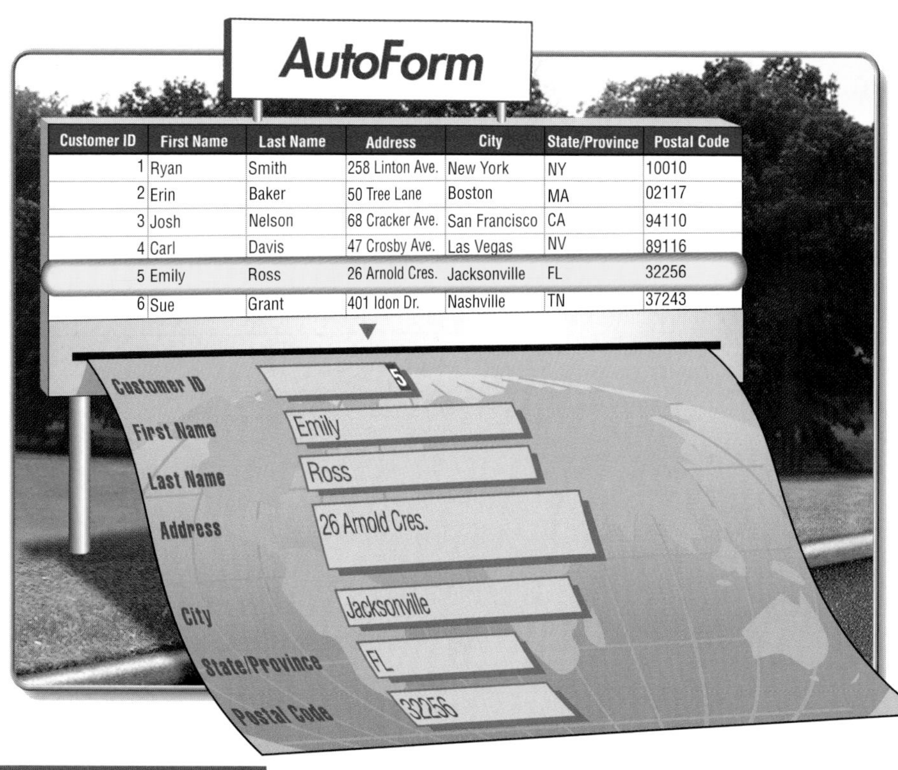

AutoForm
Customer ID
First Name
Last Name
Address
City
State/Province
Postal Code
1 Ryan Smith 258 Linton Ave. New York NY 10010
2 Erin Baker 50 Tree Lane Boston MA 02117
3 Josh Nelson 68 Cracker Ave. San Francisco CA 94110
4 Carl Davis 47 Crosby Ave. Las Vegas NV 89116
5 Emily Ross 26 Arnold Cres. Jacksonville FL 32256
6 Sue Grant 401 Idon Dr. Nashville TN 37243
Emily
Ross
26 Arnold Cres.
Jacksonville
FL
32256

A form presents data from a table in an attractive, easy-to-use format. You can use a form to view, enter and change data in a table.

CREATE A FORM USING AN AUTOFORM

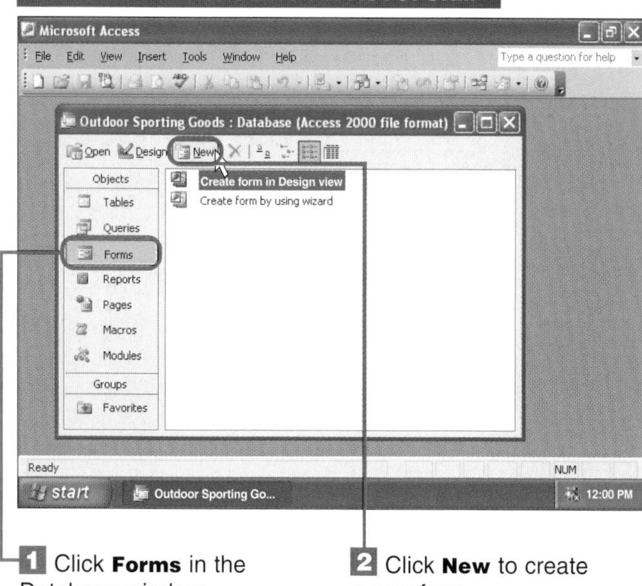

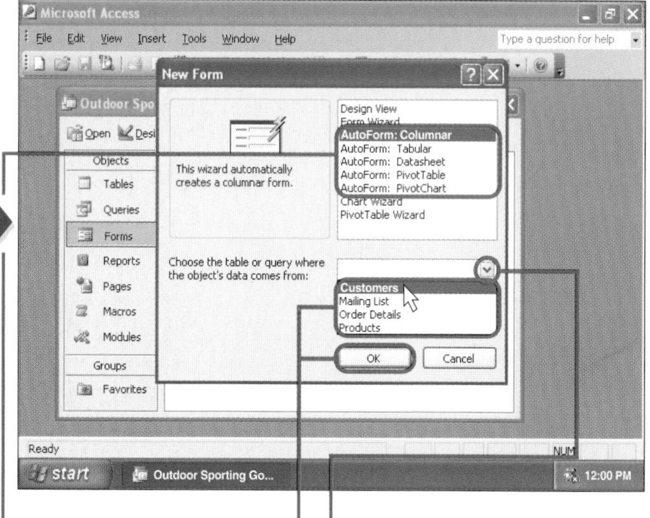

1 Click **Forms** in the Database window.

2 Click **New** to create a new form.

■ The New Form dialog box appears.

3 Click the type of AutoForm you want to create.

Note: For information on the types of AutoForms, see the top of page 137.

4 Click ▾ to display a list of the tables in your database.

5 Click the table that contains the information you want to display on your form.

6 Click **OK** to create your form.

What types of AutoForms can I create?

Columnar

Displays one record at a time.

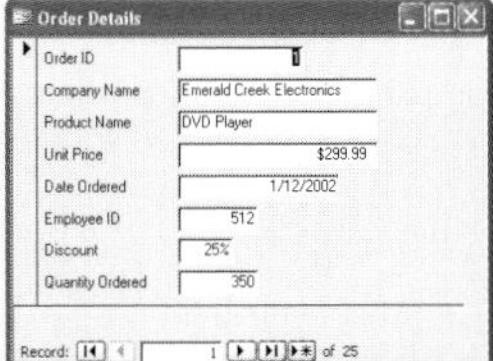

Tabular

Displays many records at a time.

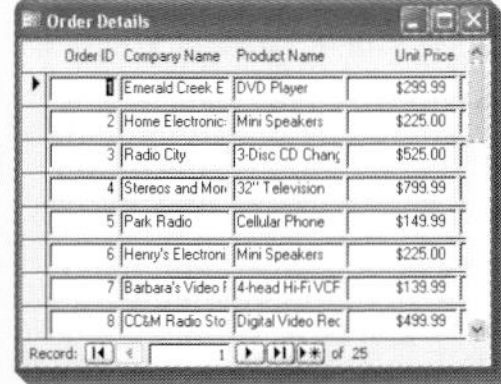

Datasheet

Displays many records at a time and resembles a table in the Datasheet view.

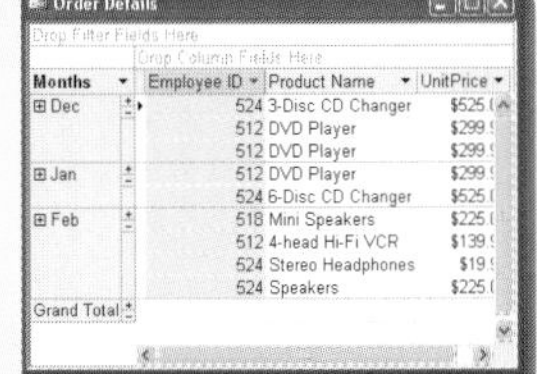

PivotTable

Allows you to summarize and analyze data.

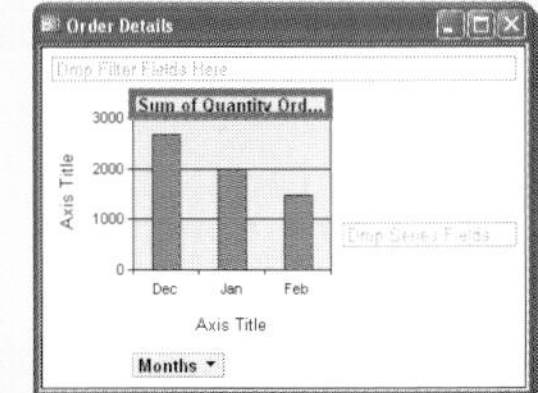

PivotChart

Allows you to display a graphical summary of data.

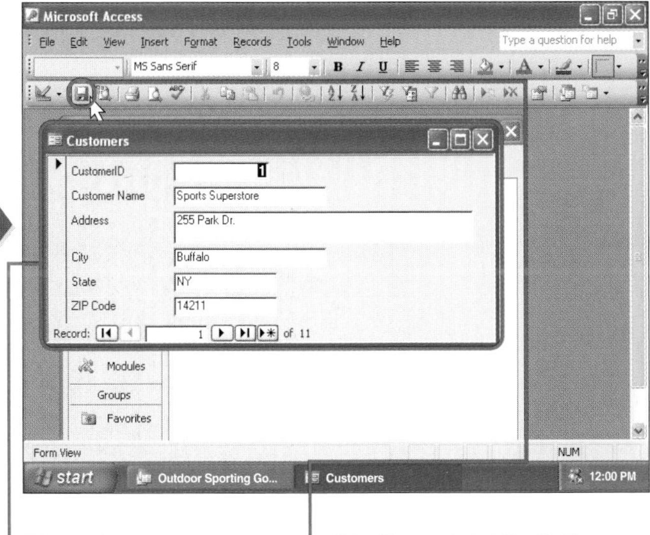

■ The form appears.

■ In this example, the form displays the field names from the table you selected and the data for the first record.

*Note: If you selected PivotTable or PivotChart in step **3**, the PivotTable or PivotChart initially appears empty so you must add the fields you want to display. For information on using the PivotTable or PivotChart, see pages 232 and 238.*

7 Click the save button to save your form.

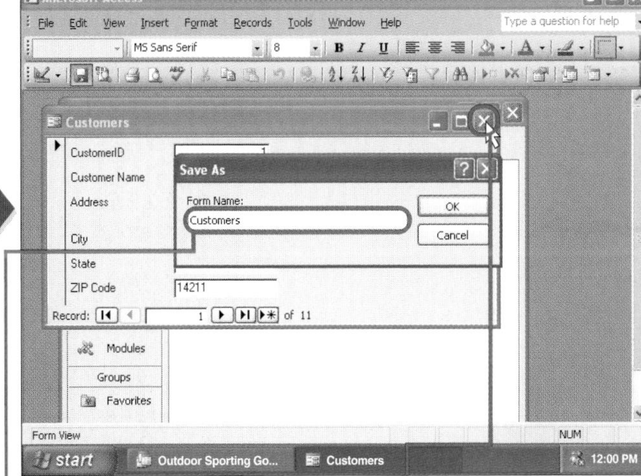

■ The Save As dialog box appears.

8 Type a name for your form and then press the Enter key.

9 When you finish reviewing the form, click the close button to close the form.

CREATE A FORM USING THE FORM WIZARD

You can use the Form Wizard to create a form that displays information from one or more tables in your database. The wizard asks you a series of questions and then sets up a form based on your answers.

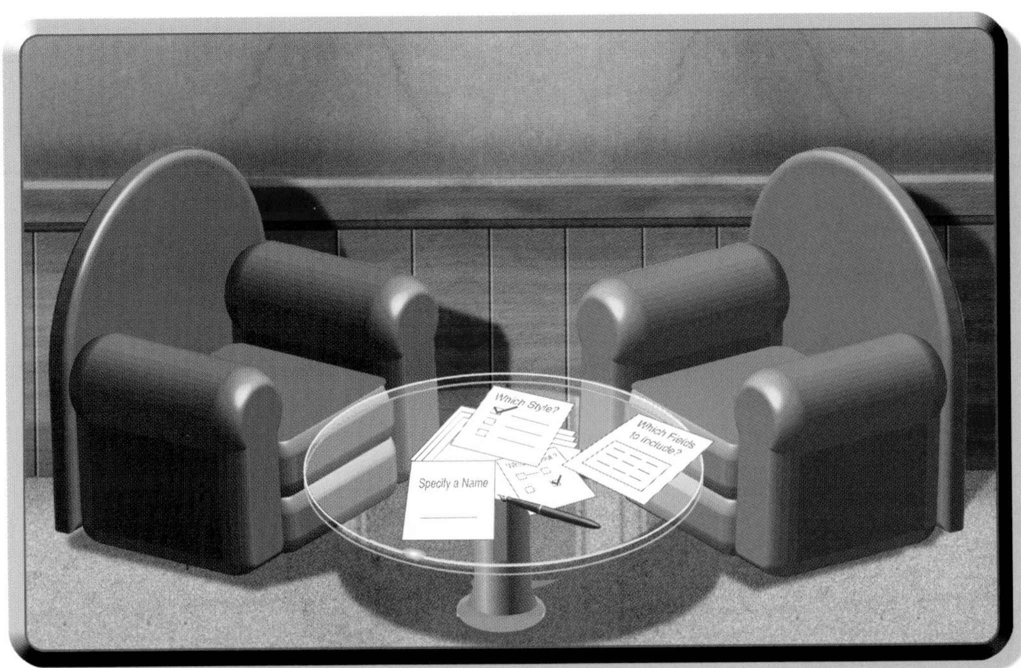

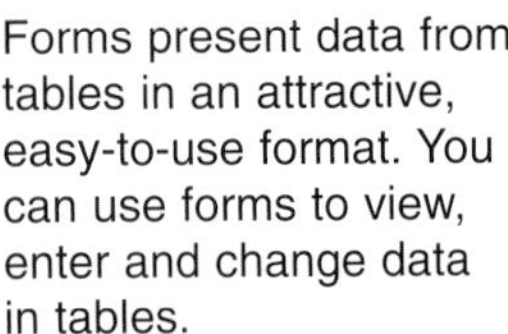

Forms present data from tables in an attractive, easy-to-use format. You can use forms to view, enter and change data in tables.

CREATE A FORM USING THE FORM WIZARD

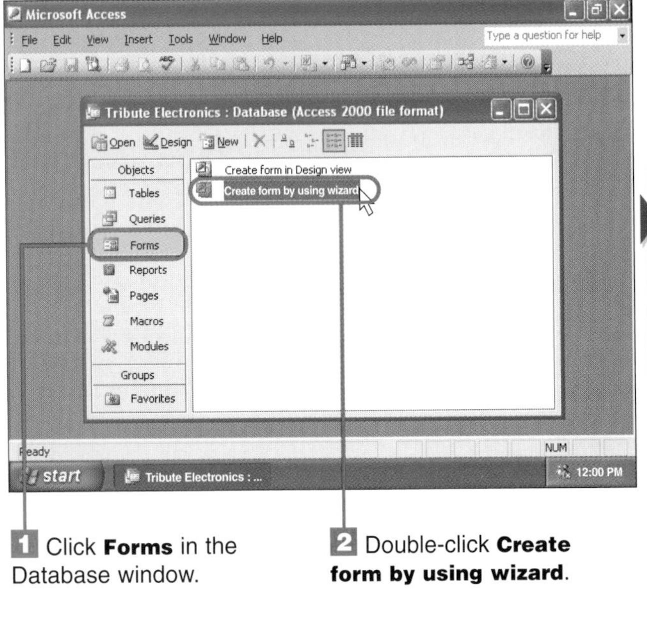

1 Click **Forms** in the Database window.

2 Double-click **Create form by using wizard**.

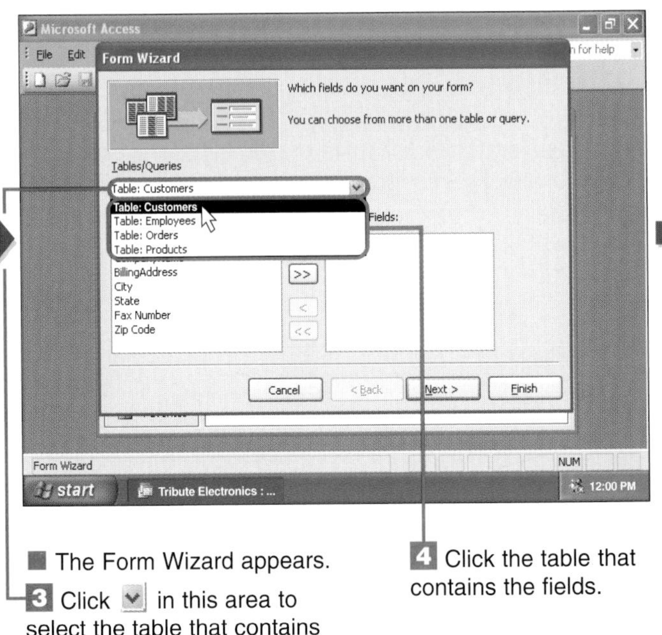

■ The Form Wizard appears.

3 Click ▾ in this area to select the table that contains the fields you want to include on your form.

4 Click the table that contains the fields.

Which tables in my database can I use to create a form?

You can use any table in your database to create a form. When creating a form that uses information from more than one table, relationships must exist between the tables so Access can bring together the information in the tables. For information on relationships, see page 128.

In what order will the fields I select appear on my form?

When you select fields in the Form Wizard, the order in which you select the fields determines the order in which the fields will appear on your form. Make sure you select the fields in the order you want them to appear on your form.

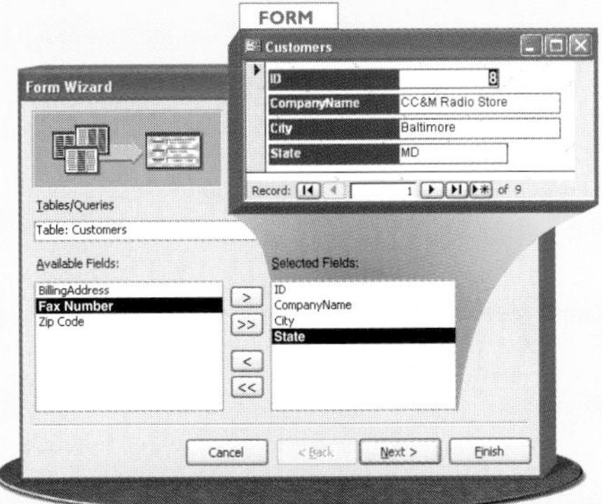

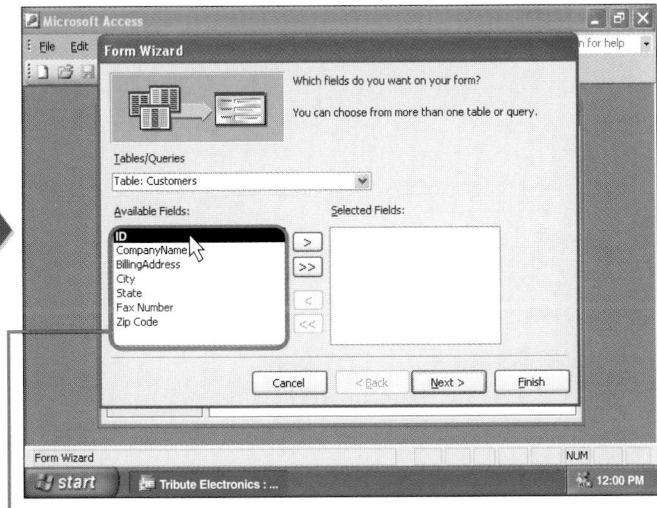

- This area displays the fields from the table you selected.

5 Double-click each field you want to include on your form.

Note: To add all the fields from the table at once, click >> .

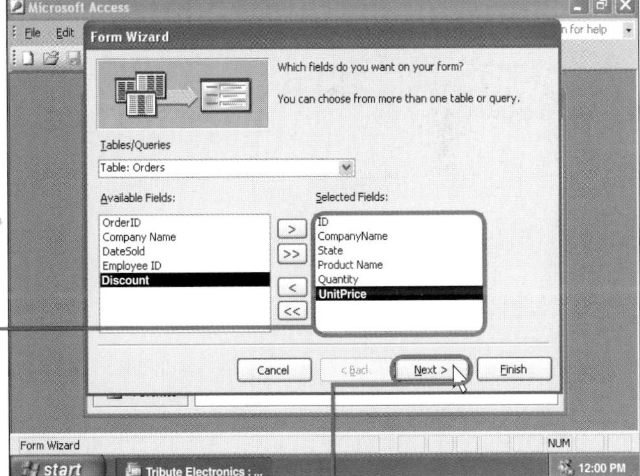

- Each field you select appears in this area.

6 To remove a field you accidentally selected, double-click the field in this area.

Note: To remove all the fields at once, click << .

7 To include fields from other tables in your database, repeat steps **3** to **5** for each table.

8 Click **Next** to continue.

CONTINUED

CREATE A FORM USING THE FORM WIZARD

When creating a form that uses data from more than one table, you can choose the way you want to view the data on the form.

You can choose to view the data from each table separately or together on a form.

CREATE A FORM USING THE FORM WIZARD (CONTINUED)

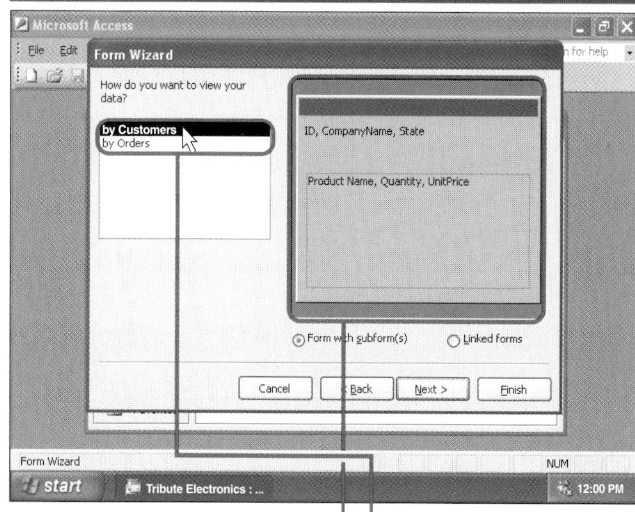

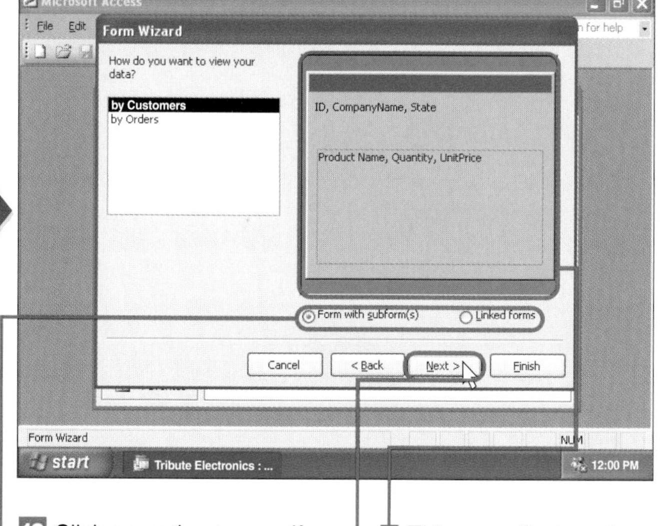

■ If you selected fields from more than one table, you can select the way you want to view the data on your form.

*Note: If this screen does not appear, skip to step **12**.*

9 Click the way you want to view the data on your form. You can view the data from each table separately or together.

■ This area displays the way the data will appear on your form.

10 Click an option to specify if you want to create a form with a subform or a linked form (○ changes to ◉). For more information, see the top of page 141.

*Note: If you selected to view the data from each table together in step **9**, these options are not available.*

■ This area displays the way the data will appear.

11 Click **Next** to continue.

How can I organize the data from multiple tables on a form?

If you choose to view the data from each table separately on a form, the Form Wizard offers two ways that you can organize data on the form.

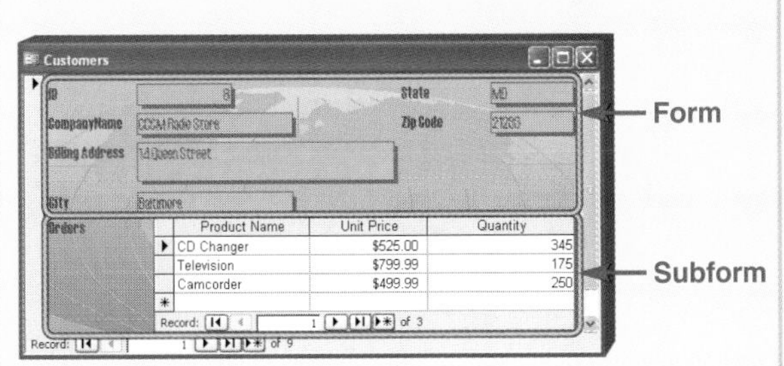

Form with subform(s)

The data from each table appears in one window.

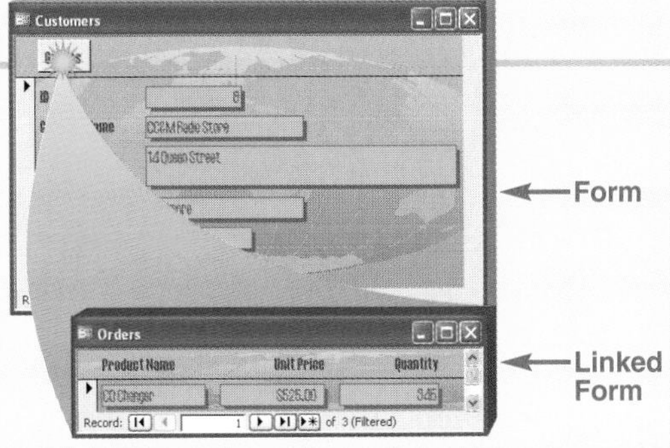

Linked forms

The data from each table appears in separate windows. You can click a button on the form to view the data on the linked form.

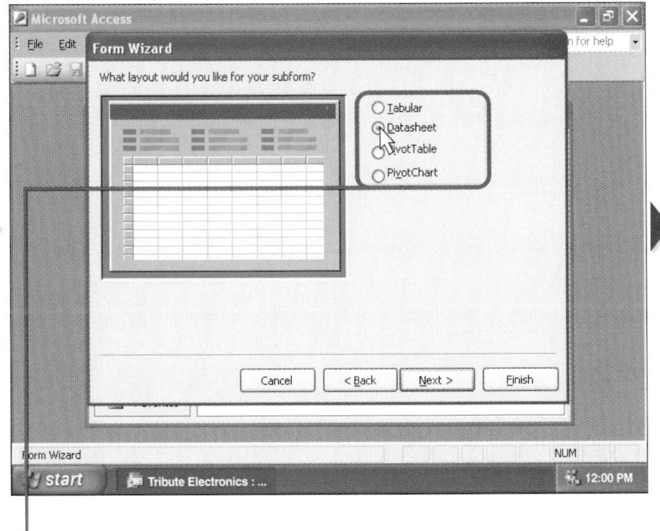

12 Click the layout you want to use for your form or subform (○ changes to ◉). For information on the available layouts, see the top of page 137.

*Note: The available layout options depend on the selections you made in steps **9** and **10**. If this screen does not appear, skip to step **14**.*

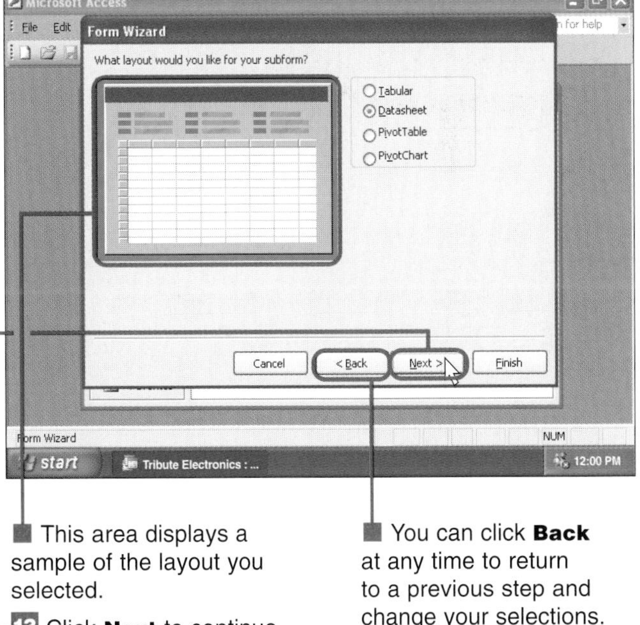

■ This area displays a sample of the layout you selected.

13 Click **Next** to continue.

■ You can click **Back** at any time to return to a previous step and change your selections.

CONTINUED

CREATE A FORM USING THE FORM WIZARD

You can choose the style you want your form to display. Access provides several styles, such as Blends, International and Ricepaper.

You may want to use the same style for every form in your database to give the database a consistent appearance.

CREATE A FORM USING THE FORM WIZARD (CONTINUED)

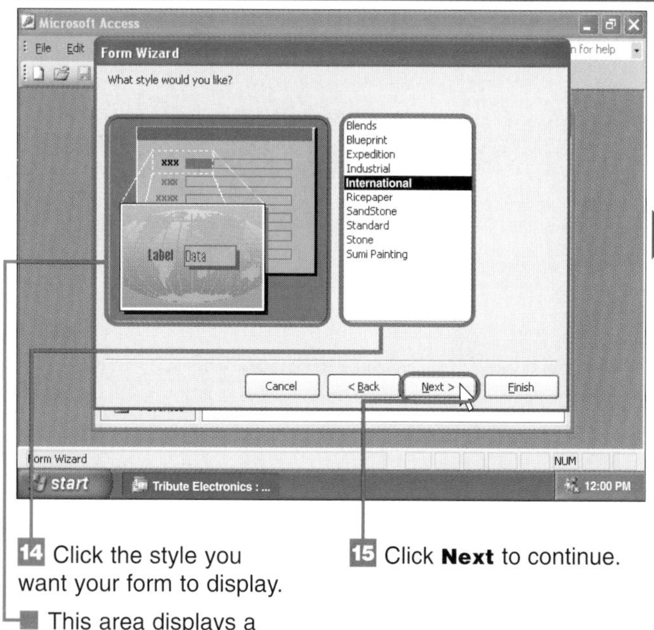

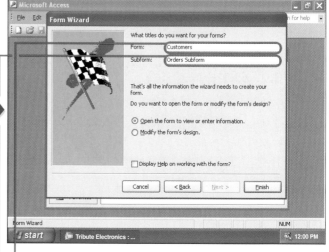

14 Click the style you want your form to display.

■ This area displays a sample of the style you selected.

15 Click **Next** to continue.

16 Type a name for your form.

17 If your form includes fields from more than one table, you can also specify a name for your subform or linked form. To specify a name, press the Tab key and then type a name for the subform or linked form.

*Note: If you selected to view the data from each table together in step **9**, you do not need to perform step **17**.*

How will my new form appear in the Database window?

The name of every form you create will appear in the Database window. If you created a form with a subform or a linked form, the subform or linked form will also appear in the Database window. You must open the main form to work with the contents of both the main form and the subform or linked form.

How do I move through the information in a subform?

When you move through the information in the main form, the information in the subform automatically changes. For example, when you display the name and address of a customer, Access automatically displays the orders for the customer in the subform. To move through records in a form, see page 145.

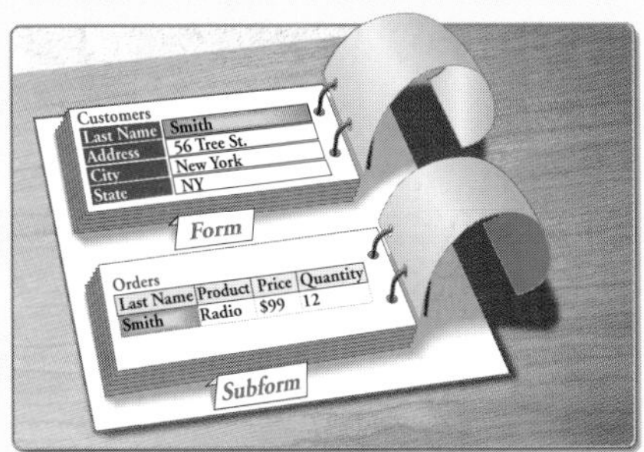

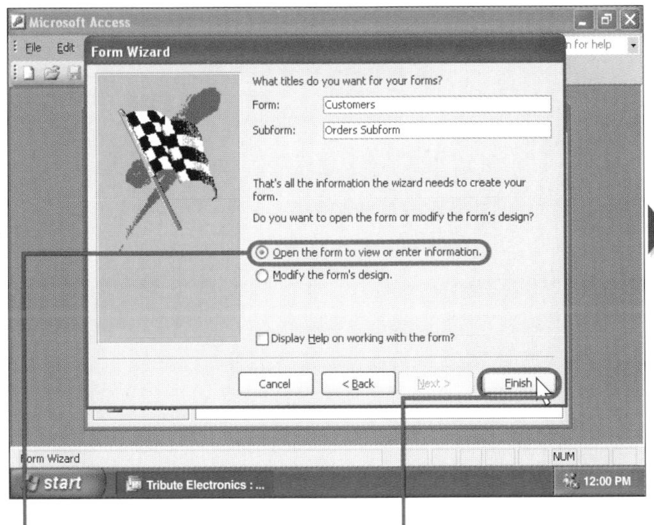

18 Click this option to open the form so you can review and enter information in the form (○ changes to ◉).

19 Click **Finish** to create your form.

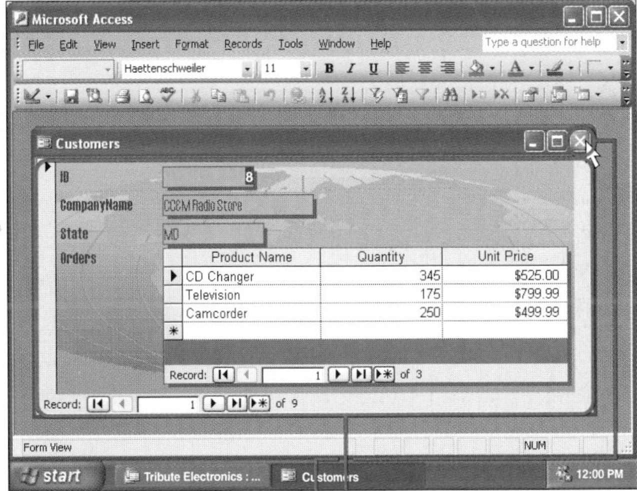

■ The form appears.

Note: The appearance of your form depends on the options you selected while creating the form.

■ In this example, the form displays the information for one customer on the main form and the orders for the customer in the subform.

20 When you finish reviewing the form, click ☒ to close the form.

OPEN A FORM

You can open a form to display its contents on your screen. Opening a form allows you to review and make changes to the form.

OPEN A FORM

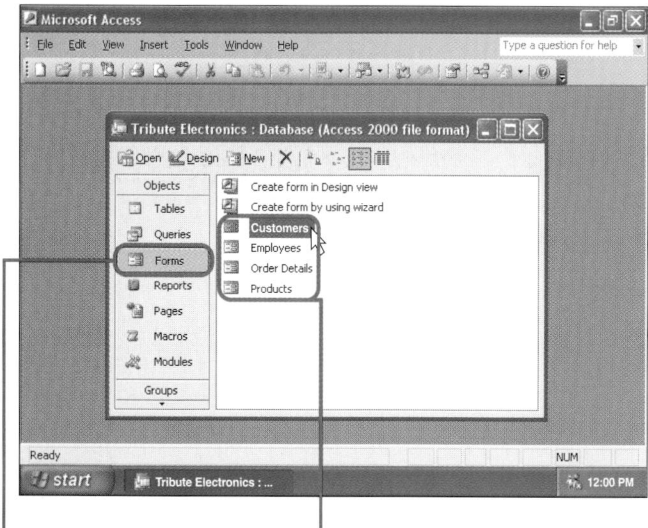

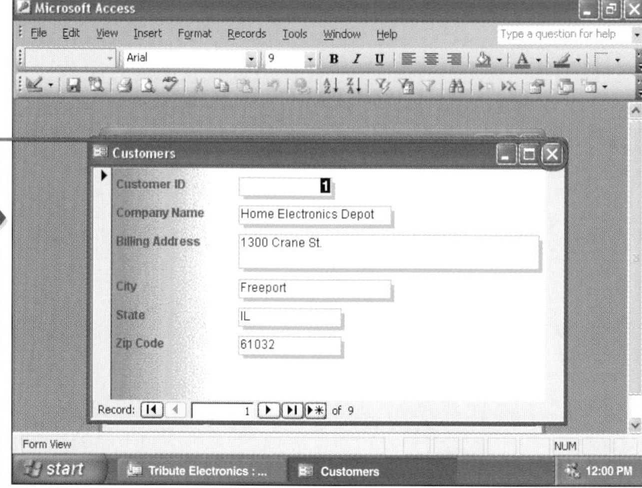

1 Click **Forms** in the Database window.

■ This area displays a list of the forms in your database.

2 Double-click the form you want to open.

■ The form opens. You can now review and make changes to the form.

■ When you finish working with the form, click ☒ to close the form.

Note: A dialog box will appear if you did not save changes you made to the design of the form. Click ***Yes*** *or* ***No*** *to specify if you want to save the changes.*

MOVE THROUGH RECORDS

You can move through the records in a form to review and edit information.

MOVE THROUGH RECORDS

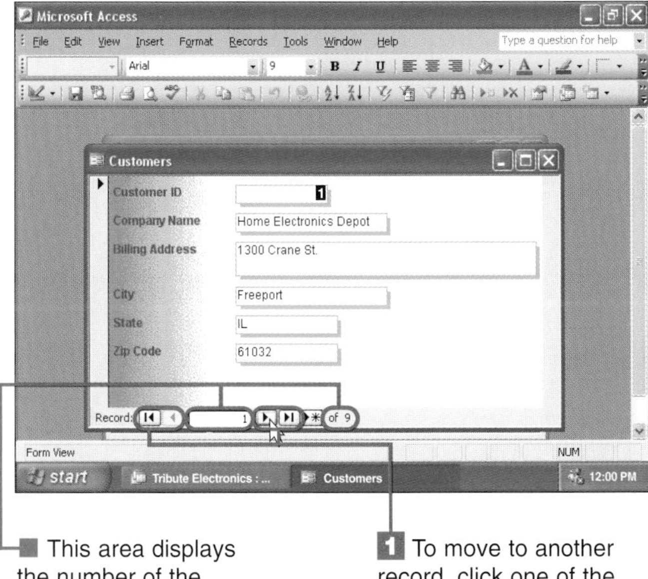

■ This area displays the number of the current record and the total number of records.

1 To move to another record, click one of the following buttons:

- ⏮ First record
- ◀ Previous record
- ▶ Next record
- ⏭ Last record

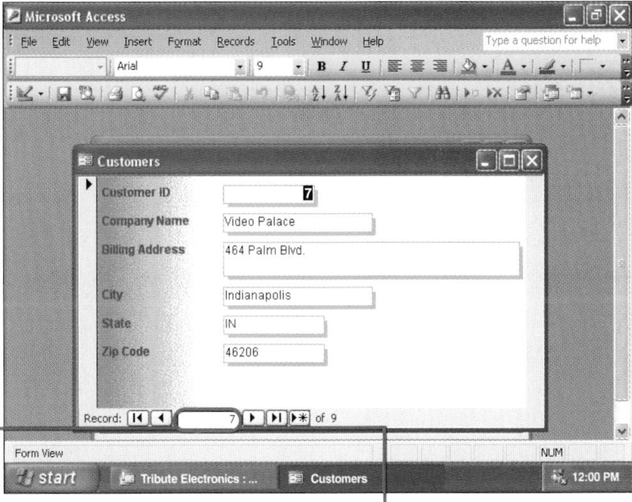

MOVE TO A SPECIFIC RECORD

1 To quickly move to a specific record, drag the mouse I over the number of the current record. The number is highlighted.

2 Type the number of the record you want to move to and then press the Enter key.

EDIT DATA

You can edit the data displayed on a form to correct a mistake or update data.

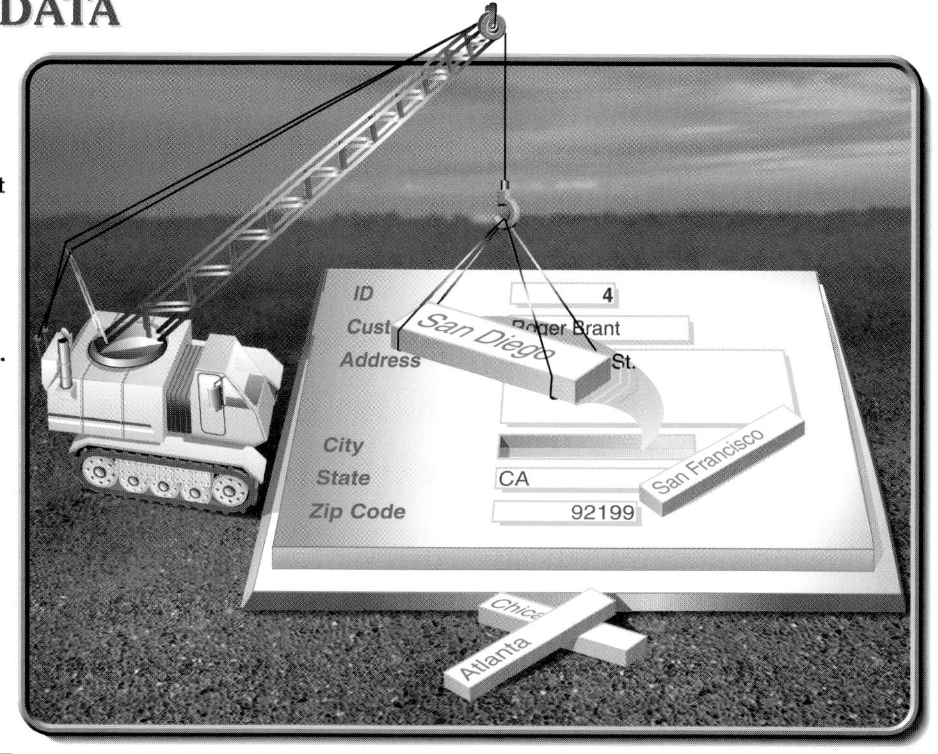

Access automatically saves the changes you make to the data displayed on a form.

When you change data on a form, Access will also change the data in the table you used to create the form.

EDIT DATA

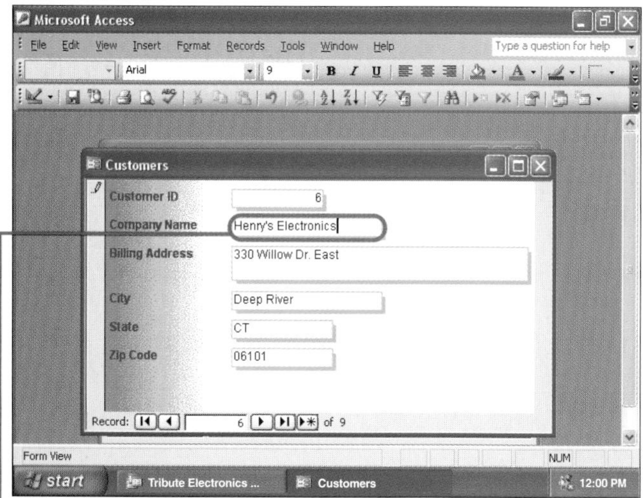

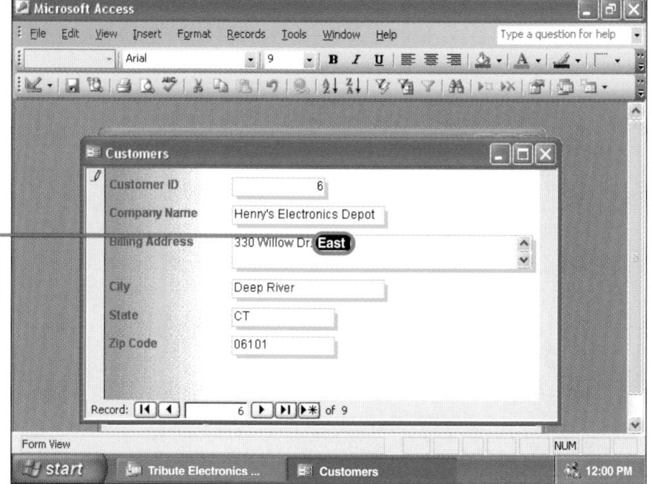

INSERT DATA

1 Click the location in the cell where you want to insert data.

■ A flashing insertion point appears in the cell, indicating where the data you type will appear.

Note: You can press the ← or → key to move the insertion point.

2 Type the data you want to insert.

DELETE DATA

1 To delete data, drag the mouse I over the data until you highlight the data you want to delete.

2 Press the Delete key to delete the highlighted data.

Note: To delete a single character, position the insertion point to the right of the character you want to delete and then press the ←Backspace key.

Why does the existing data disappear when I type new data?

When **OVR** appears at the bottom right corner of your screen, the Overtype feature is on. When this feature is on, the data you type will replace the existing data. To turn off the Overtype feature, press the Insert key.

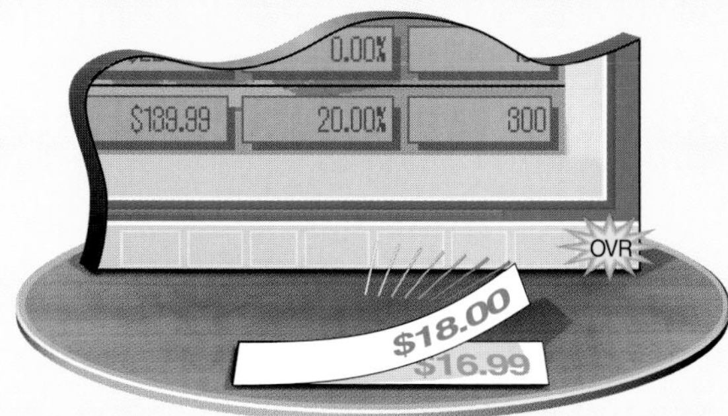

Why can't I edit the data in a cell?

You may be trying to edit data in a field that has the AutoNumber data type. A field that has the AutoNumber data type automatically numbers each record for you to uniquely identify each record. For more information on data types, see page 82.

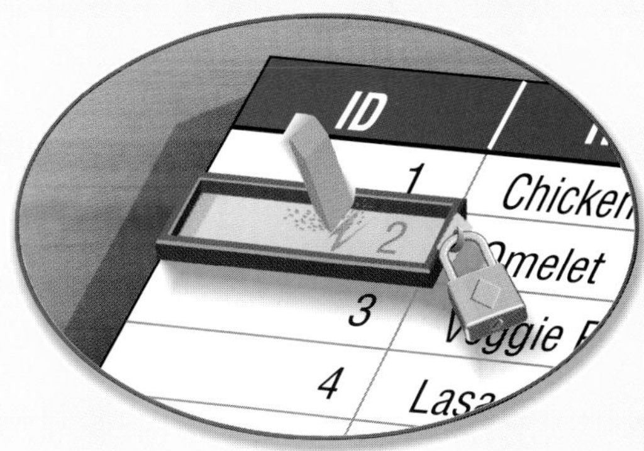

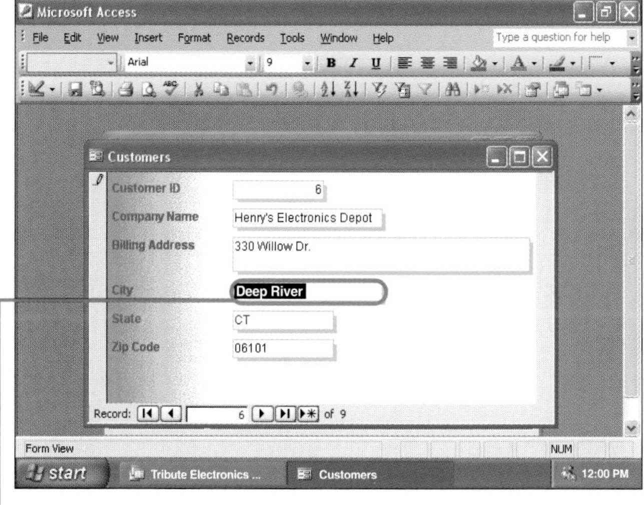

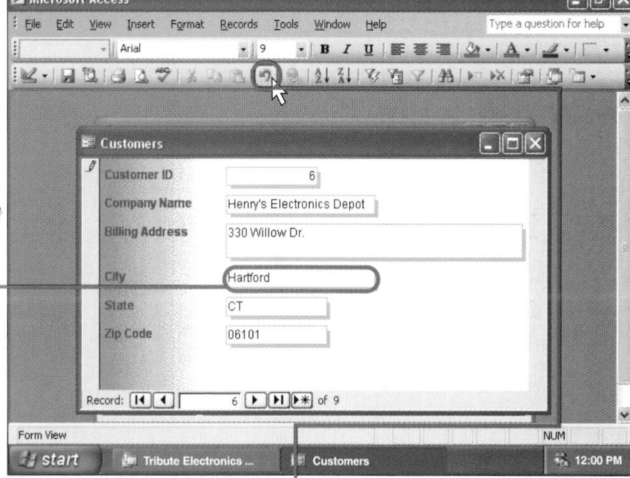

REPLACE ALL DATA IN A CELL

1 To replace all the data in a cell with new data, drag the mouse over the data until you highlight all the data in the cell.

Note: In some forms, you can click the name of the field to quickly highlight all the data in a cell.

2 Type the new data.

■ The data you type replaces the data in the cell.

UNDO CHANGES

1 Click to immediately undo your most recent change.

Note: If you move to another cell and then click , Access will undo all the changes you made to the entire record.

ADD A RECORD

You can add a new record to a form to insert additional information into your database. For example, you can add information about a new customer.

Access automatically saves each new record you add to a form.

When you add a record to a form, Access also adds the record to the table you used to create the form.

ADD A RECORD

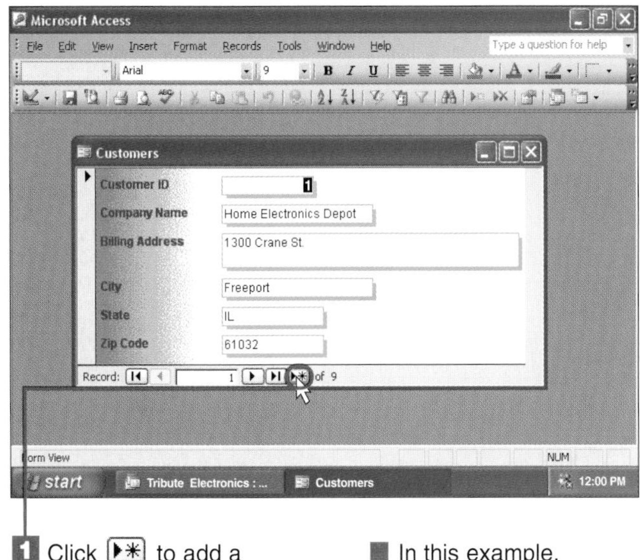

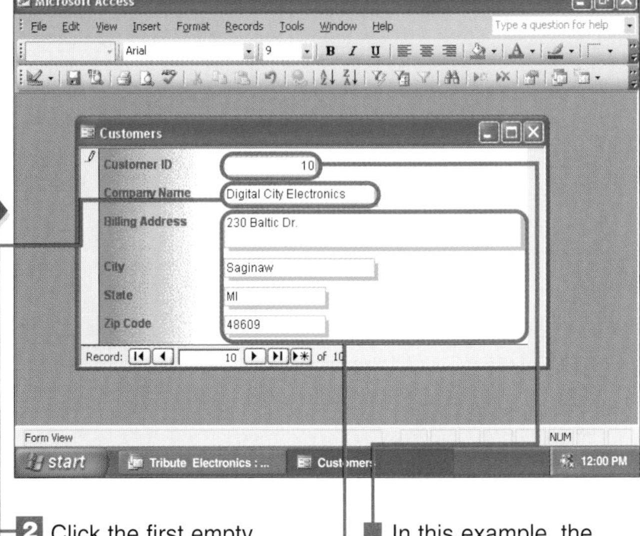

1 Click ▶* to add a new record to your form.

■ In this example, a blank form appears.

2 Click the first empty field in the form.

3 Type the data that corresponds to the field and then press the Tab key to move to the next field.

■ In this example, the ID field automatically adds a number for the new record.

4 Repeat step **3** until you finish entering all the data for the record.

DELETE A RECORD

You can delete a record displayed in a form to permanently remove information you no longer need. For example, you may want to remove information about a customer who no longer orders your products.

When you delete a record displayed in a form, Access also removes the record from the table you used to create the form.

Deleting records saves storage space on your computer and keeps your database from becoming cluttered with unnecessary information.

DELETE A RECORD

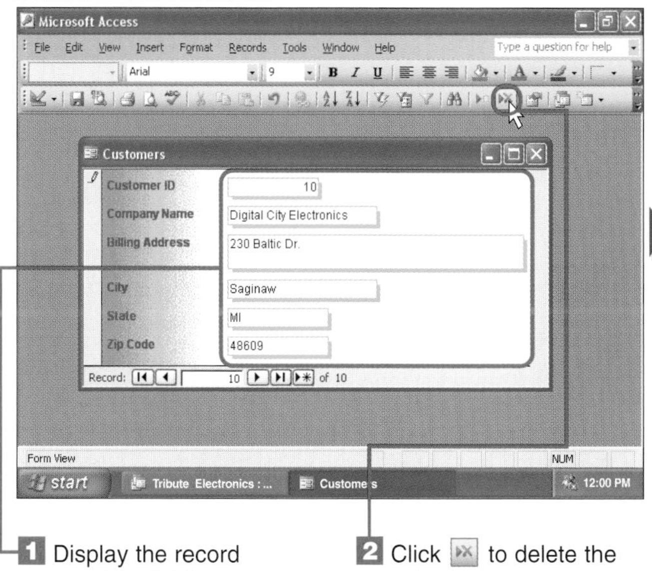

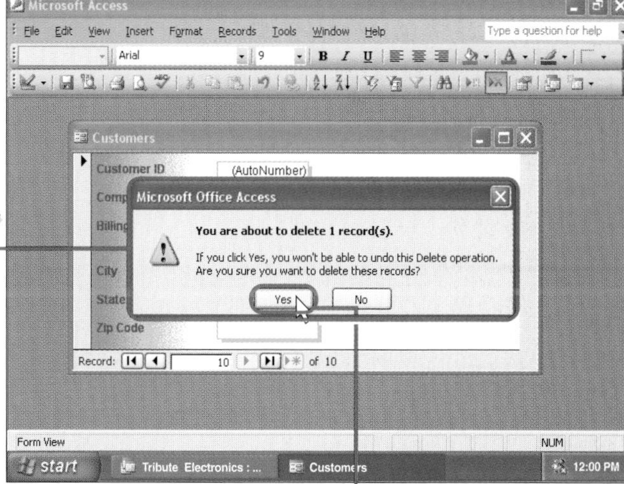

1 Display the record you want to delete.

Note: For information on moving through records in a form, see page 145.

2 Click ⊠ to delete the record.

■ The record disappears from the form.

■ A warning dialog box appears.

3 Click **Yes** to permanently delete the record.

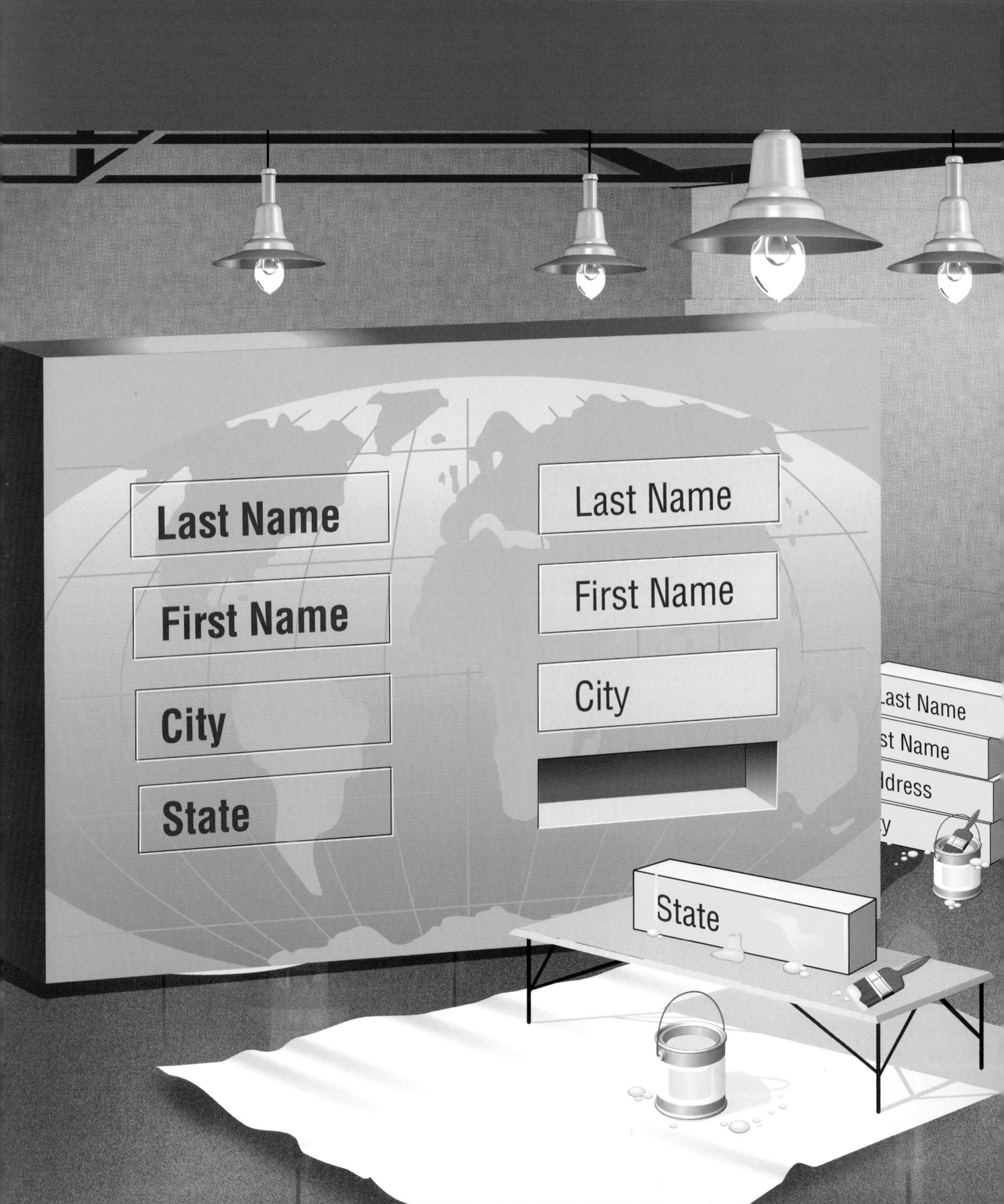

Last Name
First Name
City
State
Last Name
First Name
City
State

CHAPTER 7

Design Forms

Are you interested in customizing the layout and design of your forms? This chapter shows you how to move or resize items, change the appearance of data, undo changes, add a picture to a form and more.

CHANGE THE VIEW OF A FORM

You can view a form in five different ways. Each view allows you to perform different tasks.

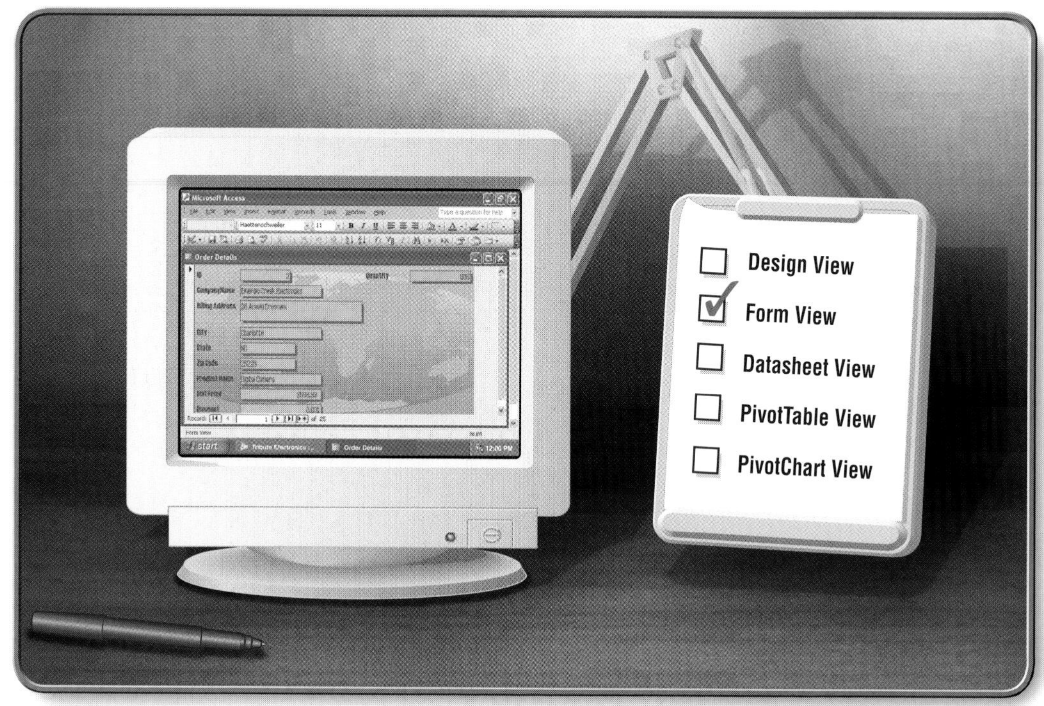

CHANGE THE VIEW OF A FORM

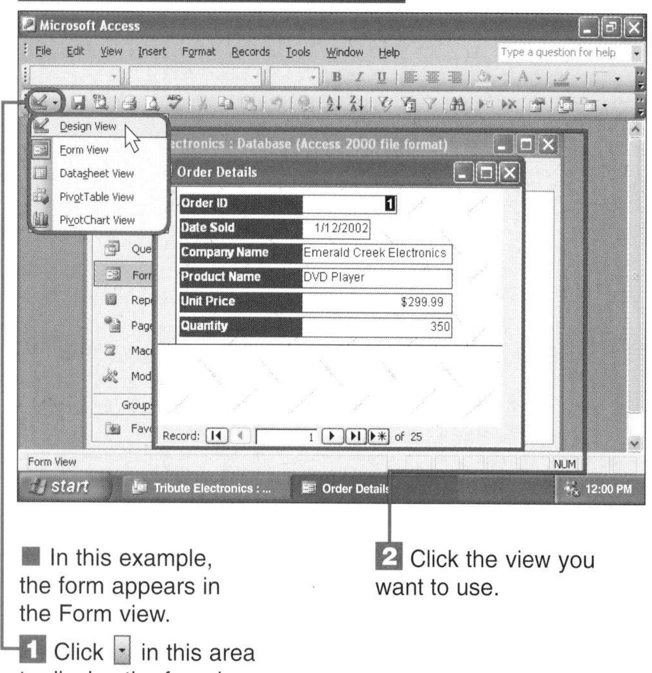

■ In this example, the form appears in the Form view.

1 Click ▾ in this area to display the form in a different view.

2 Click the view you want to use.

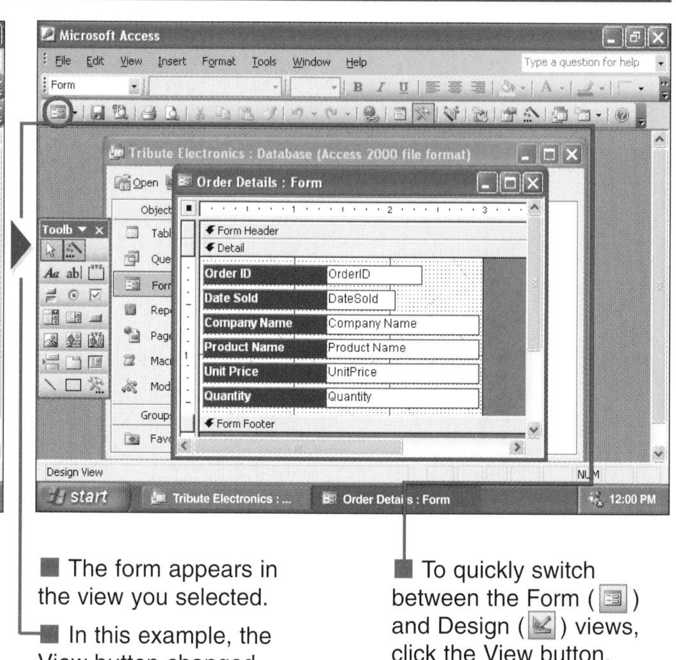

■ The form appears in the view you selected.

■ In this example, the View button changed from ( ) to ( ).

■ To quickly switch between the Form ( ) and Design ( ) views, click the View button.

THE FORM VIEWS

Design View

The Design view allows you to change the layout and design of a form. You can customize a form to make the form easier to use or to enhance the appearance of the form.

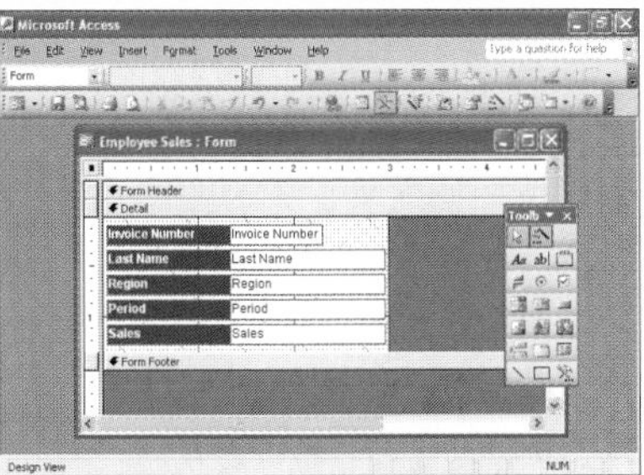

Form View

The Form view usually displays one record at a time in an organized and attractive format. You can use this view to review, enter and edit information.

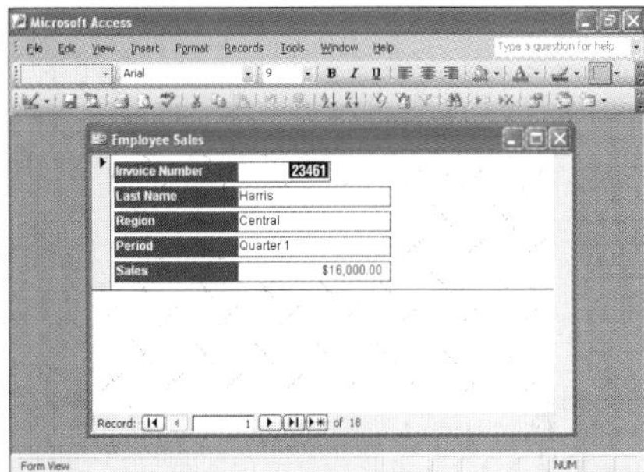

Datasheet View

The Datasheet view displays all the records in rows and columns. The field names appear across the top of the window and the information for one record appears in each row. You can review, enter and edit information in this view.

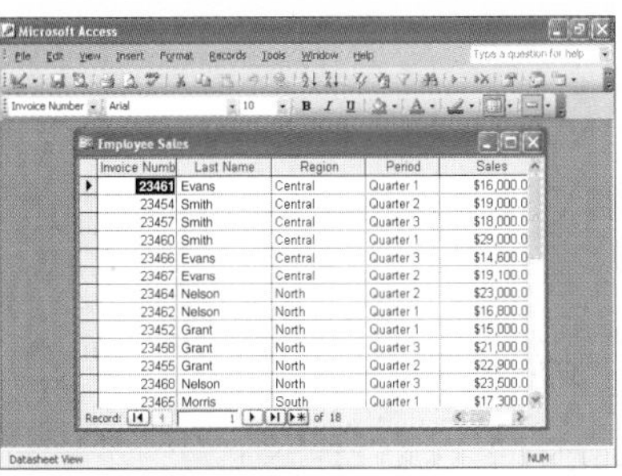

PivotTable View

The PivotTable view allows you to summarize and analyze the data in a form. When you first display a form in this view, the PivotTable is empty and you must add the fields you want the PivotTable to display. For information on using the PivotTable view, see page 232.

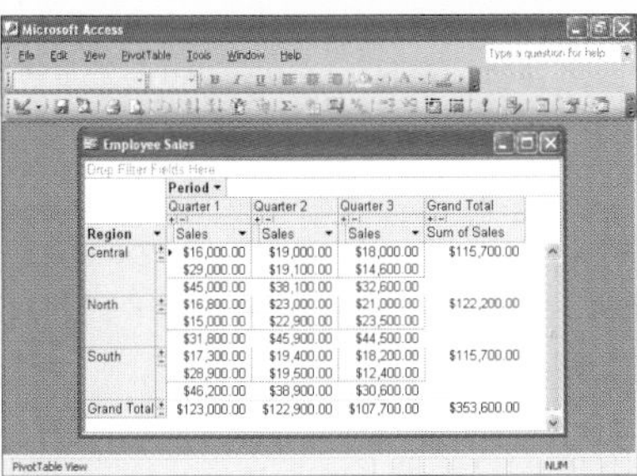

PivotChart View

The PivotChart view allows you to display a graphical summary of the data in a form. When you first display a form in this view, the PivotChart is empty and you must add the fields you want the PivotChart to display. For information on using the PivotChart view, see page 238.

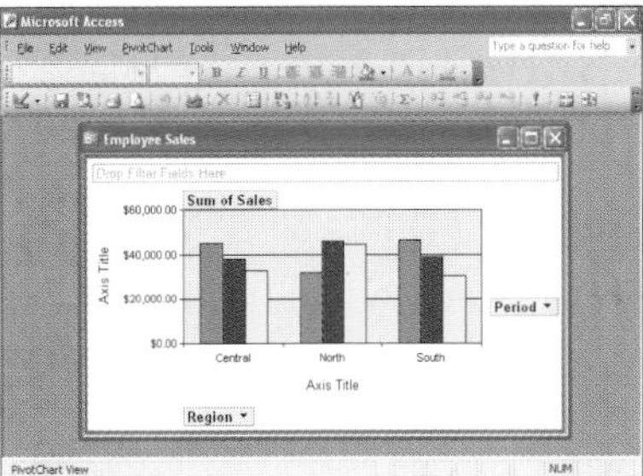

MOVE OR RESIZE A CONTROL

You can change the location and size of a control on a form.

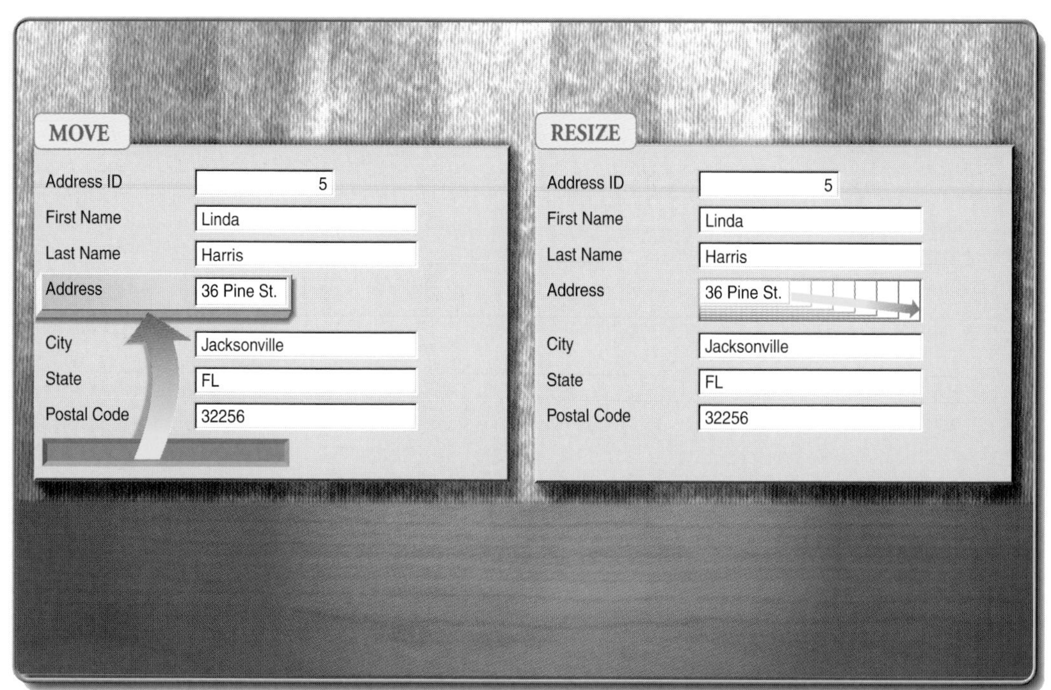

Moving a control allows you to change the order of information on a form. Resizing a control allows you to display more or less information in a control.

A control is an item on a form, such as a label that displays a field name or a text box that displays data from a field.

MOVE A CONTROL

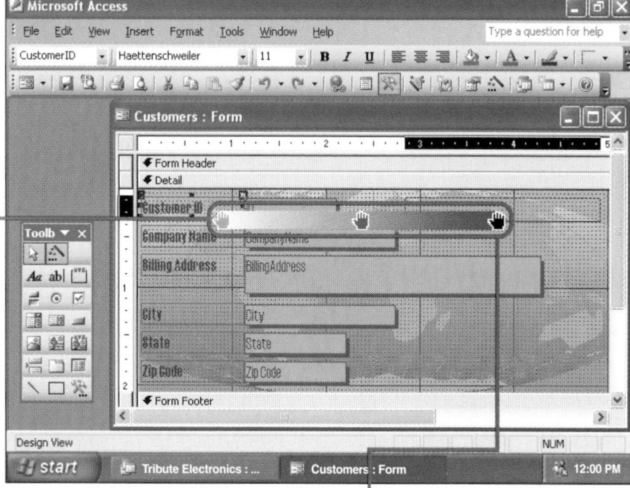

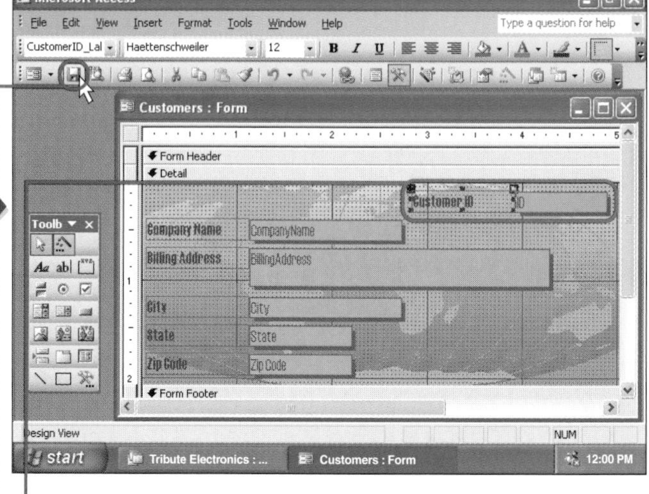

1 Display the form you want to change in the Design view. To change the view of a form, see page 152.

2 Click the control you want to move. Handles (■) appear around the control.

3 Position the mouse over the border of the control (changes to) and then drag the control to a new location on the form.

■ In this example, the label and corresponding text box appear in the new location.

4 Click to save your change.

■ To move a label or text box individually, perform steps **1** to **3**, except position the mouse over the large handle (■) at the top left corner of the control in step **3** (changes to).

Tip

How can I quickly resize a label to fit its contents?

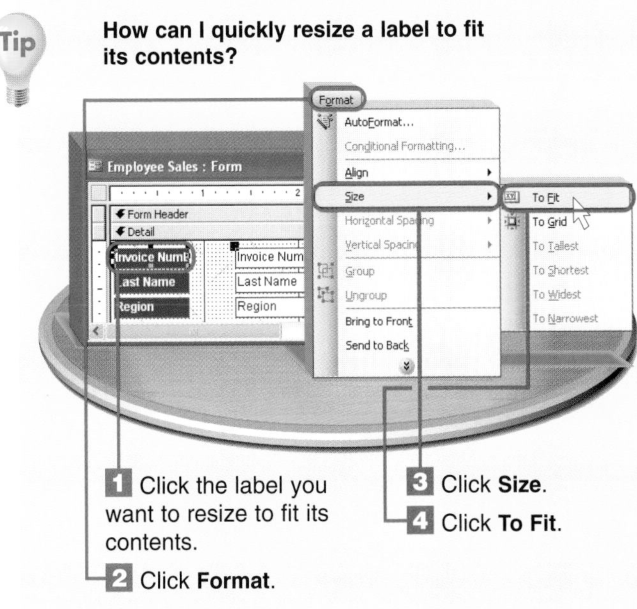

1 Click the label you want to resize to fit its contents.

2 Click **Format**.

3 Click **Size**.

4 Click **To Fit**.

Tip

How can I make small changes to the size of a control?

To make small changes to the size of a control, click the control you want to resize and then press and hold down the 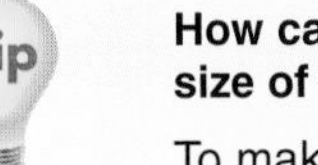 key as you press the ↑, ↓, ← or → key.

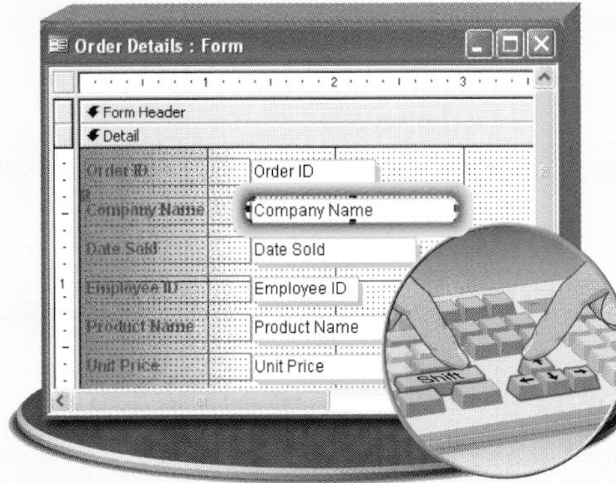

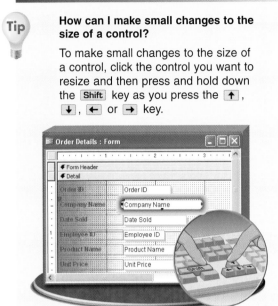

RESIZE A CONTROL

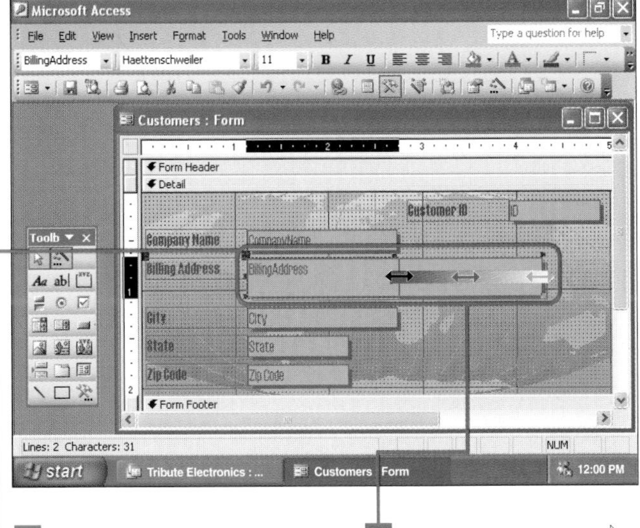

1 Display the form you want to change in the Design view. To change the view of a form, see page 152.

2 Click the control you want to resize. Handles (■) appear around the control.

3 Position the mouse over a handle (pointer changes to ↔, ↕, ↘ or ↗) and then drag the handle until the control is the size you want.

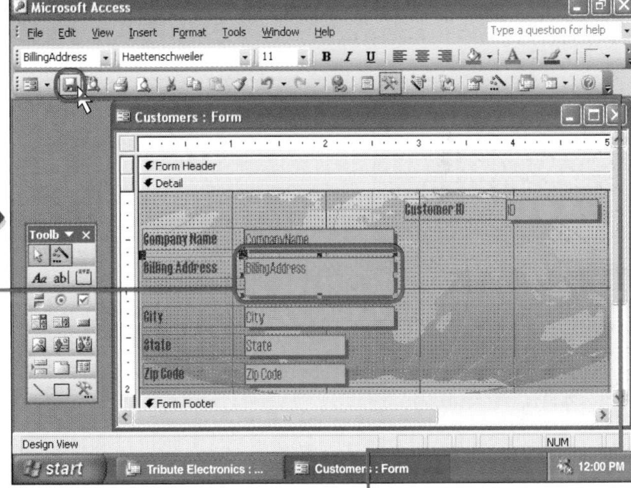

■ The control appears in the new size.

4 Click the save button to save your change.

DELETE A CONTROL

You can delete a control you no longer want to appear on a form.

A control is an item on a form, such as a label that displays a field name or a text box that displays data from a field.

DELETE A CONTROL

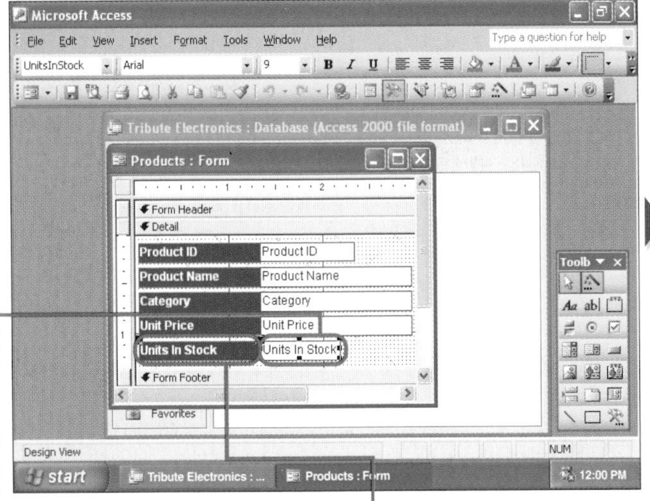

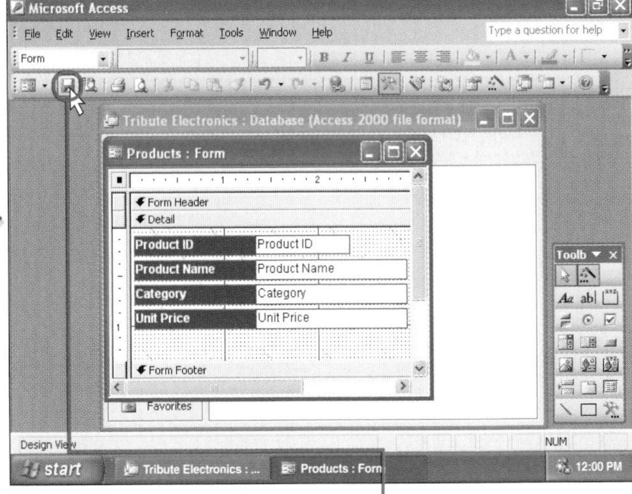

1 Display the form you want to change in the Design view. To change the view of a form, see page 152.

2 To delete a text box and its corresponding label, click the text box. Handles (■) appear around the text box.

■ To delete only a label, click the label. Handles (■) appear around the label.

3 Press the Delete key.

■ In this example, the text box and its corresponding label disappear.

4 Click 💾 to save your change.

CHANGE THE SIZE OF A FORM

You can change the size of an entire form. Increasing the size of a form can give you more room to add information such as a new field or a picture.

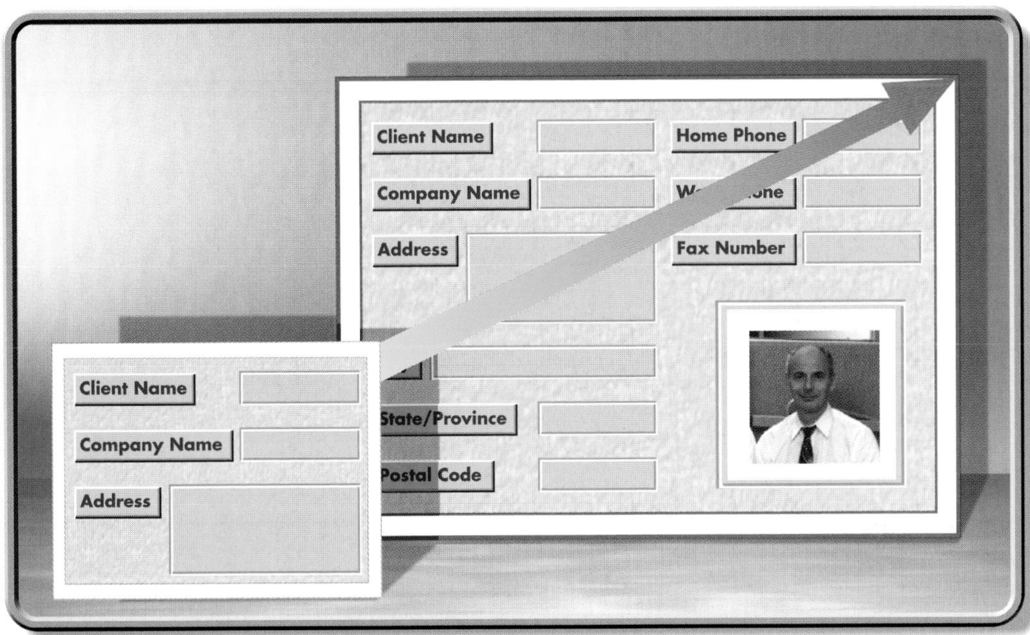

CHANGE THE SIZE OF A FORM

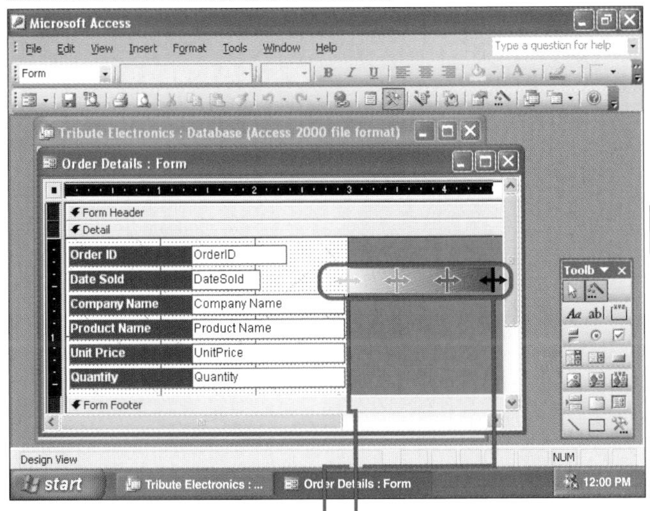

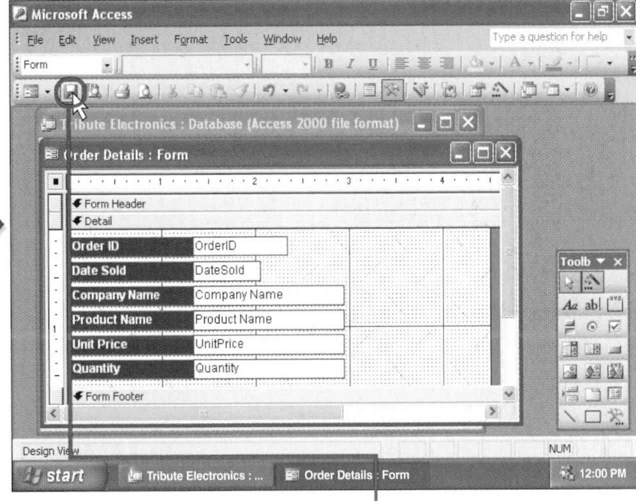

1 Display the form you want to change in the Design view. To change the view of a form, see page 152.

2 Position the mouse ↖ over the right or bottom edge of the form (↖ changes to ✛ or ✛).

3 Drag the edge of the form to the size you want.

■ The form changes to the new size.

4 Click 💾 to save your change.

ADD A FIELD

You can add a field to a form when you want the form to display additional information.

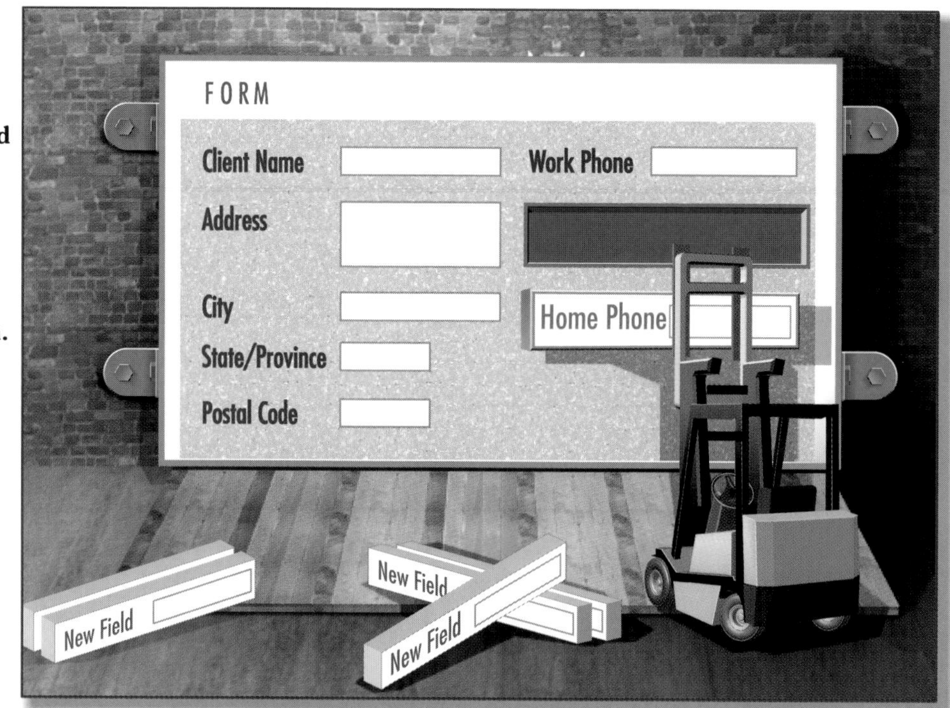

For example, you may want to add a Telephone Number field to a form that displays customer addresses.

Adding a field to a form is useful if you did not include all the fields from a table when you created a form.

ADD A FIELD

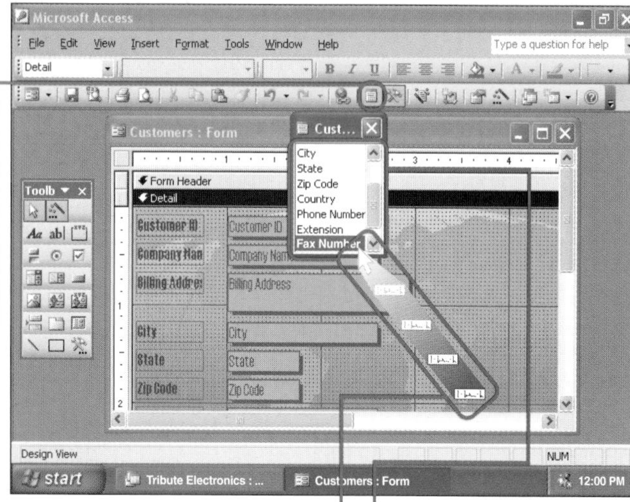

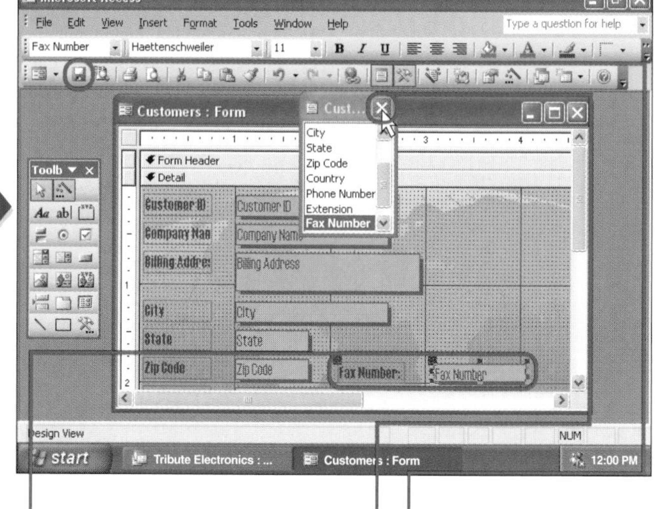

1 Display the form you want to change in the Design view. To change the view of a form, see page 152.

2 Click [icon] to display a list of fields from the table you used to create the form.

3 Position the mouse over the field you want to add to your form.

4 Drag the field to where you want the field to appear on your form.

■ The label and corresponding text box for the field appear on your form.

Note: To move or resize the label or text box, see page 154.

5 Click [icon] to save your change.

6 To hide the box displaying the list of fields, click [icon].

ADD A LABEL

You can add a label that you want to appear for each record on a form. Labels are useful for displaying important information.

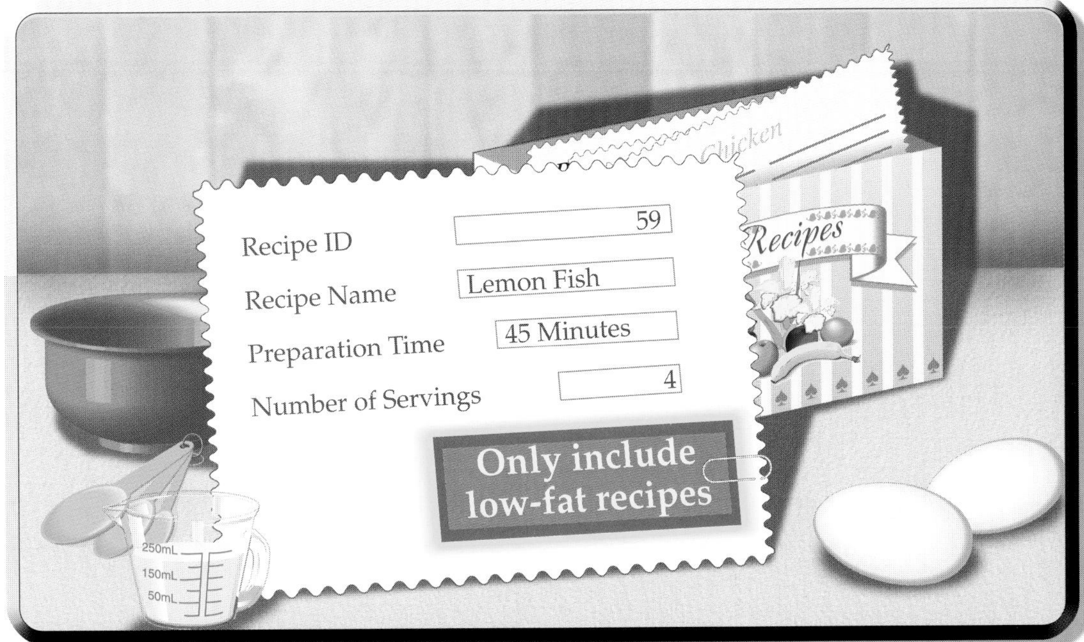

ADD A LABEL

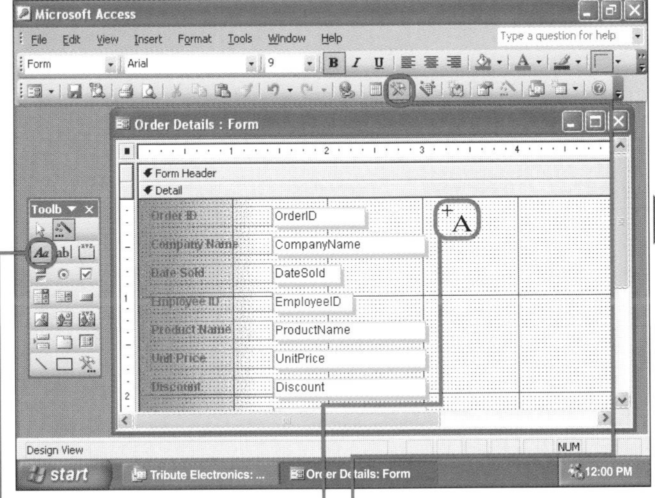

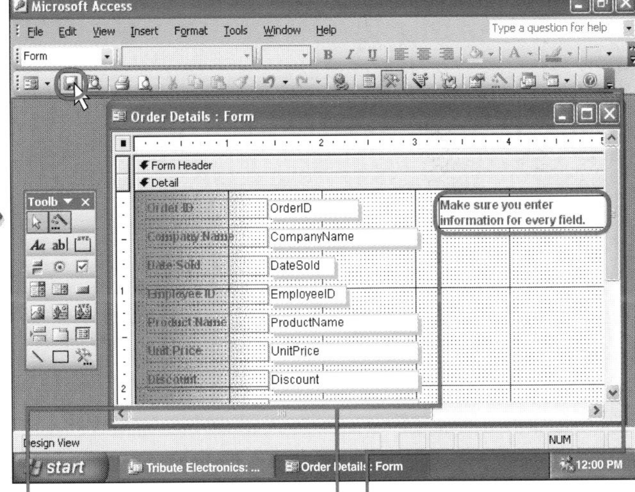

1 Display the form you want to change in the Design view. To change the view of a form, see page 152.

2 Click [Aa] on the Toolbox toolbar to add a label to your form.

■ If the Toolbox toolbar is not displayed, click [toolbox] to display the toolbar.

3 Click the location on your form where you want the top left corner of the label to appear.

4 Type the text for the label and then press the Enter key.

Note: If the Error Checking button ([◇]) appears beside the label, click the button and then click ***Ignore Error*** *to remove the button from your screen.*

5 Click [save] to save your change.

Note: To move or resize the label, see page 154.

■ To delete a label from a form, click the label and then press the Delete key.

CHANGE LABEL TEXT

You can change the text displayed in a label to make the label more descriptive.

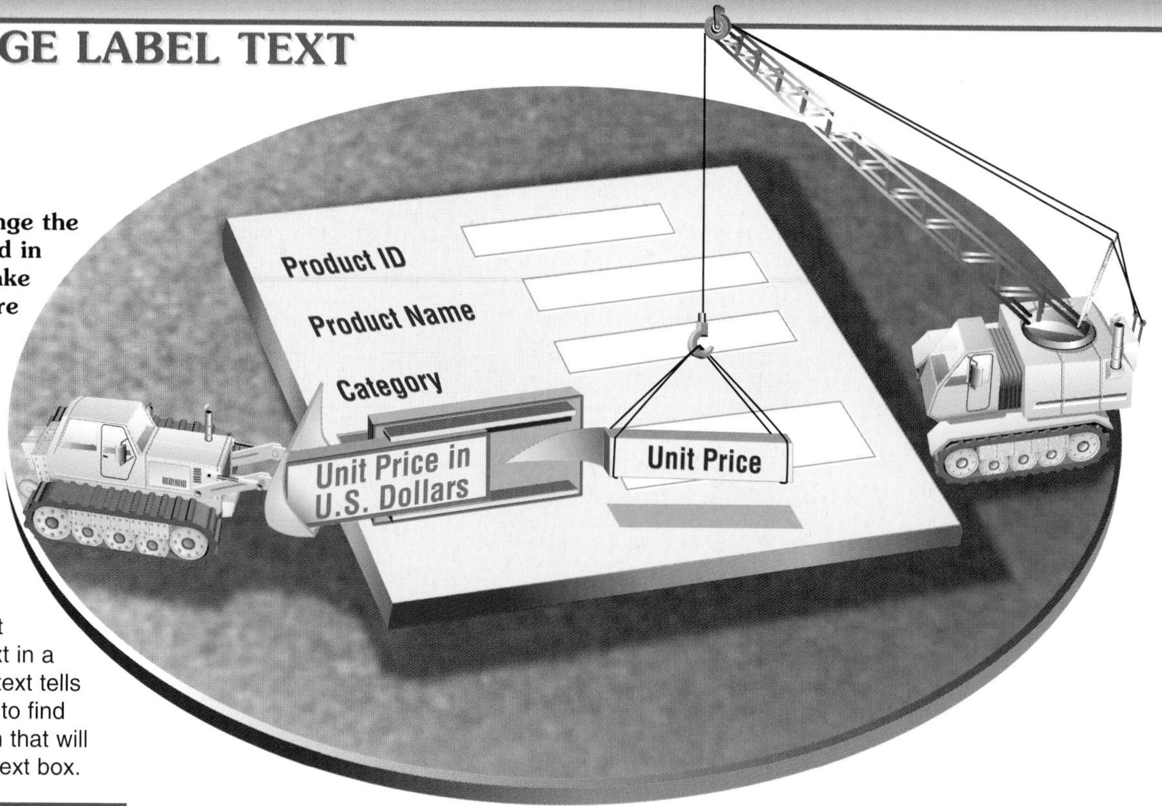

You should not change the text in a text box. This text tells Access where to find the information that will appear in the text box.

CHANGE LABEL TEXT

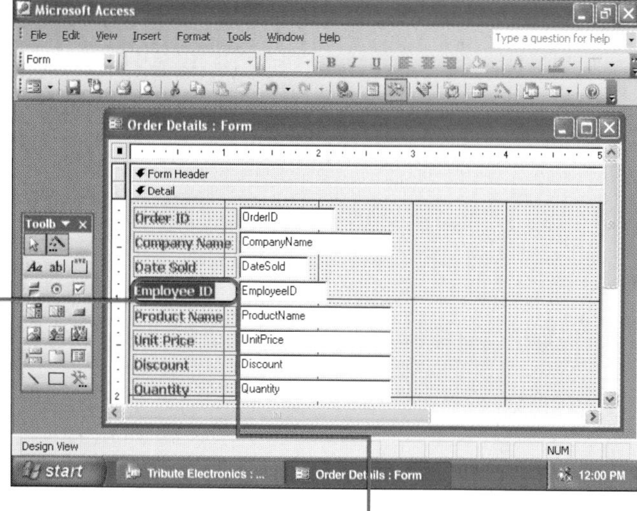

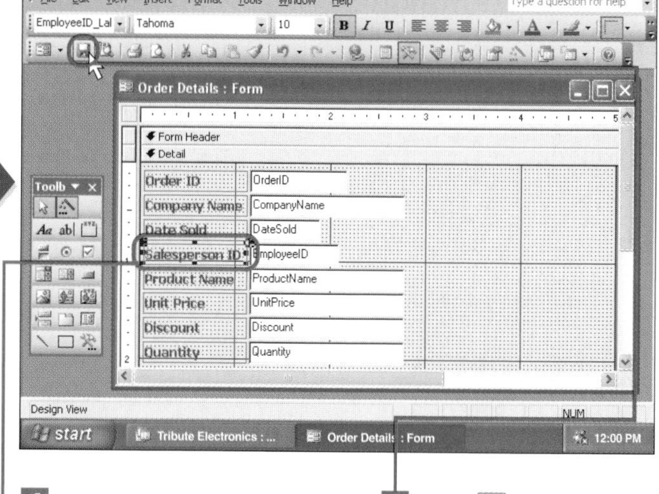

1 Display the form you want to change in the Design view. To change the view of a form, see page 152.

2 Click the label you want to change.

3 To select all the text in the label, drag the mouse ⌶ over the text until you highlight all the text.

4 Type the new text for the label and then press the **Enter** key.

5 Click 🖫 to save your change.

BOLD, ITALICIZE OR UNDERLINE DATA

You can bold, italicize or underline data on a form to emphasize information.

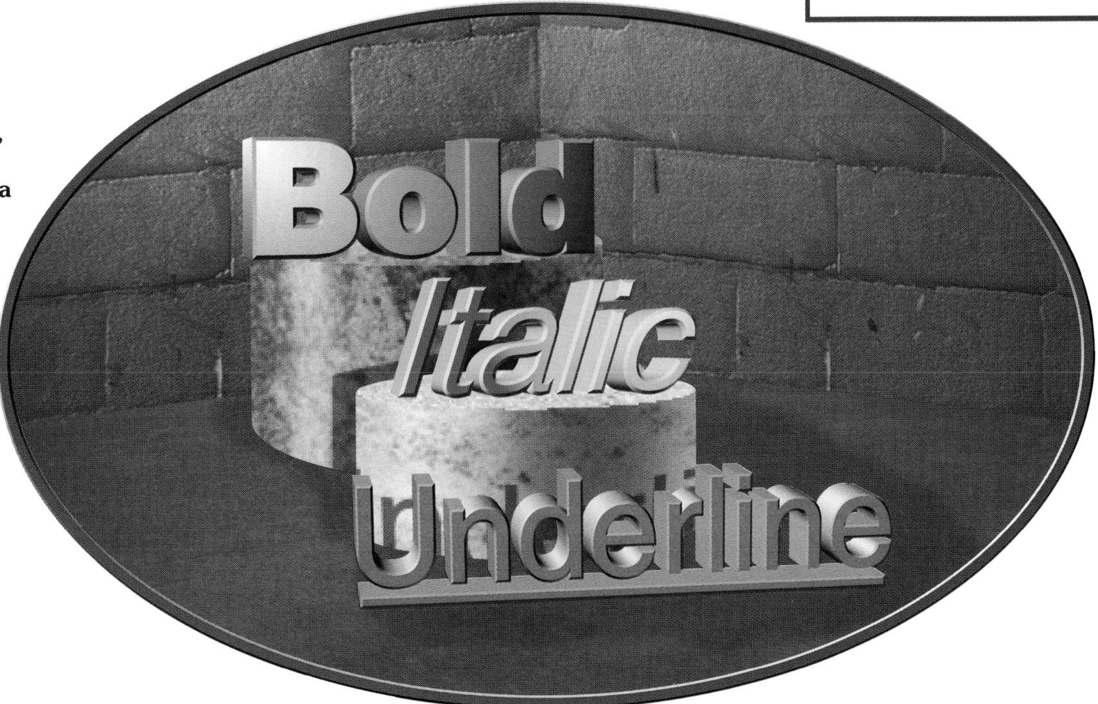

BOLD, ITALICIZE OR UNDERLINE DATA

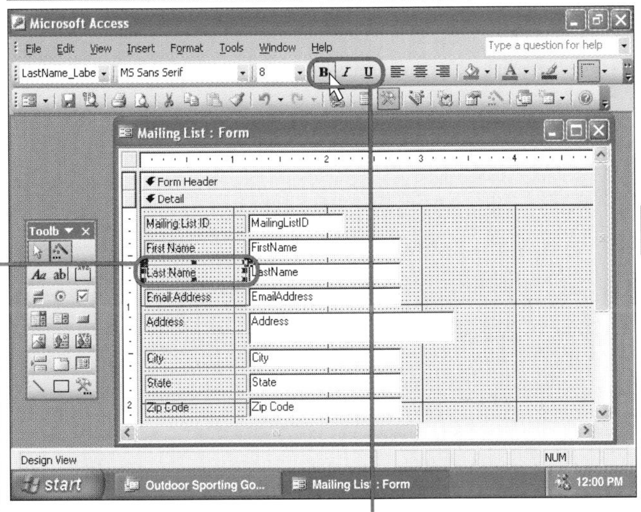

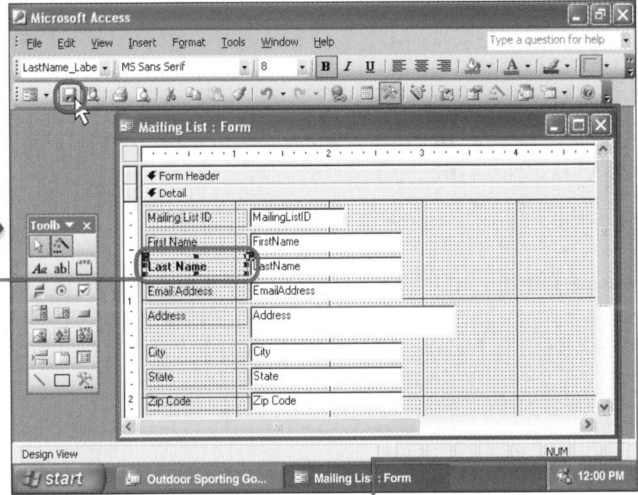

1 Display the form you want to change in the Design view. To change the view of a form, see page 152.

2 Click the control that displays the data you want to bold, italicize or underline.

3 Click one of the following buttons.

- B Bold
- I Italic
- U Underline

■ The data in the control appears in the new style.

Note: If the control is not large enough to display all the data, you can increase the size of the control. To resize a control, see page 155.

4 Click the save button to save your change.

■ To remove a bold, italic or underline style from data, repeat steps 1 to 4.

CHANGE THE FONT OF DATA

You can change the font of data in a control to enhance the appearance of a form.

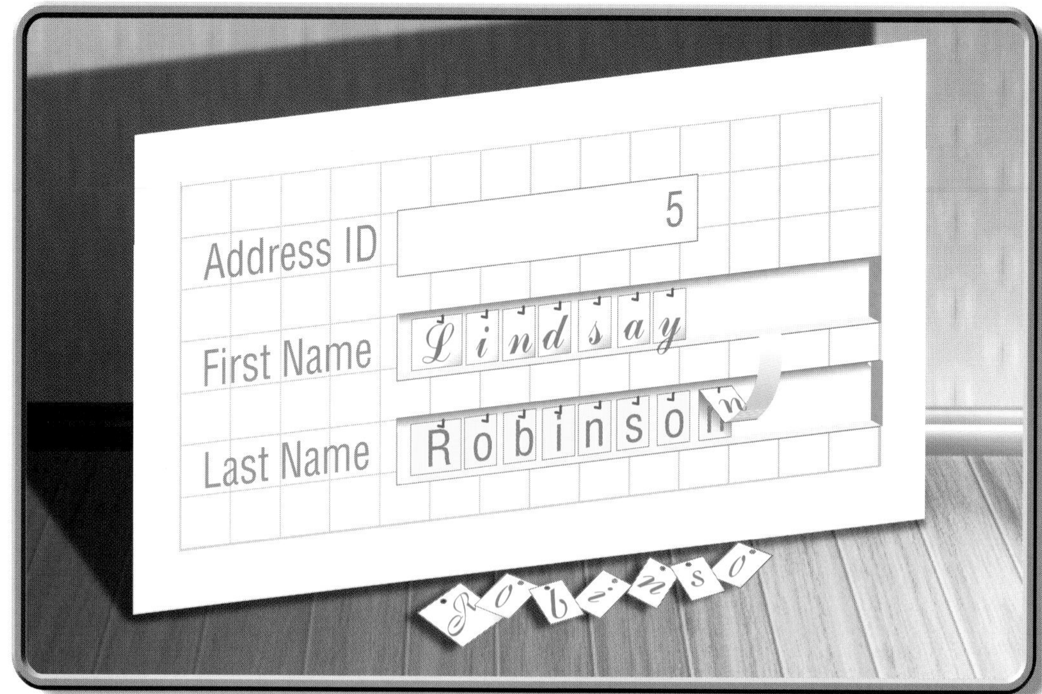

A control is an item on a form, such as a label that displays a field name or a text box that displays data from a field.

CHANGE THE FONT OF DATA

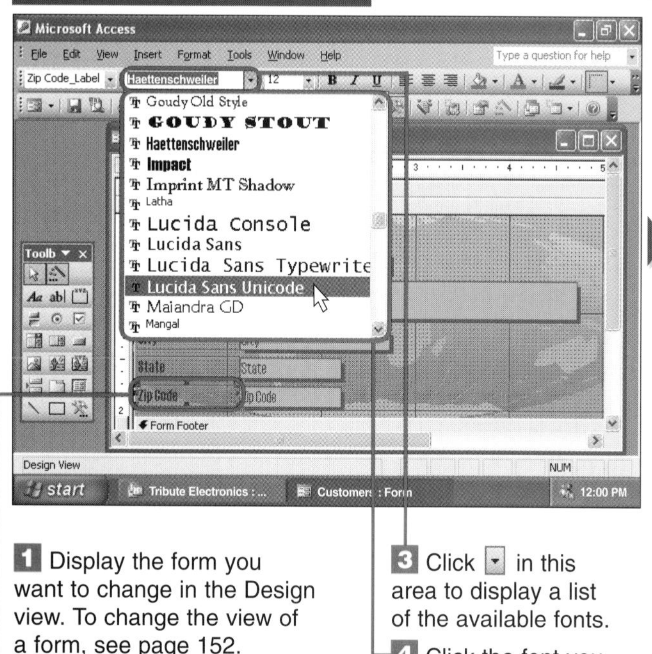

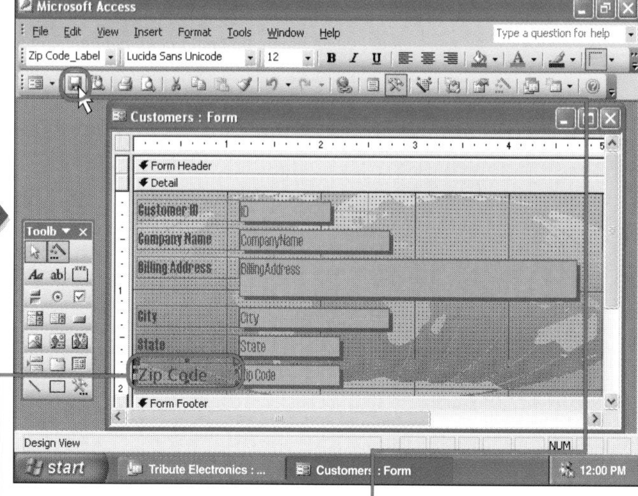

1 Display the form you want to change in the Design view. To change the view of a form, see page 152.

2 Click the control that displays the data you want to change to a different font.

3 Click ▾ in this area to display a list of the available fonts.

4 Click the font you want to use.

■ The data changes to the font you selected.

Note: If the control is not large enough to display all the data, you can increase the size of the control. To resize a control, see page 155.

5 Click 💾 to save your change.

CHANGE THE SIZE OF DATA

You can increase or decrease the size of data in a control.

Access measures the size of data in points. There are 72 points in an inch.

A control is an item on a form, such as a label that displays a field name or a text box that displays data from a field.

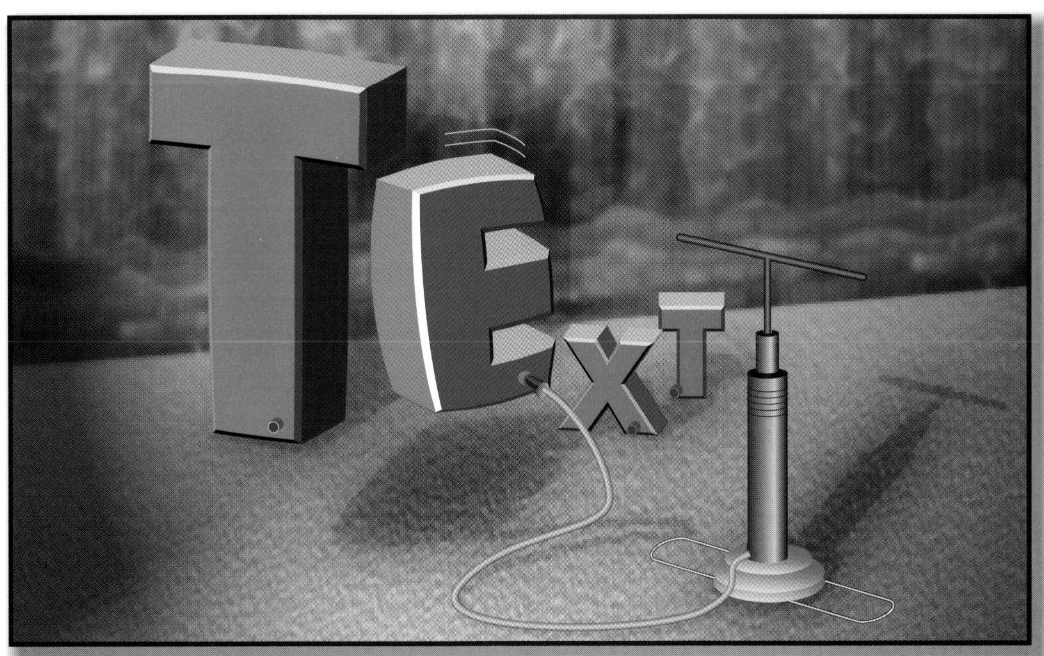

CHANGE THE SIZE OF DATA

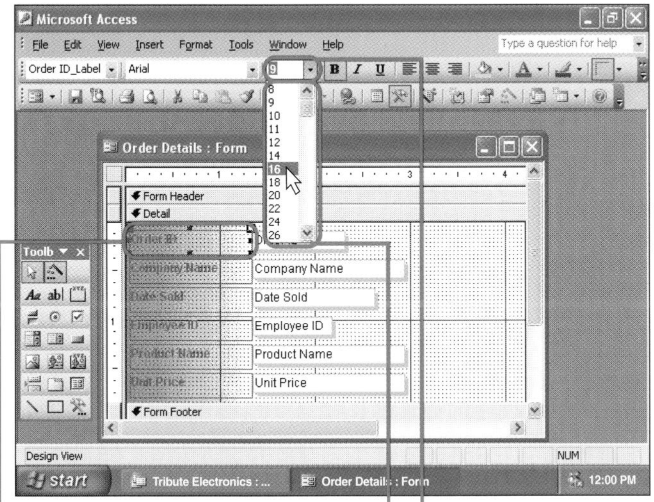

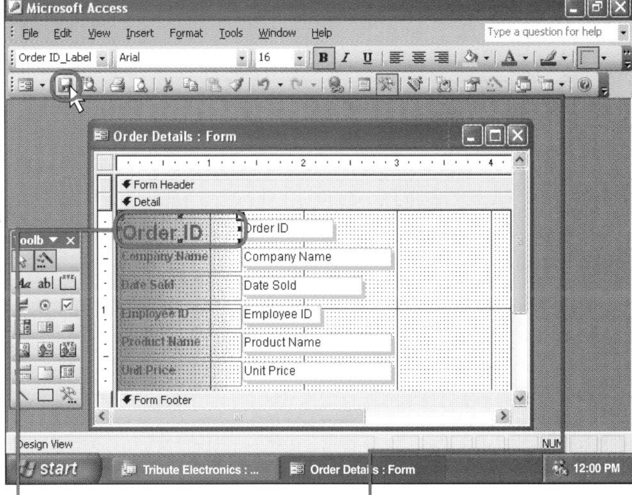

1 Display the form you want to change in the Design view. To change the view of a form, see page 152.

2 Click the control that displays the data you want to change to a new size.

3 Click ▾ in this area to display a list of the available sizes.

4 Click the size you want to use.

■ The data changes to the size you selected.

Note: If the control is not large enough to display all the data, you can increase the size of the control. To resize a control, see page 155.

5 Click 💾 to save your change.

CHANGE THE COLOR OF A CONTROL

You can change the background color and text color of a control to emphasize information on a form.

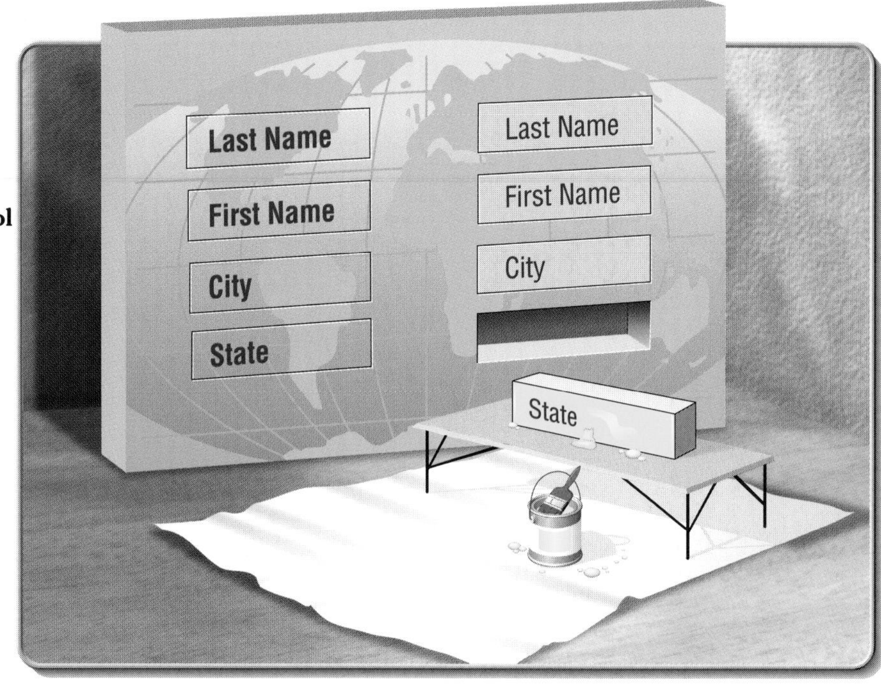

Make sure you select background and text colors that work well together. For example, red text on a blue background can be difficult to read.

A control is an item on a form, such as a label that displays a field name or a text box that displays data from a field.

CHANGE THE BACKGROUND COLOR

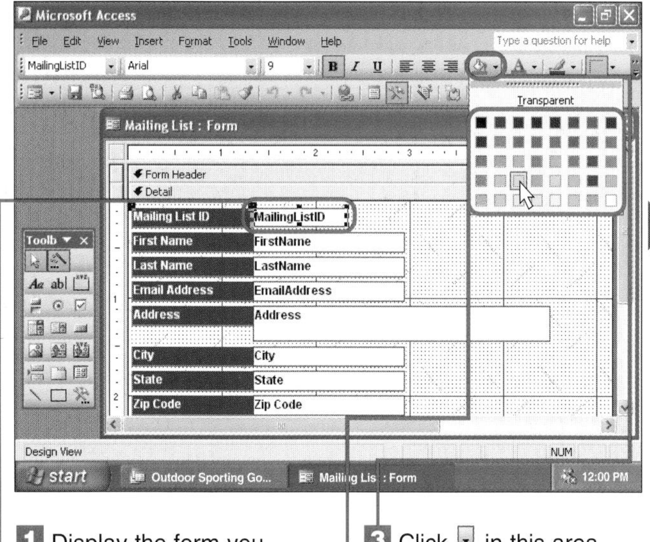

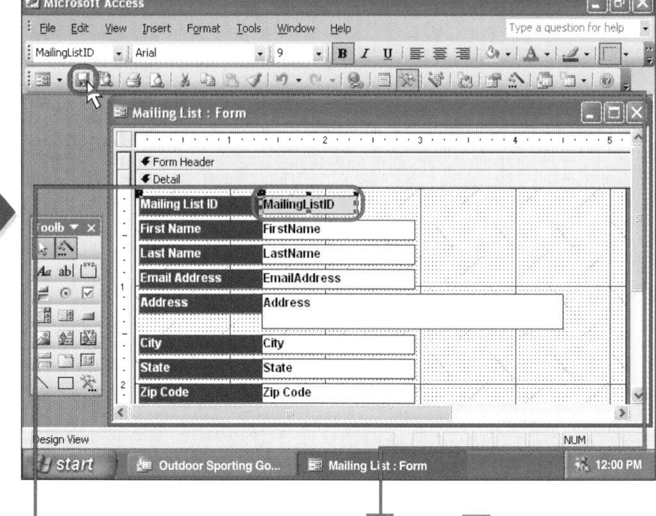

1 Display the form you want to change in the Design view. To change the view of a form, see page 152.

2 Click the control you want to change to a different background color.

3 Click ▾ in this area to display the available background colors.

4 Click the background color you want to use.

■ The control displays the background color you selected.

5 Click 💾 to save your change.

Can I change the color of several controls at once?

Yes. To select each control you want to change to a different color, hold down the Shift key as you click each control. Handles (■) appear around each control you select. To select the background color or text color you want to use, perform steps 3 and 4 below.

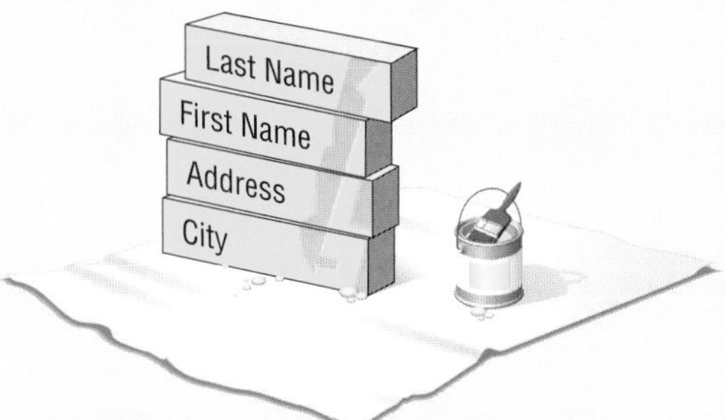

How can I quickly reapply the last color I used?

The Fill Color (🖌) and Font Color (A) buttons show the last background and text color you used. To reapply the last background or text color you used, click the control you want to change and then click the Fill Color (🖌) or Font Color (A) button.

CHANGE THE TEXT COLOR

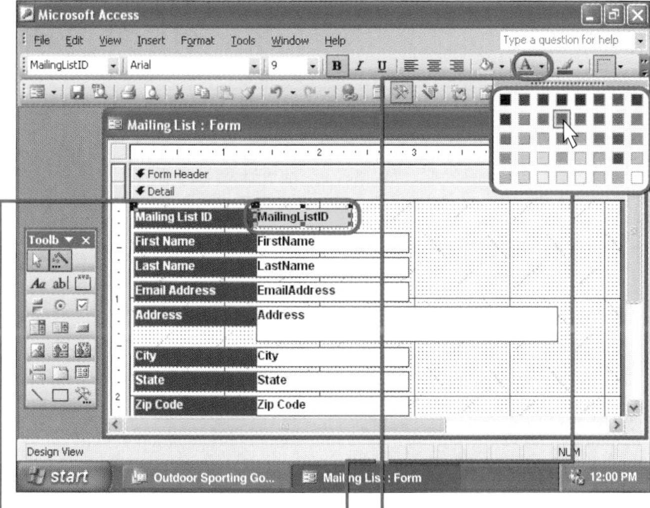

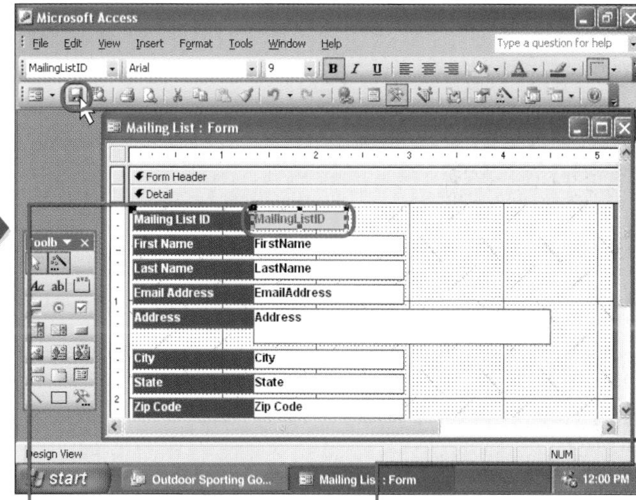

1 Display the form you want to change in the Design view. To change the view of a form, see page 152.

2 Click the control that displays the text you want to change to a different color.

3 Click ▾ in this area to display the available text colors.

4 Click the text color you want to use.

■ The text in the control displays the color you selected.

5 Click 💾 to save your change.

CHANGE THE ALIGNMENT OF DATA

You can align data on a form in three different ways.

When a form is displayed in the Form view, Access automatically left aligns text and right aligns numbers and dates on the form.

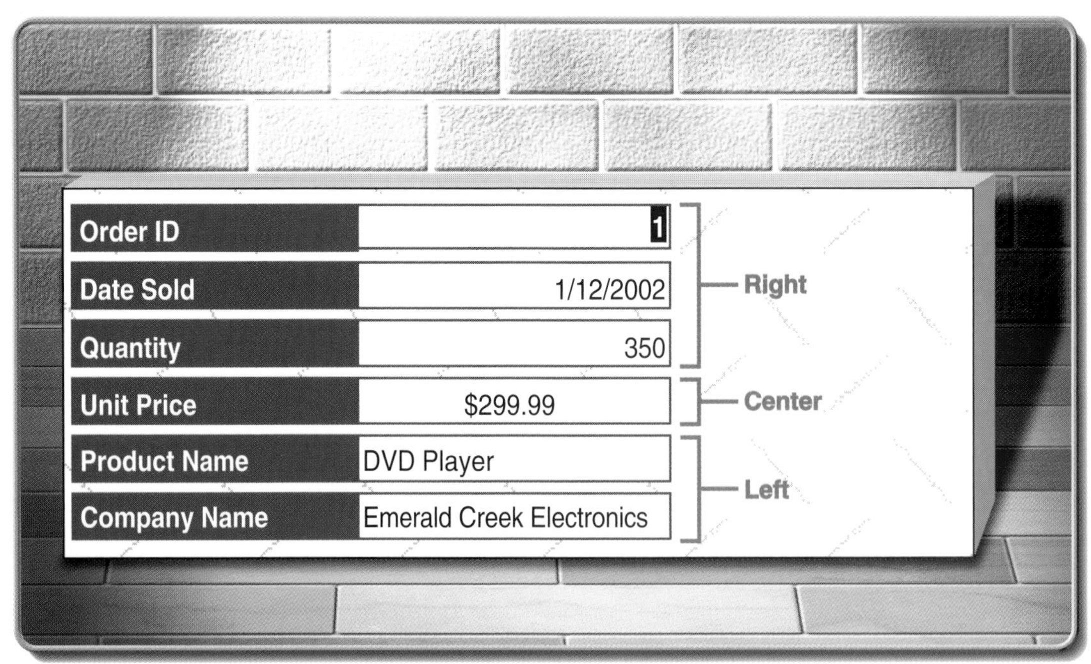

Order ID
1
Date Sold
1/12/2002
Quantity
350
Right
Unit Price
$299.99
Center
Product Name
DVD Player
Company Name
Emerald Creek Electronics
Left

CHANGE THE ALIGNMENT OF DATA

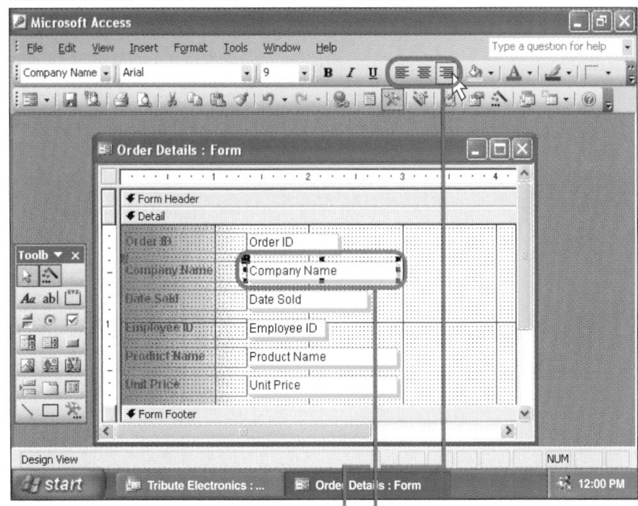

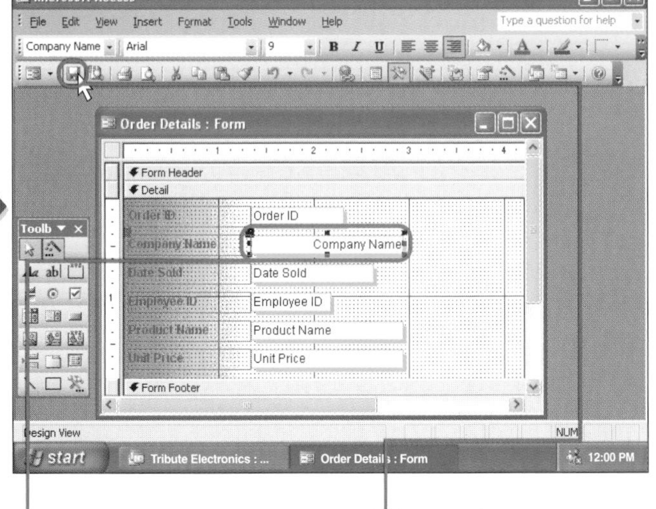

1 Display the form you want to change in the Design view. To change the view of a form, see page 152.

Note: When a form is displayed in the Design view, all data initially appears left aligned.

2 Click the control that displays the data you want to align differently.

3 Click one of the following buttons.

- Left align
- Center
- Right align

■ The data in the control appears in the alignment you selected.

4 Click to save your change.

UNDO CHANGES

Access remembers the last changes you made to a form. If you regret these changes, you can cancel them by using the Undo feature.

Access can only undo changes you made since you last opened the form.

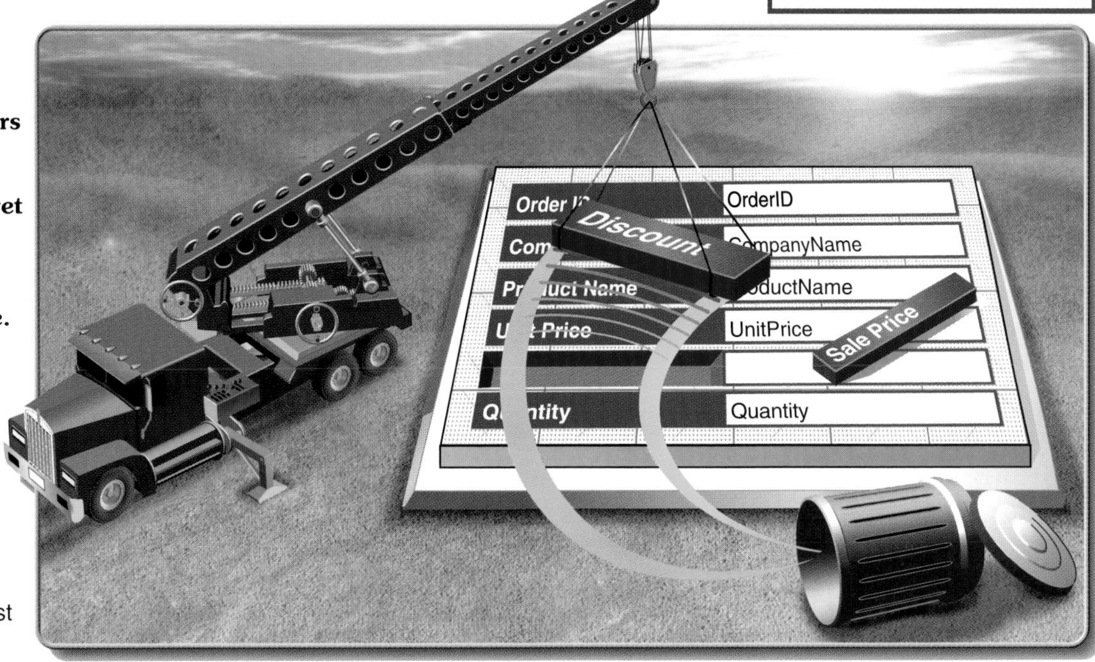

UNDO CHANGES

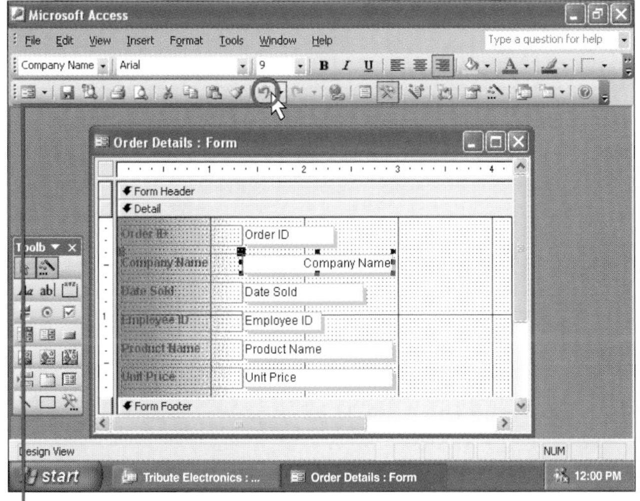

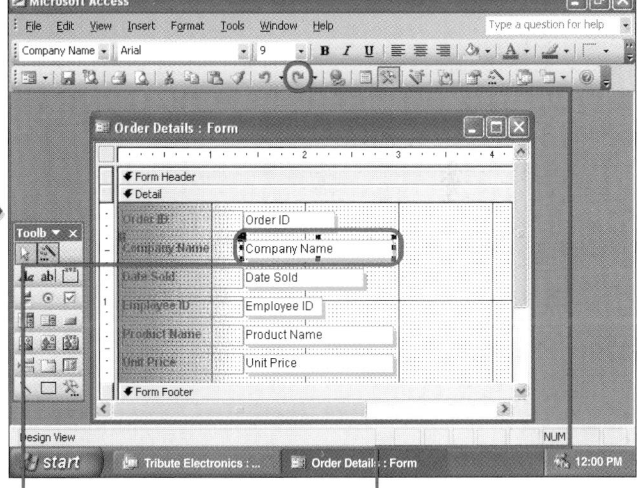

1 When working with a form in the Design view, click ↶ to undo the last change you made to your form.

Note: To change the view of a form, see page 152.

■ Access cancels the last change you made to your form in the Design view.

■ You can repeat step **1** to cancel previous changes you made to your form in the Design view.

■ To reverse the results of using the Undo feature, click ↷.

ADD A PICTURE

You can add a picture to a form to make the form more appealing or to help illustrate your data.

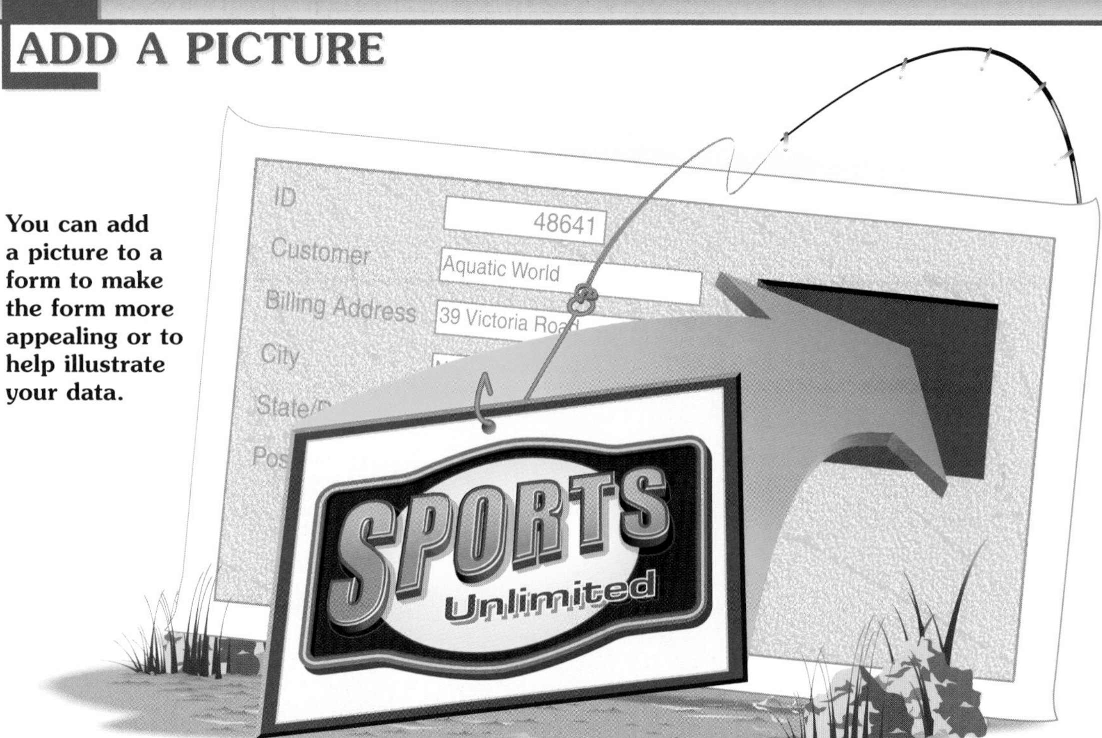

You can add a picture such as your company logo, a colorful design or a picture of your products.

If you want to display a different picture for each record, such as a picture of each employee, see page 102.

ADD A PICTURE

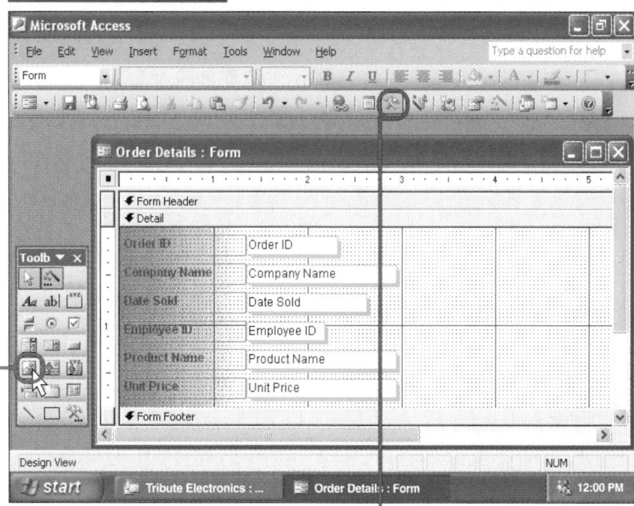

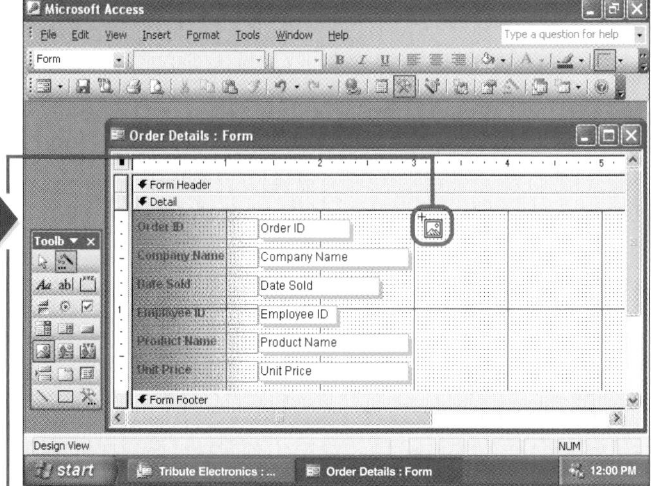

1 Display the form you want to add a picture to in the Design view. To change the view of a form, see page 152.

2 Click on the Toolbox toolbar to add a picture to your form.

■ If the Toolbox toolbar is not displayed, click to display the toolbar.

3 Click the location on your form where you want the top left corner of the picture to appear.

■ The Insert Picture dialog box appears.

Where can I obtain pictures that I can add to my forms?

You can use a drawing program to create your own pictures or use a scanner to scan existing pictures into your computer. You can also buy a collection of pictures, called clip art, at stores that sell computer software. Many pages on the Web also offer pictures that you can use.

How can I delete a picture I added to a form?

To delete a picture you no longer want to appear on a form, click the picture and then press the Delete key. Access will remove the picture from the form, but will not remove the original picture from your computer.

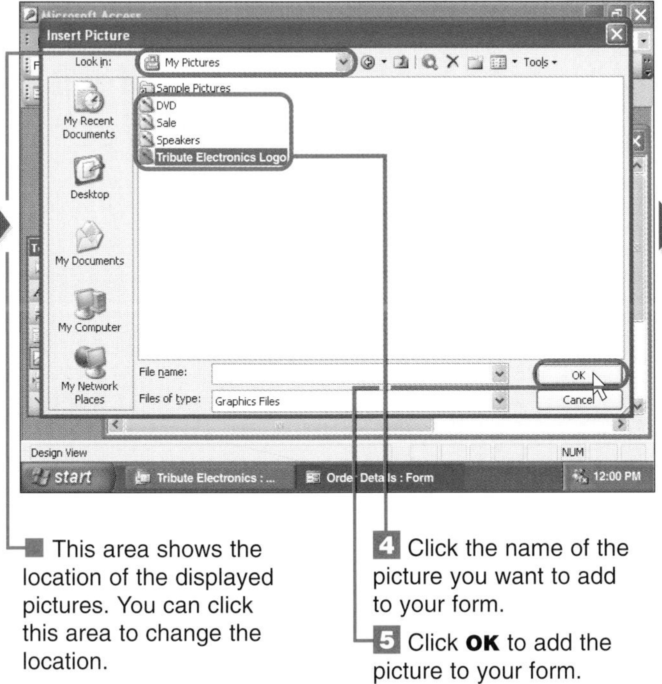

- This area shows the location of the displayed pictures. You can click this area to change the location.

4 Click the name of the picture you want to add to your form.

5 Click **OK** to add the picture to your form.

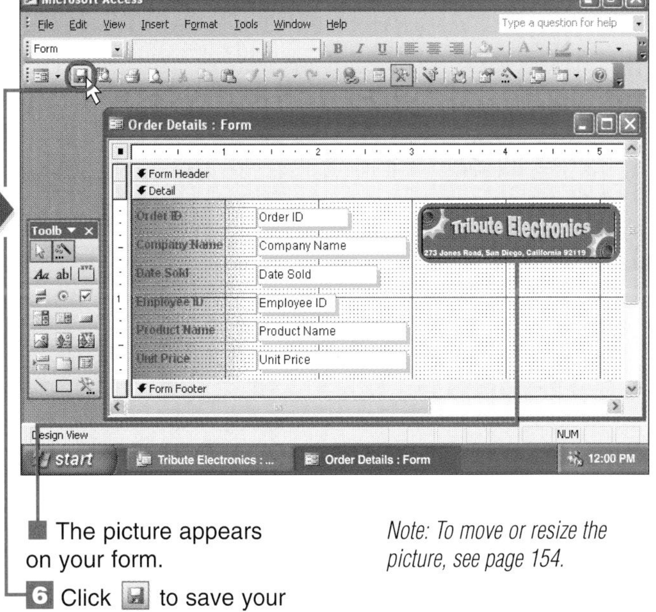

- The picture appears on your form.

6 Click the Save button to save your change.

Note: To move or resize the picture, see page 154.

APPLY CONDITIONAL FORMATTING

You can have Access apply special formatting to data in a field when the data meets a condition you specify. Applying conditional formatting to data in a field allows you to easily monitor data of interest.

For example, when the number of units in stock for a product falls below 10, you can have the number appear in red.

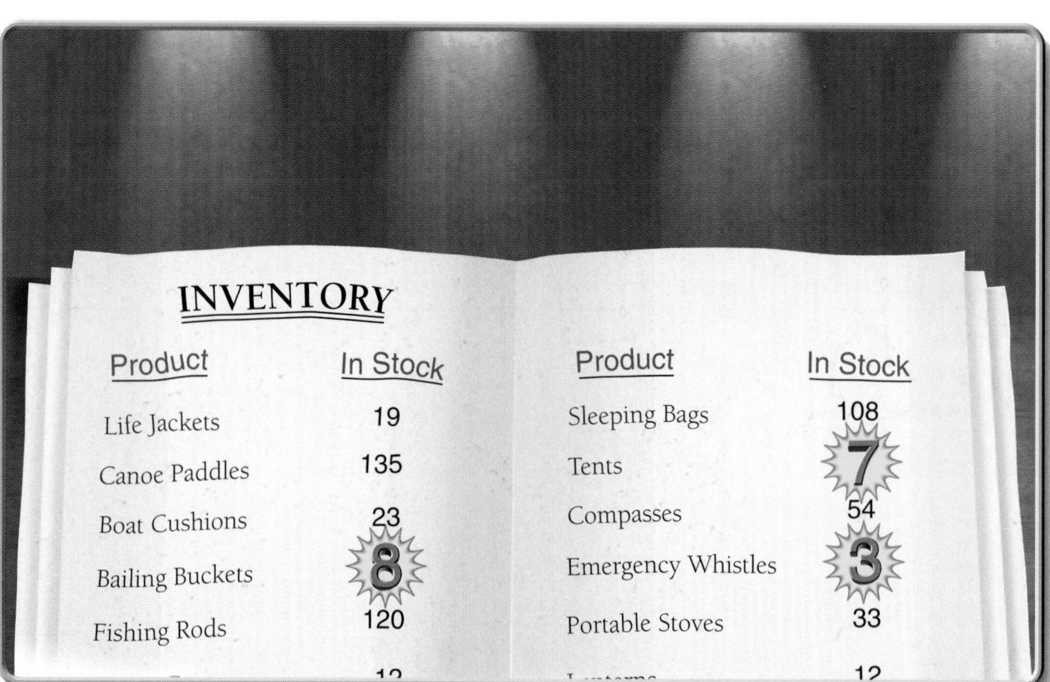

APPLY CONDITIONAL FORMATTING

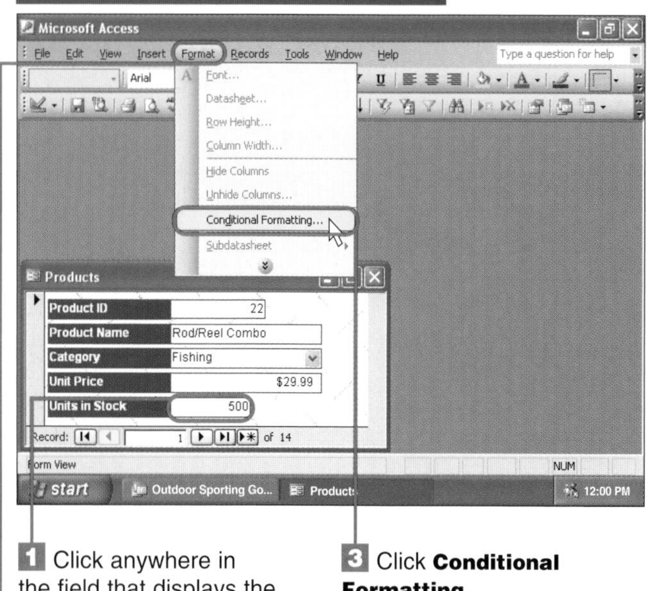

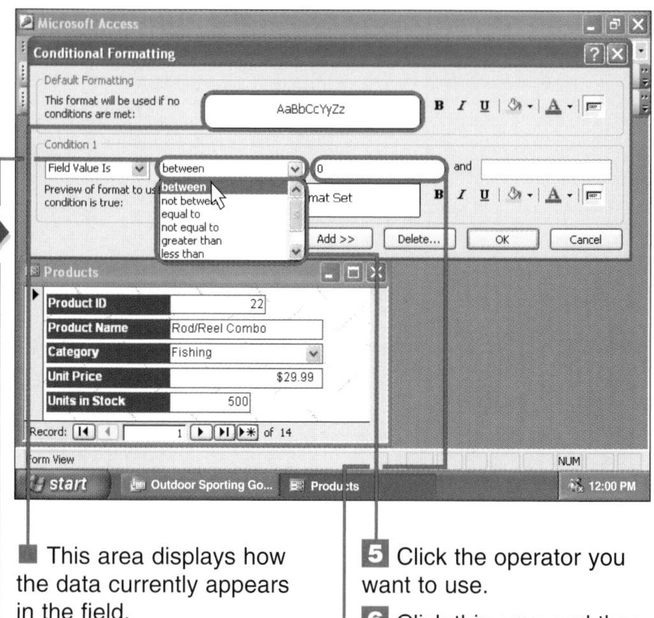

1 Click anywhere in the field that displays the data you want to apply conditional formatting to.

2 Click **Format**.

3 Click **Conditional Formatting**.

■ The Conditional Formatting dialog box appears.

■ This area displays how the data currently appears in the field.

4 Click this area to select the operator you want to use to specify the data you want to apply conditional formatting to.

5 Click the operator you want to use.

6 Click this area and then type the value that specifies the data you want to apply conditional formatting to.

What operators can I use?

Operator	Result
between 100 and 200	Formats data between 100 and 200.
not between 100 and 200	Formats data not between 100 and 200.
equal to 100	Formats data equal to 100.
not equal to 100	Formats data not equal to 100.
greater than 100	Formats data greater than 100.
less than 100	Formats data less than 100.
greater than or equal to 100	Formats data greater than or equal to 100.
less than or equal to 100	Formats data less than or equal to 100.

Tip

How do I remove conditional formatting from a field?

In the Conditional Formatting dialog box, click **Delete**. In the Delete Conditional Format dialog box that appears, click **Condition 1** (☐ changes to ☑) and then press the Enter key.

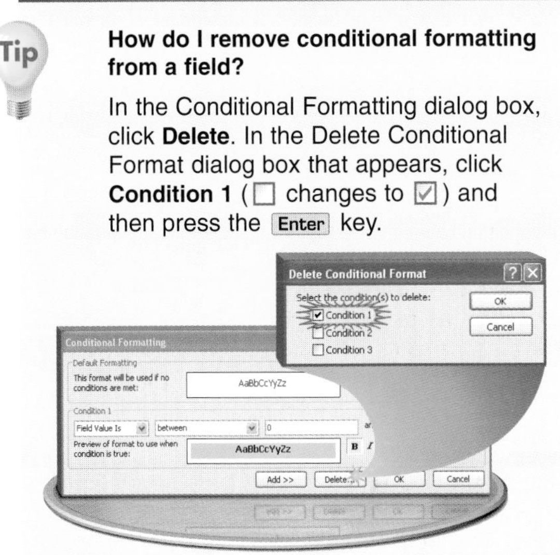

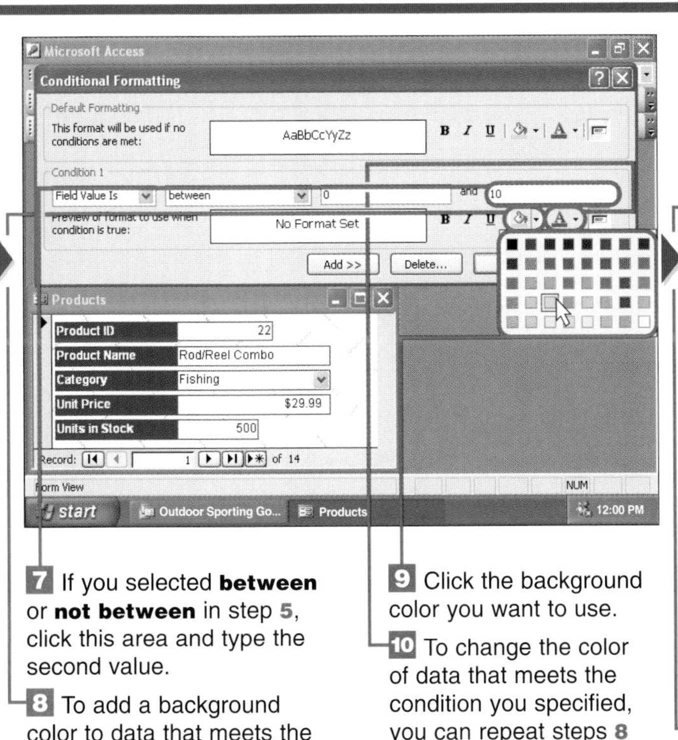

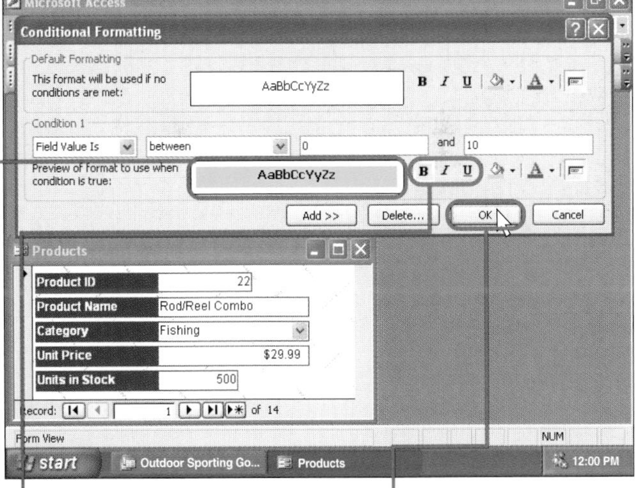

7 If you selected **between** or **not between** in step **5**, click this area and type the second value.

8 To add a background color to data that meets the condition you specified, click ▾ in this area.

9 Click the background color you want to use.

10 To change the color of data that meets the condition you specified, you can repeat steps **8** and **9** in this area.

11 To bold (**B**), italicize (*I*) or underline (U) data that meets the condition you specified, click the appropriate button.

■ This area displays how the data that meets the condition you specified will appear on your form.

12 Click **OK** to confirm your changes.

■ When data in the field meets the condition you specified, the data will display the format you specified.

APPLY AN AUTOFORMAT

You can apply an autoformat to quickly change the overall appearance of a form.

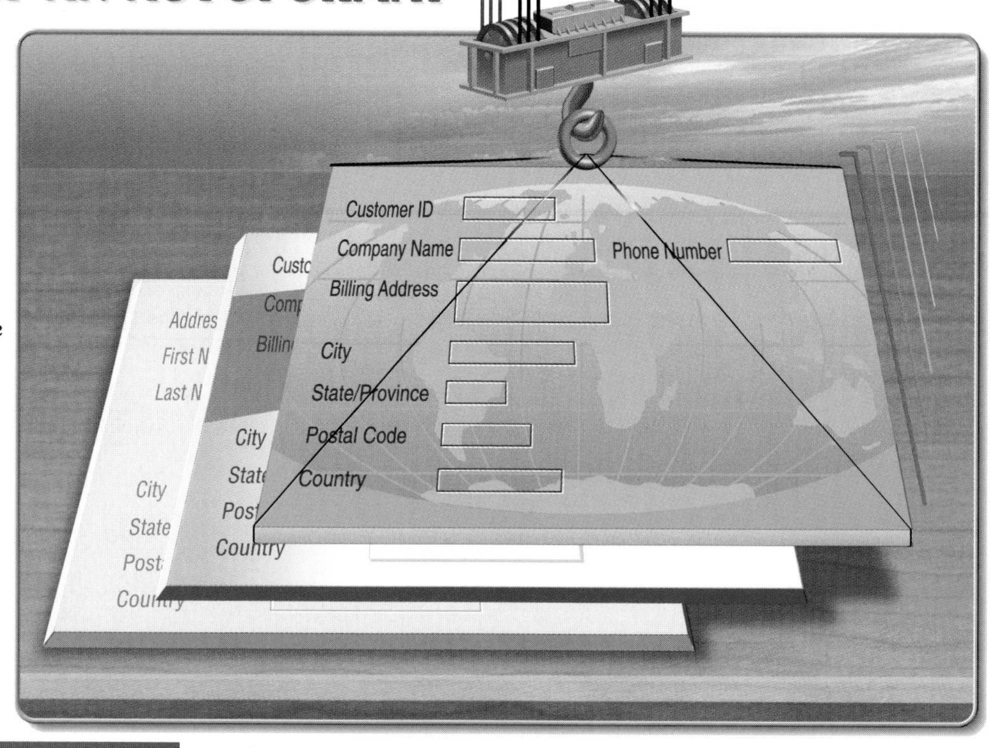

You may want to use the same autoformat for every form in your database to give your database a consistent appearance.

APPLY AN AUTOFORMAT

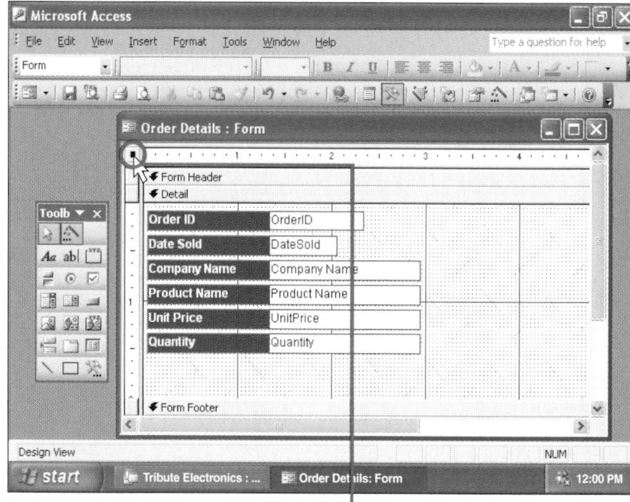

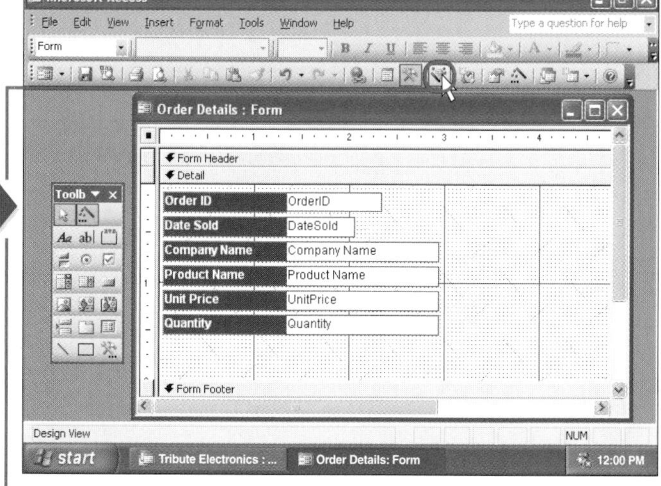

1 Display the form you want to change in the Design view. To change the view of a form, see page 152.

2 Click ▢ to select the form (▢ changes to ■).

3 Click ▢ to select an autoformat for the form.

■ The AutoFormat dialog box appears.

Why didn't my entire form change to the new autoformat?

If your form contains a subform, the appearance of the subform will not change when you apply an autoformat to the form. A subform displays information from a related table in your database. To apply an autoformat to a subform, open the subform as you would open any form and then perform the steps shown below. To open a form, see page 144.

Note: If your subform appears in the Datasheet layout, applying an autoformat to the subform will have no effect on the appearance of the subform.

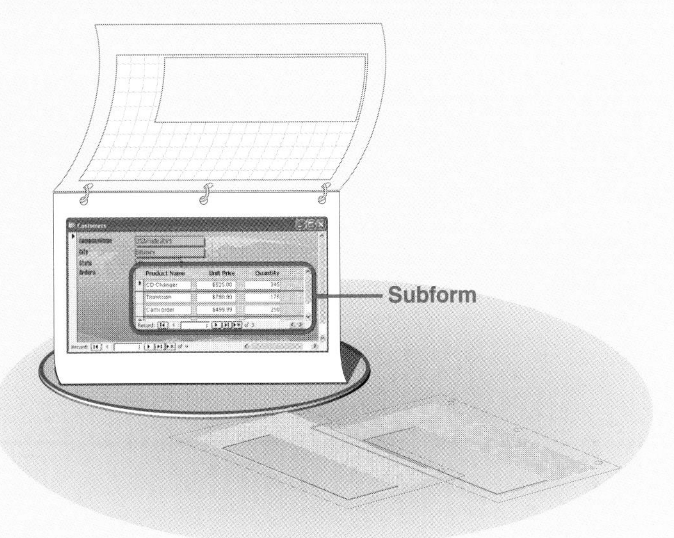

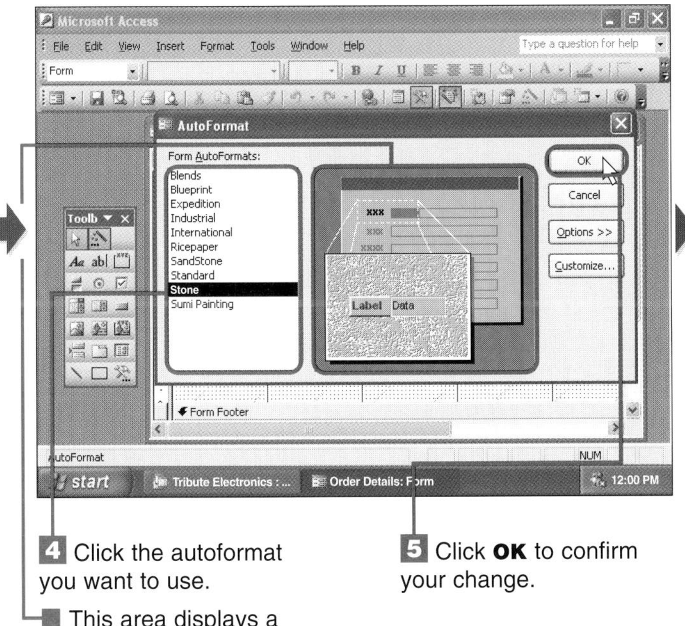

4 Click the autoformat you want to use.

■ This area displays a sample of the autoformat you selected.

5 Click **OK** to confirm your change.

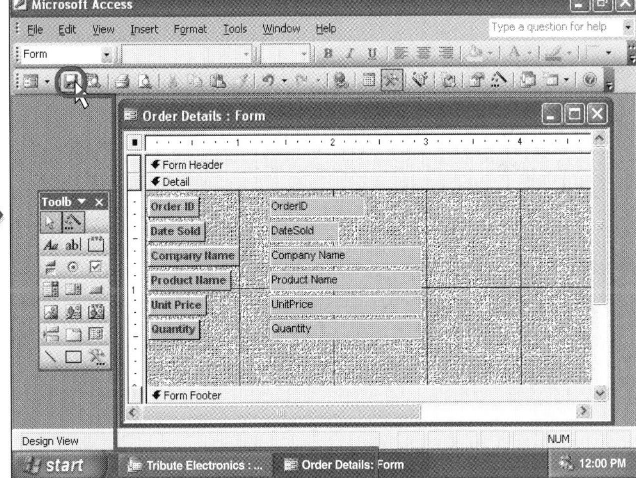

■ The form displays the new autoformat.

6 Click (save icon) to save your change.

Pages
Year Published
1990
1994
2001
400
315
360
4
Still Waters Run Deep
1996
375
5
The Tourist
2001
545
Julie Simak
906 Blue St.
Los Angeles, CA
90009
Harvey Carroll
146 Spectacular Rd.
Foster City, CA
Jeff Thomas
14 Memory Lane
Burbank, CA
91504
1 Spaceships in Orbit
5 The Tourist
8 The Magical Lilac Tree

CHAPTER 8

Find Data

Do you often need to find specific data in your database? In this chapter, you will learn how to sort, find, replace and filter data.

	Title	Year Published	Pages
	2001 360	2001	360
2	Escape from Reality	1990	400
3	Hugh's Haunted Castle	1994	315
4	Still Waters Run Deep	1996	375
	2001 545	2001	545
6	The Cowboy Invasion	1993	250
7	My Clandestine Ways	1991	325
	2001 425	2001	425

SORT RECORDS

You can change the order of records in a table, form or in the results of a query. Sorting records can help you find, organize and analyze data.

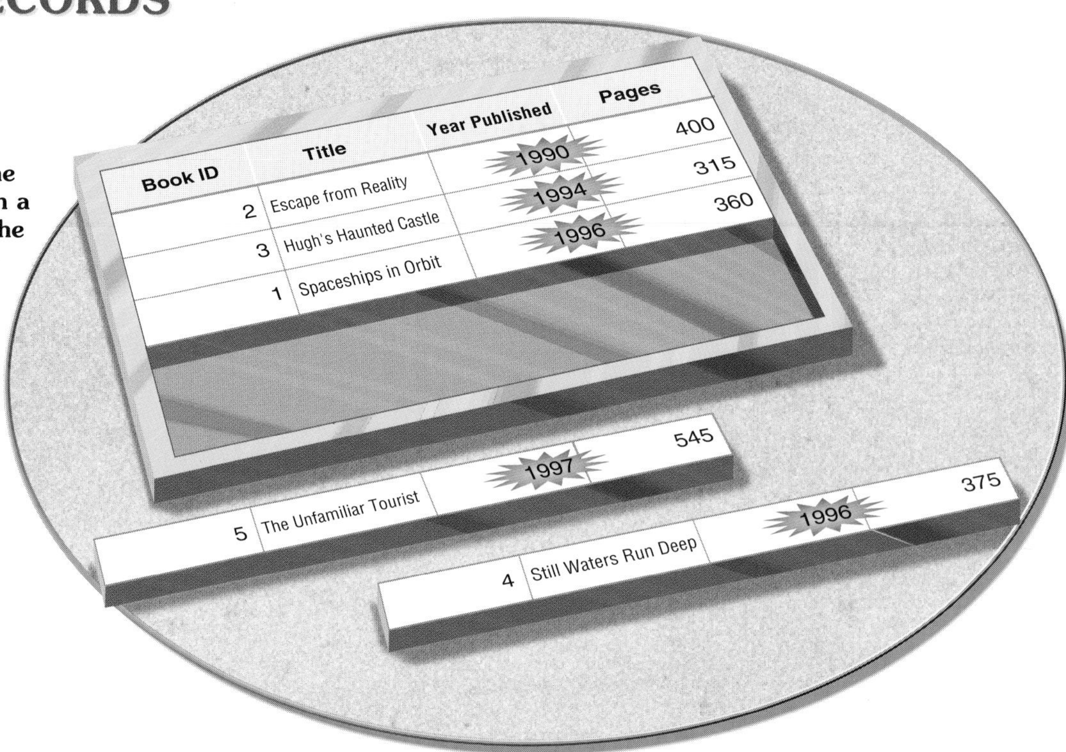

SORT RECORDS

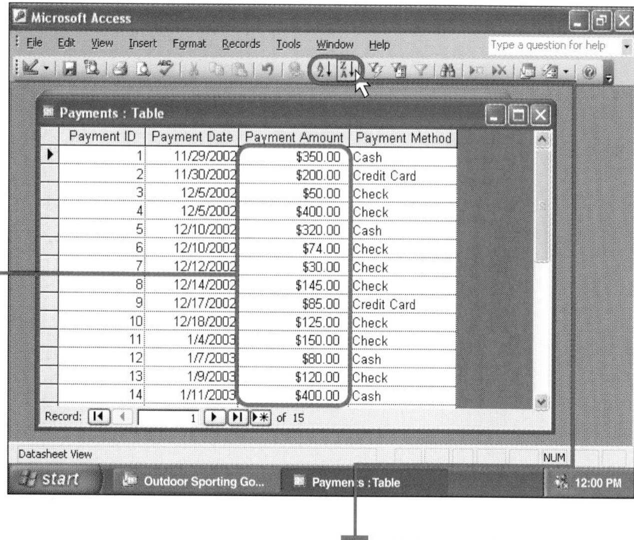

Payment ID	Payment Date	Payment Amount	Payment Method
1	11/29/2002	$350.00	Cash
2	11/30/2002	$200.00	Credit Card
3	12/5/2002	$50.00	Check
4	12/5/2002	$400.00	Check
5	12/10/2002	$320.00	Cash
6	12/10/2002	$74.00	Check
7	12/12/2002	$30.00	Check
8	12/14/2002	$145.00	Check
9	12/17/2002	$85.00	Credit Card
10	12/18/2002	$125.00	Check
11	1/4/2003	$150.00	Check
12	1/7/2003	$80.00	Cash
13	1/9/2003	$120.00	Check
14	1/11/2003	$400.00	Cash

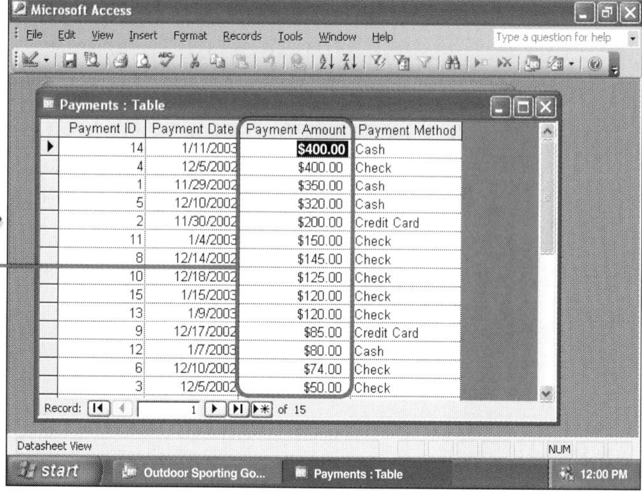

Payment ID	Payment Date	Payment Amount	Payment Method
14	1/11/2003	$400.00	Cash
4	12/5/2002	$400.00	Check
1	11/29/2002	$350.00	Cash
5	12/10/2002	$320.00	Cash
2	11/30/2002	$200.00	Credit Card
11	1/4/2003	$150.00	Check
8	12/14/2002	$145.00	Check
10	12/18/2002	$125.00	Check
15	1/15/2003	$120.00	Check
13	1/9/2003	$120.00	Check
9	12/17/2002	$85.00	Credit Card
12	1/7/2003	$80.00	Cash
6	12/10/2002	$74.00	Check
3	12/5/2002	$50.00	Check

SORT BY ONE FIELD

1 Click anywhere in the field you want to use to sort the records.

2 Click one of the following buttons.

- Sort A to Z, 1 to 9
- Sort Z to A, 9 to 1

■ The records appear in the new order. In this example, the records are sorted by payment amount.

How do I remove a sort from my records?

After sorting records, you can return your records to the original sort order at any time.

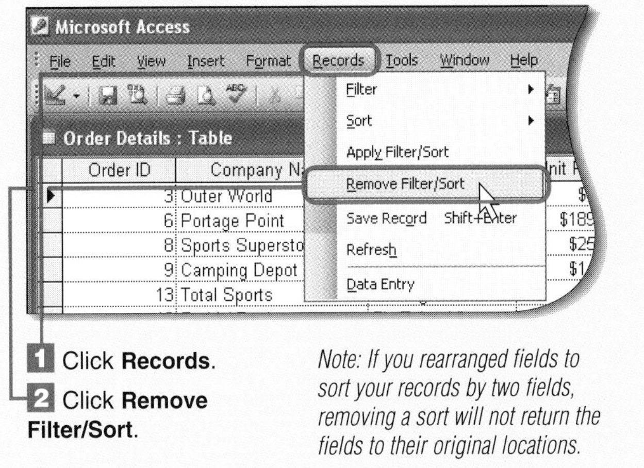

1 Click **Records**.

2 Click **Remove Filter/Sort**.

Note: If you rearranged fields to sort your records by two fields, removing a sort will not return the fields to their original locations.

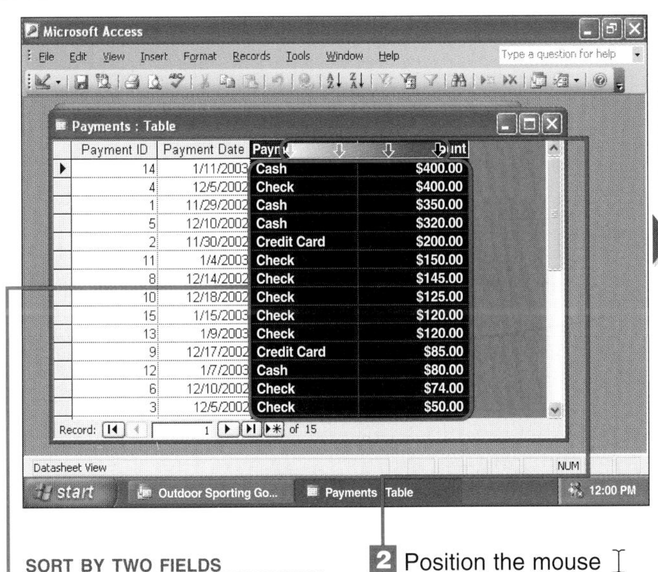

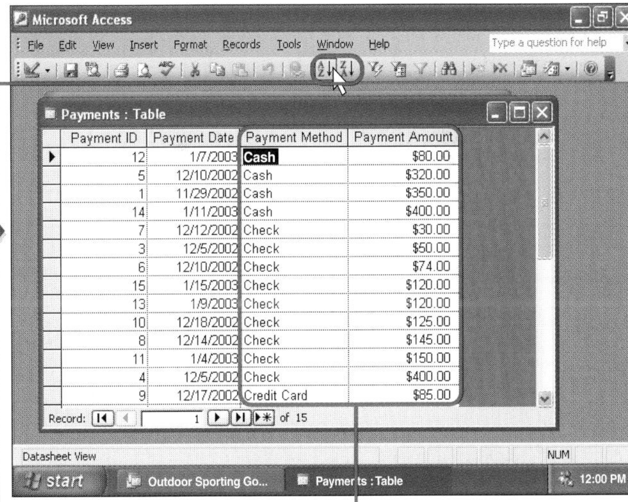

SORT BY TWO FIELDS

1 Place the fields you want to use to sort the records side by side and in the order you want to perform the sort. Access will sort the leftmost field first. To rearrange fields, see page 45.

2 Position the mouse I over the name of the first field you want to use to sort the records (I changes to ⬇). Then drag the mouse ⬇ until you highlight the second field.

3 Click one of the following buttons.

Sort A to Z, 1 to 9

Sort Z to A, 9 to 1

■ The records appear in the new order. In this example, the records are sorted by payment method. All records with the same payment method are also sorted by payment amount.

FIND DATA

You can search for data of interest in a table, form or in the results of a query.

FIND DATA

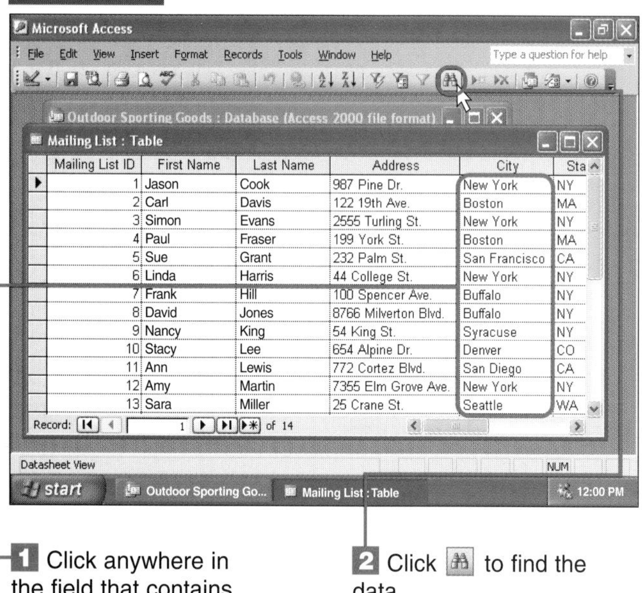

1 Click anywhere in the field that contains the data you want to find.

2 Click to find the data.

■ The Find and Replace dialog box appears.

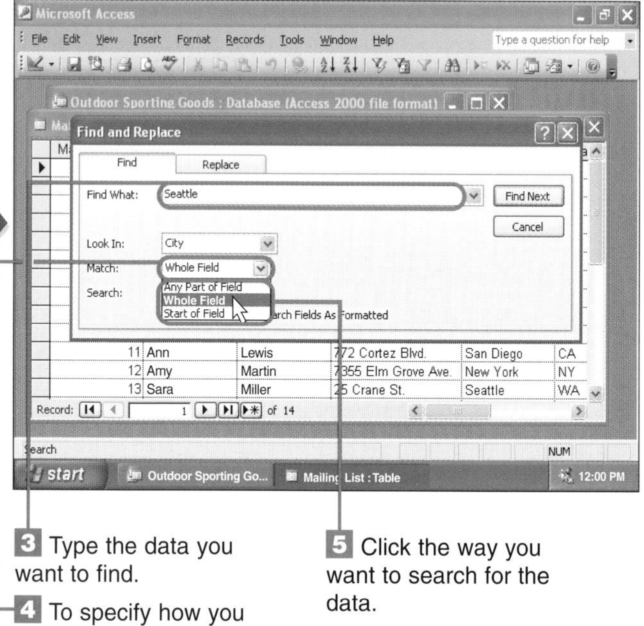

3 Type the data you want to find.

4 To specify how you want to search for the data, click this area.

5 Click the way you want to search for the data.

Note: For information on the ways you can search for data, see the top of page 179.

How can I search for data in a field?

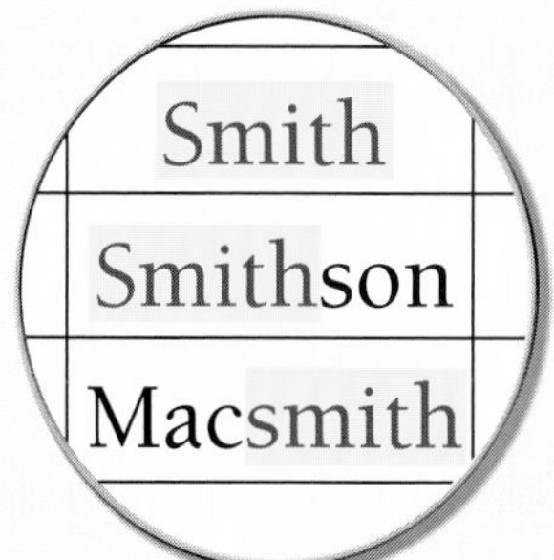

Any Part of Field

Finds data anywhere in a field. For example, a search for **smith** finds **Smith**, **Smithson** and **Macsmith**.

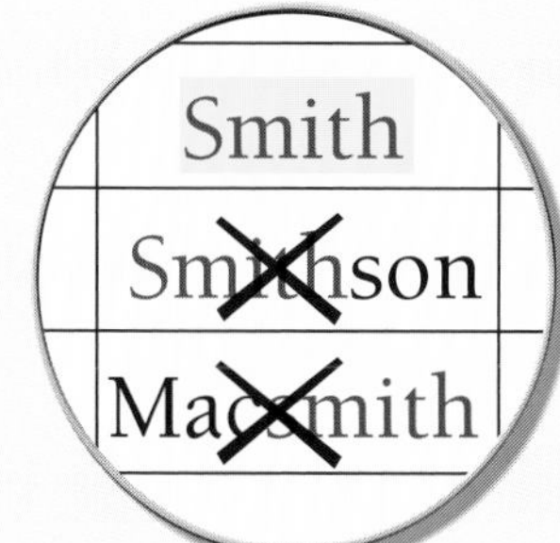

Whole Field

Finds data that exactly matches the data you specify. For example, a search for **smith** finds **Smith**, but not **Smithson** or **Macsmith**.

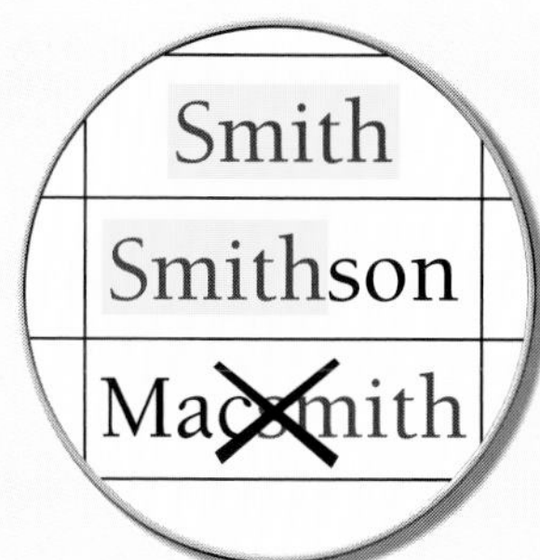

Start of Field

Finds data only at the beginning of a field. For example, a search for **smith** finds **Smith** and **Smithson**, but not **Macsmith**.

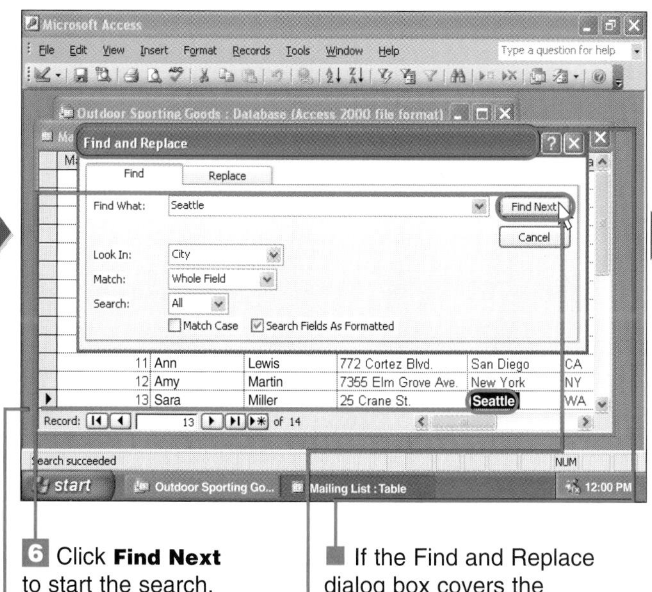

6 Click **Find Next** to start the search.

■ Access highlights the first instance of matching data in the field.

■ If the Find and Replace dialog box covers the highlighted data, position the mouse over the title bar and then drag the dialog box to a new location.

7 Click **Find Next** to find the next instance of matching data in the field.

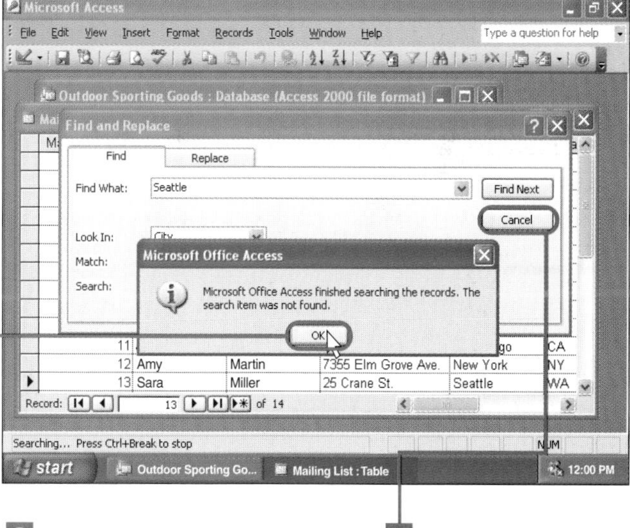

8 Repeat step 7 until a dialog box appears, telling you the search is complete.

9 Click **OK** to close the dialog box.

10 To close the Find and Replace dialog box, click **Cancel**.

REPLACE DATA

You can find and replace data in a table, form or in the results of a query. The Replace feature is useful when you want to make the same change to many records.

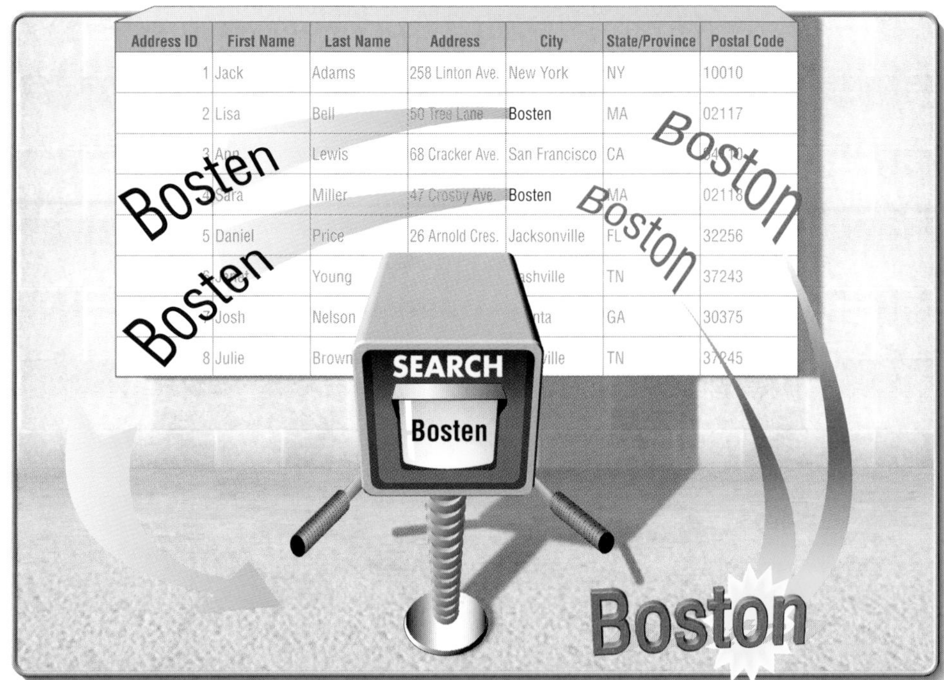

REPLACE DATA

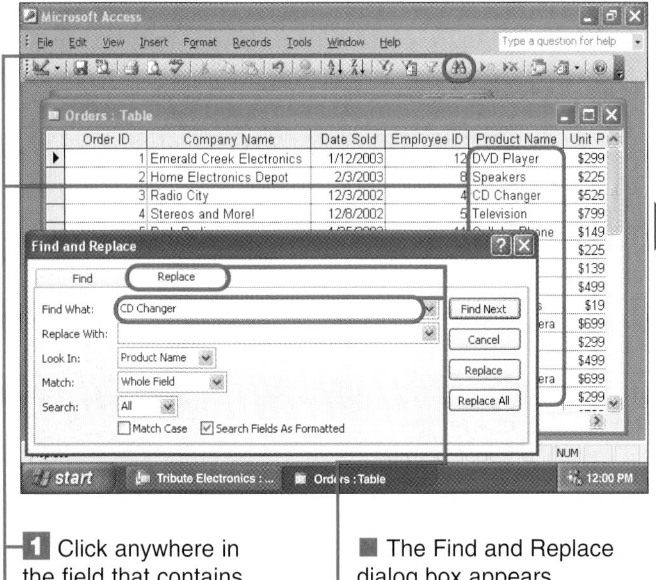

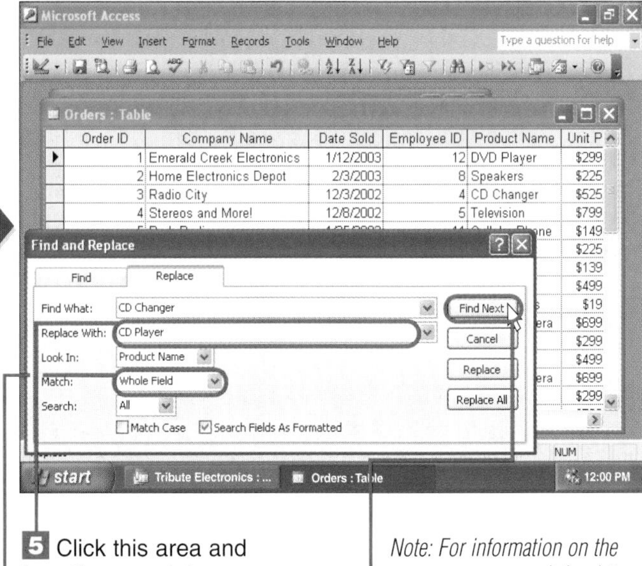

1 Click anywhere in the field that contains the data you want to replace with new data.

2 Click 🔍.

■ The Find and Replace dialog box appears.

3 Click the **Replace** tab.

4 Type the data you want to replace with new data.

5 Click this area and type the new data.

■ This area indicates how Access will search for the data. You can click this area to change how Access will search for the data.

Note: For information on the ways you can search for data, see the top of page 179.

6 Click **Find Next** to start the search.

How do I move the Find and Replace dialog box?

To move the Find and Replace dialog box so you can clearly view the data in your table, form or query, position the mouse over the title bar of the dialog box and then drag the dialog box to a new location.

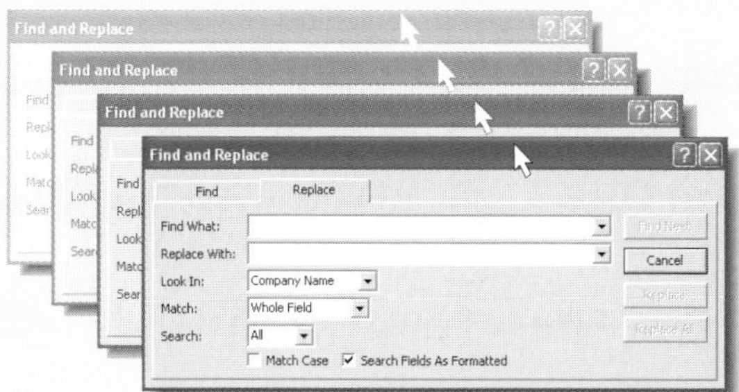

How can the Replace feature help me quickly enter data?

You can type a short form of a word or phrase, such as MA, when entering data in a field. You can then use the Replace feature to replace the short form with the full word or phrase, such as Massachusetts.

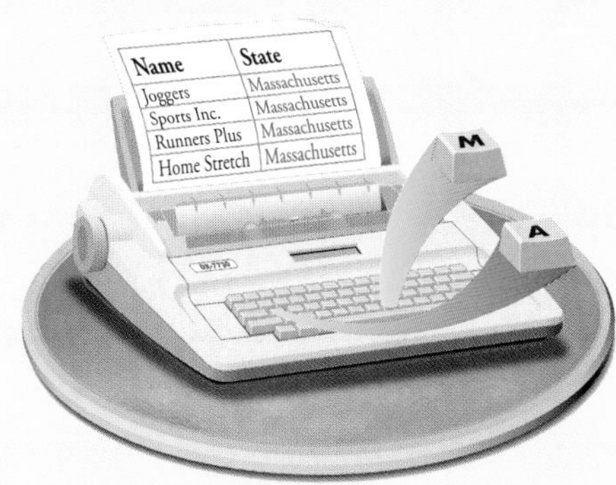

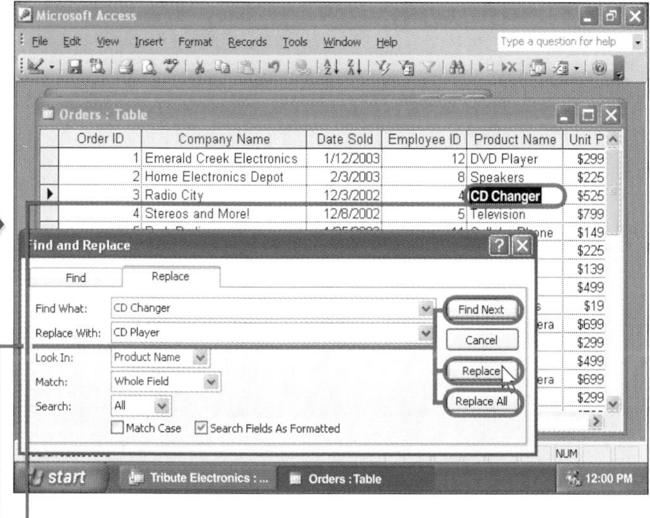

■ Access highlights the first instance of matching data in the field.

7 Click one of the following options.

Find Next - Skip the data and find the next instance of matching data in the field.

Replace - Replace the data.

Replace All - Replace the data and all other instances of matching data in the field.

*Note: If you select **Replace All**, a dialog box will appear. Click **Yes** to continue.*

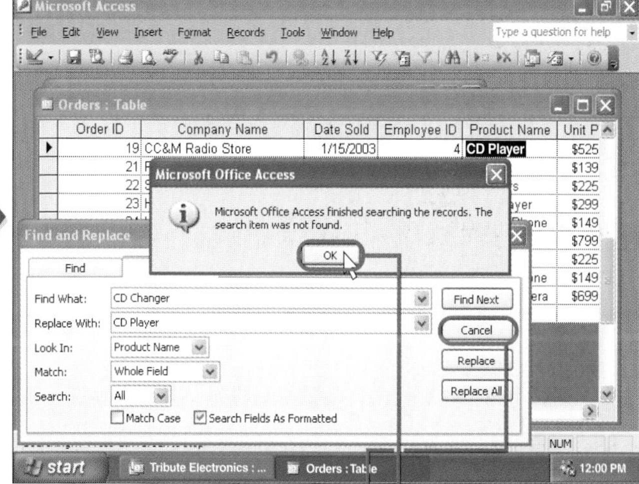

■ In this example, Access replaces the data and searches for the next instance of matching data in the field.

8 Repeat step **7** until a dialog box appears, telling you the search is complete.

9 Click **OK** to close the dialog box.

10 To close the Find and Replace dialog box, click **Cancel**.

FILTER BY SELECTION

You can filter records in a table, form or in the results of a query to display only the records that contain data of interest. Filtering records can help you review and analyze information in your database.

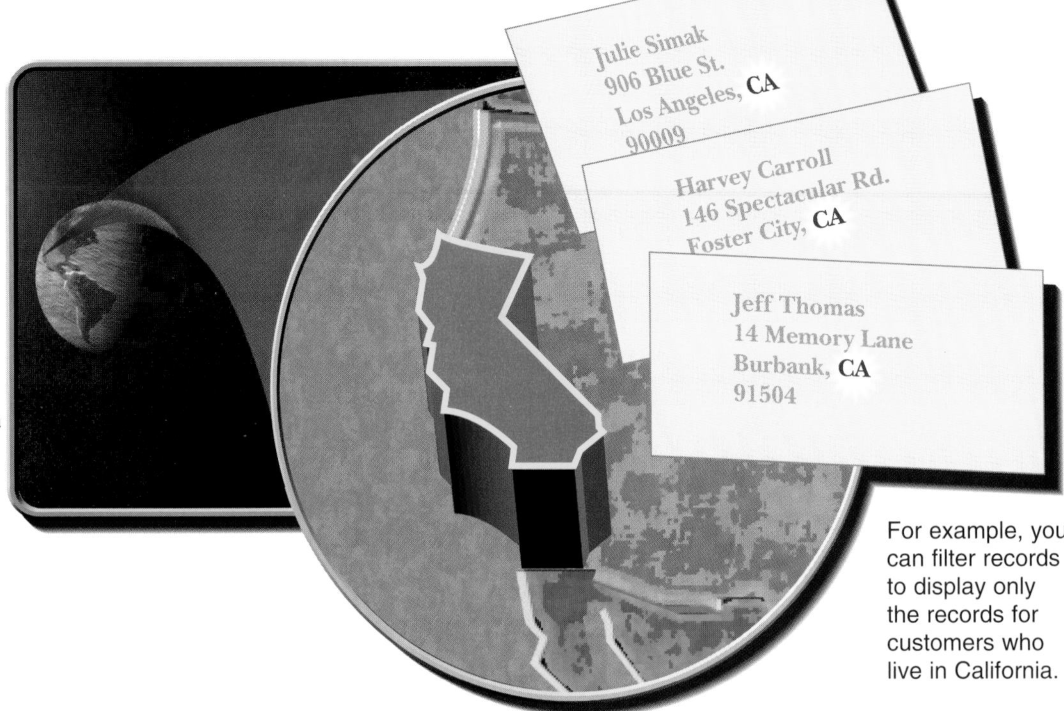

For example, you can filter records to display only the records for customers who live in California.

FILTER BY SELECTION

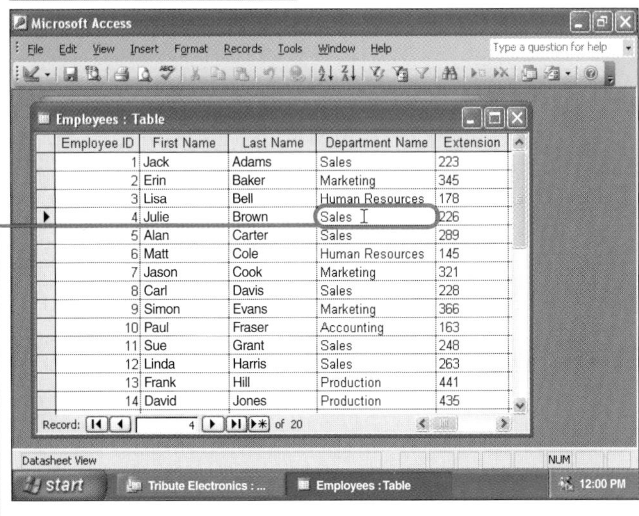

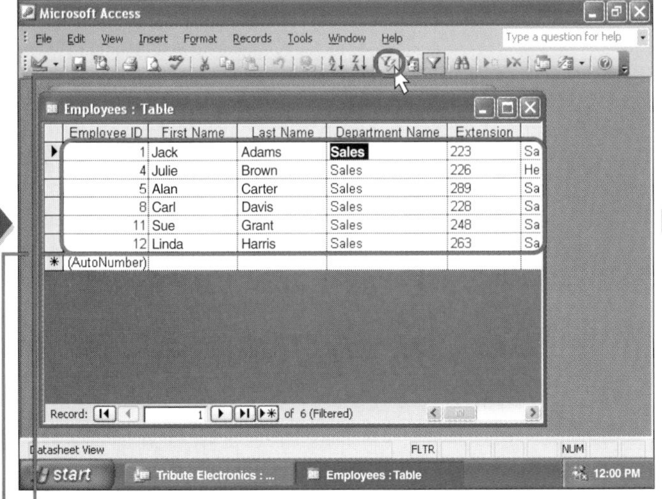

1 Click the data you want to use to filter the records. Access will display only the records that contain exactly the same data.

Note: You can select data to change the way Access filters records. For more information, see the top of page 183.

2 Click (filter by selection icon) to filter the records.

■ Access displays only the records that contain the same data. All other records are temporarily hidden.

■ In this example, Access displays only the employees in the Sales department.

How can I change the way Access filters records?

You can select data to change the way Access filters records. To select data, see page 55.

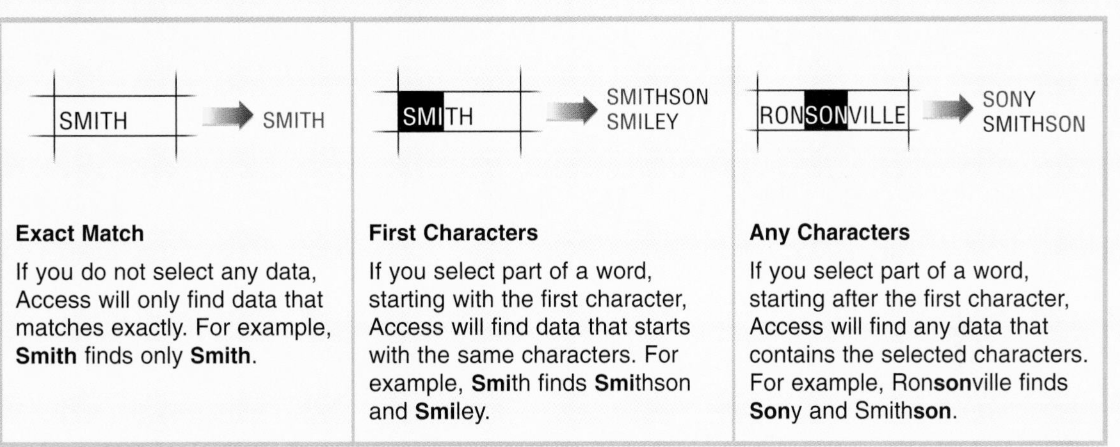

Exact Match

If you do not select any data, Access will only find data that matches exactly. For example, **Smith** finds only **Smith**.

First Characters

If you select part of a word, starting with the first character, Access will find data that starts with the same characters. For example, **Smi**th finds **Smi**thson and **Smi**ley.

Any Characters

If you select part of a word, starting after the first character, Access will find any data that contains the selected characters. For example, Ron**son**ville finds **Son**y and Smith**son**.

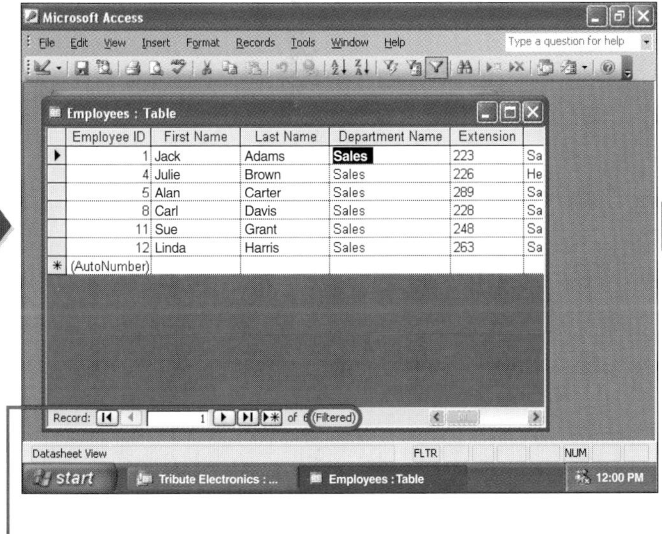

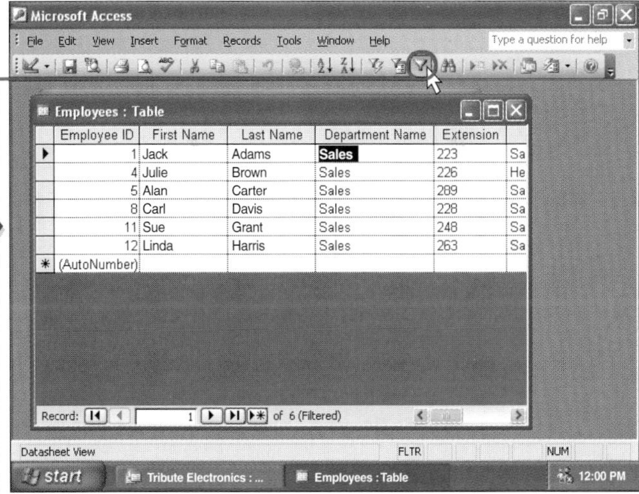

■ The word **Filtered** appears in this area to indicate that you are viewing filtered records.

■ To further filter the records, you can repeat steps **1** and **2**.

3 When you finish reviewing the filtered records, click [filter icon] to once again display all the records.

FILTER BY INPUT

You can filter records in a table, form or in the results of a query by entering criteria. Criteria are conditions that identify which records you want to display.

For example, you can enter criteria to display only the records for customers who made purchases of more than $500.

FILTER BY INPUT

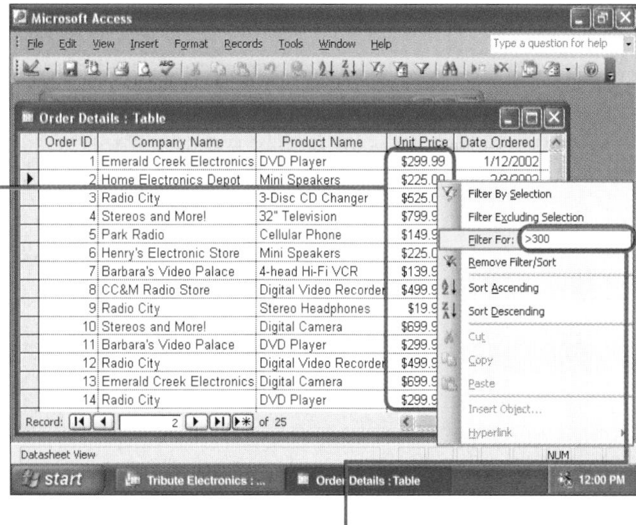

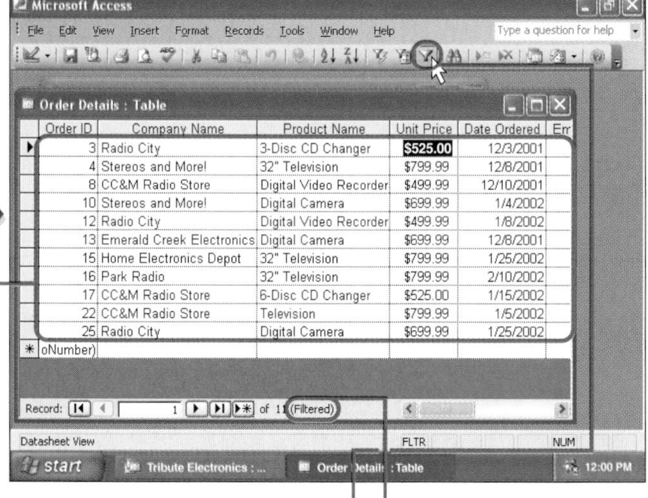

1 Right-click anywhere in the field you want to use to filter the records. A menu appears.

2 Click the area beside **Filter For:**.

3 Type the criteria you want to use to filter the records. Then press the Enter key.

Note: For examples of criteria you can use, see page 187.

■ Access displays only the records that meet the criteria you specified. All other records are temporarily hidden.

■ In this example, Access displays orders over $300.

■ The word **Filtered** appears in this area to indicate that you are viewing filtered records.

4 When you finish reviewing the filtered records, click [Remove Filter] to once again display all the records.

FILTER BY EXCLUSION

You can filter records in a table, form or in the results of a query to hide records that do not contain data of interest.

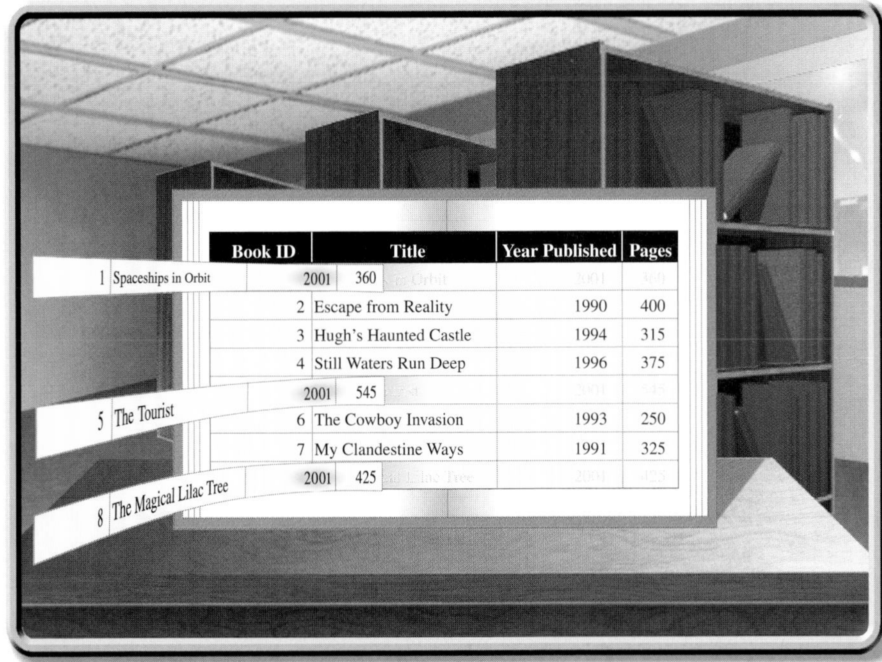

Book ID
Title
Year Published
Pages
1 Spaceships in Orbit 2001 360
2 Escape from Reality 1990 400
3 Hugh's Haunted Castle 1994 315
4 Still Waters Run Deep 1996 375
5 The Tourist 2001 545
6 The Cowboy Invasion 1993 250
7 My Clandestine Ways 1991 325
8 The Magical Lilac Tree 2001 425

For example, you can filter records to hide the records for all books published in 2001.

FILTER BY EXCLUSION

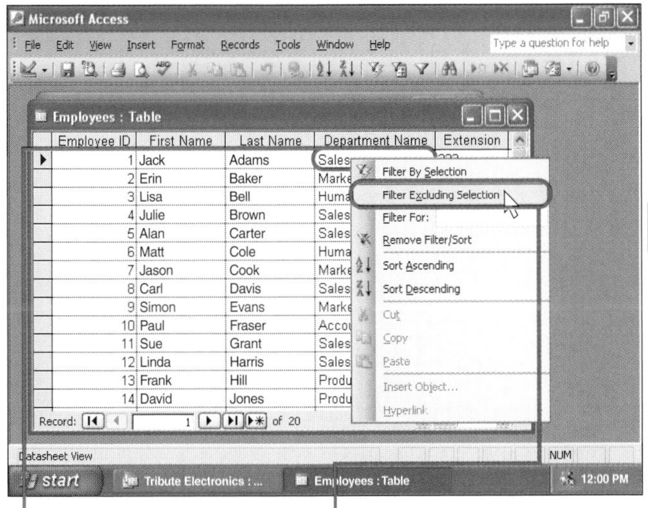

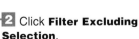

1 Right-click the data you want to use to filter the records. Access will hide all the records that contain exactly the same data.

■ A menu appears.

2 Click **Filter Excluding Selection**.

■ Access temporarily hides the records that contain the data you specified.

■ In this example, Access hides the employees in the Sales department.

■ The word **Filtered** appears in this area to indicate that you are viewing filtered records.

■ To further filter the records, you can repeat steps **1** and **2**.

3 When you finish reviewing the filtered records, click [Y] to once again display all the records.

FILTER BY FORM

You can use the Filter by Form feature to find and display records of interest in a table, form or in the results of a query.

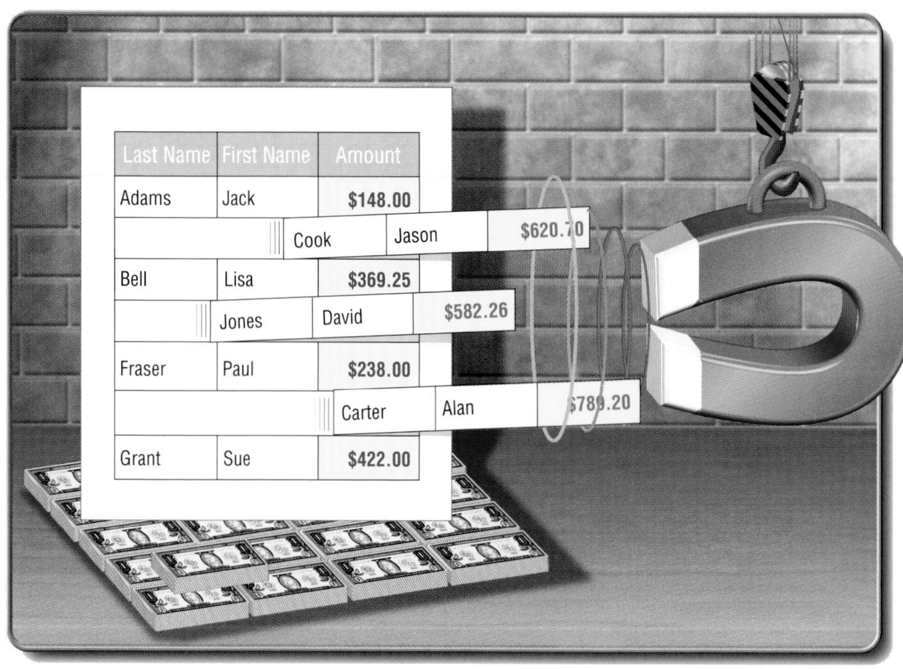

When you filter by form, you need to specify the criteria that records must meet to appear in the results. For example, you can specify criteria to display only the records for customers who purchased less than $500 of your products.

FILTER BY FORM USING ONE CRITERIA

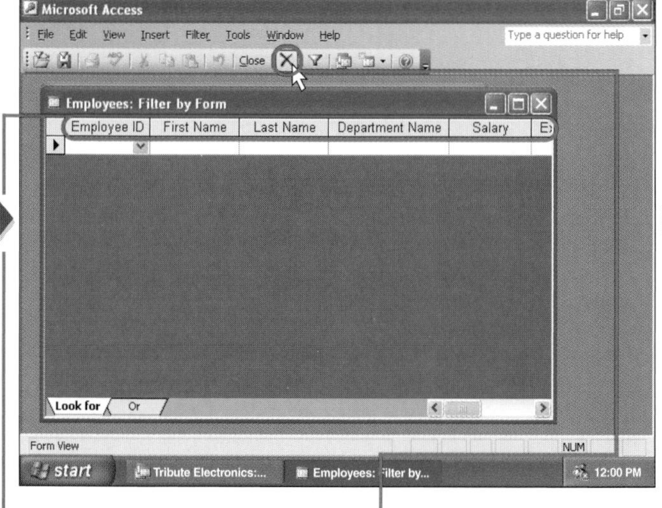

1 Click to filter your records by form.

■ The Filter by Form window appears.

■ This area displays the field names from your table, form or query results.

2 To clear any information used for your last filter, click ☒.

What criteria can I use to filter records?

Here are some examples of criteria you can use to filter records. For more examples, see page 214.

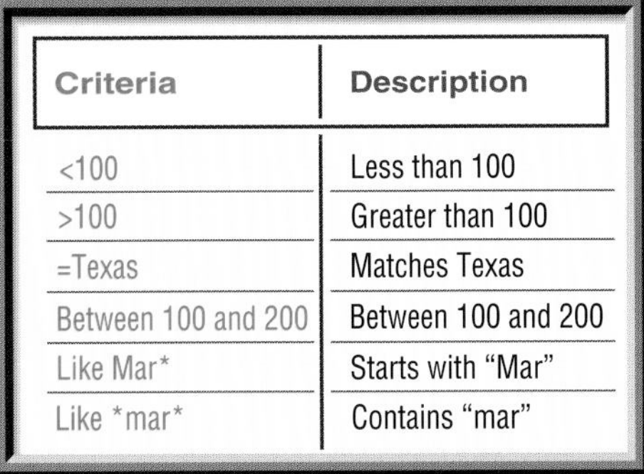

Criteria	Description
<100	Less than 100
>100	Greater than 100
=Texas	Matches Texas
Between 100 and 200	Between 100 and 200
Like Mar*	Starts with "Mar"
Like *mar*	Contains "mar"

Is there another way to enter the criteria I want to use to filter records?

Yes. To enter criteria, you can perform steps 1 to 3 below and then click the arrow ( ) that appears in the area. A list of all the values in the field appears. Click the value you want to use to filter the records.

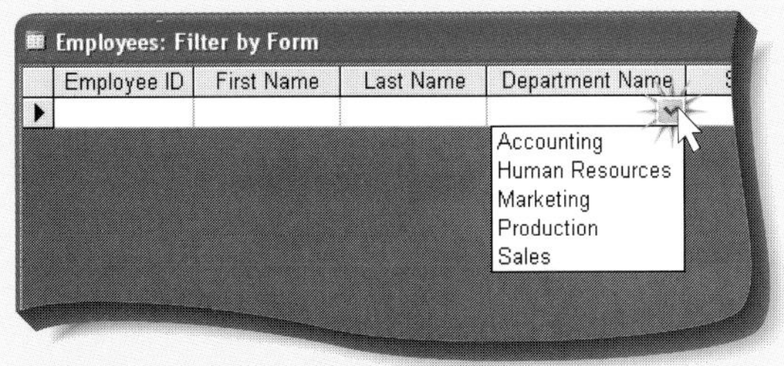

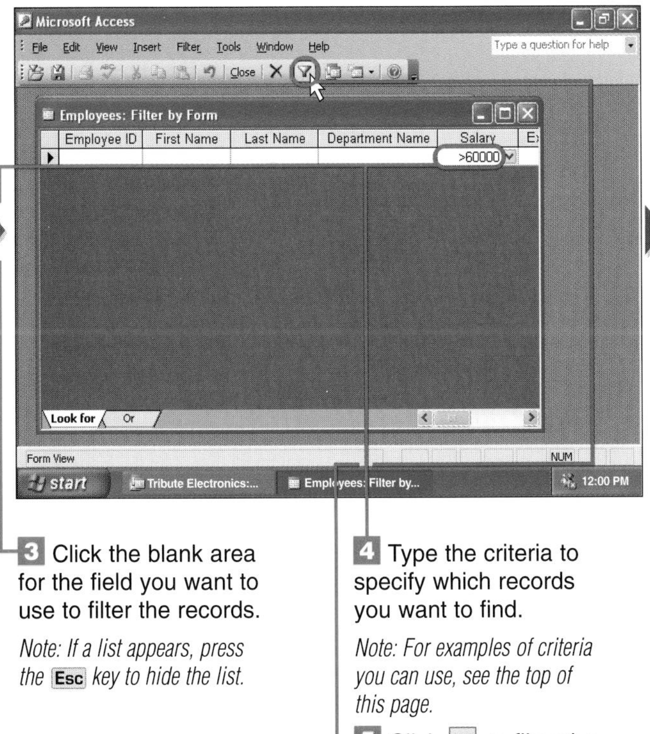

3 Click the blank area for the field you want to use to filter the records.

Note: If a list appears, press the Esc key to hide the list.

4 Type the criteria to specify which records you want to find.

Note: For examples of criteria you can use, see the top of this page.

5 Click to filter the records.

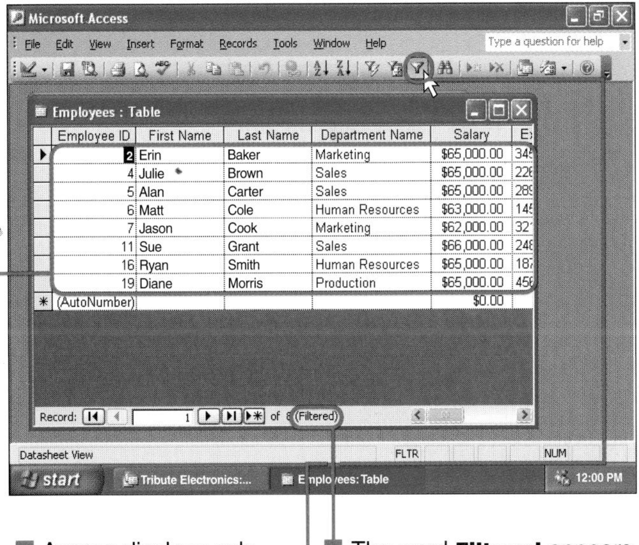

■ Access displays only the records that meet the criteria you specified.

■ In this example, Access displays employees who earn more than $60,000.

■ The word **Filtered** appears in this area to indicate that you are viewing filtered records.

6 When you finish reviewing the filtered records, click to once again display all the records.

CONTINUED

FILTER BY FORM

When using the Filter by Form feature, you can use multiple criteria to filter your records. Access will find and display records that meet the criteria you specify.

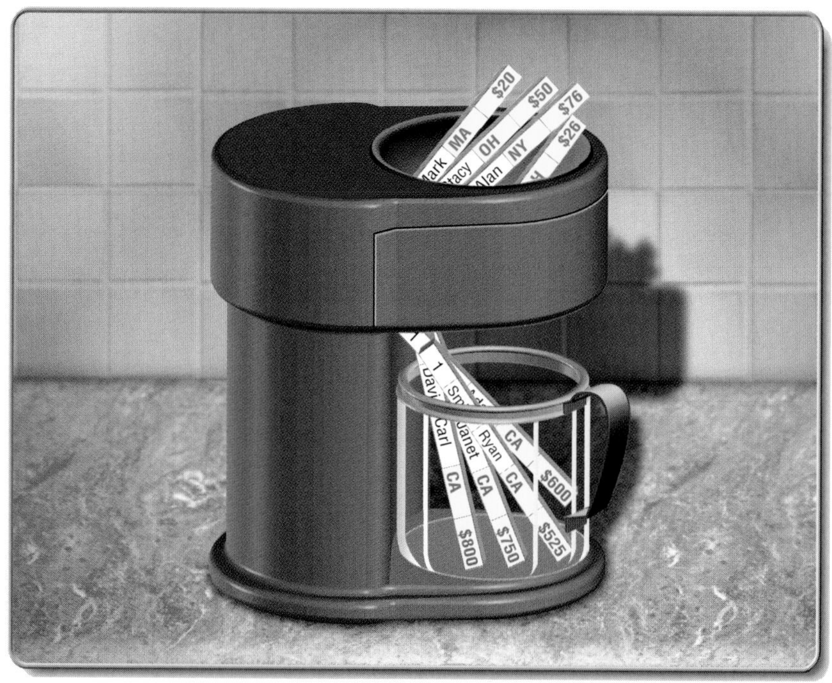

Criteria are conditions that identify which records you want to appear in the results. For example, you can specify criteria to display customers living in California who purchased more than $500 of your products. For examples of criteria, see page 214.

FILTER BY FORM USING MULTIPLE CRITERIA

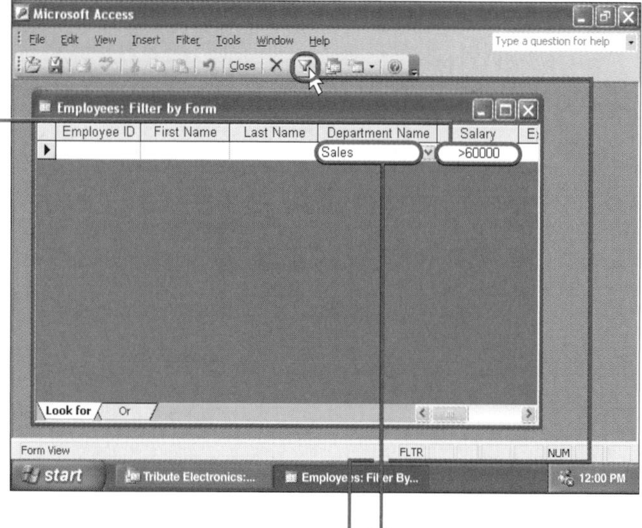

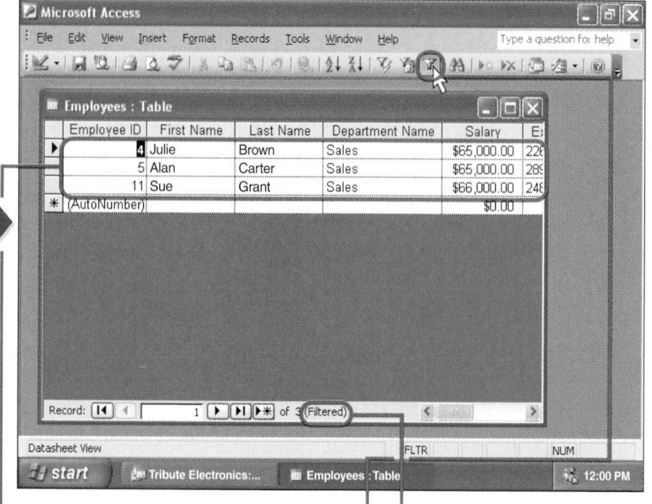

USING "AND"

1 To enter the first criteria you want to use to filter the records, perform steps 1 to 4 starting on page 186.

2 To enter the second criteria, click the blank area for the other field you want to use to filter the records. Then type the second criteria.

3 Click the filter button to filter the records.

■ Access displays the records that meet both of the criteria you specified.

■ In this example, Access displays employees in the Sales department who earn more than $60,000.

■ The word **Filtered** appears in this area to indicate that you are viewing filtered records.

4 When you finish reviewing the filtered records, click the filter button to once again display all the records.

How can I use multiple criteria to filter records?

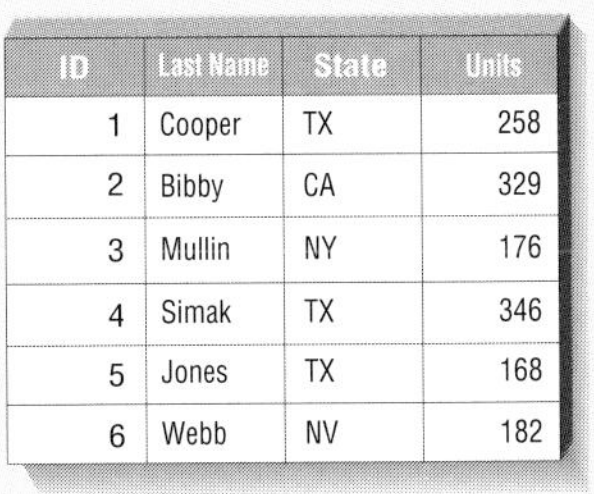

ID	Last Name	State	Units
1	Cooper	TX	258
2	Bibby	CA	329
3	Mullin	NY	176
4	Simak	TX	346
5	Jones	TX	168
6	Webb	NV	182

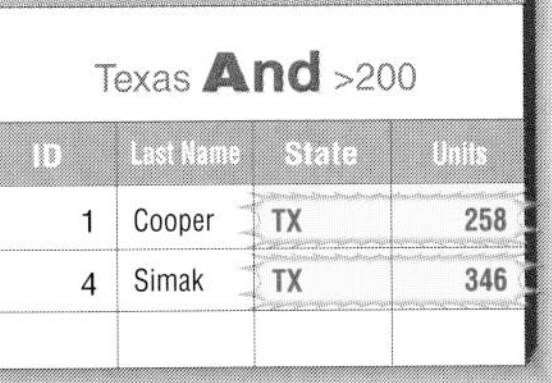

Texas **And** >200

ID	Last Name	State	Units
1	Cooper	TX	258
4	Simak	TX	346

Filter records using "And"

Displays records that meet all of the criteria you specify. For example, **Texas and >200** displays only customers living in Texas who purchased more than 200 units.

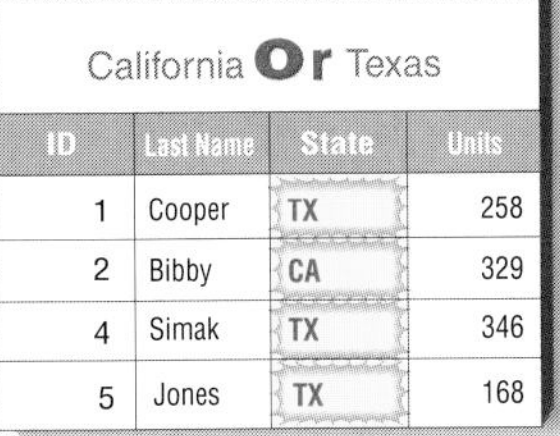

California **Or** Texas

ID	Last Name	State	Units
1	Cooper	TX	258
2	Bibby	CA	329
4	Simak	TX	346
5	Jones	TX	168

Filter records using "Or"

Displays records that meet at least one of the criteria you specify. For example, **California or Texas** displays customers who live in California or Texas.

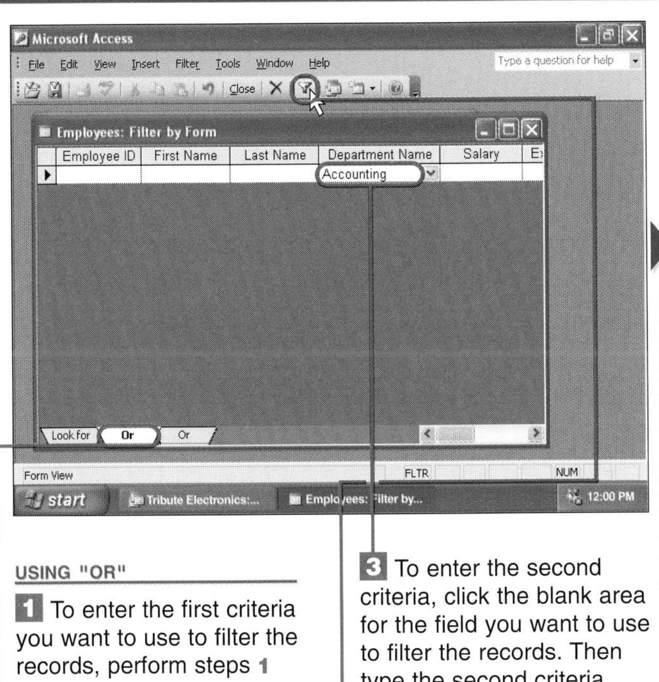

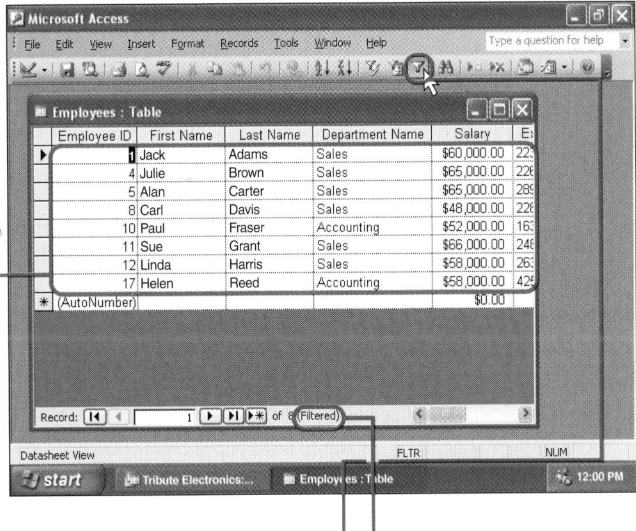

USING "OR"

1 To enter the first criteria you want to use to filter the records, perform steps 1 to 4 starting on page 186.

2 Click the **Or** tab.

3 To enter the second criteria, click the blank area for the field you want to use to filter the records. Then type the second criteria.

4 Click [filter icon] to filter the records.

■ Access displays the records that meet at least one of the criteria you specified.

■ In this example, Access displays employees in the Sales or Accounting department.

■ The word **Filtered** appears in this area to indicate that you are viewing filtered records.

5 When you finish reviewing the filtered records, click [filter icon] to once again display all the records.

What were the top five selling products this week?
Product ID | Product | Quantity
1 | Water-skis | 120
5 | Bike | 245
13 | Tennis racquet | 250
18 | Basketball | 264
23 | Running shoes | 364
Query

CHAPTER 9

Create Queries

Would you like to create queries to find information of interest in your database? This chapter shows you how.

CREATE A QUERY IN THE DESIGN VIEW

You can create a query to find information of interest in your database.

Creating a query allows you to find information that meets certain criteria in your database. Criteria are conditions that identify which records you want to find.

CREATE A QUERY IN THE DESIGN VIEW

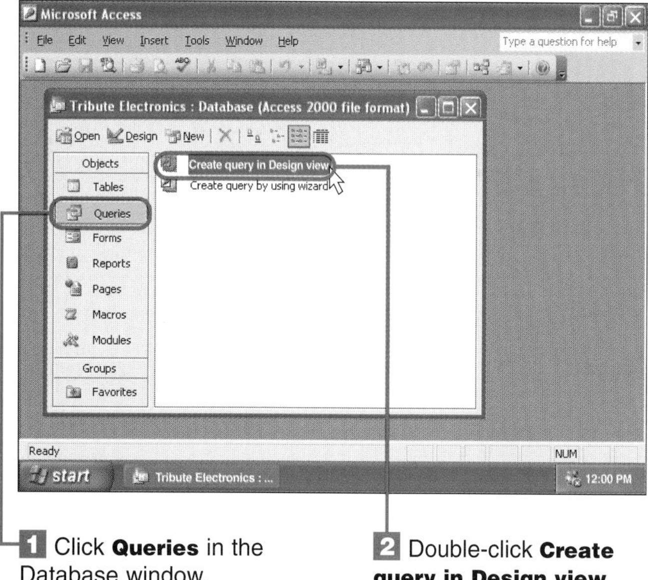

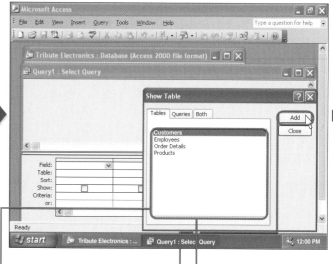

1 Click **Queries** in the Database window.

2 Double-click **Create query in Design view**.

■ The Select Query window and the Show Table dialog box appear.

■ This area lists all the tables in your database.

3 Click a table that contains information you want to use in your query.

4 Click **Add** to add the table to your query.

Why does a line appear between the tables in the Select Query window?

If the tables you select to use in a query are related, Access displays a line joining the related fields in the tables. When creating a query that uses information from more than one table, the tables should be related so that Access can bring together the information in the tables. For information on relationships, see page 128.

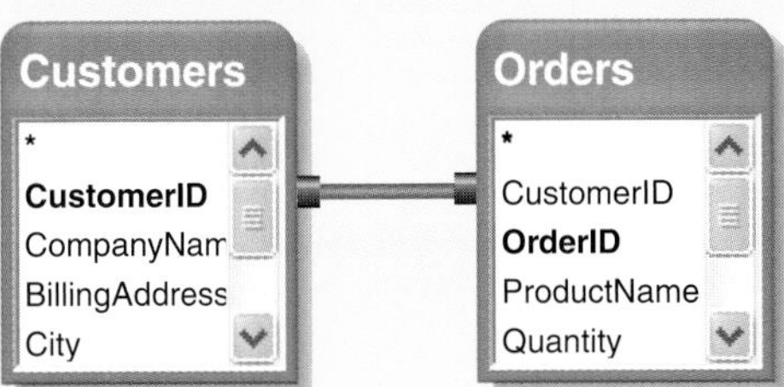

How do I add another table to my query?

To add another table to your query, click the Show Table button to redisplay the Show Table dialog box. Then perform steps 3 and 4 on page 192 to add another table to your query.

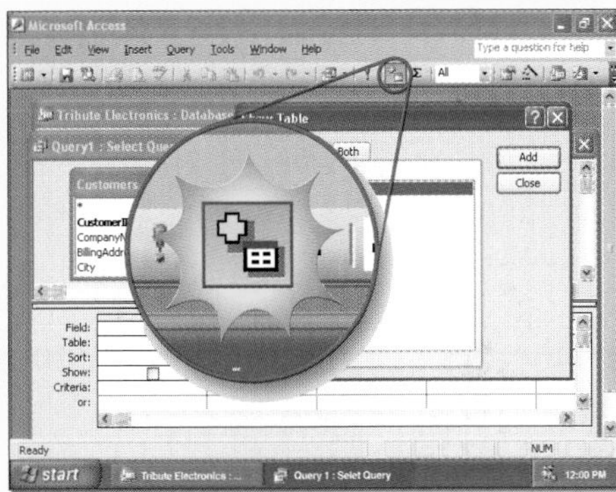

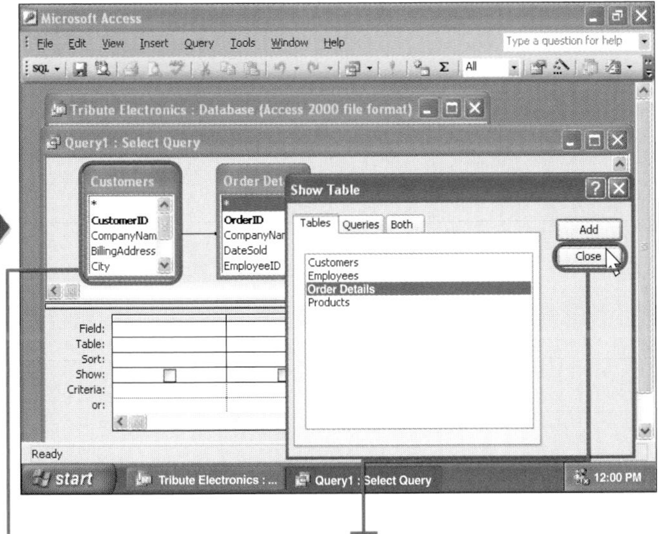

■ A box appears in the Select Query window, displaying the fields for the table you selected.

5 To add another table to your query, repeat steps 3 and 4 for each table.

6 Click **Close** to hide the Show Table dialog box.

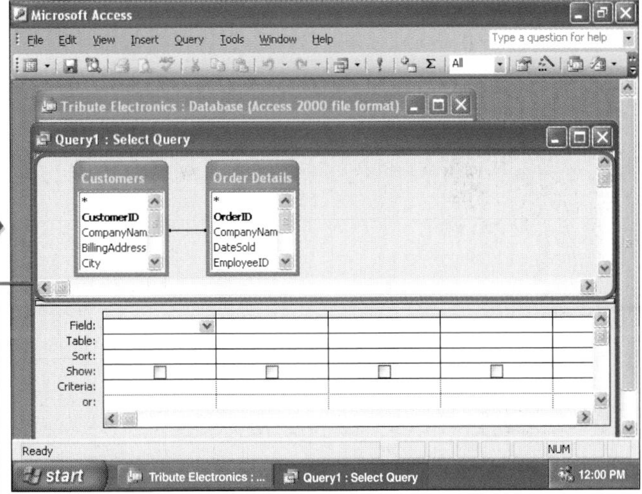

■ Each box in this area displays the fields for one table.

■ If you accidentally added a table to the query, click the box displaying the fields for the table and then press the Delete key. Access will remove the table from the query, but will not remove the table from the database.

CONTINUED

CREATE A QUERY IN THE DESIGN VIEW

You can select which fields from your tables you want to include in your query.

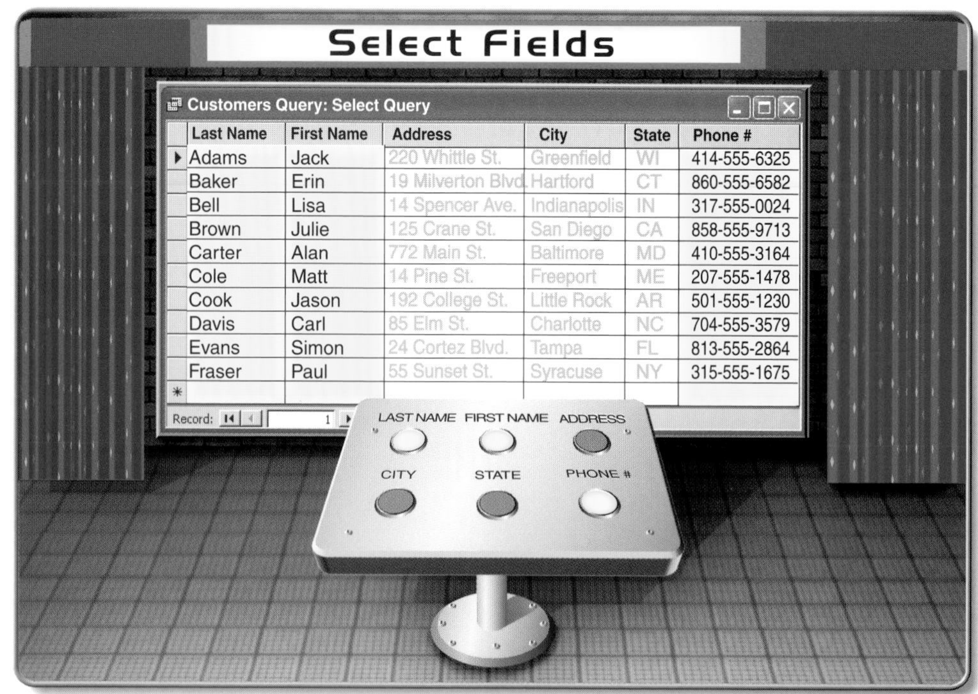

For example, you may want to include only the name and phone number of each customer.

CREATE A QUERY IN THE DESIGN VIEW (CONTINUED)

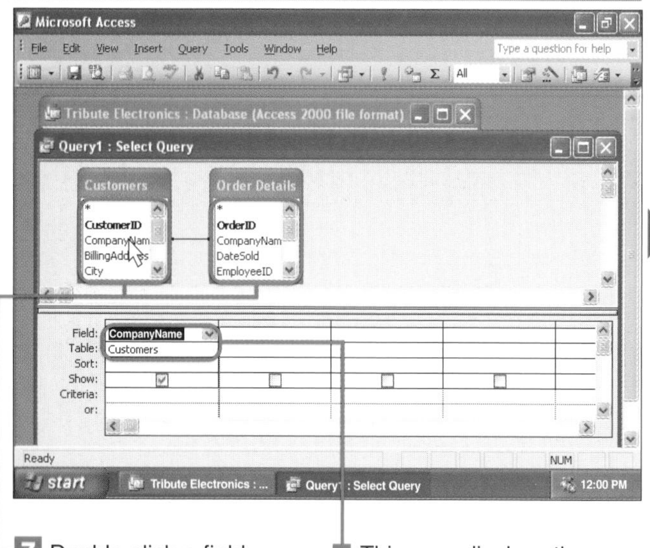

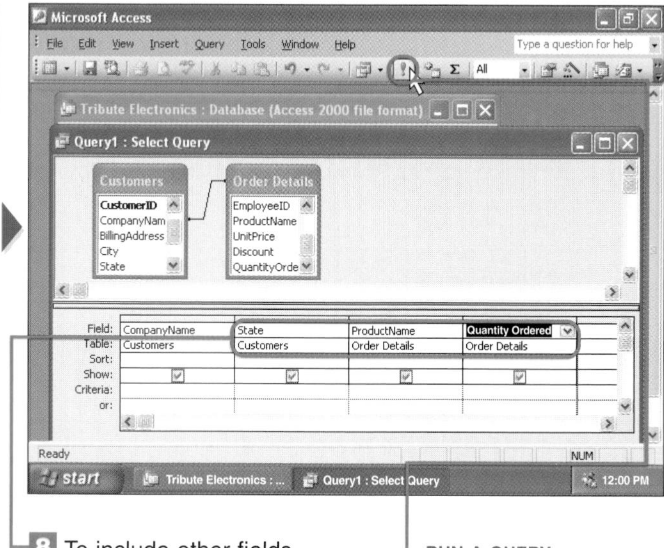

7 Double-click a field you want to include in your query.

■ This area displays the field you selected and the table that contains the field.

8 To include other fields in your query, repeat step 7 for each field you want to include.

Note: To quickly select all the fields in a table, see page 206.

RUN A QUERY

1 Click ! to run the query.

Does a query store data?

No. When you save a query, Access saves only the design of the query. Each time you run a query, Access gathers the most current data from your database to determine the results of the query. For example, you can run the same query each month to display the top sales representatives for the month.

Can I change information displayed in the results of my query?

Yes. You can edit data displayed in the results of a query as you would edit data in a table. If you change the data displayed in the query results, the data will also change in the table used to create the query. To edit data in a table, see page 56.

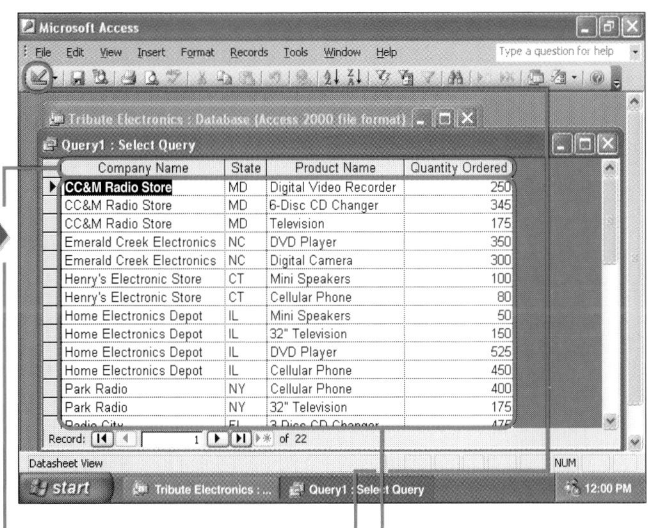

- The results of the query appear.
- This area displays the names of the fields you included in the query.
- The records that meet the conditions you specified appear in this area. In this example, all the records from the table(s) are displayed.
- To return to the Design view, click the View button.

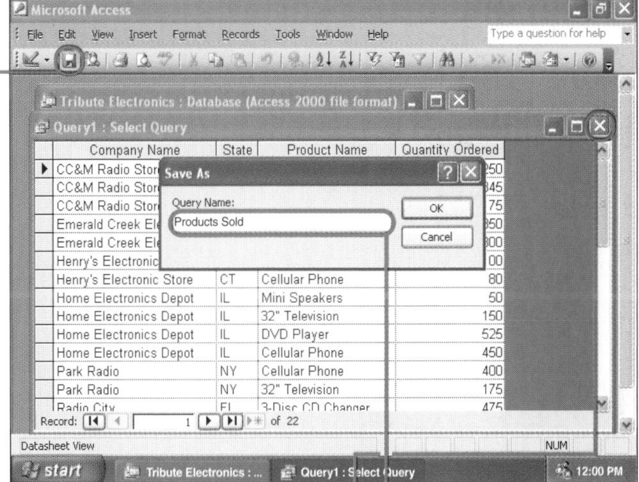

SAVE A QUERY

1. Click the Save button to save your query so you can run the query again later.
   - The Save As dialog box appears.
2. Type a name for your query and then press the Enter key.
3. When you finish working with your query, click the Close button to close the query.

CREATE A QUERY USING THE SIMPLE QUERY WIZARD

You can use the Simple Query Wizard to create a query. A query allows you to find and analyze information of interest in your database.

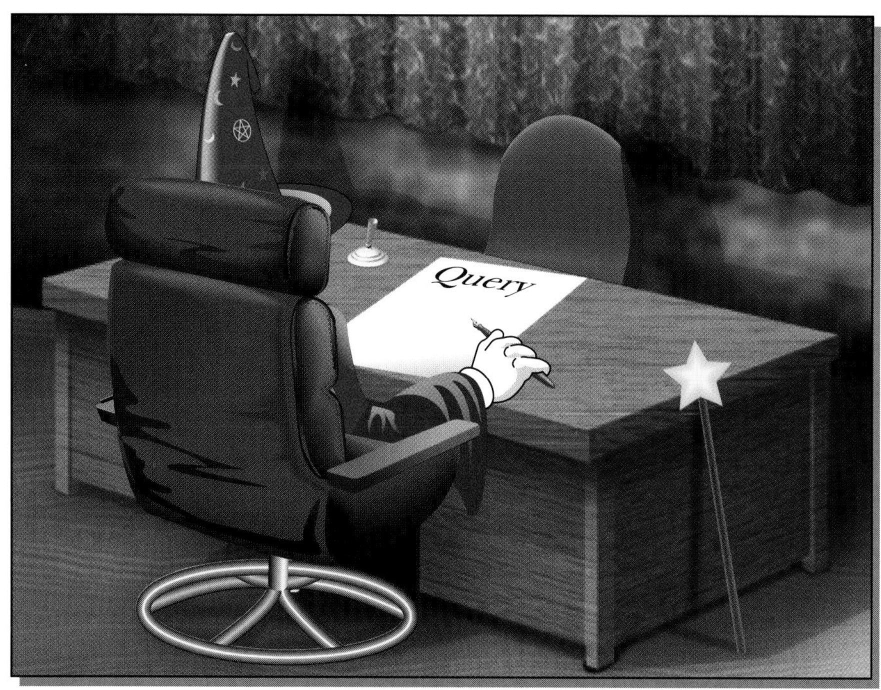

The Simple Query Wizard will ask you a series of questions and then set up a query based on your answers.

CREATE A QUERY USING THE SIMPLE QUERY WIZARD

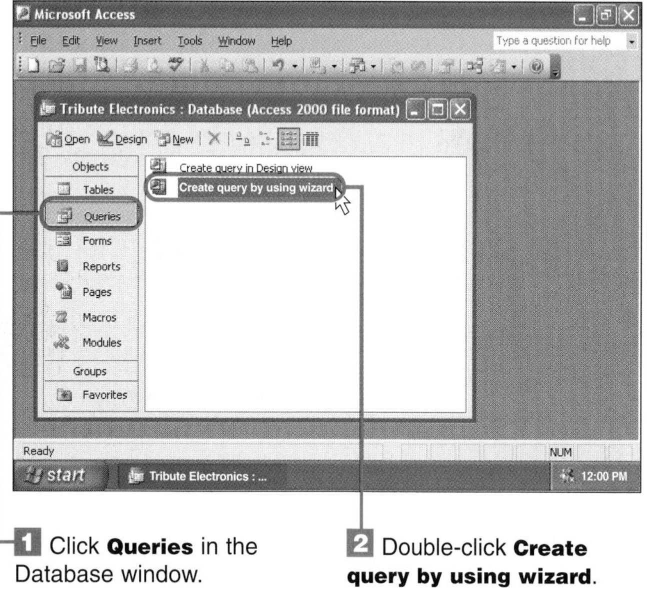

1 Click **Queries** in the Database window.

2 Double-click **Create query by using wizard**.

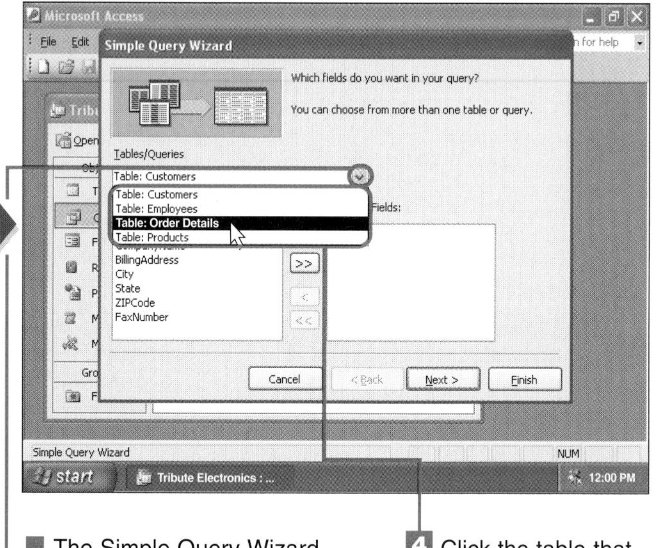

■ The Simple Query Wizard appears.

3 Click ⌄ in this area to select the table that contains the fields you want to include in your query.

4 Click the table that contains the fields.

Which tables in my database can I use to create a query?

You can use any table in your database to create a query. When creating a query that uses information from more than one table, relationships must exist between the tables so that Access can bring together the information in the tables. For information on relationships, see page 128.

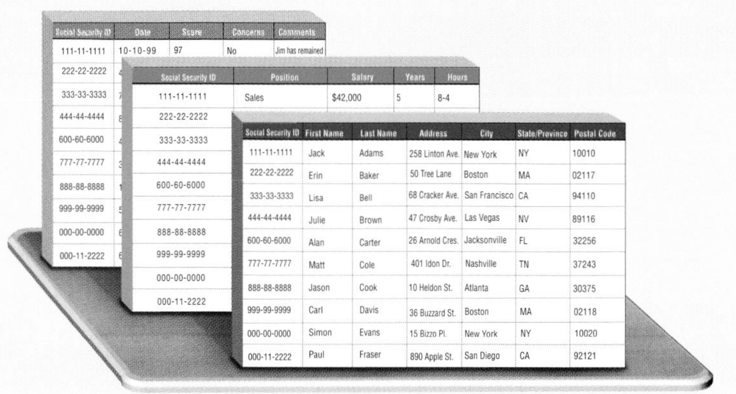

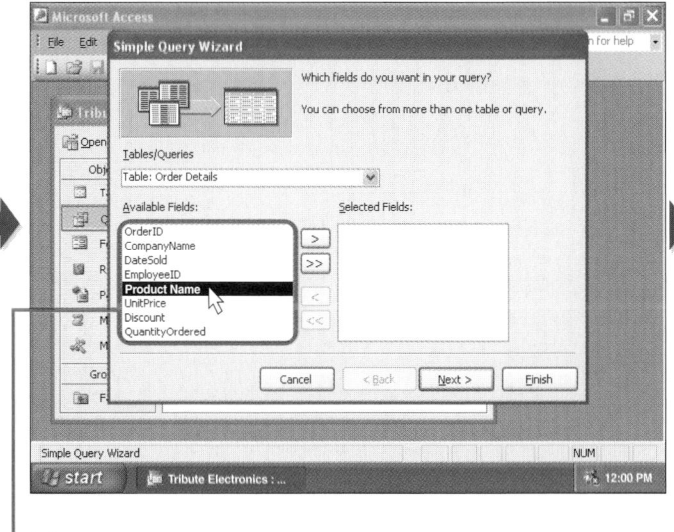

■ This area displays the fields from the table you selected.

5 Double-click each field you want to include in your query.

Note: To add all the fields from the table at once, click >> .

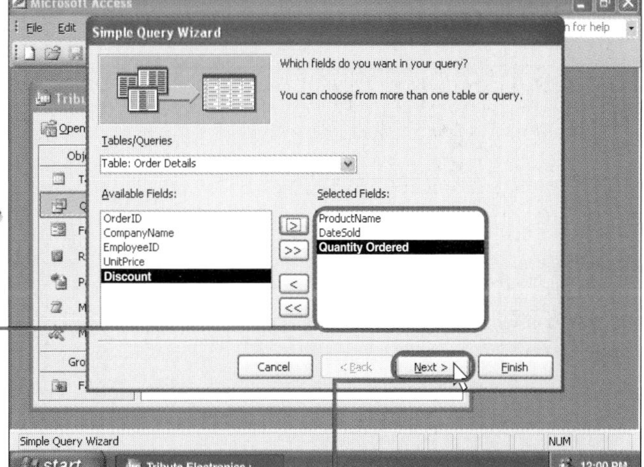

■ Each field you select appears in this area.

■ To remove a field you accidentally selected, double-click the field in this area.

Note: To remove all the fields at once, click << .

6 To include fields from other tables in your database, repeat steps **3** to **5** for each table.

7 Click **Next** to continue.

CONTINUED

CREATE A QUERY USING THE SIMPLE QUERY WIZARD

If your query contains information that Access can summarize, you can choose to show all the records or just a summary of the records in the results of your query.

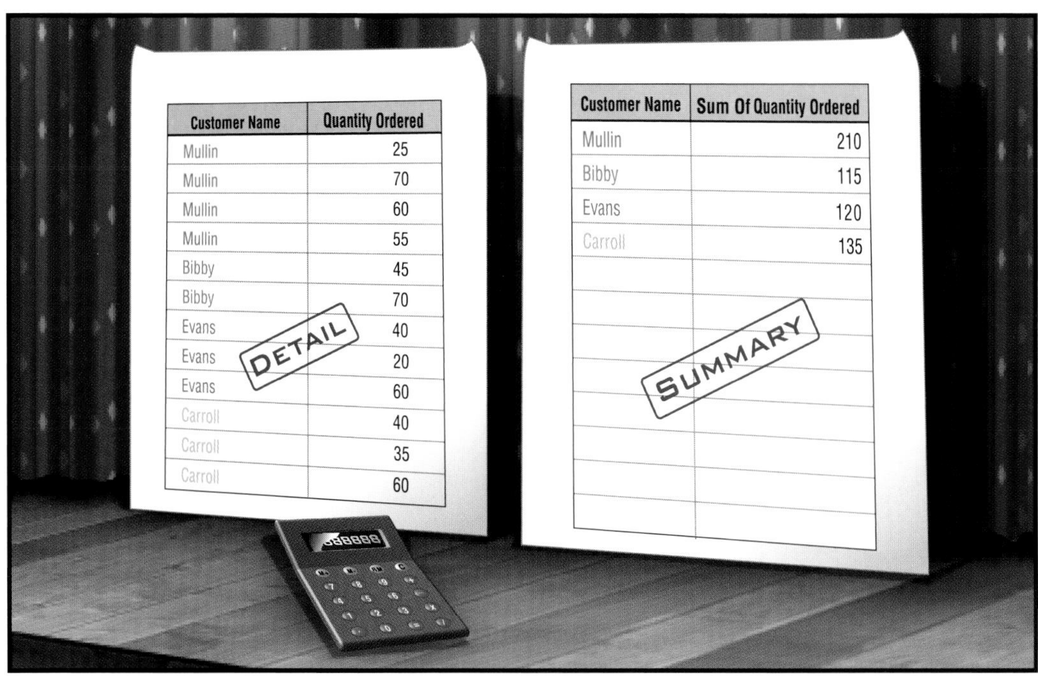

Customer Name
Quantity Ordered
Mullin 25
Mullin 70
Mullin 60
Mullin 55
Bibby 45
Bibby 70
Evans 40
Evans 20
Evans 60
Carroll 40
Carroll 35
Carroll 60
DETAIL
Customer Name
Sum Of Quantity Ordered
Mullin 210
Bibby 115
Evans 120
Carroll 135
SUMMARY

CREATE A QUERY USING THE SIMPLE QUERY WIZARD (CONTINUED)

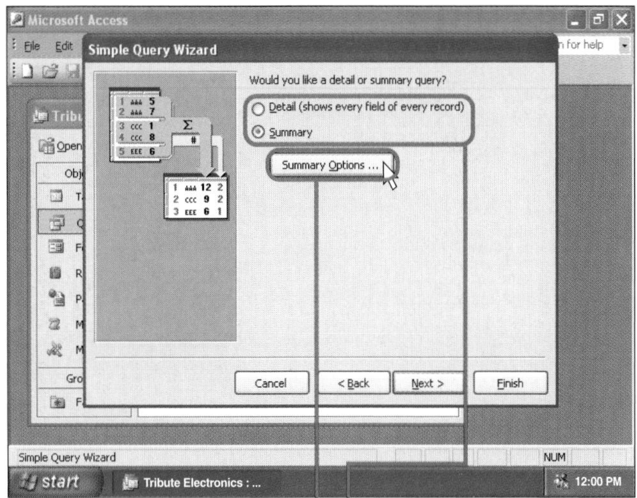

■ This screen appears if your query contains information that Access can summarize.

*Note: If this screen does not appear, skip to step **16**.*

8 Click the way you want to display the information in the results of your query (○ changes to ◉).

9 If you selected Summary in step **8**, click **Summary Options**.

*Note: If you selected Detail in step **8**, skip to step **15**.*

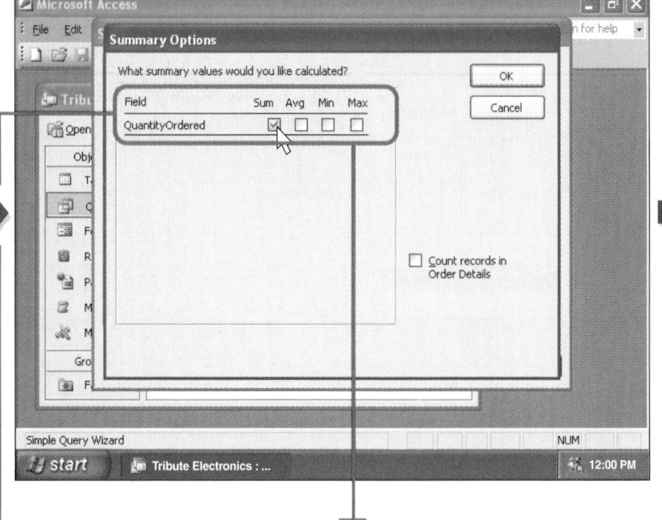

■ The Summary Options dialog box appears.

■ This area displays the fields you can summarize.

10 Click the box (☐) for each calculation you want to perform (☐ changes to ☑).

Note: For information on the calculations you can perform, see the top of page 199.

What calculations can Access perform to summarize data in my query?

Sum	**Avg**	**Min**	**Max**	**Count records**
Adds the values.	Calculates the average value.	Finds the smallest value.	Finds the largest value.	Counts the number of records.

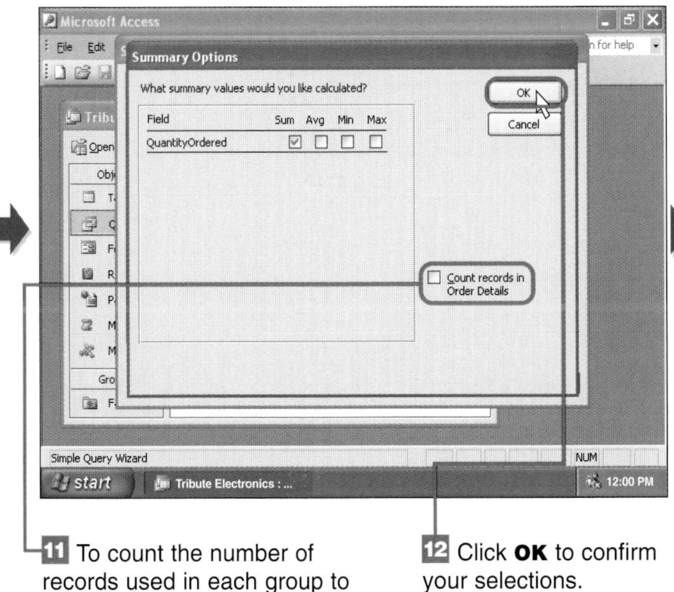

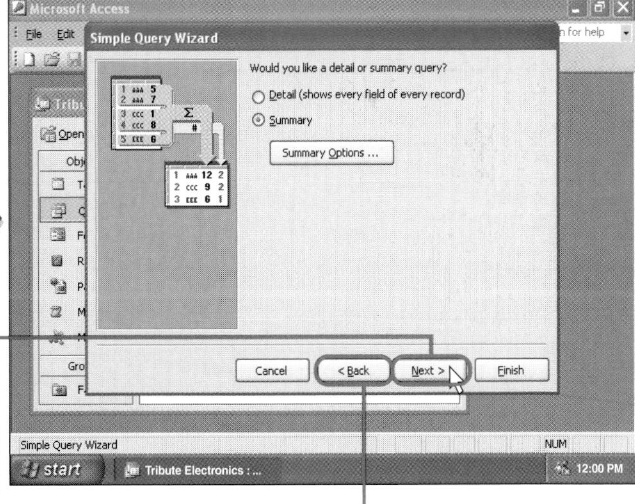

11 To count the number of records used in each group to perform the calculations, click this option (☐ changes to ☑).

12 Click **OK** to confirm your selections.

13 Click **Next** to continue.

■ You can click **Back** at any time to return to a previous step and change your selections.

CONTINUED

CREATE A QUERY USING THE SIMPLE QUERY WIZARD

If a field in your query contains dates, you can specify the way you want to group the dates in your query.

You can group dates by day, month, quarter or year.

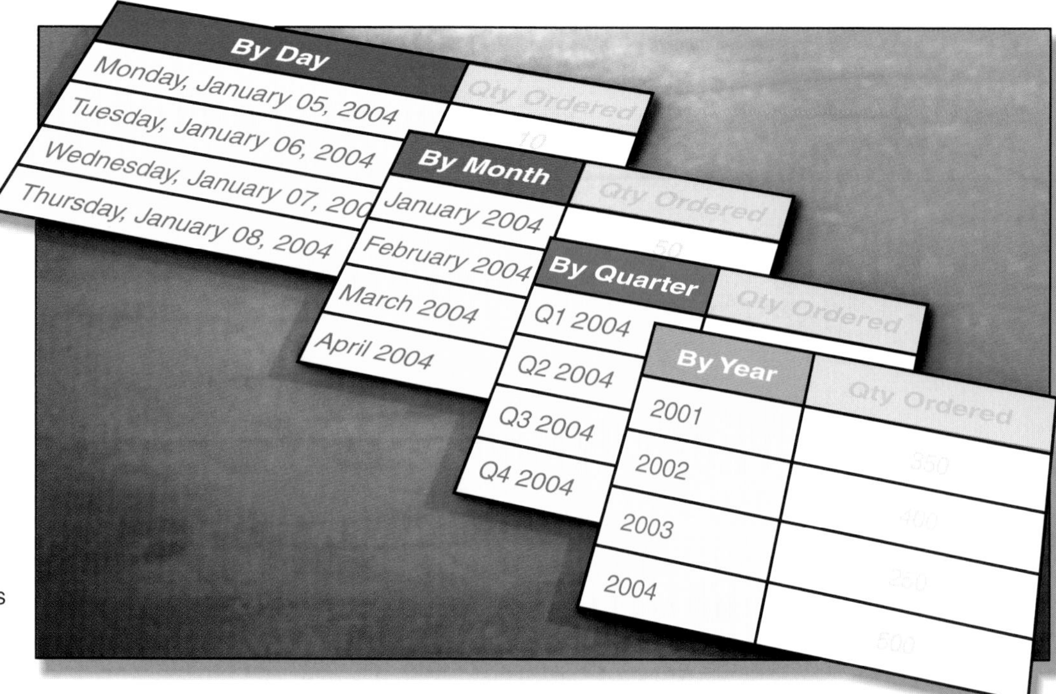

CREATE A QUERY USING THE SIMPLE QUERY WIZARD (CONTINUED)

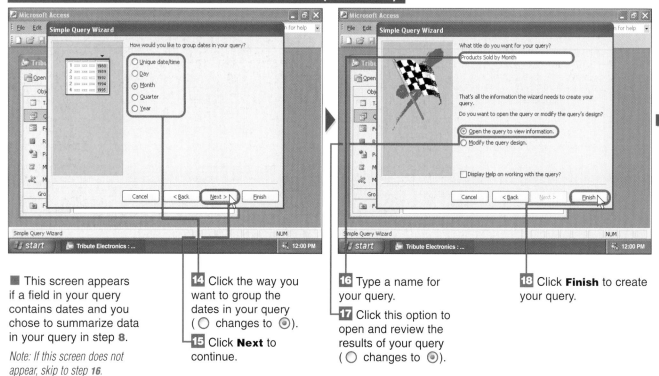

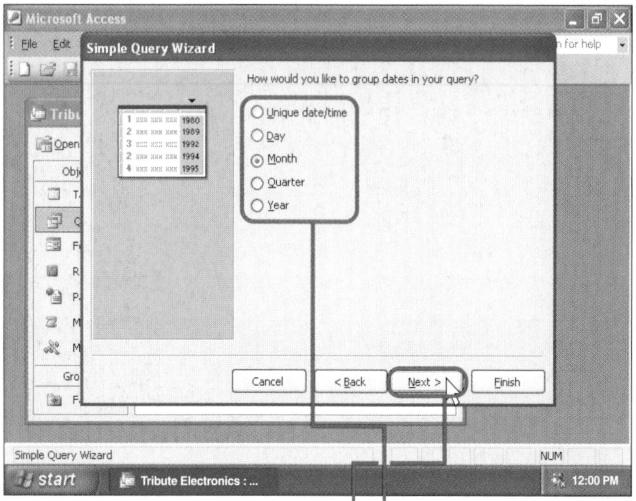

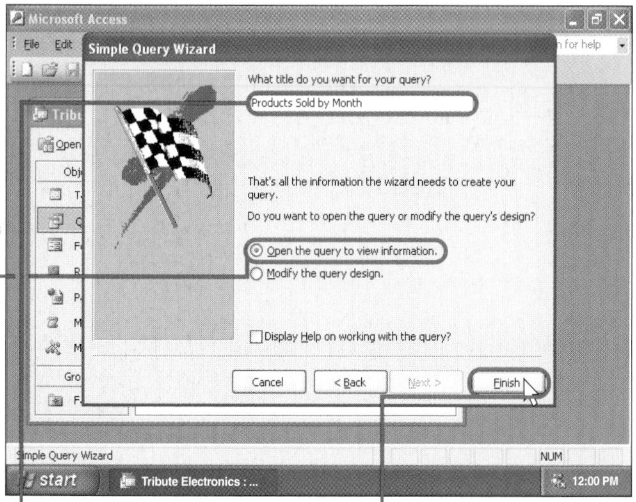

■ This screen appears if a field in your query contains dates and you chose to summarize data in your query in step **8**.

*Note: If this screen does not appear, skip to step **16**.*

14 Click the way you want to group the dates in your query (○ changes to ◉).

15 Click **Next** to continue.

16 Type a name for your query.

17 Click this option to open and review the results of your query (○ changes to ◉).

18 Click **Finish** to create your query.

Why didn't my query summarize data the way I expected?

To ensure that Access will properly summarize data in your query, make sure you include only the fields you need to summarize data. For example, to determine the total number of units sold by each employee, you should include only the Employee and Units Sold fields.

Employee	Units Sold
Abbott	8,800
Carey	7,400
Davis	3,900
Jones	3,700
Lance	7,700
McMillan	8,800

Can I make changes to a query I created using the Simple Query Wizard?

Yes. You can use the Design view of a query to make changes to any query you create. For example, you can sort records and add and remove fields. To display a query in the Design view, see page 202.

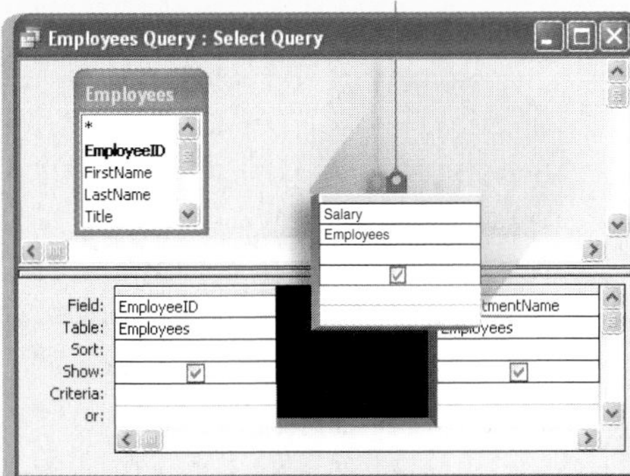

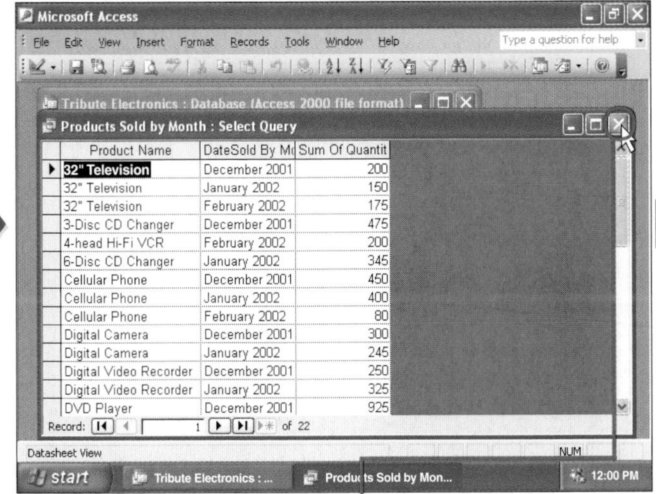

■ The results of your query appear.

19 When you finish reviewing the results of your query, click ☒ to close the query.

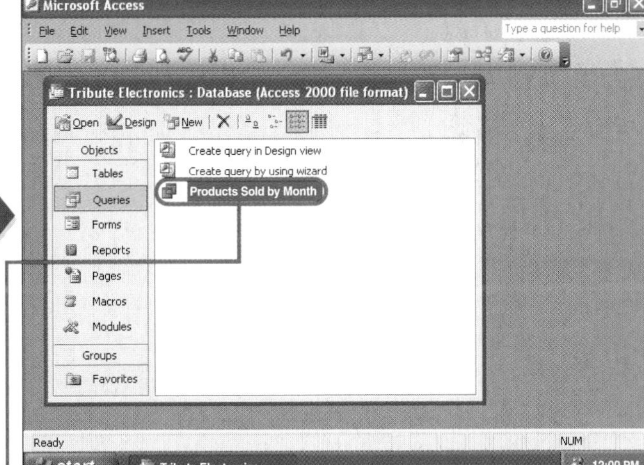

■ The query appears in the Database window.

■ To once again open the query to review the results of the query, double-click the query in the Database window.

Note: Each time you open a query, Access will use the most current data from your database to determine the results of the query.

CHANGE THE VIEW OF A QUERY

You can view a query in five different ways. Each view allows you to perform different tasks.

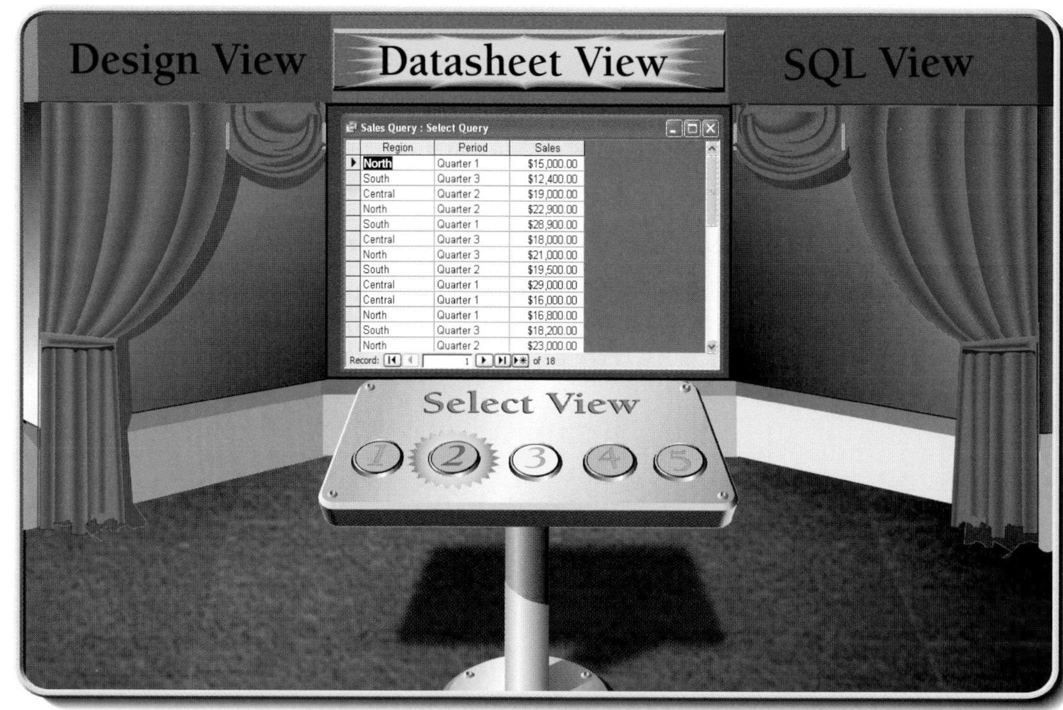

CHANGE THE VIEW OF A QUERY

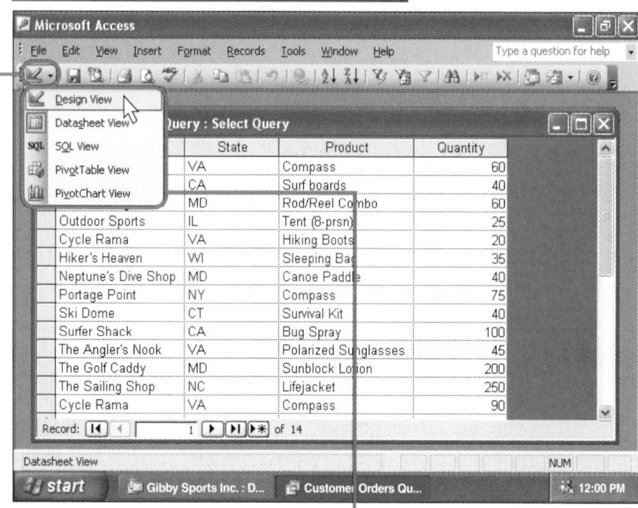

■ In this example, the query appears in the Datasheet view.

1 Click ▾ in this area to display the query in a different view.

2 Click the view you want to use.

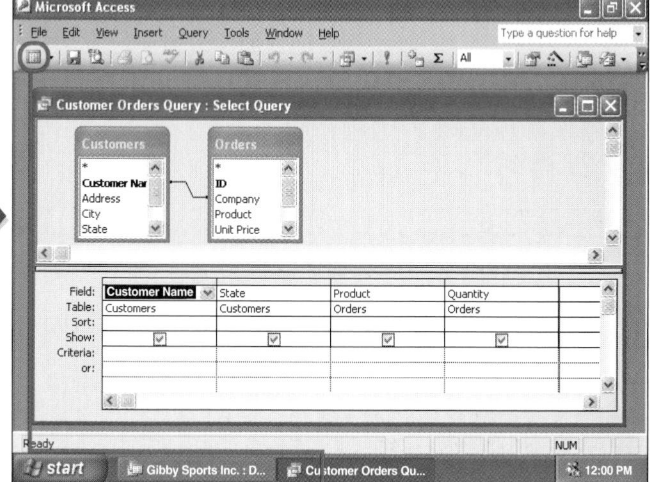

■ The query appears in the view you selected.

■ In this example, the View button changed from ✎ to ▦.

■ To quickly switch between the Datasheet (▦) and Design (✎) views, click the View button.

THE QUERY VIEWS

Design View

The Design view allows you to plan your query. You can use this view to specify the data you want to find, where Access can find the data and how you want to display the results.

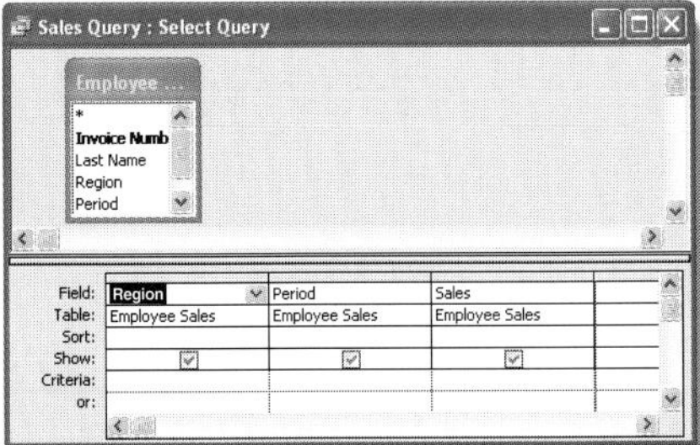

Datasheet View

The Datasheet view displays the results of your query. The field names appear across the top of the window. Each row shows the information for one record that meets the conditions you specified.

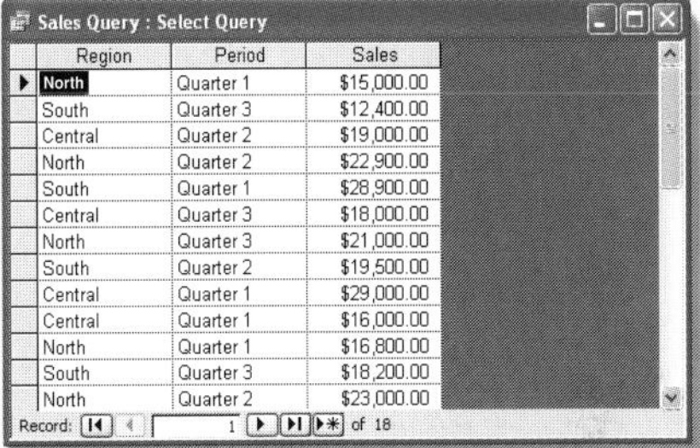

SQL View

The SQL view displays the SQL statements for your query. SQL (Structured Query Language) is a computer language used to work with the information in a database. When you create a query, Access creates the SQL statements that describe your query.

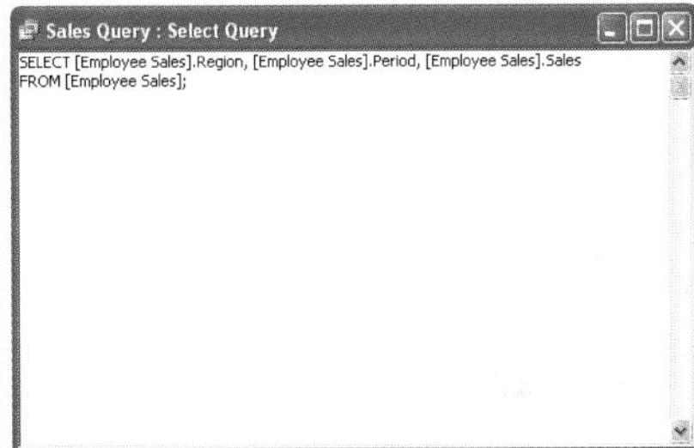

PivotTable View

The PivotTable view allows you to summarize and analyze the results of your query. When you first display your query results in this view, the PivotTable is empty and you must add the fields you want the PivotTable to display. For information on using the PivotTable view, see page 232.

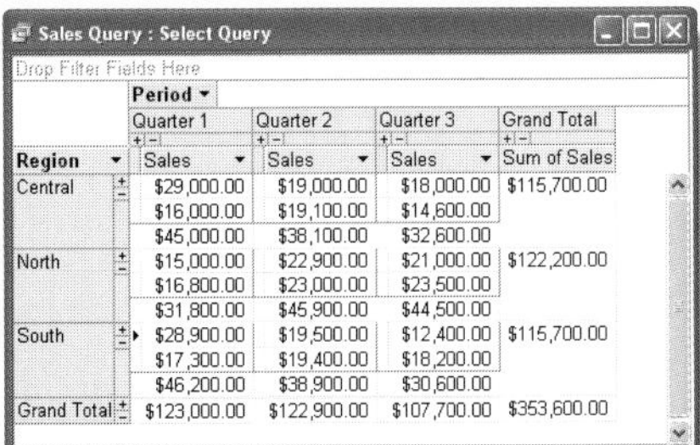

PivotChart View

The PivotChart view allows you to display a graphical summary of the results of your query. When you first display your query results in this view, the PivotChart is empty and you must add the fields you want the PivotChart to display. For information on using the PivotChart view, see page 238.

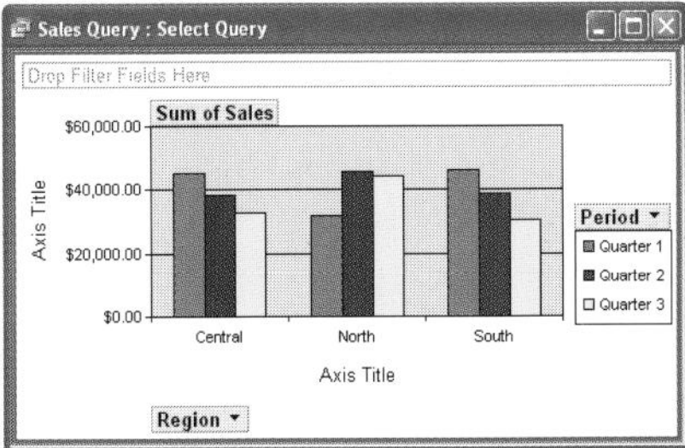

OPEN A QUERY

You can open a query to display the results of the query on your screen. Opening a query allows you to review and make changes to the query.

Each time you open a query, Access will use the most current data from your database to determine the results of the query.

OPEN A QUERY

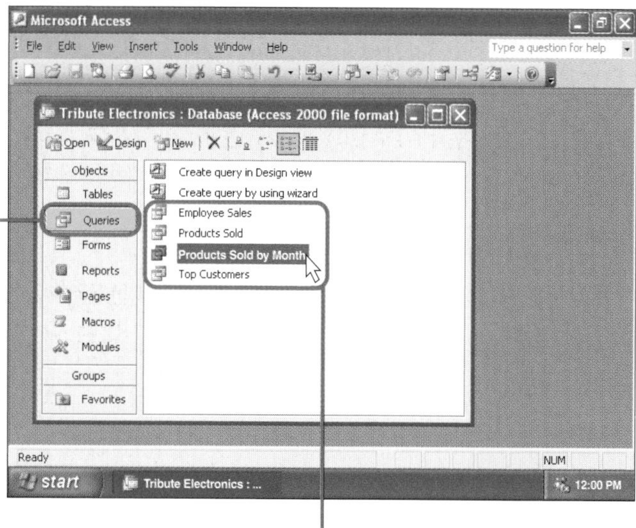

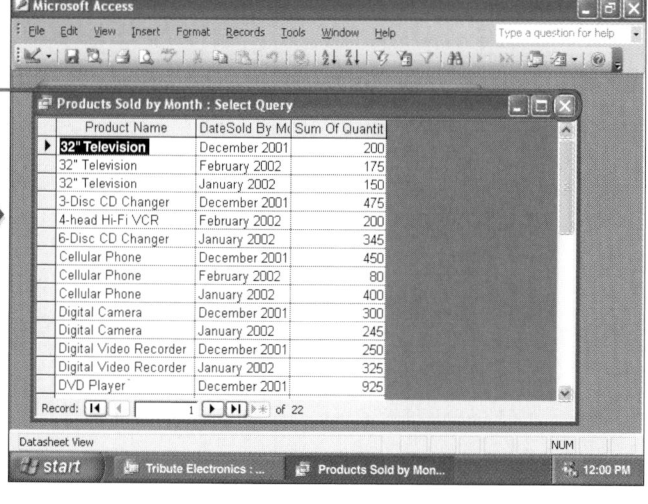

1 Click **Queries** in the Database window.

■ This area displays a list of the queries in your database.

2 Double-click the query you want to open.

■ The query opens, displaying the results of the query.

■ When you finish reviewing and working with the query, click ☒ to close the query.

*Note: A dialog box will appear if you did not save changes you made to the design of the query. Click **Yes** or **No** to specify if you want to save the changes.*

REARRANGE FIELDS

You can change the order of fields in a query. Rearranging fields in a query will affect the order in which the fields will appear in the query results.

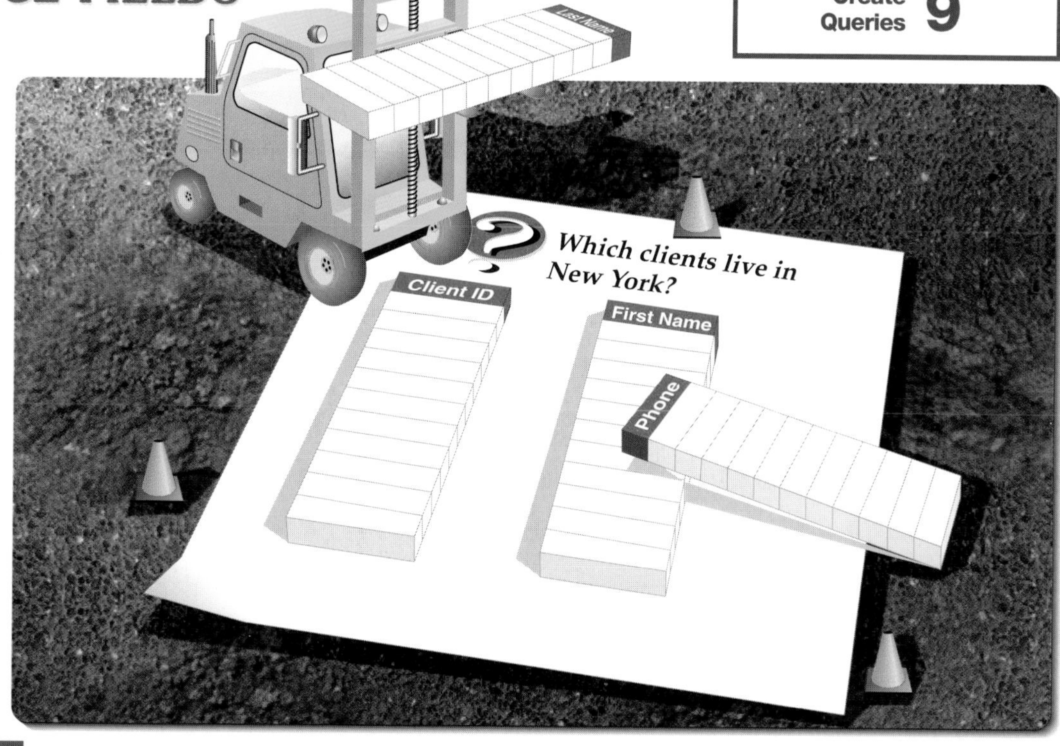

REARRANGE FIELDS

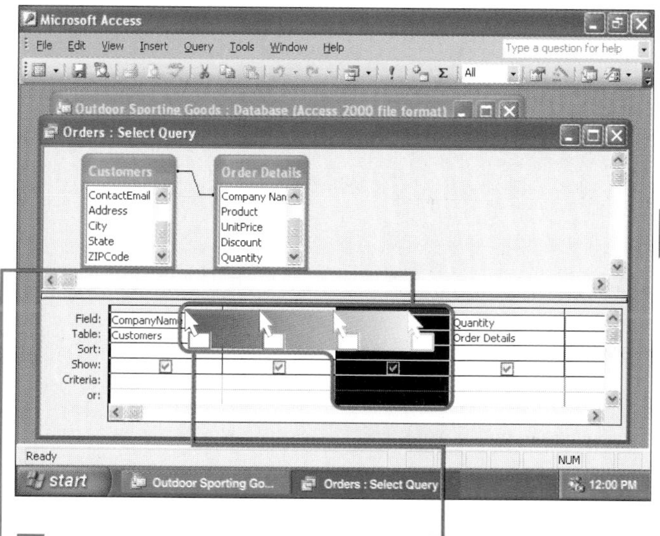

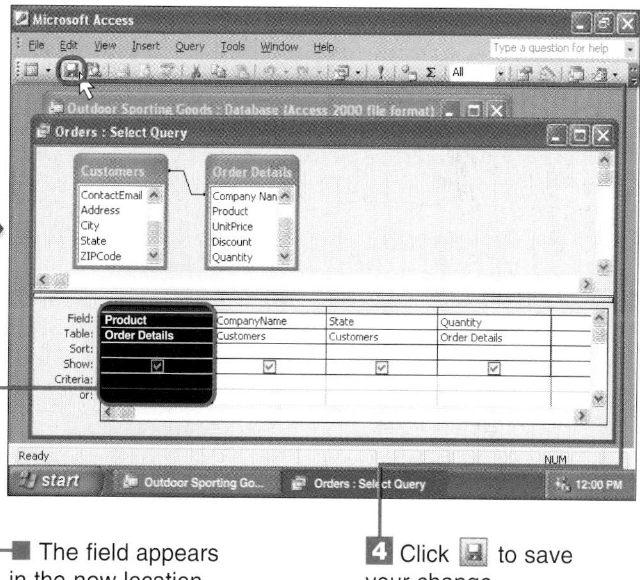

1 Display the query you want to change in the Design view. To change the view of a query, see page 202.

2 Position the mouse directly above the field you want to move (changes to ⬇) and then click to select the field. The field is highlighted.

3 Position the mouse directly above the selected field and then drag the field to a new location.

Note: A thick line shows where the field will appear.

■ The field appears in the new location.

4 Click to save your change.

ADD FIELDS

You can add one or all the fields in a table to a query. All the fields you add will appear in the results of the query.

Adding a field to a query is useful if you did not include a field from a table when you created a query.

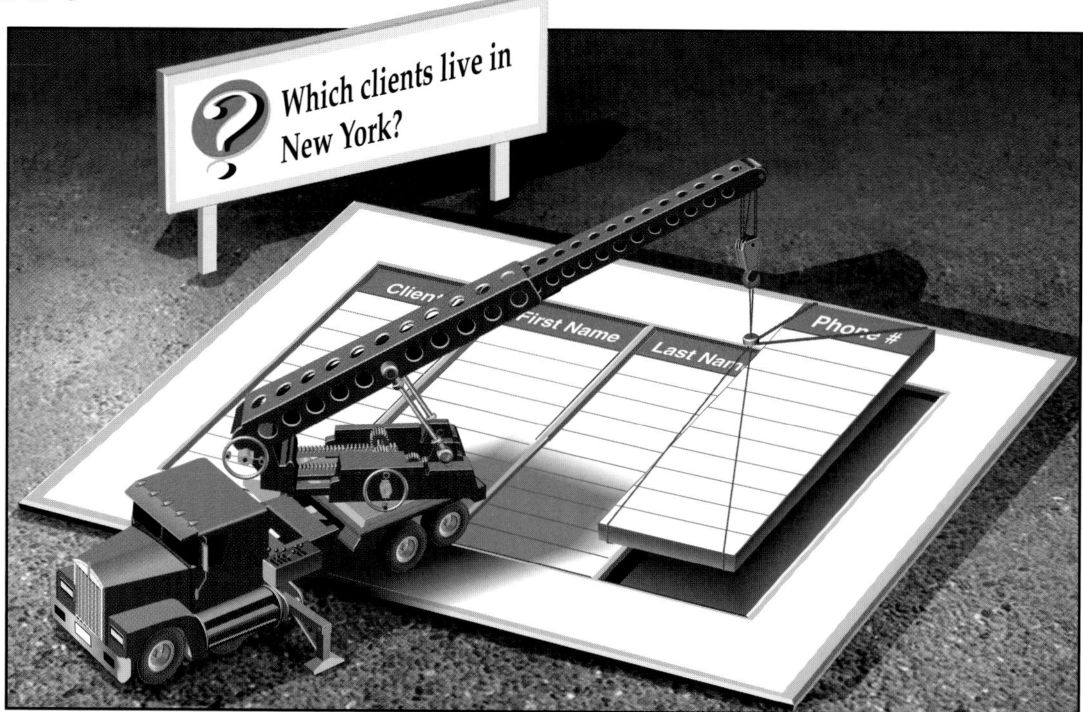

ADD ONE FIELD

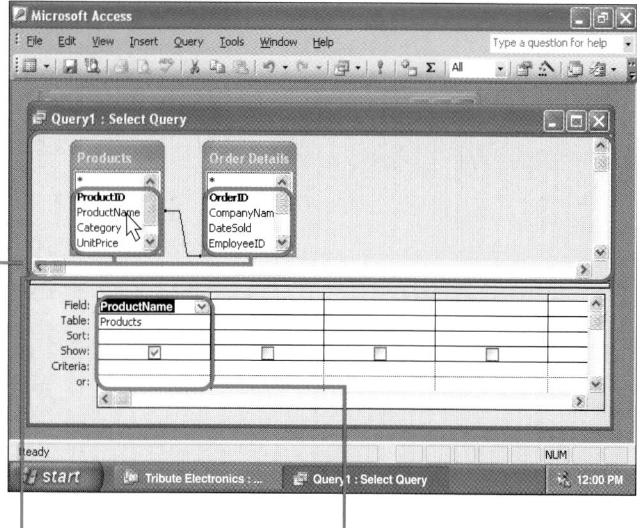

■ Each box in this area displays the fields for one table.

1 Double-click the field you want to add to your query.

■ The field you select and the table that contains the field appear in a column.

ADD ALL FIELDS

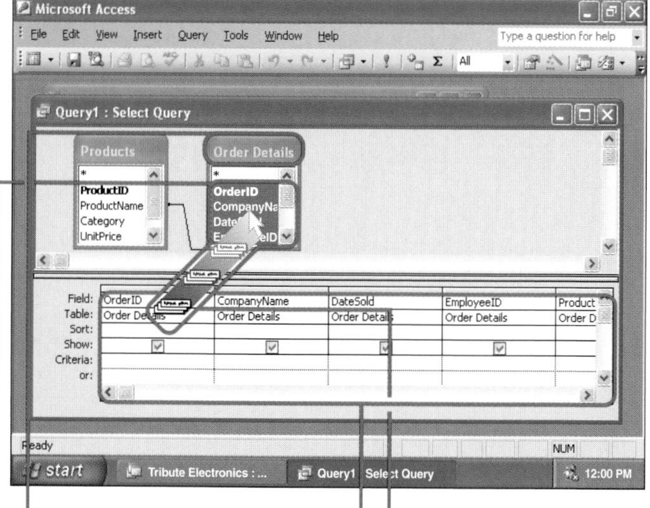

1 Double-click the heading of the box for the table that contains the fields you want to add to your query.

■ All the fields in the table are selected.

2 Position the mouse over the selected fields and then drag the fields to the first empty column.

■ Each field from the table appears in its own column.

Why would I use the asterisk (*) to add all the fields in a table to a query?

If you may later add or delete fields from a table used in a query, you may want to use the asterisk (*) to add all the fields in the table to the query. When you add or delete a field from the table, Access will automatically add or delete the field from the query.

How can I clear a query to start over?

If you make mistakes while adding fields to a query, you can start over by clearing the query.

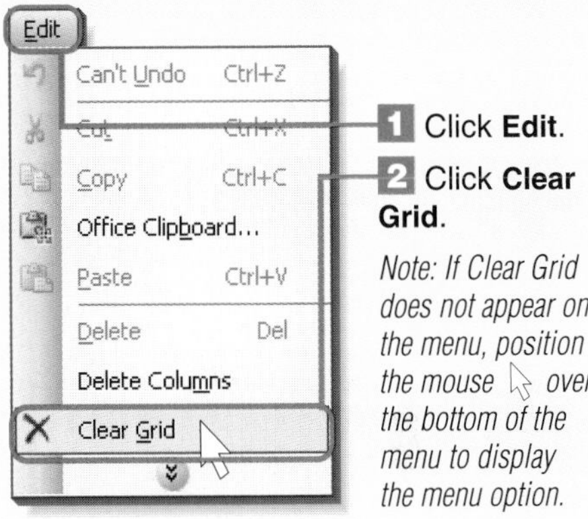

1 Click **Edit**.

2 Click **Clear Grid**.

Note: If Clear Grid does not appear on the menu, position the mouse over the bottom of the menu to display the menu option.

ADD ALL FIELDS USING THE ASTERISK (*)

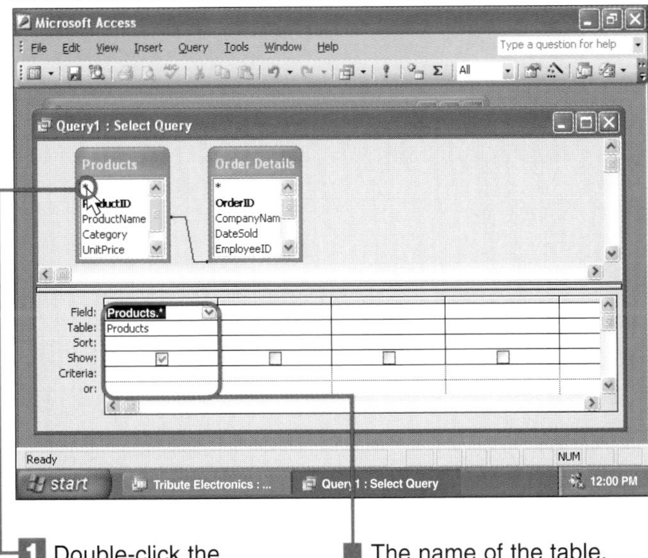

1 Double-click the asterisk (*) in the box for the table containing the fields you want to add to your query.

■ The name of the table, followed by an asterisk (*), appears in a column. All the fields in the table will appear in the results of your query.

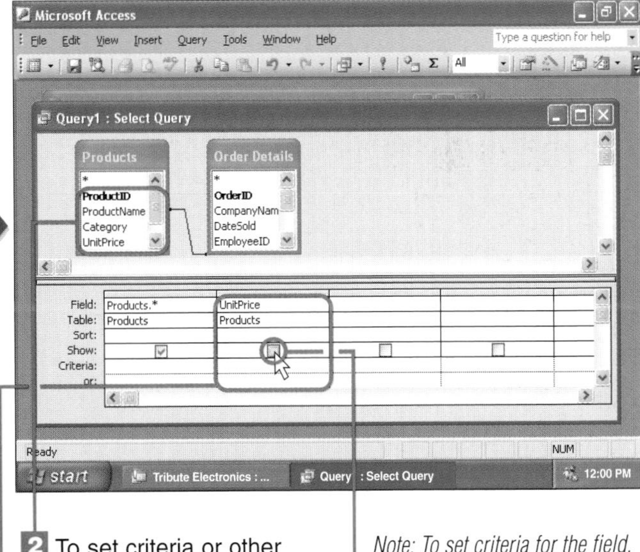

2 To set criteria or other options for one field in the table, double-click the field to place the field in a separate column.

■ The field appears in a separate column in the query.

Note: To set criteria for the field, see page 211.

3 To ensure the field will not appear twice in the query results, click the **Show** box for the field (☑ changes to ☐).

DELETE A FIELD

You can delete a field you no longer want to include in your query.

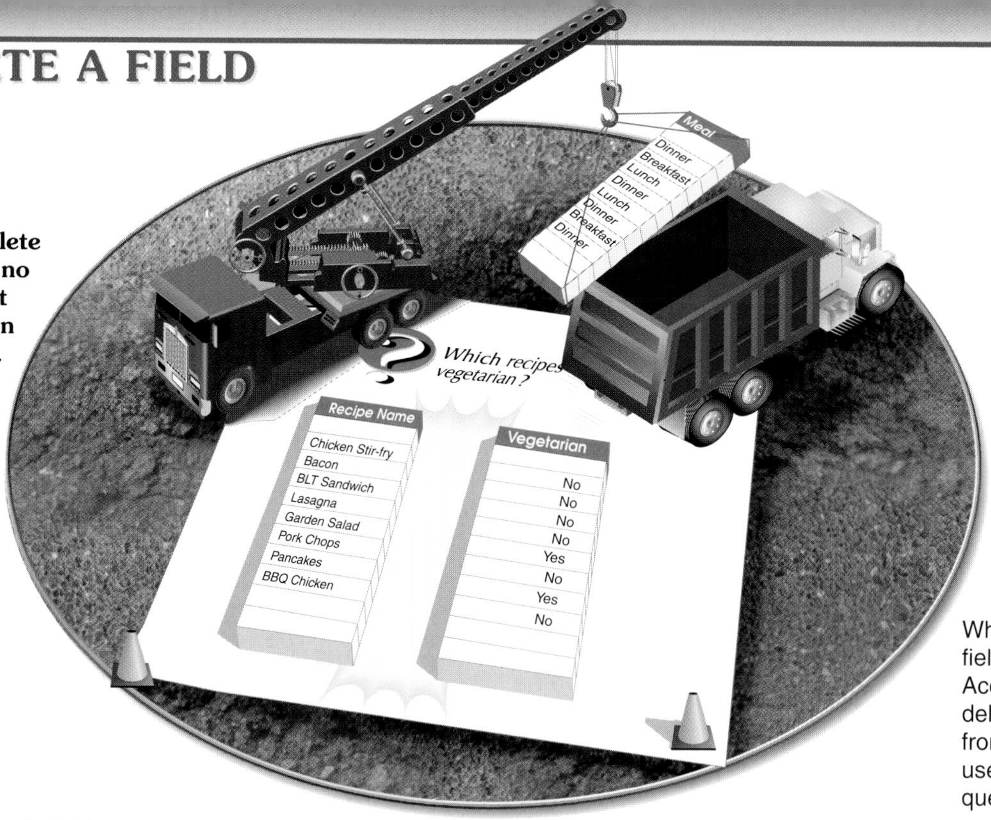

When you delete a field from a query, Access will not delete the field from the table you used to create the query.

DELETE A FIELD

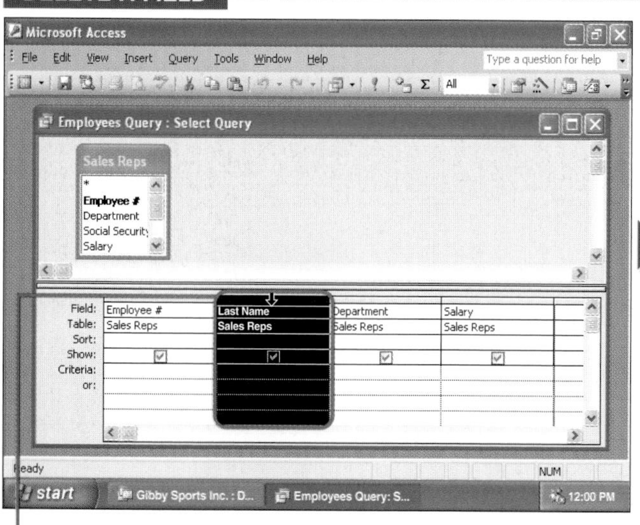

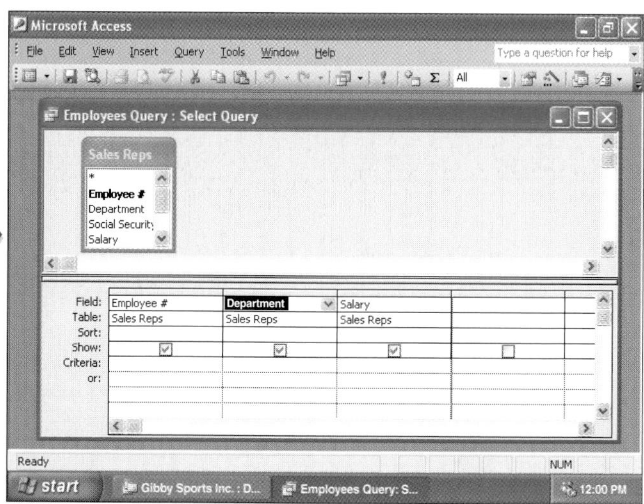

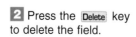

1 To select the field you want to delete, position the mouse directly above the field (changes to ⬇) and then click to select the field. The field is highlighted.

2 Press the Delete key to delete the field.

■ The field disappears from your query.

HIDE A FIELD

You can hide a field used in a query. Hiding a field is useful when you need a field to find information in your database, but do not want the field to appear in the results of your query.

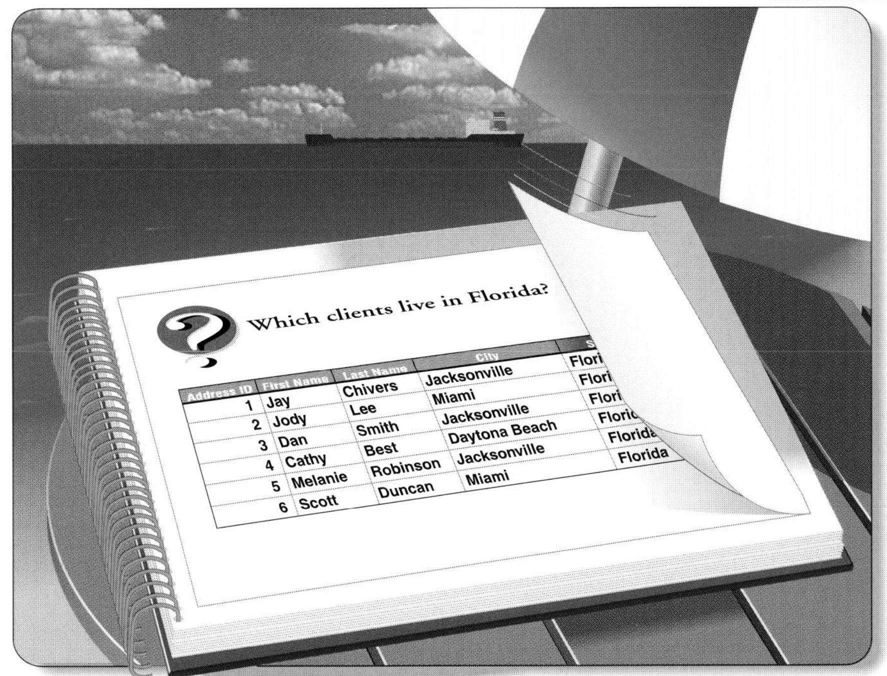

For example, you can use the State field in a query to find all your clients in Florida, but hide the State field in the query results.

HIDE A FIELD

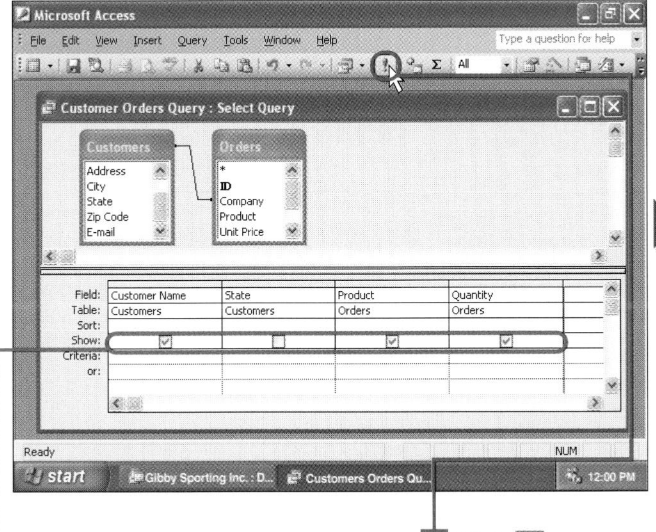

Microsoft Access

Customer Orders Query : Select Query

Customer Name	Product	Quantity
Cycle Rama	Compass	60
Surfer Shack	Surf boards	40
Reel Fishing	Rod/Reel Combo	60
Outdoor Sports	Tent (8-prsn)	25
Cycle Rama	Hiking Boots	20
Hiker's Heaven	Sleeping Bag	35
Neptune's Dive Shop	Canoe Paddle	40
Portage Point	Compass	75
Ski Dome	Survival Kit	40
Surfer Shack	Bug Spray	100
The Angler's Nook	Polarized Sunglasses	45
The Golf Caddy	Sunblock Lotion	200
The Sailing Shop	Lifejacket	250
Cycle Rama	Compass	90

Record: 1 of 14

Datasheet View

■ Each field that displays a check mark (☑) will appear in the results of your query.

1 If you do not want a field to appear in the results of your query, click the **Show** box for the field (☑ changes to ☐).

2 Click ! to run the query.

■ The field does not appear in the results of the query.

■ To return to the Design view, click the Design View button.

■ If you no longer want to hide a field in the results of your query, repeat step 1 (☐ changes to ☑).

You can sort the results of a query to better organize the results. Sorting the query results can help you quickly find information of interest.

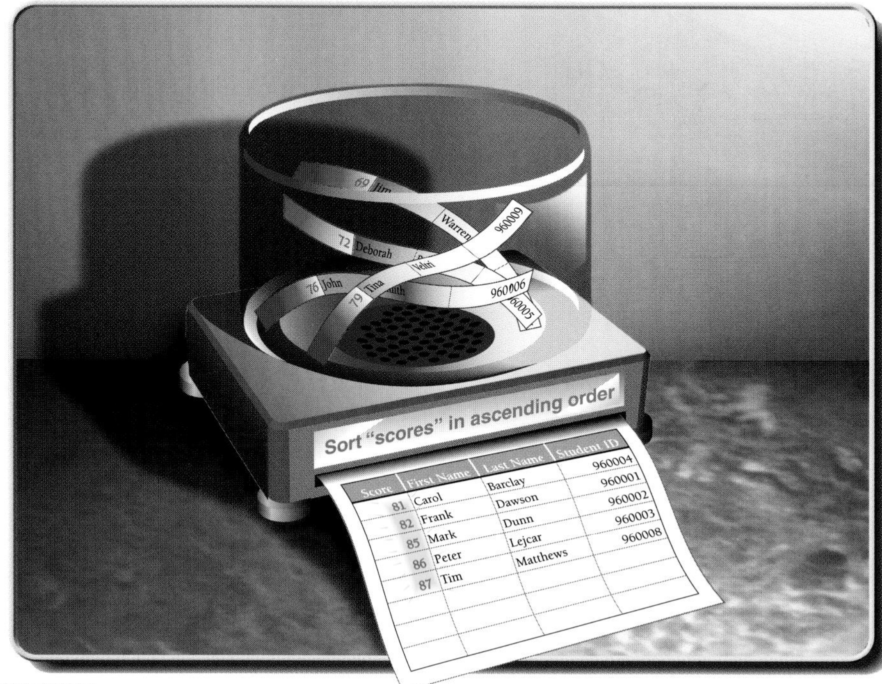

You can sort the results of a query in two ways.

Ascending
Sorts A to Z, 1 to 9

Descending
Sorts Z to A, 9 to 1

SORT QUERY RESULTS

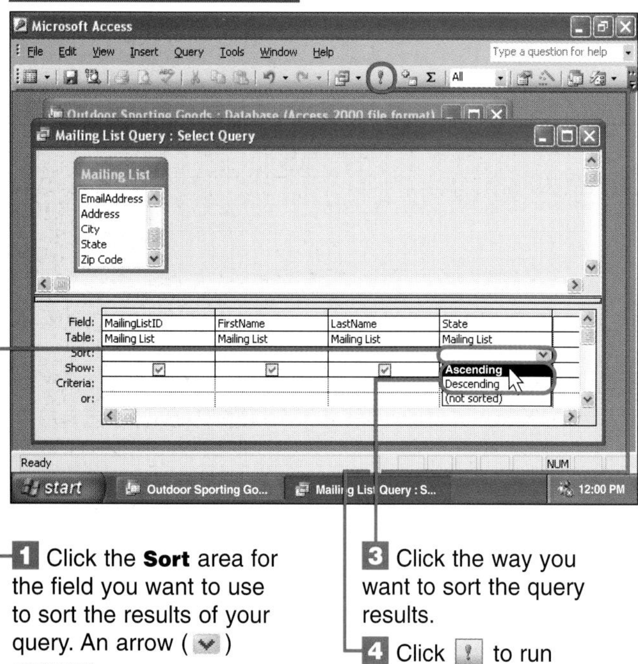

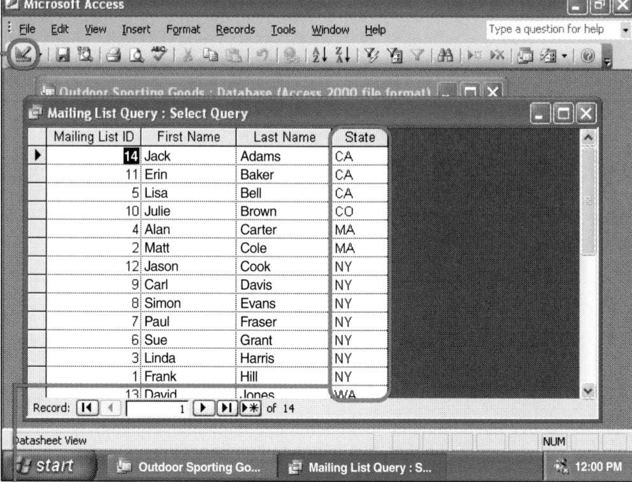

1 Click the **Sort** area for the field you want to use to sort the results of your query. An arrow ( ) appears.

2 Click the arrow ( ) to list the available sort options.

3 Click the way you want to sort the query results.

4 Click to run the query.

■ The records appear in the order you specified. In this example, the records are sorted alphabetically by state.

■ To return to the Design view, click .

■ If you no longer want to use a field to sort the query results, repeat steps 1 to 3, selecting **(not sorted)** in step 3.

USING CRITERIA TO FIND RECORDS

You can use criteria to find specific records in your database. Criteria are conditions that identify which records you want to find.

For example, you can use criteria to find all of your customers who live in California.

USING CRITERIA TO FIND RECORDS

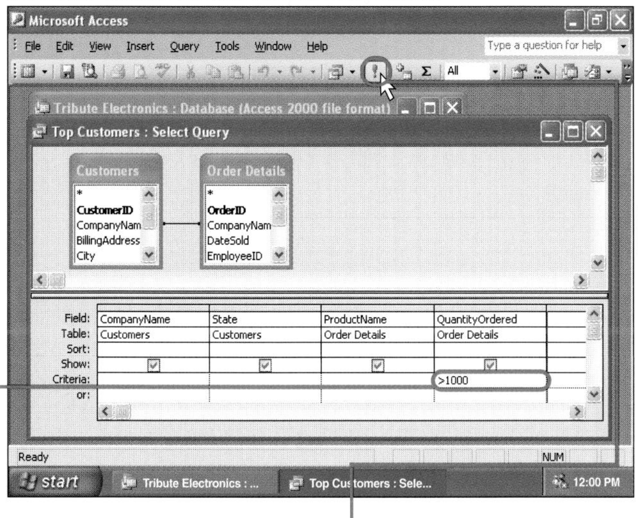

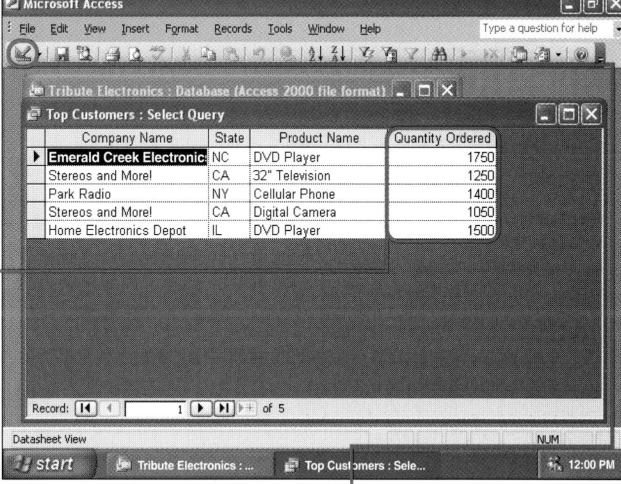

1 Click the **Criteria** area for the field you want to use to find specific records.

2 Type the criteria and then press the Enter key. Access may add quotation marks (" ") or number signs (#) to the criteria you type.

Note: For examples of criteria you can use, see page 214.

3 Click ! to run the query.

■ The results of the query appear.

■ In this example, Access found customers who ordered more than 1000 units.

■ To return to the Design view, click the Design View button.

USING MULTIPLE CRITERIA TO FIND RECORDS

You can use multiple criteria to find specific records in your database.

Criteria are conditions that identify which records you want to find. For examples of criteria that you can use, see page 214.

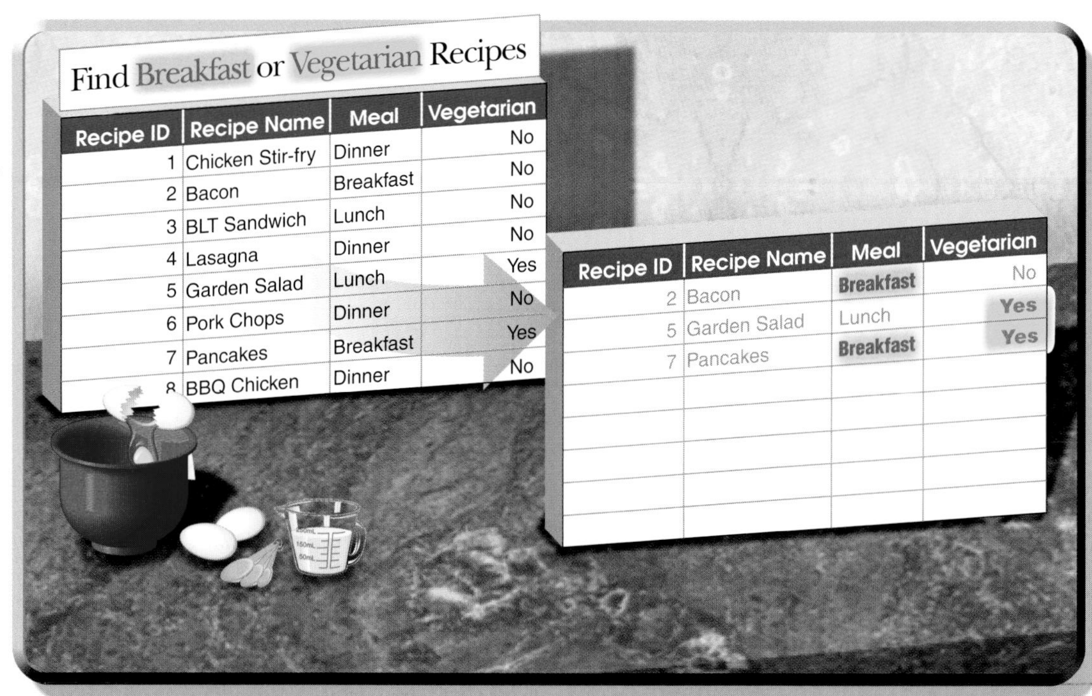

Find Breakfast or Vegetarian Recipes
Recipe ID | Recipe Name | Meal | Vegetarian
1 Chicken Stir-fry Dinner No
2 Bacon Breakfast No
3 BLT Sandwich Lunch No
4 Lasagna Dinner No
5 Garden Salad Lunch Yes
6 Pork Chops Dinner No
7 Pancakes Breakfast Yes
8 BBQ Chicken Dinner No
Recipe ID | Recipe Name | Meal | Vegetarian
2 Bacon Breakfast No
5 Garden Salad Lunch Yes
7 Pancakes Breakfast Yes

USING MULTIPLE CRITERIA WITH "OR"

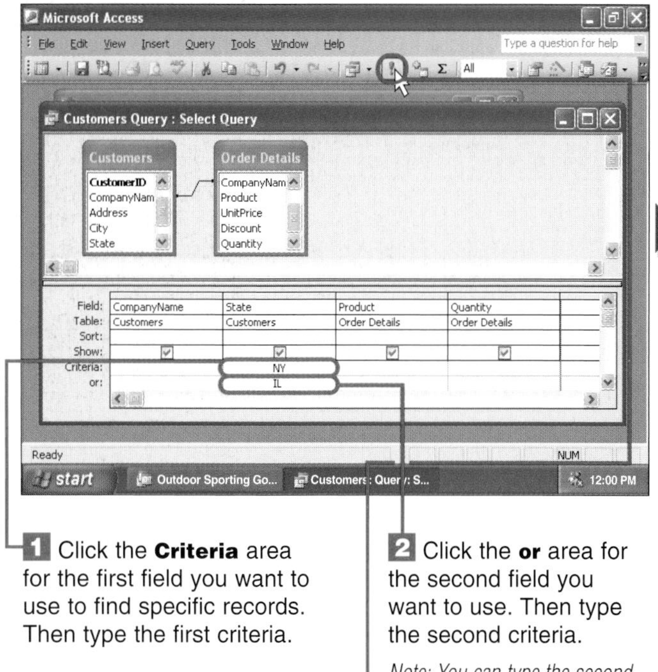

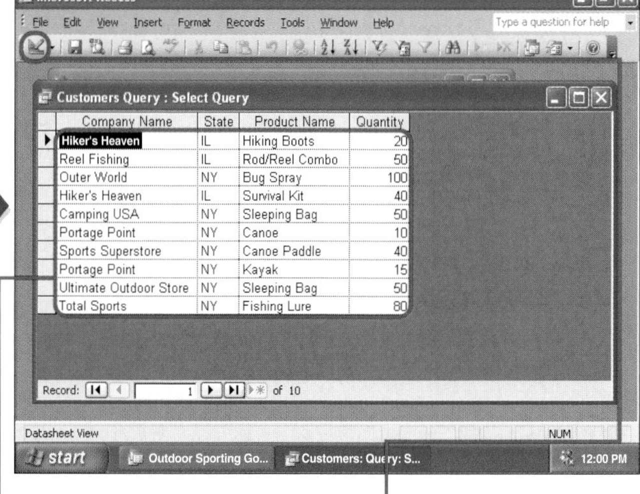

1 Click the **Criteria** area for the first field you want to use to find specific records. Then type the first criteria.

2 Click the **or** area for the second field you want to use. Then type the second criteria.

*Note: You can type the second criteria in the **or** area of the same field or a different field.*

3 Click ! to run the query.

■ The results of the query appear.

■ In this example, Access found customers who live in New York or Illinois.

■ To return to the Design view, click the Design View button.

How can I use multiple criteria to find specific records in my database?

You can use the **Or** operator to find records that meet at least one of the criteria you specify. For example, you can find employees in the Sales or Accounting department.

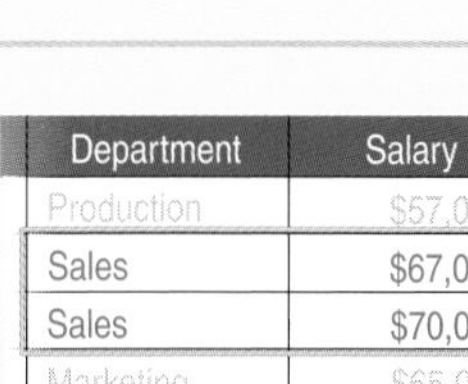

You can use the **And** operator to find records that meet all of the criteria you specify. For example, you can find employees in the Sales department who earn more than $60,000.

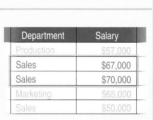

Department	Salary
Production	$57,000
Sales	$67,000
Sales	$70,000
Marketing	$65,000
Sales	$50,000

How do I use the "And" operator in one field?

In the Criteria area for the field, type the first criteria you want to use. Then type **And** followed by the second criteria. For example, to find customers who purchased more than 100 units and less than 200 units, type **>100 And <200** in the Quantity field.

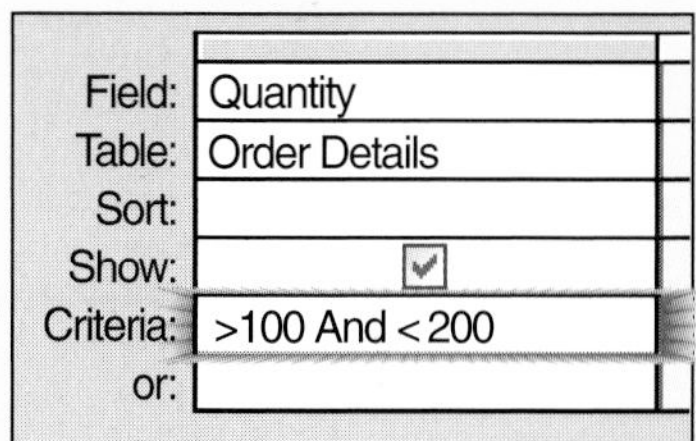

USING MULTIPLE CRITERIA WITH "AND"

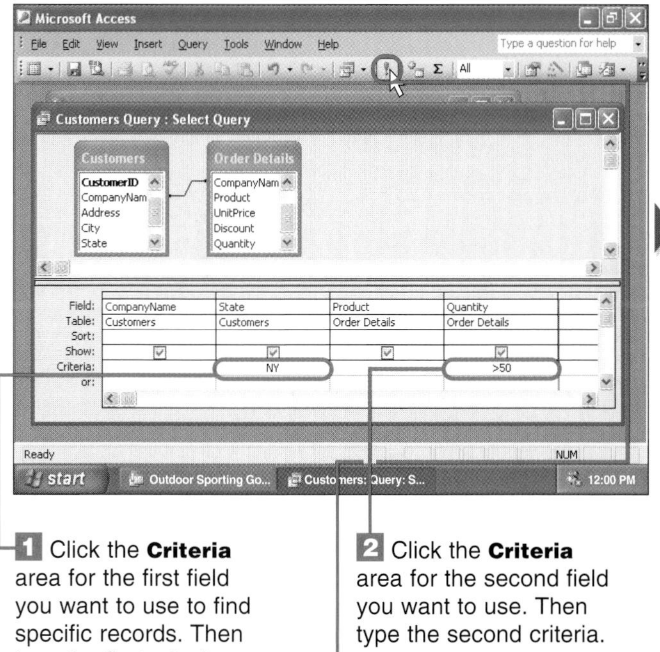

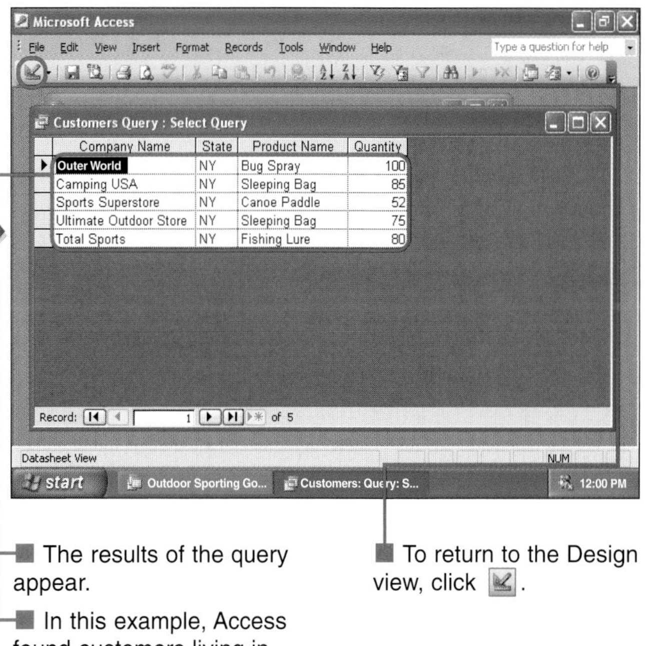

1 Click the **Criteria** area for the first field you want to use to find specific records. Then type the first criteria.

2 Click the **Criteria** area for the second field you want to use. Then type the second criteria.

3 Click ! to run the query.

■ The results of the query appear.

■ In this example, Access found customers living in New York who purchased more than 50 units.

■ To return to the Design view, click the Design View button.

EXAMPLES OF CRITERIA

Here are examples of criteria that you can use to find records in your database. Criteria are conditions that identify which records you want to find.

Exact matches

=100	Finds the number 100.
=California	Finds California.
=3/6/2004	Finds the date 6-Mar-04.
=Date( )	Finds today's date.

Note: You can leave out the equal sign (=) when searching for an exact match.

Less than

<100	Finds numbers less than 100.
<N	Finds text starting with the letters A to M.
<3/6/2004	Finds dates before 6-Mar-04.

Less than or equal to

<=100	Finds numbers less than or equal to 100.
<=N	Finds the letter N and text starting with the letters A to M.
<=3/6/2004	Finds dates on and before 6-Mar-04.

Greater than

>100	Finds numbers greater than 100.
>N	Finds text starting with the letters N to Z.
>3/6/2004	Finds dates after 6-Mar-04.

Greater than or equal to

>=100	Finds numbers greater than or equal to 100.
>=N	Finds the letter N and text starting with the letters N to Z.
>=3/6/2004	Finds dates on and after 6-Mar-04.

Does not match

Not 100	Finds numbers that do not match 100.
Not California	Finds text that does not match California.
Not 3/6/2004	Finds dates that do not match 6-Mar-04.

Empty fields

Is Null	Finds records that do not contain data in the field.
Is Not Null	Finds records that contain data in the field.

Find list of items

In (100,101)	Finds the numbers 100 and 101.
In (California,CA)	Finds California and CA.
In (#3/6/2004#, #3/7/2004#)	Finds the dates 6-Mar-04 and 7-Mar-04.

Between...And...

Between 100 And 200	Finds numbers from 100 to 200.
Between A And D	Finds the letters A and D and text starting with the letters A to C.
Between 3/6/2004 And 3/12/2004	Finds dates on and between 6-Mar-04 and 12-Mar-04.

Wildcards

The asterisk (*) wildcard represents one or more characters.
The question mark (?) wildcard represents a single character.

Like Br*	Finds text starting with **Br**, such as **Br**enda and **Br**own.
Like *ar*	Finds text containing **ar**, such as **Ar**nold and M**ar**c.
Like *th	Finds text ending with **th**, such as Smi**th** and Griffi**th**.
Like Wend?	Finds 5-letter words starting with **Wend**, such as **Wend**i and **Wend**y.

Note: You can leave out "Like" when using wildcard characters.

DISPLAY HIGHEST OR LOWEST VALUES

In the results of a query, you can have Access display only the records with the highest or lowest values in a field.

For example, you can display the five largest orders or the ten lowest-selling products.

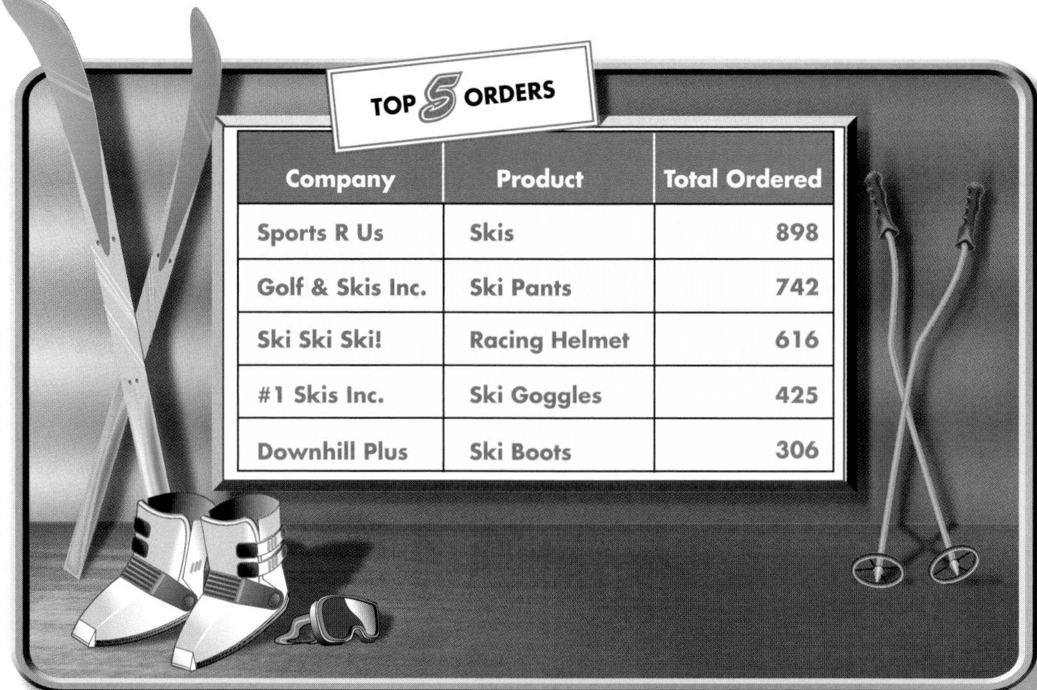

TOP 5 ORDERS
Company
Product
Total Ordered
Sports R Us
Skis
898
Golf & Skis Inc.
Ski Pants
742
Ski Ski Ski!
Racing Helmet
616
#1 Skis Inc.
Ski Goggles
425
Downhill Plus
Ski Boots
306

DISPLAY HIGHEST OR LOWEST VALUES

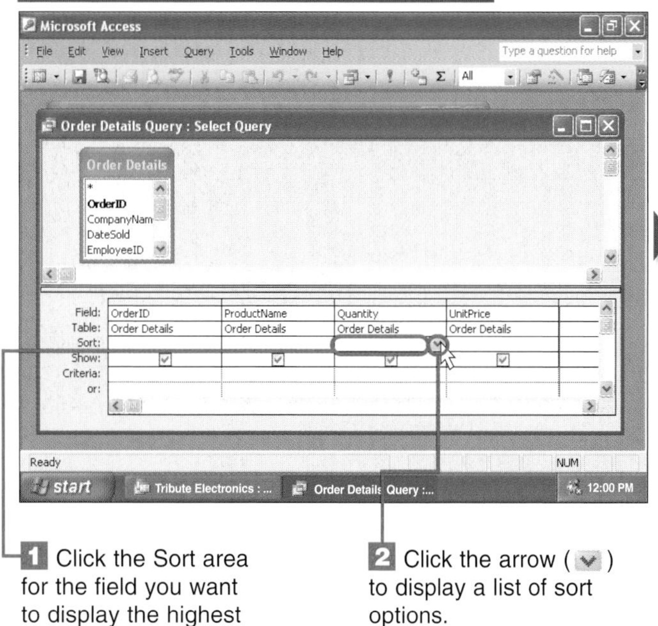

1 Click the Sort area for the field you want to display the highest or lowest values for. An arrow ( ) appears.

2 Click the arrow ( ) to display a list of sort options.

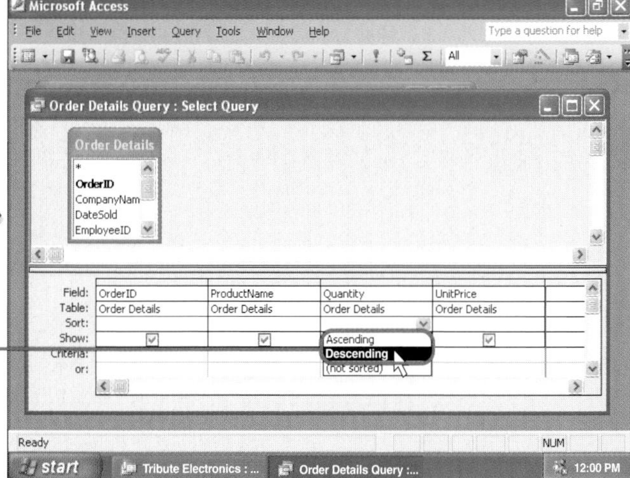

3 Click the way you want to sort the records.

Ascending
Display lowest values

Descending
Display highest values

Why didn't the results of my query appear the way I expected?

If you have set up other fields to sort the results of your query, Access may not display the highest or lowest values in a field properly. To remove a sort from a field, perform steps **1** to **3** below, selecting **(not sorted)** in step **3**.

Find Top 5 Products Sold

NOT SORTED

SORTED

Product	Units Sold
Superior Race Top	4,068
Extreme Socks	3,749
Baldwin Shorts	2,562
Stay Cool Hat	2,378
Dual Purpose Shades	1,584

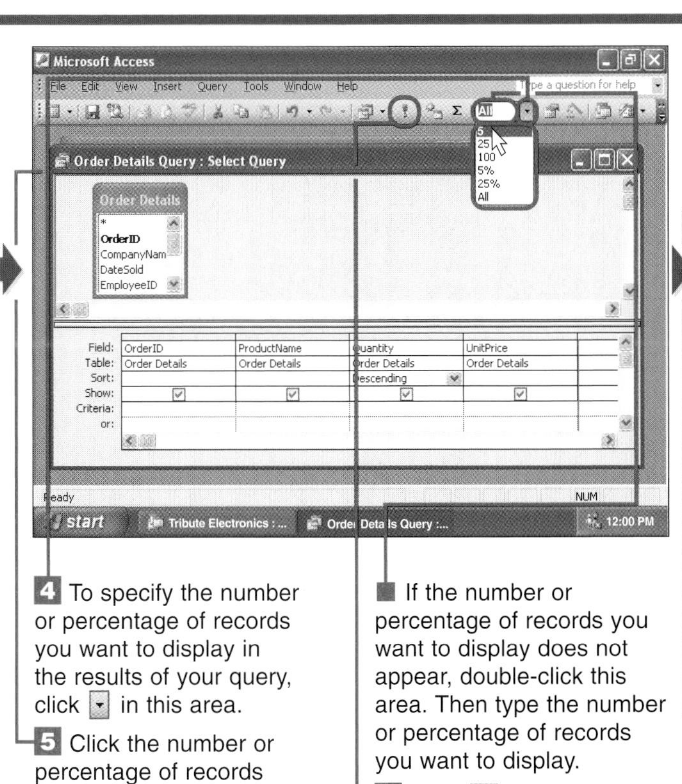

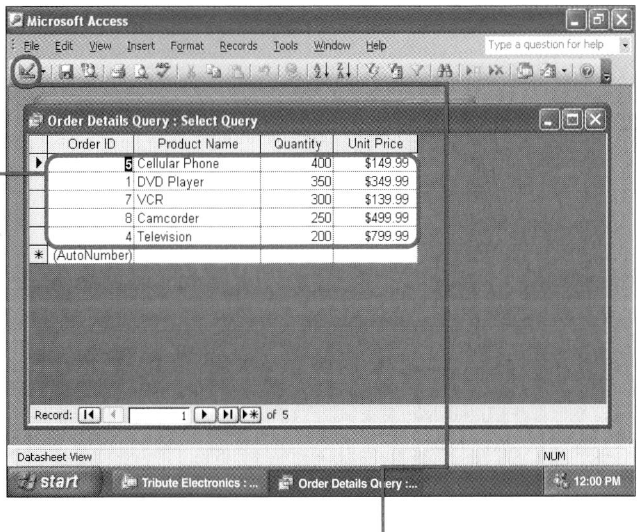

4 To specify the number or percentage of records you want to display in the results of your query, click ▾ in this area.

5 Click the number or percentage of records you want to display.

■ If the number or percentage of records you want to display does not appear, double-click this area. Then type the number or percentage of records you want to display.

6 Click ! to run the query.

■ The number or percentage of records you specified appear in the results of your query.

■ In this example, the records with the five highest values in the field appear.

■ To return to the Design view, click ✎.

■ To once again display all the records in the results of the query, repeat steps **4** and **5**, selecting **All** in step **5**.

PERFORM CALCULATIONS

You can perform a calculation on each record in a query. You can then review and analyze the results.

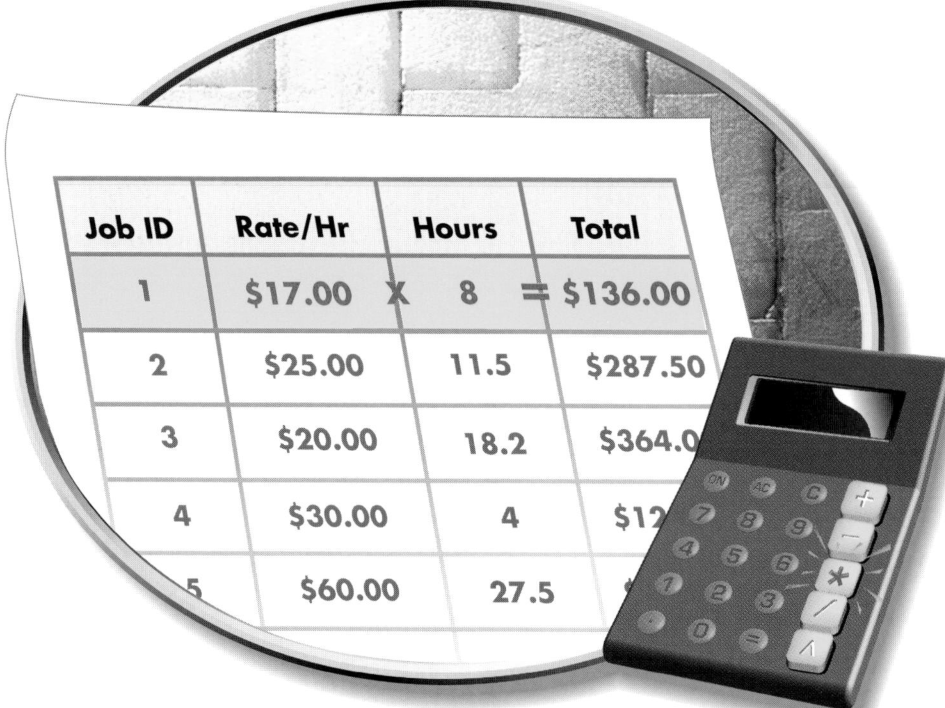

Job ID
Rate/Hr
Hours
Total
1
$17.00
8
$136.00
2
$25.00
11.5
$287.50
3
$20.00
18.2
4
$30.00
4
5
$60.00
27.5

You can use these operators to perform calculations.

+ Add

- Subtract

* Multiply

/ Divide

^ Raise to a power

PERFORM CALCULATIONS

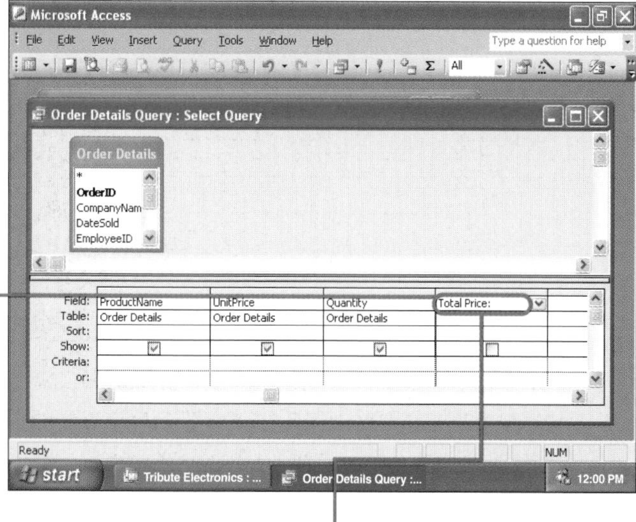

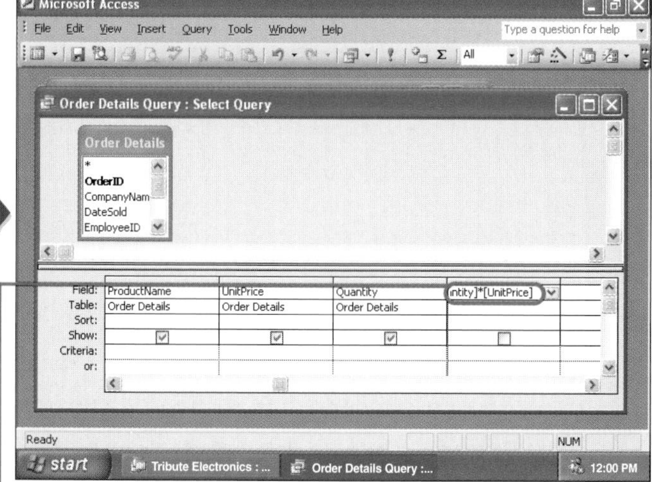

1 Click the **Field** area in the first empty column.

2 Type a name for the field that will display the results of the calculations, followed by a colon (:). Then press the **Spacebar** to leave a blank space.

3 Type an expression that describes the calculation you want to perform. In this example, type the expression **[Quantity]*[UnitPrice]**. For information on entering expressions, see the top of page 219.

Note: If the expression you type is too long to fit in the cell, you can zoom into the cell to display the contents of the entire cell. To zoom into a cell, see page 58.

How do I enter an expression to perform a calculation?

[Quantity]*[Price]

To enter fields in an expression, type the field names in square brackets. Make sure you type the field names exactly.

[Orders]![Quantity]*[Orders]![Price]

If a field exists in more than one table, you need to type the name of the table that contains the field in square brackets followed by an exclamation mark (!). Then type the field name in square brackets. Make sure you type the table and field names exactly.

Orders		
Quantity	Price	Total
100	$42	$4,200
50	$50	$2,500
70	$75	$5,250
30	$36	$1,080
90	$45	$4,050

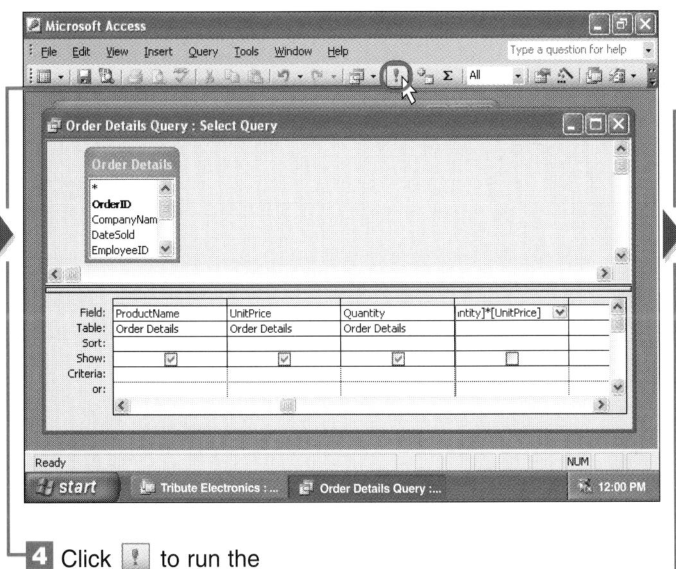

4 Click to run the query.

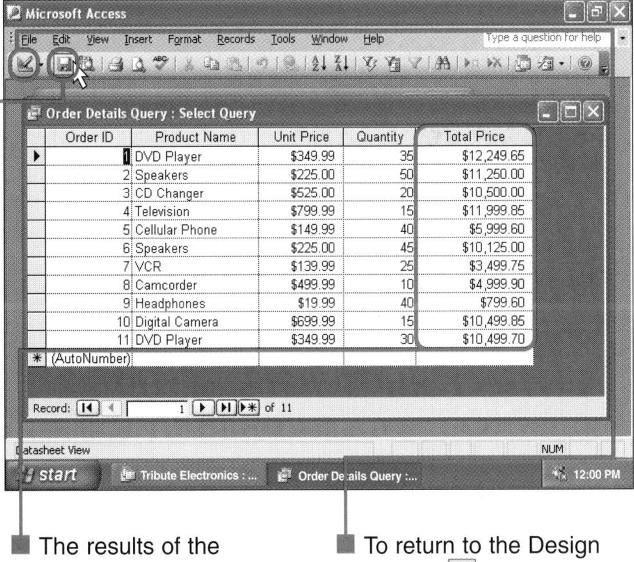

- The results of the calculations appear. The field name you specified appears at the top of the column.

5 To save the changes you made to your query, click .

- To return to the Design view, click .

Note: Access does not store the results of calculations in your database. Each time you run a query, Access will use the most current data in your database to perform the calculations.

USING PARAMETERS

You can use a parameter to be able to specify the information you want to find each time you run a query.

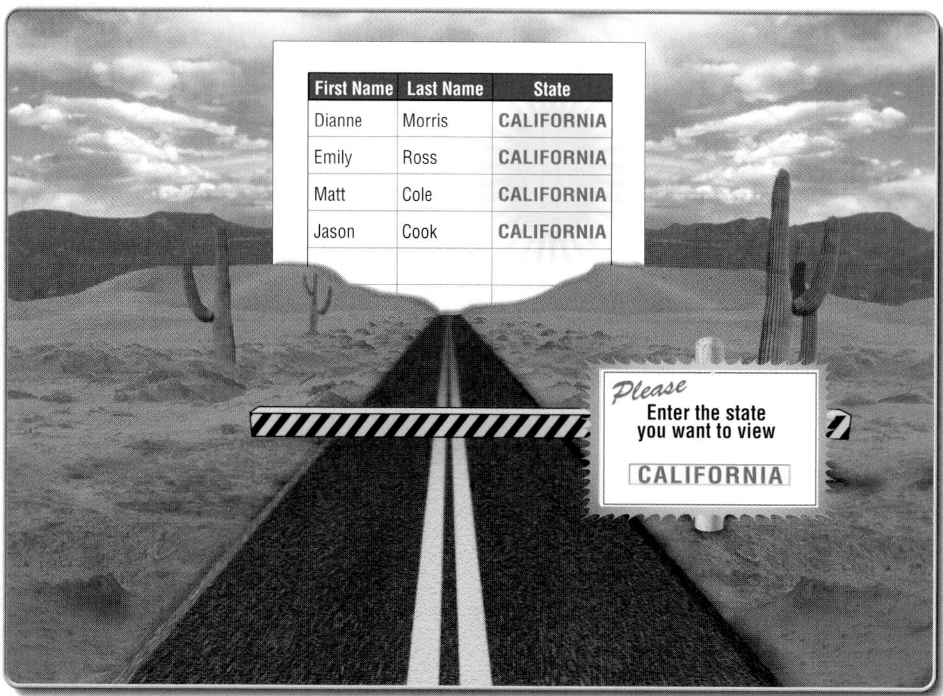

For example, you can use a parameter to have Access request the name of the state you want to find each time you run a query.

USING PARAMETERS

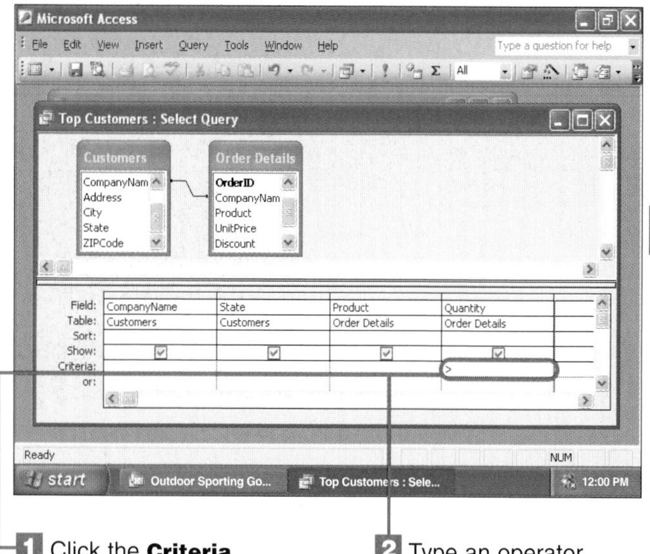

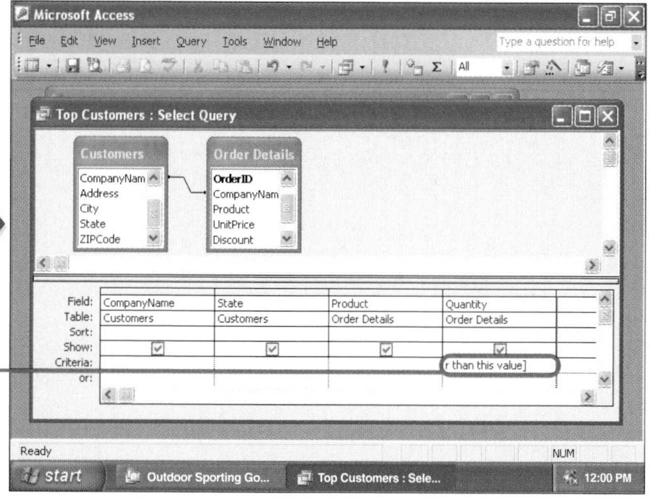

1 Click the **Criteria** area for the field you want to use a parameter.

2 Type an operator for the parameter.

Note: For examples of operators you can use, see the top of page 221.

3 Type the message you want Access to display when you run the query. Enclose the message in square brackets [ ].

Note: If the message you type is too long to fit in the cell, you can zoom into the cell to display the contents of the entire cell. To zoom into a cell, see page 58.

When entering a parameter, what operators can I use?

Operator	Result
=	Finds data equal to the value you enter.
>	Finds data greater than the value you enter.
>=	Finds data greater than or equal to the value you enter.
<	Finds data less than the value you enter.
<=	Finds data less than or equal to the value you enter.
<>	Finds data not equal to the value you enter.

Can I use more than one parameter?

Yes. You can enter a parameter for each field you want to use a parameter. When you run the query, Access will display the Enter Parameter Value dialog box for each parameter you entered. For example, you can enter one parameter that requests a company name and a second parameter that requests the number of orders for the company greater than a certain value.

Company	Orders
Portage Point	70
Portage Point	78
Video Place	90
Portage Point	104
Park Radio	63

Enter Parameter Value
Display records about this company
Portage Point
OK Cancel

Enter Parameter Value
Display orders greater than this value
75
OK Cancel

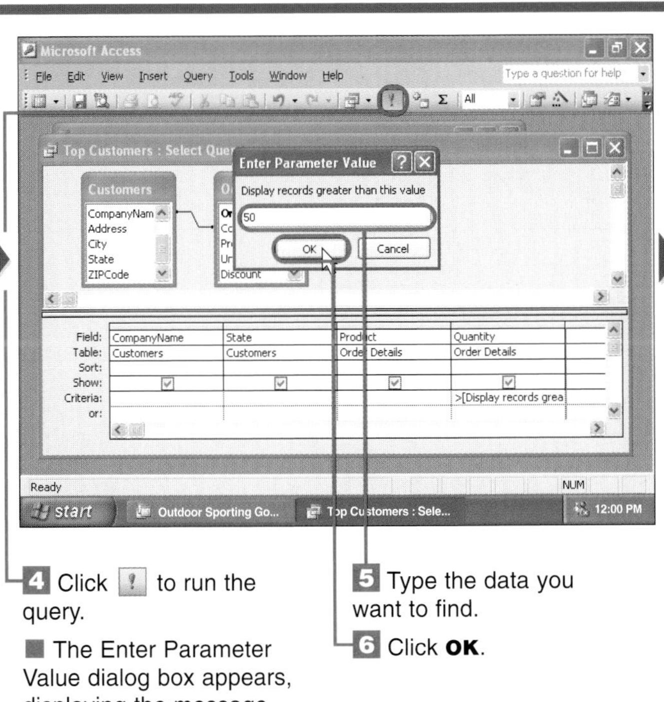

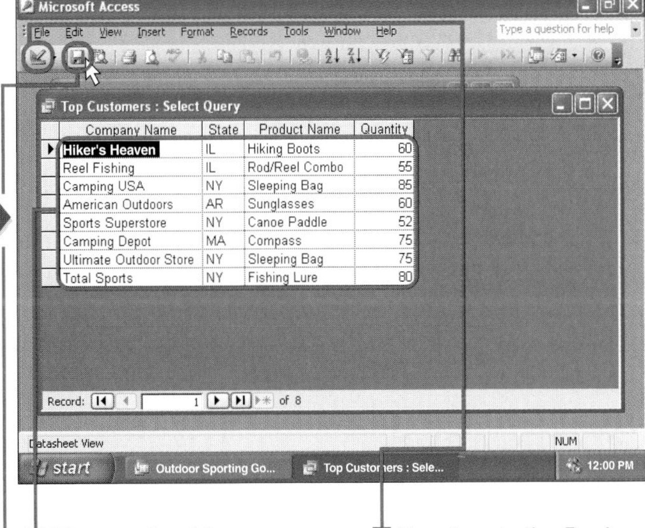

4 Click ! to run the query.

■ The Enter Parameter Value dialog box appears, displaying the message you typed in step **3**.

5 Type the data you want to find.

6 Click **OK**.

■ The results of the query appear. In this example, Access found customers who ordered more than 50 units.

7 To save the changes you made to your query, click 💾.

■ To return to the Design view, click ✎.

■ Each time you run or open the query, the Enter Parameter Value dialog box will appear, asking you to type the data you want to find.

You can summarize the data in a field to help you analyze the data.

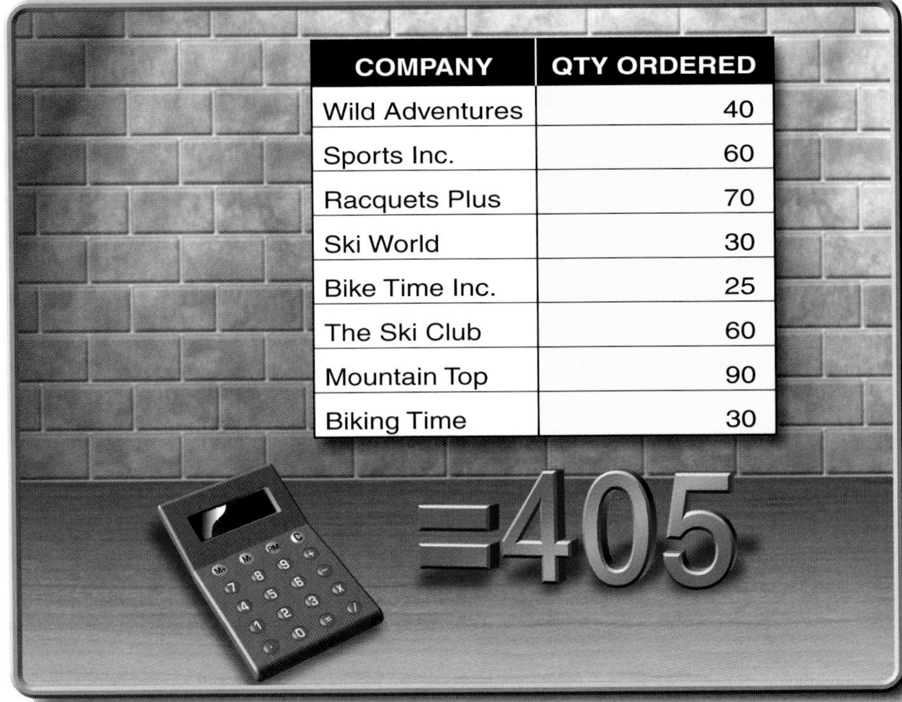

COMPANY	QTY ORDERED
Wild Adventures	40
Sports Inc.	60
Racquets Plus	70
Ski World	30
Bike Time Inc.	25
The Ski Club	60
Mountain Top	90
Biking Time	30

For example, you can summarize the data in the Quantity Ordered field to determine the total number of products ordered.

SUMMARIZE DATA FOR ONE FIELD

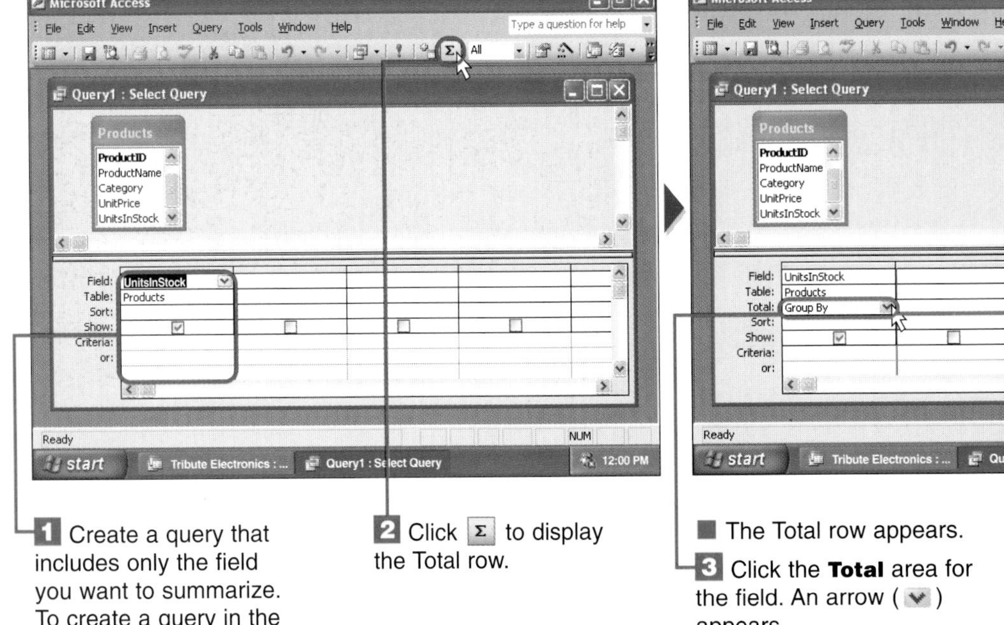

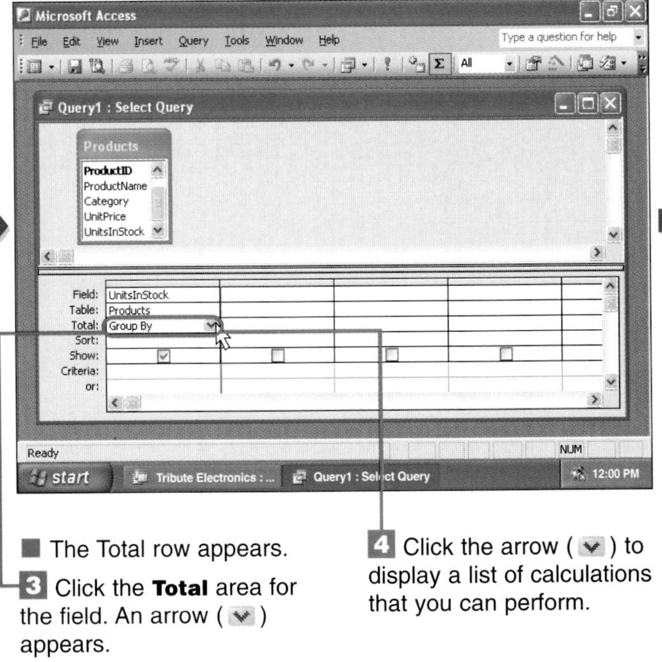

1 Create a query that includes only the field you want to summarize. To create a query in the Design view, see page 192.

2 Click Σ to display the Total row.

■ The Total row appears.

3 Click the **Total** area for the field. An arrow (▾) appears.

4 Click the arrow (▾) to display a list of calculations that you can perform.

What are some of the calculations I can perform to summarize data?

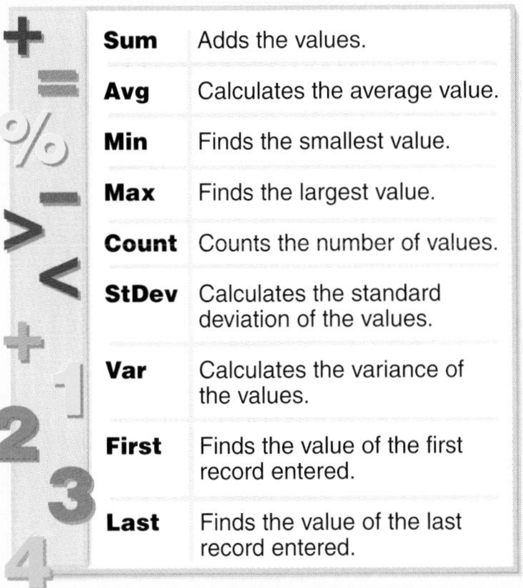

Sum	Adds the values.
Avg	Calculates the average value.
Min	Finds the smallest value.
Max	Finds the largest value.
Count	Counts the number of values.
StDev	Calculates the standard deviation of the values.
Var	Calculates the variance of the values.
First	Finds the value of the first record entered.
Last	Finds the value of the last record entered.

Can I summarize the data for more than one field?

Yes. You can summarize the data for more than one field. For example, you can summarize the data for both the Units in Stock and Units on Order fields. When creating your query, make sure you include each field you want to summarize and specify the calculations you want to perform on the data in each field.

Product	Units in Stock	Units on Order
Hockey Gloves	25	15
Hockey Stick	125	59
Hockey Helmet	50	10
Hockey Shin Pads	21	5
Skates	45	15
Putter	33	25
Golf Driver	21	9
Golf Glove	45	23
Skis	22	10
Ski Poles	24	12
Ski Boots	35	8
	=446	=191

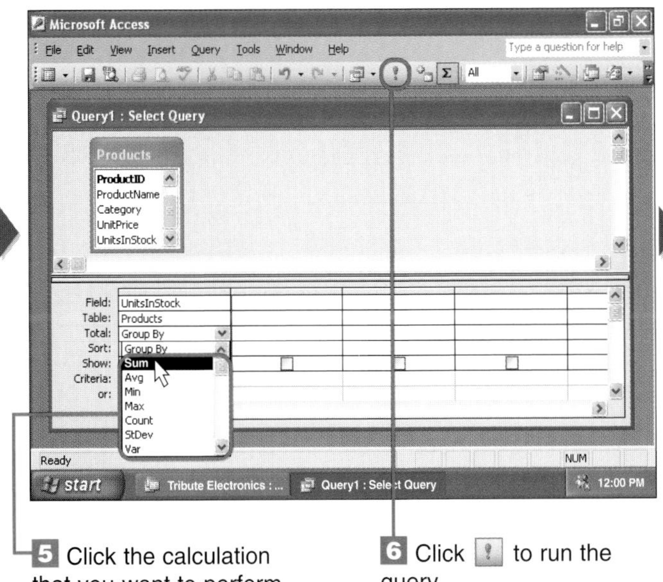

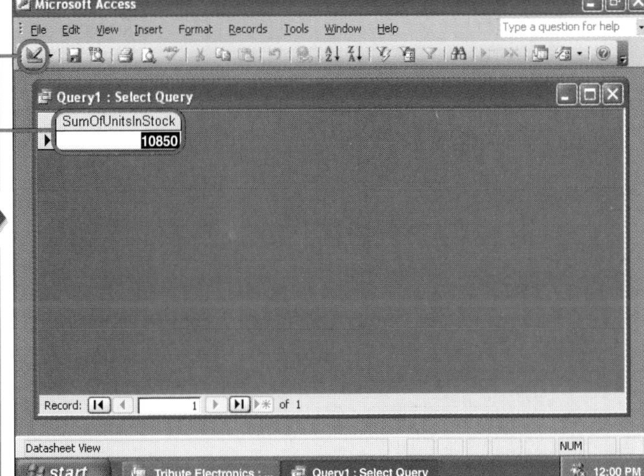

5 Click the calculation that you want to perform on the data in the field.

Note: For information on some of the calculations that you can perform, see the top of this page.

6 Click ! to run the query.

■ The result of the calculation appears.

■ In this example, Access calculates the total number of units in stock for all products.

■ To return to the Design view, click the Design View button.

■ If you no longer want your query to summarize the data in a field, repeat step **2** to remove the Total row from your query.

CONTINUED

SUMMARIZE DATA

You can group records in your database and summarize the data for each group.

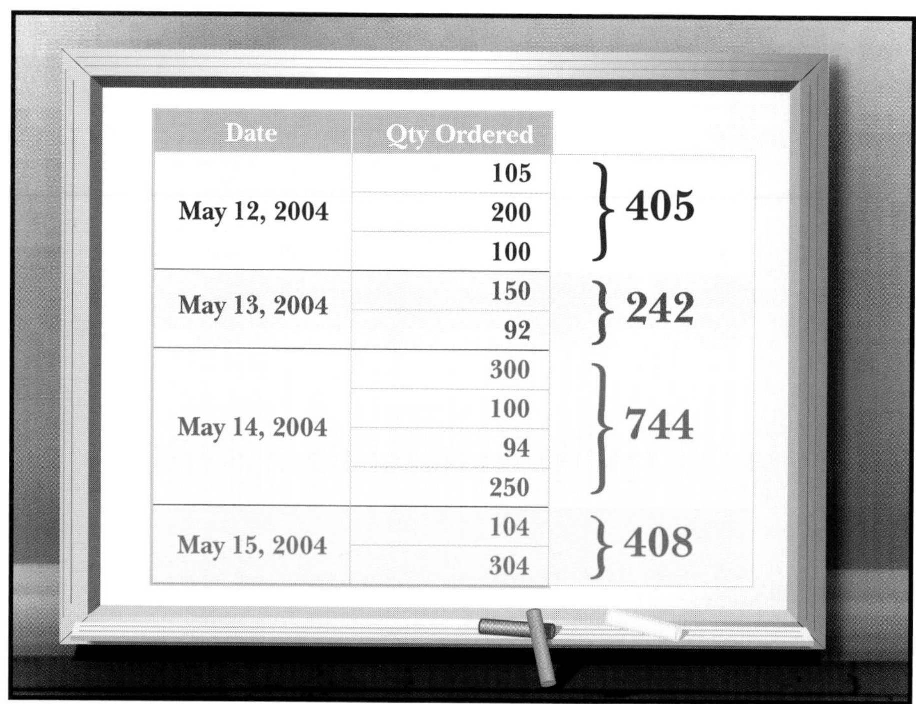

Date
Qty Ordered
May 12, 2004
105
200
100
405
May 13, 2004
150
92
242
May 14, 2004
300
100
94
250
744
May 15, 2004
104
304
408

For example, you can group records by date and determine the total number of orders for each day.

SUMMARIZE DATA FOR GROUPED RECORDS

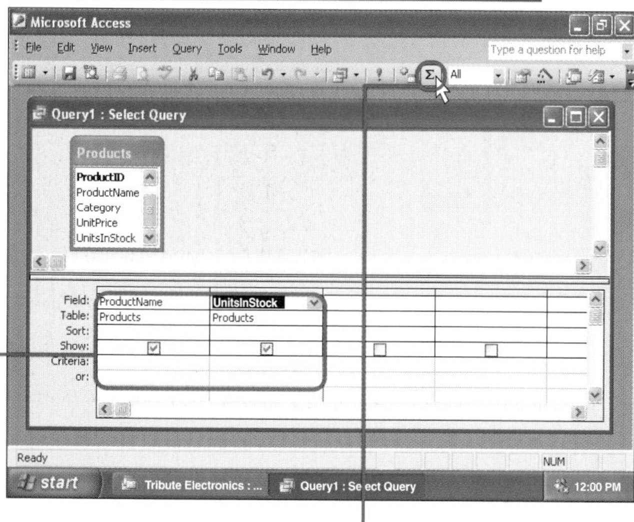

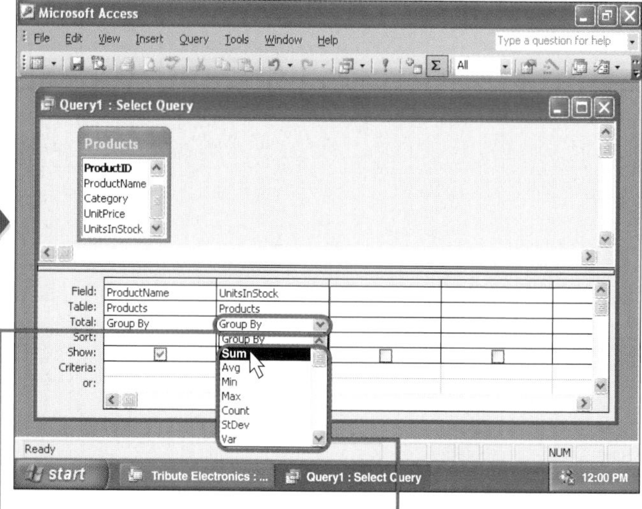

1 Create a query that includes only the field you want to use to group your records and the field you want to summarize.

To create a query in the Design view, see page 192.

2 Click Σ to display the Total row.

■ The Total row appears.

3 Click the **Total** area for the field you want to summarize. An arrow (▼) appears.

4 Click the arrow (▼) to display a list of calculations that you can perform.

5 Click the calculation that you want to perform on the data in the field.

Note: For information on some of the calculations that you can perform, see the top of page 223.

Can I use more than one field to group records?

Yes. You can group records using more than one field. For example, to determine the total amount of each product purchased by each company, use the Company and Product fields to group records and the Quantity Ordered field to summarize data. When creating your query, make sure you place the fields in the order that you want to group the records. Access will group the records using the fields from left to right.

COMPANY	PRODUCT	QUANTITY ORDERED
Fitness Minds	A	40
Fitness Minds	B	60
Racquets Plus	A	80
Racquets Plus	B	30
Ski World	A	25
Ski World	B	60
SportStop	A	90
SportStop	B	100

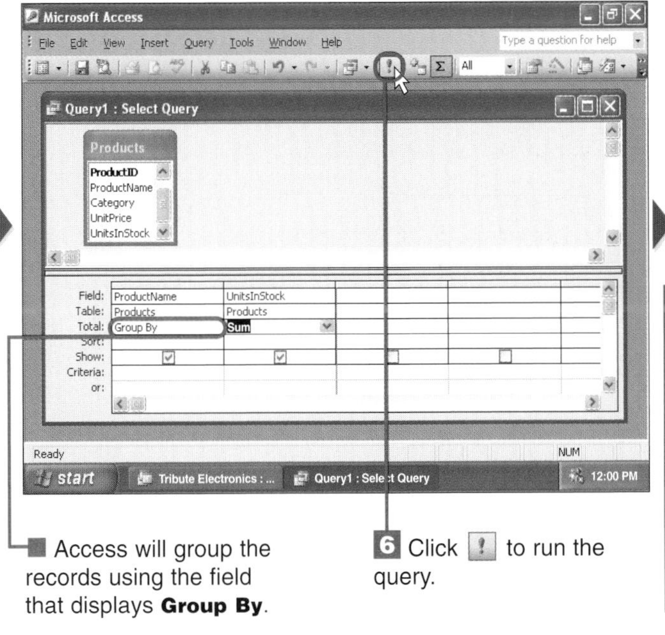

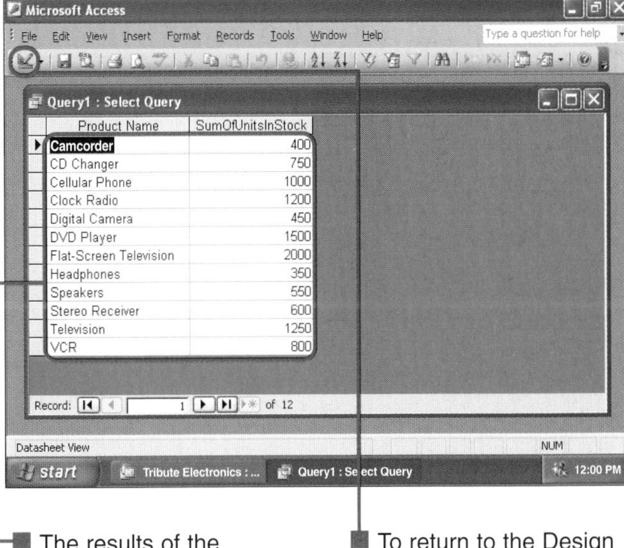

■ Access will group the records using the field that displays **Group By**.

6 Click ! to run the query.

■ The results of the calculations appear.

■ In this example, Access calculates the total number of units in stock for each product.

■ To return to the Design view, click .

■ If you no longer want your query to summarize the data for grouped records, repeat step **2** to remove the Total row from your query.

FIND UNMATCHED RECORDS

You can use the Find Unmatched Query Wizard to find records in one table that do not have matching records in another table.

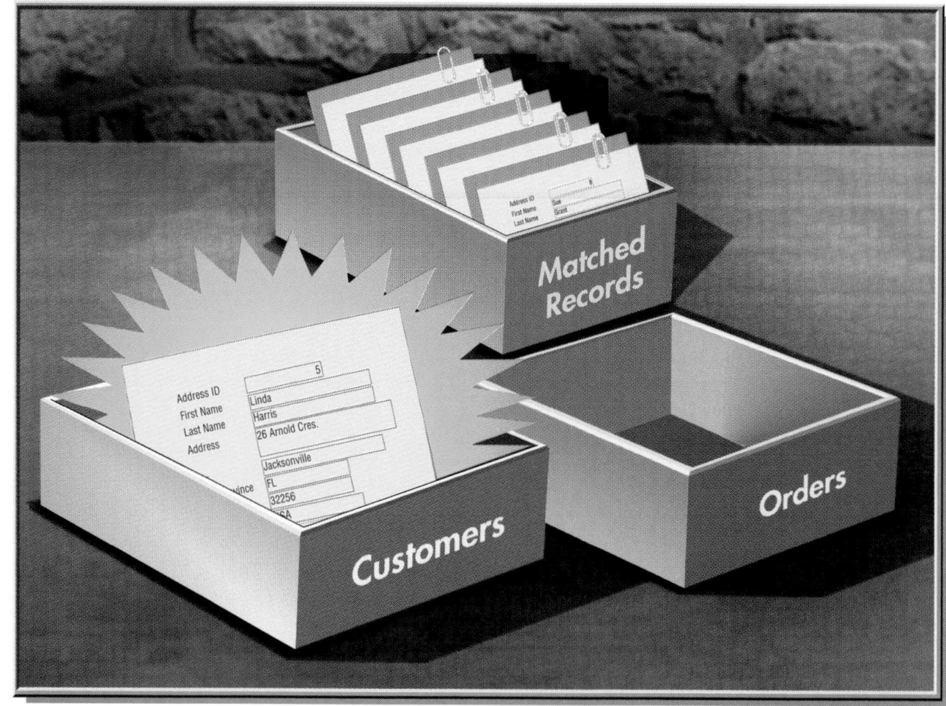

For example, you can find all customers who have not placed an order.

FIND UNMATCHED RECORDS

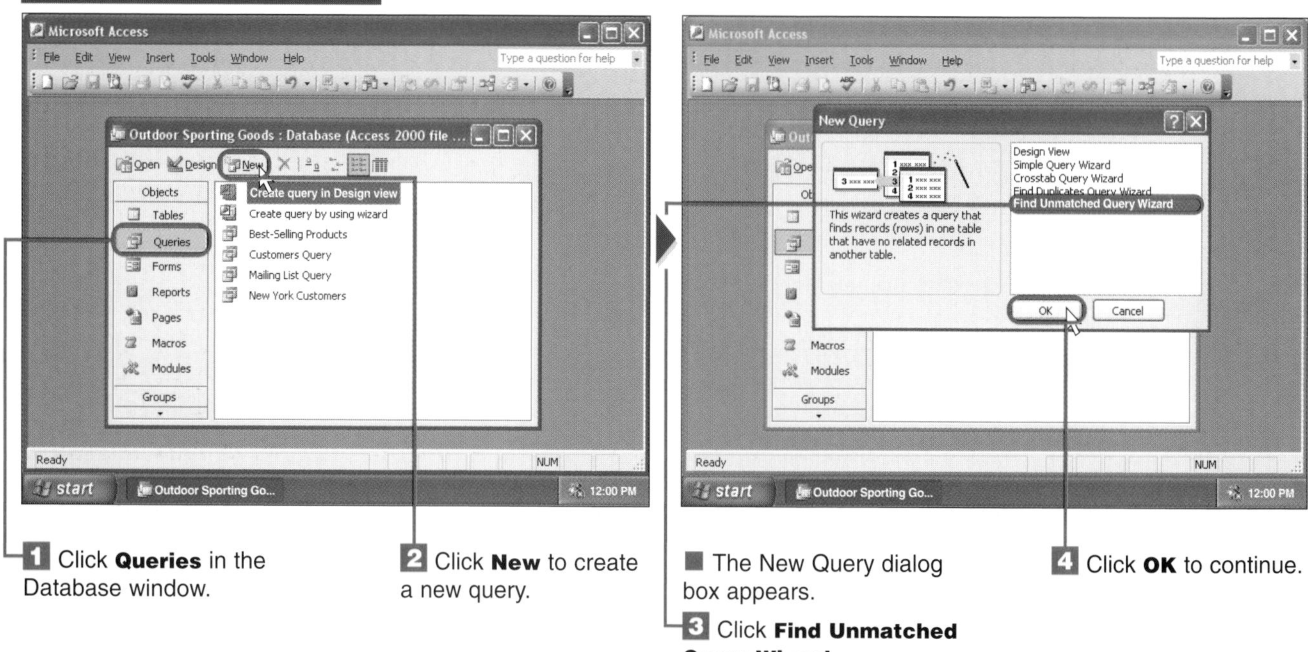

1 Click **Queries** in the Database window.

2 Click **New** to create a new query.

■ The New Query dialog box appears.

3 Click **Find Unmatched Query Wizard**.

4 Click **OK** to continue.

Why does a dialog box appear when I select the Find Unmatched Query Wizard?

When you select the Find Unmatched Query Wizard for the first time, a dialog box appears, stating that the wizard is not installed on your computer. To install the wizard, click **Yes**.

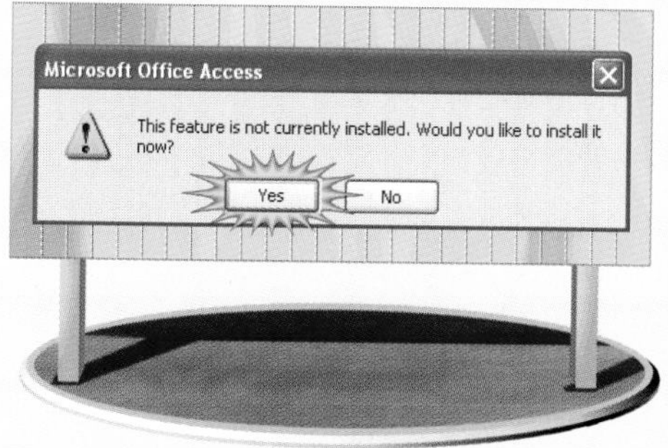

How can I prevent unmatched records from being entered in two tables?

You can enforce referential integrity between two tables to prevent you from entering a record in one table if a matching record does not exist in a related table. For example, if a customer does not exist in the Customers table, you will not be able to enter an order for the customer in the Orders table. For more information on referential integrity, see page 132.

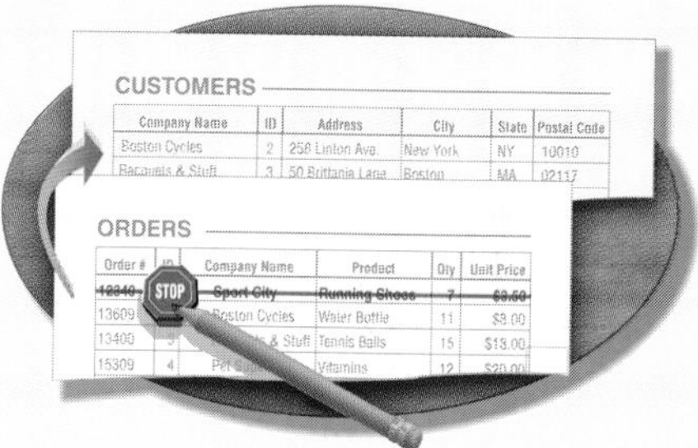

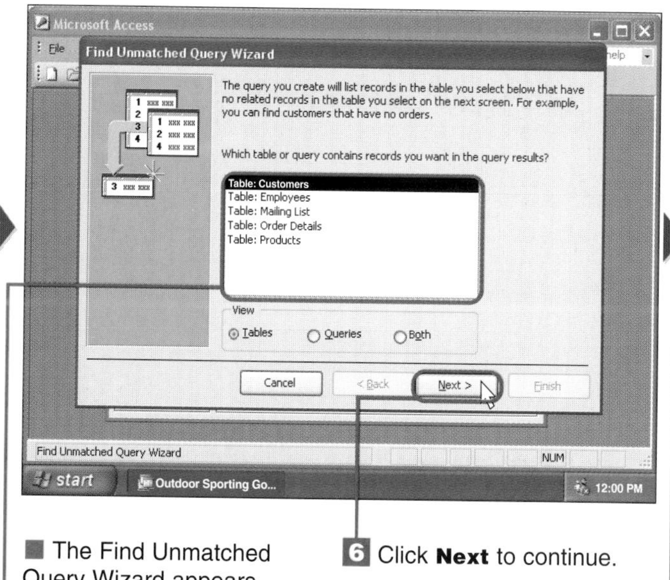

■ The Find Unmatched Query Wizard appears.

5 Click the table that contains the records you want to display in the query results if another table does not have matching records.

6 Click **Next** to continue.

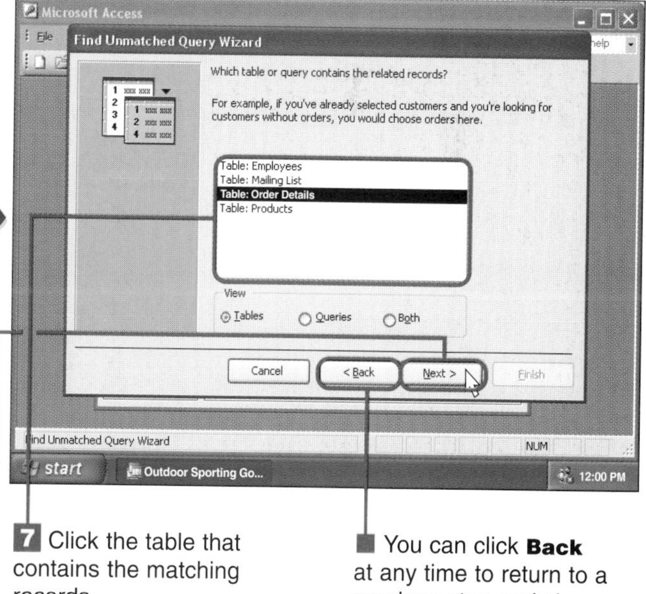

7 Click the table that contains the matching records.

8 Click **Next** to continue.

■ You can click **Back** at any time to return to a previous step and change your selections.

CONTINUED

FIND UNMATCHED RECORDS

When using the Find Unmatched Query Wizard, you need to select the field that appears in both tables so Access can compare the data in the tables.

For example, you can select the Customer ID field in the Customers and Orders tables.

FIND UNMATCHED RECORDS (CONTINUED)

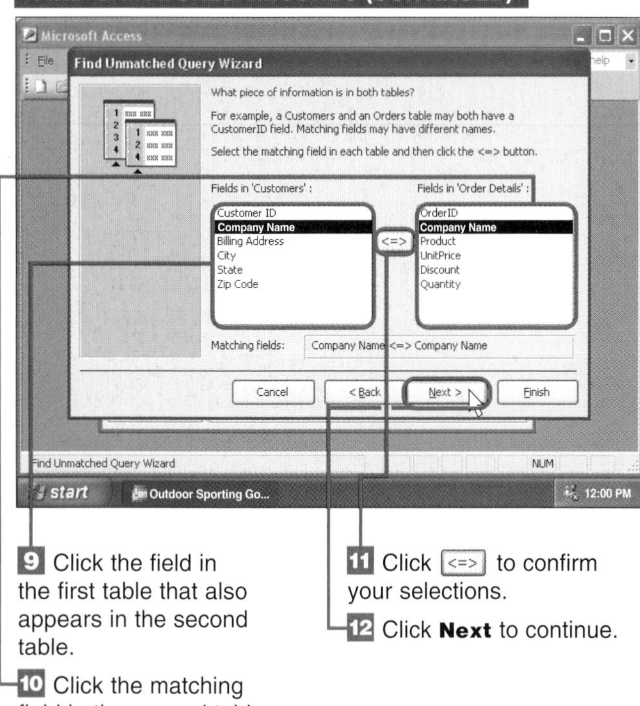

9 Click the field in the first table that also appears in the second table.

10 Click the matching field in the second table.

Note: The matching fields will usually have the same name.

11 Click [<=>] to confirm your selections.

12 Click **Next** to continue.

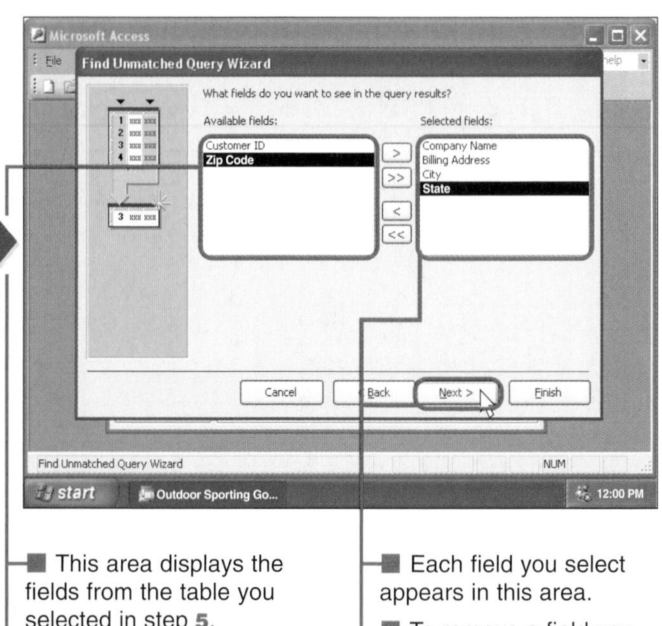

■ This area displays the fields from the table you selected in step **5**.

13 Double-click each field you want to appear in the results of your query.

Note: To add all the fields in the table at once, click [>>].

■ Each field you select appears in this area.

■ To remove a field you accidentally selected, double-click the field in this area.

14 Click **Next** to continue.

Do I have to recreate a query each time I want to find unmatched records in the tables?

No. Each time you open a query you created using the Find Unmatched Query Wizard, Access will use the most current data from the tables you specified to determine if any unmatched records exist in the tables.

Can I change data displayed in the results of my query?

Yes. You can change data displayed in the results of a query as you would edit data in a table. If you change the data displayed in the query results, the data will also change in the table you used to create the query. To edit data in a table, see page 56.

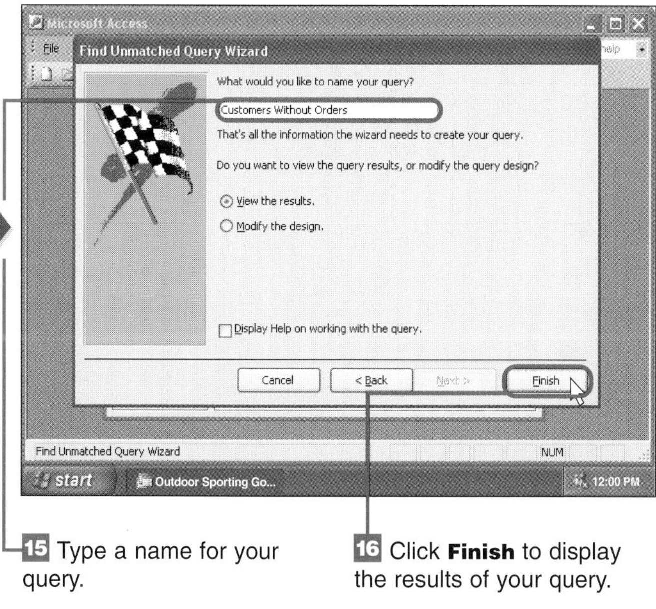

15 Type a name for your query.

16 Click **Finish** to display the results of your query.

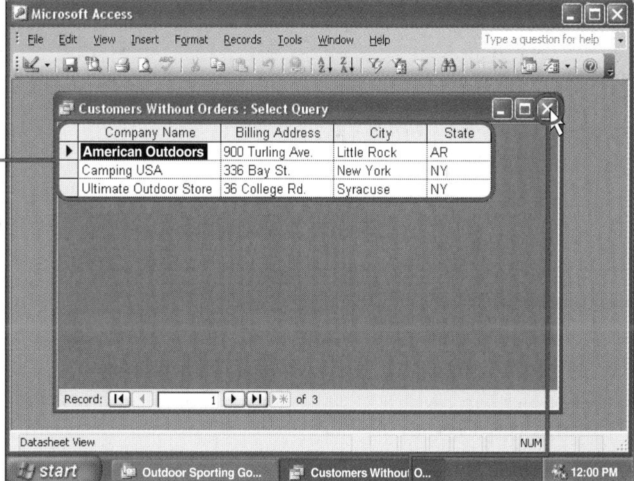

■ The results of your query appear.

■ In this example, Access displays information about each customer who has not placed an order.

17 When you finish reviewing the results of your query, click ☒ to close the query.

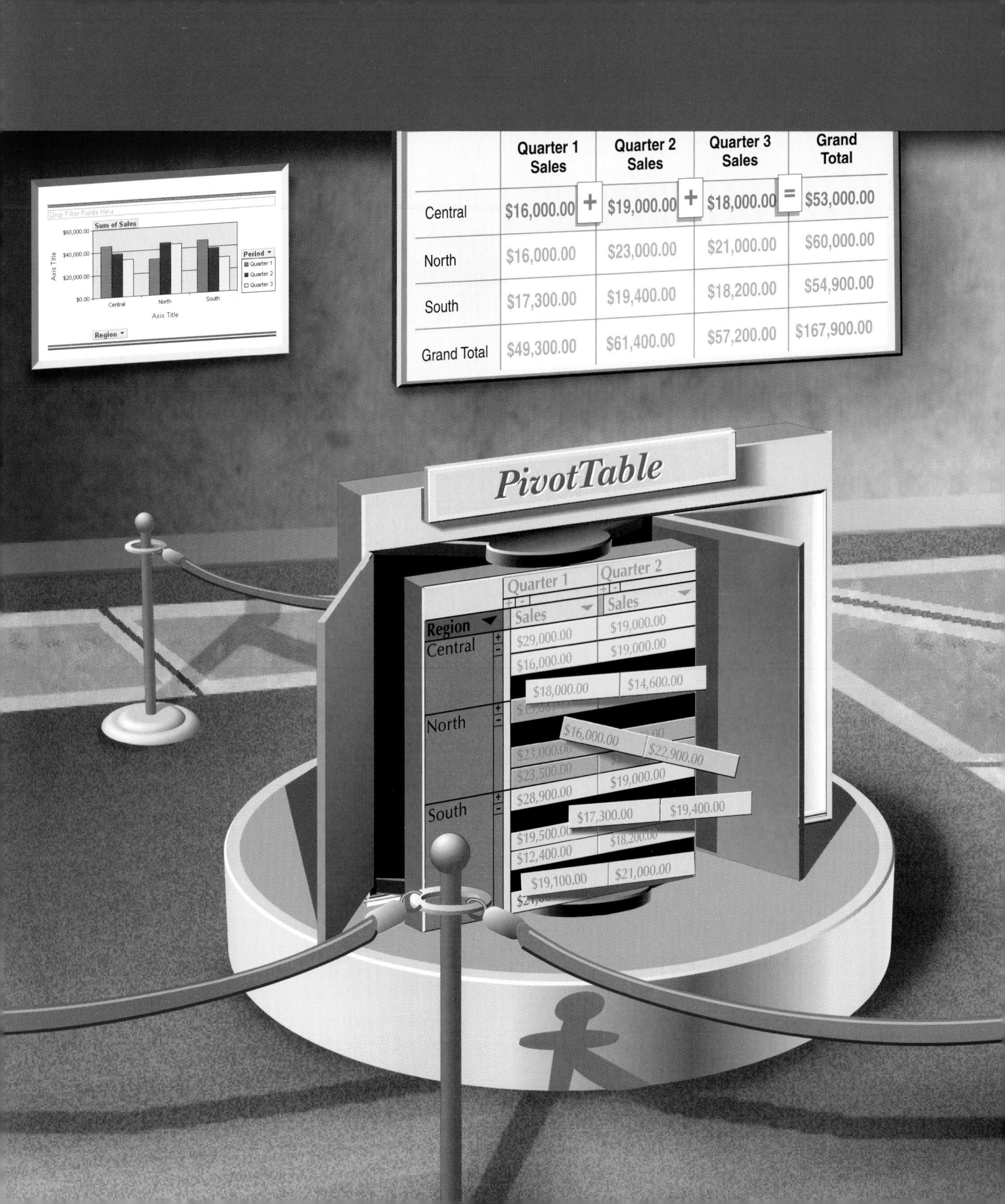

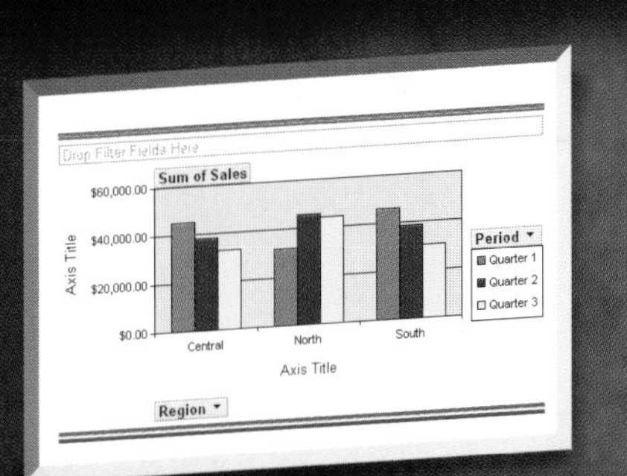

Drop Filter Fields Here
Sum of Sales
$60,000.00
$40,000.00
$20,000.00
$0.00
Axis Title
Central
North
South
Axis Title
Period
Quarter 1
Quarter 2
Quarter 3
Region
Quarter 1 Sales
Quarter 2 Sales
Quarter 3 Sales
Grand Total
Central $16,000.00 + $19,000.00 + $18,000.00 = $53,000.00
North $16,000.00 $23,000.00 $21,000.00 $60,000.00
South $17,300.00 $19,400.00 $18,200.00 $54,900.00
Grand Total $49,300.00 $61,400.00 $57,200.00 $167,900.00
PivotTable
Quarter 1
Quarter 2
Sales
Sales
Region
Central
North
South
$29,000.00
$19,000.00
$16,000.00
$19,000.00
$18,000.00
$14,600.00
$16,000.00
$22,900.00
$23,000.00
$23,500.00
$19,000.00
$28,900.00
$17,300.00
$19,400.00
$19,500.00
$18,200.00
$12,400.00
$19,100.00
$21,000.00

CHAPTER 10

Using the PivotTable and PivotChart Views

Are you interested in analyzing and summarizing data in your database? In this chapter, you will learn how to use the PivotTable and PivotChart views to work with your data.

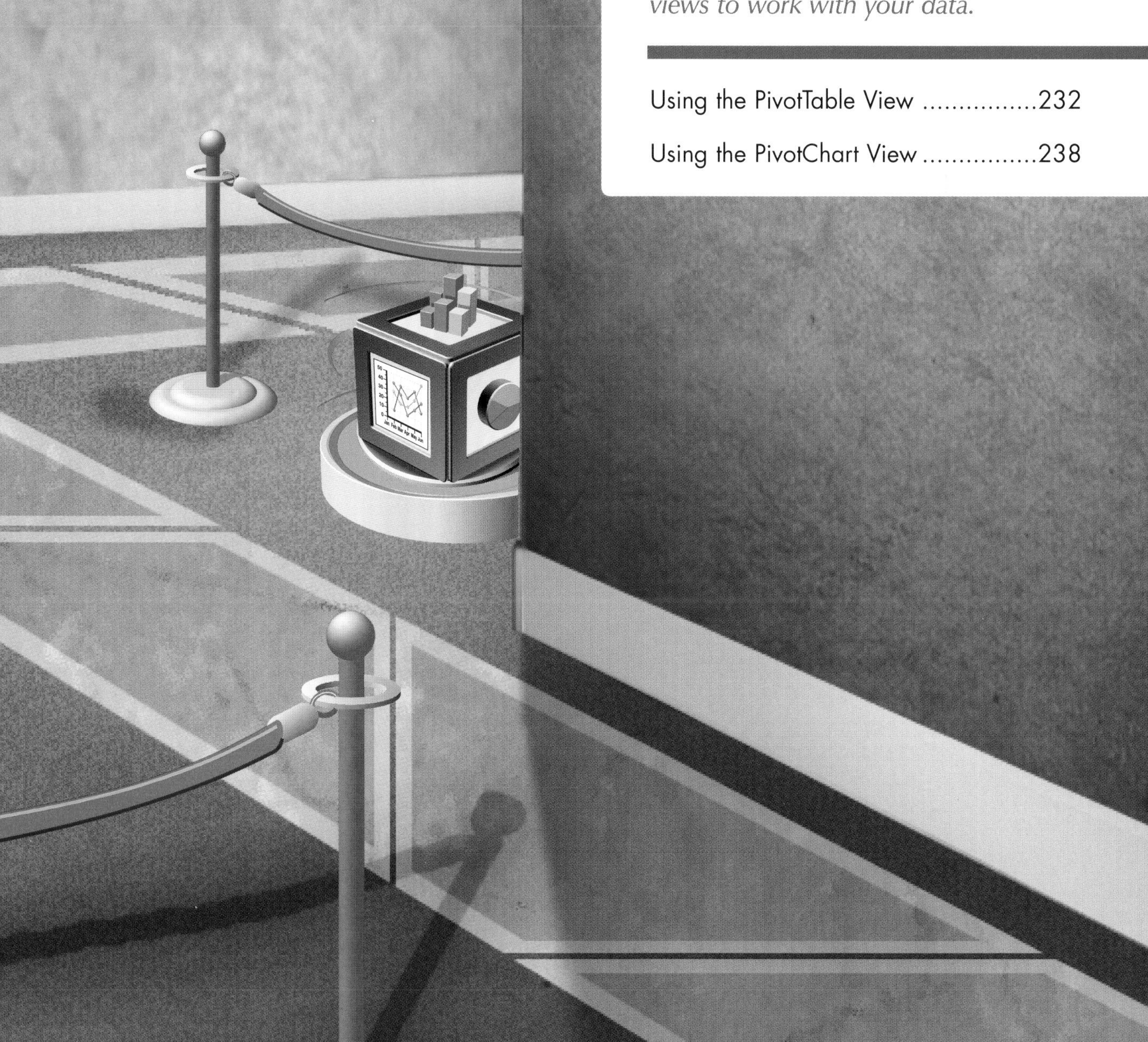

USING THE PIVOTTABLE VIEW

You can use the PivotTable view to summarize and analyze the data in a table, form or the results of a query.

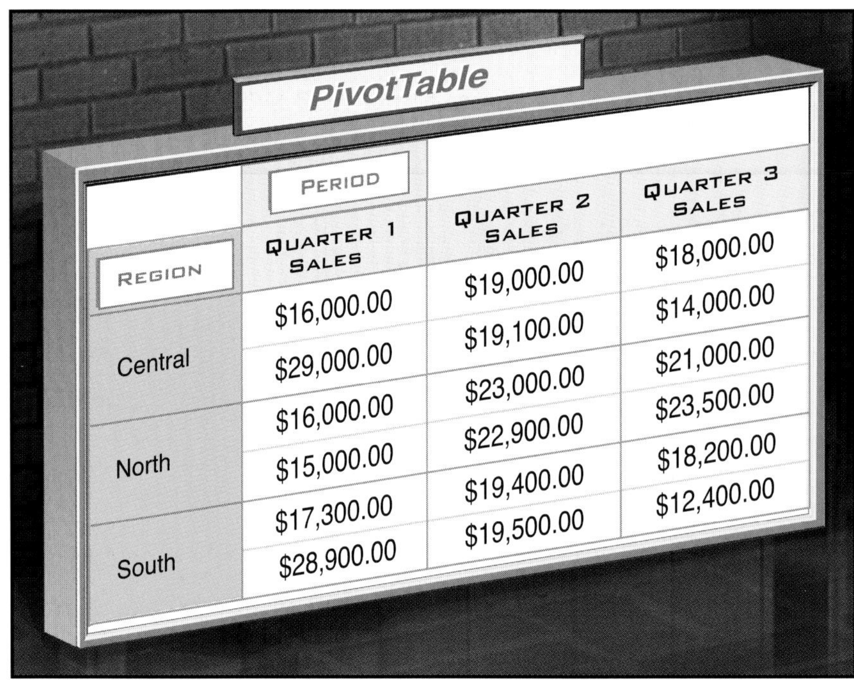

When you first display a table, form or query in the PivotTable view, the PivotTable may appear empty. You may need to add the fields you want to display to the PivotTable.

If you have previously displayed the table, form or query in the PivotChart view, the PivotTable will display the fields you added to the PivotChart. For information on the PivotChart view, see page 238.

USING THE PIVOTTABLE VIEW

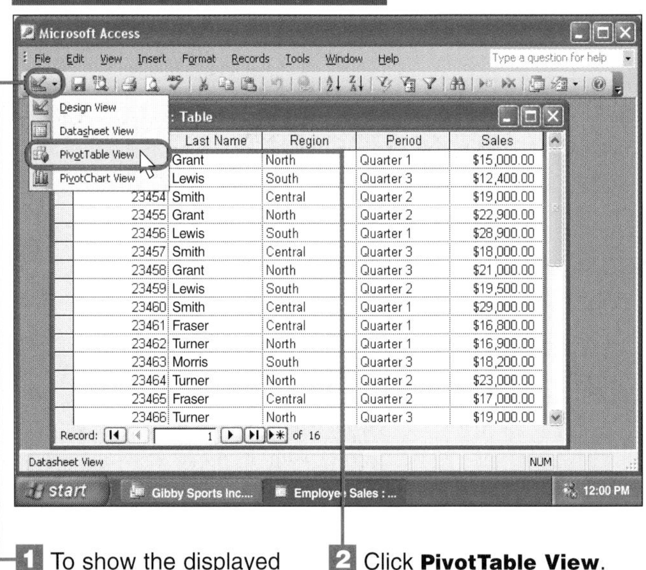

1 To show the displayed table, form or query in the PivotTable view, click ▾ in this area.

2 Click **PivotTable View**.

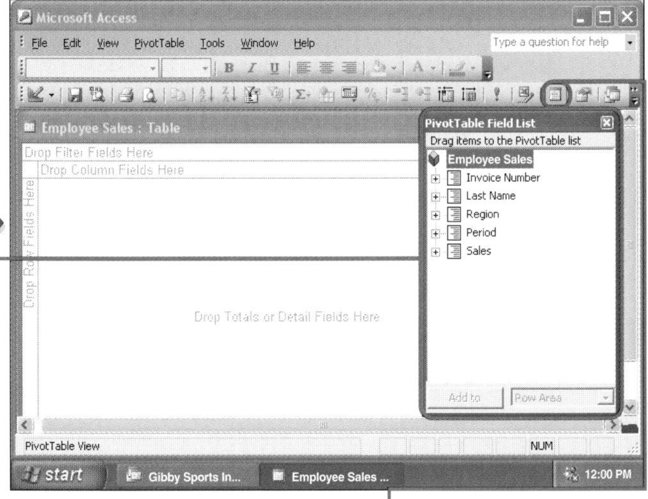

■ The table, form or query appears in the PivotTable view.

■ The PivotTable Field List dialog box also appears, displaying the name of each field in your table, form or query.

■ If the PivotTable Field List dialog box does not appear, click ▤ to display the dialog box.

Tip

What fields do I need to add to create a PivotTable?

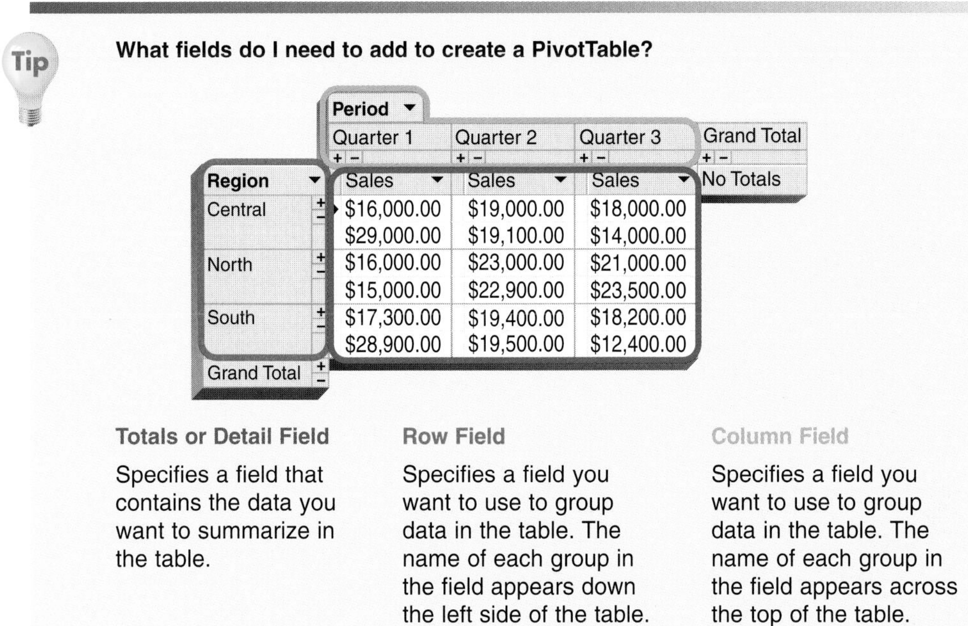

Period				
	Quarter 1	Quarter 2	Quarter 3	Grand Total
Region	Sales	Sales	Sales	No Totals
Central	$16,000.00	$19,000.00	$18,000.00	
	$29,000.00	$19,100.00	$14,000.00	
North	$16,000.00	$23,000.00	$21,000.00	
	$15,000.00	$22,900.00	$23,500.00	
South	$17,300.00	$19,400.00	$18,200.00	
	$28,900.00	$19,500.00	$12,400.00	
Grand Total				

Totals or Detail Field

Specifies a field that contains the data you want to summarize in the table.

Row Field

Specifies a field you want to use to group data in the table. The name of each group in the field appears down the left side of the table.

Column Field

Specifies a field you want to use to group data in the table. The name of each group in the field appears across the top of the table.

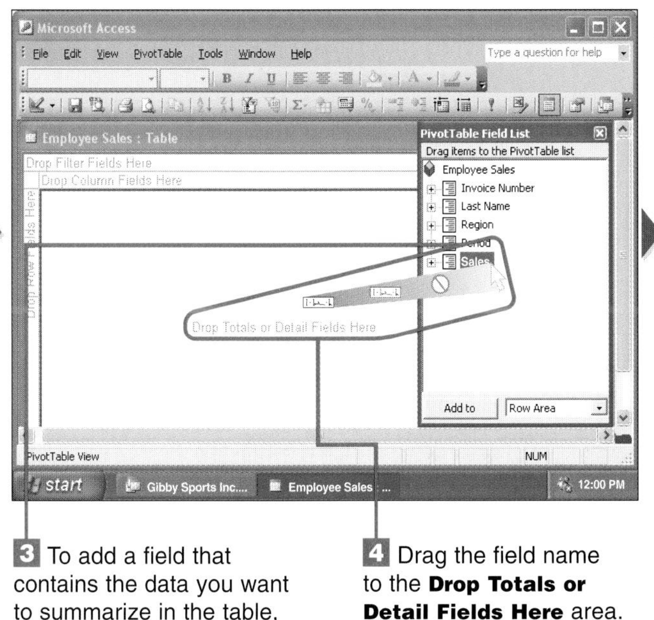

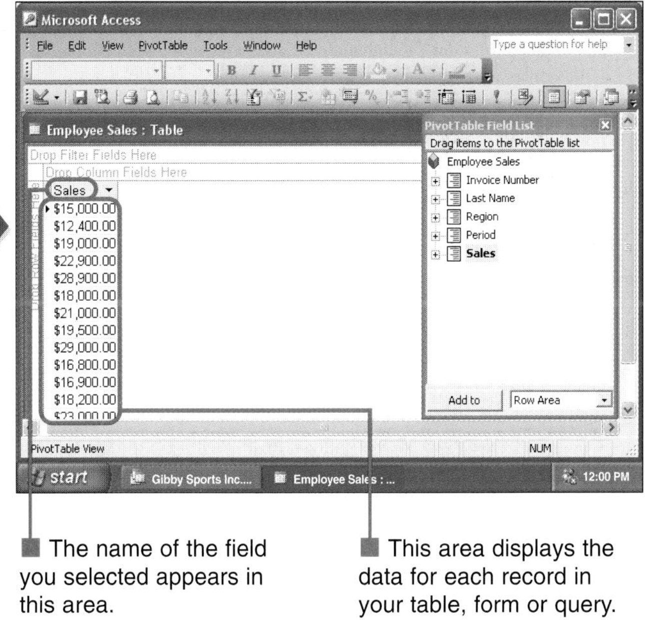

3 To add a field that contains the data you want to summarize in the table, position the mouse over the name of the field in this area.

4 Drag the field name to the **Drop Totals or Detail Fields Here** area.

■ The name of the field you selected appears in this area.

■ This area displays the data for each record in your table, form or query.

CONTINUED

When using the PivotTable view, you can select the fields you want to use to group the data in the PivotTable.

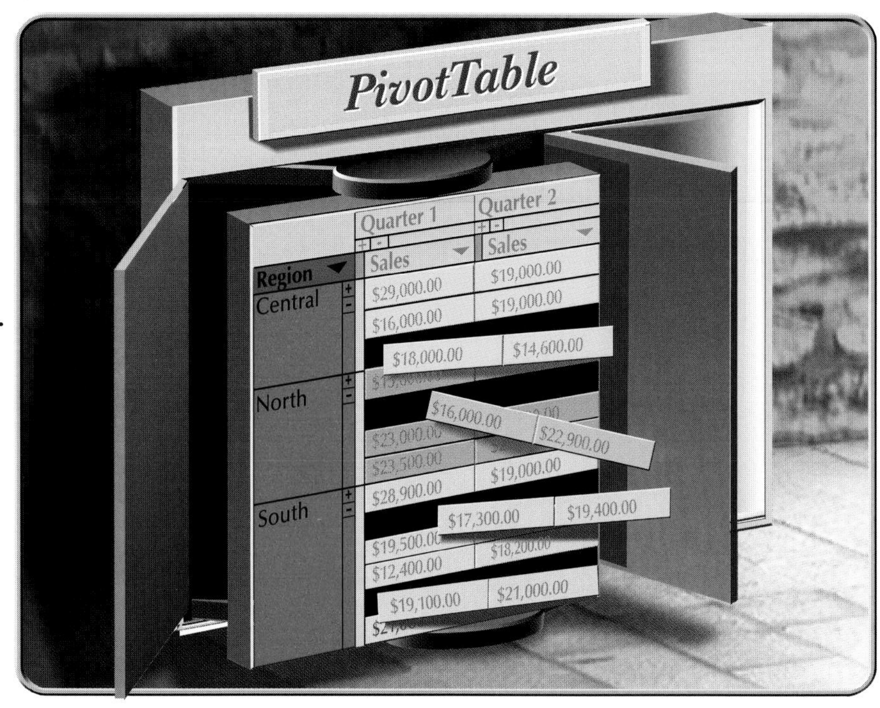

For example, you can use the Region field to group the data by region in the PivotTable.

USING THE PIVOTTABLE VIEW (CONTINUED)

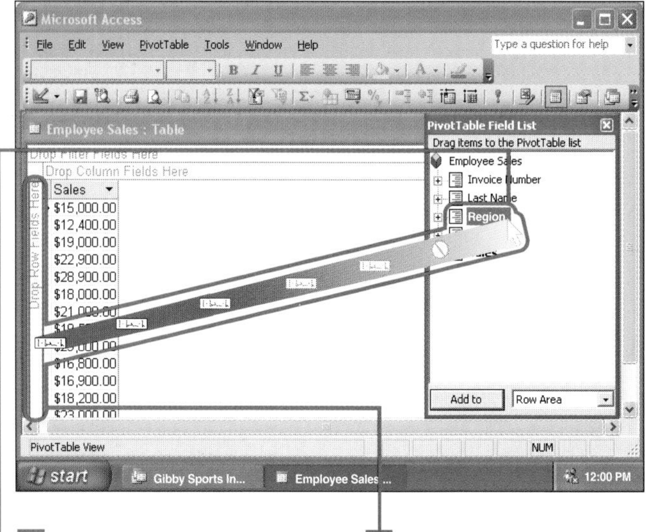

5 To add the field you want to use to group the data in the table, position the mouse over the name of the field in this area.

6 Drag the field name to the **Drop Row Fields Here** area.

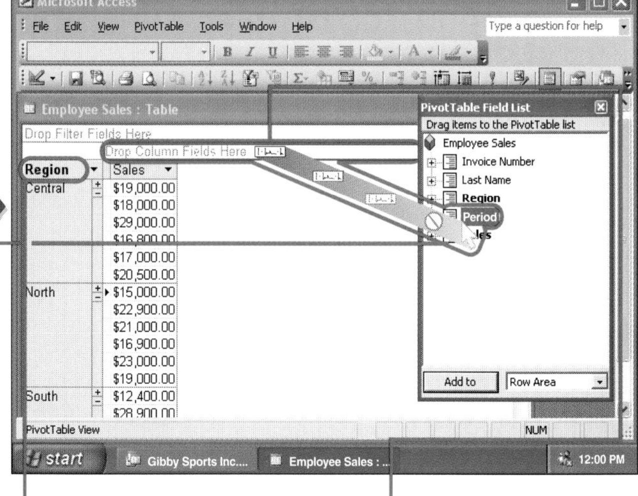

■ The name of the field you selected appears in this area. The name of each group in the field appears down the left side of the table.

7 To add another field you want to use to group the data in the table, position the mouse over the name of the field in this area.

8 Drag the field name to the **Drop Column Fields Here** area.

Can I remove a field from a PivotTable?

Yes. You can remove any field you added to a PivotTable. Removing a field from a PivotTable will not remove the field from the table, form or query used to create the PivotTable. To remove a field from a PivotTable, click the name of the field in the PivotTable and then press the Delete key.

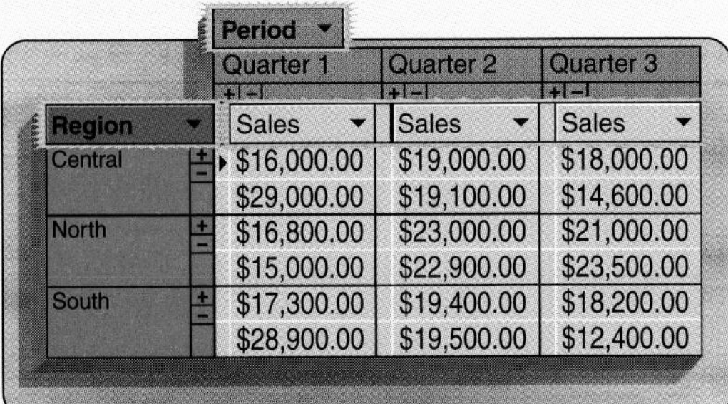

How can I move the PivotTable Field List dialog box so it does not cover my PivotTable?

To move the PivotTable Field List dialog box, position the mouse over the title bar of the dialog box and then drag the dialog box to a new location.

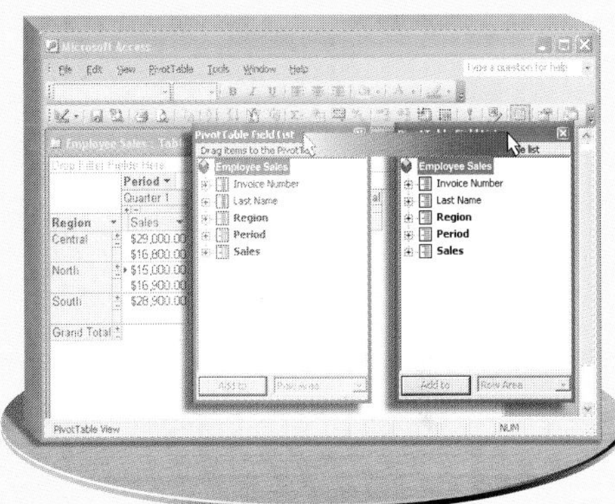

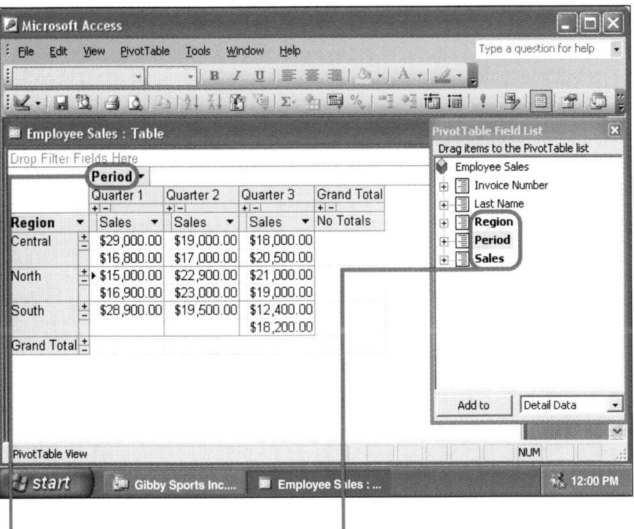

■ The name of the field you selected appears in this area. The name of each group in the field appears along the top of the table.

■ The name of each field you added to the table appears in **bold** in the PivotTable Field List dialog box.

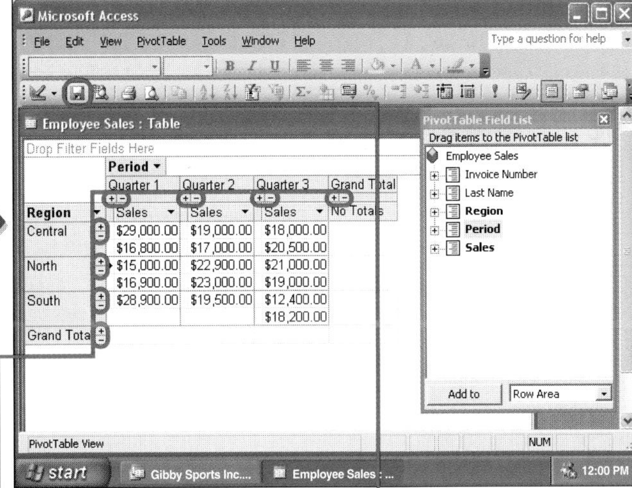

■ Each group of data displays a plus sign (+) and a minus sign (−).

■ To hide the data in a group, click a minus sign (−).

Note: To once again display the data in a group, click a plus sign (+).

9 To save all the changes you made in the PivotTable view, click the save button.

Note: Access automatically saves changes you make to a form displayed in the PivotTable view.

CONTINUED

You can perform calculations on the data displayed in a PivotTable to help you analyze the data.

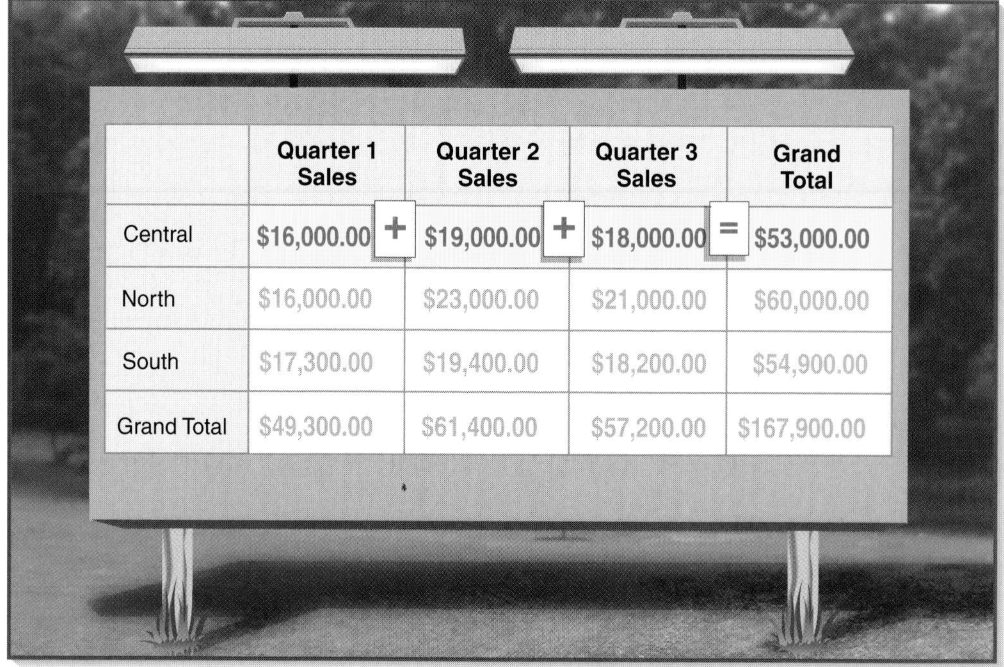

Quarter 1 Sales
Quarter 2 Sales
Quarter 3 Sales
Grand Total
Central $16,000.00 + $19,000.00 + $18,000.00 = $53,000.00
North $16,000.00 $23,000.00 $21,000.00 $60,000.00
South $17,300.00 $19,400.00 $18,200.00 $54,900.00
Grand Total $49,300.00 $61,400.00 $57,200.00 $167,900.00

PERFORM CALCULATIONS

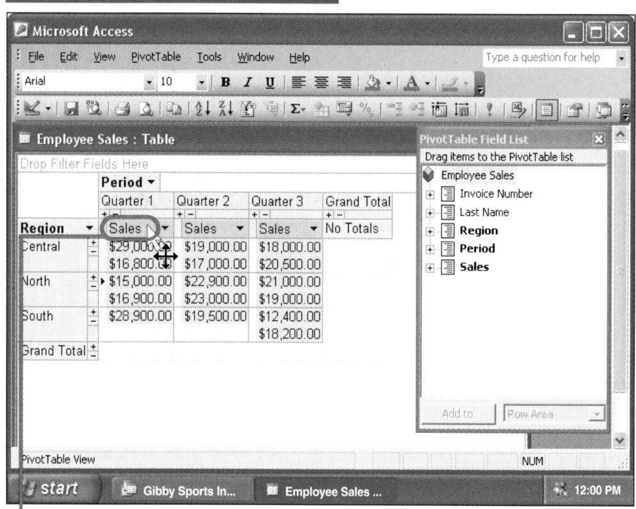

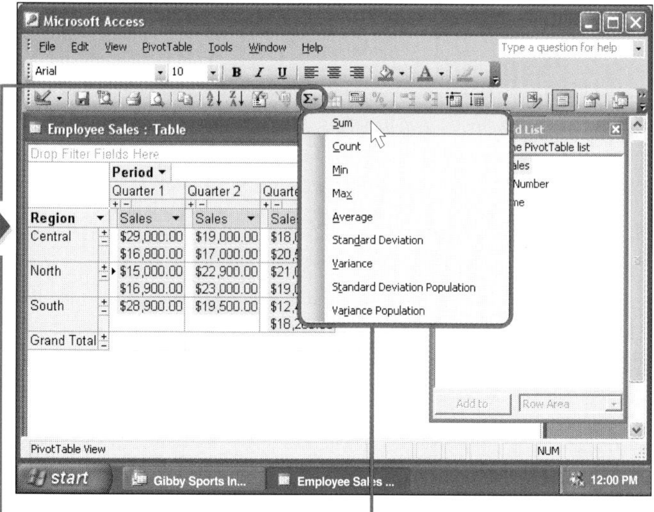

1 Click the name of the field in the table that contains the data you want to perform calculations on.

■ The data in the field is highlighted.

2 Click Σ to display a list of the calculations that you can perform.

3 Click the calculation you want to perform.

Note: For information on the calculations that you can perform, see the top of page 237.

Tip

What calculations can I perform on the data in a PivotTable?

Calculation:	Result:
Sum	Adds the values.
Count	Counts the number of values.
Min	Finds the smallest value.
Max	Finds the largest value.
Average	Calculates the average value.
Standard Deviation	Calculates the standard deviation of the values.
Variance	Calculates the variance of the values.
Standard Deviation Population	Calculates the population standard deviation of the values.
Variance Population	Calculates the population variance of the values.

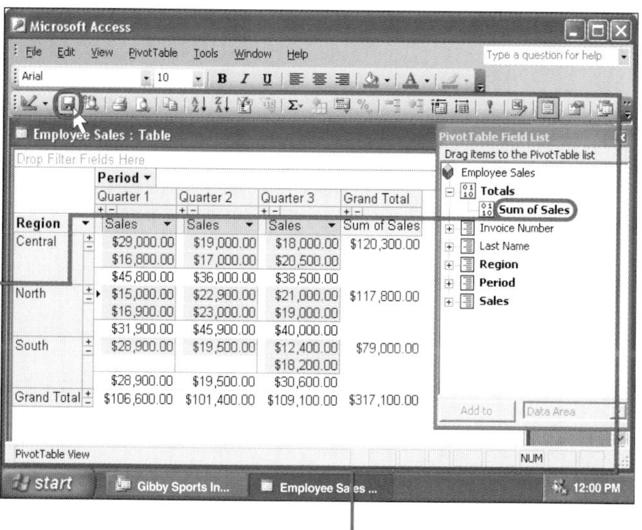

■ The table displays the subtotals and grand totals for the calculation you selected.

■ The name of the new total field appears at the top of the PivotTable Field List dialog box.

4 To save the change you made in the PivotTable view, click [save icon].

Note: Access automatically saves changes you make to a form displayed in the PivotTable view.

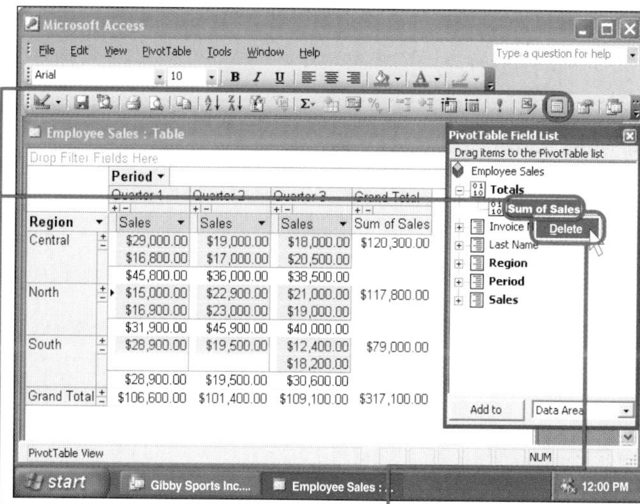

REMOVE CALCULATIONS

1 To remove calculations from a table, right-click the name of the total field in the PivotTable Field List dialog box. A menu appears.

■ If the PivotTable Field List dialog box does not appear, click [field list icon] to display the dialog box.

2 Click **Delete**.

■ The field will disappear from the PivotTable Field List dialog box and the calculations will disappear from the table.

USING THE PIVOTCHART VIEW

You can use the PivotChart view to display a graphical summary of the data in a table, form or the results of a query.

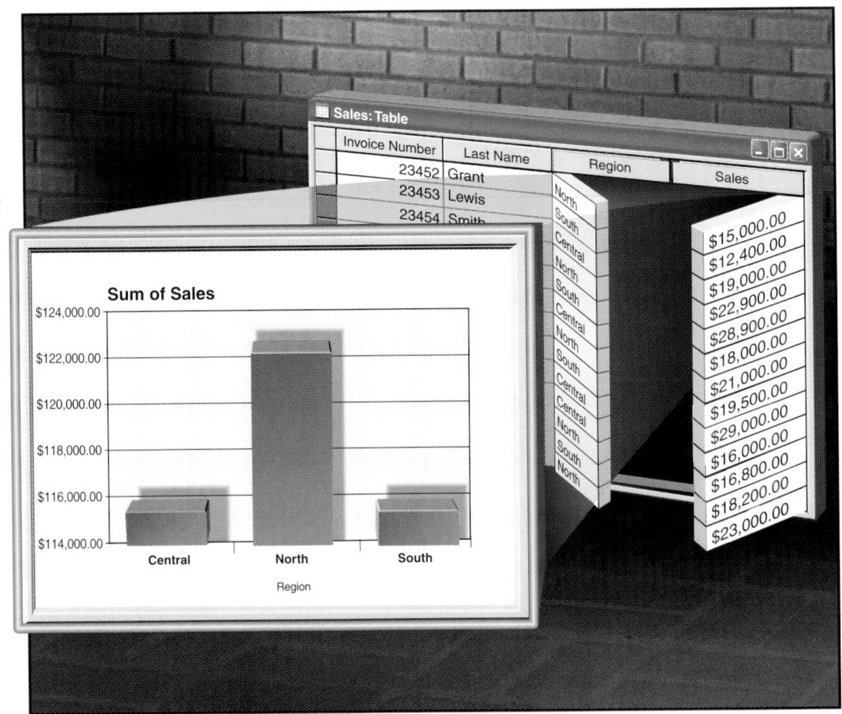

When you first display a table, form or query in the PivotChart view, the PivotChart may appear empty. You may need to add the fields you want to display to the PivotChart.

If you have previously displayed the table, form or query in the PivotTable view, the PivotChart will display the fields you added to the PivotTable. For information on the PivotTable view, see page 232.

USING THE PIVOTCHART VIEW

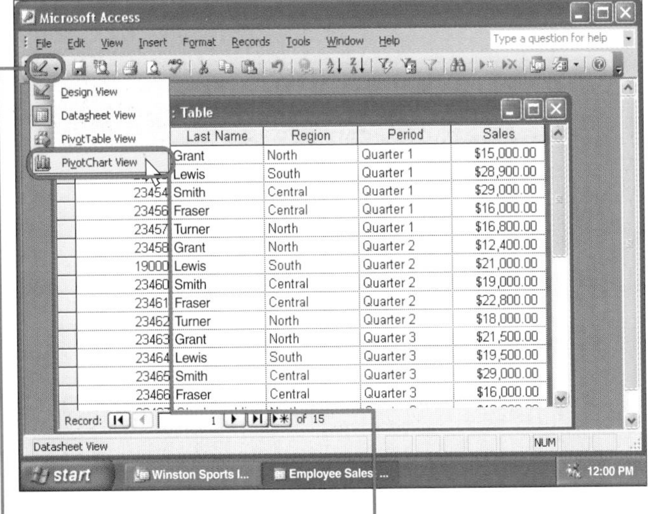

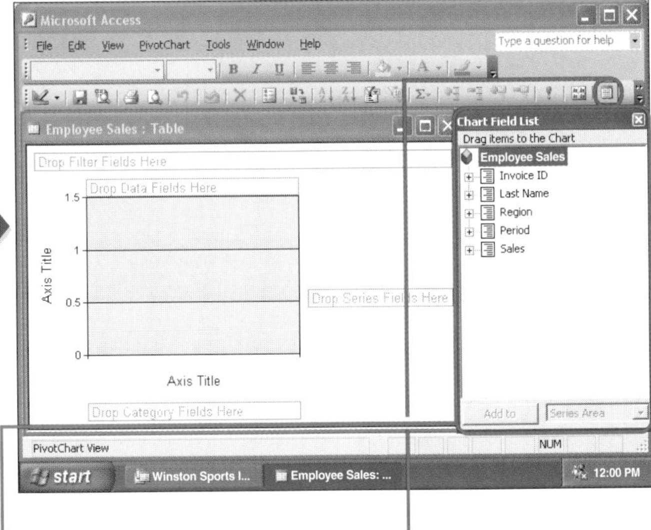

1 To show the displayed table, form or query in the PivotChart view, click ▾ in this area.

2 Click **PivotChart View**.

■ The table, form or query appears in the PivotChart view.

■ The Chart Field List dialog box also appears, displaying the name of each field in your table, form or query.

■ If the Chart Field List dialog box does not appear, click ▤ to display the dialog box.

Note: If ▤ is not displayed, click ▾ on the PivotChart toolbar to display the button.

What fields do I need to add to create a PivotChart?

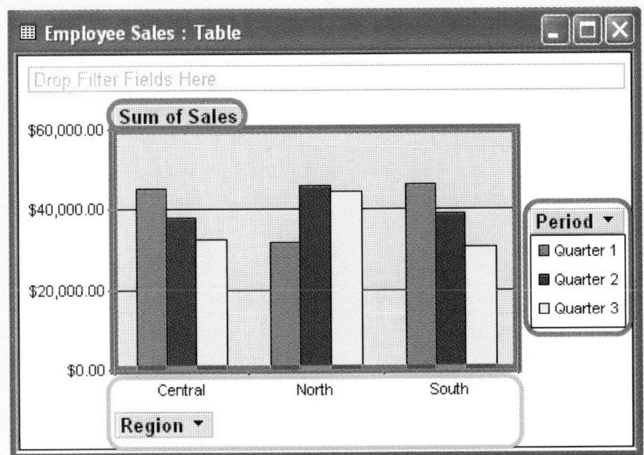

Category Field

Specifies a field you want to use to group data in the chart. The name of each group in the field appears along the bottom of the chart.

Series Field

Specifies a field that contains the data you want to display as separate data series in the chart. Each data series is represented by a specific color, which is identified in the legend.

Data Field

Specifies a field that contains the data you want to summarize in the chart. Access will plot the summary of the data in the chart.

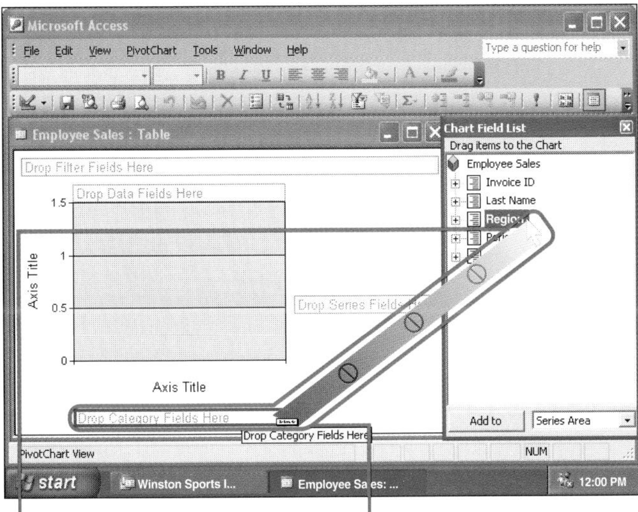

3 To add the field you want to use to group data in the chart, position the mouse over the name of the field in this area.

4 Drag the field name to the **Drop Category Fields Here** area.

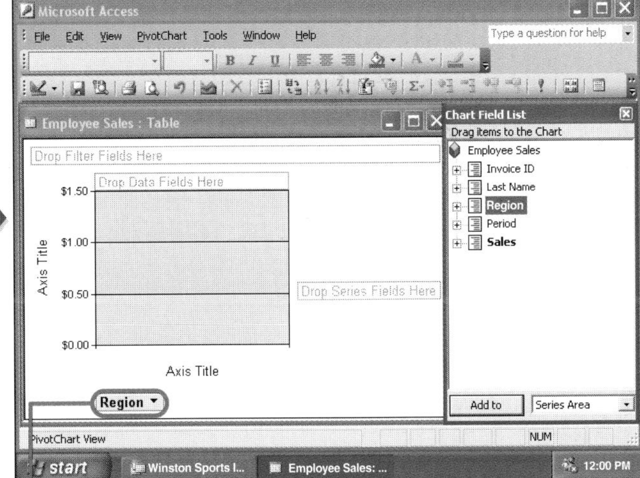

- The name of the field you selected appears in this area.
- The name of each group in the field may appear along the bottom of the chart.

*Note: The name of each group in the field may not appear in the chart until after you perform step **6**.*

CONTINUED

When using the PivotChart view, you can select the field that contains the data you want to summarize in the PivotChart.

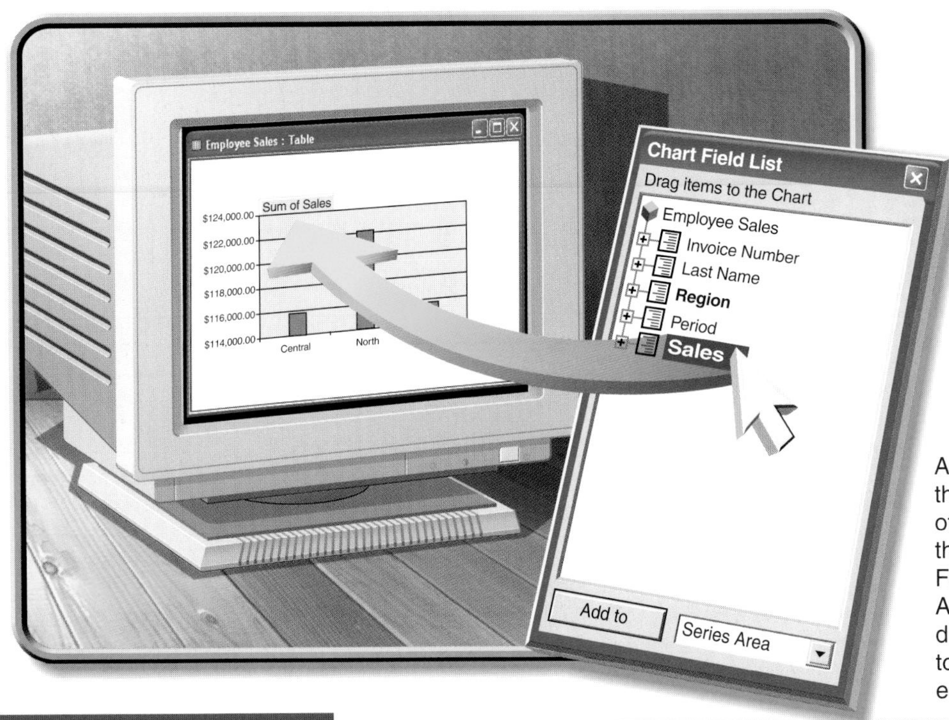

Access will plot the summary of the data in the PivotChart. For example, Access will display the total sales for each region.

USING THE PIVOTCHART VIEW (CONTINUED)

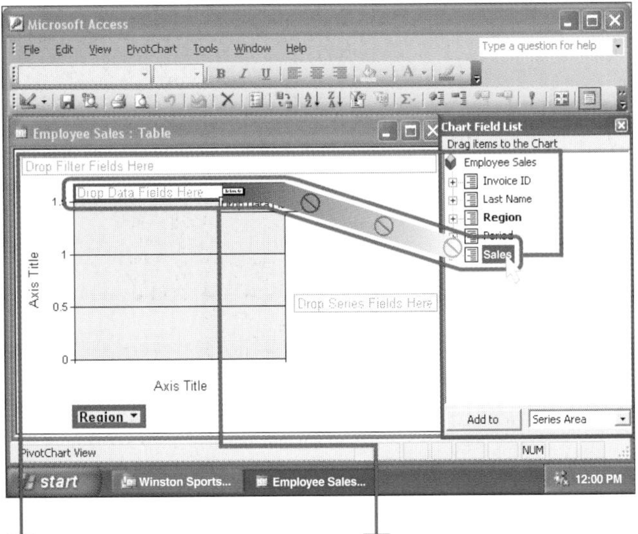

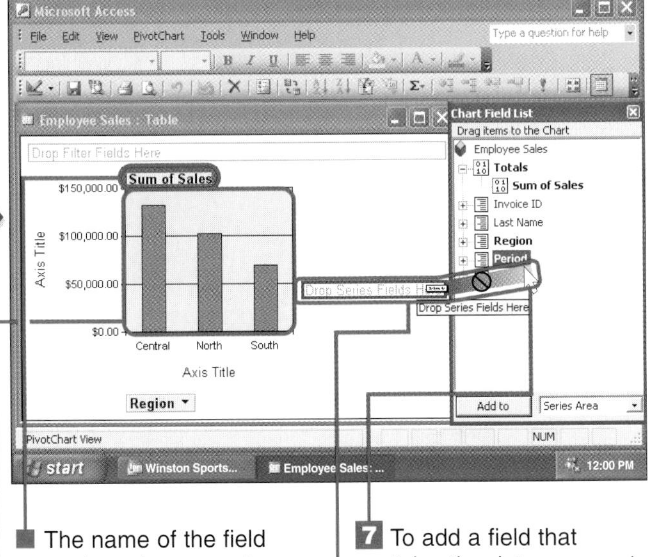

5 To add the field that contains the data you want to summarize in the chart, position the mouse over the name of the field in this area.

6 Drag the field name to the **Drop Data Fields Here** area.

- The name of the field you selected appears in this area.
- Access summarizes the data for each group in the chart.

7 To add a field that contains the data you want to display as separate data series in the chart, position the mouse over the name of the field in this area.

8 Drag the field name to the **Drop Series Fields Here** area.

Can I remove a field from a PivotChart?

Yes. You can remove any field you added to a PivotChart. Removing a field from a PivotChart will not remove the field from the table, form or query used to create the PivotChart. To remove a field from a PivotChart, click the name of the field in the PivotChart and then press the Delete key.

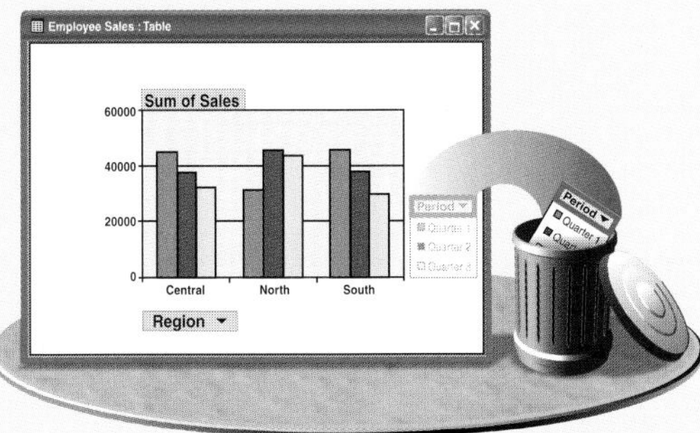

How can I move the Chart Field List dialog box so it does not cover my PivotChart?

To move the Chart Field List dialog box, position the mouse over the title bar of the dialog box and then drag the dialog box to a new location.

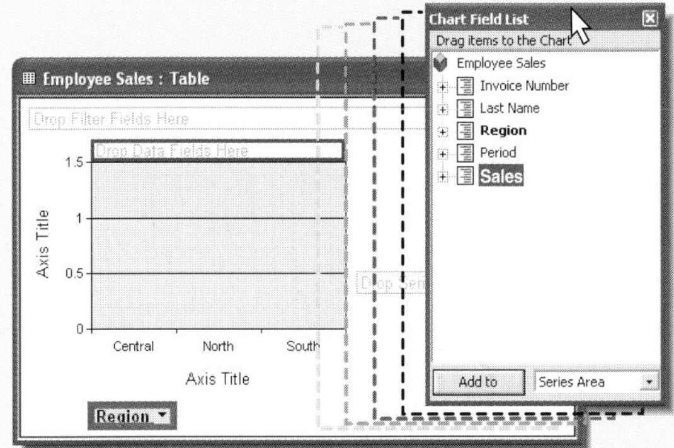

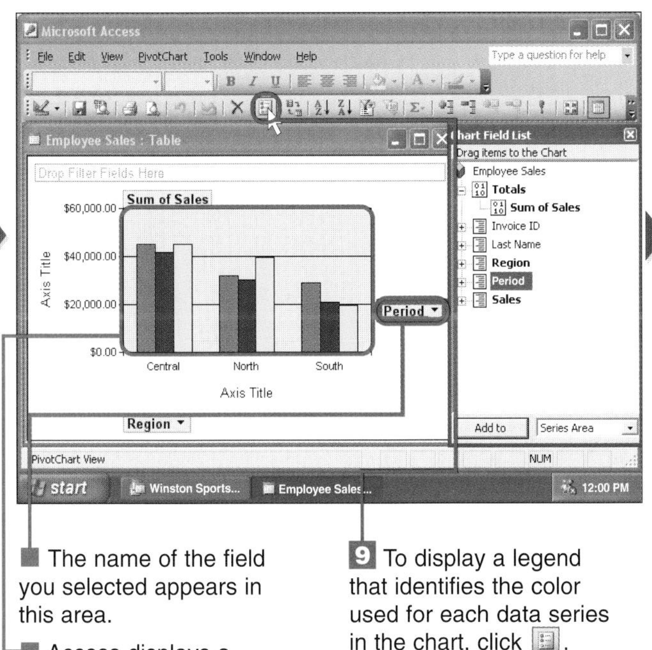

■ The name of the field you selected appears in this area.

■ Access displays a data series for each group of data in the field.

9 To display a legend that identifies the color used for each data series in the chart, click .

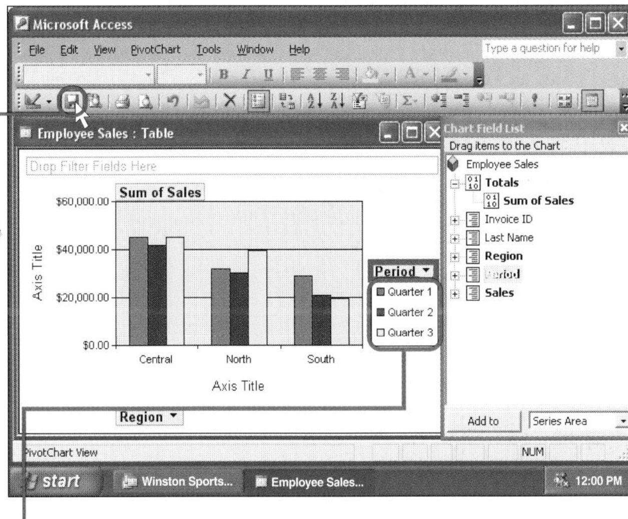

■ The legend appears.

Note: To remove the legend, click again.

10 To save all the changes you made in the PivotChart view, click .

Note: Access automatically saves changes you make to a form displayed in the PivotChart view.

CONTINUED

USING THE PIVOTCHART VIEW

You can change the chart type of a PivotChart to present your data more effectively.

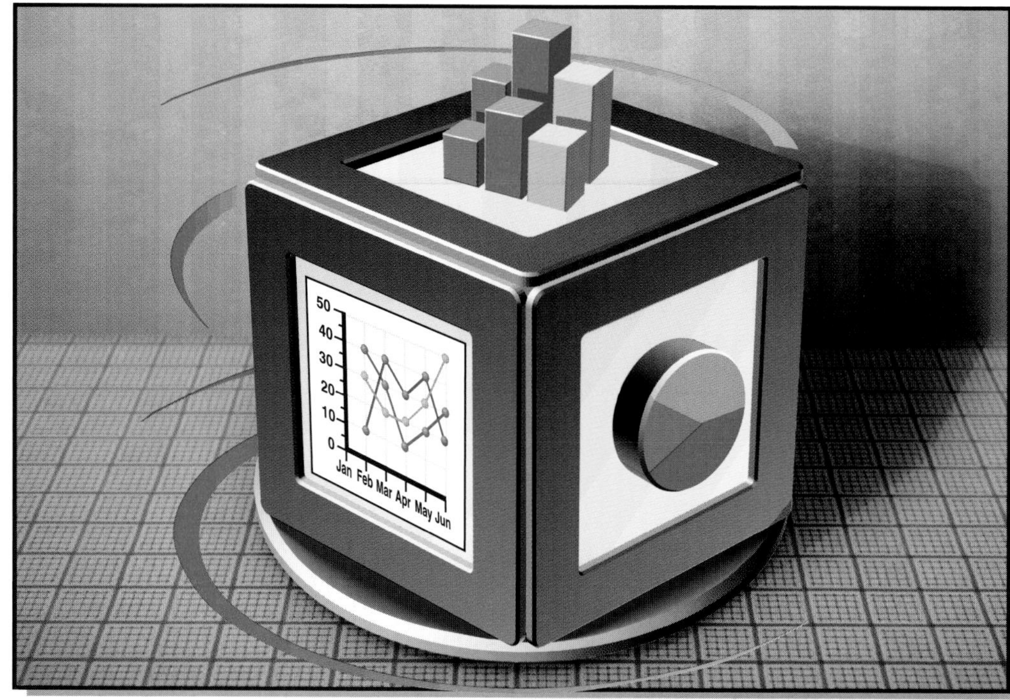

CHANGE THE CHART TYPE

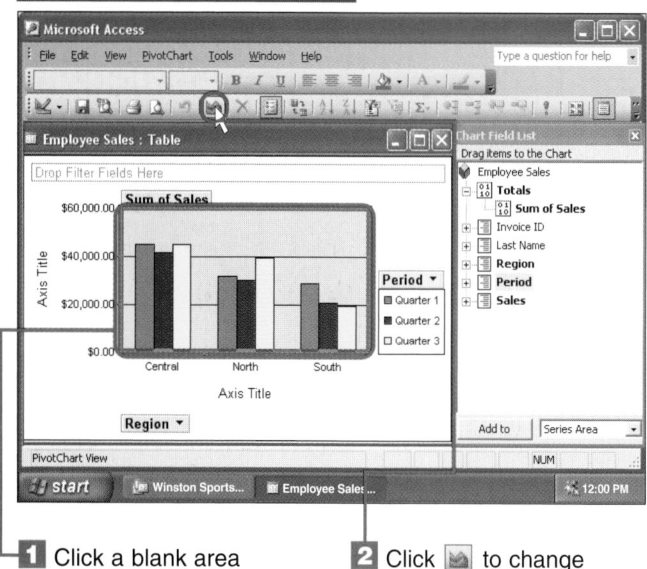

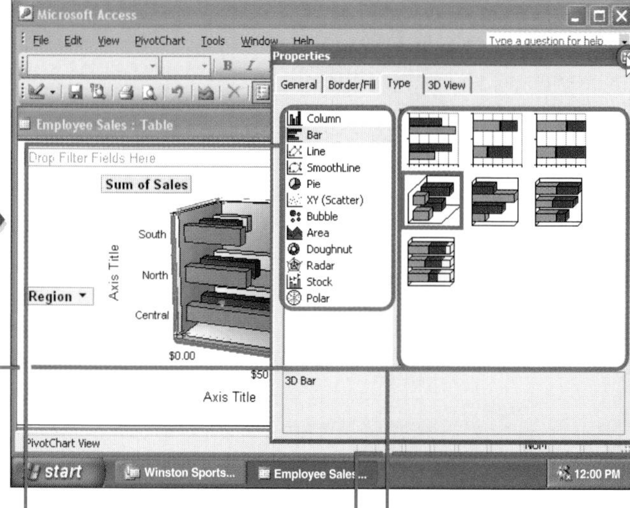

1 Click a blank area in the chart you want to change to a different chart type.

2 Click (icon) to change the chart type.

■ The Properties dialog box appears.

3 Click the type of chart you want to use.

■ This area displays the available chart designs for the type of chart you selected.

4 Click the chart design you want to use.

■ Access changes the chart type of the chart.

5 Click (close icon) to close the Properties dialog box.

You can change the type of calculation that Access performs on the data in a PivotChart to help you better analyze the data.

For example, Access can calculate the average value for each group in a PivotChart.

CHANGE THE CALCULATION PERFORMED

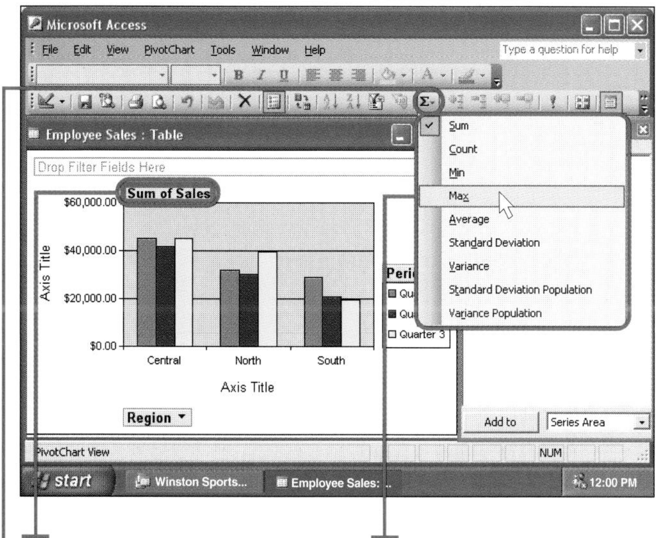

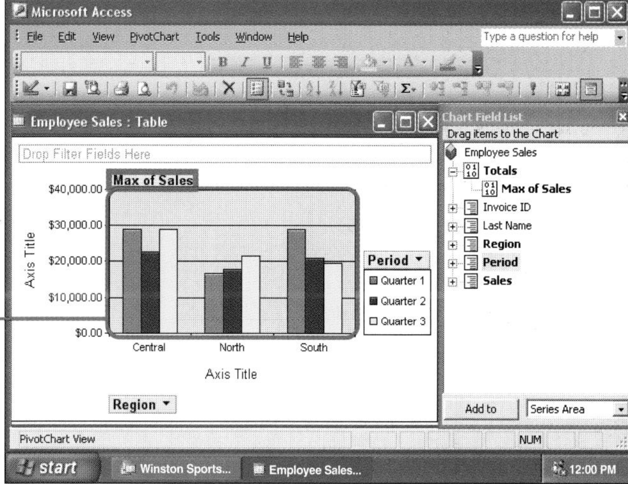

1 Click the name of the field in the chart that contains the data that Access has summarized in the chart.

2 Click Σ to display a list of the calculations that you can perform.

3 Click the calculation you want to perform.

Note: For information on the calculations that you can perform, see the top of page 237.

■ The chart shows the results of the calculation you specified.

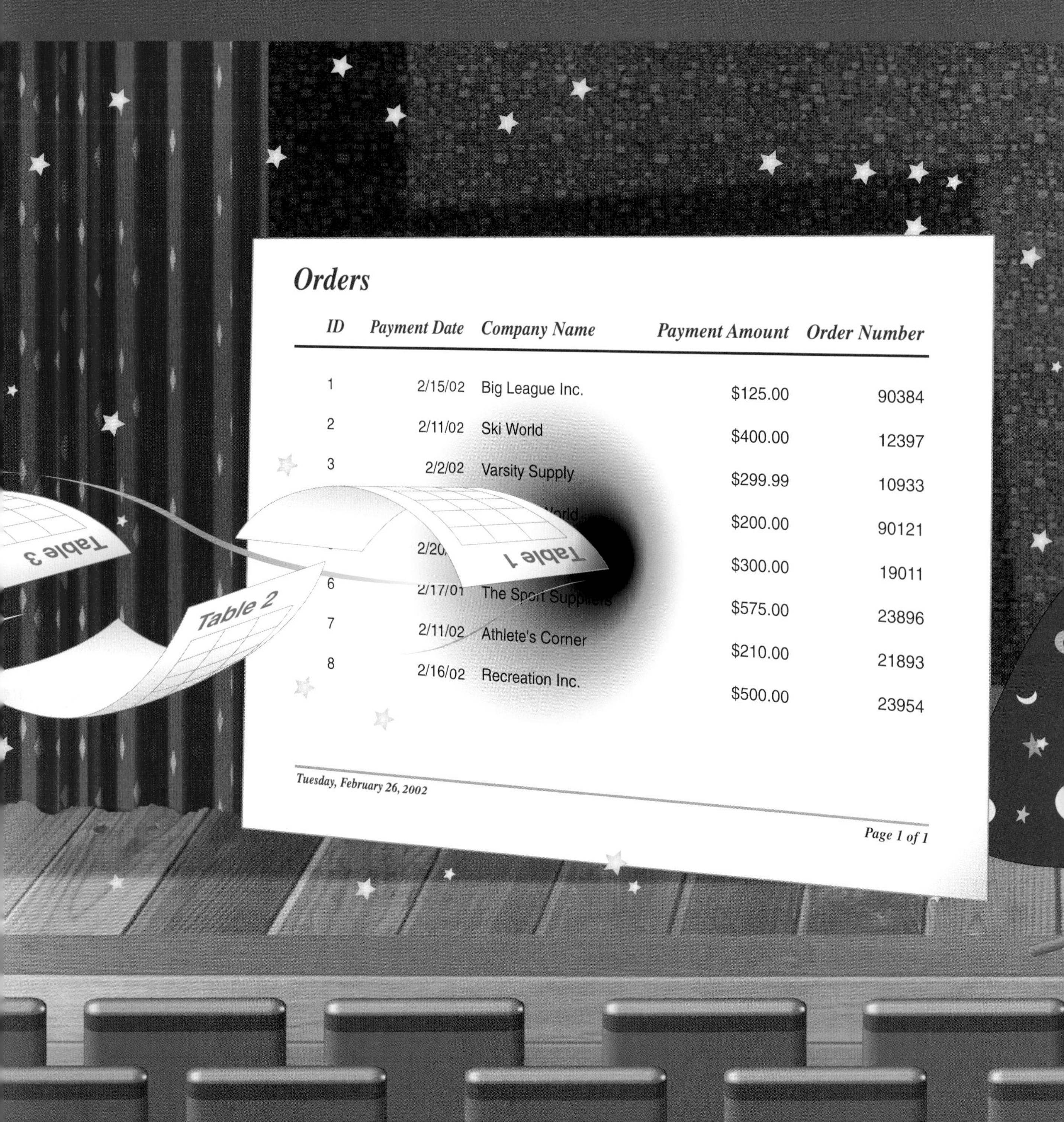
Orders
ID
Payment Date
Company Name
Payment Amount
Order Number
1
2/15/02
Big League Inc.
$125.00
90384
2
2/11/02
Ski World
$400.00
12397
3
2/2/02
Varsity Supply
$299.99
10933
$200.00
90121
$300.00
19011
6
2/17/01
$575.00
23896
7
2/11/02
Athlete's Corner
$210.00
21893
8
2/16/02
Recreation Inc.
$500.00
23954
Tuesday, February 26, 2002
Page 1 of 1
Table 1
Table 2
Table 3

CHAPTER 11

Create Reports

Would you like Access to help you present your data in a neatly organized report? This chapter teaches you how to create and work with reports.

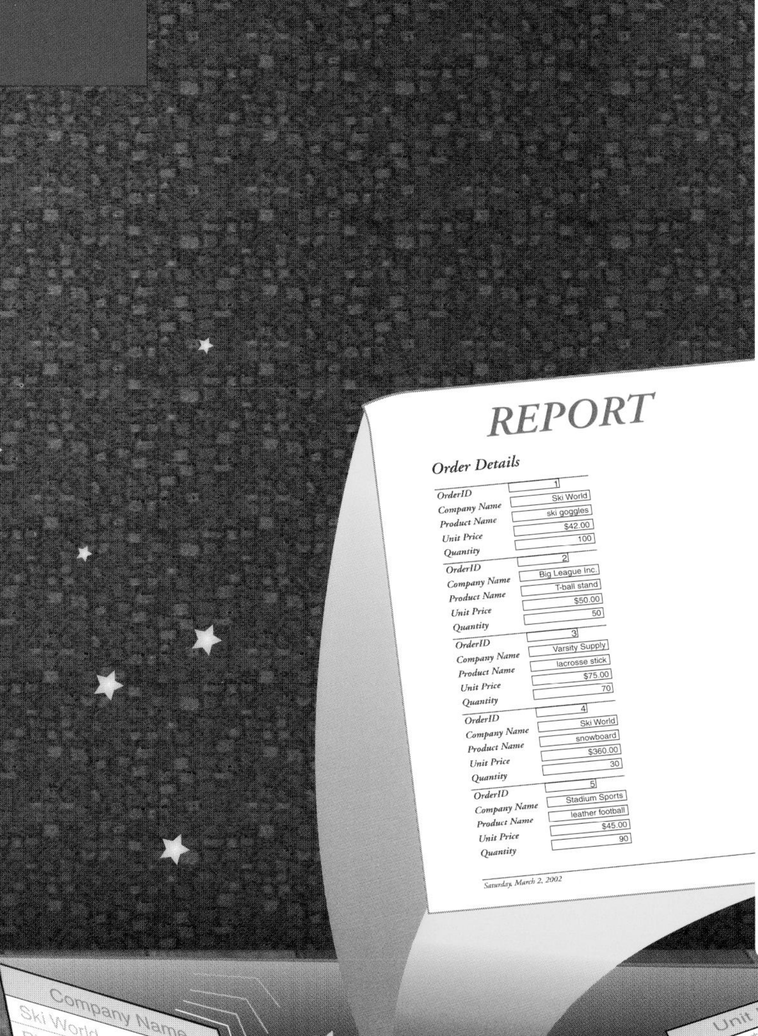

CREATE A REPORT USING THE REPORT WIZARD

You can use the Report Wizard to create a professionally designed report that summarizes data in your database.

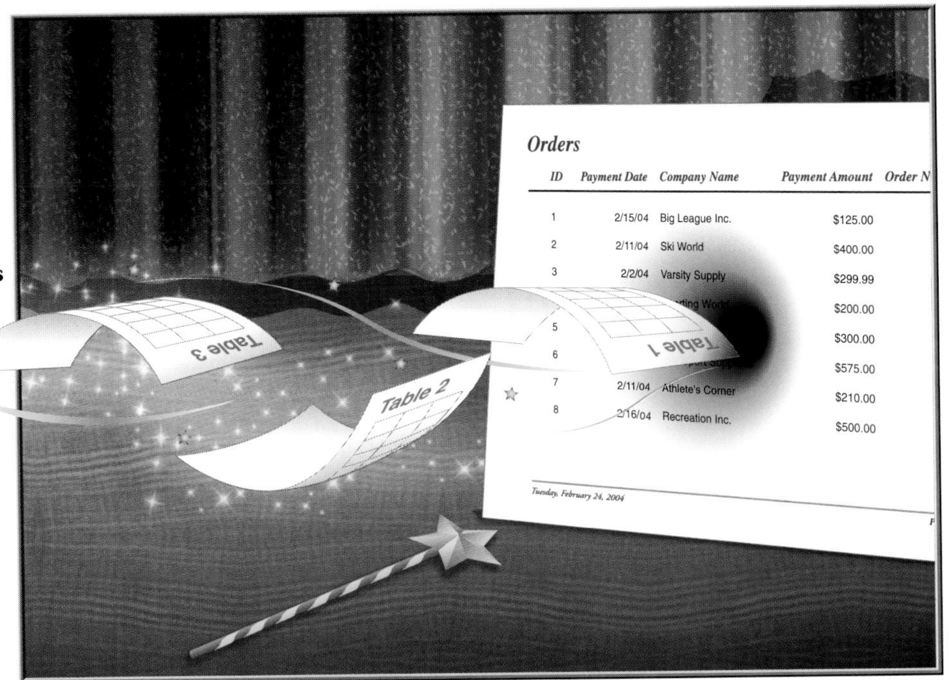

The Report Wizard asks you a series of questions and then creates a report based on your answers.

CREATE A REPORT USING THE REPORT WIZARD

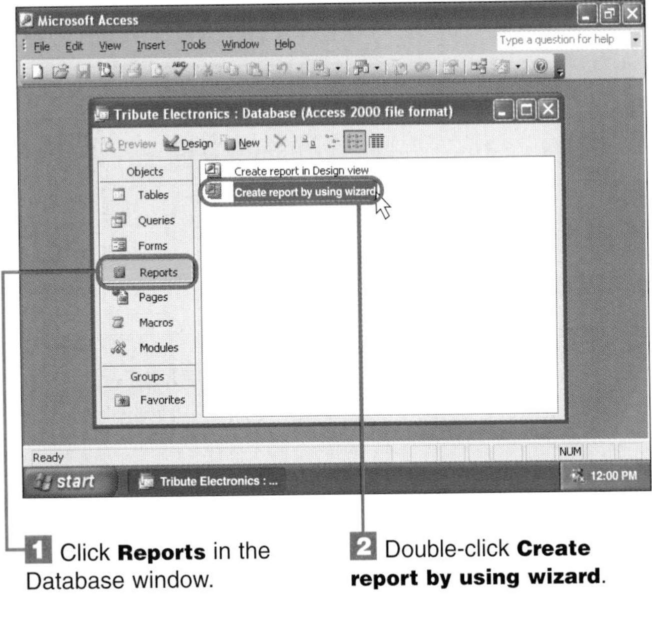

1 Click **Reports** in the Database window.

2 Double-click **Create report by using wizard**.

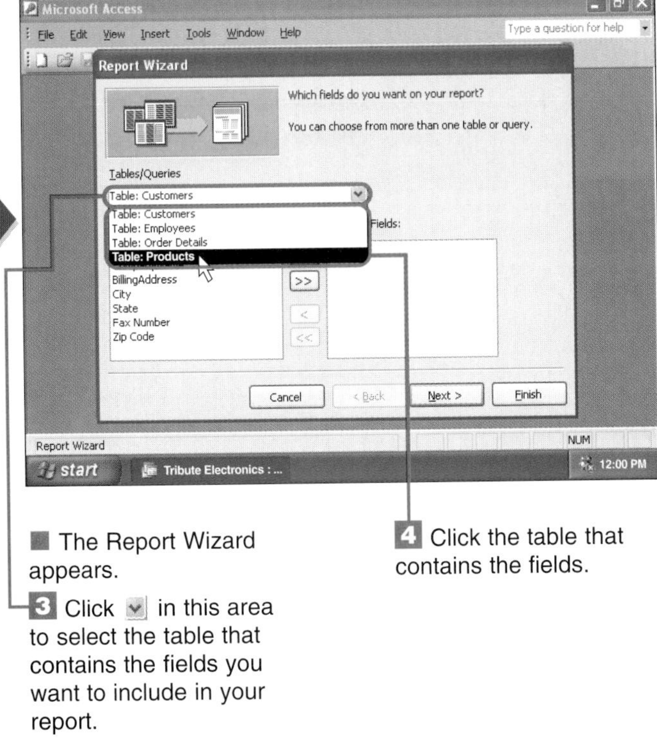

■ The Report Wizard appears.

3 Click ▼ in this area to select the table that contains the fields you want to include in your report.

4 Click the table that contains the fields.

Which tables in my database can I use to create a report?

You can use any table in your database to create a report. When creating a report that uses information from more than one table, relationships must exist between the tables so that Access can bring together the information in the tables. For information on relationships, see page 128.

Can I create a report using data from a query?

Yes. When creating a report, you can use data from queries. The Report Wizard allows you to select the fields you want to include from queries as you would select the fields you want to include from tables. For information on queries, see pages 192 to 229.

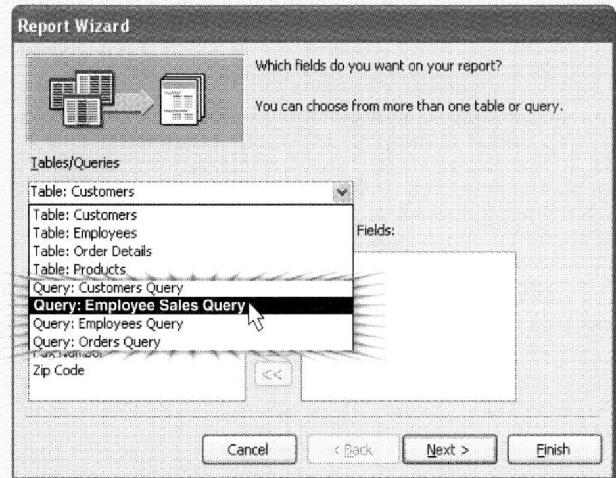

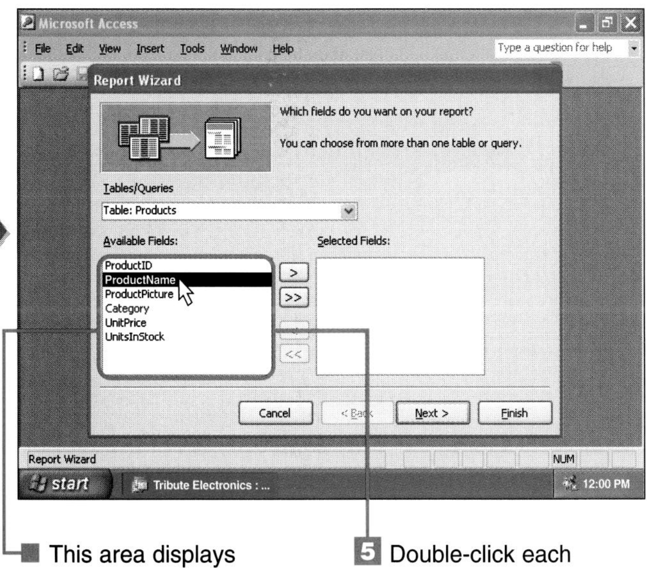

■ This area displays the fields from the table you selected.

5 Double-click each field you want to include in your report.

Note: To add all the fields in the table at once, click >> .

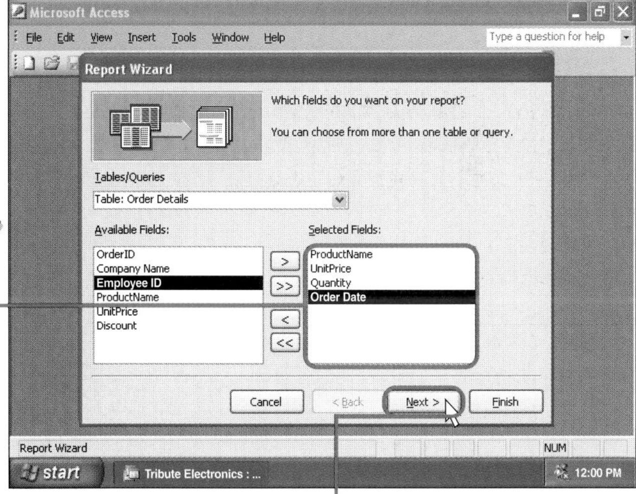

■ Each field you select appears in this area.

■ To remove a field you accidentally selected, double-click the field in this area.

Note: To remove all the fields at once, click << .

6 To include fields from other tables in your database, repeat steps 3 to 5 for each table.

7 Click **Next** to continue.

CONTINUED

CREATE A REPORT USING THE REPORT WIZARD

You can choose how you want to group data in your report. Grouping data helps you organize and summarize the data in your report.

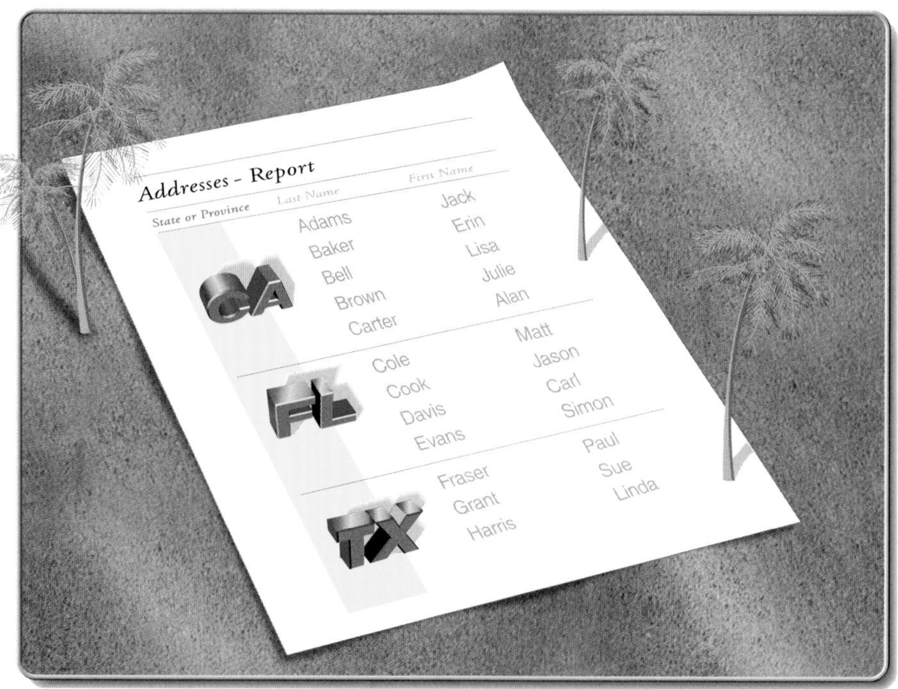

For example, you can group data by the State field to place all the customers from the same state together in your report.

CREATE A REPORT USING THE REPORT WIZARD (CONTINUED)

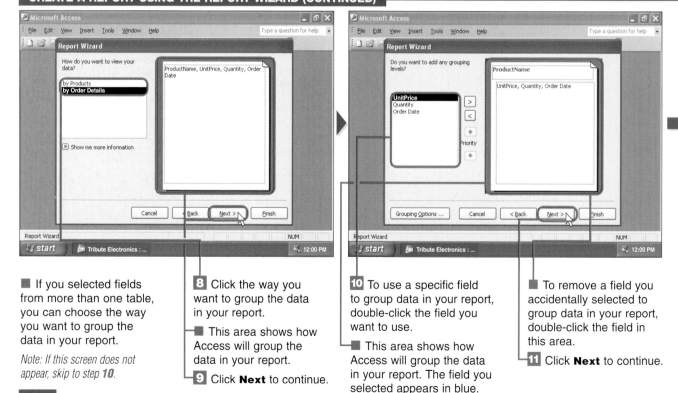

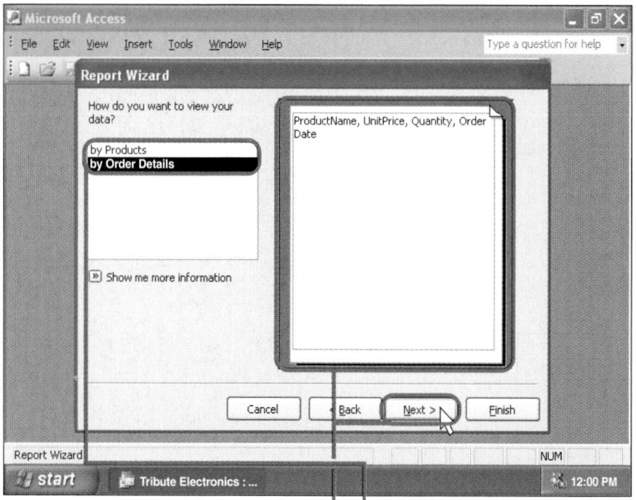

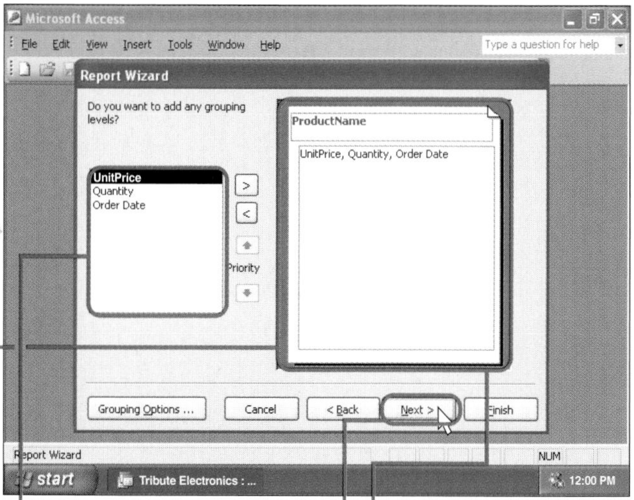

■ If you selected fields from more than one table, you can choose the way you want to group the data in your report.

*Note: If this screen does not appear, skip to step **10**.*

8 Click the way you want to group the data in your report.

■ This area shows how Access will group the data in your report.

9 Click **Next** to continue.

10 To use a specific field to group data in your report, double-click the field you want to use.

■ This area shows how Access will group the data in your report. The field you selected appears in blue.

■ To remove a field you accidentally selected to group data in your report, double-click the field in this area.

11 Click **Next** to continue.

Why would I sort the records in my report?

You can sort the records in your report to better organize the data. For example, you can sort records alphabetically by the Last Name field to make it easier to find customers of interest. If the same last name appears more than once in the field, you can sort records by a second field, such as First Name, to further organize the data. You can use up to four fields to sort the records in a report.

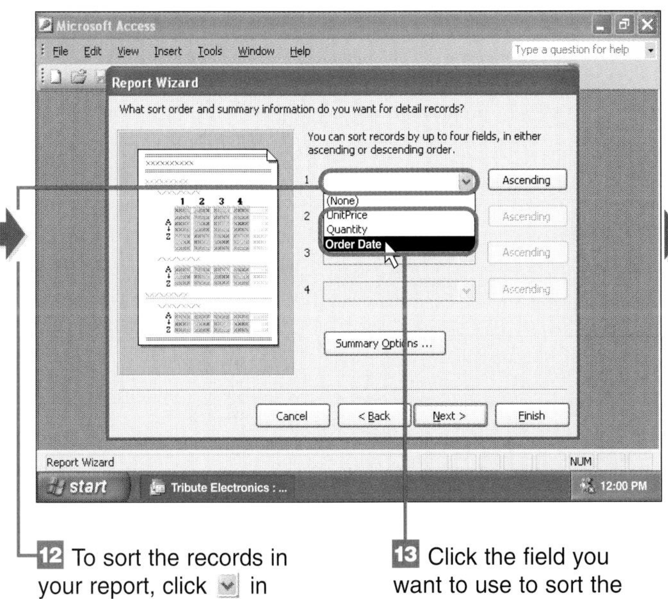

12 To sort the records in your report, click ▾ in this area.

Note: For information on sorting, see the top of this page.

13 Click the field you want to use to sort the records.

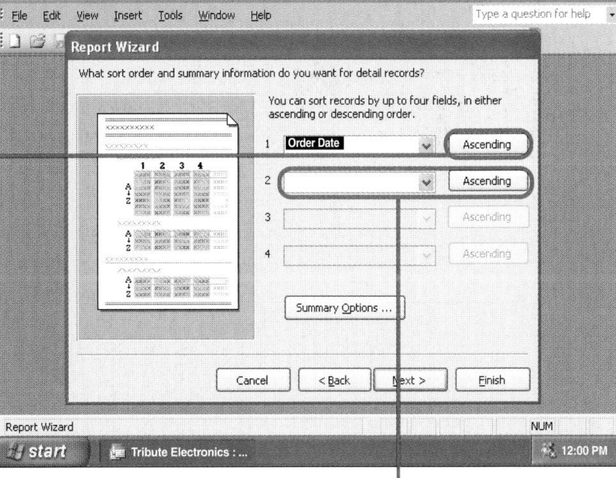

14 Click this button until the button displays the way you want to sort the records.

Ascending–Sorts A to Z, 1 to 9

Descending–Sorts Z to A, 9 to 1

15 To sort by a second field, repeat steps **12** to **14** in this area.

CONTINUED

You can perform calculations to summarize the data in your report.

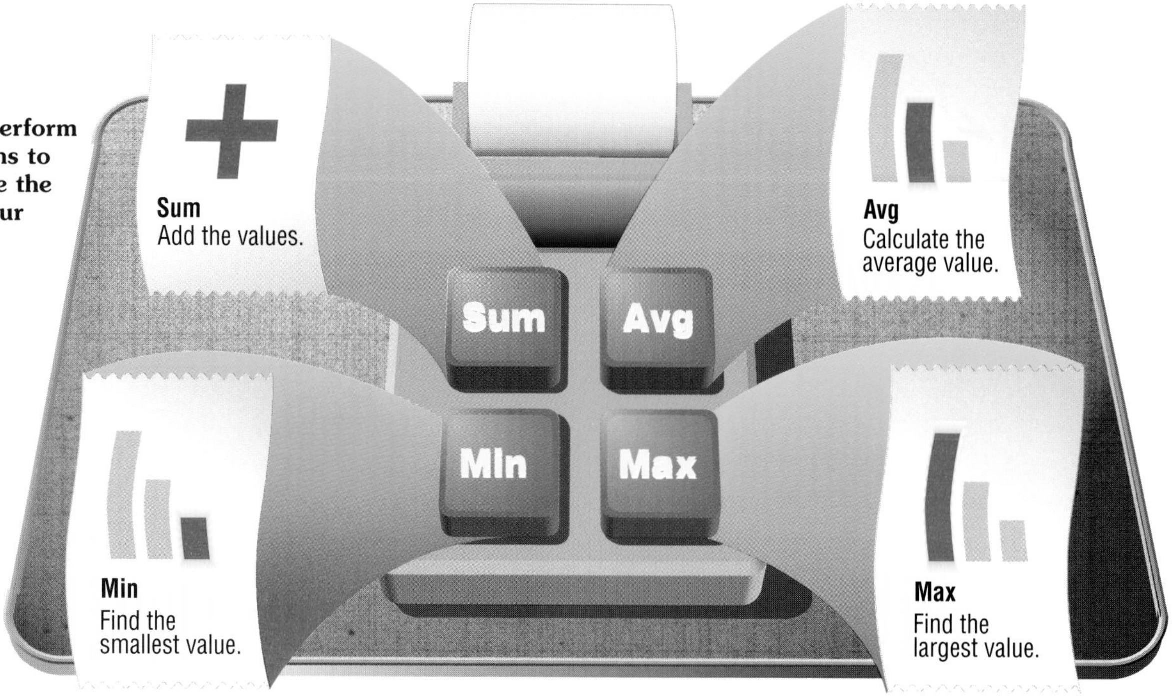

Sum
Add the values.

Avg
Calculate the average value.

Min
Find the smallest value.

Max
Find the largest value.

CREATE A REPORT USING THE REPORT WIZARD (CONTINUED)

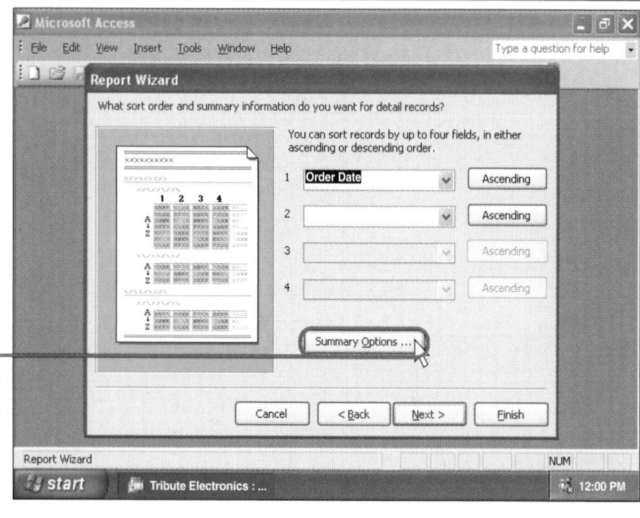

16 To perform calculations in your report, click **Summary Options**.

*Note: If you chose not to group data in your report, Summary Options will not be available. If Summary Options is not available, skip to step **21**.*

■ The Summary Options dialog box appears.

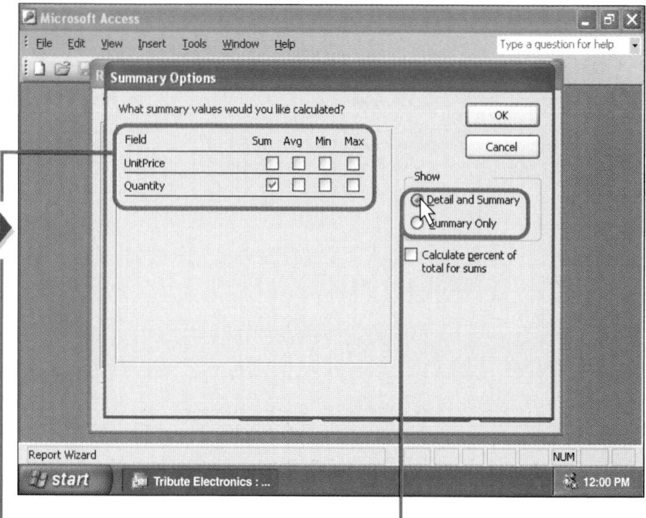

■ This area displays the fields you can perform calculations on.

17 Click the box (☐) for each calculation you want to perform (☐ changes to ☑).

18 Click an option to specify if you want the report to display all the records and the summary information or just the summary (○ changes to ◉). For more information, see the top of page 251.

When performing calculations in my report, what information can I display?

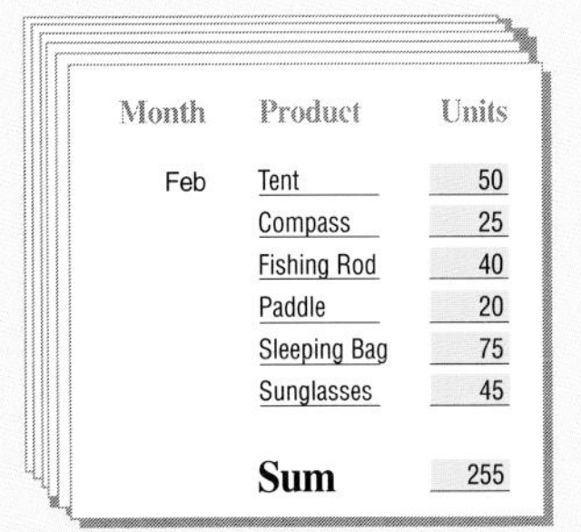

Detail and Summary

Display all the records and the summary information. For example, show all the orders and the total orders for each month.

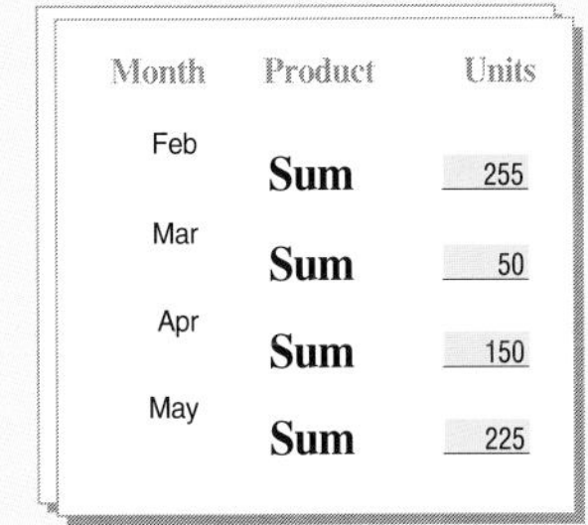

Summary Only

Display only the summary information. For example, show only the total orders for each month.

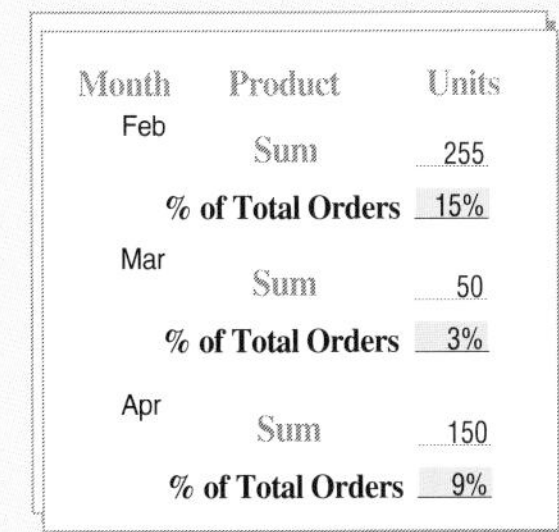

Calculate percent of total for sums

Display the percentage of the total that each group represents. For example, show the percentage of the total orders that each month represents.

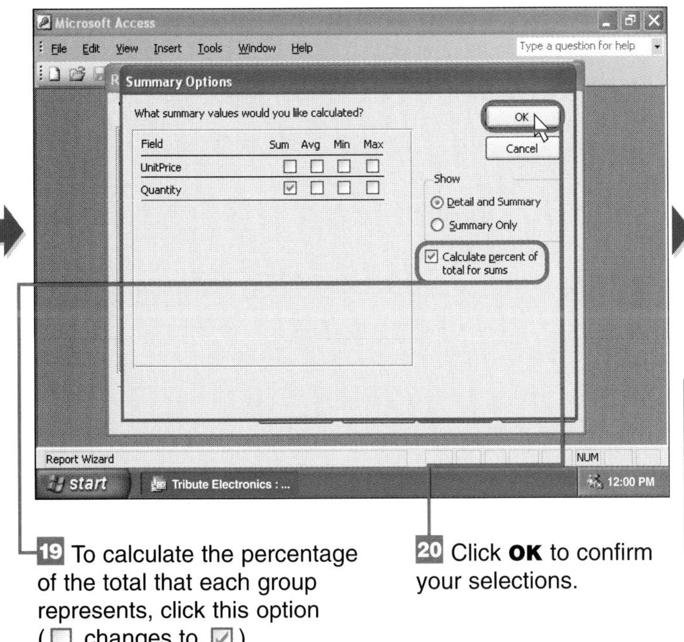

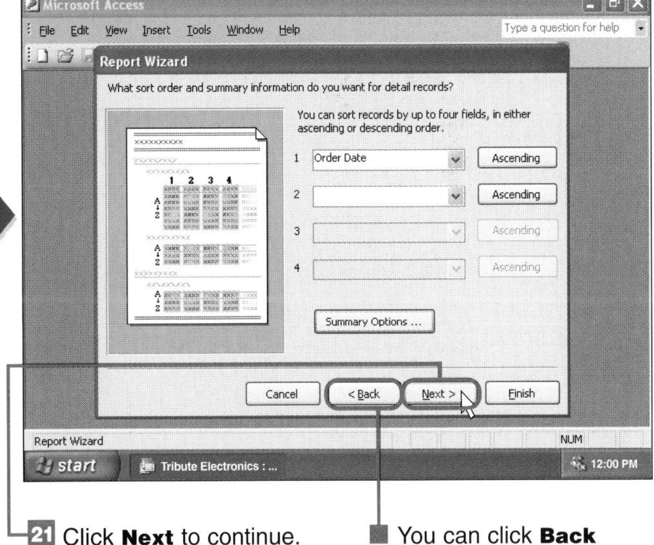

19 To calculate the percentage of the total that each group represents, click this option (☐ changes to ☑).

20 Click **OK** to confirm your selections.

21 Click **Next** to continue.

■ You can click **Back** at any time to return to a previous step and change your selections.

CONTINUED

You can choose from several layouts for your report. The layout you choose determines the arrangement of information in your report.

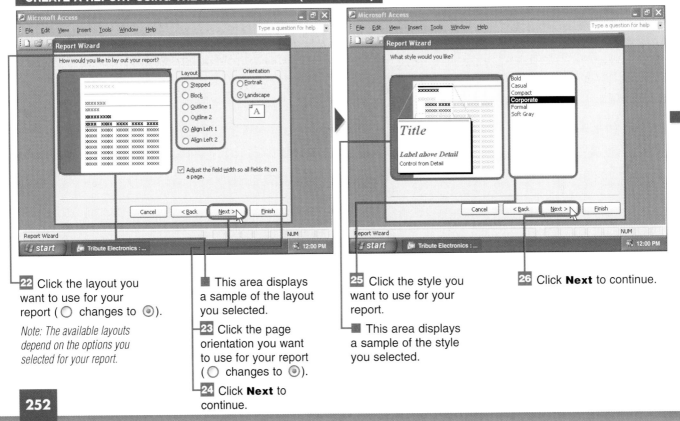

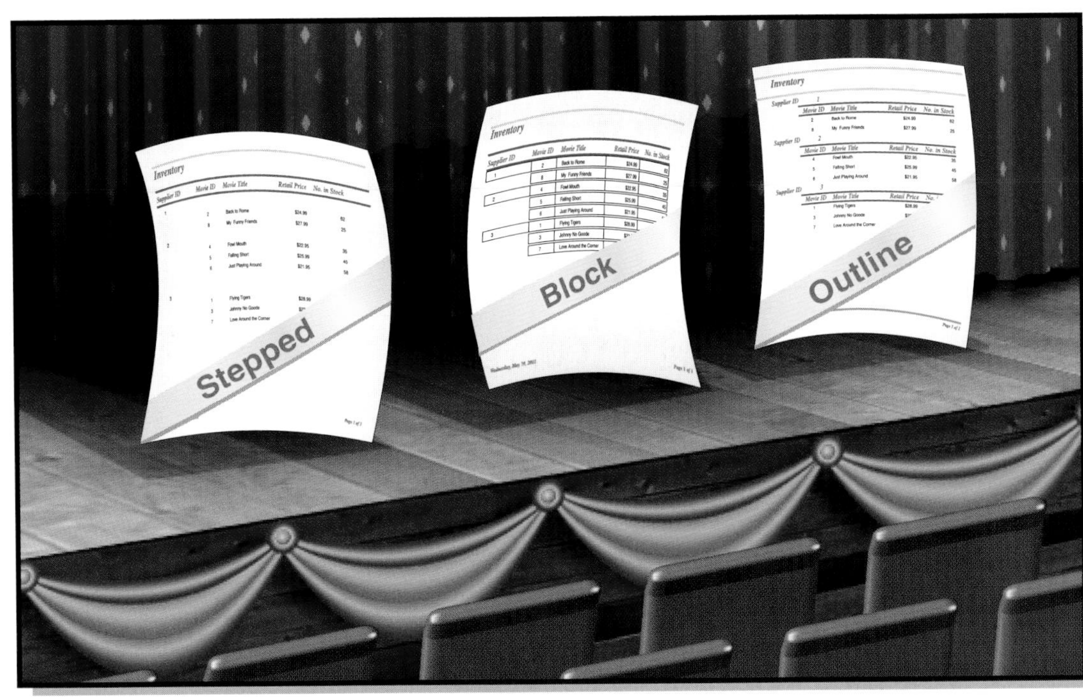

CREATE A REPORT USING THE REPORT WIZARD (CONTINUED)

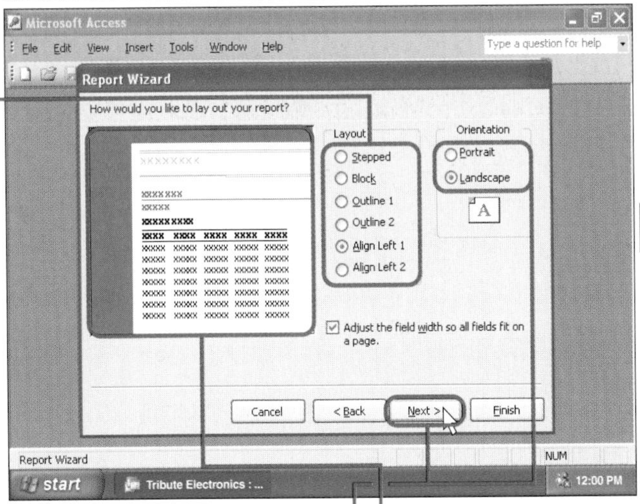

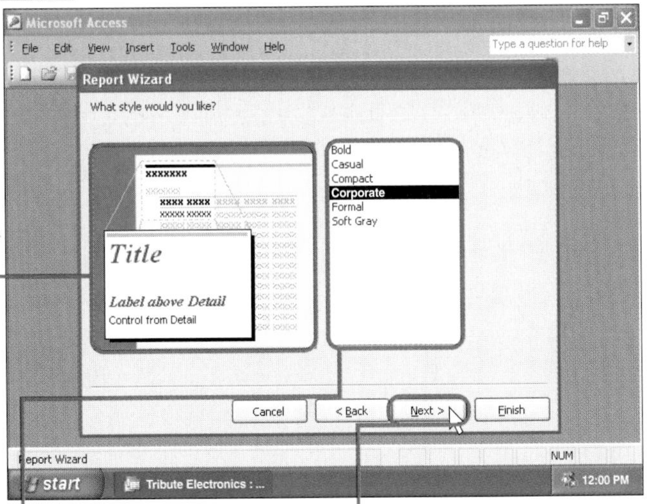

22 Click the layout you want to use for your report (○ changes to ◉).

Note: The available layouts depend on the options you selected for your report.

■ This area displays a sample of the layout you selected.

23 Click the page orientation you want to use for your report (○ changes to ◉).

24 Click **Next** to continue.

25 Click the style you want to use for your report.

■ This area displays a sample of the style you selected.

26 Click **Next** to continue.

Which page orientation should I use for my report?

The portrait orientation is the standard orientation and prints data across the short side of a page. The landscape orientation prints data across the long side of a page and can be useful when a report contains many fields.

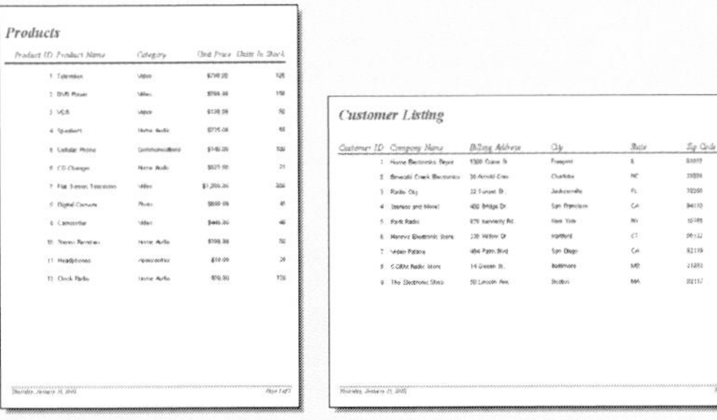

Portrait **Landscape**

Do I need to create a new report each time I change the data in my database?

No. Each time you open a report, Access will automatically gather the most current data from your database to create the report. This ensures that the report will always display the most up-to-date information. Access will also update the date displayed in the report. To open a report, see page 256.

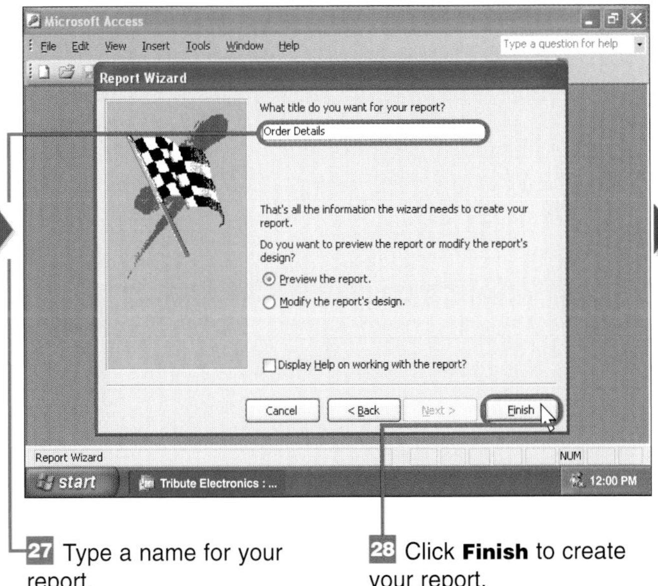

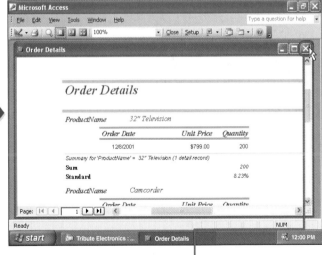

27 Type a name for your report.

28 Click **Finish** to create your report.

■ A window appears, displaying your report.

Note: To move through the pages in a report, see page 257.

29 When you finish reviewing your report, click ☒ to close the report.

CREATE A REPORT USING AN AUTOREPORT

You can use the AutoReport Wizard to quickly create a report that displays the information from one table in your database.

A report summarizes the data from your database in a professional-looking document.

CREATE A REPORT USING AN AUTOREPORT

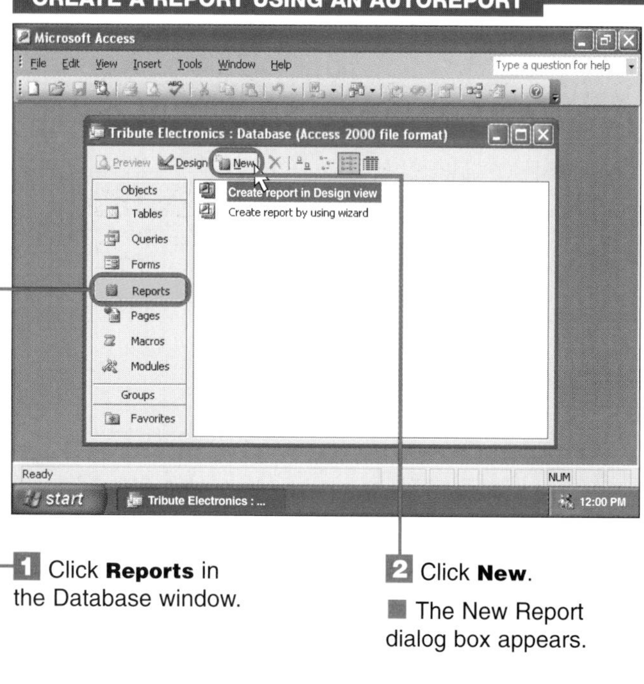

1 Click **Reports** in the Database window.

2 Click **New**.

■ The New Report dialog box appears.

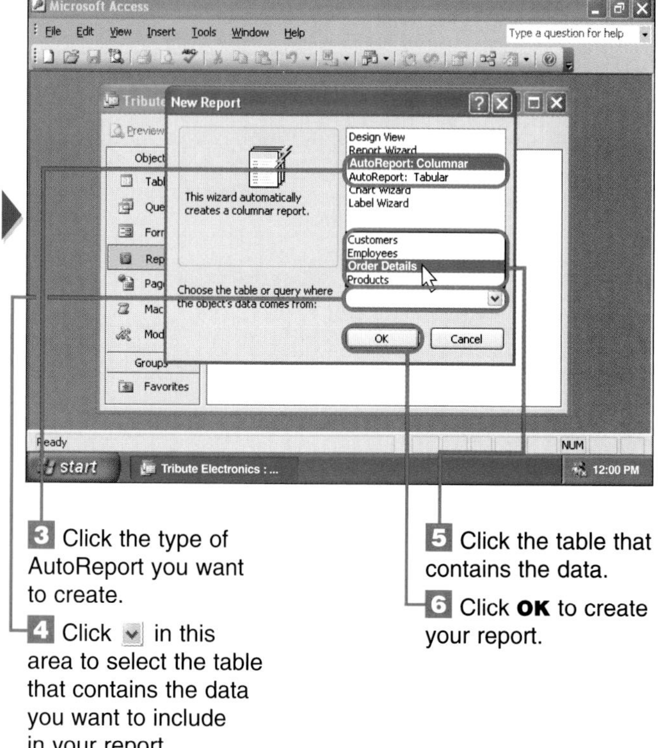

3 Click the type of AutoReport you want to create.

4 Click ▾ in this area to select the table that contains the data you want to include in your report.

5 Click the table that contains the data.

6 Click **OK** to create your report.

What types of AutoReports can I create?

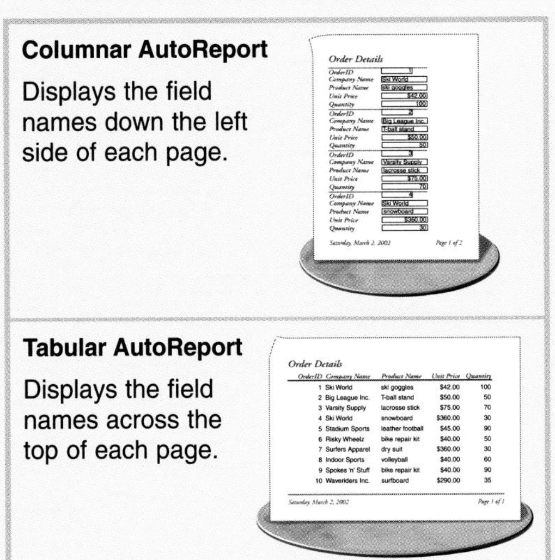

Columnar AutoReport

Displays the field names down the left side of each page.

Tabular AutoReport

Displays the field names across the top of each page.

Can I change the data displayed in a report?

If you want to make changes to the data displayed in a report, you must change the data in the table you used to create the report. Changes you make to data in the table will automatically appear in the report the next time you open the report.

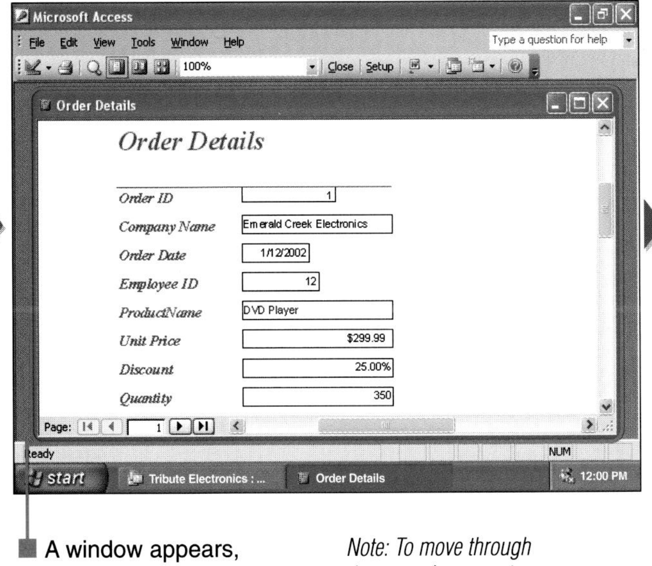

■ A window appears, displaying your report.

Note: To move through the pages in a report, *see page 257.*

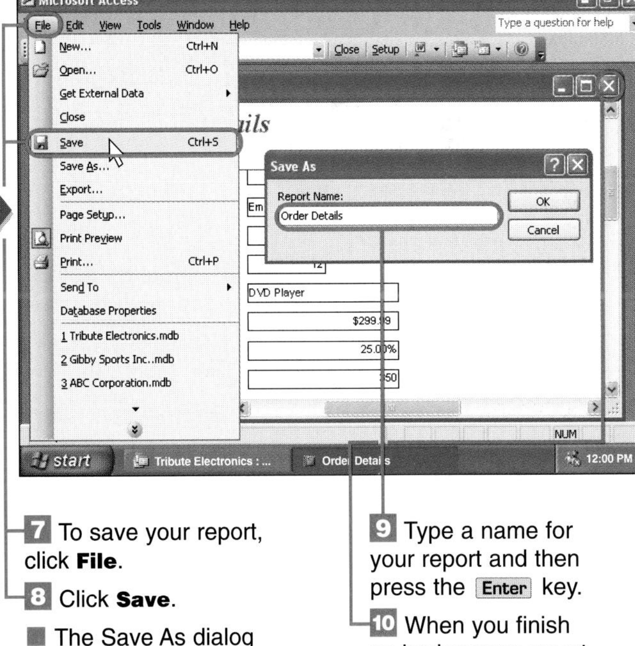

7 To save your report, click **File**.

8 Click **Save**.

■ The Save As dialog box appears.

9 Type a name for your report and then press the Enter key.

10 When you finish reviewing your report, click ☒ to close the report.

OPEN A REPORT

You can open a report to display the contents of the report on your screen. Opening a report allows you to review and make changes to the report.

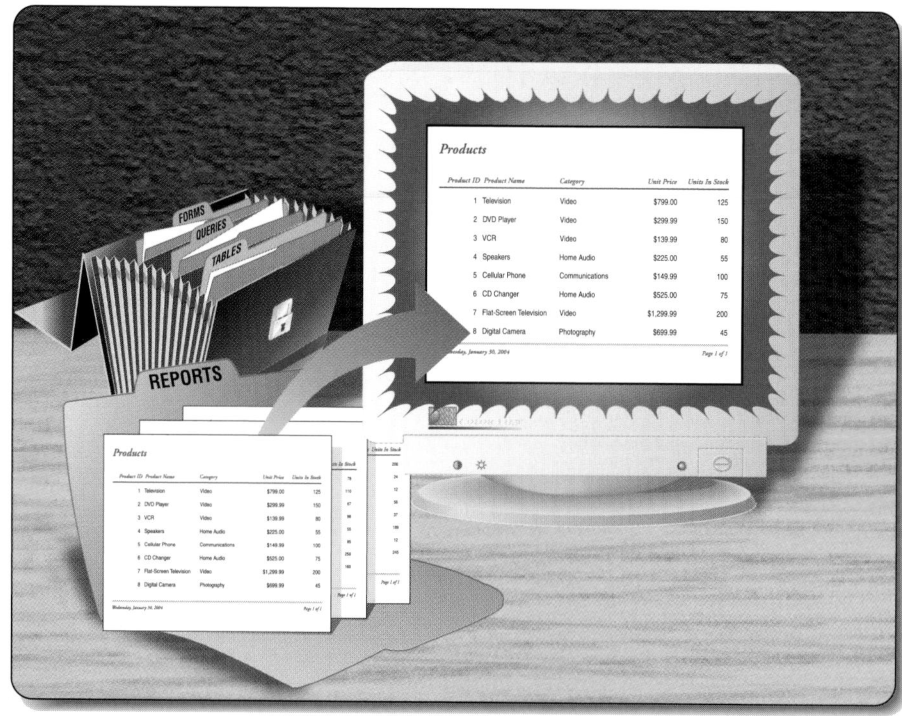

Each time you open a report, Access uses the most current data from your database to create the report.

OPEN A REPORT

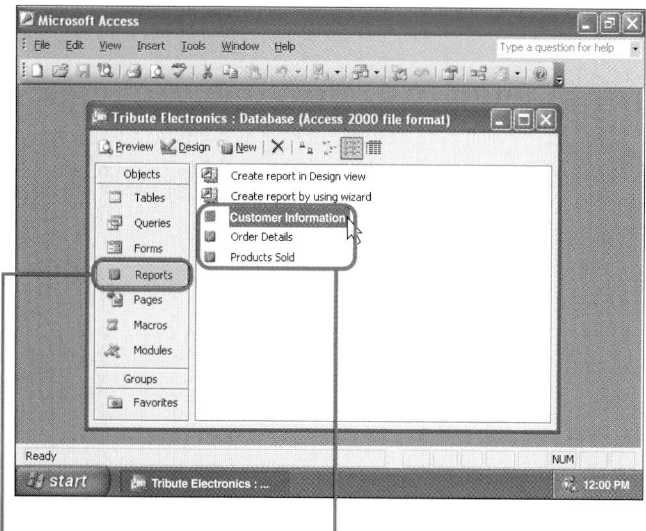

1 Click **Reports** in the Database window.

■ This area displays a list of the reports in your database.

2 Double-click the report you want to open.

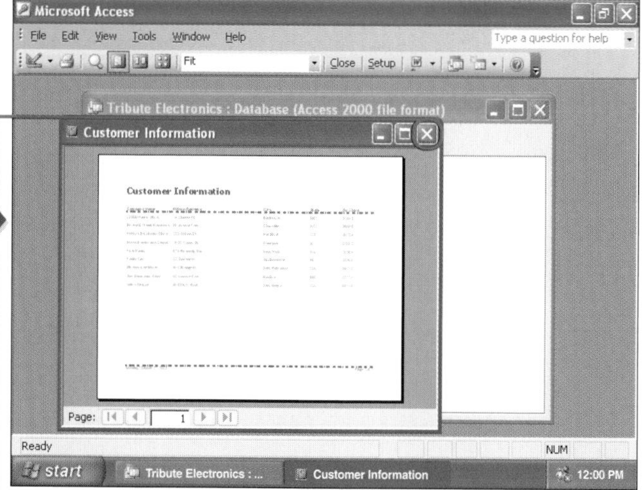

■ The report appears. You can now review and make changes to the report.

■ When you finish reviewing the report, click ☒ to close the report.

*Note: A dialog box will appear if you did not save changes you made to the design of the report. Click **Yes** or **No** to specify if you want to save the changes.*

MOVE THROUGH PAGES

If your report contains more than one page, you can move through the pages to review all the information in the report.

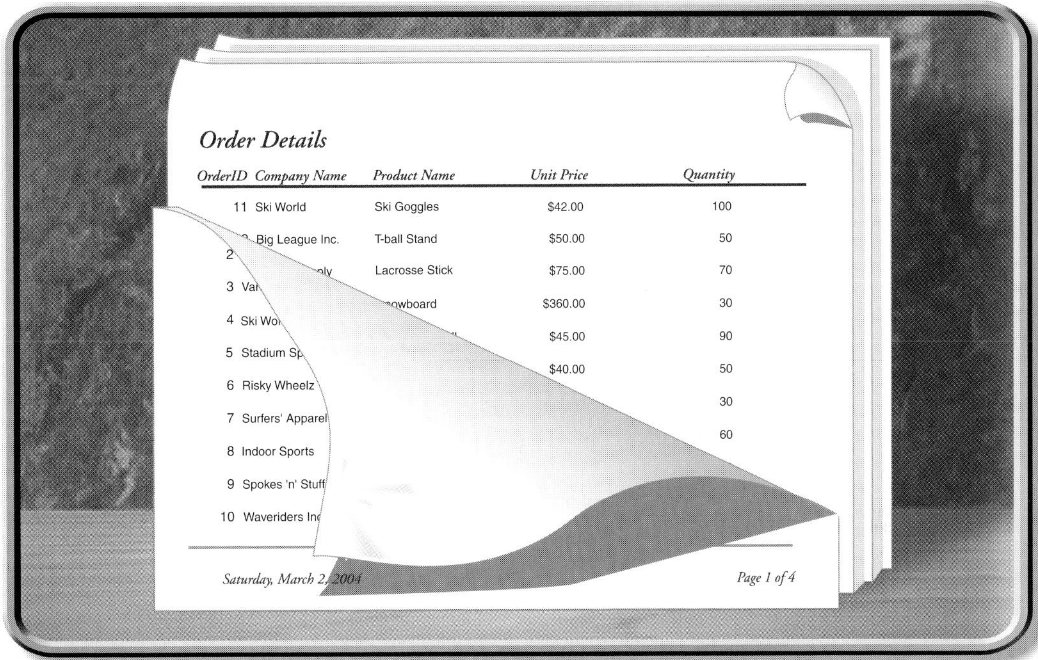

MOVE THROUGH PAGES

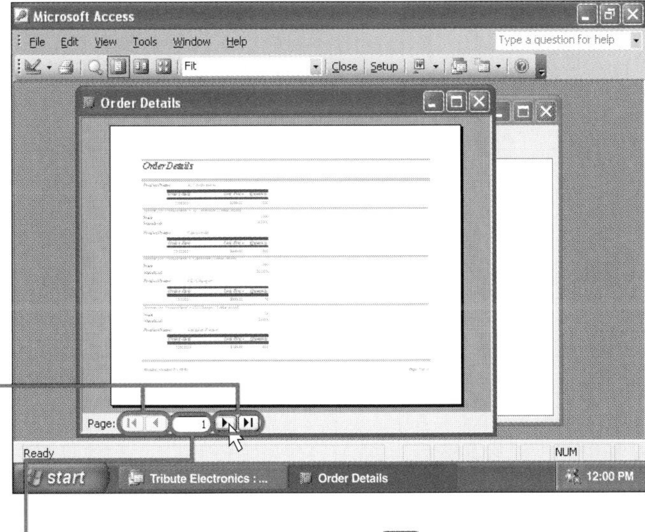

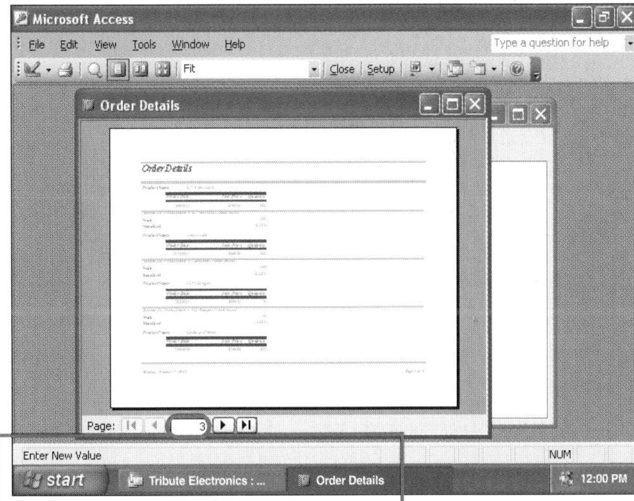

■ This area displays the number of the page displayed on your screen.

1 If your report contains more than one page, click one of the following buttons to display another page.

- First page
- Previous page
- Next page
- Last page

Note: If a button is dimmed, you cannot currently display that page.

MOVE TO A SPECIFIC PAGE

1 To quickly move to a specific page in your report, double-click the current page number. The page number is highlighted.

2 Type the number of the page you want to display and then press the Enter key.

CHANGE THE VIEW OF A REPORT

You can view a report in three different ways. Each view allows you to perform different tasks.

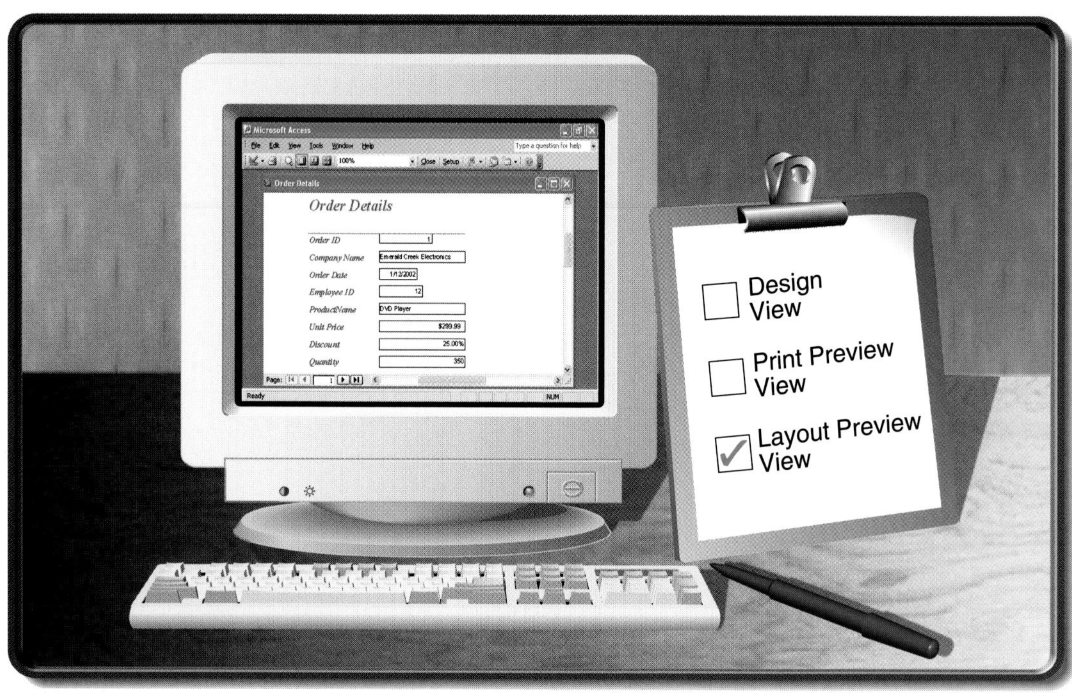

CHANGE THE VIEW OF A REPORT

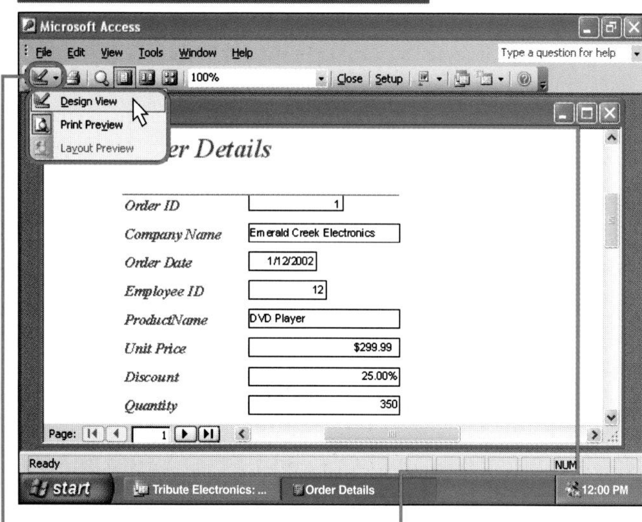

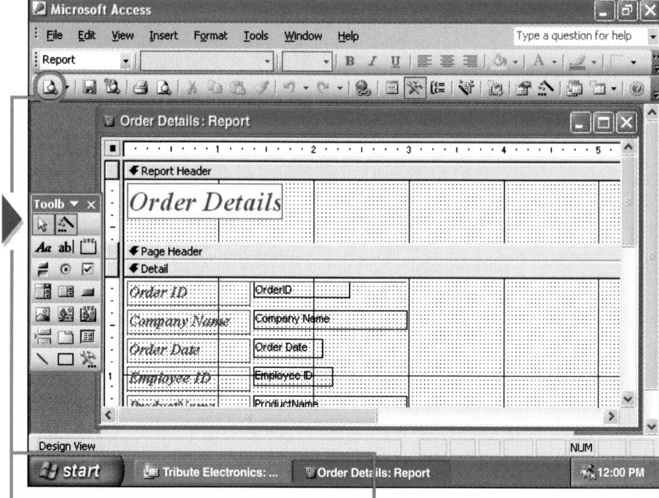

■ In this example, the report appears in the Print Preview view.

1 Click ▾ in this area to display the report in another view.

Note: The available views depend on the view you are currently using.

2 Click the view you want to use.

Note: If the view you want to use does not appear on the menu, position the mouse over the bottom of the menu to display all the views.

■ The report appears in the view you selected.

■ In this example, the View button changed from 📐 to 🔍.

■ To quickly switch between the Print Preview (🔍) and Design (📐) views, click the View button.

THE REPORT VIEWS

Design View

The Design view allows you to change the layout and design of a report. This view displays a grid of small, evenly spaced dots to help you line up the items in a report. Information in this view appears in several sections, such as the Report Header and Page Footer sections.

Print Preview View

The Print Preview view allows you to see how a report will look when printed. You can use this view to move through the pages in a report and examine how each page will print.

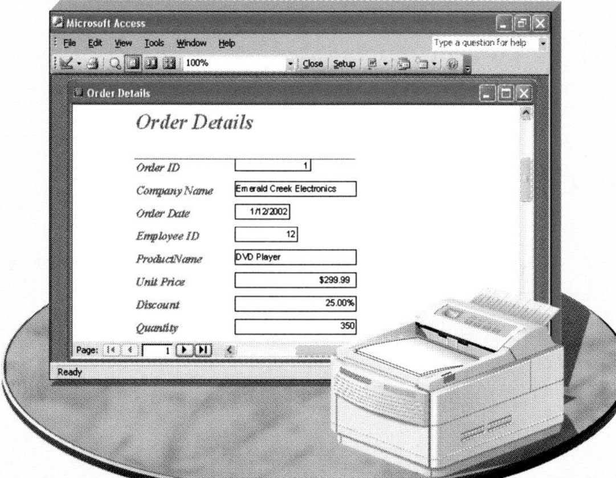

Layout Preview View

The Layout Preview view allows you to quickly view the layout and style of a report. This view is similar to the Print Preview view, but allows you to see only a few records in a report.

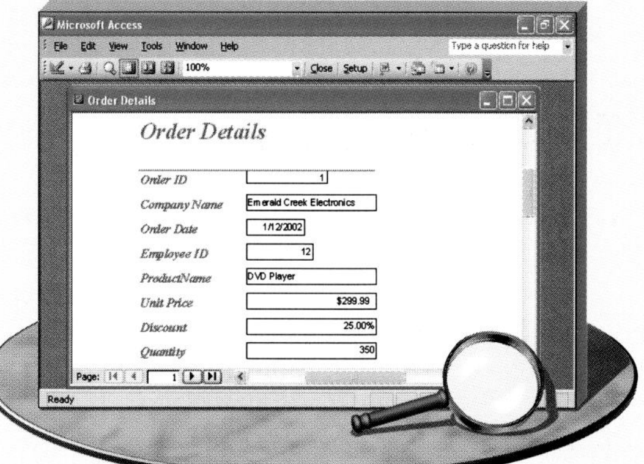

ZOOM IN OR OUT

When viewing a report, you can magnify an area of a page to view the area in more detail. You can also display an entire page in a report to view the overall appearance of the page.

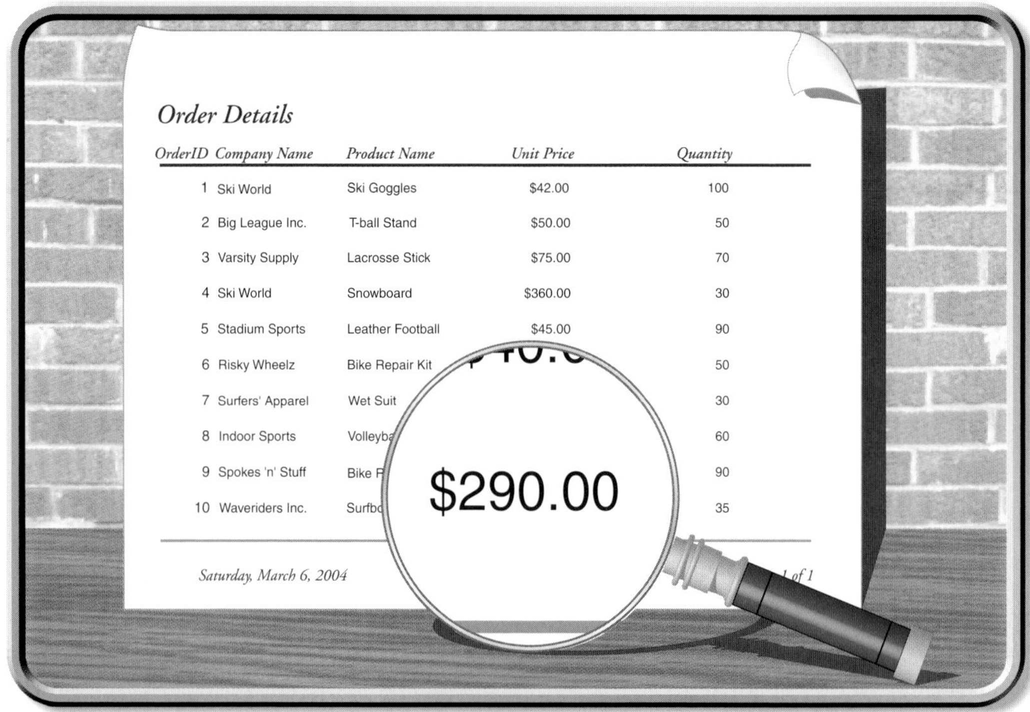

Order Details

OrderID	Company Name	Product Name	Unit Price	Quantity
1	Ski World	Ski Goggles	$42.00	100
2	Big League Inc.	T-ball Stand	$50.00	50
3	Varsity Supply	Lacrosse Stick	$75.00	70
4	Ski World	Snowboard	$360.00	30
5	Stadium Sports	Leather Football	$45.00	90
6	Risky Wheelz	Bike Repair Kit		50
7	Surfers' Apparel	Wet Suit		30
8	Indoor Sports	Volleyba		60
9	Spokes 'n' Stuff	Bike R		90
10	Waveriders Inc.	Surfbo		35

Saturday, March 6, 2004 — *1 of 1*

ZOOM IN OR OUT

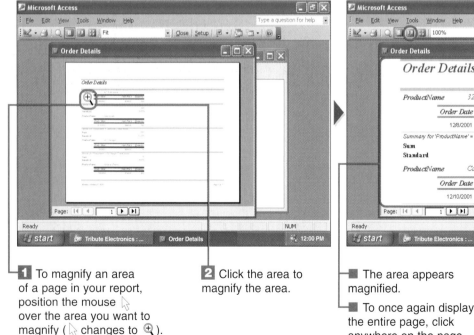

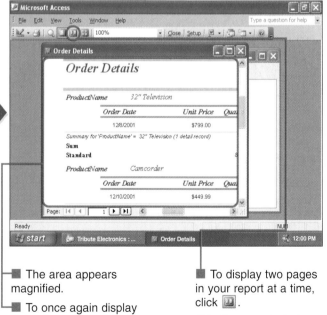

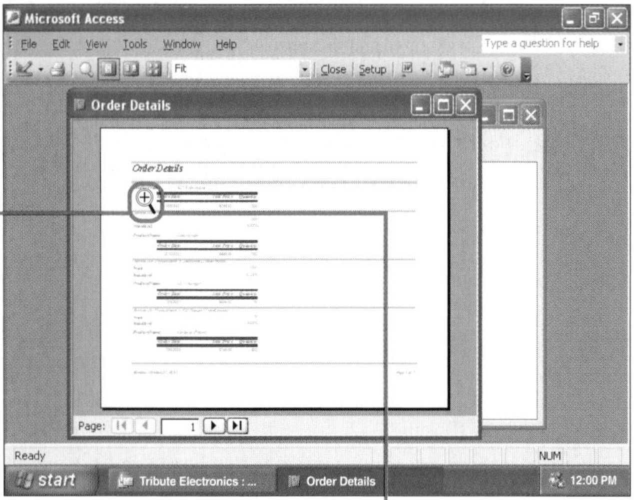

1 To magnify an area of a page in your report, position the mouse over the area you want to magnify (changes to 🔍).

2 Click the area to magnify the area.

■ The area appears magnified.

■ To once again display the entire page, click anywhere on the page.

■ To display two pages in your report at a time, click ▣.

Note: To once again display only one page in your report at a time, click ▣.

APPLY AN AUTOFORMAT

You can apply an autoformat to a report to quickly change the overall appearance of the report.

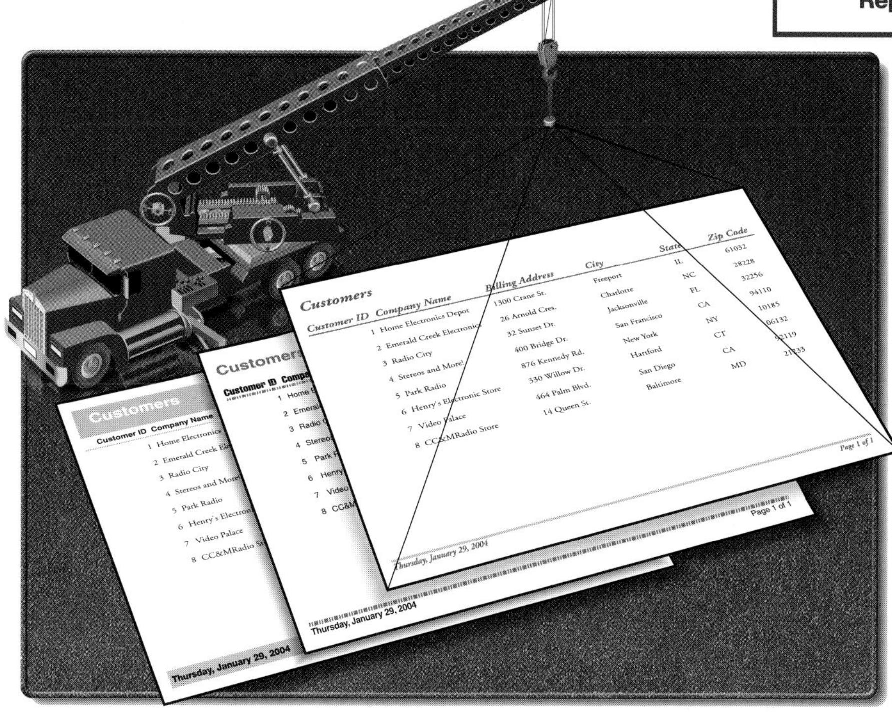

You may want to use the same autoformat for every report in your database to give your reports a consistent appearance.

APPLY AN AUTOFORMAT

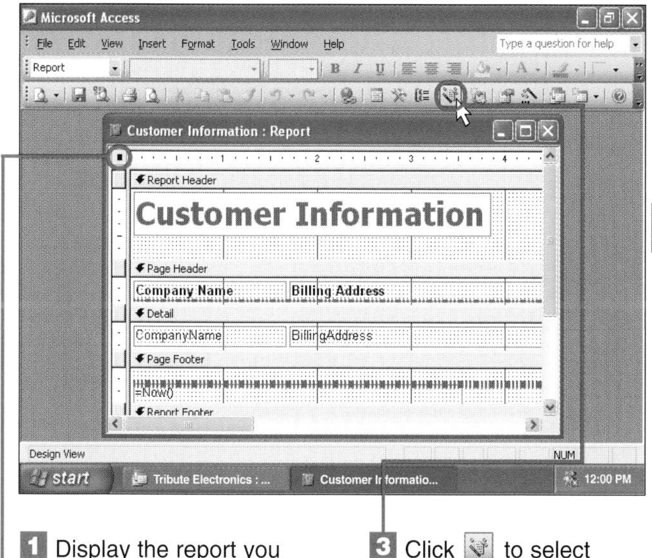

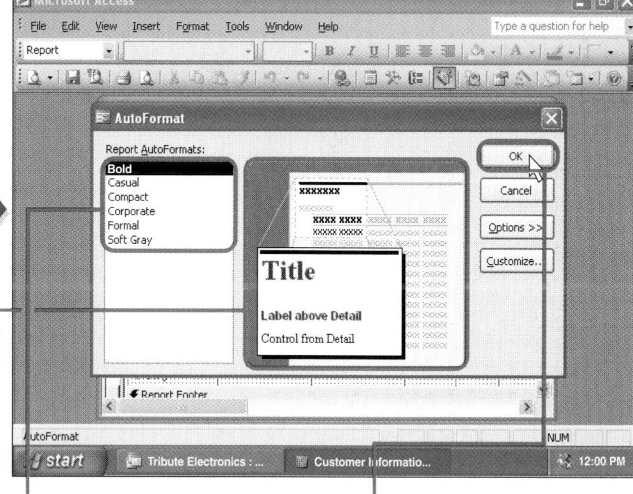

1 Display the report you want to change in the Design view. To change the view of a report, see page 258.

2 Click ▢ to select the entire report (▢ changes to ■).

3 Click ▢ to select an autoformat for the report.

■ The AutoFormat dialog box appears.

4 Click the autoformat you want to use.

■ This area displays a sample of the autoformat you selected.

5 Click **OK** to confirm your change.

■ The report will display the new autoformat.

ADD A PICTURE

You can add a picture to a report to enhance the appearance of the report.

You can add a picture to a report, such as a picture of your products or your company logo.

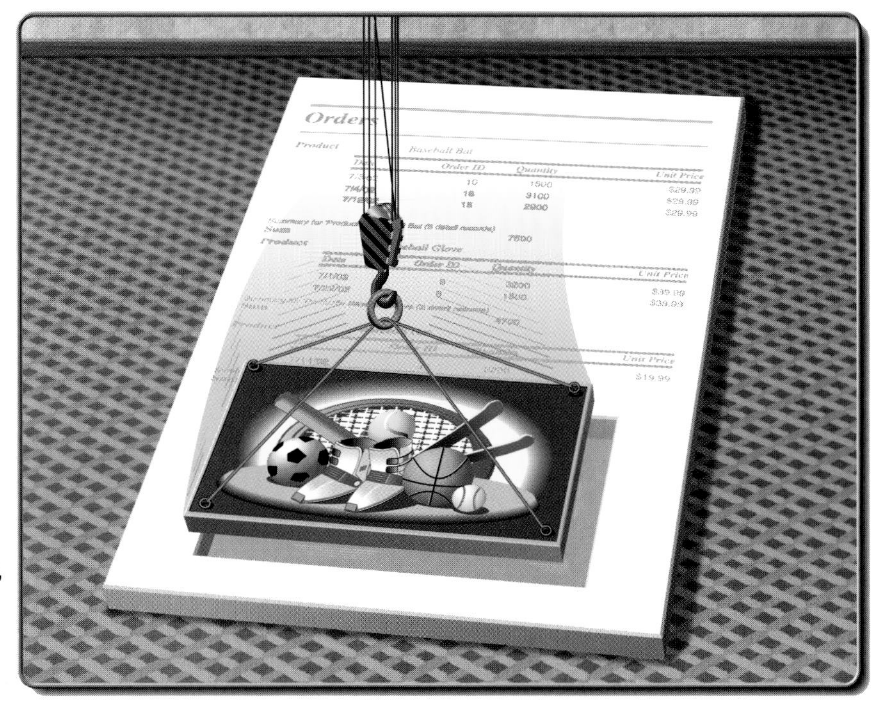

You can use a drawing program to create your own picture or use a scanner to scan an existing picture into your computer. You can also buy pictures at stores that sell computer software or obtain pictures on the Internet.

ADD A PICTURE

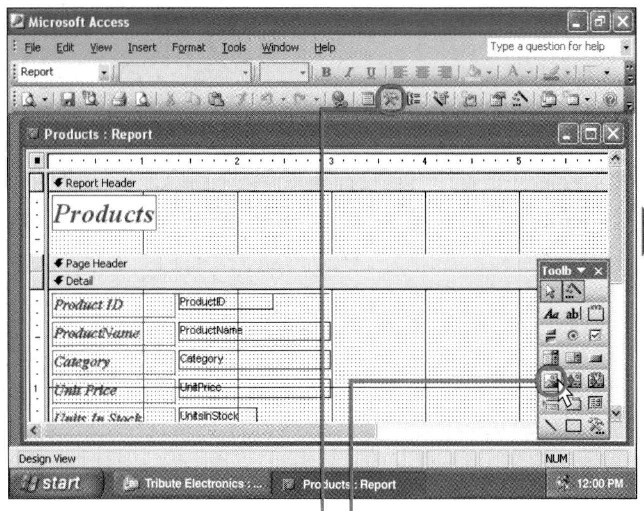

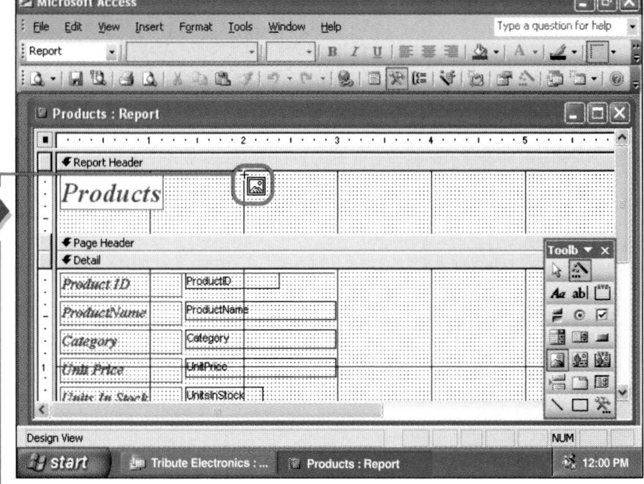

1 Display the report you want to add a picture to in the Design view. To change the view of a report, see page 258.

2 Click [picture icon] on the Toolbox toolbar to add a picture to your report.

■ If the Toolbox toolbar is not displayed, click [toolbox icon] to display the toolbar.

3 Click the location in your report where you want the top left corner of the picture to appear.

■ The Insert Picture dialog box appears.

What section of a report can I add a picture to?

You can add a picture to any section of a report. In most cases, you will want to add a picture to the Report Header section, which will display the picture at the top of the report.

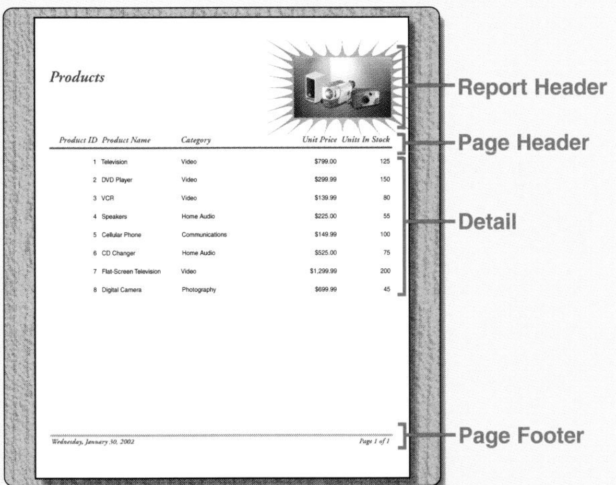

How can I delete a picture I added to a report?

To delete a picture you no longer want to appear in a report, click the picture and then press the Delete key. Access will remove the picture from the report, but will not remove the original picture from your computer.

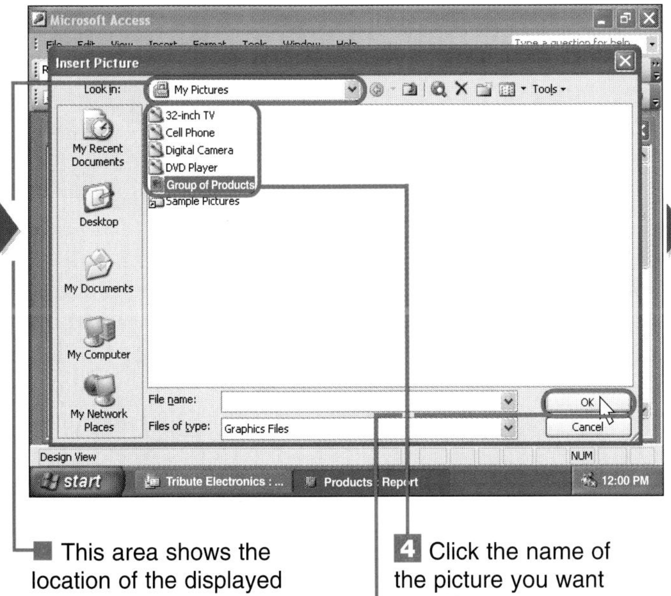

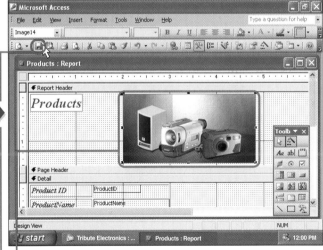

■ This area shows the location of the displayed pictures. You can click this area to change the location.

4 Click the name of the picture you want to add to your report.

5 Click **OK** to add the picture to your report.

■ The picture appears in your report.

6 Click the save button to save the change you made to your report.

Note: You can move or resize a picture in a report as you would move or resize a control on a form. To move or resize a control on a form, *see page 154.*

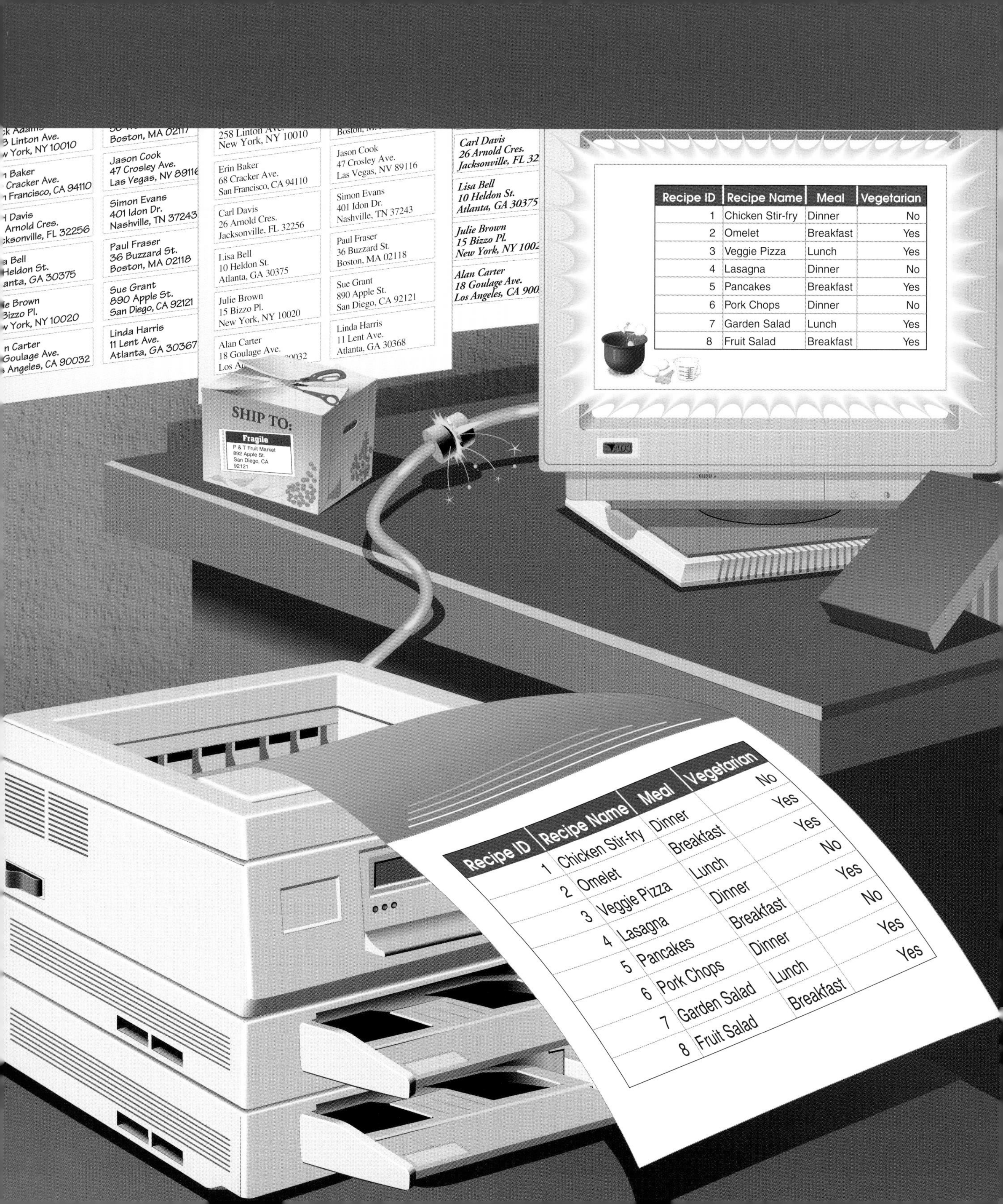

Boston, MA 02117
Jason Cook
47 Crosley Ave.
Simon Evans
401 Idon Dr.
Nashville, TN 37243
Paul Fraser
36 Buzzard St.
Boston, MA 02118
Sue Grant
890 Apple St.
San Diego, CA 92121
Linda Harris
11 Lent Ave.
Atlanta, GA 30367
258 Linton Ave.
New York, NY 10010
Erin Baker
68 Cracker Ave.
San Francisco, CA 94110
Carl Davis
26 Arnold Cres.
Jacksonville, FL 32256
Lisa Bell
10 Heldon St.
Atlanta, GA 30375
Julie Brown
15 Bizzo Pl.
New York, NY 10020
Alan Carter
18 Goulage Ave.
Jason Cook
47 Crosley Ave.
Las Vegas, NV 89116
Simon Evans
401 Idon Dr.
Nashville, TN 37243
Paul Fraser
36 Buzzard St.
Boston, MA 02118
Sue Grant
890 Apple St.
San Diego, CA 92121
Linda Harris
11 Lent Ave.
Atlanta, GA 30368
Carl Davis
26 Arnold Cres.
Lisa Bell
10 Heldon St.
Atlanta, GA 30375
Julie Brown
15 Bizzo Pl.
Alan Carter
18 Goulage Ave.
SHIP TO:
Fragile
P & T Fruit Market
892 Apple St.
San Diego, CA
92121
Recipe ID | Recipe Name | Meal | Vegetarian
1 | Chicken Stir-fry | Dinner | No
2 | Omelet | Breakfast | Yes
3 | Veggie Pizza | Lunch | Yes
4 | Lasagna | Dinner | No
5 | Pancakes | Breakfast | Yes
6 | Pork Chops | Dinner | No
7 | Garden Salad | Lunch | Yes
8 | Fruit Salad | Breakfast | Yes

CHAPTER 12

Print Information

Are you ready to print the information in your database? In this chapter, you will learn how to preview your data before printing, change the way the data will appear on a printed page and create mailing labels.

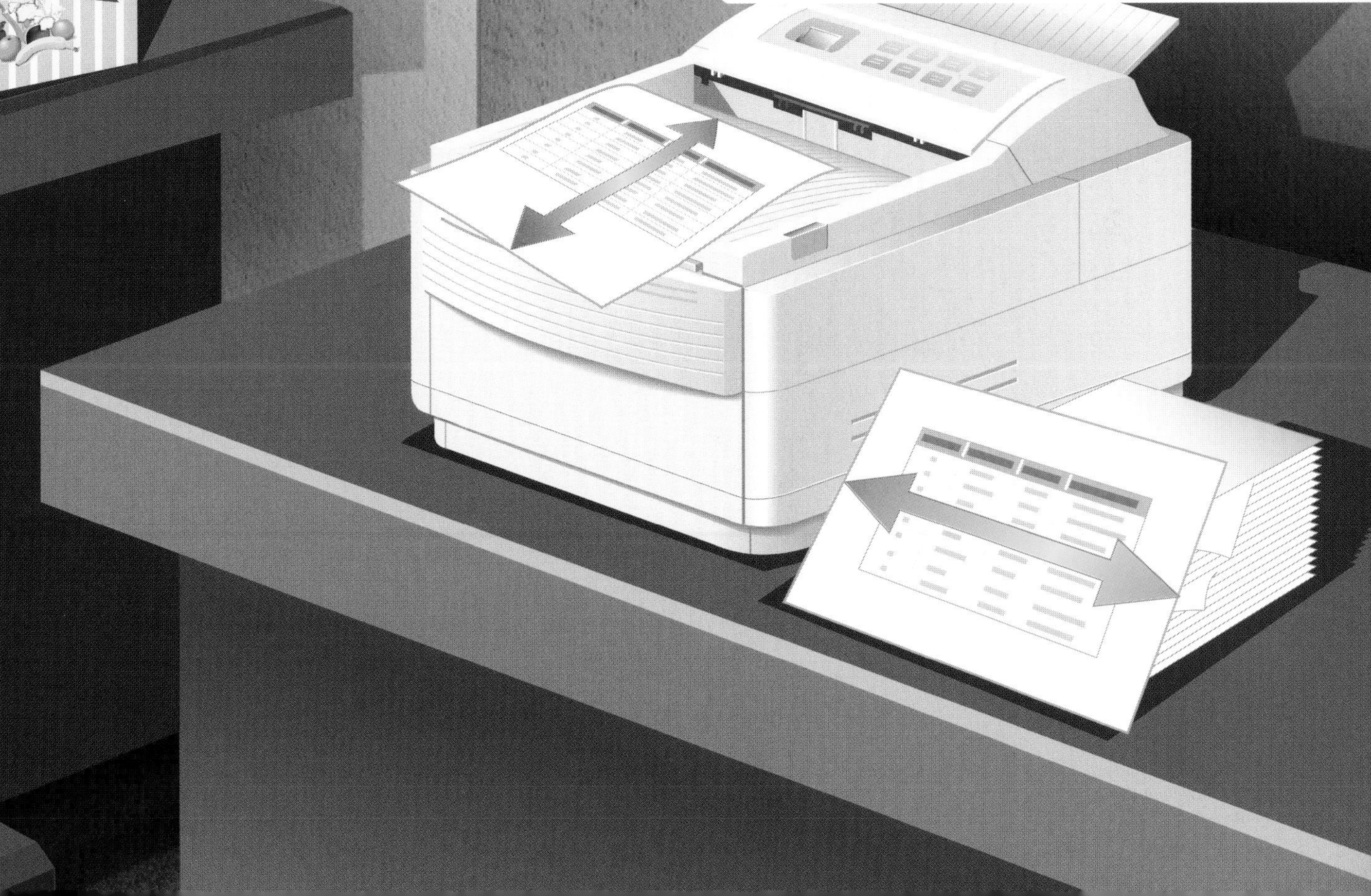

PREVIEW BEFORE PRINTING

You can use the Print Preview feature to see how a table, query, form or report will look when printed.

The Print Preview feature can help you confirm that your printed pages will appear the way you want.

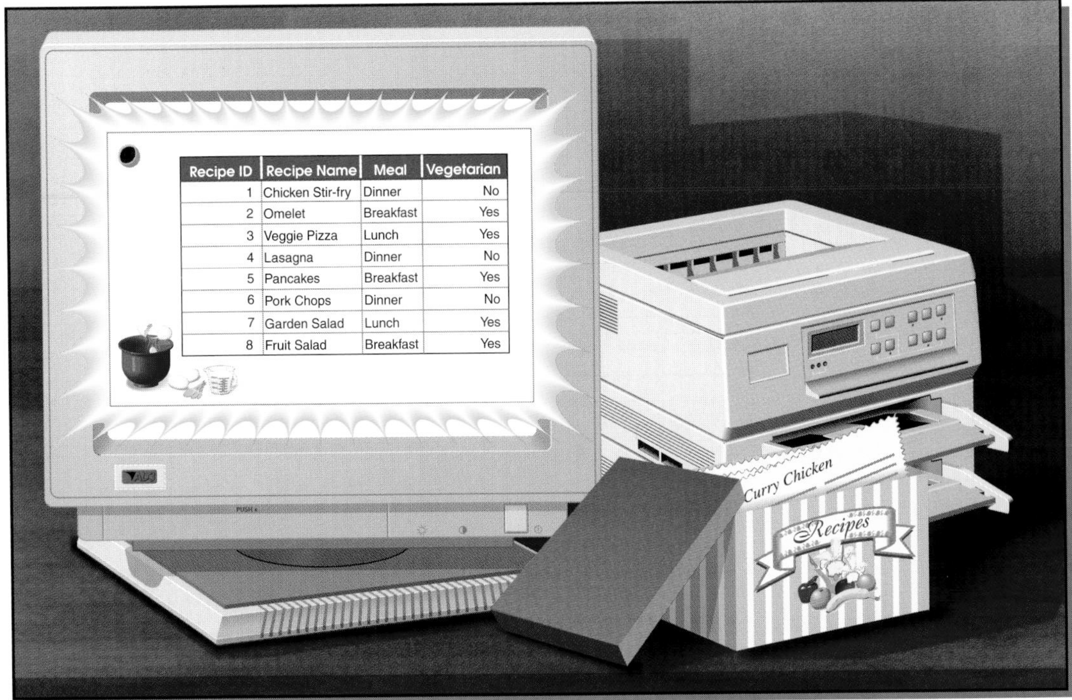

PREVIEW BEFORE PRINTING

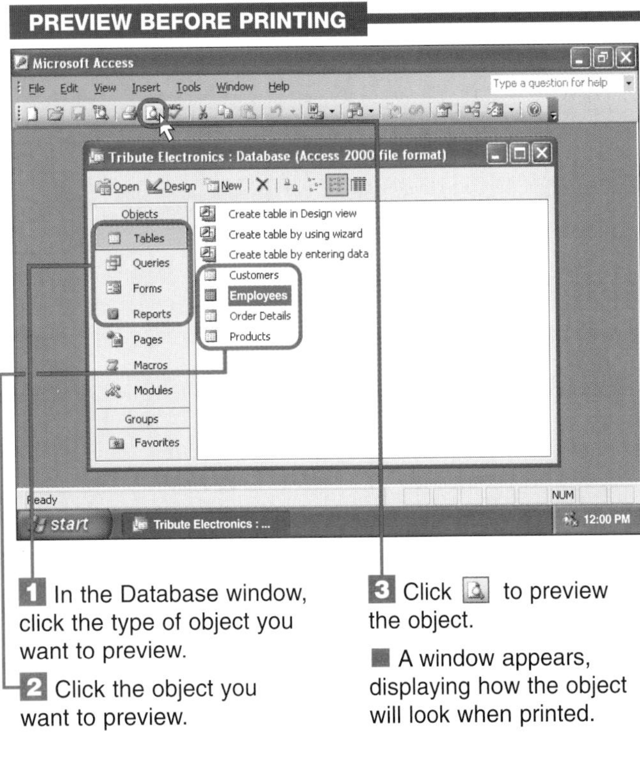

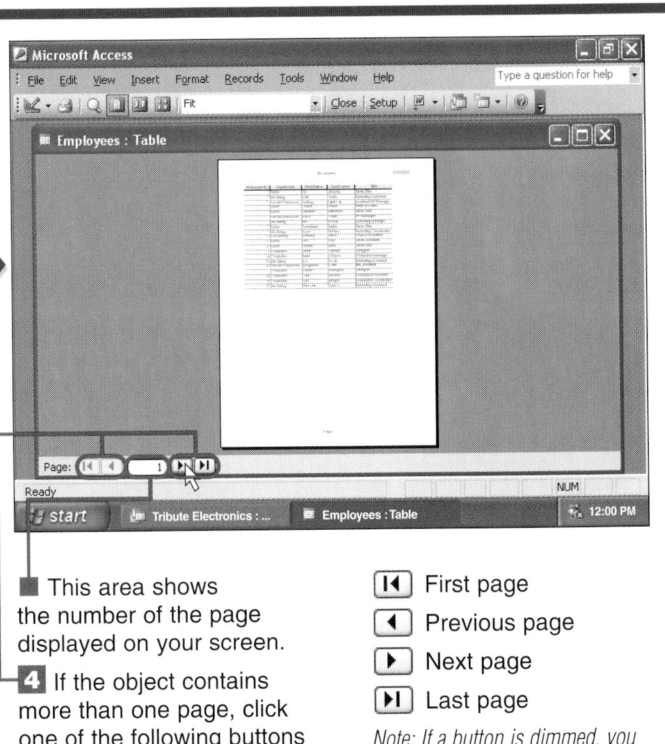

1 In the Database window, click the type of object you want to preview.

2 Click the object you want to preview.

3 Click 🔍 to preview the object.

■ A window appears, displaying how the object will look when printed.

■ This area shows the number of the page displayed on your screen.

4 If the object contains more than one page, click one of the following buttons to display another page.

⏮ First page

◀ Previous page

▶ Next page

⏭ Last page

Note: If a button is dimmed, you cannot currently display that page.

How can I display two pages at once while previewing an object?

To display two pages at once, click the Two Pages button ( ). To once again display only one page at a time, click the One Page button ( ).

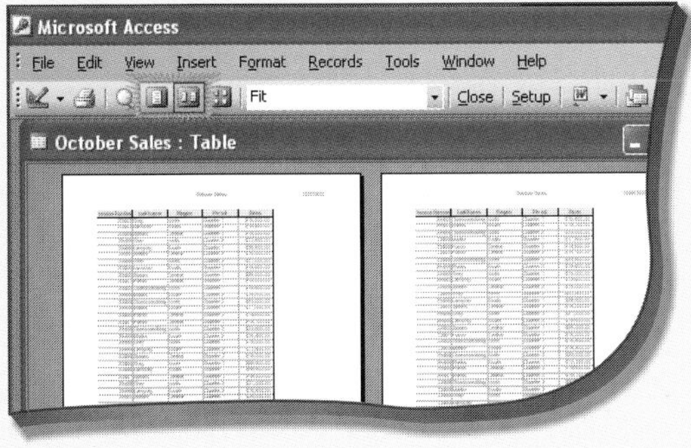

Can I see how an object will print in different views?

Yes. To see how an object will print in a specific view, display the object in the view of interest and then click the Print Preview button ( ). For example, you can display a table in the Datasheet, PivotTable or PivotChart view. To change the view of an object, see pages 74, 152, 202 and 258.

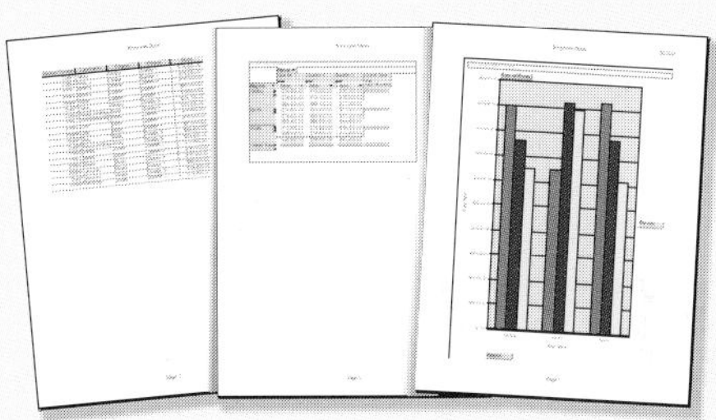

Datasheet PivotTable PivotChart

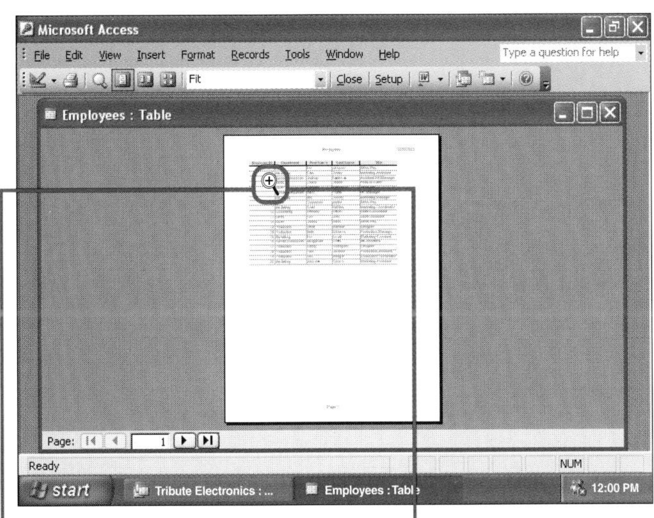

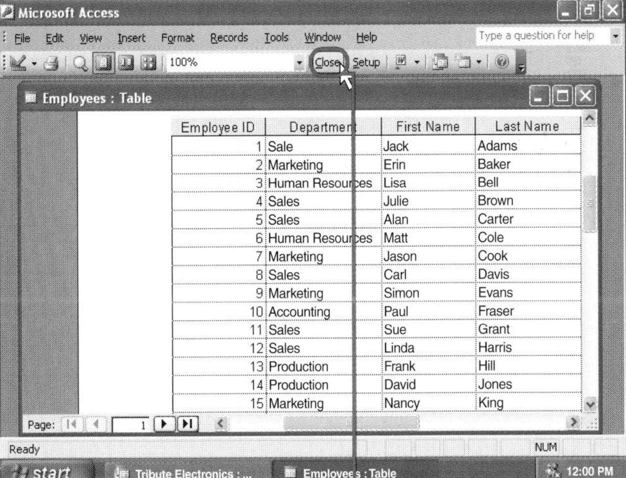

MAGNIFY AN AREA OF A PAGE

1 To magnify an area of a page, position the mouse over the area you want to magnify (changes to).

2 Click the area to magnify the area.

■ A magnified view of the area appears.

■ To once again display the entire page, click anywhere on the page.

CLOSE PRINT PREVIEW

1 When you finish previewing the object, click **Close** to close the preview window.

CHANGE PAGE SETUP

You can change the way information appears on a printed page.

Access stores the page setup options you specify for forms and reports so you need to specify the options only once for each form or report. For tables and queries, you must specify the page setup options every time you want to print a table or query.

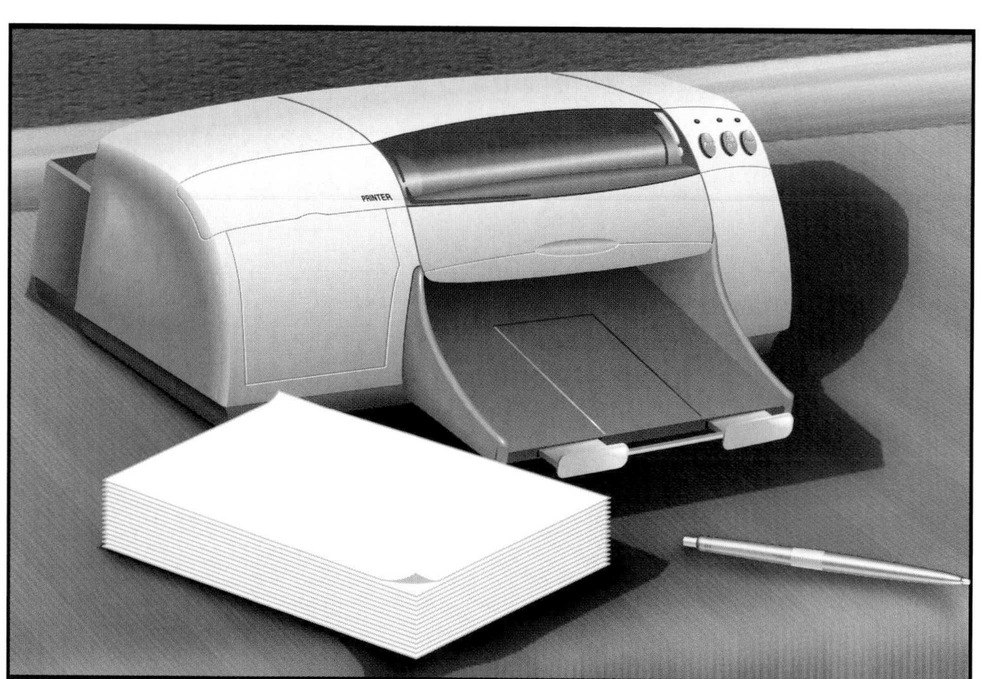

CHANGE PAGE SETUP

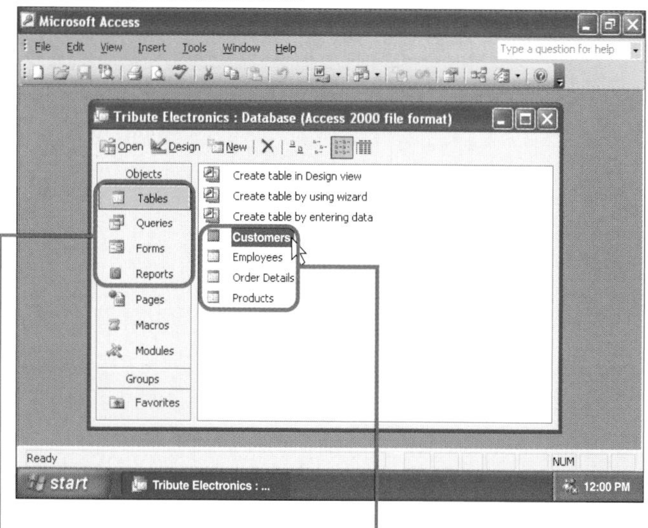

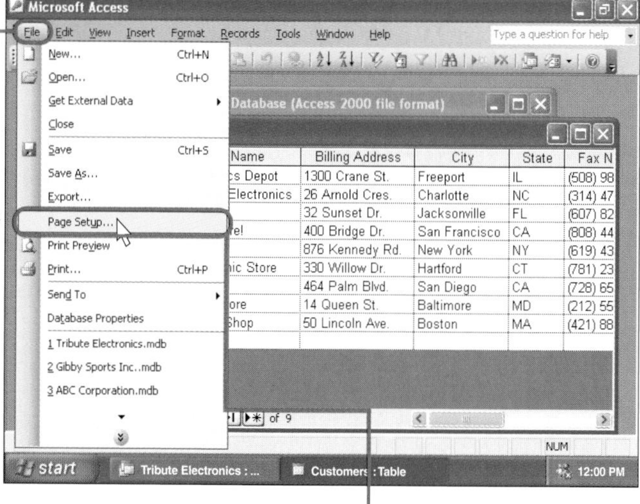

1 In the Database window, click the type of object you want to use different page setup options.

2 Double-click the object you want to use different page setup options.

■ The object opens and appears on your screen.

3 Click **File**.

4 Click **Page Setup**.

■ The Page Setup dialog box appears.

What page setup options can I change?

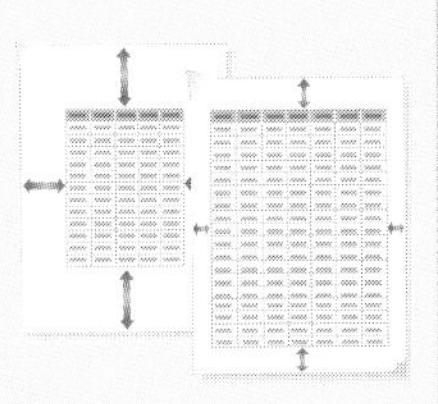	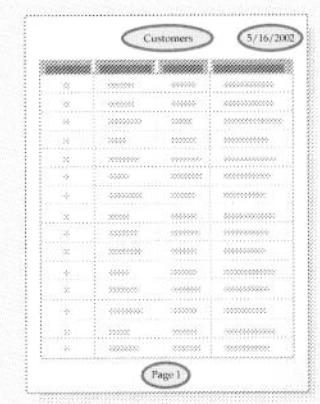	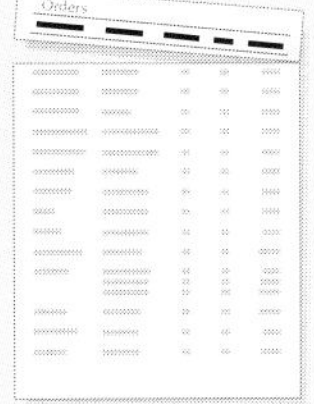	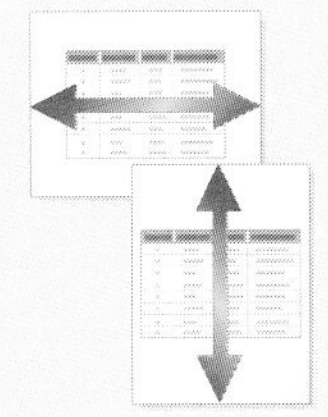	
Margins Determines the amount of space between data and the edges of each page.	**Print Headings** Prints headings, which include the title, date and page numbers. This option is only available for tables and queries.	**Print Data Only** Prints only the data. This option is only available for forms and reports.	**Orientation** Determines which direction information prints on each page.	**Paper Size and Source** Specifies the paper size and the location of the paper that you want to use in the printer.

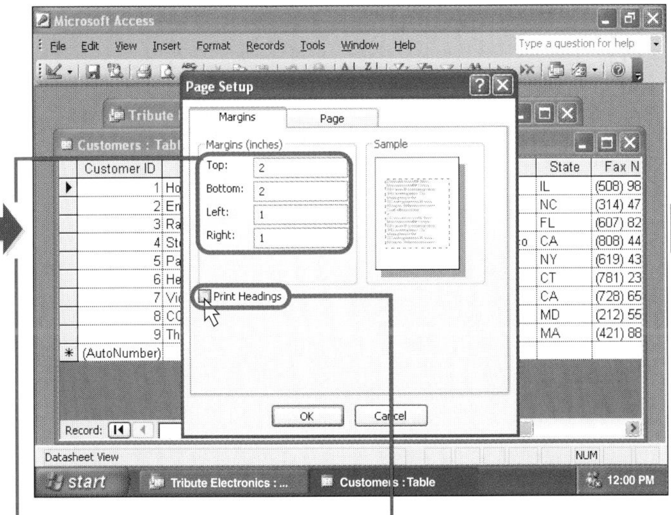

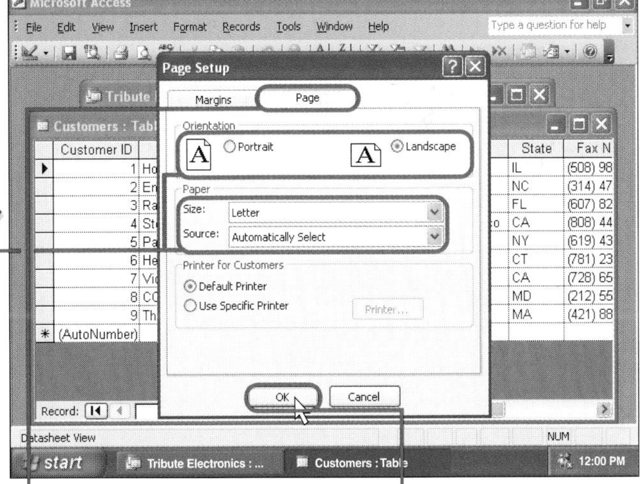

■ This area displays the margins for each page.

5 To change a margin, double-click the box beside the margin and then type a new margin.

6 If you do not want to print the title, date and page numbers, click **Print Headings** (☑ changes to ☐).

*Note: For forms and reports, the **Print Data Only** option appears instead. To print only the data in the form or report, click the option (☐ changes to ☑).*

7 Click the **Page** tab.

8 Click the page orientation you want to use (○ changes to ◉).

9 These areas display the paper size and source. You can click an area to change the paper size or source.

10 Click **OK** to confirm your changes.

Note: You can use the Print Preview feature to see how the printed pages will appear. To use the Print Preview feature, see page 266.

PRINT INFORMATION

You can produce a paper copy of a table, query, form or report.

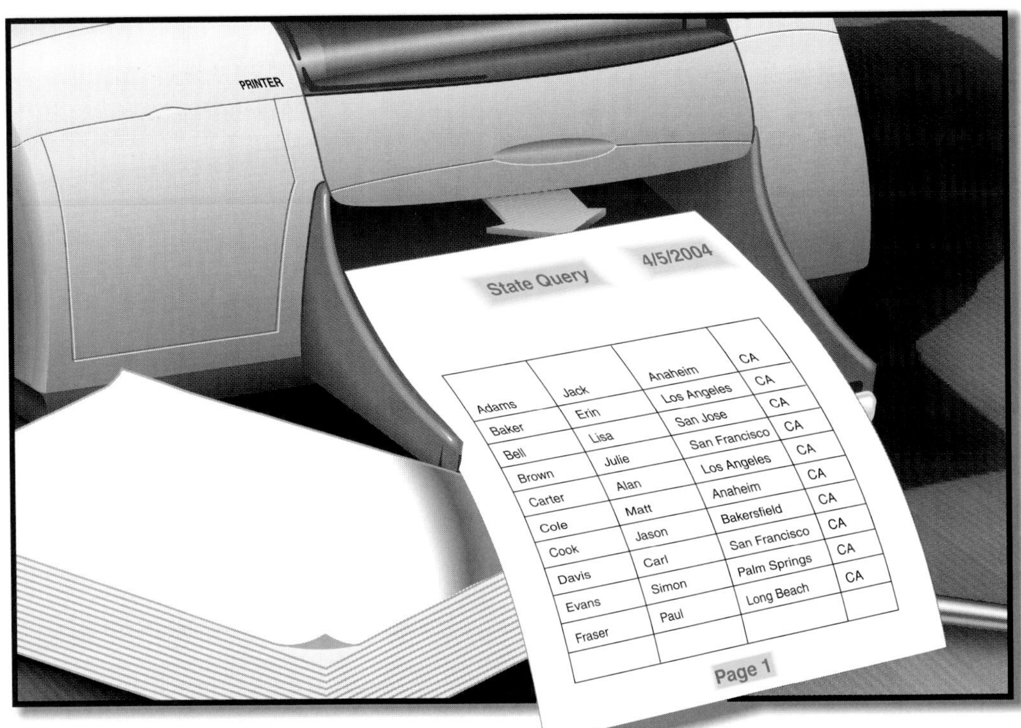

When you print a table, query or report, Access prints the title, date and page number on each page.

Before printing, make sure your printer is turned on and contains paper.

PRINT INFORMATION

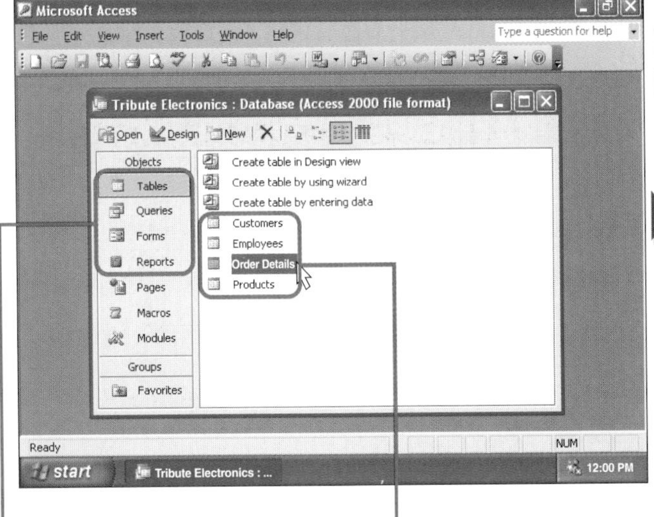

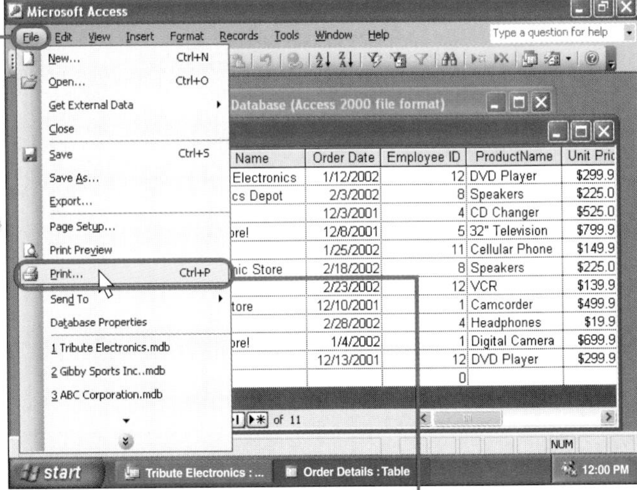

1 In the Database window, click the type of object you want to print.

2 Double-click the object you want to print.

■ The object opens and appears on your screen.

■ If you want to print only one record or a few records, select the record(s) you want to print. To select records, see page 54.

3 Click **File**.

4 Click **Print**.

■ The Print dialog box appears.

What print options can I use?

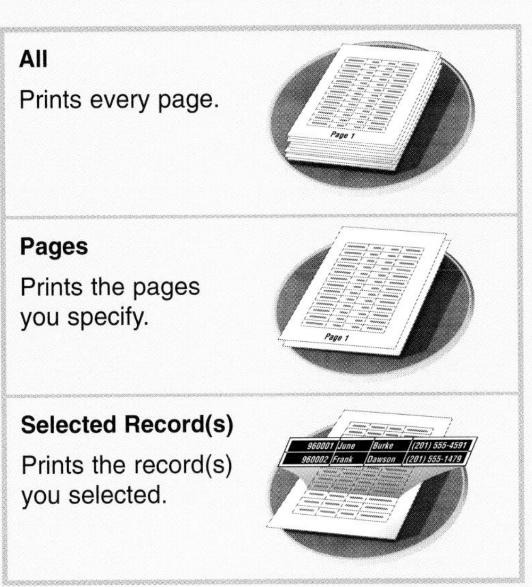

All

Prints every page.

Pages

Prints the pages you specify.

Selected Record(s)

Prints the record(s) you selected.

Can I print an object in a different view?

Yes. Before you print an object, make sure you display the object in the view you want to print the object. For example, you can display a table in the Datasheet, PivotTable or PivotChart view. To change the view of an object, see pages 74, 152, 202 and 258.

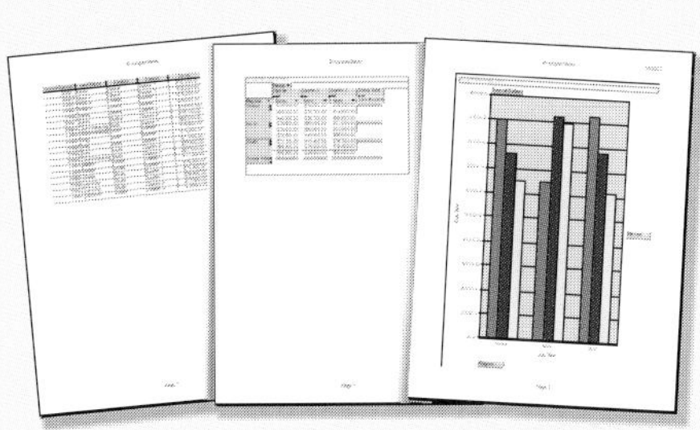

Datasheet **PivotTable** **PivotChart**

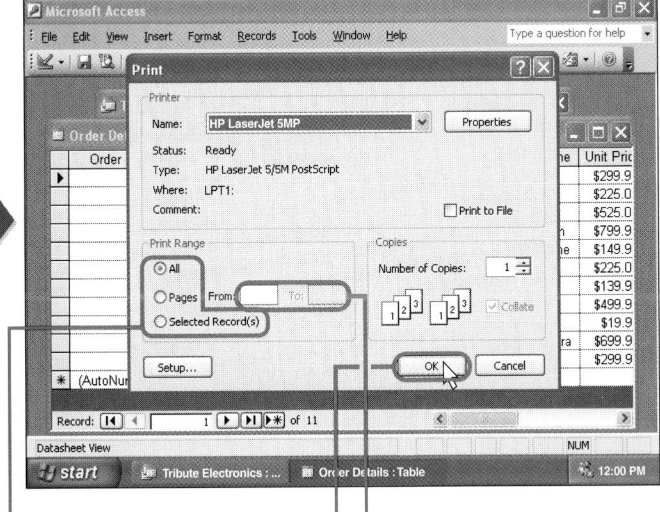

5 Click the print option you want to use (○ changes to ◉).

Note: For information on the print options, see the top of this page.

■ If you selected Pages in step **5**, type the number of the first page you want to print. Press the Tab key and then type the number of the last page you want to print.

6 Click **OK**.

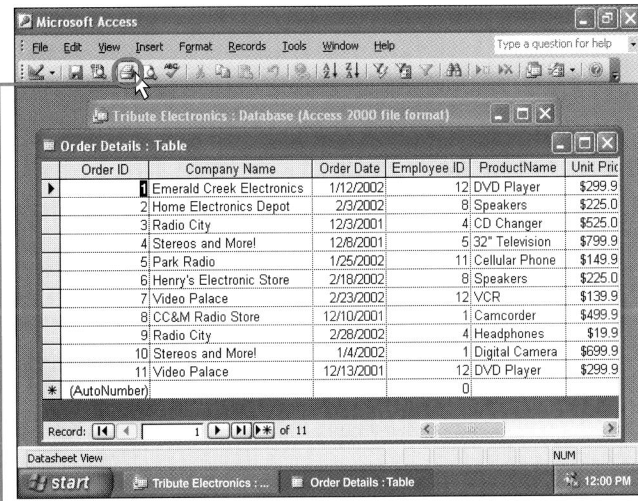

Order ID	Company Name	Order Date	Employee ID	ProductName	Unit Pric
1	Emerald Creek Electronics	1/12/2002	12	DVD Player	$299.9
2	Home Electronics Depot	2/3/2002	8	Speakers	$225.0
3	Radio City	12/3/2001	4	CD Changer	$525.0
4	Stereos and More!	12/8/2001	5	32" Television	$799.9
5	Park Radio	1/25/2002	11	Cellular Phone	$149.9
6	Henry's Electronic Store	2/18/2002	8	Speakers	$225.0
7	Video Palace	2/23/2002	12	VCR	$139.9
8	CC&M Radio Store	12/10/2001	1	Camcorder	$499.9
9	Radio City	2/28/2002	4	Headphones	$19.9
10	Stereos and More!	1/4/2002	1	Digital Camera	$699.9
11	Video Palace	12/13/2001	12	DVD Player	$299.9
(AutoNumber)			0		

QUICKLY PRINT ALL RECORDS

1 Click 🖨 to quickly print all the records.

CREATE MAILING LABELS

You can create a mailing label for every person in a table. You can use mailing labels for addressing envelopes and packages, labeling file folders and creating name tags.

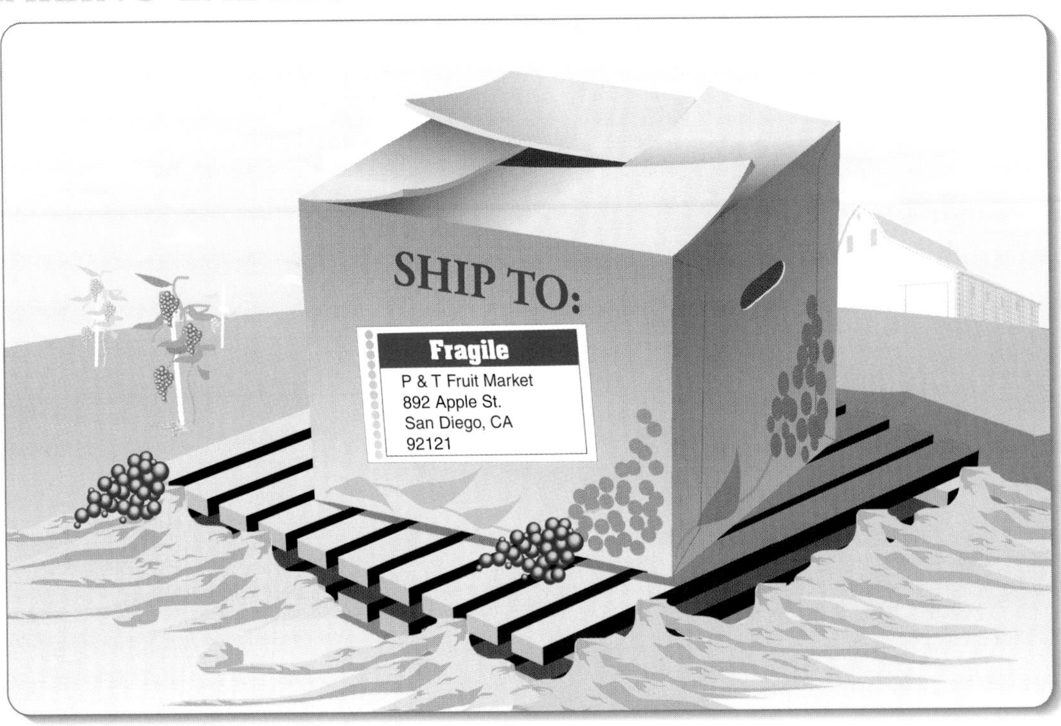

The Label Wizard asks you a series of questions and then creates mailing labels based on your answers.

CREATE MAILING LABELS

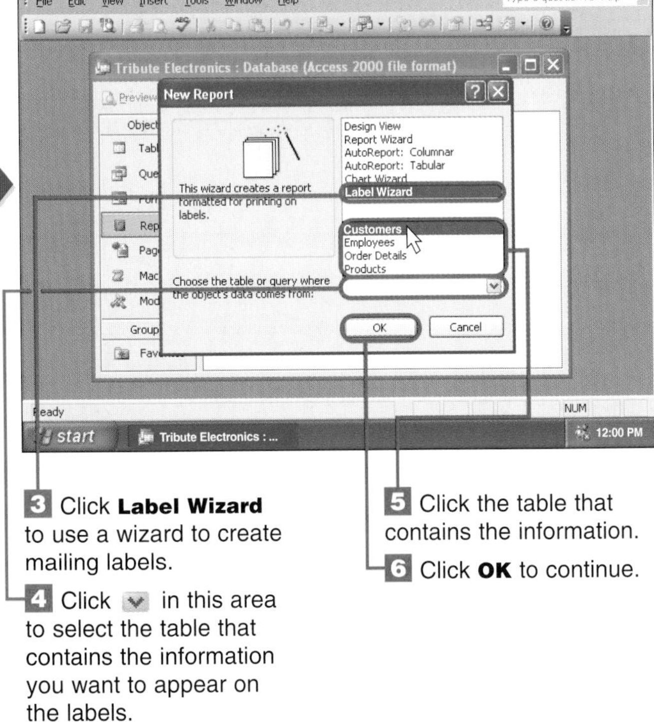

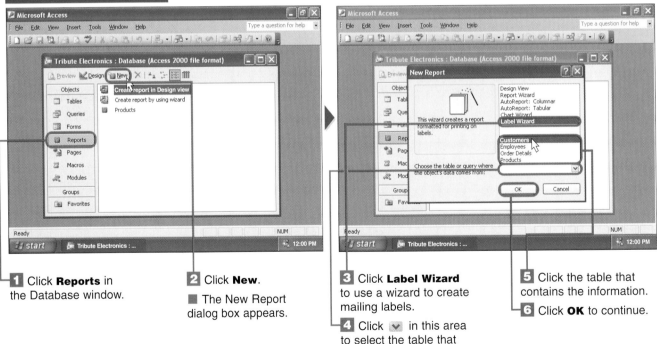

1 Click **Reports** in the Database window.

2 Click **New**.

- The New Report dialog box appears.

3 Click **Label Wizard** to use a wizard to create mailing labels.

4 Click ▾ in this area to select the table that contains the information you want to appear on the labels.

5 Click the table that contains the information.

6 Click **OK** to continue.

What information must I specify when creating mailing labels?

When creating mailing labels, you must specify the manufacturer, type and size of labels you want to use.

Manufacturer

You can select from several different label manufacturers, such as Avery, CoStar and Herma.

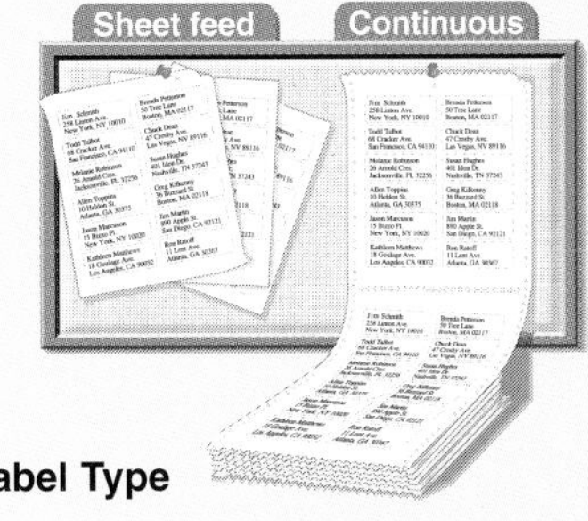

Label Type

You can choose between sheet feed and continuous labels. Sheet feed labels are individual pages of labels. Continuous labels are connected pages of labels, usually with holes punched along each side.

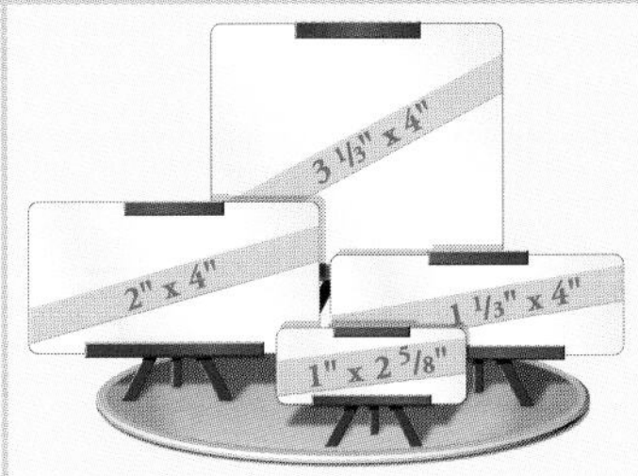

Label Size

You can select a label size to specify the dimensions of each label and the number of labels that will print across each page.

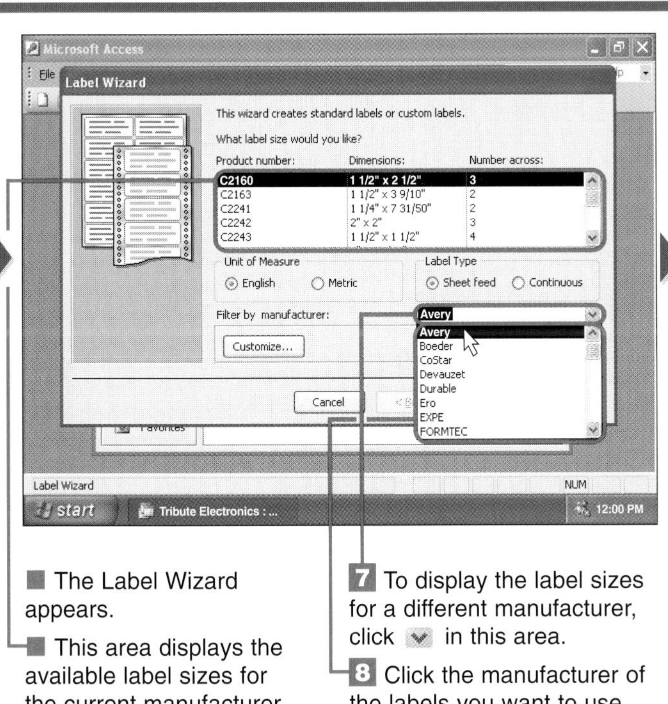

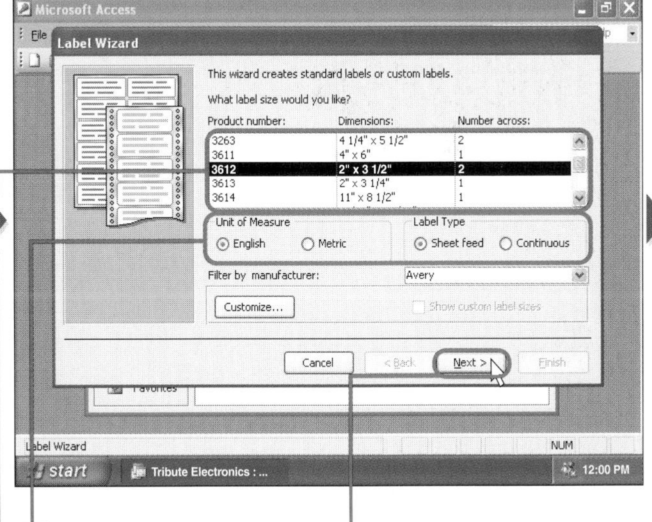

■ The Label Wizard appears.

■ This area displays the available label sizes for the current manufacturer.

7 To display the label sizes for a different manufacturer, click ▾ in this area.

8 Click the manufacturer of the labels you want to use.

9 To change the unit of measure or type of label displayed, click the appropriate options (○ changes to ◉).

10 Click the label size you want to use.

Note: You can check your label packaging to determine which label size to select.

11 Click **Next** to continue.

CONTINUED

You can change how text will appear on your mailing labels.

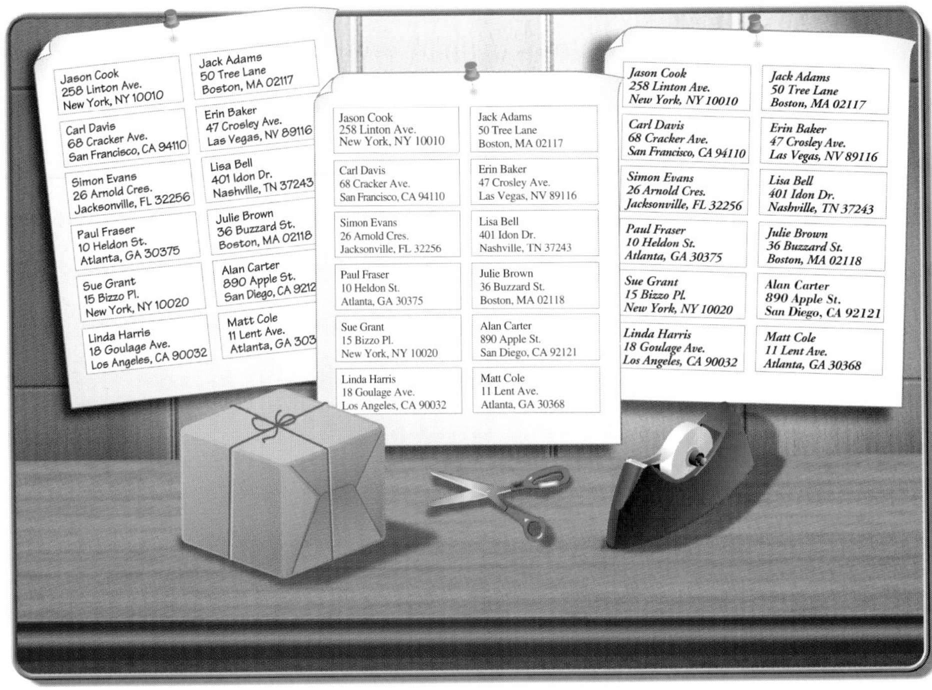

The changes you make to the appearance of text on your mailing labels will affect all the text on every label. You cannot change the appearance of text for part of a label or only some labels.

CREATE MAILING LABELS (CONTINUED)

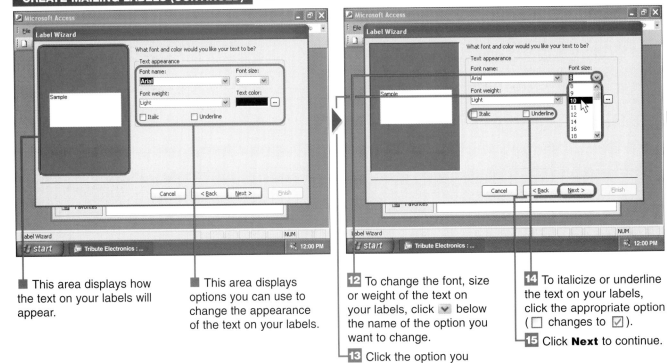

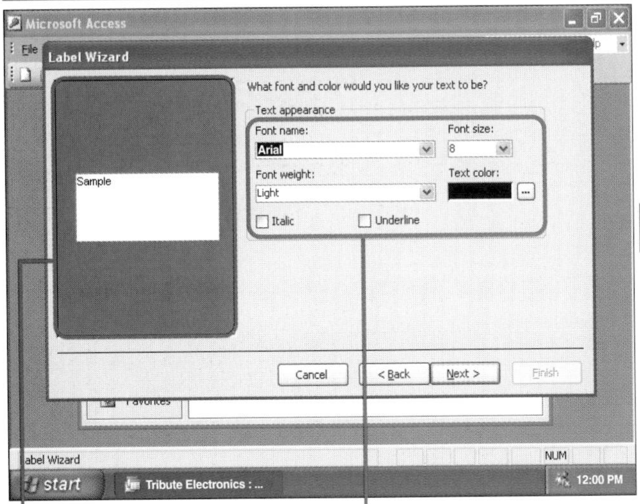

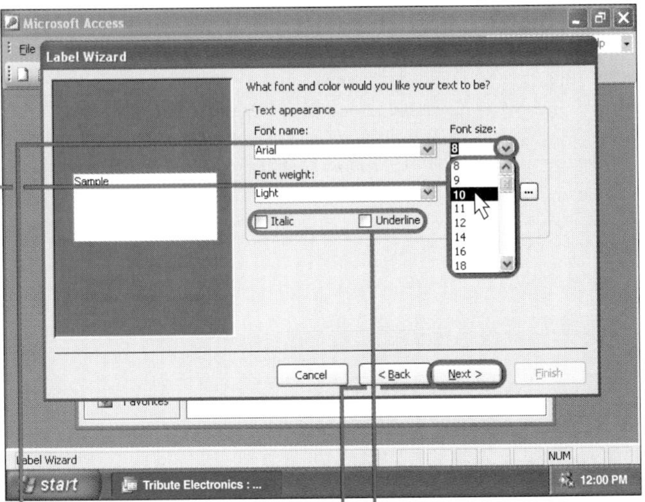

■ This area displays how the text on your labels will appear.

■ This area displays options you can use to change the appearance of the text on your labels.

12 To change the font, size or weight of the text on your labels, click ⌄ below the name of the option you want to change.

13 Click the option you want to use.

14 To italicize or underline the text on your labels, click the appropriate option (☐ changes to ☑).

15 Click **Next** to continue.

How can I select a different text color for my mailing labels?

In the Label Wizard, click the button (...) beside the Text color box. In the dialog box that appears, click the color you want to use for the text and then press the Enter key. You need a color printer to be able to print the text on your mailing labels in color.

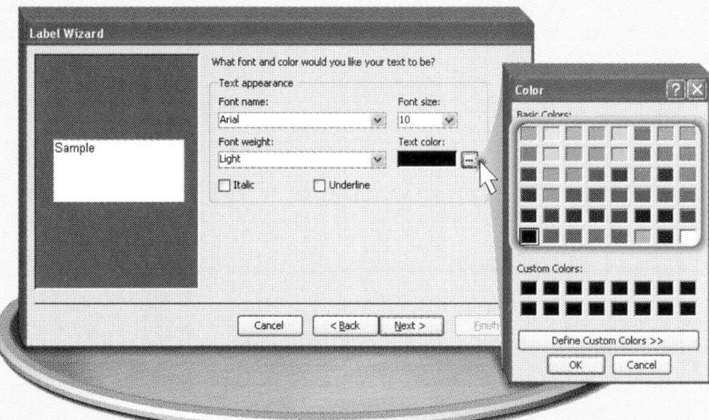

Can I display the same text on every mailing label?

Yes. You can display text, such as "Confidential" or "Important", on every mailing label. After you add the fields you want to display on the mailing labels in the Label Wizard, type the text you want to appear on every mailing label in the Prototype label area.

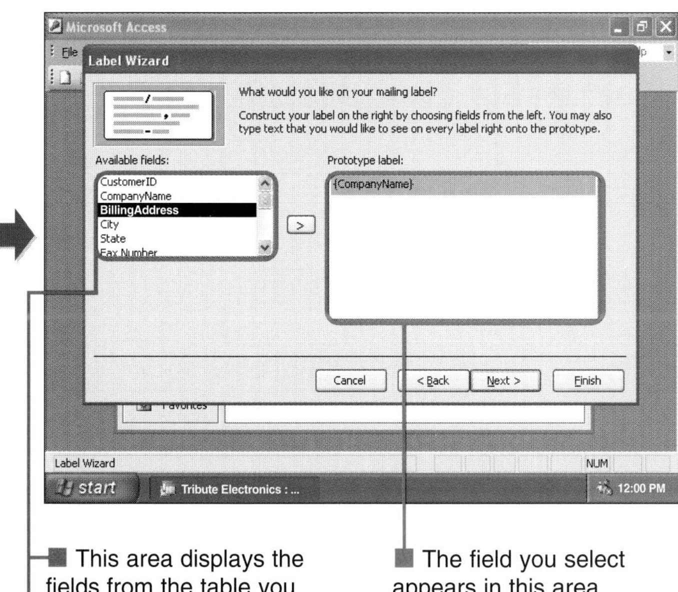

- This area displays the fields from the table you selected in step **5**.

16 Double-click a field you want to appear on the labels.

- The field you select appears in this area.

17 To add a blank space, press the **Spacebar**. To move to the next line, press the Enter key.

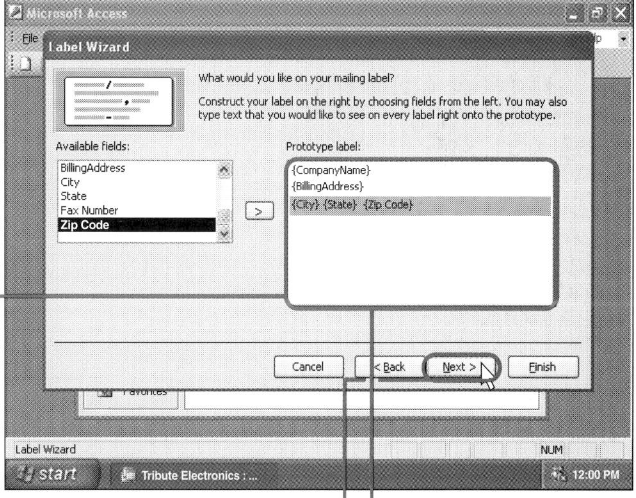

18 Repeat steps **16** and **17** until this area displays all the fields you want the labels to display.

Note: The fields should appear the same way you want them to print on your labels. Make sure you add spaces and commas (,) where needed.

- To remove a field you accidentally selected, click the field in this area and then press the Delete key.

19 Click **Next** to continue.

CONTINUED

CREATE MAILING LABELS

You can sort your mailing labels to better organize the labels.

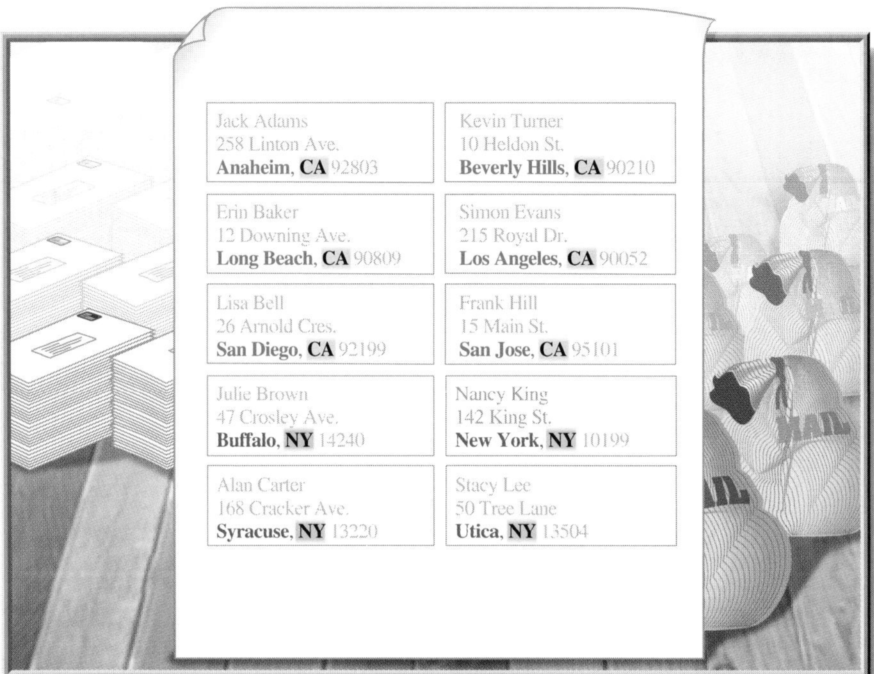

For example, you can sort your mailing labels by state to place all the labels for the same state together. If the same state appears on several labels, you can sort your labels by a second field, such as city, to further organize the labels.

CREATE MAILING LABELS (CONTINUED)

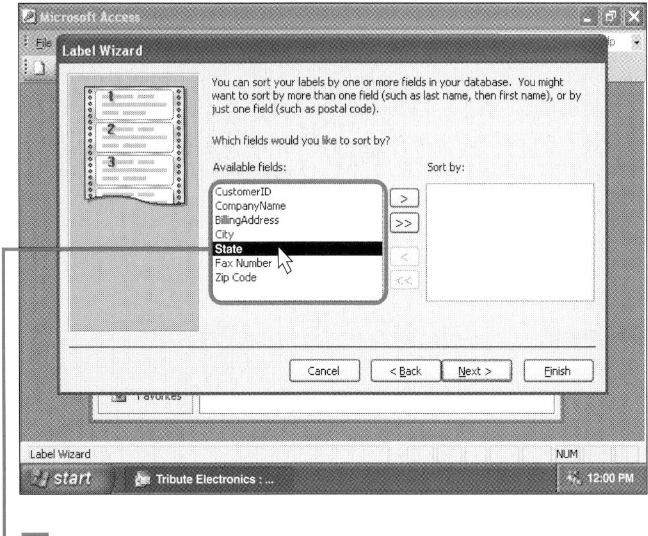

20 To sort your labels, double-click the field you want to use to sort the labels.

*Note: If you do not want to sort your labels, skip to step **21**.*

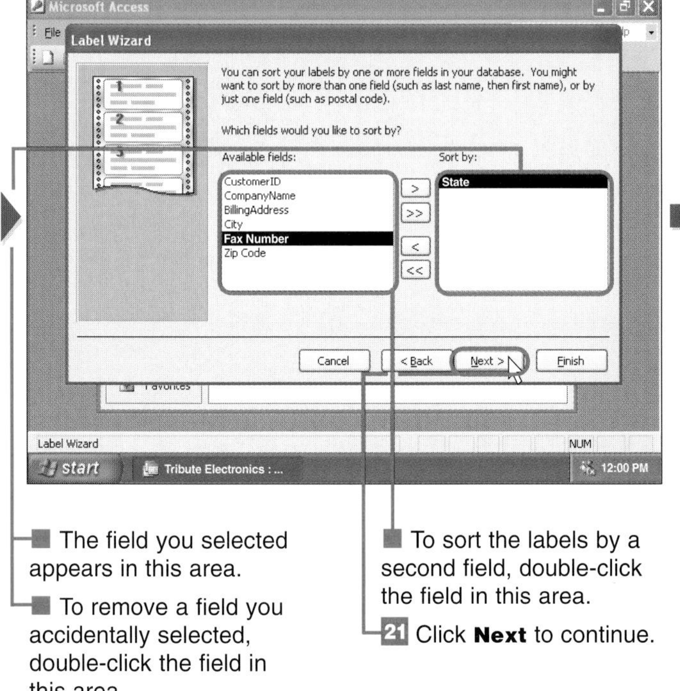

- The field you selected appears in this area.
- To remove a field you accidentally selected, double-click the field in this area.
- To sort the labels by a second field, double-click the field in this area.

21 Click **Next** to continue.

How do I print the mailing labels I created?

When viewing your mailing labels, click the Print button ( ) to print all the labels. Before printing your mailing labels, make sure your printer is turned on and the labels are in the printer. For more information on printing, see page 270.

How do I edit the mailing labels I created?

To edit mailing labels, you must change the data in the table you used to create the labels. Changes you make to the data in the table will automatically appear in the labels the next time you open the report containing the labels.

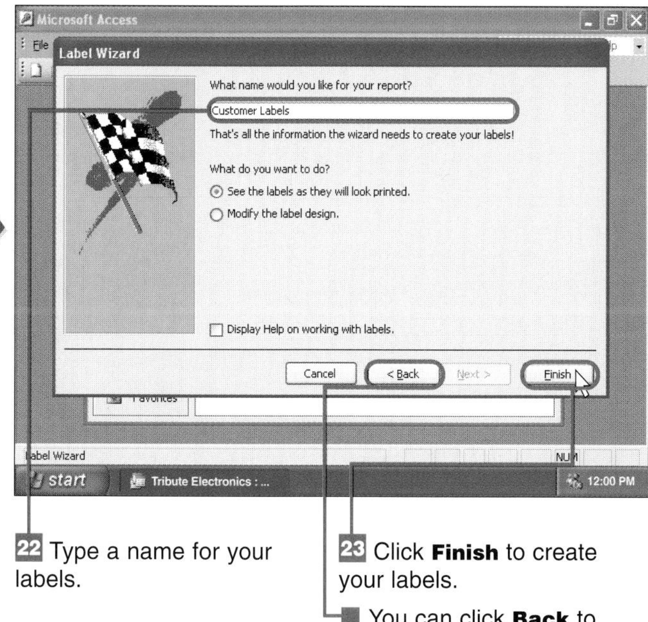

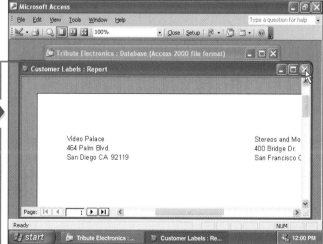

22 Type a name for your labels.

23 Click **Finish** to create your labels.

■ You can click **Back** to return to a previous step and change your selections.

■ A window appears, displaying a personalized label for each person in your table.

24 When you finish reviewing the labels, click ☒ to close the window.

■ Access stores your labels as a report. To later open a report so you can once again review and print your labels, see page 256.

Order Details
Order ID
Company Name:
Date Sold
Product Name:
Microsoft Access
File Edit View Insert Format Tools Window Help
Type a question for help
Customers
Customer Name: Cycle Rama
Address: 22 Whittle St.
City: Falls Church
State: VA
Zip Code: 22040
Customers 1 of 11
Ready
CompanyName Reel Fishing
BillingAddress 76 Haverly Lane
City Los Angeles
StateOrProvince CA
PostalCode 90012
Customers 3 of 4
CompanyName Reel Fishing
BillingAddress 76 Haverly Lane
City Los Angeles
Reel Fishing
76 Haverly Lane
Los Angeles
CA
90012
Customers 1 of 4

CHAPTER 13

Create Data Access Pages

Are you wondering how you can use Access to share data with other people on the Internet? This chapter shows you how to create and work with data access pages for the Web.

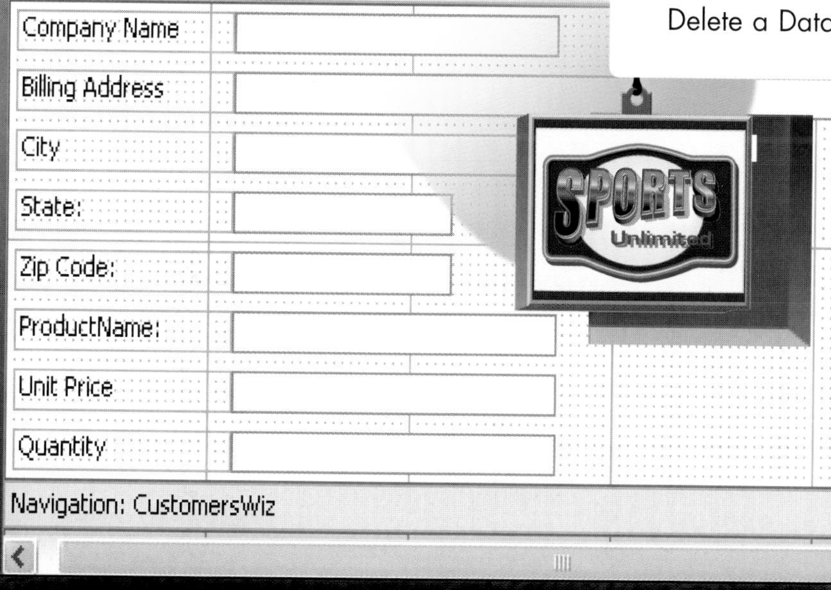

CREATE A DATA ACCESS PAGE

You can use the Page Wizard to create a data access page, which is a Web page that connects directly to the data in your database.

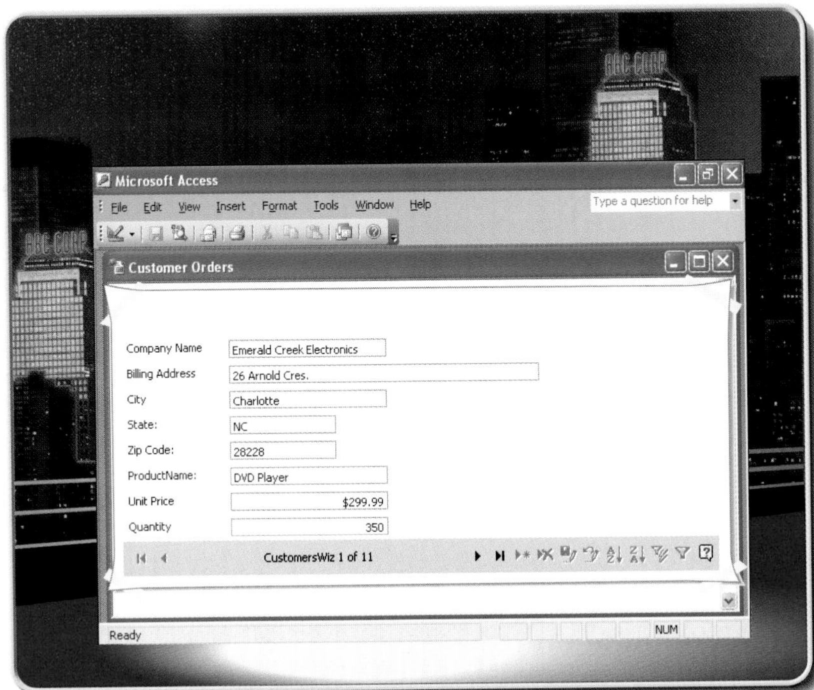

You can use a data access page to view and edit the data in your database on the Internet or your company's intranet. An intranet is a small version of the Internet within a company.

The Page Wizard will ask you a series of questions and then set up a data access page based on your answers.

CREATE A DATA ACCESS PAGE

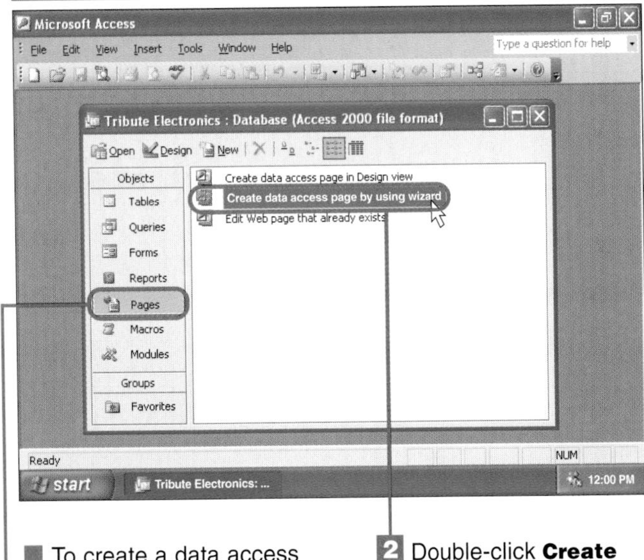

■ To create a data access page, you must have Internet Explorer 5.01 with Service Pack 2 (or a later version) installed on your computer.

1 Click **Pages** in the Database window.

2 Double-click **Create data access page by using wizard**.

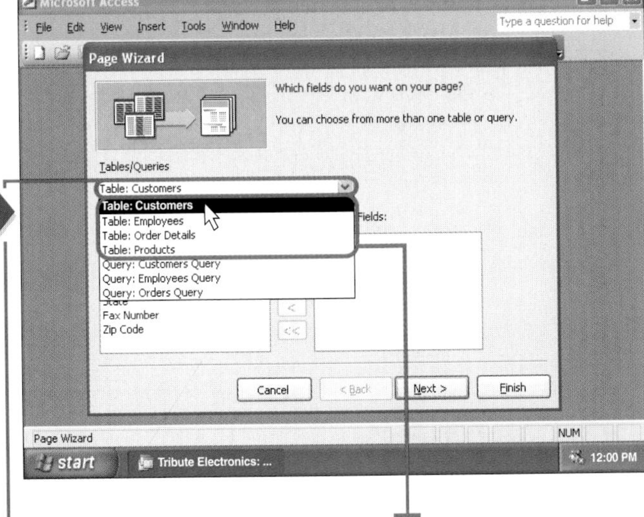

■ The Page Wizard appears.

3 To select the table that contains the fields you want to include in your page, click ▾ in this area.

4 Click the table that contains the fields.

Which tables in my database can I use to create a data access page?

You can use any table in your database to create a data access page. When creating a data access page that uses information from more than one table, relationships must exist between the tables so that Access can bring together the information in the tables. For information on relationships, see page 128.

Can I create a data access page using data from a query?

Yes. The Page Wizard allows you to select the fields you want to include from queries as you would select the fields you want to include from tables. For information on queries, see pages 192 to 229.

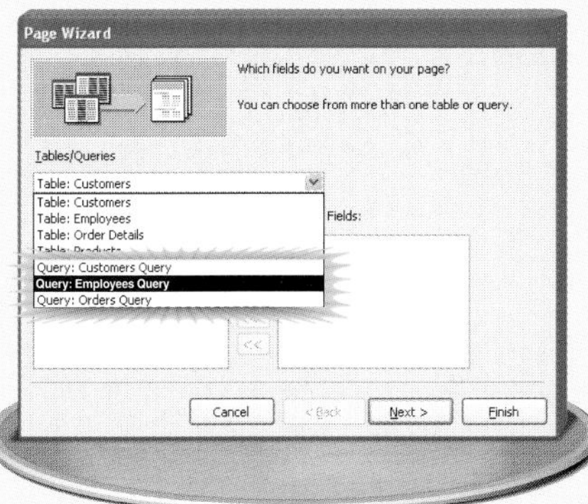

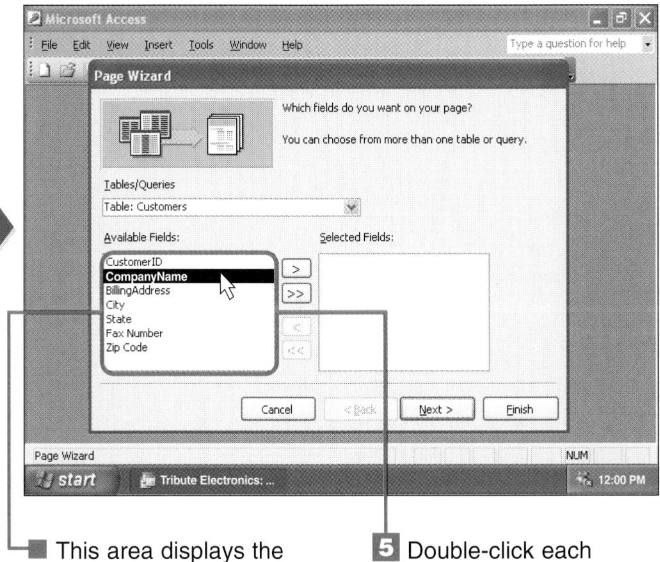

■ This area displays the fields from the table you selected.

5 Double-click each field you want to include in your page.

Note: To add all the fields in the table at once, click >>.

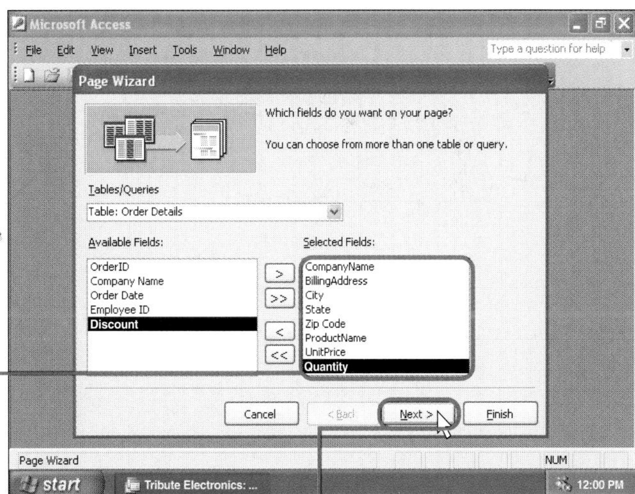

■ Each field you select appears in this area.

■ To remove a field you accidentally selected, double-click the field in this area.

Note: To remove all the fields at once, click <<.

6 To include fields from other tables in your database, repeat steps **3** to **5** for each table.

7 Click **Next** to continue.

CONTINUED

You can group the data in your data access page to place related information together. Grouping data helps you organize the data in your page.

For example, you can group all the customers from the same state together in your data access page.

CREATE A DATA ACCESS PAGE (CONTINUED)

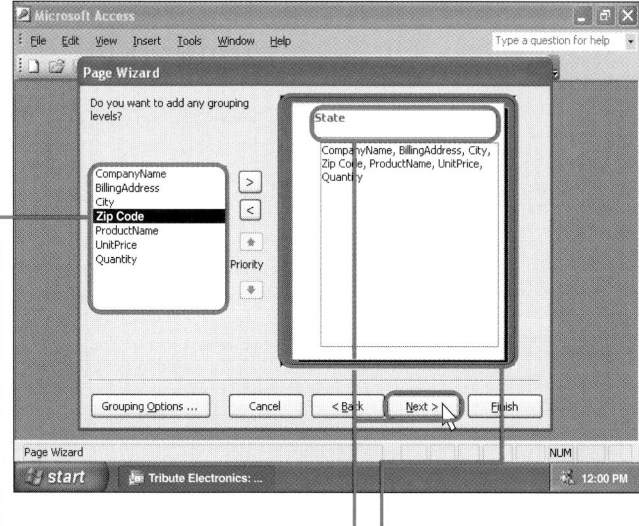

■ This area displays all the fields you selected to include in your page.

8 If you want to group data in your page, double-click the field you want to use to group the data.

■ This area shows how Access will group the data in your page.

■ To remove a field you selected to group data in your page, double-click the field in this area.

9 Click **Next** to continue.

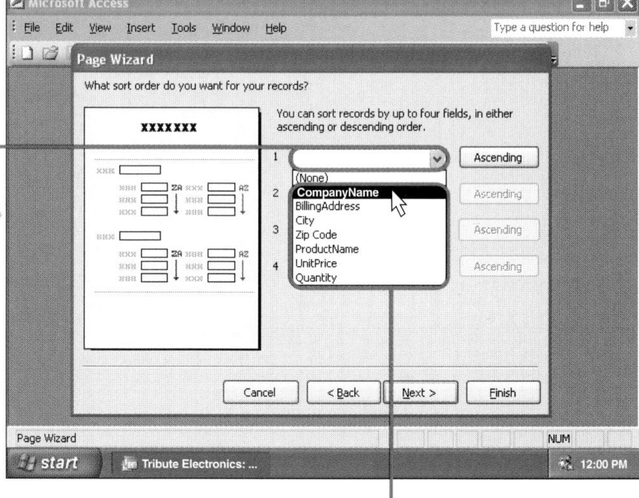

10 To sort the records in your page, click ⌄ in this area.

Note: For information on sorting, see the top of page 283.

11 Click the field you want to use to sort the records.

Why would I sort the records in my data access page?

You can sort the records in your data access page to better organize the records. For example, you can sort records alphabetically by the Last Name field to make it easier to find customers of interest. If the same last name appears more than once in the field, you can sort records by a second field, such as First Name, to further organize the records. You can use up to four fields to sort the records in a data access page.

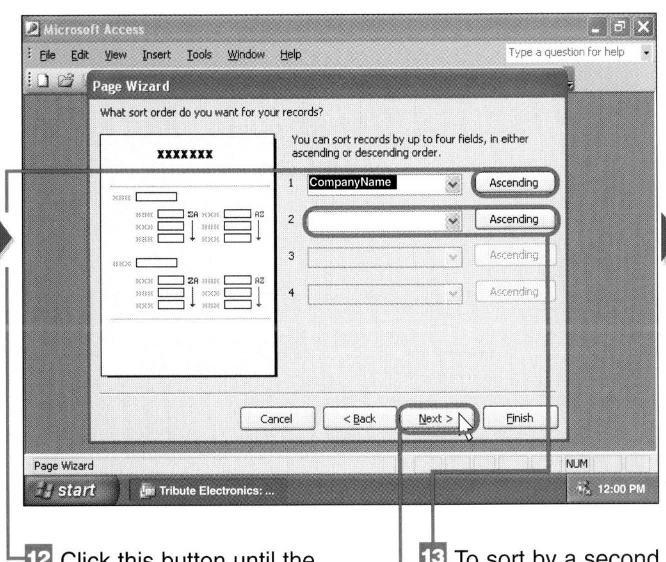

12 Click this button until the button displays the way you want to sort the records.

Ascending–Sorts A to Z, 1 to 9

Descending–Sorts Z to A, 9 to 1

13 To sort by a second field, repeat steps **10** to **12** in this area.

14 Click **Next** to continue.

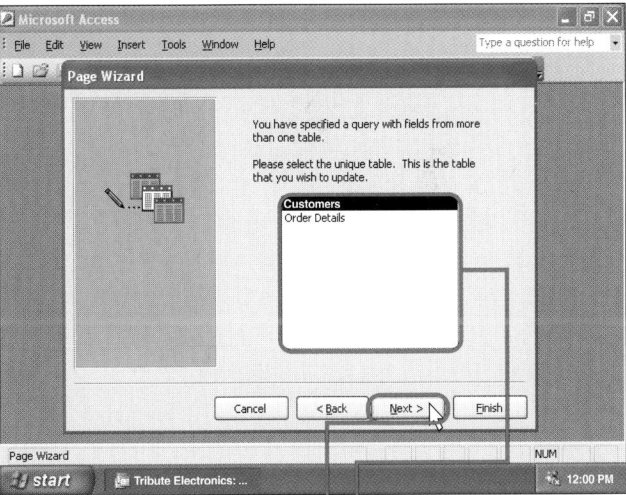

■ If you included fields from more than one table and you chose not to group data in step **8**, this screen appears.

*Note: If the screen does not appear, skip to step **17**.*

15 Click the table you want to be able to edit.

Note: You will not be able to edit data in the other table(s).

16 Click **Next** to continue.

CONTINUED

CREATE A DATA ACCESS PAGE

When creating a data access page, you can give the page a descriptive title.

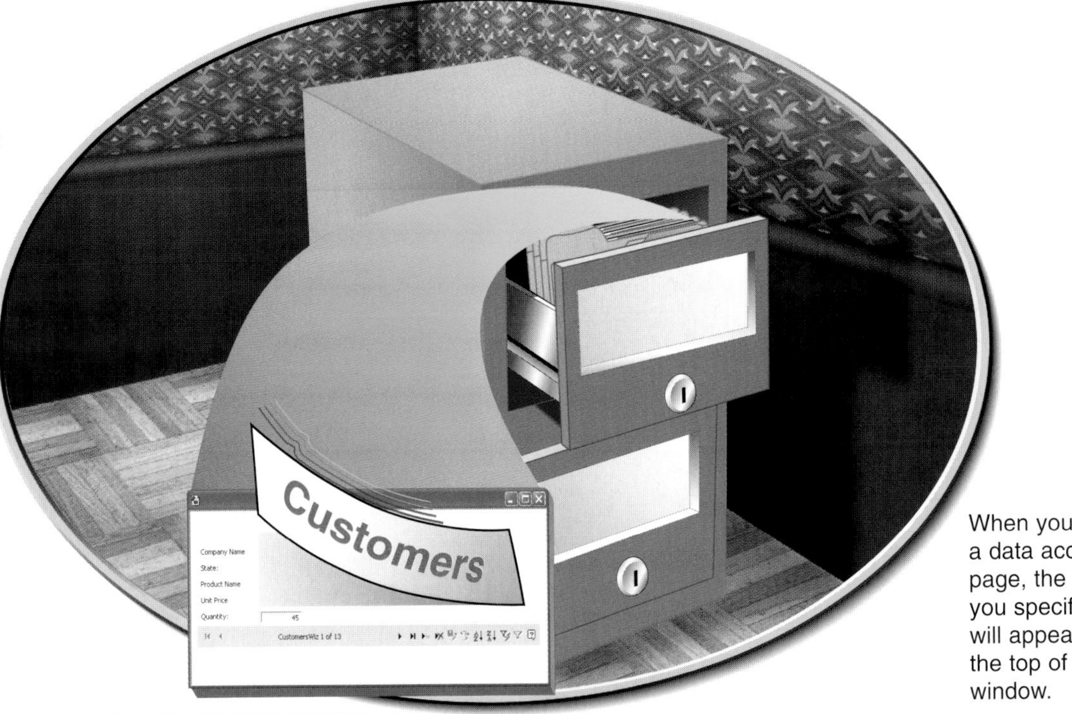

When you view a data access page, the title you specify will appear at the top of the window.

CREATE A DATA ACCESS PAGE (CONTINUED)

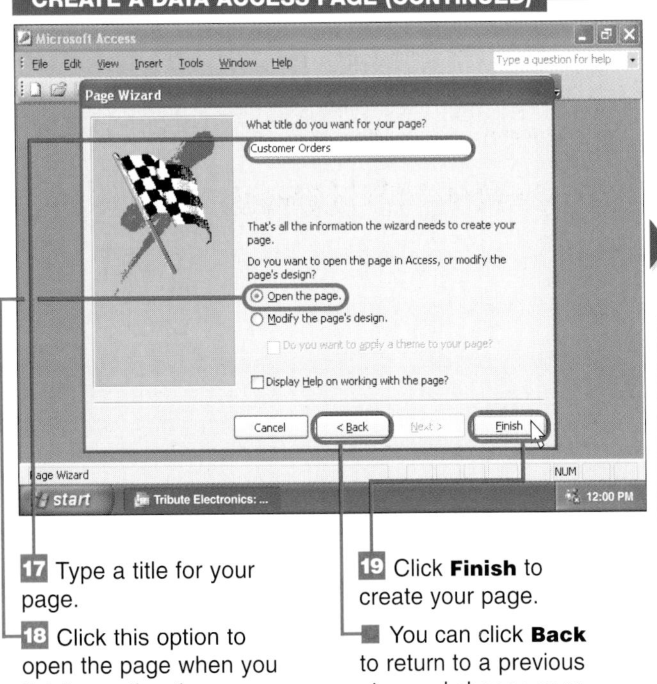

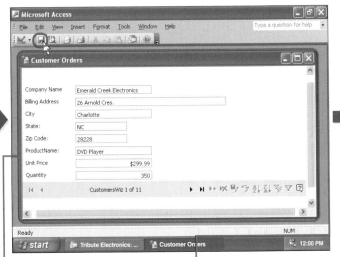

17 Type a title for your page.

18 Click this option to open the page when you finish creating the page (○ changes to ◉).

19 Click **Finish** to create your page.

■ You can click **Back** to return to a previous step and change your selections.

■ The page appears, displaying the information for the first record.

■ If the information for the record does not appear, click **+** beside the first field on the data access page to display the information (**+** changes to **−**).

Note: To move through records in a data access page, see page 290.

20 Click the Save button to save your page.

Where does Access store a data access page I create?

Access stores a data access page as a separate file outside of your database and displays a shortcut to the file in the Database window. To use the shortcut to open a data access page within Access, see page 288.

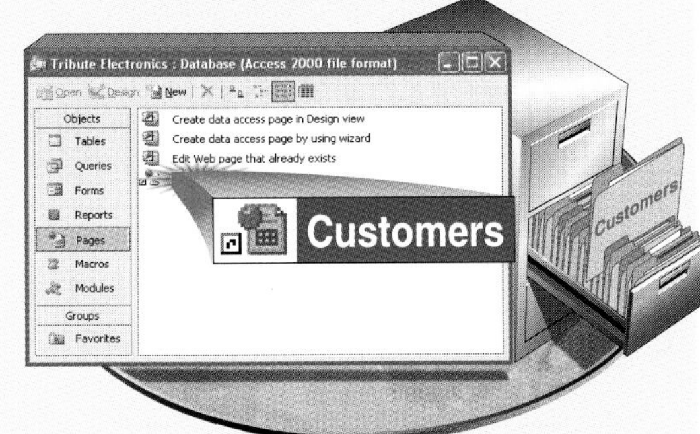

How do I make my data access page available for other people to view?

To make a data access page available on the Internet or your company's intranet, you need to transfer the page to a Web server. A Web server is a computer that stores Web pages and makes the pages available for other people to view. For information on publishing a data access page to a Web server, contact your Web server administrator.

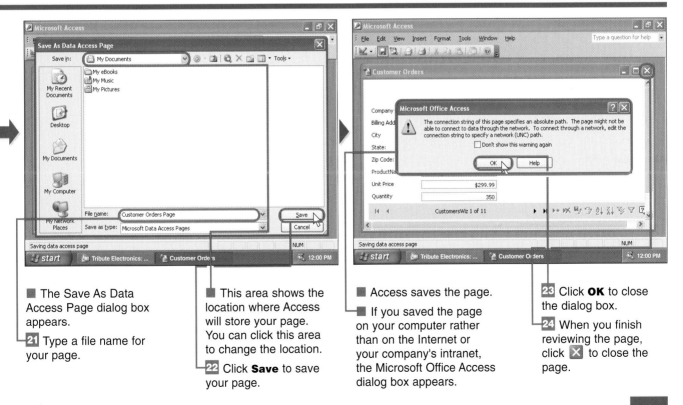

■ The Save As Data Access Page dialog box appears.

21 Type a file name for your page.

■ This area shows the location where Access will store your page. You can click this area to change the location.

22 Click **Save** to save your page.

■ Access saves the page.

■ If you saved the page on your computer rather than on the Internet or your company's intranet, the Microsoft Office Access dialog box appears.

23 Click **OK** to close the dialog box.

24 When you finish reviewing the page, click ☒ to close the page.

CHANGE THE VIEW OF A DATA ACCESS PAGE

You can view a data access page in three different ways. Each view allows you to perform different tasks.

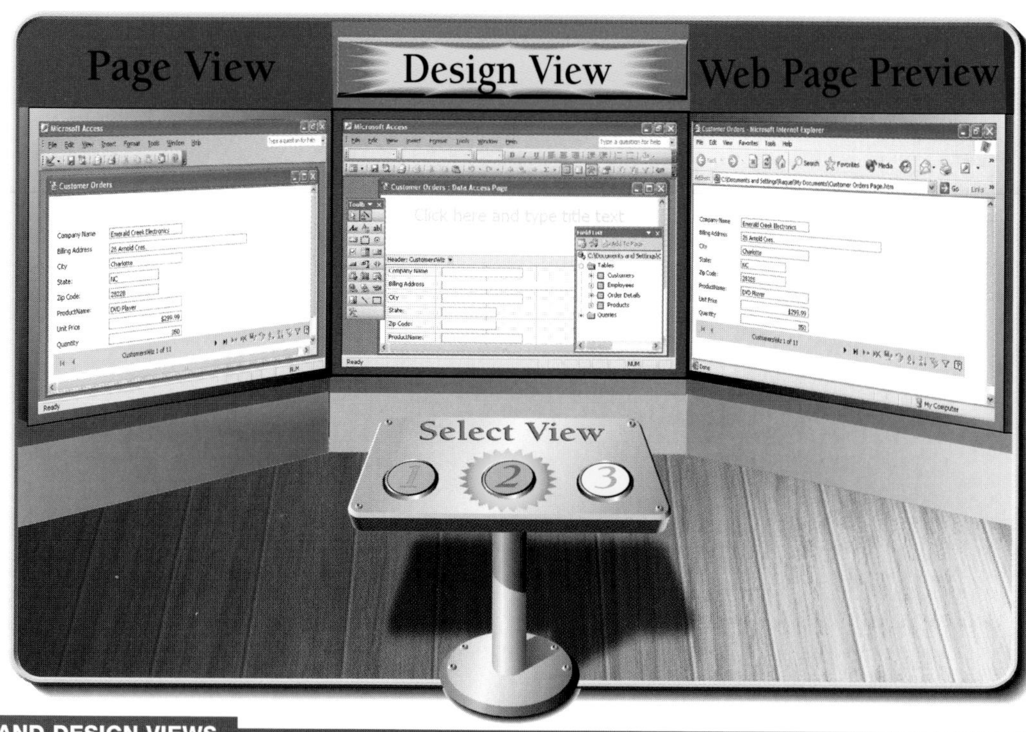

USING THE PAGE AND DESIGN VIEWS

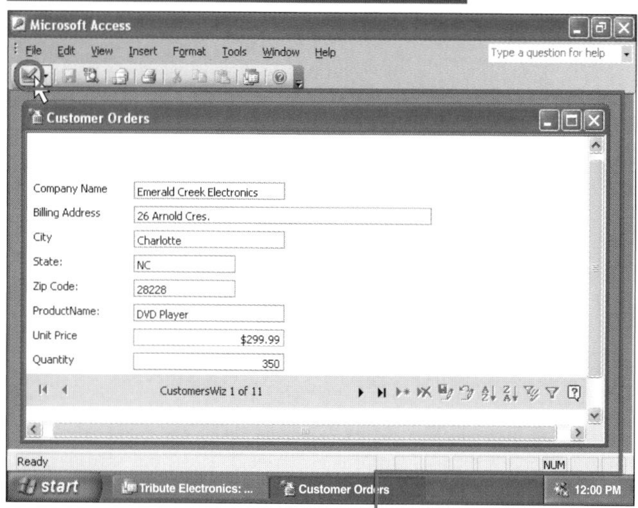

■ In this example, the data access page appears in the Page view.

1 Click [icon] to display the data access page in the Design view.

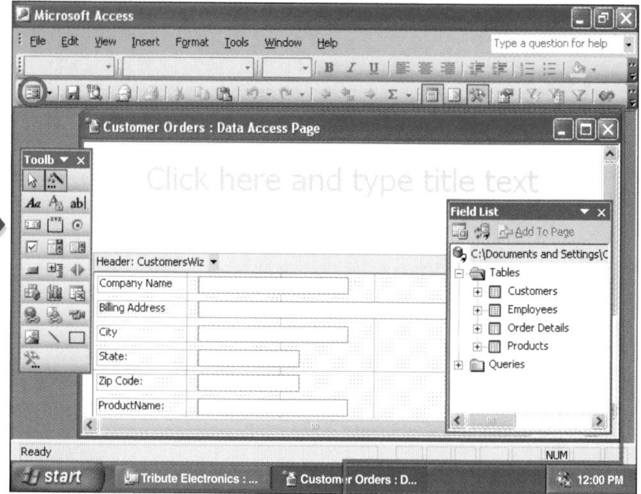

■ The data access page appears in the Design view.

■ The View button changed from [icon] to [icon].

■ To quickly switch between the Page ([icon]) and Design ([icon]) views, click the View button.

How can I view a data access page?

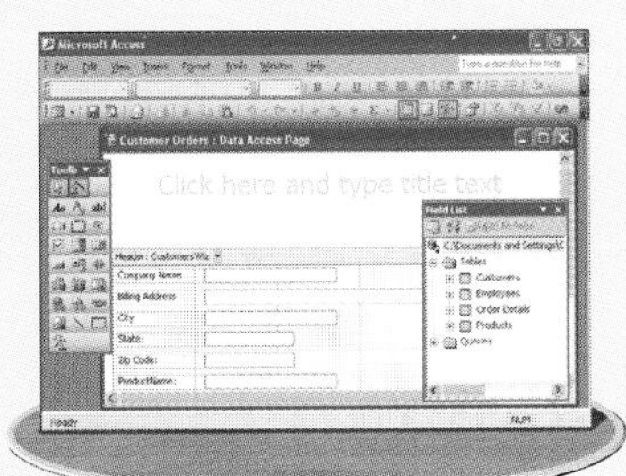

Design View

The Design view allows you to change the layout and design of a data access page to make the page easier to use or to enhance the appearance of the page.

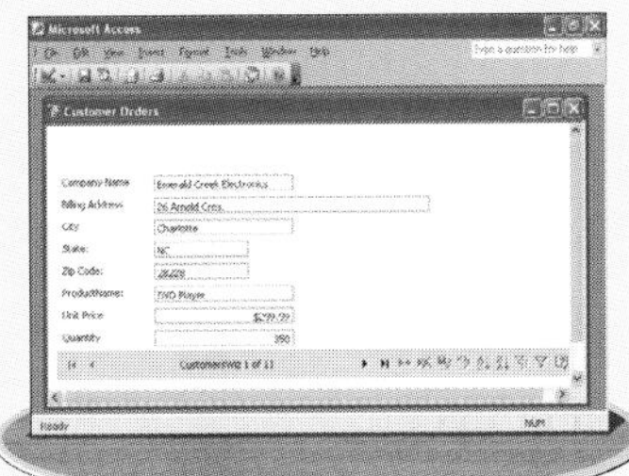

Page View

The Page view allows you to review, enter and edit information displayed in a data access page.

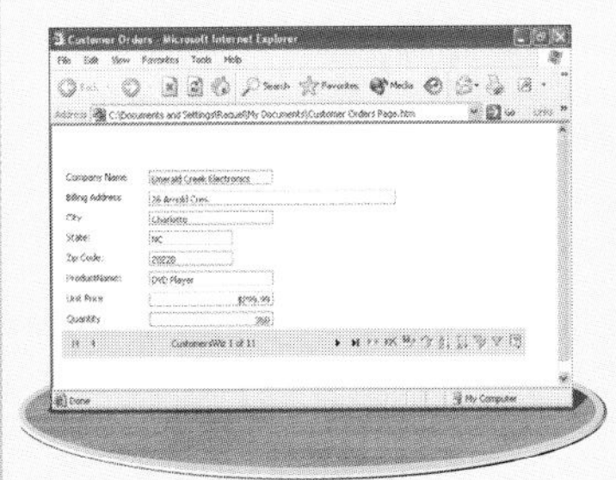

Web Page Preview

The Web Page Preview view allows you to display a data access page in your Web browser so you can see how the page will appear on the Web or on your company's intranet.

USING THE WEB PAGE PREVIEW VIEW

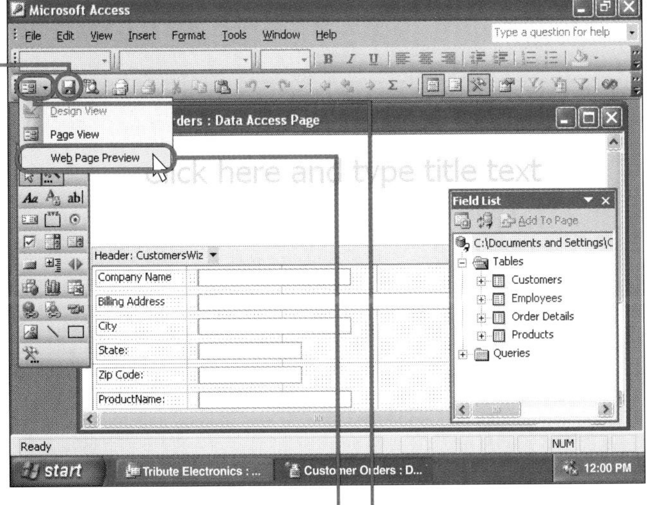

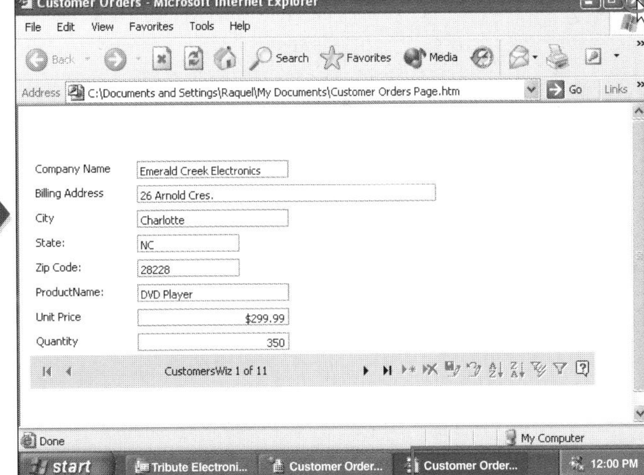

■ Before you can display your data access page in a Web browser, you must save any changes you made to the page.

1 Click 💾 to save any changes you made to the data access page.

2 Click ▾ in this area to display the data access page in a different view.

3 Click **Web Page Preview**.

■ The Microsoft Internet Explorer window appears, displaying the page as it will appear on the Web or on your company's intranet.

4 When you finish reviewing the page, click ✕ to close the page.

OPEN A DATA ACCESS PAGE

You can open a data access page to display the contents of the page on your screen. Opening a data access page allows you to review and make changes to the page.

Each time you open a data access page, Access will display the most current data from your database in the page.

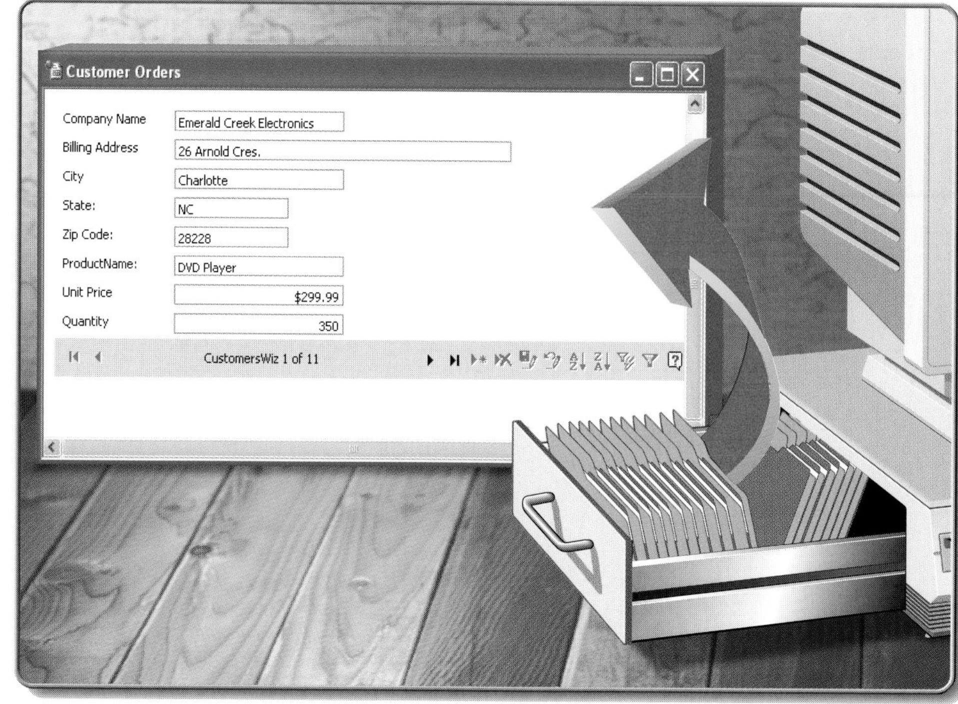

OPEN A DATA ACCESS PAGE

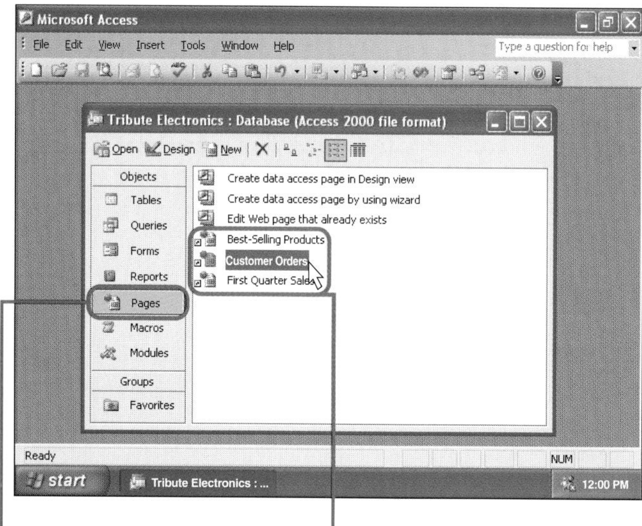

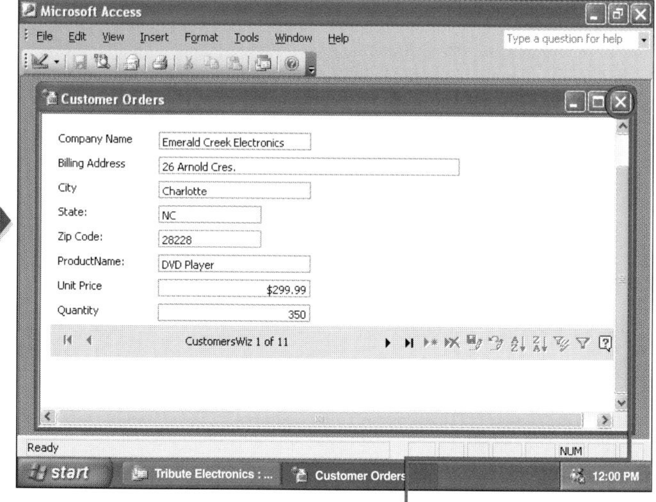

1 Click **Pages** in the Database window.

■ This area displays a list of the data access pages you have created in the database.

2 Double-click the data access page you want to open.

■ The data access page opens. You can now review and make changes to the page.

■ When you finish reviewing and working with the data access page, click ☒ to close the page.

ADD A TITLE

You can add a title to a data access page to describe the information displayed in the page.

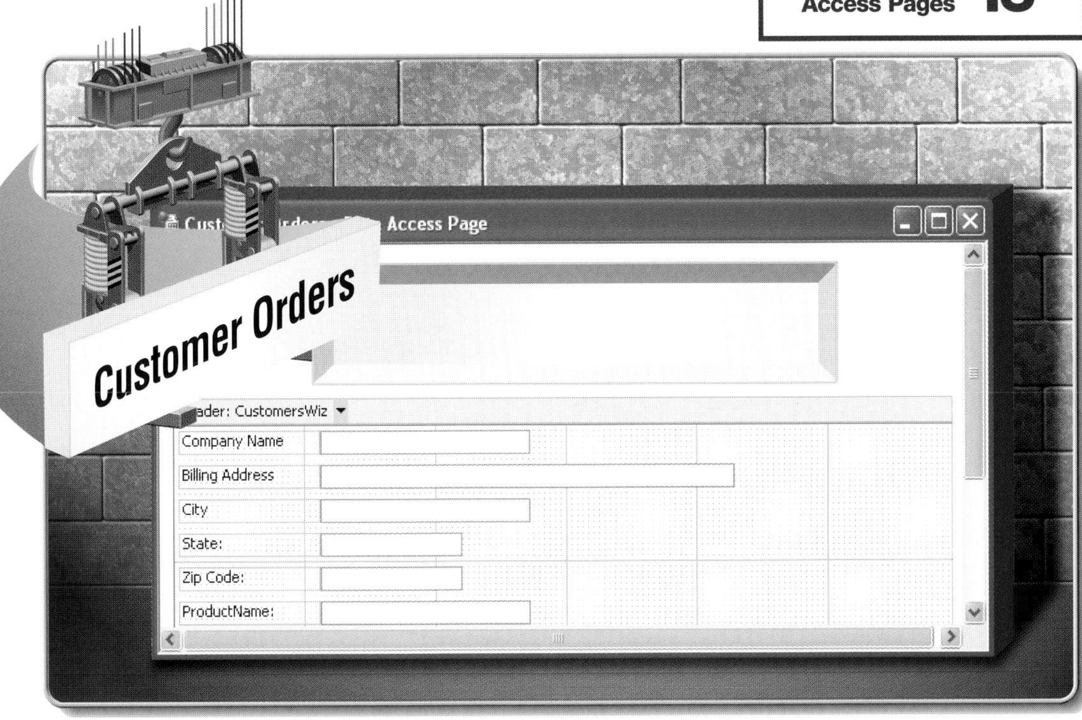

ADD A TITLE

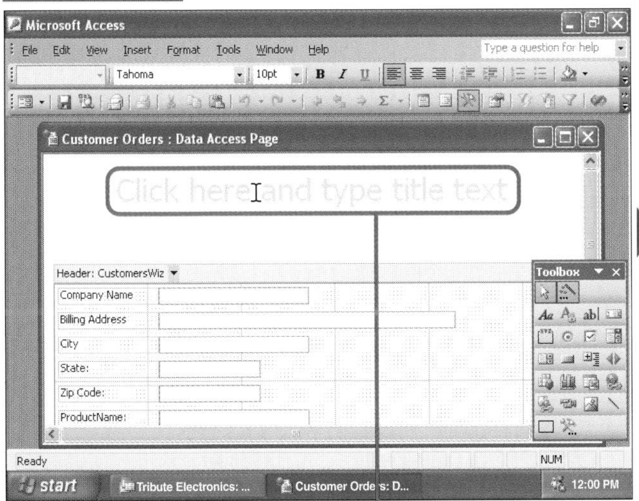

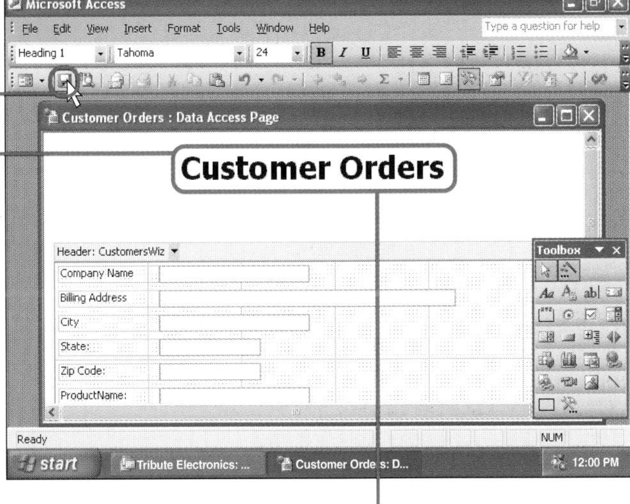

1 Display the data access page you want to add a title to in the Design view. To change the view of a data access page, see page 286.

2 Click this area to add a title to the data access page.

■ A flashing insertion point appears in the area.

3 Type a title for your data access page.

4 Click the Save button to save your change.

■ To remove a title from a data access page, drag the mouse I over the title until you highlight the entire title and then press the Delete key.

MOVE THROUGH RECORDS

You can move through the records in a data access page to review and edit information.

MOVE THROUGH RECORDS

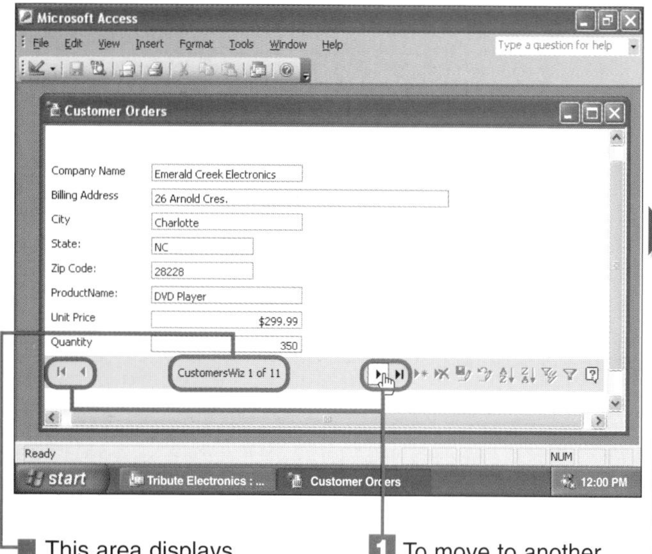

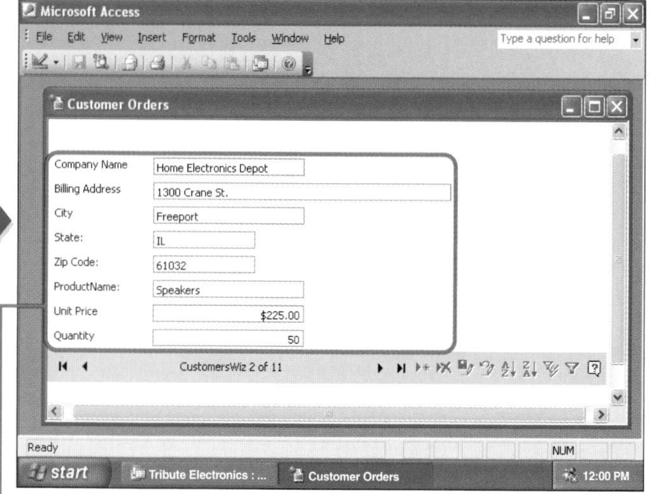

■ This area displays the number of the current record and the total number of records.

1 To move to another record, click one of the following buttons.

- First record
- Previous record
- Next record
- Last record

■ The information for the record you specified appears.

Can I edit the data in my data access page?

Yes. You can edit the data in a data access page as you would edit data on a form. To edit data on a form, see page 146. After you finish making changes to data, click in the data access page to save your changes. When you change data in a data access page, Access will also change the data in the table you used to create the page.

If your data access page displays information from more than one table, you may not be able to edit data in the page.

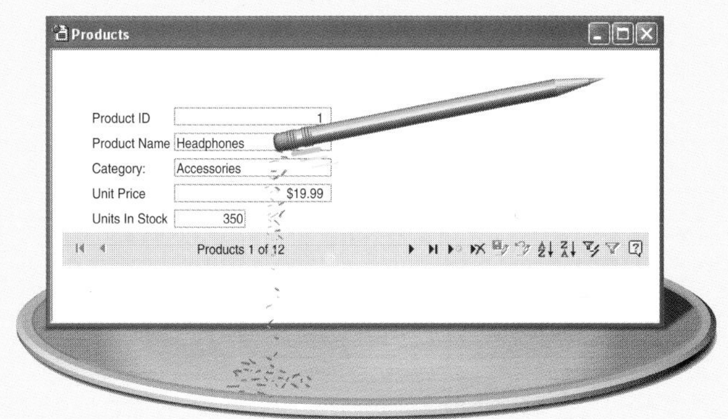

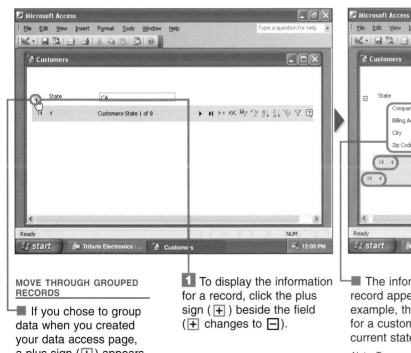

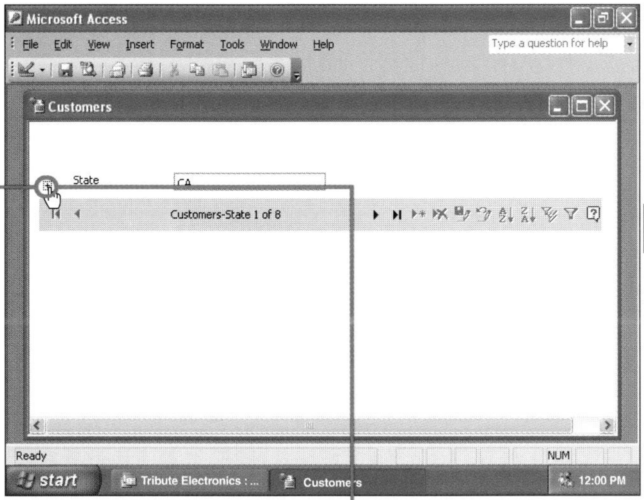

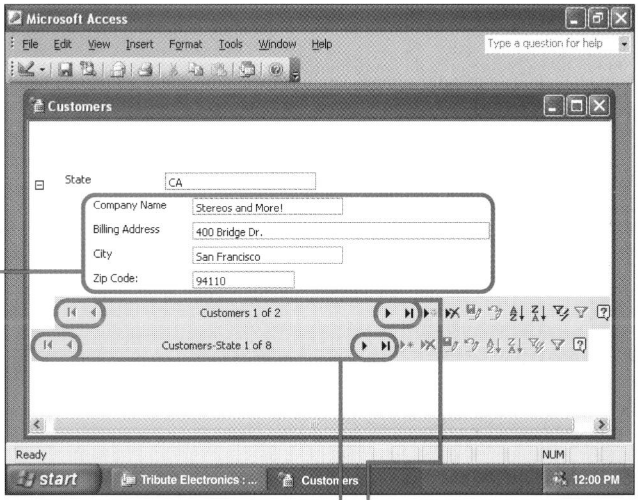

MOVE THROUGH GROUPED RECORDS

■ If you chose to group data when you created your data access page, a plus sign (⊞) appears beside the field you used to group the data. In this example, the records are grouped by state.

1 To display the information for a record, click the plus sign (⊞) beside the field (⊞ changes to ⊟).

■ The information for one record appears. In this example, the information for a customer from the current state appears.

Note: To once again hide the information for the record, click the minus sign (⊟) beside the field.

■ To move through the records in the current group, use these buttons.

■ To move through the field used to group the records, use these buttons.

APPLY A THEME

Access offers many ready-to-use designs, called themes, that you can use to enhance the overall appearance of a data access page.

A theme includes a group of design elements including fonts, horizontal lines, links, bullets and background pictures.

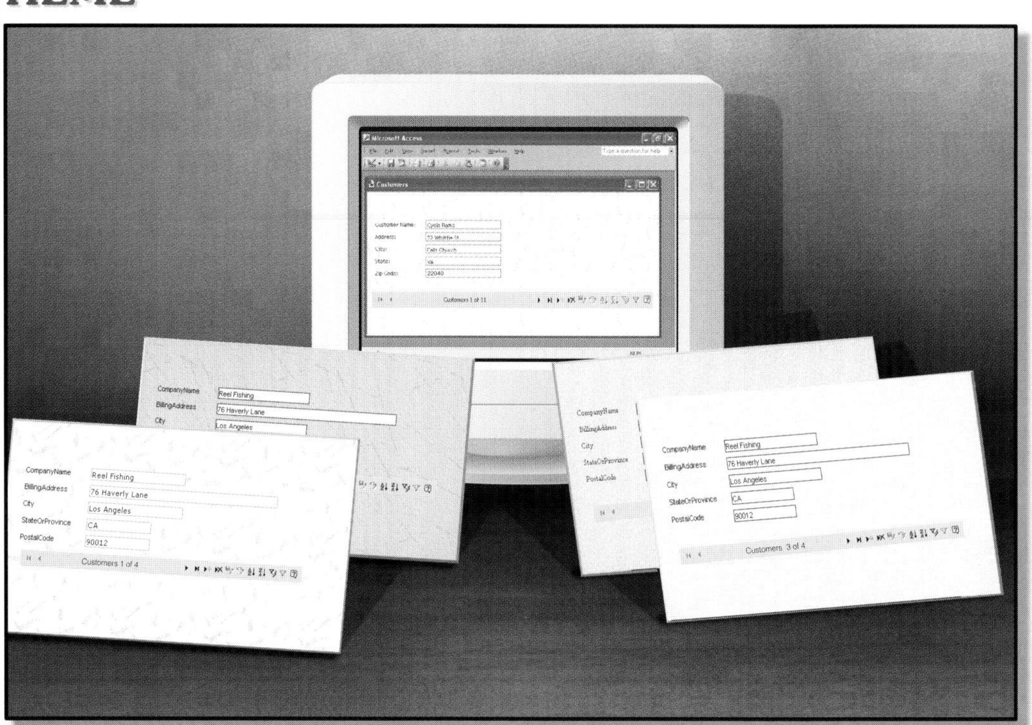

APPLY A THEME

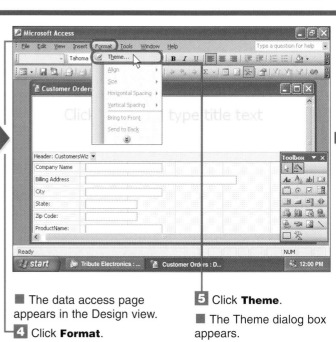

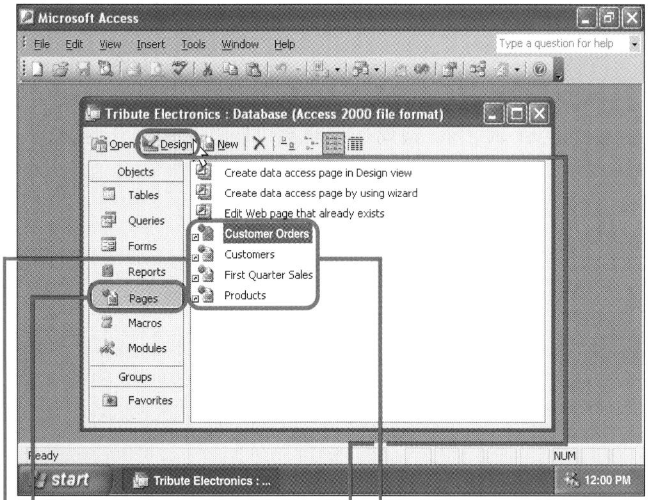

1 Click **Pages** in the Database window.

■ This area displays a list of the data access pages you have created in the database.

2 Click the data access page you want to apply a theme to.

3 Click **Design** to open the data access page in the Design view.

■ The data access page appears in the Design view.

4 Click **Format**.

5 Click **Theme**.

■ The Theme dialog box appears.

Why didn't a sample of the theme I selected appear?

If a sample of the theme you selected does not appear, the theme is not installed on your computer. To install the theme, click **Install** in the Theme dialog box.

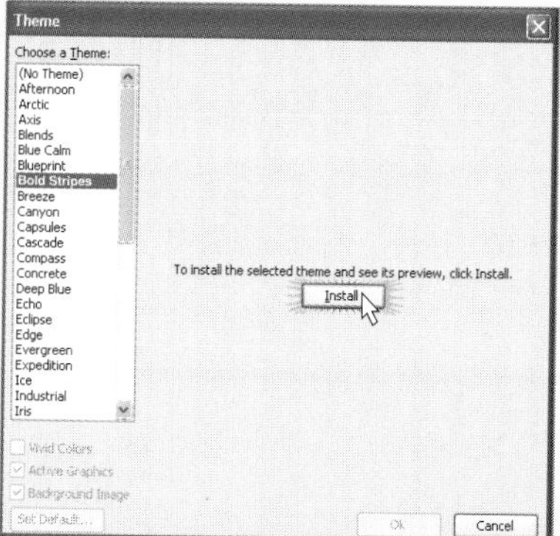

Are there other ways I can change the appearance of a data access page?

When you display a data access page in the Design view, you can change the design of the page as you would change the design of a form. For example, you can bold text, change the font and color of text and add a picture to the page. To change the design of a form, see pages 154 to 169.

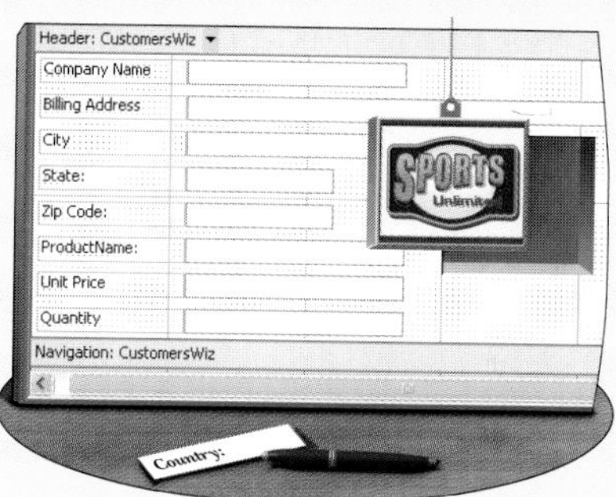

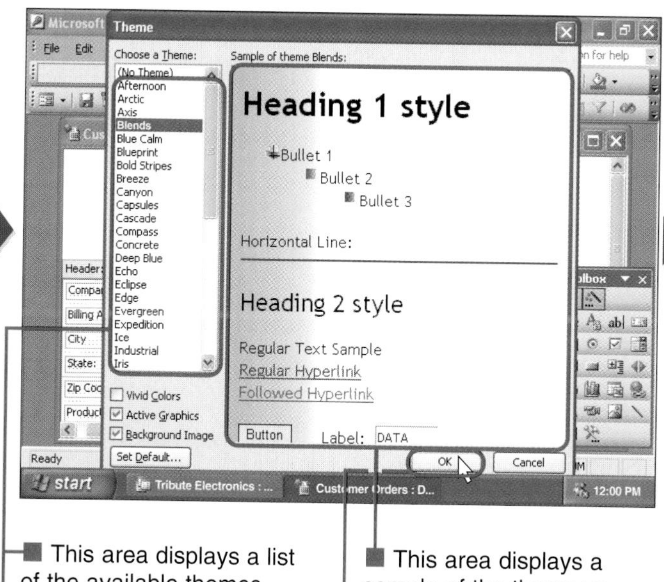

■ This area displays a list of the available themes.

6 Click the theme you want to apply to your data access page.

■ This area displays a sample of the theme you selected.

Note: If a sample does not appear, see the top of this page.

7 Click **OK** to apply the theme to your data access page.

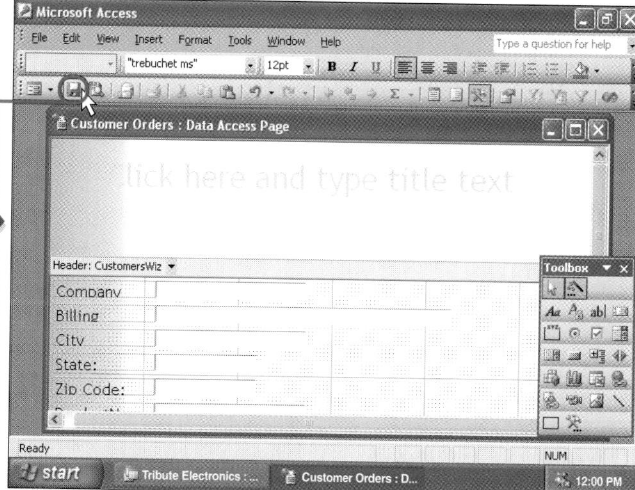

■ The data access page displays the theme you selected.

8 Click [save icon] to save your change.

■ To remove a theme, repeat steps 1 to 8, selecting **(No Theme)** in step 6.

RENAME A DATA ACCESS PAGE

You can change the name of a data access page to better describe the information displayed in the page.

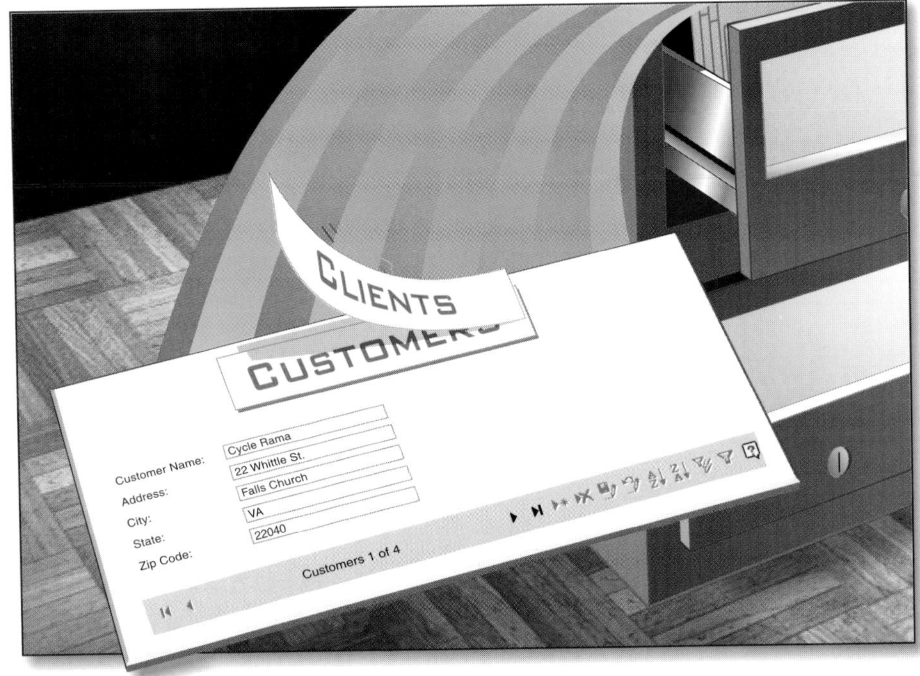

Each data access page in your database must have a unique name.

RENAME A DATA ACCESS PAGE

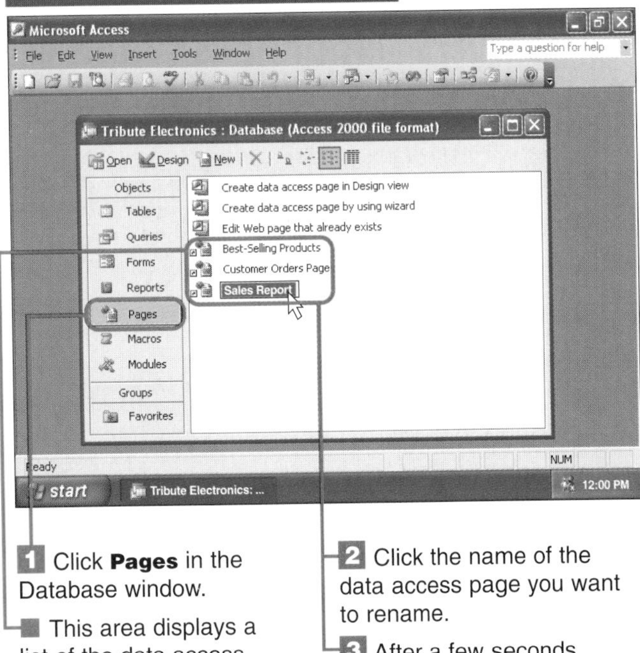

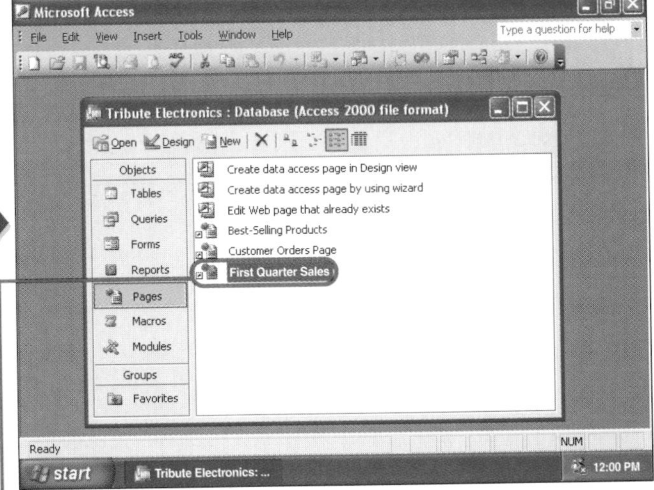

1 Click **Pages** in the Database window.

■ This area displays a list of the data access pages you have created in the database.

2 Click the name of the data access page you want to rename.

3 After a few seconds, click the name again or press the F2 key. A black border appears around the name.

Note: If you accidentally double-click the name of the data access page, the page will open.

4 Type a new name for the data access page and then press the Enter key.

■ The data access page displays the new name.

Note: Access stores a data access page as a separate file outside of your database. Renaming a data access page in Access renames the shortcut to the file, but does not rename the file itself.

DELETE A DATA ACCESS PAGE

If you no longer need a data access page, you can permanently delete the page from your database.

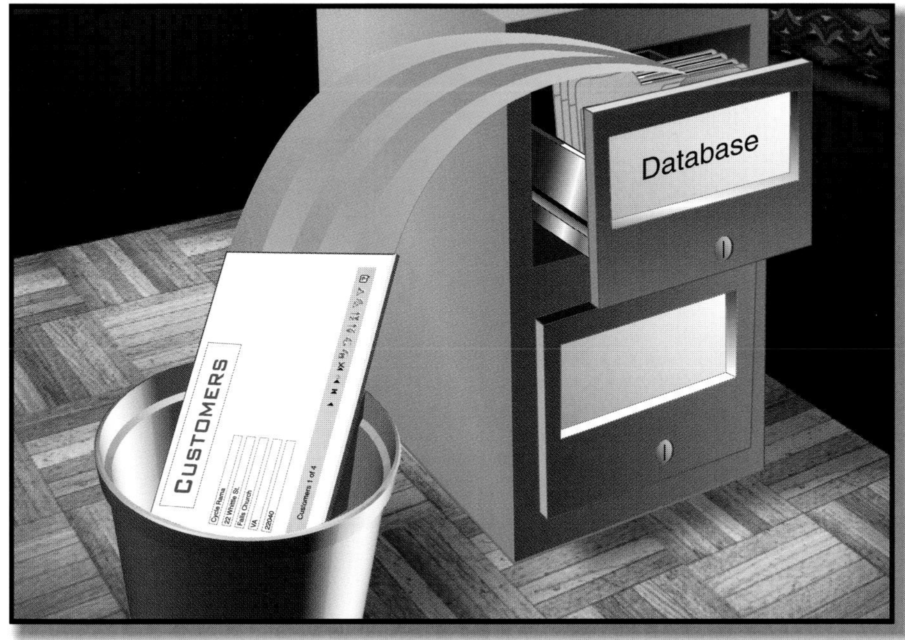

Access stores a data access page as a separate file outside of your database and displays a shortcut to the file in the Database window. When deleting a data access page, you can delete both the shortcut to the file and the file itself or just the shortcut.

DELETE A DATA ACCESS PAGE

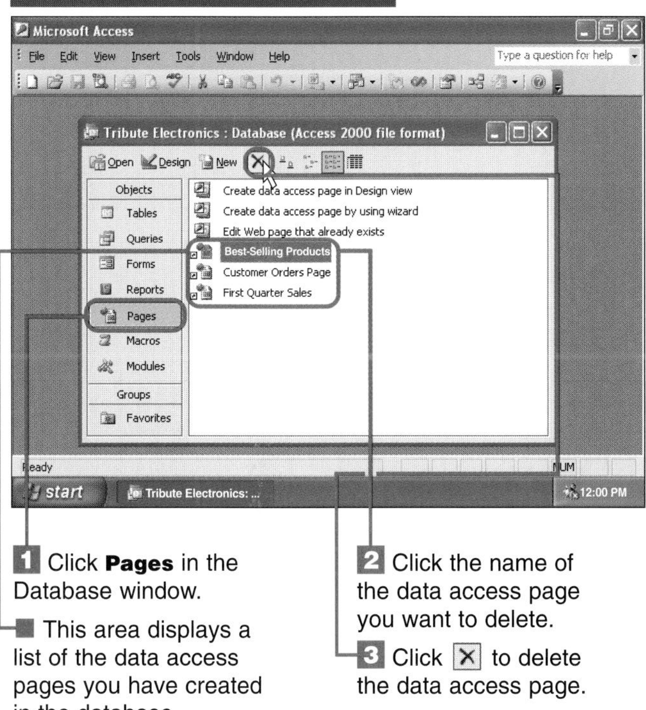

1 Click **Pages** in the Database window.

■ This area displays a list of the data access pages you have created in the database.

2 Click the name of the data access page you want to delete.

3 Click ☒ to delete the data access page.

■ A confirmation dialog box appears.

4 Click a button to specify if you want to delete both the shortcut to the file and the file itself or just the shortcut.

*Note: If you select **Delete Link and Files** in step **4**, the Confirm File Delete dialog box will appear. Click **Yes** to delete the file.*

INDEX

Symbols

A

B

C

D

INDEX

E

F

N

O

P

Q

R

S

T

U

V

W

Y

Z

maran illustrated PIANO

MARAN ILLUSTRATED™ Piano is an information-packed resource for people who want to learn to play the piano, as well as current musicians looking to hone their skills. Combining full-color photographs and easy-to-follow instructions, this guide covers everything from the basics of piano playing to more advanced techniques. Not only does MARAN ILLUSTRATED™ Piano show you how to read music, play scales and chords and improvise while playing with other musicians, it also provides you with helpful information for purchasing and caring for your piano.

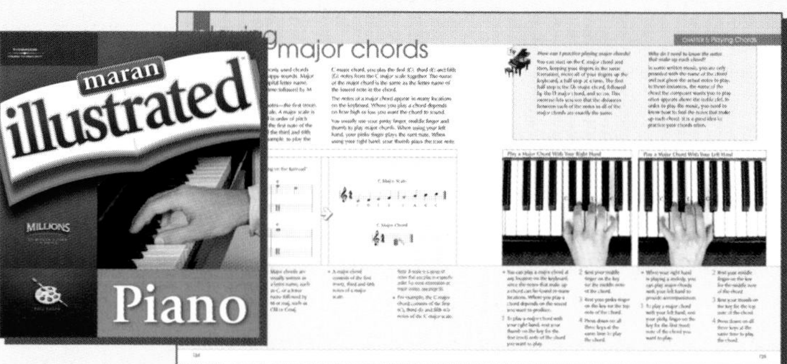

ISBN: 1-59200-864-X
Price: $24.99 US; $33.95 CDN
Page count: 304

maran illustrated DOG TRAINING

MARAN ILLUSTRATED™ Dog Training is an excellent guide for both current dog owners and people considering making a dog part of their family. Using clear, step-by-step instructions accompanied by over 400 full-color photographs, MARAN ILLUSTRATED™ Dog Training is perfect for any visual learner who prefers seeing what to do rather than reading lengthy explanations.

Beginning with insights into popular dog breeds and puppy development, this book emphasizes positive training methods to guide you through socializing, housetraining and teaching your dog many commands. You will also learn how to work with problem behaviors, such as destructive chewing.

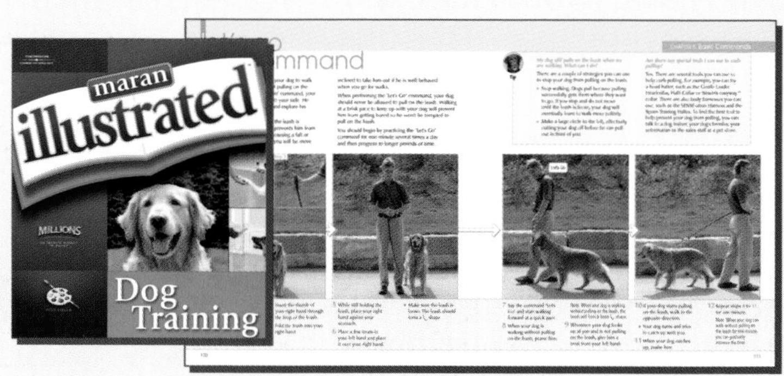

ISBN: 1-59200-858-5
Price: $19.99 US; $26.95 CDN
Page count: 256

maran illustrated KNITTING & CROCHETING

MARAN ILLUSTRATED™ Knitting & Crocheting contains a wealth of information about these two increasingly popular crafts. Whether you are just starting out or you are an experienced knitter or crocheter interested in picking up new tips and techniques, this information-packed resource will take you from the basics, such as how to hold the knitting needles or crochet hook, to more advanced skills, such as how to add decorative touches to your projects. The easy-to-follow information is communicated through clear, step-by-step instructions and accompanied by over 600 full-color photographs—perfect for any visual learner.

ISBN: 1-59200-862-3
Price: $24.99 US; $33.95 CDN
Page count: 304

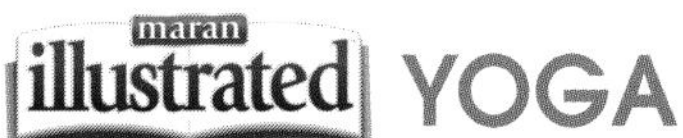

YOGA

MARAN ILLUSTRATED™ Yoga provides a wealth of simplified, easy-to-follow information about the increasingly popular practice of Yoga. This easy-to-use guide is a must for visual learners who prefer to see and do without having to read lengthy explanations.

Using clear, step-by-step instructions accompanied by over 500 full-color photographs, this book includes all the information you need to get started with yoga or to enhance your technique if you have already made yoga a part of your life. MARAN ILLUSTRATED™ Yoga shows you how to safely and effectively perform a variety of yoga poses at various skill levels, how to breathe more efficiently and much more.

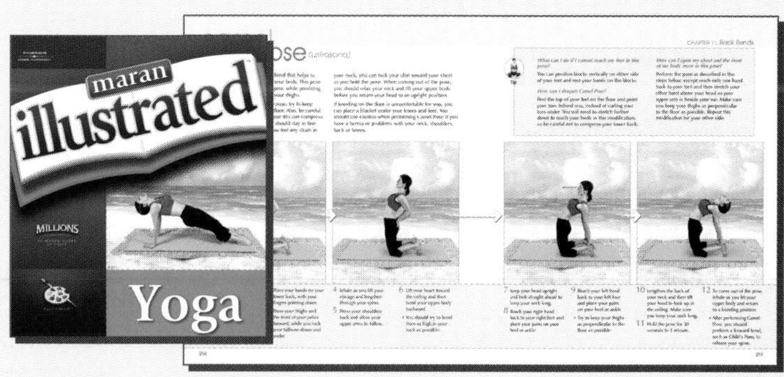

ISBN: 1-59200-868-2
Price: $24.99 US; $33.95 CDN
Page count: 320

maran illustrated WEIGHT TRAINING

MARAN ILLUSTRATED™ Weight Training is an information-packed guide that covers all the basics of weight training, as well as more advanced techniques and exercises.

MARAN ILLUSTRATED™ Weight Training contains more than 500 full-color photographs of exercises for every major muscle group, along with clear, step-by-step instructions for performing the exercises. Useful tips provide additional information and advice to help enhance your weight training experience.

MARAN ILLUSTRATED™ Weight Training provides all the information you need to start weight training or to refresh your technique if you have been weight training for some time.

ISBN: 1-59200-866-6
Price: $24.99 US; $33.95 CDN
Page count: 320

maran illustrated GUITAR

MARAN ILLUSTRATED™ Guitar is an excellent resource for people who want to learn to play the guitar, as well as for current musicians who want to fine tune their technique. This full-color guide includes over 500 photographs, accompanied by step-by-step instructions that teach you the basics of playing the guitar and reading music, as well as advanced guitar techniques. You will also learn what to look for when purchasing a guitar or accessories, how to maintain and repair your guitar, and much more.

Whether you want to learn to strum your favorite tunes or play professionally, MARAN ILLUSTRATED™ Guitar provides all the information you need to become a proficient guitarist.

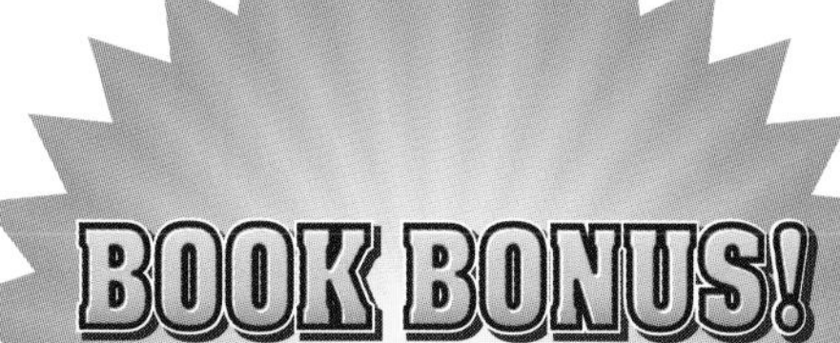

Visit www.maran.com/guitar to download MP3 files you can listen to and play along with for all the chords, scales, exercises and practice pieces in the book.

ISBN: 1-59200-860-7

Price: $24.99 US; $33.95 CDN

Page count: 320

Did you like this book? MARAN ILLUSTRATED™ offers books on the most popular computer topics, using the same easy-to-use format of this book. We always say that if you like one of our books, you'll love the rest of our books too!

Here's a list of some of our best-selling computer titles:

Guided Tour Series - 240 pages, Full Color

MARAN ILLUSTRATED's Guided Tour series features a friendly disk character that walks you through each task step by step. The full-color screen shots are larger than in any of our other series and are accompanied by clear, concise instructions.

	ISBN	Price
MARAN ILLUSTRATED™ Computers Guided Tour	1-59200-880-1	$24.99 US/$33.95 CDN
MARAN ILLUSTRATED™ Windows XP Guided Tour	1-59200-886-0	$24.99 US/$33.95 CDN

MARAN ILLUSTRATED™ Series - 320 pages, Full Color

This series covers 30% more content than our Guided Tour series. Learn new software fast using our step-by-step approach and easy-to-understand text. Learning programs has never been this easy!

	ISBN	Price
MARAN ILLUSTRATED™ Windows XP	1-59200-870-4	$24.99 US/$33.95 CDN
MARAN ILLUSTRATED™ Office 2003	1-59200-890-9	$29.99 US/$40.95 CDN
MARAN ILLUSTRATED™ Excel 2003	1-59200-876-3	$24.99 US/$33.95 CDN
MARAN ILLUSTRATED™ Access 2003	1-59200-872-0	$24.99 US/$33.95 CDN

101 Hot Tips Series - 240 pages, Full Color

Progress beyond the basics with MARAN ILLUSTRATED's 101 Hot Tips series. This series features 101 of the coolest shortcuts, tricks and tips that will help you work faster and easier.

	ISBN	Price
MARAN ILLUSTRATED™ Windows XP 101 Hot Tips	1-59200-882-8	$19.99 US/$26.95 CDN